Applied Psychology

SECOND EDITION

HUGH COOLICAN

HODDER
EDUCATION
AN HACHETTE UK COMPANY

Applied Psychology

SECOND EDITION

Orders: please contact Bookpoint Ltd, 130 Milton Park, Abingdon, Oxon OX14 4SB. Telephone: (44) 01234 827720. Fax: (44) 01235 400454. Lines are open from 9.00–5.00, Monday to Saturday, with a 24 hour message answering service. You can also order through our website www.hoddereducation.co.uk

British Library Cataloguing in Publication Data

A catalogue record for this title is available from the British Library

ISBN: 978 0 340 92745 8

First Published 2007
Impression number   10 9 8 7 6 5 4
Year   2012 2011 2010

Hodder Education's policy is to use papers that are natural, renewable and recyclable products and made from wood grown in sustainable forests. The logging and manufacturing processes are expected to conform to the environmental regulations of the country of origin.

Cover: © Matthew Spolin/Photo Alto/Getty Images.

Typeset by Phoenix Photosetting, Chatham, Kent.
Printed in Great Britain for Hodder Education, an Hachette UK company,
338 Euston Road, London NW1 3BH by the MPG Books Group

Contents

Acknowledgments

The author and publishers would like to thank the following for the use of photographs in this volume:
p. 22 PA Photos; p.31, p.40 (bottom) © University of Pennsylvania Archives; p.40 (top) Corbis; p.63 © Bob Daemmrich/The Image Works/TopFoto; p.80 Sipa Press/Rex Features; p.82 © Gideon Mendel/Corbis; p.98 © Janine Wiedel Photolibrary/Alamy; p.101 © Gideon Mendel/Corbis; p.131 © Mary Evans Picture Library/Alamy; p.137 © 2003 Topham Picturepoint; p.149 © B.KRAFT/I./CORBIS SYGMA; p.150 (left) © SOQUI TED/CORBIS SYGMA; p.150 (right) © Reuters/CORBIS; p.171 (both) Food Standards Agency; p.190 © The Baker Library, Harvard Business School; p.205 CNN via Getty Images; p.239 © Stephen Hird/Reuters/CORBIS

Every effort has been made to trace and acknowledge ownership of copyright. The publishers will be glad to make suitable arrangements with any copyright holders whom it has not been possible to contact.

Contributors

Professor Tony Cassidy is currently Head of Psychology at the University of Limerick, having previously headed departments at Thames Valley and De Montfort Universities. He is a Chartered Psychologist in Health and Sport & Exercise Psychology, and has authored books on Environmental Psychology and Stress. His recent research has covered topics such as dealing with suicide in prisons, stress and health in young carers, bullying in school and child health psychology.

Hugh Coolican is a Chartered Psychologist and holds an MSc in occupational psychology. He was the lead author for the first edition of this book and retains the role for this second edition. He has also written *Psychology in Practice: Organisations* (2001), but is better known for his work on research methods, especially *Research Methods and Statistics in Psychology* (fourth edition, 2004). Hugh is currently Principal Lecturer in Psychology at Coventry University, and teaches research methods, occupational psychology, cross-cultural psychology and philosophical principles of psychology.

Dr Orla Dunn is a Chartered Health Psychologist and committee member of the Division of Health Psychology of the British Psychological Society. She is Course Director of the MSc Health Psychology at Coventry University and teaches health psychology on the undergraduate programme. Current research interests in health behaviour change lie in the areas of breastfeeding, childhood obesity and teenage sexual health.

Dr Julie Harrower is a Chartered Forensic Psychologist and the author of *Applying Psychology to Crime* (1998) and *Psychology in Practice: Crime* (2001). Prior to becoming a lecturer, Head of the Psychology Department at Coventry University, and now Associate Dean on the Faculty of Human and Life Sciences she was a Probation Officer, Divorce Court Welfare Officer and Child Protection Officer. She teaches forensic psychology to undergraduates and postgraduates, and is particularly interested in the relationship between gender and crime, and media influences on crime. She is the Chair of the Division of Forensic Psychology Board of Assessors.

Applied Psychology

Dr Rob Sharp is a Chartered Psychologist and an Associate Fellow of the British Psychological Society. His research in child development at the University of London's Institute of Education was concerned with the influence of language on early learning. He is currently the Specialist Senior Educational Psychologist for children with physical and neurological impairment in Hertfordshire. Previously, he lectured in further and higher education, and has practised as part of a multi-professional assessment team at the Wolfson Centre, Institute of Child Health.

Dr Katherine Simons is a Chartered Psychologist and a senior lecturer in Psychology at Coventry University. Prior to becoming a lecturer, she has worked in an Adult Psychological Service, a Student Counselling Service and Substance Misuse Service. She teaches clinical psychology, counselling psychology and health psychology to undergraduate and postgraduate students.

Dr Jeremy Tudway is a Chartered Clinical and Forensic Psychologist and Director of Phoenix Psychological Services, Warwickshire. He is an honorary lecturer in forensic psychology at the University of Birmingham and an external examiner in clinical psychology at Exeter and Leicester Universities. He has specialised in mentally disordered offenders, particularly cognitive behaviour therapy and risk assessment, and was lead psychologist at the National High Secure Service for People with Learning Disabilities, Rampton Hospital and research liaison tutor in clinical psychology at Coventry University. He has published various studies relating to intellectual disabilities and mental health.

Tony Westbury is a BASES accredited Sport and Exercise Psychologist. He lectures at Napier University, Edinburgh. In his applied practice, Tony works with sport performers in a range of sports, from grass roots to Olympic athletes. He has also worked as a sport psychology consultant to elite teams, including the Scotland Rugby Team and several English county cricket teams. He has written extensively on sport psychology in sport publications and peer-reviewed journals.

Preface

This book is about the world of psychology outside the research laboratory, or at least outside academics' work rooms and offices. It has two main purposes in telling you about the world of applied psychology. First it has a practical side: it attempts to give clear guidance to those who might be interested in a career in applied psychology. For each applied area it tells you what an applied psychologist in that area *does*, including a diary for 'A Day in the Life of' that psychologist. It tells you what is involved, who the psychologist tends to work alongside, what training is required and how to go about getting that training. Second, it has a theoretical side: it tells you what theories applied psychologists use, what they have discovered, what theories they themselves have invented and what kinds of research have been conducted with what results. It should therefore be of use to a student simply studying 'applied psychology' in some kind of academic context, perhaps on the first year of a degree or even at A Level. For those new to the general world of academic psychology Chapter 10 gives an overview and explanation of the main theoretical approaches (or 'schools') in psychology, whilst Chapter 11 is a brief summary of major research methods used by psychologists.

This book is not just about how psychologists apply psychological findings to the real world of people's aspirations and problems. If you are already familiar with mainstream psychology you might be surprised to find just how much of that mainstream theory was kicked off by psychologists originally working in an applied context. The most obvious case in point would be the entire edifice of psycho-analytic theory which was constructed on the work of Freud, a doctor not a psychologist, and his work with a small number of mentally disturbed patients. The study of small group structures, norms and compliance, central to basic social psychology, was prompted in large part by the famous studies of work behaviour by industrial psychologists at the Hawthorne Electrical works near Chicago in the 1920s. Through initial work on road traffic accidents Elizabeth Loftus developed her now famous cognitive psychological studies of eyewitness testimony which are a core element in forensic psychology but will also be found prominently discussed in any general psychology textbook. The ideas of Carl Rogers, who worked with clients in therapy, and of Abraham Maslow, who worked with the industry investigating work motivation, form the two main pillars of the humanistic movement in psychology.

Applied psychologists then do not just take psychology and apply it to people's problems; they *make* psychology, and they make it through the practice of psychology as both a science and an art. This book, then, does not confine itself to describing 'how psychology is applied to real life', as though there were an independent body of psychological knowledge on the shelf waiting to be used. There is in fact a two-way street: principles from 'pure' psychological research are taken out into the community to solve problems, and discoveries in applied research and practice are fed back into mainstream psychology.

Applied psychologists are out in the community working alongside and sometimes trying to convince other professionals. Forensic psychologists work with the police, health psychologists with nurses and doctors, clinical psychologists and counsellors with NHS professionals and private clinics, educational psychologists with social workers and headteachers, occupational psychologists with managers and workers, sports psychologists with players and trainers. In this edition we have included a new chapter on counselling psychology since this area has grown significantly since the first edition. Counselling psychologists too will work with doctors, social workers and almost anywhere that people need to discuss personal problems.

We hope you enjoy reading this book and gain knowledge from it. If it prompts you into becoming an applied psychologist then we'd certainly love to know and wish you well in a wisely chosen career!

We would like to thank Emma Woolf and Nina Hyland from Hodder Arnold, and Alison Thomas for copyediting the manuscript.

Hugh Coolican
Tony Cassidy
Orla Dunn
Julie Harrower
Rob Sharp
Katherine Simons
Jeremy Tudwell
Tony Westbury

Introduction to Applied Psychology

When I switched from physics and maths to psychology and philosophy in the first year of my university career, friends and family retorted with: 'That's all very well, but what can you do with it?' At the time, the only applied psychology I could have imagined would have been a bearded Freud asking his supine patient about all manner of normally taboo personal secrets. Until just after the Second World War it would have been unusual to encounter an applied psychologist working independently outside a university. The number of professional psychologists helping clients with problems gradually increased in the years that followed, but it was in the last years of the twentieth century and the first years of the twenty-first that numbers rose significantly, as will be detailed below. It is still possible to say, then, that now is a good time to think about becoming an applied psychologist, and this book is all about what you can do with psychology should you decide to earn your living by applying psychological knowledge to human problems. A large part of the book also covers the kind of content you will find in many undergraduate and other courses in applied psychology, with the emphasis here being on how psychology can be applied to everyday life and problems. So let us expand on what we mean by applied psychology.

WHAT IS APPLIED PSYCHOLOGY?

Applied psychology is the use of theory and findings in psychology to solve practical problems in important areas of the human environment, including education, health, the workplace, and so on.

It is customary to think of an applied science as the already established theories and findings of 'pure' or 'real' science being applied to practical problems in the everyday world. Physicists develop theories of mechanics; engineers apply these principles to the building of bridges. Box 1 provides a fictitious example of what might be considered the ideal of applied science.

Box 1 How application might work in the 'hard' sciences – a cereal submarine

Imagine that the projects manager at Cereal Toys plc is given a problem one morning. 'Look, Julia, we've got a great design, but we need some scientific input on this one. We need an object which is safe if it is accidentally eaten. What we would really like it to do, however, is to sit in the kiddy's bowl of milk until the surface dissolves and it then looks like a submarine and starts to chug around the bowl. Can you get the boffins downstairs on to this one in a hurry?' The 'boffins' will work in an entirely systematic and scientific manner, drawing on a store of known properties of chemicals and, in the case of some projects, theories of why some matter behaves as it does. The theories employed are usually tested so accurately that predictions can be made and progress achieved quite rapidly, so long as the problems require no breaking of new frontiers. There is no *single* correct path here either. The scientists may have *several* possible solutions, but each one will be effective – it *will* work.

Even in the 'hard' sciences, the traffic is not always one-way like in Box 1; it is not always a case of applying existing theory and findings to a new practical problem. It is frequently the case that a discovery 'in the field' leads to the development of new theory and research directions. A medical team may come across a new form of a disease, or an unexpected effect of brain damage, for example, which would mean a dash back to the laboratory to check out the implications for existing theory, and perhaps, eventually, to change it. Note though, that the dash is indeed very often back to the rarefied atmosphere of the laboratory. Psychologists do not often work in laboratories, and when they do they are likely to be accused of producing findings that hardly apply to 'real life' – more of that debate later.

In psychology the traffic has always been very much two-way. There is not really an independent body of theory and research which can be taken down from the shelf by the applied psychologist who

needs to deal with a specific problem. Much of the theory and research that applied psychologists use was originally created or stimulated by people we would now call 'applied psychologists', and quite a bit of that only subsequently worked its way into the mainstream content that is covered in general psychology courses. In the early days, many psychologists were out in the field, working in applied areas, and they *created* many of the basic concepts and general theories that we read about today. Although these theories and concepts may have been significantly modified, the development of early psychology itself often went hand in hand with improvements psychologists were trying to make in the fields of education, mental health, organisational change or personnel relations (see Box 2 for a few examples).

Box 2 The role of applied psychology in general theory development

➠ Intelligence tests, and the whole subsequent theory of general intelligence and its factors, started with an attempt by Binet to respond to the French government's appeal for a way to identify and deal with children with learning difficulties in the normal school system (Binet and Simon 1915).

➠ The famous research methods concept of the 'Hawthorne effect' was a product of an expansive series of work-psychology studies conducted by Mayo (1927) at the Hawthorne Electrical plant near Chicago, which investigated, among other things, the effects of environmental and social changes on worker productivity.

➠ Hovland and his colleagues (1949) developed an original and influential model of attitude change during the Second World War, while working on the practical matters of altering US citizens' attitudes towards eating offal (meat became scarce), cleaning teeth and helping the government to persuade US fighting forces to accept that the war in South East Asia might be prolonged.

➠ Freud's construction of the psychoanalytic understanding of the human psyche was achieved on the basis of the work of a few doctors working with psychologically disturbed patients.

➠ Bowlby (1980) was working with delinquent children when he promoted his famous and controversial theory linking the strength of attachment of children to their mothers with a raft of later behaviour and personality disturbances.

Psychology as a less than perfect science

In psychology, then, the situation could never be as clear-cut as in the Cereal Toys problem (see Box 1). There is very little theory or factual knowledge within psychology which will guarantee that a solution to a problem will 'work' every time it is tried, or that it will 'work' on identified individuals. Some psychotherapies are found to be generally better than others, but none can be absolutely guaranteed to have a positive effect on all those to whom it is administered. Similarly, there are popular ways to motivate a workforce or attempt to change attitudes on health issues, but people are just not much like those little submarines in the cereal product problem – each person will not behave in the same way as another, even though external circumstances are almost identical. Cereal toys vary ever so slightly, but not enough to upset the outcome of well-calculated equations. People vary enormously and psychologists' ability to predict performance from a known history, with control over several current variables, is exceedingly crude compared with the control that cereal toy boffins can exert over edible chemicals. Furthermore, there are relatively few reliable 'facts' of psychology and there is no one theory that is absolutely 'correct', nor even a general approach that is universally accepted. Physicists and chemists, despite the fact that their knowledge is not perfect, can use known theory to make fairly precise predictions. The calibre of predictive accuracy in mainstream psychological research is just not in the same category.

How is psychology applied?

Does this mean that psychological science cannot really be applied? There are several answers to this, the first of which concerns just what kind of science psychology is. We shall expand this concept below, but for now, the first important point to note is that psychology is a social science. Most of the research knowledge in mainstream psychology is based on studies of groups of people rather than individuals. Usually we cannot predict that a memorising technique will produce improvement in any particular individual, but we can be fairly confident that the overall performance of a group, say 15–20 people, will be higher when using the technique than when not. We cannot predict which individuals will stop smoking as a result of a health-based advertising campaign, but we can be almost certain that a significant number of people *will* stop as a result of it.

Second, working with and studying people is not like studying chemicals. People react; people know they are under study; people have freewill and can change their mind or behaviour as a result of knowing what is expected of them, either to conform or to be contrary. Third, and related to this, psychologists are not working with phenomena that the lay person does not understand or is not familiar with. Before psychology was born as a research subject there were plenty of managers and leaders able to control people effectively, plenty of sports trainers, plenty of observers of the 'criminal mind'. Applied psychologists often have to work with professionals who already know a lot about their fields, so they need to add something in order to be taken seriously and to generate credibility in their particular field.

A question we can ask, then, is how can the applied psychologist convince professionals in their field that they have something to add, that they are better informed than any thoughtful person who uses 'common sense'? What sets the psychologist apart from the manager or the journalist in describing and explaining behaviour, especially when (as is often the case in applied psychology) the focus is on an individual and not a group?

THE ROLE AND CREDIBILITY OF THE APPLIED PSYCHOLOGIST

The professional psychologist

Anyone can put up a plaque outside their door and call themselves a 'psychologist'. It is not illegal to do so, even if you have never formally studied psychology. The fact that a charlatan might use the term 'psychologist' may have some weight in a civil court case involving more general fraud, but the simple act of claiming to be a psychologist is not in itself a crime. Calling yourself a doctor when you are not would certainly put you in line for criminal proceedings. The British Psychological Society (BPS) has long sought some kind of statutory status for practising psychologists of the type that doctors and nurses enjoy. In spring 2005, in response to

BPS representations, the government issued a consultation document on statutory regulation, which proposed that psychologists should be regulated by the Health Professions Council (HPC). The BPS raised several serious objections, not least being the fact that most psychologists work outside the NHS. In September 2006 the BPS issued a statement to members arguing that two recent government reports on the matter still approached psychologist regulation from an NHS perspective and still proposed the HPC as regulator. The BPS is arguing for a new, more appropriate regulatory body.

In the meantime, however, applied psychologists do have *some* formal status – wrongly calling oneself a 'Chartered Psychologist' *would* have legal implications. What the BPS has achieved, since 1987, is the establishment of a Register of Chartered Psychologists. These are psychologists who have undergone a rigorous programme of training and practical experience, which satisfies criteria laid down by the BPS, and which usually involves at least three years of learning and practising alongside qualified supervisors. Hence, chartered status is a form of kitemark for psychologists which should reassure the public that they are consulting a competent, experienced and professional practitioner.

A chartered psychologist is entitled to use the title 'C. Psychol' and can be described as a:

➡ Chartered Clinical Psychologist;
➡ Chartered Counselling Psychologist;
➡ Chartered Educational Psychologist;
➡ Chartered Forensic Psychologist;
➡ Chartered Health Psychologist;
➡ Chartered Occupational Psychologist.

Training for clinical and educational psychologists currently includes the acquisition of a doctorate, so these chartered psychologists will also use the letters PhD and be titled 'Doctor'. Chartered status is granted by the BPS, but professional psychologists are likely to belong to the BPS whether or not they are chartered. The BPS has been growing fast since the first edition of this book was published in 1996. At that time, within the British Psychological Society there were 14 sections, just 5 divisions and 4 special groups. The greatest change has been among the divisions, which now number 10 in all, the newcomers being Health, Neuropsychology, Sport and Exercise, Teachers and Researchers, and Occupational. A 'division' is defined by the British Psychological Society as a grouping which caters for the professional interests of members; a 'section' is defined as being available to members with an interest in an area of psychology; and a 'special group' is designated as a forum for professional work that is at present insufficiently debated. With this in mind, it is to be noted from Table 1.1 that Health Psychology was a Special Group in 1996, with 858 members, but by the end of 2005 it was a Division, with 1156 members. During the same period, Occupational Psychology moved from a Section to a Division, with an increase in membership from 2398 to 3259. The membership of the Division of Clinical Psychology increased from 3474 to 5884, while Counselling Psychology membership increased from 1126 to 1738. The most interesting change, however, was the establishment, in the early twenty-first century, of the Special Group in Coaching Psychology, which now boasts nearly 2000 members. These do not all, as it might sound, belong within a sport and exercise psychology context, but might be members from the Divisions of Occupational, Educational and Child or Counselling Psychology who are interested in training and personal development.

Working in a scientific manner

Most psychologists would agree that their approach to research and the investigation of problems is scientific, although there are disagreements about which methodology is appropriate and the extent to which psychology should try to mimic the physical sciences (see the debate about quantitative and qualitative methods in Chapter 11). However, most would probably agree that there is a logical procedure for testing hypotheses which are generated when trying to explain human behaviour. Table 1.2 overleaf outlines these hypothesis-testing procedures, providing an example (column 2) that might occur in purely academic psychology, and then utilising the same procedure to tackle a practical problem that might be faced by an occupational psychologist (column 3).

In lines one and two of the table a hypothesis is proposed. A hypothesis is a claim about the world that is then investigated by trying to find evidence

DIVISIONS		SECTIONS	
Clinical (DCP)	5884	Education	531
		Social	495
Education & Child (DECP)	1343	Developmental	591
Occupational (DOP)	3259	Cognitive	487
Forensic (DFP)	1604	Maths, Stats & Computing	147
		History & Philosophy	190
Scottish Education (SDEP)	246	Psychobiology	175
Counselling (DCoP)	1738	Psychotherapy	573
Teachers & Research (DTRP)	383	Transpersonal	366
		Psychology of Women	337
Health (DHP)	1156	Consciousness & Experiential Psychology	275
Neuropsychology (DoN)	809	Lesbian & Gay	263
Sport & Exercise (DSEP)	592	Qualitative Research Methods	1575

SPECIAL GROUPS	
Psychologists and Social Services	131
Coaching Psychology	1977

Table 1.1 Membership of BPS Divisions, Sections and Special Groups, end of 2005
Courtesy of Graham Bennell, Business Information Manager, British Psychological Society

which supports it. In the pure theory example, the hypothesis is generated from questioning the explanation of an observed laboratory effect – is competition necessary for social facilitation to occur? The second hypothesis is generated in the process of trying to explain differences in job attitudes. In each case, a possible test of the hypothesis is devised and a clear rationale is produced which states what result would be expected for support of the hypothesis under test, for example: 'If competition is not necessary for social facilitation to occur, and observation alone produces the effect, then we would expect the group performing in front of an audience to produce higher task performance.'

The research design is then devised, paying careful attention to any variables that might confuse the result – often referred to as possible *confounding variables* (see Chapter 11). The *design* is the overall structure of the research study, and dictates how data are gathered and in what form. The idea is to obtain data in as clear and unambiguous a manner as possible. For instance, we would want to ensure that the high and low democratic leaders were not also different in the level of their aggression, or in any other characteristic that is likely to lower job satisfaction among team members. If they *did* differ in this way, the difference would *confound* any effects of democratic style, and we might conclude that low staff involvement caused dissatisfaction when the actual cause was the aggression of the team leaders. We would have a flawed design.

An important feature of this scientific approach is that the hypothesis is tested using *clear and observable measures* of performance. In the pure theory example there is such a measure of performance – number of 'e's crossed out in a set time. In the job satisfaction example we encounter one of the particular strengths of a psychological approach. Whereas charlatans might produce a poorly designed questionnaire, psychologists use a long-established and rich tradition of good scale design in the form of *psychometric tests* (see Chapter 11).

Finally, when a result occurs in the predicted direction, psychologists never talk about 'proving' anything. They do not claim, for example, that they

	Pure theoretical approach	Investigation of field problem
Observation	Previous research shows that people work harder when in competition with others, but could the increased performance ('social facilitation') be caused solely by the *presence* of others?	Workers in some departments of a company are more motivated and have higher job satisfaction.
Hypothesis generation	Participants observed by an audience work harder than participants working alone.	Team leaders who involve the whole team in decision-making have more satisfied staff.
Hypothesis test	Ask participants to cross out all letter 'e's in a newspaper article; one group works alone, another group is observed by six students.	Measure satisfaction of teams with more and less democratic leaders, using well-established psychometric tests and/or careful observations.
Careful research design	E.g. ensure observers behave in exactly the same way for all participants.	E.g. ensure more and less democratic leaders are not different on other significant qualities.
Result (operational measures)	Participants working with an audience cross out more 'e's in a set time than participants working alone.	More democratic leaders do have more satisfied team members.
Interpretation	Supports hypothesis that an audience alone will improve performance – but were the two groups of participants equivalent on the task to start with? Do the findings also support other theories?	Supports original hypothesis – but did the two teams work under similar conditions? Are there other explanations of why the two types of team differ?

Table 1.2 Use of scientific method in general and specific research

have 'proved' that an audience improves performance. They would claim only that they have provided evidence which *supports* this hypothesis. After all, some other feature of the experimental situation might be responsible. In the work-psychology example, the teams led by low democratic leaders might also have been working in more stressful or frustrating work situations, and this might be the real cause of the observed differences in job satisfaction.

The features of a scientific, or at least an objective approach by applied psychologists include:

⬛➡ planning a fair test of a hypothesis;
⬛➡ conducting as unambiguous a research design as possible;
⬛➡ careful observation and measurement of variables;
⬛➡ unbiased collection of data;
⬛➡ careful and appropriate analysis of results;
⬛➡ keeping an open mind about interpretations of those results, and being ready to accept and test alternative explanations;
⬛➡ publishing the results of investigations in a public forum (e.g. psychological journals and conferences).

These features would apply when qualitative as well as quantitative work is being conducted, except that there may be no hypothesis test and no specific measurement of variables. *Qualitative work* (see Chapter 11) is becoming increasingly popular as a methodological approach within applied psychology. It refers to the gathering of data which are not numerical measures, but which (very often) consist of verbal data from interviews, discussions or observations, and sometimes pictorial data such as murals, drawings or graffiti. The data are frequently used to construct a thorough and meaningful model of a phenomenon, such as people's perceptions of the causes of their smoking habit or how they view physical abuse.

Adherence to a professional Code of Ethics

In 2006 the BPS published a new *Code of Ethics and Conduct*, which covers both research with human participants and practice with clients. This and several other ethical papers are available at: http://www.bps.org.uk/the-society/ethics-rules-charter-code-of-conduct/code-of-conduct/code-of-conduct_home.cfm

Research ethics are discussed fully in Coolican (2004), but the basic principles are as follows:

➡ to leave the participant in the same state as they were in at the beginning;
➡ to respect privacy and confidentiality;
➡ to treat people with sensitivity, respect and dignity;
➡ to foster trust, generally, rather than any suspicion, in the authenticity of psychological research and practice.

This marks a clear distinction between the professional applied psychologist and the journalist or charlatan. Becoming chartered means accepting these standards, as does simply being accepted as a member of the British Psychological Society. Anyone found to have violated the Code can have their chartered status removed and, ultimately, can be expelled from the Society.

Being a practitioner-researcher

We have emphasised that being an applied psychologist does not simply involve applying existing psychological knowledge to human problems. Ideally, the full role involves the application and *creation* of knowledge. By applying psychological knowledge to (or by initial investigation of) a human problem, applied psychologists can contribute to knowledge, and, as has often been the case in the past, initiate a whole new theoretical context (see the examples in Box 2 on p. 2).

The ideal role of the applied psychologist is both as *practitioner* – in the field, using knowledge of psychology to solve human problems – and as *scientific researcher* – conducting research investigations in the field or laboratory to provide evidence to support hypotheses or to generate new concepts. In some fields, especially clinical psychology, this has become known as the *scientist-practitioner* model. As indicated above, scientific research can be undertaken at a rather general level or implemented in a single case – for instance, using hypothesis testing to figure out what precise events trigger an outburst in a child with poor classroom behaviour. Practical programmes for change implemented for clients by applied psychologists are known as *interventions* – they are like experiments, but are carried out not simply to gain knowledge or test a hypothesis, but to produce change in humans for what is considered to be the humanly better. Quite often an intervention is implemented not by psychologists but by other professionals (e.g. nursing staff), and the applied psychologist's role is to *evaluate* the programme, for example, by taking before and after measures of people's adherence to a course of medication. As a research design this would be referred to as a *quasi-experiment* (see Chapter 11) because the variables are not controlled by the psychologist who takes measures and analyses findings.

The point to emphasise here is that we would expect a practising chartered psychologist to incorporate scientific thinking into their practice, even though the interpretations of 'science' might be quite broad. We would expect that they would operate according to the basic principles of research ethics listed above. We would expect that, when planning any treatment of, or problem-solving with clients, they would make thorough use of published research in drawing up their plan of action. Charlatans standing outside shopfronts in London streets may call you in to undergo a 'scientific' test of personality, and they might claim to be using scientific thinking and research in their costly programmes. However, you will probably find that the kind of 'science' they operate with has a closed system. Any results that conflict with the theory might be conveniently ignored, or simply incorporated with an 'additional' (but gratuitous) explanation. For example, a person whose behaviour is extroverted, yet who scores as an introvert, might be accused of presenting a 'false' personality. This is the difference between charlatanism and a scientific approach: in a truly scientific approach, evidence can be contrary to existing patterns, and theories are permitted to compete with one another; the emphasis is on open, public research and the weighing of findings in terms of their apparent support for one theory or another. Rather than worrying about the hard-edged sound of the term 'science', we can consider that a scientific approach in applied psychology demonstrates this willingness to allow conflicting theories and to always consider all available evidence.

Tensions in the practitioner–researcher role

It is a fairly common complaint of professional applied psychologists that they get precious little time to indulge in research since they spend so much of their working day with clients, especially in clinical and educational psychology. Norcross, Brust and Dryden (1992) found that most clinical psychologists published no research work in any one year and that just 8 per cent published over half of all research articles. In 2003 a survey found that clinical psychologists in only 19 out of 371 equivalent full-time posts in Scotland were involved in research and audit.[1] We can see from the quotation on p. 188 (Chapter 8) that Fletcher (2003) believes that few occupational psychologist practitioners are actively involved in research, but for very different reasons from those working as clinical psychologists in the NHS. For the latter, reasons stated are often to do with the pressures of waiting lists and face-to-face client contact, along with the perception that research is not valued by NHS organisations.[2] For occupational psychologists, not conducting full research can be a matter of commercial survival. Companies may see occupational psychologists as providing a useful service in areas such as the provision of training, team building, evaluating an incentive scheme or assessing work motivation. If the occupational psychologist demands that interventions are run as full scientific experiments, which would require random selection of employees into control and experimental groups (see Chapter 11), few employers would be prepared to spare the

resources. Doyle (2003: 39) reports a colleague's comment: 'If I tell my clients that I *must* evaluate my interventions in their organisation, they'll just get out Yellow Pages and look up the nearest management consultant.'

Anderson, Herriot and Hodgkinson (2001: 392) argue that the gap between practitioner and researcher in occupational psychology is growing wider, even though work psychology, throughout its history, has benefited from a strong research-practice link, with 'robust research [informing] best professional practice, whilst simultaneously informed practice in the field has stimulated new direction for research and theories [in work psychology]'.

Although their model is developed within the context of work psychology, it can be considered here as applicable to all applied disciplines, though each will have different levels of practitioner-researcher divide and different reasons for the gap. What Anderson et al. propose is that we look at the divide along two dimensions. The first they call 'methodological rigour'. This refers to the extent to which any research or intervention is conducted along rigorous scientific lines, with careful control of conditions, allocation of participants to treatments, well-standardised or piloted measures, and so on (see Chapter 11). The other dimension is one of 'practical relevance', being the degree to which the research carried out is applicable and obviously relevant to practical problems which a practitioner might encounter in their everyday activities. At the extreme opposite end of this dimension, work is perhaps valid, but bears no resemblance to real-life problems. In mainstream psychological research of the past, examples of 'impractical' or unrealistic research might be the learning of nonsense syllables or the simulation of 'social loafing', using a task where 11- and 14-year-old children 'share the job' of counting tones played into headphones.

Four different cells are produced when we assess each piece of research as either high or low on rigour and either high or low on relevance. These are shown in Table 1.3. Anderson et al. argue that *pragmatic science*, where rigour and practical relevance are both high, should dominate in work psychology, and presumably in any applied field.

---

[1] Referred to in conference notes: *Psychology into Practice: Developing a Framework to Support the Improvement of Health.* Report of a national conference, October 2005, NHS Education for Scotland, available at: http://www.nes.scot.nhs.uk/psychology/Conference%20Documents/documents/Confreport-final.doc

[2] Ibid.

Methodological rigour

		Low	High
Practical relevance	High	Popularist science	Pragmatic science
	Low	Puerile science	Pedantic science

Table 1.3 Types of research, high or low in rigour and practical relevance
Source: Adapted from Anderson et al. (2001)

A drift towards *popularist science* is found where researchers rush to publish in order to provide some semblance of legitimacy for their work. The work may be published in journals that do not have articles carefully reviewed by other academics (known as 'peer review'). Claims may be made for the effectiveness of team-building procedures, for example, when little evidence has actually been found to support them. *Pedantic science* occurs where academics conduct research in areas that are likely to produce significant results, and therefore be published in good journals, but where the work conducted has little if any relevance for practitioners working in the field with clients. There may be a concentration on the replication of previous studies with slightly different participant groups, or on increasingly technical and statistical detail, appreciated only by small groups of similarly oriented experts. Finally, *puerile science* occurs where there is neither rigour in the method nor relevant application of the content. Anderson et al. claim that, thankfully, in their field of occupational psychology, most such studies are blocked by editorial boards (of journals) and that few clear examples exist. However, the growing pressures on university staff to increase their levels of publication, the existence of publications which the general public might take as more prestigious than is the case, and the tendency for the media to overdramatise 'scientific breakthroughs' make it necessary for applied psychologists to be alert to the quality of research published in their field.

Evidence-based practice

There have been developments which might help to ensure that Anderson et al.'s pragmatic science remains the priority in applied psychology. The most important of these is probably the emphasis given to what is termed *evidence-based practice*. Harper, Mulvey and Robinson (2003: 162) state that:

> Evidence based practice represents an approach to decision-making about the most effective intervention that is transparent and accountable. It focuses on the current best evidence about the effects of particular interventions in both the short and the longer term

The key terms here are 'effective', 'transparent' and 'accountable'. An applied psychologist wishing to implement some kind of programme to improve a situation in the health or educational arenas, for instance, will need to convince other professionals involved, and often the clients for whom it is intended, that the planned intervention is feasible. It will need to be obvious (*transparent*) to them, therefore, why it has been chosen, that it has some chance of succeeding and that it is not impractical, or even dangerous. Psychologists working in the public sector will need to convince managers that the programme is affordable and will produce results that are financially as well as humanly worthwhile. This is the issue of *accountability*, which has risen to prominence in public services since the last decades of the twentieth century; but psychologists working with or in private companies too will need to convince money managers that their planned projects are commercially viable.

In order to justify their planned interventions to those who will fund them or permit them to go ahead, psychologists need to be armed with evidence about *effectiveness*. This means, in a narrow sense, does the programme work? To answer this, it is necessary to gather together as much convincing evidence as possible that such schemes do work, how many they work for and under what circumstances. This burden of evidence is particularly acute where there are alternative interventions being proposed, perhaps by competing providers. Here, of course, we run into a dilemma. On the one hand, the scientific training of psychologists will make them prefer the best intervention based on previous scientific evidence and an argument that the proposed programme is most likely to be effective in the given circumstances. These circumstances are often unique, so that the proposed action is something of an 'experiment'. On the other hand, commercial interests might lean towards a cheaper solution or a 'quick fix' (Briner 1998; Doyle 2003), which is an approach that looks good on the surface, is speedy and economical, and is therefore pleasing to finance managers. However, quick fixes are often hard to evaluate because of their short duration, and it is possible for all concerned to believe that they *must* have done some good, when in fact they are quite ineffective.

What is effective?

Harper et al. (2003) also raise the question of what counts as effectiveness? As far as narrow psychological research methods are concerned, this might be assessed simply in terms of: 'Is there a significant change in behaviour?' and 'Is this effect found consistently?' – the issues of *validity* and *reliability* respectively (see Chapter 11). However, effectiveness might also be assessed, for example, in terms of ethical appropriateness and client satisfaction. To take a crude and melodramatic example, it might be that smoking can be stopped, at least temporarily, by use of electric shocks, but is this ethical and is it in the client's best interests in the long term? A school's academic achievement might be raised by an intense training programme in subjects relevant to SATs (maths, science, English), but what is the effect on children of being deprived of other subjects?

INTERVENTIONS AND THEIR EVALUATION

We have mentioned the fact that applied psychologists carry out interventions and that these are rather like research projects, except that they are aimed primarily at human problem solution. They will also provide valuable research findings once they have been evaluated. Quite often psychologists are involved in an intervention only after it has been carried out; their role is the narrower, but vital one of evaluating the project's outcomes. When they are involved in the creation, implementation and management of an intervention, however, the following stages will commonly occur:

➡ contact with the client;
➡ assessment;
➡ diagnosis or formulation;
➡ design of the intervention programme;
➡ implementation of the intervention programme;
➡ evaluation.

Contact with the client (individual or organisation)

The client may come hesitantly to the psychologist, as when the clinical psychologist acts as therapist. The client may expect a service without question, as in the case of special needs assessment by an educational psychologist. The client might be a company consulting an occupational psychologist on a commercial basis. The psychologist may get involved as a member of a team (of health professionals tackling a public health awareness programme, for instance), through an aspect of their academic research, or because they are already employed by the organisation requiring an intervention.

Assessment

Having discussed and considered with the client(s) the general problem to be tackled, the applied psychologist will set about an initial assessment of the difficulties and issues. This may include:

➡ Discussion of the problem as seen by the client, and consideration of whether there really *is* a problem.
➡ Initial data collection through any of the methods outlined in Chapter 11(interviews, observation, psychological tests, etc.), in order to assess the current situation. This should be a relatively unbiased recording, for example of present levels of job satisfaction or all relevant behaviour patterns of a child with reported behaviour problems.
➡ Analysis of problematic behaviour or systems (for instance, comparison with normal levels of job satisfaction in an equivalent job context; a description of events which have triggered or preceded aggressive or destructive behaviour).

Diagnosis or formulation

It is at this point that the applied psychologist's background in scientific method, psychology and research becomes of crucial importance. Previous similar cases will be compared, and successful treatments or interventions analysed for their relevance to the present case. The *scientific* aspect of the scientist-practitioner model includes the application of a *model* (working theory or preferred approach) and the generation of hypotheses. Having formed such hypotheses, predictions might be made and initial tests of confirmation applied. For instance, the clinical or educational psychologist might predict the circumstances provoking violent behaviour and await the next outbreak for confirmation. The occupational psychologist might consider changes to the level of independence and control given to employees in their jobs, or to different kinds of incentive schemes.

Design of the intervention programme

Here is where the implications of the analysis already carried out are put into practical terms. The psychologist, other team members and the client (in most cases) draw up a specific course of action to be taken, which is intended to resolve a problem or improve a situation. It is very important at this stage to define exactly what will be counted as showing that the intervention 'worked'. This is done by specifying desired or expected *outcomes* – what it is hoped will be achieved. These *must be operationally defined* (see Chapter 11) so that the evaluation stage (see below) can provide clear and unambiguous evidence of improvement and therefore of the success of the intervention. For instance, 'aggression' reduction in a disturbed child might be specified as an 80 per cent drop in the child's hitting rate. Increased athlete motivation might be measured in a percentage of performances above the current average. Worker satisfaction might be measured by questionnaire or by increased positive statements made at weekly appraisal sessions.

Implementation of the intervention programme

Implementation may involve a lot of people in quite different roles. It will almost certainly involve consideration of a number of ethical and practical issues too detailed to discuss thoroughly here. However, some main features of this stage can be listed for reference and further thought. Here, the 'change-agent' is either the psychologist or a team of professionals implementing change; and the 'client group' is made up of those people who are the focus of intended change (e.g. a departmental workforce or some children whose behaviour is difficult to handle). In this sense, the 'client group' could be just one individual, as is often the case in clinical psychology.

Information and consent

The direct client might be an employer or representatives of a health trust, and if the client group is a number of employees or a group of patients, it is important that these people are fully consulted and informed at some stage. In some cases, the client group is too large for this to occur, as when a campaign is launched to increase the reporting of sexually transmitted diseases; but where there is a focused client group, ethical principles require their *informed consent*. It might be problematic, initially, to give *full* information on a project. For example, if a group of employees given a certain type of training know they are expected to do better than a control group, they might just do better anyway, motivated by the expectation. However, participants can be given general information about the project and their likely experience, and should be fully debriefed *after* the intervention is complete. There will also be an extent to which information can be made available to the client group as the project progresses, and this will also apply to other people working or associated with them, such as the family or care staff working with a child with severe learning difficulties.

Ethics

These decisions about information and consent bring in the general issue of research and professional ethics (the BPS *Code of Ethics and Conduct* was mentioned earlier). During the intervention, the applied psychologist needs to keep a check on the level of comfort experienced by participants with what is happening to them. It is not enough to say 'no one complained'. People often find it hard to complain. In some cases, a careful watch must be kept on the extent to which the intervention is resisted or rejected.

Confidentiality of any information gathered is extremely important. If not completely confidential, then where findings are published, participants need to remain anonymous. The psychologist may discover a personal conflict of interest, for instance, an employer's ulterior motive (perhaps to fire staff using intervention findings) may only be revealed when a programme is already under way, where the declared aim was to improve staff morale and efficiency.

Contracts

Partly to answer these ethical points, but also to ensure that all those involved are informed, committed and agreed, the change-agents and client group would usually draw up and agree contracts on all the important stages, terms and principles of the intervention.

Monitoring and feedback

A constant watch must be kept on progress. It must be agreed clearly, in advance, at what point certain aspects of the intervention will be brought to an end, or at what point new measures will be taken or new stages implemented. This depends very strongly on the agreed outcome measures.

Unexpected outcomes

As a result of close monitoring, any unexpected changes in client group behaviour or other outcome measures will need to be dealt with. Children's behaviour might unexpectedly deteriorate because of an unanticipated variable – they might 'rebel' against a scheme of withdrawing privileges, for instance. Workers may collectively slow down production in the presence of 'alien' observers. Appropriate and previously unplanned responses to these outcomes must be produced quickly, while remaining in the spirit of the original model on which the intervention is based.

Evaluation

At some point, a decision must be made about whether the intervention has achieved what it was meant to achieve. Did it work? How well did it work? If outcome measures were clearly specified at the start, these decisions will be much easier. Further very important questions remain. The answers to these serve as valuable means with which to increase general knowledge in the psychologist's area of expertise and to guide solutions to similar problems in the future:

➡ What were the overall *costs* and *benefits* of the intervention?

➡ Were particular individuals helped, and/or was the intervention beneficial to the whole client group?

➡ What implications are there for the *model* on which the intervention was based? Do we have further support or contradiction of the background theory? If the latter, how can further research help clarify any conflict in results?

➡ What was the particular value of the *psychological* aspects of this intervention?

➡ What is the next step for the client (group)? Should the intervention strategy continue? Is there another step with which to make progress?

➡ What *practical and ethical issues* have arisen from which learning has occurred? How will this be *transmitted* to other practitioners and agents of change (e.g. through a journal article)?

AREAS OF OVERLAP IN APPLIED PSYCHOLOGY WORK

As applied psychology increases in importance, as each specialism grows and expands to deal with an ever wider range of problems and issues, it is inevitable that previously distinct applied areas will begin to overlap. For instance, educational psychology was once pretty much confined to the testing and assessment of children in a mainstream educational context. Today, however, educational psychologists will be engaged in the 'statementing' of children with special educational needs. For a long time there has been cooperation with therapeutic services such as the Child Guidance Service. Though this kind of cooperation continues, some educational psychologists today will *themselves* be engaged in the creation, management and operation of therapy programmes with children who are difficult to manage in the school setting. Similarly, clinical psychologists might work inside hospitals alongside health psychologists. Occupational psychologists can be involved in counselling employees, or in health-related programmes such as the provision of stress-reduction programmes within a large company. Counselling psychologists can work with athletes. Forensic psychologists might be involved in prison education programmes, or in what amounts to therapy with offenders, and so on.

THEORETICAL PERSPECTIVES IN APPLIED PSYCHOLOGY

A majority of research in psychology has been carried out within a framework of thinking provided by one of a few overarching schools of psychological thought. These are often known as 'approaches', 'perspectives' or, at times, just 'theories'. Some of the more prevalent of these are behaviourism, the psychoanalytic movement, humanism, the cognitive schools and the emphasis on physiological explanations of human behaviour.

The reader who has tackled no psychology at all before reading this book might like to consult a general textbook in order to become familiar with the major schools of thought in the history of psychology's 100 years or so of development as a theoretical and scientific research discipline. A full description of each perspective is not possible here, but, as with research methods, to appreciate the general outline of the approaches, and to refresh those psychology students who do not wish to consult old notes or other texts (and to save our authors repeating themselves in each chapter!), we have provided a brief outline of major approaches and general theoretical issues in psychology in Chapter 10.

Clinical Psychology

INTRODUCTION

Various definitions of clinical psychology exist, and the choice depends on certain key aspects, some of which will become clear later in the chapter. A generalised definition is that this is the application of psychological theory to human distress, manifested as psychological problems. Therefore, clinical psychology is a profession primarily concerned with the alleviation of psychological problems. Notwithstanding, it can hardly lay claim to being the sole source of support for individuals presenting with psychological problems, and there is a wide variety of practitioners, some of whom are also Chartered Applied Psychologists. Of the non-medical professions primarily concerned with the alleviation of psychological distress, clinical psychologists represent one group – albeit a relatively large one – although it is important to note that counselling and health psychologists also play a vital role in the application of psychological therapy, alongside psychotherapists, counsellors, social workers, specialist nurses (e.g. community psychiatric and learning disability nurses). Indeed, although clinical psychologists possess a wide range of therapeutic skills, their training is not primarily that of a therapist, although many pursue additional post-qualification training in specific therapies, including cognitive behavioural, systemic, existential, psychodynamic and integrative, in addition to those who undertake more detailed specialist training in a particular area of expertise (e.g. clinical neuropsychology).

CLINICAL PSYCHOLOGY IN THE BRITISH PSYCHOLOGICAL SOCIETY (BPS)

Clinical psychology represents the largest single division within the BPS, and arguably constitutes the largest number of Chartered Psychologists holding a Practising Certificate within the United Kingdom. In 2005, those with membership of the Division of Clinical Psychology (DCP) constituted approximately 52 per cent of the entire register of Chartered Psychologists. Not all qualified, or even practising, psychologists in the United Kingdom are members of the BPS, however, and so these figures should be considered with some caution. Nevertheless, it remains true that clinical psychology is a particularly large and significant force within the BPS and represents the largest single applied group of psychologists, with whom most people will have a professional contact.

The DCP has a number of special interest groups and faculties operating within it, including Children and Young people, Learning Disabilities, Sexual Health and HIV, Addictions, Clinical Health Psychology, Eating Disorders and Forensic. As a very influential component, DCP has been actively involved in discussions in the early twenty-first century regarding key legislation about the assessment of *capacity* (the ability by which individuals can enter into agreements), which has very clear implications regarding the ability of people to make critical decisions regarding their future. Similarly, the division has been involved in very long-term discussions surrounding amendments to key mental health legislation operating within the United Kingdom, and particularly that with special reference to people presenting with personality disorders.

PRINCIPLES OF CLINICAL PSYCHOLOGY

Clinical psychologists are, first and foremost, applied psychologists and therefore provide interventions to clients based on psychological theory – for example, how the actor-observer effect influences our attributions about other people's motivations, or cognitive dissonance as a framework to explain the effect of discovering something contrary to our beliefs. They then apply this theory to a range of psychological problems with various therapeutic techniques. Although not dissimilar to the main aim of contemporary mental health work in the UK, clinical psychology is bound by the overriding principle that intervention and clinical practice must be based on:

➡ empirically-tested evidence subjected to peer scrutiny;
➡ an evidence base published in the public domain;
➡ the process of theory or practice development being credible and open to replication;

➡ collaboratively generated hypotheses about client problems;
➡ empowerment of clients.

In addition to this, clinical psychologists may work directly with clients, within systems, indirectly through others or by teaching, training or research activity, which covers a wide span of activities. Clinical psychologists are also bound by a strict professional code of conduct, and, while not all qualified clinical psychologists are Chartered with the BPS, this remains a very self-critical profession. In the late twentieth and early twenty-first century, the process of *reflective practice* has become an increasing element of professional life for the clinical psychologist. Reflective practice is a way of approaching psychological practice; it is an active process by which we attempt to consider what it is about our own experience and values that might explain why we react in certain ways. This can occur at various stages throughout life, but for clinical psychologists the crucial element is that through becoming aware of our own experience, we can begin to consider how this may influence our work with clients. Training and practice now include significant elements of peer assessment and development, as this enables standards and working practices to be considered by our peers, particularly those qualities that add to or detract from effective clinical work. Developing reflective practice necessarily involves learning through experience (both personal and professional) and then considering what has happened, how we reacted to it and, most importantly, exactly what has been learned. Although very diverse in terms of processes, the core theme of reflective practice remains the same: examination of experience, awareness of reactions and learning, changing our ways of behaving, and considering how this influences our deeply held values. Although breaches of professional etiquette and conduct do take place, these are relatively rare among clinical psychologists.

How is clinical psychology different from psychiatry?

Although often confused by clients and their carers, clinical psychology and psychiatry are very distinct indeed. The primary difference between the two is that psychiatry is a branch of medicine, so practitioners are medically qualified prior to undertaking training in psychiatry, whereas clinical psychology is a branch of applied social science, and therefore practitioners have all received a basic training in psychology and social science methodology prior to undertaking training in applied clinical psychology. The distinction between psychiatry and psychology does not end here, however, as psychiatrists currently act as the legally responsible medical officer for those clients under their care, and are able to prescribe medication or invoke legal powers of compulsory (and largely medical) treatment and detention under the Mental Health Act (1983). There has been considerable interest in the revised Mental Health Bill (2005), under which clinical psychologists would likely be granted a range of new legislative powers, particularly in respect to compulsory treatment, under the clinical supervisor role. The clinical supervisor is a new concept that is unique to the proposed revision, and replaces the existing role of 'registered medical practitioners' in decision-making regarding compulsory 'treatment'. The proposed bill suggested that the clinical supervisor would be responsible for the delivery of care in conjunction with a multidisciplinary team. This means that clinical psychologists would potentially be placed in a lead role regarding the supervision of clients in the community, whether considered 'potentially dangerous' or not. The new bill also involved a range of very significant changes that tended to emphasise protection of the public from aggression and this was the cause of considerable opposition. At the time of writing (2006), the proposed bill has not progressed and therefore this distinction (the compulsory power of detention and 'treatment') remains a very fundamental one between the two professions.

Some clinical psychologists describe psychiatry in very negative terms, concluding that it represents a very fundamental aspect of state control (e.g. Szasz 1960) or that it is primarily concerned with biological and reductionist models of mental health. Others tend to view each as separate components of a comprehensive and multidisciplinary approach to mental health difficulties in which psychiatry represents a medical option, and, increasingly, psychiatrists are developing a very sophisticated understanding of clinical psychology.

WHAT A CLINICAL PSYCHOLOGIST DOES

Following the closure programmes of large hospitals and the development of community mental health care services in the 1980s (although recommendations for such services date back to the early 1970s!), services have tended to form into multidisciplinary teams (MDT). Anyone experienced in working within an MDT framework will be aware of the significant challenges and benefits inherent in this model. Initially, these teams comprised the same professionals who had worked in hospitals and it was simply that the setting had changed. In many cases, the goals and objectives of these teams were not discussed or agreed in any formal way. The MDT has become the dominant way in which care for people with complex needs is delivered throughout the UK. Interestingly, research undertaken by Bebbington, Johnson and Thornicroft (2002) on the use of such teams has identified that these are often very dependent on local elements (e.g. established practice among professionals, available resources and cultural elements) and not based on clear guidelines or nationally accepted standards and practice. (Rather ironically, empirical research into the impact of this change to the community teams is very limited.) With so many different forms of practice and delivery, it is particularly difficult to assess the impact of different models. Perhaps an issue of greater importance is the fact that there is very little meaningful input into the design, practice or even recruitment of professionals into these teams from those people for whom the services are intended.

Increasingly, a role for the clinical psychologist has been to introduce theoretical psychological frameworks to enable the teams to understand the subtle psychological processes that operate on the teams themselves (e.g. social psychology theories about group processes and decision-making). Some researchers (e.g. Brallier and Tsukuda 2002) have argued that it is essential to consider the structure and processes of teams in order for them to deliver a service to clients effectively. If the various professionals have a very different understanding of how they fit together or what their respective roles are, this reflects in the response of the team and will undermine how effectively they react to client needs. Similarly, if there is disagreement about who can make key decisions about care, or how these decisions are made, risk and responses become vague – even unsafe.

Clinical psychologists have developed unique roles within teams, as therapist, counsellor, scientist-practitioner, applied psychologist, supervisor and researcher, and it is possible to consider three general models of clinical psychology practice: the independent practitioner, the consultant practitioner and the consultant supervisor.

The independent practitioner

In this model of practice, the clinical psychologist only accepts specific referrals to work with clients – primarily from psychiatrists or GPs, although sometimes from the client, or even organisations – based on an identified problem, such as anxiety, depression or difficulties associated with childhood sexual abuse. As such, this model of practice is to offer individual sessions to clients and provide a report or summary to the source of the referral. This model has tended to reflect more strictly psychotherapeutic approaches, often found in independent practice as opposed to National Health Service (NHS) based services. As this model is usually only open to referrals from other sources (GPs, psychiatrists, etc.), it is sometimes viewed as restrictive, given the full range of skills and techniques that clinical psychologists have at their disposal. Also, this model of clinical practice tends to have a one-to-one client basis, rather than being within a multidisciplinary team, and therefore it can be an isolated existence. Finally, this model does not provide a broader perspective, which is gained through input from a wider set of opinions drawn from colleagues with different experiences, perspectives and relationships with the client.

The consultant practitioner

This model of practice involves working as part of a specialist team of health professionals, offering advice on referrals from a wide variety of sources and engaging in joint decision-making about the choice of intervention and the key clinician best able to address these needs. As such, practice tends to involve a considerable amount of individual therapeutic work, usually alone, but also with colleagues from different disciplines. This model often tends to operate in community teams, including more specialised services such as Personality Disorder Services or Assertive Outreach, which helps people with severe mental health problems to manage daily life at home.

The consultant supervisor

In this model, the clinical psychologist also tends to work as part of a multidisciplinary team, but provides a more central role in the decision-making about the appropriateness of referrals and requests for assessments by the team. Within this framework, the dominant model of delivery involves care based around agreed areas of responsibility (for example, daily living skills, medication, psychological therapy, risk assessment, etc.) and a package of intervention agreed with the client. Key workers are allocated to be the point of contact between the client and their care team. This allocation is based on either a 'best fit' of the person (which may be influenced by a range of issues, including gender or ethnic group) or the professional (which may reflect the nature of difficulties, including psychological difficulties or daily living problems), and depends somewhat on the structure of the specific team. Within this model, the clinical psychologist will often provide or organise systems for clinical supervision to other professionals in the team. This supervision enables careful consideration of the entire process of care, allowing professionals to change their input depending on a variety of factors – for example, if a client is beginning to react differently, or the practitioner is experiencing something in his or her own life that may influence practice, or there is a particular aspect of psychological theory that may assist in the work. This often concentrates on the way in which the team works with the client, and the clinical psychologist will usually provide a lead role in the problem formulation and measurement of the effectiveness of the intervention. In addition to this role, clinical psychologists tend to have an individual caseload of clients who are highly complex, and they are often found working with offenders who have mental health problems (Forensic Mental Health) and children and young people with mental health problems (Child and Adolescent Mental Health Services).

What sort of psychological problems do clinical psychologists deal with?

Although clinical psychologists work within the psychiatric system and encounter a wide variety of psychological problems, it is beyond the scope of this chapter to provide a comprehensive introduction to abnormal psychology, and interested readers are directed to the introductory text, *Abnormal Psychology* (Oltmanns and Emery 2006).

Psychological models of mental health and ill-health differ significantly from psychiatric diagnosis – hence the use of psychological *formulation* (explained later in the chapter). Nevertheless, it is useful to consider the two dominant diagnostic systems currently employed by psychiatry, known respectively as the *International Classification of Diseases*, 10th Edition (ICD-10) and the *Diagnostic and Statistical Manual of Mental Disorders*, 4th Edition (DSM-IV).

The World Health Organization (WHO) assumed responsibility for a classification system originally conceived in the 1850s, known as the *International List of Causes of Death*. This system is now referred to as the *International Classification of Diseases* (ICD) and was developed in 1948, with the most current version (version 10) being endorsed by the 43rd World Health Assembly in May 1990. This version was introduced into WHO member states from 1994 onwards and acts as an international standard for diagnostic classification, including psychiatric symptoms. It also provides statistical data regarding prevalence and incidence of various disorders.

The ICD-10 contains 22 chapters, of which Chapter 5 refers specifically to mental and behavioural disorders (classification numbers F00–F99), and this is subsequently divided into the following groups:

- F00–F09 Organic, including symptomatic mental disorders;
- F10–F19 Mental and behavioural disorders due to psychoactive substance use;
- F20–F29 Schizophrenia, schizotypal and delusional disorders;
- F30–F39 Mood [affective] disorders;
- F40–F49 Neurotic, stress-related and somatoform disorders;
- F50–F59 Behavioural syndromes associated with physiological disturbances and physical factors;
- F60–F69 Disorders of adult personality and behaviour;
- F70–F79 Mental retardation;
- F80–F89 Disorders of psychological development;
- F90–F98 Behavioural and emotional disorders with onset usually occurring in childhood and adolescence;
- F99 Unspecified mental disorders.

Alternatively, the DSM-IV is published by the American Psychiatric Association and forms the basis of the psychiatric diagnostic structure used in the USA. DSM-IV is more specific than the ICD-10 and, since its first publication in 1952, it has gone through five revisions, with the next due for publication around 2010.

The DSM was originally developed to create a more objective diagnostic system to enable psychiatric research, as there was considerable variation in both the frequency and the nature of diagnosis during the 1950s. Both the criteria and the classification system had been defined through a process of consultation committee meetings, involving a wide range of mental health professionals (although these were primarily psychiatrists). As such, the system has been criticised as being a subjective representation of primarily biological models of mental illness.

In its earliest conceptualisation, DSM was influenced primarily by psychodynamic thinking, although by the 1980s this was abandoned in favour of a biomedical model that introduced the clear distinction between 'normal' and 'abnormal'. The DSM also abandoned theory relating to psychiatric 'illness', as it was not considered necessary to provide an aetiology for mental disorders, but merely an expansion from the research diagnostic criteria that had been developed in the 1970s. In its present structure, DSM is separated into five axes, ranging from the major mental disorders, developmental disorders and learning disabilities (Axis I), through underlying pervasive or personality conditions, including mental retardation (Axis II), to non-psychiatric medical conditions (Axis III), social functioning and impact of symptoms (Axis IV) and, finally, clinical assessment of functioning (Axis V). As such, common Axis I disorders might include depression, anxiety, schizophrenia and bipolar (manic) depression, whereas Axis II disorders include personality disorders and mental retardation (learning disabilities).

It is noteworthy that a central tenet of both DSM and ICD is the distinction between the so-called neurotic and psychotic syndromes, of which the psychoses are generally considered to represent more restrictive disorders, associated with an impaired capacity to discriminate 'real' and 'imagined' experiences. Individuals with psychosis suffer a major disruption in thinking processes and emotional responses. In addition, the *psychoses* are associated with a gradual decline in functioning. These are often referred to by more specific names, such as *schizophrenia*, *manic depression* and *delusional disorders*, and are characterised by periods of hallucination and unusual or irrational reasoning, and at the more extreme end can be associated with long-term attention and memory problems. As such, these are often described as severe and enduring mental health problems.

Box 1

Schizophrenia is a psychiatric diagnosis, characterised by impairments in the perception or expression of reality, and by significant social or occupational dysfunction. A person experiencing schizophrenia is typically characterised as demonstrating thought disorder and as experiencing delusions or auditory hallucinations.

Manic depression (or bipolar depression) is associated with mood swings, from 'highs' of excessive energy and elation, to 'lows' of utter despair and lethargy. At times this is also associated with strong delusions or hallucinations that can have a severe impact on daily functioning.

Conversely, the *neurotic* conditions tend to be characterised by a restriction of the individual's ability to function, but without distortion of basic reality discrimination. These include the anxiety disorders (agoraphobia, *a fear of being in open and usually public spaces*, generalised anxiety disorder and panic attacks), along with adverse reactions to life-threatening events (post-traumatic stress disorder), so-called neurotic depression and reactive depression.

Box 2

Agoraphobia is an anxiety disorder consisting of the fear of experiencing a difficult or embarrassing situation from which you cannot escape. This may be associated with panic attacks when trapped or out of control, and, in some cases, those suffering from the condition may be confined to specific parts of their homes. Agoraphobia is characterised by extreme sensitisation to physiological sensations, which are then interpreted as an indication of impending panic.

General anxiety disorder (GAD) is an anxiety disorder characterised by excessive and uncontrollable worry about everyday things. As with all anxiety disorders, the worry is disproportionate to either the source or the probability of the feared event occurring, and interferes with everyday functioning.

Post-traumatic stress disorder (PTSD) refers to a reactive condition that may occur after experiencing (or witnessing) life-threatening events. PTSD is characterised by a difficulty in adjusting to such situations even after the passage of time, and this may even worsen without therapeutic input. PTSD is often associated with reliving an experience, with flashbacks and sleep disorders, and can significantly impair daily functioning.

Reactive depression is a depression that is triggered by a traumatic, difficult or stressful event, after which people will feel low, anxious, irritable and even angry. Reactive depression can also follow a prolonged period of stress, sometimes beginning after the stress has ceased.

Neurotic depression is a depression that is not always triggered by an upsetting or stressful event and is sometimes called the 'common cold of mental illness'. This is often associated with clear physical symptoms (weight change, tiredness, sleep problems), along with low mood, concentration problems and low self-esteem.

In addition to these, most classification systems acknowledge organic disorders, including neurological damage that is gradual (e.g. Alzheimer's disease and dementia) or acquired (e.g. alcohol-related problems such as Korsakoff's syndrome); also included are developmental disorders such as learning disabilities and the autistic spectrum disorders.

Historically, clinical psychologists would spend considerable time developing treatment interventions that were specific to particular disorders or met the requirements of specific services. These were often developed to reflect broad classifications around these distinctions, for example, adult mental health, learning disabilities, child and services for older adults. Indeed, there were also services that were sub-specialisms of these, such as psychiatric rehabilitation services, which aimed to enable people with serious and enduring mental health problems to return to the community and live more independent lives; and primary care services, which worked with referrals from GPs to provide services to people outside the traditional 'psychiatric' umbrella, but within adult mental health, offering psychological services to people with severe and enduring mental health problems or neurotic disorders.

What is normal and what is abnormal?

As previously noted, it is not the purpose of this chapter to provide an overview of abnormal psychology, but it would be remiss not to consider some of the major debates within the field of psychiatry. The most obvious of these relates to concepts of normality versus abnormality. Our definitions of normality acquire a veil of scientific credibility when recourse is made to statistical judgements, and therefore those aspects considered too far outside the average range may be referred to as 'abnormal'. But when does eccentric or highly individual behaviour and attitude constitute an abnormality that warrants description and definition as a mental illness? Unusual methods of verbal communication may simply be that – unusual communication – and not necessarily suggestive of mental health difficulties. More importantly, the description of psychological features or symptoms indicative of the underlying pathology or disease cannot necessarily be considered to represent evidence of any hypothesised underlying disorder. In themselves, these symptoms represent the only evidence for such a disorder, so does the absence of such symptoms necessarily indicate that the disorder no longer exists? The effect of having such systems diagnosed as 'abnormal' is usually very traumatic.

Despite the clear need for sensitive psychiatric services, the experience of becoming an in-patient remains very distressing and has a psychological impact at a very fundamental level. Indeed, Jackson et al. (2005) showed that pertinent in-groups and out-groups for in-patient service users mainly centred around the context of being an in-patient (being 'unwell', 'victimised' or 'not as bad as them'), but were also influenced by non-mental health service group membership ('like you professionals' or 'ordinary'), and their desire to return to the non-psychiatric client group, suggesting that one part of the psychological impact of 'becoming a mental health in-patient' is that it challenges the sense of self by associating the individual with membership of a low-desirability group.

User empowerment

As models of mental health have evolved, services for people with mental health problems have developed a greater emphasis on the involvement of those people receiving such services. As such, service users have become an important source of consultation in the development of new initiatives, and a greater emphasis is placed on the notion of 'doing with', in collaboration, as opposed to 'doing to', under duress. The notion of user empowerment encompasses this principle, and is a broad description of methods for enabling those who have traditionally not been able to make themselves heard, or who have simply been ignored, to gain access to a platform for expression and influence.

Interested readers might wish to consider the work of Marius Romme and Sonia Escher (2000), who questioned the central assumptions about the abnormality of hallucination experience, suggesting that many people experience such 'hallucinations', yet do not become engaged with psychiatric services and are not considered 'odd', 'dangerous' or even 'unwell'. The work of Romme and Escher inspired the development of the **hearing voices network**, a self-help group of people previously diagnosed with schizophrenia, providing an alternative explanation for their experiences, and a network of support and advocacy for those people traditionally disempowered by psychiatric services. Similarly, within the field of learning disability, the increasing power of clients has systematically changed the language used to describe people (people with Down's syndrome used to be referred to as 'mongols', and the terms 'cretin', 'moron' and 'imbecile' were originally psychological terms used to describe people whose IQ was estimated to be lower than average); it has also challenged highly restrictive service provision. It should be noted, however, that conditions for some clients with learning disabilities remain woefully inadequate and characterised by a brutalising treatment. It is shocking that in the early twenty-first century we can still find examples of maltreatment of the most vulnerable people in society. Buddock Learning Disability Hospital in Cornwall was the subject of such a scandal in 2006.

Pathologising normal behaviour

Another significant issue to be considered when discussing the concept of mental ill-health is that of pathologising certain behaviours, beliefs or legitimate emotional reactions to aversive life conditions (e.g. classifying non-compliant behaviour as symptomatic of a more generalised psychological disorder when this behaviour occurs in an undervalued group). An example would be young men from minority ethnic groups being suspicious of the motives of predominantly white practitioners and this being considered as evidence of 'paranoia', or considering that sexual orientation is indicative of an enduring mental health problem. Indeed, homosexuality was considered to be a mental illness that required treatment into the 1970s. Feminist psychologists routinely commented on the process by which women's emotional reactions to their political and domestic status may more readily have accounted for the overprescription of medications for anxiety and depression, as opposed to considering any underlying psychiatric vulnerability. For example, is it really evidence for a mental health problem if women present with low mood and lack of motivation to undertake domestic tasks such as hoovering and dusting, or does this reflect genuine dissatisfaction with the division of labour, economic status and lack of support from male partners?

More recently, increasing controversy has centred round the development of 'personality disorder', and particularly the notion of dangerous and severe personality disorder.

Box 3 Michael Stone

Figure 2.1 Michael Stone
Michael Stone, who had a long history of drug addiction and violent behaviour, was convicted of the murders of Lin and Megan Russell in 1996. He was diagnosed with a severe personality disorder. Five days before attacking his victims, Stone told his community psychiatric nurse that he wanted to kill someone. This case has provided impetus for reforms of the Mental Health Act (1983), particularly the proposal to allow people like Stone to be detained indefinitely *before* they commit any crimes. In addition to this, the increasing influence of personality disorder as a diagnostic category has shaped the development of many specialist services in the community, to provide treatment for individuals deemed to be suffering from disorders that manifest in self-defeating or 'out-of-control' behaviour.

In conjunction with this, a number of similar descriptions have been applied to very young children, the most contentious being oppositional defiant disorder (ODD), which is described as being seen characteristically in children below the age of 9 or 10 years, and is defined by the *presence* of markedly defiant, disobedient, provocative behaviour, and by the *absence* of more severe dissocial or aggressive acts that violate the law or the rights of others. It is important to note that the frequency of the observed behaviour has to be in excess of that expected by the child's peer group.

The concept of personality disorder has been subjected to some criticism, as an oversimplification of the complexity of what psychological researchers have spent many years defining, and is over-reliant on the influence of trait theories of personality (e.g. enduring and fundamental aspects of personal style) in favour of state theories of personality (e.g. reacting to environmental factors). A particularly cynical observer might note that the dimensions used to describe personality disorder are all behaviours found to be toxic or obnoxious to others; behaviours that are ignored are those that are equally dysfunctional for the individual performing them, but are pleasant, even helpful, to the recipient. As such, the concept of personality disorder may represent simply a very eloquent, technical, but nonetheless value-laden, way to call someone names.

In relation to the mental disorders, psychiatric diagnosis experiences a similar difficulty, particularly with regard to the definition of a 'delusional belief'. This is often described as a belief that is not logically consistent, yet is maintained in the face of contradictory evidence, and often associated with strange behavioural routines – for example, drawing every curtain in the house to stop the police spying, even though no police have ever been sighted near the house. Cognitive psychology has provided extensive evidence to suggest that human beings are remarkably poor at understanding the nature of statistical evaluation of probability, often demonstrating significant biases in reasoning. Many fine examples of such biases can be found in the explanations offered by people using so-called lucky charms, or those repeatedly using a special set of numbers in the national lottery, but it hardly seems reasonable to describe these as 'indicative of delusional behaviour'. One of the features inherent in the diagnosis of schizophrenia is that the sufferer is described as having little or no insight into mental health difficulties. As such, those people who do not accept that they may be suffering from mental illness can be described as presenting with no insight into their problems, and it is only when they begin to acknowledge that they have a mental illness that they can be deemed to be moving towards recovery. It is not difficult to see the circular logic involved in this conceptualisation, and it will come as no surprise that this is often cited by user groups as primary evidence of ways in which psychiatry can be abused and used to subjugate those who simply 'do not fit in'.

Although clinical psychologists may vary in their opinions regarding these issues and debates, it is generally accepted that systems of psychiatric classification alone are highly problematic, and therefore it is necessary to undertake a more specific psychological assessment in order to understand exactly which aspects are associated with most distress and to enable clients to develop a method by which they can understand their experiences and generate alternative ways of coping with them.

Race, gender and sexuality issues in clinical psychology and diagnosis

Race and ethnicity cannot be separated from issues of diagnosis and, as highlighted in the previous section, psychology has a vital role in raising awkward questions relating to the involvement of power in psychiatric diagnosis. In the mid 1990s, Cochrane and Sashidharan (1995) found black and ethnic minority in-patient admissions to be significantly higher than those for the white population. Despite various theoretical attempts, it is not possible to explain these differences as a result of biological differences or as the product of immigration. Similarly, black men are over-represented among those diagnosed with severe and enduring mental illness and tend to be over-medicated (Fernando, Ndegwa and Wilson 1998). Sadly, very little research has been conducted into the long-term effects of racism on the development of severe and enduring mental health problems, even with regard to the impact of racism on admission.

Research in psychiatry and clinical psychology tends to focus on problems, and, consequently, exploring 'problems' as these are 'observed' in particular groups. Approaching research from such a position is not free from bias, and it may tell us as much about deep-rooted biases in the world of psychiatry and clinical psychology as it does about particular 'problems' in specific communities. For example, the low rate of neurotic conditions within the Asian community is often reframed as a cultural 'problem'. Indeed, cultural practices are blamed for stopping individuals presenting for intervention for psychological problems, and it is argued that the under-representation actually indicates a resistance by the Asian community to engage with services, therefore covering up significant mental health problems. Surely it is also possible that strong community customs and structures may serve as a protective factor against the *development* of such problems? Another important issue to consider is the fact that western-based psychological therapy is firmly rooted in individualism, with an emphasis on independence and self-actualisation, whereas other cultures emphasise relationships with others, such as family duties. Approaching a problem from a Eurocentric, psychiatric disease model is only one way to consider the issues, and will not necessarily result in appropriate conclusions or theories.

Although noted within the BPS as a clear difficulty, the percentage of clinical psychologists from ethnic minorities remains very small indeed; applications to the Clearing House for Clinical Training in 2006 suggest that 91 per cent of applications were received from people recording their ethnic origin as white (Clearing House in Clinical Psychology). The slow rate of change remains a concern, as clinical psychology remains, essentially, a white professional group.

In the case of gender composition, the ratio of women to men applying for clinical training is approximately 5.6:1, and this ratio is preserved in applicants who are successful. While this represents a positive improvement in equal opportunities from that reported by Nicholson (1992), there is still considerable distance to cover, and women remain subject to long-standing gender-based expectations and restrictions, particularly in respect to their careers (e.g. despite the considerable over-representation of women to men in clinical psychology, many work part-time to support young children, unlike their male counterparts). Clinical psychology remains a very high-status profession, in which competition for places and jobs is high. Sadly, this means that it is a career choice likely to emphasise the contradictory aspects of womanhood and career.

Clinical psychology has a past based in the less savoury elements of deep-seated homophobia, particularly evident in the use of aversive behavioural methods to 'treat' homosexuality during the 1960s and 1970s. In previous years, people presenting with various difficulties associated with sexual orientation might have expressed a desire to change what was perceived as deviant. Consequently, clinical psychologists might have been prepared to offer 'treatment' without question, as a motivation to change what was considered 'deviant' was entirely understandable. Indeed, the very notion that sexual orientation is open to behavioural intervention now seems both outrageous and somewhat silly, aside from the ethical difficulties this raises.

Stages in working with individual cases

Reaching the clinical psychologist

There are several ways in which an individual might access the services of a clinical psychologist working in primary mental health services, such as those for people with neurotic or depressive symptoms, and those for individuals with learning or developmental disabilities. Indeed, it is possible for individual members of the public to refer directly to most clinical psychologists, although NHS services generally require a referral from a general practitioner, psychiatrist or community mental health team. In addition to these routes, clinical psychologists are also employed by charities and social services departments, which might also act as a means of referral. Gaining access to more specialised clinical psychology services, such as neuropsychology or clinical forensic psychology, requires a more specialised referral, usually from a psychiatrist.

Increasingly, clinical psychology services are available by independent referral, and it is also possible for individuals to access the British Psychological Society for details of the particular skills and availability of clinical psychologists who offer independent work in the individual's local area. For example, a client may refer with a difficulty in relationships, perhaps related to concerns about stress or satisfaction with their role within the relationship. Some clients may experience particular difficulties with sexual performance or very specific reactions to situations that they have become concerned about. In severe cases, this may relate to problems associated with excessive behaviours such as substance use, or recurrent thoughts that have become troubling.

At this stage, it is usual practice for the clinical psychology service, or the individual clinical psychologist, to provide an introductory letter that will explain the process of the referral and provide times for which a meeting might be arranged. The following gives a basic outline of the typical process involved in meeting with a clinical psychologist.

Initial assessment

At the first interview, the clinical psychologist will introduce themselves and provide a brief introduction to the work of a clinical psychologist, and outline how this differs from other professionals. It is during this initial session that the clinical psychologist draws on the most basic of interpersonal skills in order to establish rapport with the client. This requires active listening and core counselling skills, to create an empathetic environment in which clients can discuss difficulties, which may have become debilitating and are often a source of great embarrassment. The primary goal is to ascertain whether the client is presenting with a difficulty that can be ethically and appropriately addressed through psychological therapies. For example, individuals may wish to discuss feelings of concern that partners will reject them or perceive them as not worth bothering with, or they may become increasingly anxious or upset that they will be unable to satisfy a sexual partner.

More detailed and structured consideration of the intensity, frequency and duration of the difficulties might reveal that the anxiety generated about a potential problem is the real issue or, indeed, that the responses under consideration are perfectly usual given the situations people find themselves in. It may be the case that carers (of young children or people with learning disabilities, for instance) approach clinical psychologists, requesting intervention for behaviour they consider to be problematic, but assessment might reveal that it is the reaction of the carer that exacerbates the difficulty, and therefore intervention is most appropriately directed towards the carer, as opposed to the original target of the referral. A person with learning disabilities described by carers as 'challenging' and 'a handful', for example, on more detailed observation of frequency and intensity, may be noted to present with little or no difficulty, or indeed interaction, and then only be considered 'a challenge' when carers are required to engage with them and find that they cannot complete other tasks which they have prioritised above interaction with the client.

At this stage, the clinical psychologist will often ask a considerable number of detailed questions regarding the intensity, frequency and duration of the difficulty, and may require clients or carers to complete records of behaviour, thoughts or emotions. In addition, the clinical psychologist may decide that further information regarding the nature of the presentation would be of benefit, and therefore will request that clients complete assessments of personality and social functioning, key emotional responses or symptom checklists. In certain situations, a clinical psychologist may undertake additional and more structured formal psychometric assessments of intellectual functioning or key aspects of cognition, such as memory, to assist in the overall assessment of the difficulty.

Formulation of the problem

Given that clinical psychology is an applied social science, it is essential that practitioners apply generalised psychological models and theories to their interventions. As a consequence, the *formulation* of an individual's problem forms the basis of clinical psychology practice, providing an interface between theory and practice and embodying the principles of the scientist-practitioner model (see Chapter 1).

Formulation is a key skill of the clinical psychologist, but the subject of very little research or agreement. Essentially, a formulation is a way of understanding problems from a psychological perspective, including some rationale about how this has developed and been maintained, and, therefore, how an intervention might reduce any distress or interference in the future. For most clients coming to a psychologist, their problems appear to be a confusing mess of different elements that undermine and interfere with life and seem to occur without any reasonable explanation.

One way of understanding psychological formulations is that, as these are based on established psychological research, they reflect an attempt to test the predictions of the theory by applying it to a specific problem. It is a test of the skills of the clinical psychologist to make a formulation as simple and straightforward as possible, and include only that which is necessary to explain the client's unique problems. As a consequence, a formulation must be hypothetical and remain open to change when, or if, new information comes to light. For example, an initial formulation about someone presenting with sleep and digestive difficulties, and an excessive preoccupation about a relationship ending, might first be formulated to be overly concerned with potential negative consequences and therefore spending too much time ruminating over a fear that their relationship will end. On gathering more information, however, it may become apparent that the individual has long-standing concerns about their body image and has expended huge efforts to achieve a 'nearly perfect' body. The distorted perception they hold in regard to their own body may be linked to a global evaluation of themselves as fundamentally unappealing, and this might act as a filter, detecting any incidents of perceived 'rejection' or 'dissatisfaction' by partners, regardless of the reality of these perceptions.

Executed well, psychological formulation enables the clinical psychologist to differentiate between origin and any secondary aspects, which can reduce the perceived complexity of experience for the client. This often involves identifying similarities between an apparently wide range of diverse symptoms and problems, and making observations as to the function that these might serve. For example, if a parent is exhausted by a child who has been behaving in a particularly challenging way, there is a temptation to relax and leave the child to their own devices when all is quiet. This results in 'peace and quiet' for the parent, but may actually reinforce very noisy and challenging behaviour, as attention from the parent is very desirable for the child. Similarly, the fear invoked by appearing to be foolish may be sufficient for a client to avoid going into new social situations. By avoiding these, however, the dread of committing such a gaffe is strengthened, and the thought of happening upon a new situation becomes terrifying in and of itself. By formulating this problem, it may be possible to understand that a process of attribution of the causes of such distress (Seligman 1975) results in the development of a belief that others find them foolish and that the emotional consequence of being considered as such is linked to a core self-evaluation that they are, indeed, foolish. The discovery of this by others would be catastrophic, as it would mean that no one would want to socialise with them and they would be left alone. Thus, the different elements of the problem can be identified: the self-evaluation of foolishness, the fear of being alone, without friends and essential social contact, the attribution of negative evaluation by others and then the process of reinforcing the fear by avoidance. It may also be necessary to consider where the core evaluations originated and how the social systems in which the individual lives have further reinforced these and similar thoughts. A variety of different aspects of psychological theory can be introduced, such as attribution theory, cognitive psychology and reasoning biases, arousal theory, behavioural and reinforcement theory, and then a rationale for challenging the beliefs in therapy sessions, encouraging the client to practise methods to reduce anxiety, thereby reducing avoidance and preventing the problem from escalating, and agreeing on safe ways to change thoughts, behaviour and emotions for the future.

Formulation allows the clinical psychologist to prioritise those elements which can be dealt with first and will often enable client and psychologist to agree a strategy for intervention that is both obvious and transparent. In addition, formulation-based intervention enables the clinical psychologist to predict how the client will typically react to key situations, and therefore to identify potential pitfalls during intervention (e.g. seeing mistakes as catastrophes or underplaying achievements). Formulation, therefore, is a collaborative process between the client and the clinical psychologist, in which cause-effect and action-consequence can be separated and understood to identify what needs to change (e.g. a specific element such as thinking or behaving, or the magnitude of this) in order to reduce distress. Formulation enables clinical psychologists to make predictions about the process of change, and also provides a method for explaining why change is not taking place.

> ## Box 4 Ten tests to check a psychological formulation
>
> 1 Does it make theoretical sense?
> 2 Does it fit with the evidence gathered during the assessment?
> 3 Does it account for predisposing, precipitating and maintaining factors?
> 4 Does it make sense to peers?
> 5 Is it possible to generate predictions about the client's thoughts, emotions or behaviours?
> 6 Can you test these predictions by safe experimentation?
> 7 Does the past history fit?
> 8 Does it suggest an intervention and does this progress as the theory would predict?
> 9 Can it be used to identify future sources of risk or difficulty for this person?
> 10 Are there important factors left unexplained?

What is the difference between diagnosis and formulation?

Psychiatric diagnosis is fundamentally concerned with symptom-based models, relying on correlations between individual cases. It tends to concentrate on the individual's current symptoms, making predictions (prognoses) based on hypothetical model cases (e.g. 'classical depression'). As such, diagnosis is frequently not based on sound scientific methodology, nor is it dependent on a theory; instead, it is collected from a set of assumptions about cases that correlate, often considered as 'symptoms'. As an alternative to this, formulation is essentially 'ideographic', that is, it is designed around the unique presentation of the individual. It can account for the original onset, maintenance and future likelihood of any given presentation or set of symptoms. At its most effective level, formulation should draw on considered and established psychological research, so that it remains fundamentally theoretical in nature.

For many people experiencing psychological distress, the most fundamental difficulties are related to their apparent inability to make sense of what is often a confusing morass of symptoms. Psychiatric diagnosis can provide an instant 'explanation' of these, but may offer a longer-term problem, as it represents a label or a very disheartening future prognosis. On the other hand, a coherent and collaborative psychological formulation of these difficulties provides a theoretically guided method for structuring the information concerning an individual problem, and consequently a logical and coherent basis on which someone can make sense of their experience. Although often considered to be an empowering experience, the limited research available suggests that the psychological formulation may present a challenge (Chadwick, Williams and Mackenzie 2003), perhaps because it implies the need for individuals to change themselves, elements of the way they understand the world or the way they relate to other people.

Given that formulation is central to the work of clinical psychology, it might seem surprising that so little published work exists within the clinical psychology literature regarding methodology, impact or efficacy of such a core skill. Indeed, the available empirical evidence to suggest that interventions are demonstrably better where these are formulation-based is limited, and this remains largely an a priori assumption. From the limited literature available, individualised treatments based on unique formulations appear to be little better than off-the-shelf, 'standardised' treatments (Emmelkamp, Bowman and Blaauw 1994; Jacobson et al. 1989; Schulte 1997; Schulte et al. 1992). In the financially driven environment of health provision, it is hard to justify the luxury of a bespoke intervention plan, specifically designed to meet the needs of the individual client, if there is a readily available treatment manual that contains a step-by-step method to treat the disorder. The absence of thorough empirical studies on the efficacy of individual psychological formulation versus application of a generalised model does little to promote the value of a key clinical psychology skill.

Intervention

Following on from the formulation, the clinical psychologist devises an intervention strategy, designed to target key aspects of the difficulty and therefore reduce the subjective suffering of the individual. Sometimes formulations need to address wider elements in the life of the individual and will consequently include the family or social system within which the individual lives. Clinical psychologists introduce aspects of the psychological theory and research, and blend this with key therapeutic skills intended to maximise the likelihood of positive change. Although most clinical psychologists are broadly *multimodal* (e.g. they will have a variety of therapeutic models on which they can draw), they may favour one particular orientation over another, and this will form the basis of their intervention strategy. It is not unusual for clinical psychologists to involve clients in significant amounts of self-directed work, often referred to as 'homework'. Similarly, in the case of the client's wider social structure, the clinical psychologist may direct family, carers or other professionals working with the client to change the ways that they have become used to using in response to the individual.

In the case of working with complex systems, such as those found in residential accommodation or nursing homes, the perceived challenges posed by particular clients may actually reflect differences in the ways in which groups of carers respond to particular problems. For example, it may be the case that an individual with an alcohol-related dementia such as Korsakoff's syndrome, where memory and the acquisition of new skills are severely impaired, presents with aggressive behaviour only at certain times, which may have been explained by the care home as symptomatic of the illness and therefore beyond any therapeutic intervention. Closer analysis, however, reveals that some members of the direct care team do not introduce themselves to the client or reinforce the fact that she is now living in a nursing home. Consequently, this leads to increased confusion and aggressive behaviour as the client attempts to challenge care staff whom she mistakes for intruders in her home. In such circumstances, the clinical psychologist may design a behavioural strategy that includes a training component to encourage all staff to respond in a uniform, yet more constructive manner. Continuing with the previous example, the clinical psychologist may suggest that when staff approach the client, they use very clear cues to orient her to her surroundings and remind her that she is now living in a care home. Similarly, it may be necessary to remind the client of the date and that the people who approach her are members of staff. At times, this may be as simple as providing a clear picture board, with simple orientation information, using photographs in conjunction with words.

Clearly, in such situations, the full range of clinical psychology skills is necessary to maintain the motivation and engagement of carers, who perceive the problem as being outside of themselves. At times, this can be very difficult and may require a fundamental change of approach within the service.

Evaluation

Essentially, clinical psychology is an application of psychological theory and research to the real world of human experience, and this requires careful evaluation to address two important issues. The first of these relates to whether an intervention is effective at reducing the identified target behaviour and therefore follows the predictions made by the formulation. The second, and possibly more important issue, relates to whether intervention is ineffective and, therefore, whether the initial assessment accurately identified the nature of the problem or if the formulation requires restructuring. Restructuring a formulation might involve 'fine-tuning' to identify accurately under what conditions symptoms may worsen or ease. It may be the case that the problem presented with initially may not actually be the real difficulty, but rather a consequence of other problems. For example, someone seeking help with 'relationship problems and poor assertiveness' may report no improvement from assertiveness training, and subsequent investigation might reveal significant problems associated with a history of childhood sexual abuse that are impacting on adult relationships.

At this stage, the clinical psychologist will utilise a collaborative approach to working with the client in order to share the outcome of the intervention thus far. In the event that the intervention is clearly not impacting on the difficulty in the predicted direction, the clinical psychologist will generally raise the issue of whether there may be additional factors acting on the problem that were not discussed in the initial assessment, or if key information was not disclosed. At times, this can be a challenging process, but it may be a very necessary step in the process of positive growth for the client.

Often, the clinical psychologist will utilise a comparison of pre- versus post-intervention intensity on a range of measures, in order to demonstrate the impact (or lack of it) on the target behaviour. This might be represented in graphical form to reinforce positive progress, where appropriate.

A day in the life of a clinical psychologist

Arrive at approximately 08.30 to prepare for a clinical meeting to discuss a joint client with colleagues from another part of mental health services. Check final typed copy of the report and formulation of the particular presenting problems and summary of therapeutic input, then sign and ensure that sufficient copies are available for the meeting. Before the meeting begins, double-check with the client and their advocate that they still give consent for the nature of their difficulties to be discussed, and outline some of the basic elements of the meeting structure. At the meeting, it is necessary to chair and facilitate active involvement from both the client and their advocate. At the end of the meeting, an action plan is agreed for the transfer of the client to another service, including a clear timescale, with achievable objectives that are understood by all parties.

Immediately following this meeting, the referrals panel meets to discuss any new referrals to the service and to share information on any clinically relevant elements that may require a response. Diary dates in respect of clinically significant multidisciplinary meetings, reviews and assessments are shared, and then any forthcoming dates where psychologists will not be available are agreed. At this meeting, three new referrals are received for clinical psychology, and it is agreed that assessments will take place within the next six to eight weeks. These include an assessment of risk associated with a long-standing history of sexually aggressive behaviour, a referral for an assessment of suitability to undertake psychological therapy, and a request for a clinical psychology opinion regarding a diagnosis of possible obsessive–compulsive disorder.

The referrals meeting and a quick lunch are followed by a drive to the outpatient clinic for two appointments with long-standing clients who are engaged in psychological therapy, one for long-

standing sexual and gender identity difficulties, and another for an individual who has significant anger and personality problems.

Following these, drive to an in-patient unit appointment with another long-standing client, who is currently spending a period of respite on the in-patient acute admissions unit. This client has gradually developed trust in the service and agreed to commence psychological therapy to understand the nature of his psychotic illness and the impact of childhood sexual abuse.

At approximately 15.30, drive back to the team base to provide clinical supervision to junior colleagues and trainee clinical psychologist currently on specialist placement. In the supervision session, it is agreed that it would be particularly useful for the entire clinical psychology department to request an additional training session on the assessment of alcohol-related neuropsychological damage. It is agreed that the assistant psychologist will contact the local neuropsychology service to enquire about possible speakers. At the end of the day, it is necessary to catch up with emails, post and general administrative duties, including dictating summaries of the day's therapeutic sessions.

How would I become a clinical psychologist?

This is probably the question asked most frequently by undergraduate psychology students, and, surprisingly, the answer remains complex.

Applications to clinical psychology training courses are through the central system and not directly to courses. Although each course may have particular aspects or requirements, the following are necessary prerequisites for a successful application. An essential first step is to obtain a first degree in psychology that qualifies for Graduate Basis for Registration (GBR) of the British Psychological Society. It is very important to establish whether a first degree entitles you to GBR if you wish to pursue a career in clinical psychology before starting a programme. Some psychology degrees qualify for Graduate Membership of the BPS, but this is **not** the same as GBR. If your first degree only confers Graduate Membership, you will need to undertake additional study before being eligible to apply to courses.

Competition for places on training courses is fierce and, consequently, a strong first degree will

provide an advantage. Candidates with a 2:1 honours degree classification or above are the standard, although occasionally courses will consider applicants with a 2:2 (generally, you will be expected to demonstrate further evidence of your academic ability, such as an MSc or publications in peer-reviewed journals). There have only been six successful applications to the Clearing House from undergraduates without postgraduate experience since 2000, and therefore it is highly unlikely that candidates making an application from a first degree will be successful, unless there is something unique about the application.

It is essential that you strengthen your application by undertaking some relevant preclinical experience, as this demonstrates that you are aware of what you are applying for and that you have an idea of what is involved in the role of a clinical psychologist. To strengthen your application, it is of benefit to be able to demonstrate that you have worked in a variety of different settings, with a range of different client groups. In the financial reality of the NHS, it is often not possible to secure employment in the more traditional assistant psychologist role, and therefore other forms of caring or direct role with clients may provide experience. Overall, it remains very important to secure supervision from a qualified clinical psychologist, as they may be willing and able to provide you with a reference relating to your suitability.

In addition to the clinical experience, your application will be strengthened significantly by completion of a research project by which you can demonstrate research skills beyond your undergraduate studies. If possible, try to take part in projects that are clinically relevant and likely to result in some form of publication in a peer-reviewed journal or other credible publication.

While clinical psychology remains a profession with excellent career prospects, the centralised funding increases pressure on courses to maintain strong completion rates and this strongly influences the choice of candidates. Candidates with a record of academic achievement, established clinical skills and clear evidence of an ability to complete are significantly more likely than others to secure a place on a training course.

Where can I find jobs?

While the BPS Appointments Memorandum does advertise assistant psychologist posts, this is not the sole source, and it is important to check the NHS vacancies website, *The Guardian* and *The Independent* newspapers, and social services vacancies and voluntary sector opportunities. Owing to increased pressure on assistant psychologist posts, some services will only advertise locally, so check your local press as well.

As employees of the NHS, trainee clinical psychologists are required to undergo a Criminal Records Bureau check, because the job entails working with vulnerable people and children. Similarly, NHS salaries and conditions of service are centrally agreed and available, so candidates will know what their salary will be throughout the three years of clinical training. It is expected that trainees will conduct themselves appropriately as employees of the NHS, and attendance on training days is compulsory (with a prescribed amount of annual leave). Similarly, disciplinary regulations are also applicable to trainees.

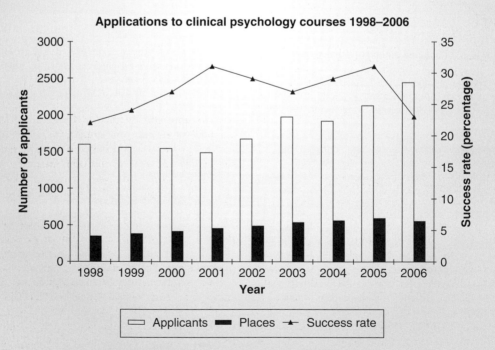

Figure 2.2 Applications to clinical psychology courses 1998–2006
Source: Clearing House for postgraduate courses in clinical psychology

How good are my chances?

In total, for the 2006 entry, 2442 people applied to undertake training in clinical psychology, with 554 places available (although this is influenced by the fact that each application includes four choices). Across all courses, the ratio of applicants to places ranged from 9:1 to 24:1, so it is essential to improve your application wherever possible. Here is a quick checklist to improve your chances:

➡ Plan time to strengthen your application.
➡ Gain experience during and after your degree (e.g. nursing assistant, befriending, youth work).
➡ Consider a clinically related undergraduate project (e.g. one that makes theoretical predictions about psychological disorders).
➡ Inform yourself about clinical psychology and read relevant journals (e.g. *British Journal of Clinical Psychology*).

For further information and applications, contact the **Clearing House for Post Graduate Courses in Clinical Psychology**, University of Leeds, 15 Hyde Terrance, Leeds, LS2 9LT. Website: http://www.leeds.ac.uk/chpccp/

Data from the Clearing House suggest that female applications to clinical courses outstrip male applications (by approximately 6:1), and the relative success of applicants reflects this ratio. The age of applicants ranges from 20 to over 50, but the majority are aged between 20 and 29 (78 per cent), and of these, only 37 per cent are aged between 20 and 24.

Figure 2.3 Lightner Witmer

DEVELOPMENT OF CLINICAL PSYCHOLOGY

The term 'clinical psychology' was first used by Lightner Witmer, who founded his psychological clinic to apply the principles of theoretical psychology, initially to education, and later to mental health problems, in Philadelphia (Pennsylvania) in 1896. Witmer was particularly interested in ways in which experimental psychology could be used to perform 'experiments' in order to understand the difficulties presented by clients. The term 'clinical method' is said to have been coined by Witmer, as a process to apply psychology to individual cases, and he was also the first to note the distinction between 'pure' and 'applied' psychology, while indicating the intimate nature of the relationship between the two, suggesting that what fosters one, fosters the other. In 1908, Witmer founded the first journal of clinical psychology, *The Psychological Clinic*.

In 1934, the first official meeting of the Pennsylvania Association of Clinical Psychologists (PACP) was held, and by 1935 over 150 psychological clinics had been established in the United States, with more developing around the world. The first formal course was established in 1904, and by the First World War clinical psychologists had developed a variety of roles and interventions, with six main activities forming distinct aspects of the work of clinical psychologists: assessment, treatment, research, teaching, counselling and management.

Following the Second World War, an increase in the demand for clinical psychologists led to the recognition that there was a need to train significantly more, and the Veterans Administration, a US Government department, defined clinical psychology as 'a profession which implies doing diagnosis, treatment and research related to adult disorders' (Compas and Gotlib 2002: 47). The Veterans Administration went on to outline the need for training to be of a sufficiently high standard and therefore required a doctoral degree, which, in turn, prompted the development of accredited clinical psychology training programmes. The Committee on Training in Clinical Psychology, led by David Shakow, recommended the following proposals, which were outlined at the 1949 Boulder (Colorado) conference – hence the model is referred to as the 'Boulder model':

1 Clinical psychologists should be primarily psychologists (i.e. a scientist with practical skills and knowledge).
2 Clinical training should be as strict as in other non-clinical fields of psychology. It should involve the setting up of standards for postgraduate training.
3 Clinical training should focus on assessment, treatment and research.

Meanwhile, in the UK, progress had been somewhat slower, and during the 1930s child guidance clinics were created, based on the American influence of applied psychology to the treatment of juvenile delinquency. These clinics included an early example of multidisciplinary working, being comprised of psychologists, psychiatrists and social workers, with specific tasks undertaken by different professionals, including the assessment, design and delivery of special educational measures for young people identified as presenting with particular difficulties. It is notable that, at this stage, these services were largely voluntary in nature. Around this time, the BPS committee of professional psychologists (Mental Health) began to coin the phrase, *clinical* when referring to psychologists working within child guidance clinics, and this became adopted as a term describing the application of psychology to mental health, as opposed to educational problems, for which the term 'educational' psychologist was used. By the 1940s, when it became clear that clinical psychology was a growing branch of applied psychology, the adult section of the BPS was formed.

It is no coincidence that in the United Kingdom clinical psychology training is centrally funded by the NHS, and the development of the profession has closely followed the development of the NHS itself (established in 1948). Just ten years after the formation of the NHS, it was agreed that an honours degree and postgraduate training in clinical psychology should constitute the basis of a separate professional group within the embryonic National Health Service, and that it would be possible to practise as a clinical psychologist only having completed such a period of training. Therefore, in 1958 the Division of Professional Psychologists (Educational & Clinical) was formed within the BPS, and in 1966 the Division of Clinical Psychology was founded. At the time, it was noted that one of the central purposes for forming such a division was to provide an organisational structure within the BPS to respond quickly to matters related to the employment of clinical psychologists within the NHS. Despite the close association between the NHS and clinical psychology, initial human resources planning omitted provision for psychologists and it was only following intervention by the BPS that a career structure was established.

In the late 1960s, clinical psychologists were considered responsible for the assessment of various aspects using psychometric tests (e.g. intelligence and personality), to assist psychiatrists in diagnosis and treatment. In addition, given the scientific background of psychology, it was assumed that clinical psychologists would also teach and undertake research into psychological problems. Not many clinical psychologists would agree with such a restrictive description of their role in the twenty-first century. Indeed, by the early 1970s, clinical psychologists were keen to emphasise their clinical role in treatment alongside their function as applied scientists.

Within the structure of the NHS, there are two key developmental stages for clinical psychology. The first was actually an oversight by the 1968 Royal Commission into the NHS, headed by Lord Zuckerman. The committee considered the roles and structures of various professions within the service and made recommendations about future planning and developments, but omitted psychology. Following this, the BPS lobbied the government and a subcommittee was formed, chaired by Professor W. Trethowan. The Trethowan committee focused exclusively on the role of psychologists in the NHS. Consequently, clinical psychologists were able to define what they did, where and to whom. In the final Trethowan Report (1977) it was argued that independent professional status should be accorded to clinical psychologists in the NHS, with the proviso that medical responsibility and treatment could not be handed over to any other profession in the service. The report also identified that research and teaching were core skills in clinical psychology. Trethowan went further to argue that a full-time psychologist be appointed centrally to the Department of Health, but while many of the recommendations of this visionary committee were established, this one was never achieved.

By the late 1980s, various changes in the structure of the NHS had resulted in considerable lapses in both the pay and conditions of service for clinical psychologists in the NHS. The Manpower Advisory Group (MPAG) Report (1990) was commissioned, and this outlined a new career structure for clinical psychologists and further established the three levels of skill (clinical, teaching and research) first acknowledged by the Trethowan Report of 1977. Since this time, clinical psychology has flourished in the NHS and the independent sector. The 2004 restructuring of the NHS saw the integration of clinical psychology into a unified structure across the entire service, in which the depth and length of training required for qualified psychologists is recognised by the grading structure.

Clinical psychology training

In terms of formal training provided to clinical psychologists, the earliest, approved schemes appeared in 1957 at the Tavistock Clinic in London and the Crichton Royal Hospital, Scotland. These both emphasised personal development and therapeutic skills alongside those of the empirical applied scientist. Between 1947 and 1966, a 13-month postgraduate training course, devised by Hans Eysenck, operated at the Institute of Psychiatry Maudsley Hospital in London, although this programme never formally received the approval of the BPS. It is of note that Eysenck was strongly opposed to clinical psychologists engaging in therapy and held that the notion of personal development through therapy was irrelevant for an applied scientist.

In 1966, the Institute of Psychiatry founded a two-year MSc degree for training in clinical psychology, and this may be considered the foundation for clinical psychology training as we know it today. In 1967, a unique joint initiative between the NHS and the BPS founded the Joint Diploma in Clinical Psychology and in-service training programmes. These required candidates to obtain a good honours degree, but then provided candidates with an NHS contract of employment, which provided trainee clinical psychologists with the same terms and conditions of employment as all other NHS salaried staff. As such, trainees were entitled to annual leave, sick pay and contributions to the NHS pension scheme, which continued throughout their employment. In addition, the rates of pay and conditions of service were included in national negotiations and standardised across the whole service to ensure fairness. This further cemented the close relationship between clinical psychology and the NHS, which remains to this day.

As the profile of clinical psychology grew, so did the range of skills and techniques used by its practitioners. The scientific basis of psychology enabled clinical psychologists to demonstrate clinical effectiveness and this led to a steady growth in demand for trained clinical psychologists. Consequently, additional programmes based at universities developed in addition to the BPS/NHS in-service training programmes throughout the 1970s and 1980s. By the mid 1970s it became evident that the requirements of clinical psychology training did not fit satisfactorily with the two-year MSc model, and that the US model of doctoral-level clinical psychology training had enabled greater development of the profession. In 1976, the University of Birmingham commenced a two-year MSc, with the option of a four-year clinical PhD, although a growing number of trainers began to lobby for three-year professional doctoral-level training in clinical psychology. Consequently, in 1992, the first three-year doctoral programmes in clinical psychology emerged in the United Kingdom, and now all programmes in clinical psychology offer the award of the degree Doctor of Clinical Psychology.

Clinical psychology has therefore been at the forefront of developing training and the professional image of applied psychology within the UK. In addition to these accolades, clinical psychology has also been very active in the development of collaborative university programmes, such as the programme jointly delivered by the Universities of Coventry and Warwick. In the early twenty-first century, clinical psychology training continues to undergo considerable development, including very close links between the NHS restructuring programme and the development of a core set of skills for clinical psychologists linked to NHS job descriptions.

RESEARCH, THEORY AND APPLICATIONS

Major therapeutic approaches in clinical psychology

Although training in clinical psychology will give some introductory training in the main therapeutic approaches to working with psychological problems, in practice, most clinical psychologists will use an integrated model, combining elements of different perspectives into their practice to achieve positive results for clients. Many clinical psychologists will subsequently undertake post-qualification training in particular methods of therapeutic work, such as cognitive behaviour therapy, systemic family therapy or psychodynamic therapy, and these often involve a significant additional commitment after completing clinical training.

In the UK, these constitute the basic aspects of the main therapeutic approaches found in clinical psychology. Although this chapter cannot hope to provide a comprehensive account of these theories and their development, it intends to provide a very basic introduction and hopes that the interested reader might seek out further study. Figure 2.4 explores the links between the general school and different orientations, and how these relate to each other.

Psychodynamic therapy

In the UK, the influence of Eysenck (1952) positioned clinical psychology as a profession that

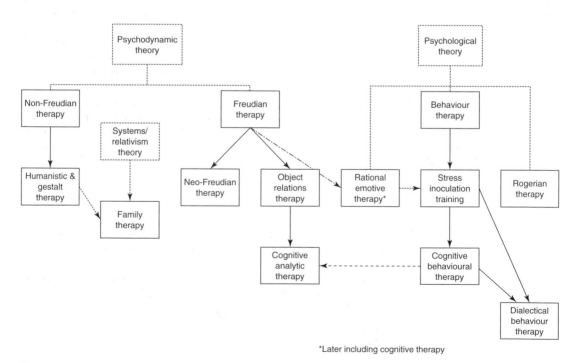

*Later including cognitive therapy

Figure 2.4 Schools and orientations in clinical psychology

was in opposition to biological psychiatry and psychotherapy, although this was more likely a reflection of Eysenck's own position than the opinions of the wider psychology community. As noted earlier in the chapter, the Tavistock clinical psychology training programme was based on a very clear psychodynamic orientation, and has enabled psychodynamic thinking to remain one of the major therapeutic considerations used within clinical psychology in the UK up to the present day.

Although it is rare for clinical psychologists to provide formal psychoanalytic psychotherapy within the NHS, owing to the constraints of time and expense, some clinical psychologists are trained in formal psychoanalysis. This means it is more likely that you will find a psychoanalytic psychotherapist in private practice rather than within the NHS. As part of their training, all psychoanalysts must experience deep analysis, which takes the form of individual therapy over a number of years.

Psychodynamic principles

Psychodynamic therapies all have their roots in Freud's thinking, although many have changed fundamentally from these origins. All *psychodynamic theory* asserts that humans strive to present a rational front, but that we frequently struggle (often using inadequate defences) against hidden conflicts that we are motivated to hide from others – or even from ourselves. Despite the rather antiquated language and form of the main principles of psychodynamic theory, it is notable that Freud formed these based on his interactions with and observations of clients. For him, the unconscious represents a series of conflicts, unacceptable wishes and suppression of traumatic events through slips of the tongue, forgetting and dream symbolism. These are repressed through defence mechanisms that are controlled by the superego and the ego, which are engaged in a tripartite struggle with the id (representing uncontrolled base urges and instincts).

Freud believed that the psyche was comprised of these three structures: the id (selfish, primitive,

childish, pleasure-oriented, with no ability to delay gratification), the superego (internalised societal and parental standards of good/bad and right/wrong behaviour) and the ego (conscious self that balances the id and the superego).

Freud believed that the id was driven by biological and instinctual impulses, and he called these aggression (or Thanatos, the death instinct), and sexuality (or Eros, the life instinct). These impulses are based on the *pleasure principle*, which requires instant gratification of desires and needs. For Freud, the ego has two basic processes, one of which is an unconscious (primary) process, in which thoughts are not coherently organised and emotions can shift, depending on circumstance; the second is a conscious (secondary) process, where thoughts are organised and strong boundaries are set. As children grow and develop, the superego is formed by parental and societal pressures and punishments. The superego consists of the conscience (the store of 'bad' behaviour relating to punishment experience) and the ego-ideal (the store of 'good' or idealised behaviour).

As the pleasure principle and id impulses are not acceptable in polite society, the ego modifies these, using the reality principle (in other words, introducing the real world), and it is the ego that deploys defence mechanisms to protect the self against unwanted or uncomfortable emotions. For example, the id may desire sex with a best friend's new boyfriend or girlfriend, but the superego introduces moral and ethical beliefs that you should respect friendships and not desire meaningless sex. In such a situation, feelings of anxiety come to the surface and defences are deployed to reduce these negative feelings.

Freudian theory argues that defence mechanisms exist as a means of protection from unconscious thoughts or feelings that the ego cannot tolerate. Defences only allow such thoughts and feelings to be expressed indirectly. Defences hide a variety of thoughts and emotions (anger, fear, competitive-ness, love, sadness, depression, greed, dependency, selfishness, helplessness, etc.).

Some examples of defensive responses to being dumped

➡ **Denial** (completely rejecting the thought or feeling): *'I'm not upset with him/her – actually I'm quite relieved!'*

➡ **Reaction formation** (turning the feeling into its opposite): *'I never really wanted to date him/her anyway!'*

➡ **Projection** (putting your feelings or thoughts onto someone else): *'She/he really loves me … a little **too** much.' 'Everyone is angry at him/her for how he/ she treated me.'*

➡ **Displacement** (redirecting feelings to another target): *'I really can't stand so-and-so.'*

➡ **Rationalisation** (developing an explanation to justify the situation): *'She/he dumped me because she/he knew I was going to go off to University, so it will be for the best in the long run.'*

➡ **Undoing** (attempting to 'undo' feelings by taking action indicating that you feel the opposite): *'I'll get him/her that top he/she wanted.'*

➡ **Regression** (reverting to old, immature behaviour): *'Let's bitch about how pointless relationships are anyway!'*

➡ **Sublimation** (redirecting feelings into a productive activity): *'I've written a song for the band about this.'*

In practice, psychodynamic therapy considers the relationship between client and therapist as a facilitative one. The therapist interprets elements of the client's behaviour and links this to long-standing conflicts, and the client responds to these interpretations.

Psychodynamic theory has developed since Freud, away from these basic instinctual (often sexual) drives. In the UK, psychodynamic thinking was strongly influenced by Fairburn (1952), Winnicott (1953) and Bowlby (1969), all of whom belong to the *object relations* school (see below). Bowlby's theories developed from his work with delinquent children; he became interested in how patterns of family interaction influenced child development. This interest led to the development of attachment theory, which focused on the effects of separation from mothers on young children, and the impact of this into adult life. For Bowlby, attachment behaviour represents an evolutionary strategy to protect infants from predators, and disruption to the attachment process can result in lifelong, problematic, anxious or aggressive behaviour. Bowlby's attachment theory was criticised extensively by Rutter (1981), particularly the assumption that children who do not make one special bond with their mother are highly likely to exhibit disturbed or even criminal behaviour. It is of interest, however, to note that within the field of working with mentally disordered offenders, patterns of poor attachment have again become the focus of psychological work (McCormack, Hudson and Ward 2002).

Object relations theory

Object relations theory is a modern adaptation of traditional psychodynamic thought that de-emphasises the basic drives as described in earlier Freudian thought, instead concentrating on the relationships between humans as the basic motivational force – contrary to Freud's main contention. As such, human beings are motivated primarily to seek relationships rather than pleasure, and therefore relationships are the main focus of psychotherapy, particularly the relationship between client and therapist.

Within the theory, the 'object' refers to anything that is the target of 'relational' needs in human development, and modern object relations theorists believe that humans have an innate drive to form and maintain relationships. Thus, objects can be people (e.g. mother or father) or things (e.g. objects of particular significance with which we form attachments, such as teddy bears). The relationship between the child and these objects becomes incorporated into the concept of the self, which is the basic 'blueprint' of the personality and manifests as the most basic tendency to look for relationships that affirm these early object relations by seeking warmth and security. The theory then postulates that the more traumatic the early self–object relations, the more rigid and resistant to change individuals become. Psychological dysfunction, therefore, can be considered as being 'stuck' at a specific stage of development, and psychological symptoms as a dysfunctional attempt to resolve early conflicts or traumas by seeking reassurance from subsequent partners, above or beyond that which is appropriate to an adult relationship.

Gestalt therapy

Gestalt therapy has three major sources: psychoanalysis (principles of inner life), humanistic and existential writings (personal experience) and gestalt psychology (concentration on interaction and process). The major influence in gestalt therapy is undoubtedly Fritz Perls, and particularly his book *Ego, Hunger and Aggression* (1969, first published 1947), which criticised psychoanalytic theory for the unnecessary importance it gave to specifically psychological developmental elements, while ignoring others that might be just as important (e.g. being able to chew food or perceive colours). The gestalt movement is characterised by collaboration, and the theory and practice of gestalt therapy is described in Perls, Hefferline and Goodman's seminal *Gestalt Therapy: Excitement and Growth in the Human Personality* (1951). Gestalt therapy places particular emphasis on an understanding of the experience of 'being' and the development of self-awareness.

Fritz Perls dismissed the psychodynamic notion of introspection (concentrating on the internal world) and suggested that the central focus of therapy should be assimilation of experience. Gestalt therapy requires that clients accept or reject their experience, but not simply adopt it wholesale; the emphasis of the gestalt therapist, therefore, is on encouragement of discovery and avoidance of interpretation.

As a consequence, gestalt therapists do not interpret, but rather lead clients towards self-discovery by various experiments that generate greater awareness and experience of personal potential. Gestalt therapists view unfinished business as unexpressed emotions towards key people in their lives, and experiments are often employed to facilitate closure of these emotions. In essence, gestalt work is based in experience rather than formal interpretation of feelings, and this is a clear departure from psychoanalytic psychotherapy

Family therapy

Family therapy is a branch of therapy based on some of the general principles of *systems theory*, which was originally developed in engineering and mathematics to explain how certain systems behaved. In the UK, contemporary family therapy is based on the *cybernetic model*, in which systems are considered to be comprised of interlinked elements and feedback loops (Bateson 1972) – similar to the idea of feedback systems in biology – and the *structural family therapy model*, in which therapy is directed towards optimising the organisation of the family, clarifying boundaries between members of the family and therefore reducing distress (Minuchin 1968). Psychological problems are considered to arise from difficulties or unmatched relationships within the system; consequently, addressing these difficulties will remove the problem. In family therapy, the family is viewed as a homoeostatic mechanism, with patterns of communication that are similar to those found in information-processing systems. In family or systemic therapy, the family is observed by therapists, and therapeutic work then takes place by consideration of the various relationships and responses to 'problems' within the family.

Behavioural therapy

Although a source of much confusion, assumption and misunderstanding – often perceived as being of little value – it was through behavioural therapy that clinical psychology in the UK developed therapeutic skills as part of the core of the profession. It is reasonable to argue that behavioural techniques remain at the very centre of clinical psychology practice, despite significant gaps in understanding of the theory, let alone any real knowledge of the research base that underpins it. Widely publicised examples of bad practice in behaviour therapy exacerbate the situation, and many psychologists hold the view that behaviour therapy was little more than a bad idea and an oversimplified way to approach clinical problems. This chapter will not provide an overview of behaviour theory (see Chapter 10), but it will be useful to have a brief reminder of some of the essential points. It is important to remember that in behaviour therapy human beings are thought to develop behaviours through three basic routes: internally, by the association of actions and events; externally, by the manipulation of events as responses to certain actions; and socially, by the observation of the results of others' behaviour.

Behaviour therapy is concerned with *maladaptive* responses, which might be excesses or deficits within the individual's behavioural repertoire. For example, excessive fear in the absence of the feared object is a maladaptive response (phobia) and is associated with wide-ranging avoidance behaviour (maladaptive excess). Psychologists such as Skinner (1955) and Wolpe (1958) argued that general behavioural principles which had been developed from intensive animal laboratory studies also applied to humans, and, consequently, could be utilised to modify unwanted responses. In behaviour therapy, therefore, the goal is to change maladaptive to adaptive behaviours.

Early behavioural conceptualisations of phobic avoidance included Mowrer's (1956) two-factor theory, in which a highly salient yet unpleasant event is associated with extreme fear and discomfort. This discomfort is so unpleasant that avoiding any future situation in which the individual is likely to encounter the feared object becomes a focus for energy. Phobias commence with classically conditioned aversive association, and are maintained by an operant negative reinforcement schedule of avoidance.

Similarly, the ritualistic behaviours demonstrated in obsessive–compulsive disorder (OCD) can be conceptualised as avoidance or safety behaviours, designed to neutralise an undesired consequence. The goal of therapy, therefore, is to address the inappropriate behaviours; this might involve using the principle of habituation, satiation or extinction, in which the consequences of responding (avoidance, in the case of phobias or OCD) are nullified.

Box 6 A simple intervention example for the banana phobia

Maintenance of the phobia is explained to the client (i.e. avoiding yellow bananas maintains the fear of them, despite the fact that this seems to be associated with reduced anxiety). A hierarchy of anxiety is then constructed and the client is taught how to reduce their arousal in the presence of the feared objects (dictated by the fear hierarchy). The client learns to maintain relaxation in the presence of the feared object (the banana).

In this way, it is not necessary to identify the original 'cause' of the problem; rather, the goal of therapy is to change the response, so therapy is conducted very much in the here-and-now.

Behaviour modification

Aversion therapy attempts to associate a highly unpleasant unconditioned stimulus (UCS), such as an unpleasant smell or an electric shock, previously able to elicit a strong unconditioned response (UCR), such as closing the eyes and moving away (avoidance) or jumping (escape), with an unwanted or problematic conditioned stimulus (CS), such as a cigarette or sexually preferred object. Pairing of the UCS and the CS will then induce a conditioned response (CR) at any future point when the CS is present. As such, smoking may be addressed by pairing a cigarette with a noxious smell that results in rapid withdrawal, a sensation of nausea and avoidance. Future presentation of the cigarette should induce the conditioned response of avoidance.

Although straightforward as a hypothesis, this very basic application of learning theory overlooks the

---

Box 5 A simple example of the two-factor theory of banana phobia

A child reaches for a nice, ripe, yellow banana, anticipating a pleasant experience. When the child holds the banana, unpeels it and moves it up towards their mouth, a spider that has been hidden in the bunch runs over the banana and across the child's hand. This causes a startle response, intense arousal and fear in the child.

The fear is associated with the sight of yellow bananas and these are avoided so as not to re-experience the intense fear from the initial exposure. This strengthens the association of yellow, banana-shaped objects with intense fear, and eventually even mention of yellow bananas is sufficient to elicit avoidance behaviour.

Consequently, the initial phase is a simple, aversive classical conditioning phase, and the avoidance phase is maintained by the negative reinforcement of reduced anxiety.

phenomenon of spontaneous recovery of previous association and learning (i.e. the association of CS and CR weakens, depending on the previous importance of the CS). Other difficulties may also arise, particularly when considering using aversion methodologies to address sexual arousal, as this may inadvertently reinforce a sexual response to the UCS. Sometimes referred to as the *blocking effect*, a very strong response to a given stimulus may undermine attempts to use aversion therapy, as the pairing with an aversive UCS may result in the UCS eliciting a similar response to that of the CS. For example, an attempt may be made to reduce sexual attraction to children by association of a noxious smell with an image of a young child. If the strength of the sexual arousal and association is not adequately understood, the noxious smell might be paired inadvertently with sexual arousal, in addition to the previous sexual arousal to young children. Owing to the largely discredited attempts to address 'problem' sexual arousal (particularly homosexuality) during the 1970s, aversive methodologies are not widely used in this area. Later behavioural researchers, such as Wolpe (1958), Meichenbaum (1977) and Bandura (1997), worked on the application of behavioural theories to a broader range of psychological and psychiatric problems.

Systematic desensitisation is based on the very simple premise that it is impossible to be both relaxed and anxious at the same time. Wolpe (1958) first reported the use of a hierarchy of anxiety relating to a feared object (e.g. a hierarchy of line drawings of spiders, through lifelike images, to small dead spiders and, at the top, a live tarantula), which is then used in conjunction with training in relaxation methods. The feared objects from this hierarchy, starting at the bottom, were then gradually introduced to the individual, who used the relaxation techniques to reduce arousal and therefore extinguish the association between the feared object and intense anxiety. An alternative, opposite form of this approach, sometimes referred to as 'flooding' or 'response-prevention', occurs when the element at the *top* of the fear hierarchy (e.g. the tarantula) is introduced *first* to the individual, who is then taught to reduce their intense anxiety. The theory predicts that this facilitates new, less anxious learning, as it weakens the association of the UCS (i.e. spiders) with the CR (intense anxiety).

Functional analysis

Undoubtedly, one of the most widespread uses of behavioural methodology has been to provide an explanatory framework for seemingly inexplicable behaviour; this is known as *functional analysis*. A thorough explanation of the model is given in Sturmey (1996), but, briefly stated, this is a methodology by which the various links between potential sources of reinforcement for a given behaviour can be isolated, thereby allowing the 'function' served by the behaviour to be identified. In some cases, extreme or aggressive behaviour may serve a function of communicating a need, in the absence of traditional methods of communication. Similarly, a functional analysis may be of use to identify why a particularly undesired behaviour persists, by identifying where, and when, potential sources of reinforcement are provided. An example might be a child who is disruptive, whose disruptive behaviour temporarily recedes when individual attention is provided, only to re-emerge when individual attention is withdrawn. A functional analysis may reveal that the majority of the time the child does not receive individual attention, and that it is only after the presentation of disruptive behaviour that he or she *does* receive individual attention. Thus the child is negatively reinforcing individual attention from the adult and the adult is positively reinforcing disruptive behaviour in the child.

Other behavioural principles used by clinical psychologists include behavioural programmes that adjust the availability of potential reinforcement to influence the frequency of behaviour. Sometimes referred to as 'differential reinforcement', these programmes dictate when reinforcement is provided, once a predetermined target behaviour has occurred (or not occurred). These can often be seen in institutional settings, such as hospitals or residential homes providing services for people who represent a challenge to existing services, or where behaviour is consistently irresponsible or illegal. In earlier forms, these were often little more than very basic *token economies*, in which individuals were 'rewarded' for behaviour with tokens that could be exchanged for a desired object. These token systems often failed, however, owing to contraband currencies in 'illegal tokens'. More commonplace was the fact that behaviour changed very rapidly in the institutional setting, but quickly deteriorated after discharge, when the very rigid structures to maintain the behaviour were absent. More modern conceptualisations of the token economy remove the token and use socialisation activities, based on the principles of social learning theory (more specifically, the concept of vicarious learning, or learning through observation and self-efficacy – the belief that one can successfully master an activity). Bandura (1997: 36) defines this in the following terms: 'Perceived self-efficacy refers to beliefs in one's own capabilities to organise and execute the courses of action required to produce given attainments'; and there is evidence that beliefs about efficacy are more predictive of behaviour change than direct measures of the self-concept (Parjares and Miller 1994). Unless individuals develop an awareness of their own capabilities and social interaction skills, they find little incentive to change their behaviour or to develop more appropriate ways of achieving their needs and goals.

Modern behavioural programmes aim to develop the individual's self-awareness of their skills, while subjectively evaluating them, in combination with modelling and problem-solving to change their behaviour.

In practice, behavioural therapy is not interested in the relationship between client and therapist, but in the predictability of behaviour, given knowledge of the contingencies underlying this. As a consequence, the therapist provides empirical evidence of behavioural frequencies and utilises specific aspects of the environment (either tangible or intangible) to facilitate client responses.

Cognitive behavioural therapy

Cognitive behavioural therapy (CBT) describes a number of branches of individual therapy which all share a principle based in psychological theory, namely that emotional responses are mediated by thought processes which are prone to systematic bias – colloquially known as 'faulty thinking'. Consequently, the extent to which we experience an emotional response is dependent on the extent to which we endorse a particular belief. Although the principles of cognitive therapies have this element in common, there are some important differences between the various branches of what is collectively referred to as CBT. Although now considered to represent a reaction against behavioural therapy, CBT has always included elements of behavioural

rehearsal to strengthen gains made by intellectual and emotional challenges in sessions, but these have become more pronounced as the theory has developed over the years. Although many have contributed to the development of CBT, the two most famous exponents of the form are Albert Ellis (rational emotive behaviour therapy) and Aaron Beck (cognitive therapy). Box 7 provides a diagram of the process of formulation in CBT.

Figure 2.5 Albert Ellis

Figure 2.6 Aaron Beck

Box 7 The UCL case formulation model (Bruch and Bond 1998: 26)

Phase 1: Definitions of problems

1 Obtain statement of the problem from those involved.
2 Clarify initial objectives of those involved.
3 On the basis of initial information received, specify problems.

Theme: A process of growing awareness aimed at a therapeutic consensus

Phase 2: Exploration

1 Hypothesis of cause and maintenance are generated.
2 Multilevel CBT assessment is conducted.
3 Data are collected to test hypotheses.

Theme: The process is one of increasing refined observations

Phase 3: Formulation

1 Formulation and intervention hypotheses are established.
2 Discussion with participants and redefinition of objectives takes place.
3 The adequacy of the hypotheses are checked and verified.

Theme: The process is one of testing the hypothesis until an adequate explanation is available

Phase 4: Intervention

1 The procedures to be used are specified.
2 An intervention contract is established.
3 The agreed programme is enacted and monitored.

Theme: The process is one of structured practice

Phase 5: Evaluation

1 Accomplished outcomes are evaluated.
2 Any gains made are supported and enhanced, the programme is optimised and further objectives, if suggested, are pursued.
3 Continuing evaluation and review. Generation of further ideas to consolidate progress.

Theme: The process is one of monitored achievement and support

Rational emotive behaviour therapy

Rational emotive behaviour therapy (REBT) was originally described and defined by Albert Ellis in his seminal work, *Reason and Mention in Psychotherapy* (1962). He observed that clients in therapy routinely displayed rigid, dogmatic and irrational thinking that was closely linked to their emotional disturbance. Influenced by his training in psychology, Ellis began to develop his therapeutic technique based on the philosophical principle of phenomenology (or individual perception of 'reality'), and spelled out the most basic form of his theory in a quote from the Stoic philosopher, Epicticus (AD 55–135): 'Men are disturbed not by things but by the views they take of them'. Thus, humans can control the extent of their emotional responses to events, but cannot necessarily control events themselves. Indeed, thinking that is based on demands to change life conditions in order to achieve happiness is destined to result in disturbed emotions. Ellis (1962) outlines what he refers to as the principles of 'Responsible Hedonism' (see Box 8) and this follows the central tenet of his theory that all human beings have a tendency to act irrationally and make mistakes (human fallibility).

Box 8 Principles of responsible hedonism in REBT

➠ *Self-interest*: It is reasonable to put one's own interests at least a little above the interests of other people. It is also reasonable to give a little to loved ones, but not so much that one feels overwhelmed.

➠ *Social interest*: It is wise to be mindful to the rights of others, as this helps to keep the peace.

➠ *Self-direction*: Although it is important to cooperate with other people, it is necessary to accept personal responsibility for one's life. One cannot *demand* or *need* excessive support or nurturance from other people.

➠ *Tolerance*: It is helpful to allow people the right to be wrong. It is not appropriate to enjoy anti-social behaviour, but it is not necessary to damn the person for doing it. In other words, dislike the behaviour, not the person.

- ➡ *Flexibility*: Rigid, biased and inflexible rules tend to reduce happiness. Flexible thinking leads to reduced distress.

- ➡ *Acceptance of uncertainty*: In general, absolute certainties *do not exist*. One can strive for a degree of order, but not demand complete predictability.

- ➡ *Contentment*: Most people tend to be happier when they are absorbed in things outside themselves. At least one strong creative interest and some significant involvement with another person seem to provide structure for a happy daily existence.

- ➡ *Self-acceptance*: Take the decision to freely accept oneself; not to measure, rate or try to prove oneself.

- ➡ *Risk-taking*: Being prepared to take some risks in life without being foolhardy.

- ➡ *Realistic expectations*: Accepting that it is unlikely to get everything one wants or to avoid everything one finds painful. Decide not to waste time striving for things that one cannot attain or for absolute perfection in life.

- ➡ *High frustration tolerance*: Recognising that there are two sorts of problems; those with and those without solutions. Develop the goal to try to change conditions that can be changed, and learn to tolerate those that cannot.

- ➡ *Self-responsibility*: Accepting responsibility for one's own thoughts, feelings and behaviours rather than blaming others, the world or fate for distress.

Box 9 Inference and Evaluation

Event
On her way to meet a group of old friends, Jane sees her friend Andrea and waves to her, but Andrea continues walking and gives no visible response to Jane. Jane is furious and decides not to go out, but returns home to pig out on ice cream, despite wanting to diet.

Inference
Andrea is ignoring me, she's NEVER liked me. Andrea's so popular, and if she doesn't like me, then none of my friends will like me.

Awfulising and demanding
This is AWFUL. Friends SHOULD be kind and not show me up. I can't stand this…

Evaluation
Andrea is a horrible person! Now everyone will think I'm worthless and unlikeable.

If Jane held a different central evaluative belief, this event would not necessarily lead to such intense anger and avoidance of the meeting.

In addition to this, Ellis draws a distinction between two types of thought: an inference (or thoughts that are couched in terms of being 'facts') and evaluations (or thoughts that relate to the worth of an individual or event). Within his theory, therefore, inferences are driven by evaluations. If an individual who endorses beliefs regarding the necessity for friendships, and creates a link between having friends and their own self-worth, believes that they have been ignored by someone they consider to be a friend, this event will be associated with a dysfunctionally strong emotional response.

Cognitive therapy

Aaron Beck first described his *cognitive therapy* in the late 1960s. Similar to Ellis, he was concerned with the link between thoughts and emotion. One important distinction to draw here, however, is that Beck approached this from the perspective of a psychiatrist, and his initial work conceptualised depression as a thought disorder (a form of psychiatric disorder similar to a delusional belief). Beck's early work was in the field of depression, and particularly in applying the *learned helplessness* model (see Box 10) to his clinical practice. The integration of psychological theory into his model produced the *triad of depression*. Essentially, it was Beck's contention that depression resulted from the negative view that individuals had of themselves, the world and the future (inspired by Seligman's (1975) work). Thus, depression *followed* this style of thinking as opposed to giving rise to it. Thinking errors are characterised by key elements and these give rise to negative automatic thoughts; commonplace thinking errors are noted in Box 11.

Similar to Ellis, Beck's therapy identifies thoughts as inferences about the world, but uses a method known as Socratic questioning, in which the therapist engages the client in exploring the evidence to support their inferences about reality, with the aim of shaking their assumption that these beliefs are accurate.

Box 10 Learned helplessness

Martin Seligman developed an already established behavioural observation that a central effect of unavoidable punishment was *behavioural supression*. Animals and humans will simply stop responding and remain passive when they cannot avoid unpleasant events which follow their behaviour. Seligman referred to this as *learned helplessness*. This provided a behavioural model of depression, where sufferers become apathetic, lethargic and unmotivated to help themselves. This became a very influential theory, which has been developed further since this basic model (although it was clearly inadequate, as not everyone becomes depressed in situations where they cannot control the outcome). Seligman developed what he referred to as *explanatory style*, as a means of explaining why some people developed learned helplessness and others did not. If the individual has a *depressive explanatory style* they will perceive aversive life events as personal, all-pervasive and permanent, whereas those with a *non-depressive explanatory style* will consider such events as non-permanent, non-pervasive and not personalised, and they are therefore less likely to become depressed.

Since the publication of his earlier work, the Beck model has been developed to include behavioural rehearsal, and the adoptive name Cognitive Behavioural Therapy (CBT) has been applied to encompass the application of both Ellis' and Becle's work to a wide range of disorders, from anxiety to schizophrenia, and clinical evidence indicates that this is a very beneficial approach. It is not without its critics, however, and some claim that CBT has been over-applied, or that clinical evidence is not as strong as the advocates of the theory would have us believe. Despite this, there is no doubt that CBT in its various forms has provided a set of highly influential models and practices to improve mental health for a wide variety of people. CBT has also applied psychological theory directly to clinical practice, unlike any other form of therapy.

Box 11 Beck's key thinking errors

Selective abstraction
Basing a conclusion on isolated details while ignoring contradictory or more salient evidence

I failed my stats exam and therefore I'm no good at exams.

Overgeneralisation
Extracting a rule on the basis of one event and applying it to other dissimilar occasions

Last time I revised nature-nurture it came up – it's always going to be in a psychology exam.

Magnification
Overestimation of the significance of undesirable consequent events

If I can't answer the first question I'll never be able to answer any of them and I'll fail my course!

Dichotomous or all-or-nothing thinking
Reasoning in extreme and absolute terms

There are simply good students who can do work and bad students who can't do work, and I'm a bad student.

Personalisation and self-reference
Egocentric interpretations of impersonal events or over-interpretation of events relating to the self

Oh no, the lecturer was referring to me when she said, 'Some of you will find this particularly hard!'

Superstitious thinking
Believing in the cause–effect relationship of non-contingent events

If I think I've done well in an exam then I'll fail, just for being too cocky!

In practice, cognitive behavioural therapy uses the relationship between client and therapist, but empowers clients to become expert in the theory, so that they can then use these new-found skills to challenge attributions about themselves and the world. Cognitive behavioural therapists encourage clients to use these skills in conjunction with behavioural exercises, to adapt to the various challenges that life presents, without recourse to unnecessary therapy. As a consequence, the therapist provides clients with methods by which they can generate their own sources of empirical evidence to facilitate change.

Example of an intervention in clinical psychology: cognitive behavioural therapy for paranoid delusions

In 1996, two UK clinical psychologists, Paul Chadwick and Peter Trower, tested the prediction that certain kinds of delusional beliefs were actually a defence against fundamentally negative views of the self, and that therapy must address issues of self-evaluation. In this paper, using a single-case experimental design, they assessed the impact of cognitive behaviour therapy techniques in challenging negative self-evaluative beliefs and paranoid delusions. They used a measure of belief-conviction and demonstrated clearly that the beliefs change and the client reported improvement. This formed the basis for their revolutionary cognitive conceptualisation of delusional beliefs, which has opened up psychological therapy to clients previously thought to be unable to work directly with psychologists. Since this highly influential study was published, they have replicated their findings with a larger number of participants (Chadwick et al. 2005).

In their study, they describe a 31-year-old man with a 9-year psychiatric history, who had previously been diagnosed as suffering from schizophrenia, and who met DSM-IV criteria for schizo-affective disorder, presenting with bizarre delusions and auditory hallucinations. In the background section they explain that he received medication to treat psychotic symptoms, and they note the extreme trauma he had been exposed to (being told by his mother that he was conceived when his father had raped her, and that this act effectively broke their marriage). On the separation of his parents, he first lived with his father, but returned to his mother and stepfather (who was physically aggressive toward him). During his late teens the client molested a young girl and had sexual contact with animals, although there had been no recurrence of either behaviour and he reported no related urges or fantasies.

The client presented with clear paranoid thinking with associated delusions, and heard frequent abusive male voices calling him names like 'pervert'. The client also experienced depressive symptoms and appeared troubled by intrusive thoughts and images that were either blasphemous or abusive, directed towards other people. It seems that he held two distinct paranoid beliefs:

1 That he was being punished by members of the public for his sexual misdemeanours; specifically, that others could read his thoughts and knew about the sexual acts – hence they tormented him, planning to expose and subsequently attack him.

2 God was punishing him, specifically by frequent and severe pressure in his head, which he attributed to physical punishment by God for blasphemy and for having broken a promise to attend church.

In addition to these thoughts, the authors identified a negative self-evaluative belief that he was a totally bad and perverted person, and this caused him the most distress.

Chadwick and Trower decided to challenge the negative self-evaluation first and used a standardised measure of depression, the Beck Depression Inventory (Beck, Steer and Brown 1996), to indicate the severity of his symptoms over the entire intervention (at selection for therapy, at the first and last sessions of the baseline phase, three times during therapy corresponding to the close of each discrete phase, and at three follow-up appointments). In addition to this, his conviction and preoccupation with the delusional beliefs were measured using a percentage rating (0 being none of the time and 100 being all of the time). Therapy took place on a weekly basis, lasting for 60 minutes, and the authors describe three stages:

➡ *Pre-baseline interviews*, in which the client was seen three times in order to identify the beliefs and begin to build a rapport.
➡ *Baseline*, in which further information was gathered about the beliefs, especially any evidence for and against.
➡ *Cognitive therapy for punishment paranoia*.

The therapy itself involves the introduction of the cognitive model and challenges the negative self-evaluative belief. Following this, the therapist conveys the insight that it is his negative self-

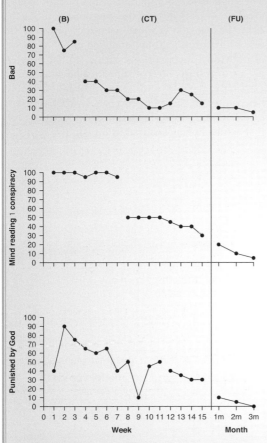

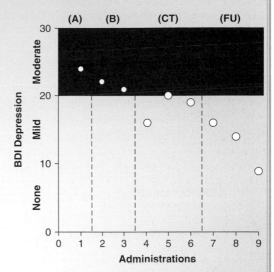

Figure 2.7 Bill's percentage conviction scores for the negative self-evaluation and two paranoid delusions during baseline (B), cognitive therapy (CT) and follow-up (FU)
Source: Chadwick and Trower (1996)

Figure 2.8 Bill's BDI scores at assessment (A), baseline (B), cognitive therapy (CT) and follow-up (FU)
Source: Chadwick and Trower (1996)

evaluation (the inescapable badness) that drives the paranoid delusion, with the themes of exposure and punishment. Finally, the therapist uses this rationale to introduce the process of challenging the delusions. Results are reported in Figure 2.7.

The intervention clearly shows that cognitive therapy is very effective in the reduction of conviction in negative self-evaluation and that this reduction is associated with a reduction in delusional beliefs. Furthermore, these effects are maintained at follow-up meetings. In addition to the conviction ratings, the authors also demonstrate that scores on the BDI are reduced in a pattern similar to that of the conviction in self-evaluation and delusional beliefs. It is notable that the DDI scores relate to symptoms of depression and are clearly related to emotion, therefore providing additional evidence for the cognitive model. The study very clearly demonstrates the need to address links between negative self-evaluation and paranoia, and for therapists to address these in addition to simply challenging the 'evidence' for delusional beliefs.

Research in clinical psychology

Clinical psychology is, essentially, an applied branch of psychology, and therefore attempts to apply scientific principles to human distress. As can be seen from Figure 2.8, the single-case experimental design is a powerful methodology. This relates to the evaluation of outcomes, and the single-case experimental design method is a very useful empirical procedure, providing a clear, objective alternative to the traditional psychoanalytic 'case study', which provided a unique account of an individual.

In addition, single-case experimental design provides a wide range of established options that are used to address specific clinical questions, and these can be applied to quantitative (or numerical) and qualitative (more descriptive) analysis. As outlined previously, clinical psychology is heavily influenced by the scientist-practitioner model, and the single-case experimental design provides a useful method by which clinical psychologists can demonstrate the effectiveness of their clinical work.

The single-case experimental design methodology is used to investigate specific presenting problems, either in one case (a more scientific version of the case study) or in a group (analysed either as a series of individual interventions with a similar problem or as a group intervention). The method is extremely flexible and it is possible to study behaviour and thought processes, as well as beliefs, emotions and physical reactions – in fact, anything that can be operationalised in measurable terms.

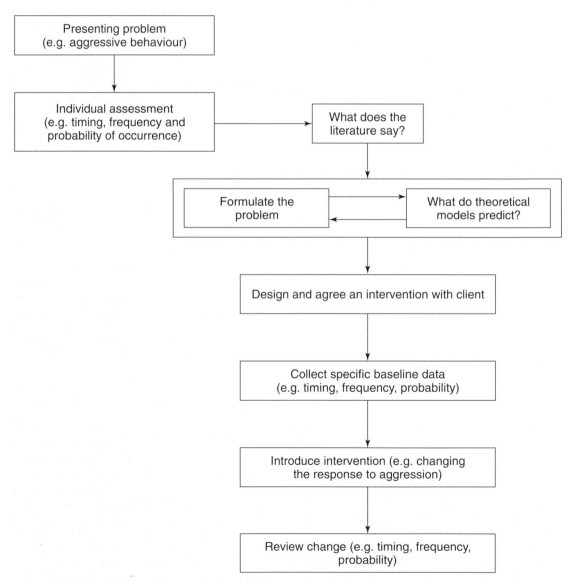

Figure 2.9 The process of single-case experimental design

Essentially, the single-case experimental design measures change in a dependent variable (thoughts, behaviours, emotions, etc.) over the time of an intervention. If the dependent variable changes systematically, this provides the first stage of evidence that the intervention has an effect, and offers an opportunity to consider exactly what was the underlying mechanism of change and how this relates to the predictions of the particular theory under consideration.

As such, single-case experimental methodology must consist of *at least* two phases. A **baseline phase**, where the target (behaviour, emotion, thought, etc.) is recorded before any intervention, is followed by a **treatment phase**, where an intervention is introduced and change is measured (e.g. aggressive behaviour is measured at five incidents per day during the baseline, and then an intervention is introduced, in which assertive behaviour is positively reinforced and the frequency of the aggression reduces to one per month). This very simple principle can be adapted into very complex and subtle versions of the same basic model. In its most basic form, as described here, it is referred to as an AB design (where A is the baseline and B is the intervention). For more complex designs, there may be two or more stages to an intervention, which might therefore involve an ABC design, where A is the baseline, B is part 1 of the intervention and C is part 2 (e.g. introducing a relaxation training phase and then a cognitive therapy stage for someone with chronic anger).

In cases where it is possible to reverse or remove an intervention, this is referred to as ABA (e.g. removing or reversing the intervention and evaluating whether the problem returns to the original frequency or intensity).

Before undertaking a single-case experimental design, it is necessary to establish whether the issue in question can be operationalised into a concise, yet intelligible format. Once satisfied that it is possible to do so, it is necessary to consider issues associated with the recruitment of potential participants. For example, if the intervention is known to be associated with a particularly rapid or slow impact on either behaviour or emotion, how might this influence the methods for recording data? Similarly, how long is the intervention intended to take? If this is a long-term intervention,

---

Box 12 Ethics

Quite apart from the feasibility of reversal (i.e. can someone really unlearn coping strategies once these have been learned?), a more critical point concerns whether it is ethical to reverse or withdraw an intervention once this has shown a positive impact on the individual. For example, under what circumstances would it be reasonable to withdraw a coping strategy for memory loss that demonstrably improves self-esteem for someone who has suffered a head injury?

Although these are serious ethical problems, it is possible to measure the impact of an intervention without withdrawal or reversal of the intervention, and therefore overcome such ethical dilemmas. The central issue for clinical psychologists is to demonstrate rigour in their application of psychological theory, in order to understand exactly how and why an intervention has either worked or not.

---

are there other ways that the effectiveness can be evaluated and these data used to modify the process? For example, in an intervention intended to address seriously irresponsible behaviour, designed to be implemented over 18 months, are there elements that can be measured to provide interim data about the effectiveness of the intervention in the meantime (e.g. reduction in the frequency of arguments or reports of problem behaviour, or variables known to be associated with irresponsible behaviour, such as self-esteem)?

Finally, the question of data analysis must be considered, and it is essential to establish what is intended as the method of measurement (e.g. average or overall level of a response; trend or direction of any change). Despite the obvious advantages of the single-case experimental design, there are significant limitations, including the fact that these do not permit a full experimental analysis, owing to other factors that influence the intervention beyond the control of the clinical psychologist. Similarly, as single-case methodology relies on data collected about the same case at different times, it is particularly susceptible to the effects of changes related to the timing of when these are collected during the baseline phase, as the intensity of the problem may vary naturally. For example, ratings of a particular problem may increase or decrease during the baseline phase, and each of these factors must be considered before embarking on such a method to evaluate an intervention.

CURRENT DIRECTIONS IN CLINICAL PSYCHOLOGY

As noted earlier in this chapter, the vast majority of clinical psychologists are currently employed within statutory services – more specifically, within the NHS. Since the early 1980s, clinical psychology has expanded from very limited, hospital-based departments into all aspects of health care provision. The number of independent psychiatric hospitals has also expanded, with an increase in clinical psychologists working within the independent sector, with a wide range of difficulties that statutory services are unable to respond to. In addition, an increasing number of clinical psychologists now work in independent practice, providing direct individual therapy on a private basis, along with consultancy to both statutory services and the court system.

Changes within the NHS, and increasing concern about financial management, have led to an increase in psychological therapies being undertaken by professionals without basic training in psychology (e.g. nurses, social workers and psychiatrists), and clinical psychologists are often required to provide training and supervision for these colleagues in order to maximise the range of psychological therapy to the greatest number of people. Although this has raised concern among clinical psychologists that it will have a negative impact on the quality of psychological therapy or the availability of clinical psychology posts, experience suggests that this has had a very positive impact, for both clients and professionals. Often referred to as the *consultancy model*, it has seen clinical psychologists involved in supervision and clinical management of colleagues. Assuming responsibility for more complex cases, and the devising of overall clinical strategies, appears to represent a 'best-value' use of what is fundamentally a very expensive resource. The clinical consultancy model means that the role of the clinical psychologist may, at times, be associated with a reduction in direct client contact and increasing involvement in management, which is often contrary to the motives that inspired people to become clinical psychologists in the first place.

As the importance and effectiveness of psychological therapies grows, clinical psychologists are increasingly working at a strategic level, to devise new services or ways of delivering psychology to an ever-expanding client population, or those with particular difficulties that challenge existing services (e.g. people with dangerous and severe personality disorders). Clinical psychologists will often be engaged in long-term research projects, and the presentation of such data at national and international levels, and to government departments. Indeed, statutory services, such as the NHS, have recognised the organisational benefits of psychological models and this has rapidly become an area in which many clinical psychologists have become involved.

The proposed new Mental Health Bill, although not yet entered onto the statute book at the time of writing (2006), raises a wide range of possible challenges and positive developments for clinical psychology. The proposed bill would replace previous legislation, specifically the Mental Health Act (1983), which provides a legal framework to address the needs of people presenting with mental health difficulties and requiring treatment when, at times, they may not consider that this is a need. The bill includes a broader context and makes changes to key definitions, including where treatment is provided and what constitutes mental disorder (including the replacement of 'psychopathic disorder' with 'personality disorder'). More controversially, it introduces the concept of 'clinical supervisor'. The latter represents a potential key change to the role of the clinical psychologist, who will be eligible to become the clinical supervisor of individuals with severe mental health difficulties in the community. The introduction of this new role has given rise to fierce debate within the clinical psychology community. Some have argued that this will force positive change, as it removes one of the last bastions of medical power and introduces a legislative need to provide psychological treatments. They claim that the absence of statutory legal duties, specifically the power to restrict freedom and impose treatments, has acted as a barrier to the development of clinical psychology as a profession. Other commentators have challenged the motivations of those in favour of such a development, as summed up by Dave Pilgrim (2003: 7):

> No matter how poorly psychiatry actually performs as a profession, the RMO role-plus-prescription pad ensure both its indispensability to services and its inflated salaries. The amount paid to locum consultant psychiatrists, for example, in some localities can now well exceed £100,000 p.a. By contrast, to date, we have been potentially dispensable and have not warranted such excessive remuneration. This is probably why legal powers, to constrain liberty and prescribe drugs, elicit an instant salivation response in the strong professionalisers in our midst. The clinical supervisor role on the horizon will encourage a convergence with medicine – for good and bad.

Indeed, there is great concern that such developments will not serve to liberalise mental health services, but rather increase the entrenchment of clinical psychology into the existing ranks of statutory services, effectively making it part of the problem and not a means by which solutions can be effected.

In addition, the Mental Capacity Act 2005 introduces changes to the assessment of capacity, and provides a legal framework to empower and protect vulnerable people who are not able to make their own decisions. Specifically, this defines who can take decisions, in which situations, and how they should go about this. It also enables people to plan ahead for a time when they may lose this capacity. It is comprised of five key principles (see Box 13). The Act requires that individuals presumed to lack capacity are assessed in very specific ways; these are reliant on clinical psychologists and therefore increase the role of the profession within a legislative context. The Act also makes very clear provision for the involvement in research of people who lack capacity. Given that many people involved in clinical psychology research are vulnerable and lack capacity, the legislation will have a significant impact on the

future development of clinical psychology. As a research-based profession that requires practitioners to complete a doctoral research project as part of their basic training, the provisions of the Act introduce a significant hurdle into what is already a very tight training schedule.

Box 13 Five key principles of the Mental Capacity Act 2005

1 Presumption of capacity: Every adult has the right to make his or her own decisions and must be assumed to have the capacity to do so unless it is proved otherwise.
2 The right to be supported to make their own decisions: Every adult must be given all appropriate help before the conclusion that they cannot make their own decisions.
3 Retain the right to make what might be seen as *eccentric* or *unwise* decisions.
4 Best interests: Anything done for or on behalf of people without capacity must be *in their best interests*.
5 Least restrictive intervention: Anything done *on behalf of* should be the *least restrictive of their basic rights and freedoms*.

RECOMMENDED FURTHER READING

Brewer, K. (2003) *Clinical Psychology*. Oxford: Harcourt Heinemann.

British Journal of Clinical Psychology

Cheshire, K. and Pilgrim, D. (2004) *A Short Introduction to Clinical Psychology*. London: Sage.

Knight, A. (2002) *How to Become a Clinical Psychologist*. Sussex: Brunner-Routledge.

Roberts, M. C. and Ilardi, S. S. (eds) (2003) *Handbook of Research Methods in Clinical Psychology*. Oxford: Blackwell.

USEFUL WEBSITES

http://www.bps.org.uk/dcp-affiliate/althandbook.cfm

Exercises

1 What are the main differences in the role of the therapeutic relationship between the psychodynamic, behavioural and cognitive behavioural orientations?

2 How would you outline the main differences between a psychiatrist and a clinical psychologist to someone who has not had any training in psychology?

3 How would you respond to the allegation, 'clinical psychology is no better than psychiatry – it is all under state control and designed to force people into one version of normality'.

4 Outline two main distinctions between a psychological formulation and a diagnosis of a psychological problem.

5 Write an introductory pamphlet to inform clients about a hypothetical clinical psychology service and what they should expect when they are given an appointment.

Counselling Psychology

INTRODUCTION

The term 'counselling' is used in a number of ways and has numerous definitions. In everyday speech it is often used to indicate advice-giving or guidance, such as debt-counselling. However, the activities of therapeutic counselling have little, if anything, to do with the giving of advice.

The British Association for Counselling (1984) provides this definition of counselling:

> The term counselling includes work with individuals and with relationships which may be developmental, crisis support, psychotherapeutic, guiding or problem solving ... The task of counselling is to give the client an opportunity to explore, discover and clarify ways of living more satisfyingly and resourcefully.
>
> (BAC 1984)

Counselling is offered in a number of different guises and is supplied by a variety of different providers. For example, psychotherapy is provided by practitioners who are highly trained specialists in their field, whereas much counselling is carried out by non-professional volunteer workers who have undertaken some form of basic counselling training. Counselling psychologists are practitioners who have an initial training in psychology, and who use psychological methods and models in their approach to counselling.

A significant difference between the work of counsellors and the work of counselling psychologists, is that the work of the counselling psychologist is concerned with the application of psychological theories and techniques.

PRINCIPLES OF COUNSELLING PSYCHOLOGY

Counselling psychology as an applied field of *psychology* aims to facilitate personal and interpersonal functioning across the life span with a focus on *emotional*, *social*, *educational*, *health-related*, *developmental* and *organisational* concerns. Through the integration of psychological theory, research and practice, counselling psychology includes a broad range of practices that help people improve their well-being, alleviate distress, resolve crises, and increase their ability to live more fulfilling lives.

Some of the objectives of the client work carried out by counselling psychologists are listed below:

⇒ **Insight**: The counselling psychologist helps the client gain insight into the origin, development and maintenance of the psychological difficulty. With insight, it is hoped that the client is better able to take control of their thoughts, emotions and behaviour and be in a better position to change them.

⇒ **Self-awareness**: Through counselling the client develops greater self-awareness and becomes aware of thoughts and feelings that have previously been denied or ignored.

⇒ **Self-acceptance**: Clients are helped to become more accepting of themselves. Through identifying factors that have led to them holding negative thoughts and ideas about themselves, the counselling psychologist and the client work around the client developing a more positive attitude towards themselves.

⇒ **Social skills training**: The type of skills in which a counselling psychologist might train a client are: assertiveness, anger management, problem-solving and relaxation techniques.

⇒ **Cognitive and behavioural change**: Counselling psychologists encourage clients to think differently. Clients are helped to identify negative or irrational thoughts and encouraged to modify or replace them. Similarly, clients are encouraged to modify or replace maladaptive behaviour.

By following these principles, a counselling psychologist aims to reduce psychological distress in people with physical, emotional and mental difficulties, improve well-being and resolve crises.

WHAT DO COUNSELLING PSYCHOLOGISTS DO?

Counselling psychology is a relatively new profession. Counselling psychologists are practitioners whose initial training is in psychology and who use methods and models which are based upon psychological theory. As applied psychologists they are concerned with the integration of psychological theory and research with therapeutic practice.

Counselling psychologists work with clients who have a variety of problems in a variety of settings. They work with people who are experiencing difficulties with everyday living, such as relationship problems or problems with substance misuse. They also work with clients who have psychological disorders, such as anxiety, depression, eating disorders and psychosis.

Counselling psychologists work in NHS services, for example, GP practices, in prison, social services, voluntary organisations, occupational health departments, student counselling services and also in private practice. They work with individual clients, couples, families or groups. Counselling psychologists might work individually with adult clients with a variety of problems and difficulties. With older adults, the issues might include retirement, bereavement, chronic illness and loss. They may work with students and young people through student counselling services focusing, for example, on relationship problems, substance misuse, career evaluation and educational guidance. Counselling psychologists working in health care settings work with clients who have chronic diseases such as cancer or AIDs, disabling conditions such as multiple sclerosis, or clients who are having medical interventions such as major surgery.

Where they work

Counselling psychologists work in almost every setting where there are people. For instance counselling psychologists are currently employed in industry, commerce, the prison service and in all areas of education from primary school to university. About half of all counselling psychologists are employed to do clinical work in health and social care settings. Other career paths can be found in teaching and research for academic institutions. Counselling psychologists can also practice privately. They may work directly with individuals, couples, families and groups, or act as consultants.

Box 1 Key tasks include:

➡ Working with individuals, groups and/or organisations, applying psychological principles and understanding, with the objective of assisting them to change, improve, understand or better manage their situation.

➡ Building relationships with clients: 'being with' rather than 'doing to' the client.

➡ Facilitating well-being in clients as opposed to responding to sickness and pathology.

➡ Offering advice on how best to work with a client, usually when employed on a consultancy basis.

➡ Undertaking research, either individually, or as part of a team.

➡ Performing assessments, including assessment of mental health needs, risk assessment and psychometric testing.

➡ Formulating psychological explanations of the cause and maintenance of psychological difficulties.

➡ Planning and implementing therapy, together with the evaluation of the outcome of therapy.

➡ Writing reports and record-keeping.

➡ Working within a multidisciplinary team of other health professionals including: consultant psychiatrists, senior house officers, clinical psychologists, occupational therapists, social workers and community psychiatric nurses.

➡ Receiving ongoing personal therapy and supervision.

The work may also involve teaching, supervising and training other counselling psychologists, applied psychologists, assistant psychologists and related professionals.

A day in the life of a counselling psychologist working in a substance misuse service

➡ 9.00: Attend weekly allocation meeting at which new referrals are discussed. Allocated four new clients, one of whom presents with dual diagnosis – i.e. substance misuse with a psychological disorder, in this case a woman who misuses alcohol and has a diagnosis of schizophrenia.

➡ 10.00: See first client. Fifth session out of planned 12. Client has responded well to CBT and has successfully reduced alcohol consumption over the five weeks. Carries out homework tasks and fills in drink diary every day. Discussion of the diary entries, such as identified triggers for drinking, and her thoughts before, during and after drinking, takes up much of the session.

➡ 11.00: See second client. Session 12. Review session. Client has made very little change, continues to drink heavily. Discussed option of in-patient detoxification due to his deteriorating physical health. Client has accessed acupuncture service, anger management course, relaxation training, outpatient psychiatric service. Discussed motivation to stop drinking. Agreed to a further six sessions in which to prepare for detoxification.

➡ 12.00: Administration hour. Write up notes of client work. Write letters and make telephone calls (letter to GP concerning referral of client for detox, phone call to social services informing them of a client who is placing her young children at risk by drinking heavily while being their sole carer.

➡ 1.00: Lunchtime

➡ 2.00: Facilitate 'New Life Group'. A cognitive behavioural therapy group for people who have stopped drinking and wish to remain abstinent. One member returned following an absence of four weeks because she had started drinking again. Group members helped to identify what had caused her relapse. Discussed coping strategies for trigger situations. Discussed assertiveness and highlighted the difference between being angry and being assertive. Group members role-played assertive behaviour.

➡ 4.00: Supervision with Senior Counselling Psychologist. Discussed difficulty of working with threatening client who becomes angry during session. Discussed issues of conflict avoidance and management of others' anger.

➡ 5.00: Finish writing up notes of client work, complete supervision log.

➡ 5.30: Check all notes and files are securely stored and leave the office.

How would I become a counselling psychologist

Training to be a counselling psychologist involves a three-year full-time postgraduate course which consists of:

➠ Core therapy training in counselling or psychotherapy (350 hours)
➠ Additional skills training in different models of counselling practice (at least 150 hours)
➠ 450 hours supervised practice in more than one placement using more than one therapeutic approach and modality (couples, groups, family)
➠ Production of a competence log book as documentary evidence of these requirements
➠ The writing of three academic papers which address therapeutic, ethical issues etc.
➠ Research dissertation (approx 15,000 words)
➠ At least 40 hours of personal therapy
➠ Reports based on work carried out at all placements after every 50 hours of supervised practice.

DEVELOPMENT OF COUNSELLING PSYCHOLOGY

Counselling psychology in the United Kingdom is a relatively new discipline. In 1982 the British Psychological Society established a Counselling Psychology Section and in 1989 it became a Special Group. The status of a Special Group lies somewhere between scientific interest group and professional body.

Later the same year, the Society, through establishing the Diploma in Counselling Psychology, provided a route to chartered status for trainees wishing to specialise in this area. The diploma in counselling psychology allowed candidates to register as Chartered Psychologists exclusively on the basis of counselling psychology qualifications. Consequently, in March 1994, the Membership of The Society voted in favour of the Special Group in Counselling Psychology being re-designated 'The Division of Counselling Psychology'. Within 12 years, counselling psychology had become a full profession of applied psychology alongside clinical, educational and occupational psychology.

The Division of Counselling Psychology (DCoP) of the British Psychological Society is devoted to furthering the development of counselling psychology, both as a body of knowledge and skills, and as a profession. Historically, counselling psychology has developed as a branch of professional psychological practice strongly influenced by human science research as well as principal psychotherapeutic traditions.

RESEARCH, THEORY AND APPLICATIONS

The four main theoretical frameworks from within which counselling psychologists work are: the Humanistic perspective, the Psychodynamic perspective, the Systemic perspective, and the Cognitive Behavioural perspective. How these theoretical models are applied in the practice of counselling psychology is discussed in the following section.

THE HUMANISTIC PERSPECTIVE

The roots of humanistic psychology are in humanism, a philosophy that attaches importance to humankind and human values. Begun in the 1950s in the USA, its major figures include Carl Rogers (1961) and Abraham Maslow (1968). It developed largely as a reaction against both psychoanalysis and behaviourism, establishing a 'third force' against both approaches. Humanists considered that in both of these approaches, human beings were seen to have no choice and no control over themselves, either driven by biological drives or simply reacting to stimuli. In contrast, the focus of humanistic psychology was on healthy, rational, higher motivations.

Carl Rogers (1961) was one of the leading humanists. He argued that human beings are positively motivated with a natural internal drive towards growth and development. This innate drive stimulates creativity and encourages individuals to pursue new challenges and learn new skills that further enhance growth. Rogers refers to this ongoing tendency as the *actualising tendency*. When an individual is in harmony with their actualising tendency it leads them towards further positive growth and happiness. However, if they are not, the consequence is sadness, depression or anxiety.

Rogers suggested that the actualising tendency continuously drives us towards our *ideal self*. The ideal self encompasses who we would like to be: the hopes and desires of our lives. The extent to which our actual self and ideal self match each other has a powerful impact upon how we feel and behave. When the two match quite closely we feel positive. However, if our actual self differs from our ideal self, we feel sad and other negative emotions and the actualising tendency becomes impeded. Rogers used the term *congruent* to describe the match between the actual self and ideal self.

According to Rogers, many individuals first experience incongruence in childhood. He argued that the manner in which parental love and approval are given has a profound effect on the developing person. Certain subtle interactions between parent and child can contribute to the development of psychological problems in adult life.

One example of this occurs when parents show their disapproval of bad behaviour and of the child ('You hit your little sister, and I don't love you when you behave in this way'). Parental love and approval is given only if the child behaves in a way that their parents want them to. The term used for this is *conditional positive regard*. The consequence for the child is that they adopt their parents' *conditions of worth*. In other words, the child comes to associate their self-worth with how they behave, and is careful to behave only in ways that are valued by their parents. The parents' aspirations become internalised into the child's ideal self, and the child strives towards achieving them rather than his or her own wishes and desires. The result of this process is to inhibit the *self-actualising tendency*.

Rogers argues that certain aspects of an individual's interactions with others can assist their move towards self-actualisation. Three of these are:

1 **Unconditional positive regard**: Acceptance and love that does not depend upon the individual behaving in a certain prescribed way. For example, 'I do not like how you behaved, but I still love you'.
2 **Genuineness**: A setting in which the individual feels able to express their own sense of self, instead of adopting a role or hiding behind a façade.
3 **Empathy:** A setting in which the individual interacts with people who are able to understand the world from the viewpoint of the individual.

Person-centred therapy

The difficulties of clients, however they may present, are understood to have come about as a result of obstruction of the actualising tendency (the innate drive towards growth and development), often due to experiencing conditional positive regard. Person-centred counselling aims to help individuals to be able to free themselves from the constraints and obstacles that do not allow them to make use of their innate ability to self-actualise.

In 1942 Rogers declared:

> Therapy is not a matter of doing something to the individual or inducing him to do something about himself. It is instead a matter of freeing him for normal growth and development so that he can again move forward.
>
> Rogers (1942: 29)

The person-centred approach to counselling psychology suggests that this freedom can be achieved through the therapeutic relationship.

The therapeutic relationship within the person-centred approach is of far greater significance than in any of the other approaches. As far as Rogers was concerned, the personal qualities of the counsellor are more important than the professional qualifications they possess. Furthermore, the relationship between client and counsellor is considered to be one of equals. As the term 'person-centred' suggests, it is the person who is at the centre of counselling not the skills or expertise of the counsellor. The counsellor does not direct the client nor the session, neither does he or she suggest interventions or employ techniques to induce change in the client. The aim of person-centred counselling is for the client to realise they can trust their own experiencing and the validity of their own perceptions. This is more likely to come about if the counsellor is not perceived by the client as the powerful expert. As Rogers says:

> It is the client who knows what hurts, what directions to go, what problems are crucial, what experiences have been deeply buried. It began to occur to me that unless I had a need to demonstrate my own cleverness and learning, I would do better to rely upon the client for the direction of movement in the process.
>
> Rogers (1961: 11–12)

Rogers saw the role of the therapist as providing the ideal conditions in which to facilitate growth within the client. In order to achieve this, the counsellor has to convey acceptance and understanding of the client. The goal of the therapist is to provide a setting in which the client is not judged and can be free to explore different ways of being. In other words, therapy provides the conditions necessary for growth identified earlier. When these conditions are created, then changes will occur in the client and the process of growth will take place. Rogers listed what he regarded as 'The necessary and sufficient conditions of therapeutic personality change' (Rogers 1957: 95):

⟹ Two persons are in psychological contact.
⟹ The first, whom we shall term the 'client', is in a state of incongruence, being vulnerable and anxious.
⟹ The second person, whom we shall term the 'therapist', is congruent or integrated in the relationship.
⟹ The therapist experiences unconditional positive regard for the client.
⟹ The therapist experiences an empathic understanding of the client's internal frame of reference and endeavours to communicate this experience to the client.
⟹ The communication to the client of the therapist's empathic understanding and unconditional positive regard is, to a minimal degree, achieved.

Rogers firmly believed that if the client experienced these six essential conditions for therapeutic growth, then nothing else is needed for change to take place in the client.

Of the six conditions, three conditions have received the most attention: empathic understanding, unconditional positive regard and congruence. Rogers and followers of the client-centred approach, regard these as the core conditions of a counselling relationship that will facilitate actualisation and growth (Patterson 1974).

Counselling psychologists draw on a number of essential skills to successfully communicate these effective therapeutic conditions to the client.

Empathy

For Rogers, empathy is a very special way of being with another person (Rogers 1975). Empathic understanding involves the ability to enter clients' worlds and to see things from their frame of reference – their way of seeing things. In empathising with a client the counsellor leaves aside their own frame of reference, so they can experience the feelings of the client *as if* they are their own.

Research suggests that basic empathy is a necessary feature of virtually all successful counselling relationships. As well as person-centred counsellors, this has been supported by psychoanalytic (Fiedler 1950), rational emotive (Ellis 1962) and behavioural (Wolpe 1969) counselling psychologists.

One of the positive effects of empathy is that it communicates the counsellor's understanding of the client, which in turn increases the client's self-esteem. The client may not have experienced such a process before.

Unconditional positive regard

Unconditional positive regard is an attitude of the counsellor which 'manifests itself in the counsellor's consistent acceptance of and enduring warmth towards her client' (Mearns and Thorne 1988: 59).

Clients typically present with a long held belief that they will only be liked and respected if they behave in a certain way. In other words, their behaviour is determined by conditions of worth.

The client, who has lived with conditions of worth imposed upon him/her, will have learned that he/she is only of value when he/she behaves in ways that fulfil others expectations. The importance of unconditional positive regard lies with the counsellor valuing the client, irrespective of the client conforming to any set 'conditions'. Ultimately the clients come to value themselves as a direct outcome of experiencing the counsellor's valuing of them, and they acknowledge the viability of such an attitude. In other words, they accept the possibility that they are of value to others.

Congruence

According to Mearns and Thorne, congruence is a 'state of being when the outward responses of the counsellor towards the client consistently match the inner feelings which she has in relation to the client' (1988: 75).

Congruence builds trust between counsellor and client and can facilitate the development of congruence in the client him/herself. The most important benefit of congruence is that it 'enhances the quality of the response which the counsellor gives to the client' (Mearns and Thorne 1988: 87). In being congruent, the counselling psychologist is demonstrating the effects which the client's behaviour has on another person, a person whose integrity can be trusted.

Sometimes a therapist is unable to feel genuinely accepting of an individual. When this is the case, for example if the counsellor is angered or irritated by the client, it is important that the counsellor is honest about these feelings towards the client. It is necessary for the counsellor to respond to the client in a genuine manner and not simply pretend to understand and accept the client.

Rogers firmly believed that if the client experienced these core conditions for therapeutic growth, then nothing else is needed for change to take place in the client. Over time, the therapeutic relationship established under these conditions can facilitate clients to live less by the externally imposed standards of others. This is thought to be achieved through a series of seven stages (Rogers, 1961) in which the client:

⮕ fails to acknowledge feelings, and considers personal relationships as dangerous
⮕ is able to describe their behaviour, but rarely their feelings, which are not 'owned'
⮕ can begin to describe their emotional reactions to past events, and recognise contradictions in their experience
⮕ develops an awareness of their current feelings, but finds it difficult to cope with them
⮕ begins to explore their inner life in a more meaningful and emotional way
⮕ is able to fully experience feelings while talking of past events
⮕ develops a basic trust in their own inner processes: feelings experienced with immediacy and intensity.

The counselling psychologist's actions facilitate each of these processes. Empathic reflection encourages the client to explore and express feelings and thoughts. Acceptance and genuineness foster trust in the self and courage in the sharing of previously withheld thoughts and feelings.

Counselling Skills

In order to communicate empathy, unconditional positive regard and congruence to the client, the counselling psychologist has to draw on a number and range of skills. The following skills are necessary for effective counselling; listening, the use of non-verbal behaviour or body language, paraphrasing and reflecting.

The next section will discuss how these counselling skills may be used to establish the core conditions of effective therapeutic practice described above.

Listening

Active listening involves showing understanding by attending to and reflecting (with your verbal, voice and body messages) the root of the meaning contained in the verbal, voice and body messages of clients.

Egan (1986) argues that complete listening involves three things: (1) observing and reading the client's non-verbal behaviour; (2) listening to and understanding the client's verbal messages; and (3) listening in an integrated way to the person in the context of both the helping process and everyday life.

The process of listening to another person is not the same as hearing. Listening involves other aspects of communication apart from what people say verbally.

Box 2 Three aspects of listening (Egan, 1986)

Linguistic aspects	Words
	Phrases
	Metaphors
Paralinguistic aspects	Timing
	Volume
	Pitch
	Accent
	'Ums and Errs'
	Fluency
Non-verbal aspects	Facial expression
	Use of gesture
	Touch
	Body position
	Proximity
	Body movement
	Eye contact

One of the main considerations when listening to another person is the behaviour that the listener adopts. Egan (1986) offers the acronym SOLER as a means of identifying the type of behaviour that promotes effective listening:

Box 3 Behavioural Aspects of Listening (Egan, 1986)

Sit squarely in relation to the person you are listening to (this does not mean directly opposite). Adopt an attentive upright position.

Maintain an **O**pen position, i.e. sit with arms and legs uncrossed.

Lean slightly towards the person. This may depend on the context and flow of the conversation as maintaining a fixed posture towards the person for long lengths of time may be intimidating.

Maintain reasonable **E**ye contact with the person. Eye contact needs to be consistent but don't stare at the other person. A fixed gaze can be unnerving for the other person.

Relax. The listener has to be relaxed to convey confidence to the client. It is important to be at ease and comfortable, although be careful not to convey a sense of boredom or an unprofessional attitude.

Patterson (1974) states that the function of the counsellor is to respond to the client. When it is predominantly the client responding to the counsellor, it can sound and feel like an interrogation. If the client only responds to the counsellor, the client may not feel free or able to talk about significant issues. As a result, the counsellor will be unable to understand what the client is really feeling and, consequently, will also be unable to demonstrate empathic understanding. Therefore, accurate listening, not only to the words of clients but also to their non-verbal behaviour, is an essential skill for counselling psychologists.

Use of non-verbal communication

Empathy, unconditional positive regard and congruence are communicated to clients partly by non-verbal communication. In addition, counsellors are more likely to understand their clients accurately if they are able to identify and respond to non-verbal, as well as verbal components of their communication. Non-verbal communication includes: gestures, head movements, posture, facial expression, eye contact, proximity, spatial position and touch.

Posture, sitting position and eye contact all convey messages about attentiveness and interest. Sitting upright with an open posture while leaning slightly forward and maintaining eye contact are all important in communicating the core conditions.

Paraphrasing

Paraphrasing is one of the component skills of how you show understanding in active listening. Paraphrasing is providing a short summary (in your own words not those of the other person) of the content of what the person has said to you or details of their experience – 'repeating back'. Examples of paraphrasing are:

➡ **Client:** I told my kids I was going to go and never come back.
➡ **Counsellor:** You told your children you were going to leave home.

➡ **Client:** I find being without a partner depressing. I'm so anxious about being on my own.
➡ **Counsellor:** You feel low and are very anxious about not being in a relationship.

Paraphrasing lets both counsellor and client know that they are communicating with and understanding each other. In particular, it lets the client know they are being listened to. The counselling psychologist uses it as a tracking device to follow what the client is both saying and feeling. An example of a basic form of paraphrasing is 'you feel … because of …'. The counselling psychologist will tend to use their own words while at the same time respecting the values and culture of the client. However, the counsellor may usefully repeat significant words or phrases used by the client. When paraphrasing, it is necessary for the counselling psychologist to ignore her own ideas, feelings and attitudes. The aim of paraphrasing is to be in touch emotionally with the client, yet at the same time to be separate and therefore avoiding over-identification.

Reflection of content

Paraphrasing involves the reflection of both content and feelings. Accurate reflection of content by the counsellor lets the client know that they are being heard. This in turn builds trust and respect. Reflection of content also provides the counselling psychologist with the opportunity to check or clarify what the client has said.

Reflection of content is also a way of improving the skill of getting into and responding from within the client's frame of reference.

Reflection of feeling

Accurate reflection of feeling demonstrates to the client that the counsellor perceives what the client is feeling, and also why he/she is experiencing those feelings. Accurate reflection is a powerful way of helping clients to feel understood and to identify and experience their emotions. In this way reflection of feeling leads towards empathic understanding of the client's world.

It is necessary for all counselling psychologists, whatever their theoretical orientation, to be adept in the skill of communicating to clients empathic understanding, unconditional positive regard and congruence. In order to do this counsellors need to draw on skills of listening to clients, understanding them and communicating back to them that they are accepted and understood.

THE PSYCHODYNAMIC PERSPECTIVE

The psychodynamic approaches to counselling psychology are based on the psychoanalytic theories and practice of Sigmund Freud. They argue that a significant part of our mental functioning is unconscious. The unconscious part of our mind contains memories, thoughts and feelings which we have repressed to avoid the pain and conflict they might cause. Although this material is buried in our unconscious, it does not mean that such matter does not affect us. On the contrary, from the psychodynamic perspective the memories and emotions we have buried in our unconscious have a significant impact on our behaviour, thoughts and feelings.

The psychodynamic approach argues that the origin of psychological problems lies in our childhood experiences. If the disturbing thoughts, feelings and memories of our childhood experiences are repressed by the unconscious processes, they are not accessible and therefore remain unresolved. The aim of psychodynamic counselling is to bring unconscious material into conscious awareness so that the client can gain insight and understanding.

The word psychodynamic comes from the two Greek words 'Psyche' meaning soul or mind, and 'Dynamic' referring to forces, often moving in different and opposing directions. Freud's model of the human mind was based on the idea that our experiences are dynamic, a result of conflicting forces, wishes, impulses and ideas.

Applying psychodynamic theory

Psychodynamic counselling aims to bring the content of the unconscious into conscious awareness. The belief is that if the conflicts underlying our troublesome thoughts and feelings can be identified and understood, we can change our behaviour. Clients are helped to see the links between past experiences and present behaviour, enabling them to integrate previously unknown parts of themselves into their present and future selves, and become more whole individuals.

The emphasis on the significance of the unconscious is specific to the psychodynamic approach and sets it apart from all other approaches. The counselling psychologist continuously attempts to understand the unconscious links between the client's past and their present. A second distinctive feature of this approach is the use of interpretation by the counsellor as a way of bringing material in the unconscious to consciousness. The techniques used by psychodynamic counsellors to enable clients to uncover unconscious matter and bring them to conscious awareness will be discussed in the next section.

Within the psychodynamic approach to counselling, an assessment is carried out to gather information which might help the counsellor establish the possible causes of clients' problems and current conflicts. Jacobs (1988) identifies a number of areas that the psychodynamic counsellor is interested in covering during the assessment:

➡ Factual material. The family history and the current life situations of the client.
➡ Presenting problems and duration. What is the problem that has brought the client to counselling and how long has it lasted?
➡ Precipitating factors. Why has the client come for help now? What has happened in the recent past? What was the trigger?
➡ Current conflicts and further problems that often emerge in later sessions.
➡ Underlying conflicts and past problems. What has happened in the past that is related to current difficulties?
➡ Goals. What does the client want to achieve?
➡ Method of referral. How did the client come to counselling? Have they been sent? Was it their own idea? Was it to please their partner?
➡ Appearance of the client and manner.

Once the assessment is completed, the therapeutic work can begin. The aim of the work is for the client to resolve current conflicts which underlie the client's presenting problems. In bringing unconscious thoughts and feelings into conscious awareness, the client is helped to make sense of their current problems and early memories. Once the client has gained insight into and has an understanding of the causes of their difficulties, they are better able to resolve their current difficulties.

Psychodynamic counselling aims to help the client recognise and understand the way they relate to others. It also helps make the client aware of how he or she relates to different parts of themselves. Being made aware of the parts of ourselves of which we have not previously been conscious, helps us to present a more integrated sense of self.

A successful outcome of psychodynamic counselling is not necessarily the solution of the presenting problem. It is anticipated that through counselling the client has gained insight and understanding and is in a stronger position to confront their problems more directly. Freud once described the psychoanalyst's job as one of replacing 'neurotic misery with ordinary unhappiness' (Breuer and Freud 1895).

Therapeutic relationship

A client will only feel able to reveal to a counsellor the troublesome thoughts, feelings and memories they have repressed if they feel safe within the therapeutic relationship. In other words, before effective work can be done, a therapeutic alliance needs to be formed. Dryden and Mytton (1999) refer to the three rules that guide the psychodynamic counsellor's attitude and style

'The rule of abstinence'

This refers to a deliberate holding back from responding to the client in the way that most people would consider normal social interactions.

'The rule of anonymity'

This refers to the fact that psychodynamic counsellors purposely reveal nothing of themselves so that the client can see them in their own particular way. 'The rule of anonymity' allows transference to take place. 'Transference' is the term Freud used to refer to circumstances where one person treats another person as if they were someone else in their lives, usually a significant person. For example, the client can see an anonymous counsellor as their father or mother. When the counsellor responds to the client as if they, the client, were someone else, this is referred to as counter-transference and it is used to gain further understanding of the client. Feelings stirred up in the counsellor by the client provide insight into how others might feel towards the client and how, in turn, the client might relate to others. For example, if the counsellor begins to feel the need to take care of the client, this might suggest that the client has a strong need to be looked after by others.

'The rule of neutrality'

This refers to the attitude that counsellors take to all clients; it reflects a commitment to discover the truth and a respect for their clients' independence. The psychodynamic counsellor reflects on what the client says. By remaining neutral the counsellor does not seek to influence the client but rather tries to help the client understand themselves more fully.

The psychodynamic counselling process

As the client proceeds through the process of therapy, the psychodynamic counsellor begins to develop ideas about why the client behaves in the way that he or she does. The counsellor offers these interpretations to the client. This sharing of the interpretations serves to bring into conscious awareness what the client is unconsciously communicating to the counsellor.

Any demonstration of transference by the client is encouraged by the counsellor. Through the experience of transference the client feels emotions from the past, often difficult ones, and attributes them to the counsellor. For example, a client's past fears about rejection or abandonment from her father may be transferred onto the counsellor. These feelings may become apparent in the reaction of the client when the counsellor announces that he/she is going on holiday for two weeks. The client may feel inappropriate anger or distress towards the counsellor. Such reactions may reflect the client's problems in relationships generally, and need to be explored and worked through.

Working through

Over time, through the process of interpretation, the client develops considerable insight into their problems. Gradually, they become aware of the factors and forces that they have repressed in their unconscious, and how these relate to their current difficulties and experiences. Acquiring insight takes place over a protracted period of time. A single interpretation offered by the counsellor is unlikely to have a major impact on the client in terms of changing his or her ways of behaving. The counsellor begins with tentative interpretations, and as the counselling process goes on, and the client reveals more information about their feelings and emotions, the counsellor develops and refines the interpretations.

THE SYSTEMIC PERSPECTIVE

The systemic perspective within counselling psychology understands families as an interacting system – one member's problems are symptomatic of problems within the system. In other words, an individual's problems are best understood through considering the interactions within an entire family (the system), because the individual's difficulty may be a symptom of a dysfunction within the family; rather than an indication of psychopathology within the individual (Goldenberg and Goldenberg 1996).

Counselling psychologists working from the family systems approach (also known as the systemic approach) hold three main assumptions about a client's problematic behaviour: (1) it may serve a function or purpose for the family; (2) it may reflect the family's inability to operate productively, particularly during times of change, such as when children leave home; and (3) it may be a symptom of dysfunctional patterns of behaviour handed down from generation to generation.

A central principle of the approach is that individuals are connected to, and are part of, living systems (such as the family) and any change in one part of the system has a knock-on effect on every other part of that system. In other words, actions by any one individual family member will influence all the others in the family and their reactions in turn will have an effect on the individual.

There are a number of different schools of family systems therapy and each has developed different methods of intervention.

Multigenerational Family Therapy (Bowen 1966, 1976) holds that a family can best be understood when it is analysed from at least a three-generation perspective, because a predictable pattern of relationships between members connects the functioning of family members across generations. In other words, what occurs in one generation will probably occur in the next, because key unresolved emotional issues tend to be played out over generations. Information about past relationships is valued as an important context from which to design interventions in the present. The genogram was devised as a way of collecting and organising important information about a family over at least three generations.

This approach focuses on the emotional cycles with one's family of origin (parents and siblings, spouse, and children). A basic assumption is that unresolved emotional fusion to one's family (in other words failure to emotionally separate) must be addressed if one hopes to achieve a mature personality. The major contributions of Bowen's theory to family therapy are the core concepts of *differentiation* of the self and *triangulation* (Bowen 1966 and 1976).

Differentiation of the self involves two processes. The first is psychological separation of intellect and emotion, and the second is independence of the self from others. Differentiated individuals are able to choose between being guided by their feelings or by their thoughts. Undifferentiated individuals often react only on the basis of feeling, rather than responding in a more rational, less emotional manner. The second process of differentiation involves separation of the self from others. In family systems theory, the key to being a psychologically healthy person includes both a sense of belonging to one's family while at the same time developing a sense of separateness and individuality.

Bowen (1976) suggests that anxiety can easily develop within intimate relationships, and that in stressful situations, two members of a family draw in or recruit a third member into the relationship to reduce the anxiety and gain stability. This is referred to as *triangulation*. Creating triangles serves to reduce or increase the emotional intensity within the family. For example, parents experiencing marital difficulties may draw in a child to diffuse the situation.

In **Structural Family Therapy**, a second school within the systemic approach, Salvador Minuchin (1974) focuses on the interactions of family members as a way of understanding the structure, or organisation, of a family. Structural family therapists concentrate on how, when and to whom family members relate. Through this information the structure of a family and the problems that bring the family into therapy can be assessed.

Structural family therapy is based on the idea that most symptoms displayed by individuals are a by-product of structural failings within the family organisation (Guerin and Chabot 1992). For example Minuchin (1974), in his work with families of anorexic girls, found that attention on the anorexic member of the family tends to function as an outlet and diversion from wider issues. This allows the family to focus on the individual's problem, rather than address difficulties operating in the whole family. The key concepts are: family structure, family sub-systems, and boundaries. Sub-systems are defined by interpersonal boundaries. Boundaries vary in their permeability: they may be diffuse or rigid. One of the characteristics of the typical 'anorexic family' identified by Minuchin, was that of 'enmeshment', where boundaries are diffuse and family members are over involved in each other's lives.

The family's sub-systems, boundaries, alignments and coalitions are studied in an attempt to understand its structure. So for example, a firm alliance between the parents prevents a child from forming an alliance with one or other of the parents and furthermore forces children into forming their own sub-systems with brothers and sisters or others of their own generation.

In a third school of systemic therapy, **Strategic Family Therapy**, the problem presented in the individual client is not addressed as a symptom of some other systemic dysfunction. The problem brought by the family is treated as 'real' and an attempt is made to 'solve' it. This practical approach involves the notion that change occurs through a family carrying out a therapist's directives and changing its transactions.

Strategic family therapists assume that people often develop problems during times of change, or transitions from one developmental stage to the next. The purpose of therapy is to help move the family forward to the appropriate stage of family life (Haley 1973). For example, starting school admits others into the family system, forcing change. Children with school phobia may be responding to the family's inability to widen the boundaries.

Strategic family therapy requires neither understanding nor insight, and neither is sought. The focus of therapy is not on growth or resolving issues from the past, but on solving problems in the present. The focus for treatment within this approach is on the whole family (the system). It will usually involve the members who live together, but might also include members who live elsewhere.

The systems therapist focuses on the here and now and on changing how the family functions. The four main aims of family therapy are:

1 Understanding the dynamics of the family.
2 Discovering and activating the psychological resources of the family.
3 Working with the family members to change their relationships with one another in order to reduce dysfunctional behavioural symptoms.
4 Helping family members develop problem-solving and coping skills.

Techniques

The primary goal in family systems therapy is to produce visible change in behaviour. A number of techniques are used by family therapists to achieve this goal.

Family sculpting

Developed by Duhl, Kantor and Duhl (1973), family sculpting enables individuals within a family to recreate the family system, representing family members' relationships to one another at a specific period of time. The family therapist can use sculpting at any time in therapy by asking family members to physically arrange the family: One family member positions the other members of the family to physically represent the emotional relationships that exist between them. Adolescents often make good family sculptors as they are provided with a chance to non-verbally communicate thoughts and feelings about the family. Family sculpting is a useful diagnostic tool and provides the opportunity for future therapeutic interventions.

Figure 3.1 A group therapy session

Strategic alliances

This technique, often used by strategic family therapists, involves meeting with one member of the family as a supportive means of helping that person change. Individual change is expected to affect the entire family system. The individual is often asked to behave or respond in a different manner. This technique attempts to disrupt a circular system or behaviour pattern. For example, if the mother usually relies on the father to discipline the children, the therapist would encourage the mother to takeover this responsibility.

Reframing

Most family therapists use reframing as a method to both join with the family and offer a different perspective on presenting problems. Specifically, reframing involves taking something out of its logical class and placing it in another category (Sherman and Fredman 1986). For example, it is possible that a mother's repeated questioning of her daughter's behaviour after a date can be seen as genuine caring and concern rather than that of a non-trusting intrusive parent. Through reframing, a negative can often be reframed into a positive.

Tracking

Most family therapists use tracking. Structural family therapists (Minuchin and Fishman 1981) see tracking as an essential part of the therapist's joining process with the family. Joining refers to the formation of a therapeutic alliance. The technique of tracking involves following the content of the family's communications and behaviour, attending to symbols, styles, language and values of the family. During the tracking process the therapist listens intently to family stories and carefully records events and their sequence. Through tracking, the family therapist is able to identify the sequence of events operating in a system to keep it the way it is. What happens between point A and point B or C to create D can be helpful when designing interventions.

The genogram

The genogram, a technique often used at the start of family therapy, provides a graphic picture of the family history. The genogram reveals the family's basic structure and demographics. (McGoldrick and Gerson 1985). Through symbols, it offers a picture of three generations. Names, dates of marriage, divorce, death and other relevant facts are included in the genogram. In addition to demographic data, the genogram also graphically illustrates family relationships. The therapist and family work together to develop the genogram and, as such, it provides an enormous amount of data and insight for the therapist and family members early in therapy.

Figure 3.1 overleaf shows an example of a genogram constructed from the information provided in the case study below:

Box 4 Case study

Christine is the only surviving child of elderly Italian parents who moved from a northern Italian village to London some 30 years ago in the hope that their children could have a 'better future'. Sadly, one year after their arrival in England, Christine's older brother was killed in a traffic accident whilst playing with neighbourhood children.

After leaving school Christine attended a community college where she trained as a Secretary. She found work easily and soon settled in at an accountancy firm within walking distance from her family home. Christine continued to live at home until she married a junior associate at her work. After they were married Christine and her husband set-up house two doors from her parents. Christine describes this as the beginning of what was to be persistent marital conflict between her and her husband.

Christine's husband was never happy with the level of involvement she maintained with her parents. She reported that in order to 'break them up', he would demand that they never include her parents in their activities and he forbade her to telephone them. The breaking point came in their relationship when he applied for, and accepted, another job in the North of England.

Christine's husband expects her to leave London with him when the time comes for him to commence work. Christine was devastated that he had made such a decision without talking to her. She sees no acceptable resolution to the dilemma that confronts her and feels like a failure, both as a daughter and as a wife.

Circular questioning

Another systemic technique consists of asking circular questions that are designed to get clients to think about the roles they play in relating to members of their family. So, for example, the counselling psychologist might ask the partner of a woman with depressive symptoms, 'Is there anything you do that might have a positive effect on Julie's mood?' and 'Is there anything you can do to make Julie's mood worse – intentionally or unintentionally? This form of questioning allows the family to experience the circularity of their interactions and it also encourages family members to move to the position of an observer of themselves and others, giving them the chance of perceiving themselves and others differently.

A counselling psychologist adopting a systemic approach in working with Christine (see case study) would undertake the following tasks:

1 Assess the current living situation and life experiences of Christine and her family.
2 Explore the history and relationships between members of the family using a genogram.
3 Encourage the family members to join Christine at counselling sessions.
4 Formulate questions and test a number of 'hypotheses' such as: How does Christine's depression affect her husband and her parents? Does her depression serve the needs of other family members? If so how? Does it distract others from problems in their intimate relationships?

Maintaining symptoms to protect other family members is not restricted to children and their parents, but may occur between marital partners as well (Wachtel and Wachtel 1986). For example, it might be that Christine's depressive symptoms are an attempt to gain her husbands' sympathy, and therefore serve the purpose of maintaining her relationship with him. Or, it might be that the depressive symptoms serve to limit the intimacy of their relationship, thereby reducing, for both of them, the stress that an intimate relationship would involve in their circumstances.

Rather than viewing the appearance of symptoms as emanating from a single 'sick' person, the counselling psychologist would try to view Christine as a symptom bearer who was expressing the family's dysfunction.

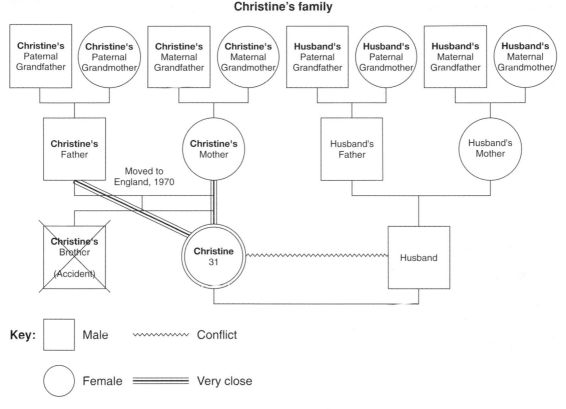

Christine's family

Key:

■ Male   ∿∿∿∿ Conflict

● Female   ════ Very close

Figure 3.2 An example of a genogram

THE COGNITIVE BEHAVIOURAL PERSPECTIVE

Cognitive behavioural therapy, often referred to as CBT, focuses on the links between what a person thinks about themselves or a situation and how this affects the way they feel and behave. As the first century Greek philosopher Epictetus suggested: *'Men are disturbed not by things, but by the views they take of them'.*

If our thoughts are too negative, it can block us seeing things or doing things that don't fit – or disconfirm – what we believe is true. In this way, we continue to hold on to the same old thoughts and fail to learn anything new. For example, a depressed woman may think, 'I can't face going to work today, I am not up to it. I won't be able to do anything right and I will feel awful.' Having these thoughts, and believing them, she phones in sick and spends the rest of the day at home in bed.

In behaving this way, she does not have the opportunity to find out that her prediction was wrong. Had she gone to work she might well have found things she could do and perhaps some things that were bearable. By not going to work and staying at home worrying about her failure to go in, she may end up thinking 'I've let everyone down, they will be angry with me. Why can't I cope like everyone else? I am so weak and pathetic.' Ruminating on these thoughts will make her feel even worse and make it even more difficult for her to return to work the next day. Thinking, behaving and feeling like this starts a downward spiral, one from which it can be very difficult to escape.

In the 1960s Aaron Beck, an American psychotherapist, first identified the significance of the link between thoughts and feelings. He coined the term 'automatic thoughts' to describe emotion-filled or 'hot' thoughts that just pop into the mind apparently from nowhere. These automatic thoughts tend to be negative and are neither realistic nor helpful. In his therapeutic work, Beck found that people were not always aware of these thoughts, but with help could learn to identify and record them. Beck found that the key to overcoming their difficulties lay with the individual successfully identifying these thoughts.

Beck suggested that our thinking patterns are formed in childhood, and become automatic and relatively fixed. A child, who received little affection from her parents but was roundly praised for school work, might come to think 'I have to do well all the time. If I don't, people will reject me'. If a person lives by such a rule, experiencing an inevitable failure may trigger automatic thoughts like 'I've completely failed. No one will like me. I can't face them'.

In CBT the client and counselling psychologist work together to help the client understand and change the ways of thinking that are causing distress or making it hard to live a normal life. The focus is on the problematic patterns of thinking that cause the problematic behaviour. Misinterpreting situations or symptoms can weaken peoples' ability to cope with life, and abnormal patterns of behaviour may be used as coping behaviour. These abnormal patterns of behaviour serve to exacerbate and reinforce these problems. For example, healthy people with panic disorder tend to interpret a rapid heart rate and tightness in the chest as a sign of an imminent and potentially fatal heart attack. This leads to a state of panic with ensuing further increase in heart rate and tightness in the chest, which causes yet heightened anxiety and panic. Typically in this situation, the client will rest or lie down to 'take the strain off the heart'.

The counselling psychologist encourages the client to identify their panic related thoughts, e.g. 'I am going to have a heart attack', 'I am going to die', 'I can't breath'. Once the client has identified their thoughts, the counselling psychologist asks them to provide evidence to support them. Usually the client has difficulty doing so, and is helped to provide counter-evidence for the thoughts. For example, the client may come to realise that the rapid heart rate may be related to excitement, worry, exercise or caffeine consumption. The client may be asked to walk briskly up and down a corridor or stairs to induce a rapid heart rate to demonstrate that it has no adverse consequences.

The aim of cognitive behavioural therapy is to break this cycle by encouraging clients to examine their thinking and assumptions. Thoughts are treated as hypotheses to be tested and challenged. The counsellor helps the client to explore alternative ways of thinking about themselves or situations. This is done by identifying and challenging the negative thoughts. The counselling psychologist will ask the client the following questions in order to get them, the client, to question their thoughts:

1 **What is the evidence?**
   What evidence do I have to support my thoughts?
   What evidence do I have against them?

2 **What alternative views are there?**
   How would someone else view this situation?
   How would I have viewed it before I got depressed?
   What evidence do I have for these alternatives?

3 **What is the effect of thinking the way I do?**
   Does it help me, or hinder me from getting what I want? How?
   What would be the effect of looking at things less negatively?

4 **What thinking error am I making?**
   Am I thinking in all or nothing terms?
   Am I condemning myself as a total person on the basis of a single event?
   Am I concentrating on my weaknesses and forgetting my strengths?
   Am I blaming myself for something which is not my fault?
   Am I taking something personally which was little or nothing to do with me?
   Am I expecting myself to be perfect?
   Am I using a double standard – how would I view someone else in my situation?
   Am I paying attention only to the darker side of things?
   Am I overstating the chances of disaster?
   Am I exaggerating the importance of events?
   Am I fretting about the way things ought to be instead of accepting and dealing with them as they come?
   Am I assuming I can do nothing to change my situation?

Am I predicting the future instead of experimenting with it?

5 **What action can I take?**

What can I do to change my situation?

Am I overlooking solutions to problems on the assumption they won't work?

What can I do to test the validity of my rational answers?

Adapted from Emery (1981)

A typical course of CBT consists of 8 to 12 sessions usually taking between three to six months. Clients attend a session a week, each session lasting about an hour. CBT has been used to treat a wide range of psychological problems, including: depression, panic disorder, anxiety disorders, eating disorders and obsessive-compulsive disorder.

CBT sessions follow a structure rather than the client talking freely about issues that come to mind. At the beginning of therapy, the client and therapist set goals for the client to work towards based on the presenting problem. The problems may be troublesome symptoms such as difficulty sleeping or inability to concentrate on work, or they could be longer-term problems, such as being unhappy at work, or being in an unhappy marriage.

The identified problems and set goals form the basis for planning the content of the sessions. Homework is typically set for clients and usually involves putting in to practice what they have learned during the session.

Homework

Homework assignments are a vital part of the therapeutic process within CBT. The homework tasks vary, but at the start of therapy usually involve diary keeping. For example, clients often keep diaries to record their negative or upsetting thoughts and disturbed feelings and the events that trigger them. Keeping a diary helps clients to note constructive changes in these thoughts and feelings over time.

A structured method of challenging irrational or negative beliefs is by encouraging clients to fill in a daily thought diary (see Table 3.1 on p. 68) based on the model of emotional disturbance proposed by Albert Ellis (1950) known as Rational Emotive Behaviour Therapy (REBT). The basic hypothesis

or REBT is that our emotions stem from our beliefs, evaluations, interpretations and reactions to life situations. Through therapy, clients learn to identify, dispute and replace irrational beliefs and change their emotional reactions to situations. It is assumed by Ellis that humans are born with the potential for both rational or straight thinking and irrational, crooked thinking. He argued that we learn irrational beliefs from significant others during childhood and create irrational dogmas and superstitions by ourselves. Through autosuggestion and self-repetition these self-defeating beliefs are continuously reinforced and irrational beliefs stay with us. Ellis identified common types of irrational beliefs, one of which emerges due to individuals' tendency to escalate desires and preferences into demands and commands: 'shoulds', 'musts' 'oughts'. He referred to this penchant as 'Mustabation'. For example: 'I must have love or approval from all the significant people in my life', 'I must perform important tasks competently and perfectly well.'

Ellis' model is known as the ABC theory of emotions:

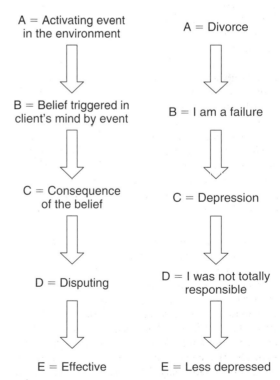

Figure 3.3 The ABC theory of emotions

Applied Psychology

In the first REBT session the focus is on building rapport and identifying problems to be targeted for exploration. The counselling psychologist might ask the client 'In what ways would you like to think, feel and act differently than you do now?'

Clients make a note of the activating event (A). That is, they are asked to describe clearly and concisely the situation that disturbed them. They then have to identify their irrational belief or beliefs (B) about the situation. The next step is to record the consequences (C) of holding the belief. What are their disturbed emotions and behaviours in the situation? Next the client has to dispute (D) their irrational beliefs. They are asked 'Where is the evidence for your beliefs?' An example of a dispute might be 'Why is it *terrible* and *horrible* if life is not the way you want it to be?' They are encouraged to ask themselves questions such as 'Why *must* people treat me fairly?', 'If life doesn't go the way I would like it to, is it so *awful*, or is it just inconvenient?'

Clients are encouraged to identify and record a different way to think about the situation through disputing their initial irrational beliefs. The final stage is to identify their new effective (E) thoughts, feelings and behaviour in the situation.

For example, the mother of a teenage boy is annoyed by his late return after an evening out with his friends. When he gets home he slams the front door and goes straight upstairs to his room (Activating event). The mother thinks what a rude and inconsiderate young man he is (Belief). She is angry and storms upstairs after him (Consequence) and they have a row leaving her upset and their relationship damaged. The mother could have thought 'perhaps something is wrong, maybe he is upset' (Dispute) and taken a cup of tea up to her son to see if he was OK and by doing so could have strengthened the relationship (Effective).

RECENT EXAMPLE OF AN INTERVENTION

Cognitive therapy vs medications in the treatment of moderate to severe depression DeRubeis et al. (2005)

There is a great deal of evidence that antidepressant medications treat moderate to severe depression effectively, but there is less research evidence for the efficacy of cognitive therapy for depression of this type.

Situation	Negative Automatic Thoughts	Emotions	Alternative and balanced thoughts	How do you feel now?
Describe clearly and concisely. Who? What? Where?	Rate believability of thoughts 0%–100% What was going through your mind?	Rate intensity of emotions 0%–100%	Rate believability of alternative thoughts 0%–100%	Re-rate intensity of emotions 0%–100%
On my own at home on Saturday night.	No one wants to be with me. I am a failure. I am going to be on my own for the rest of my life.	Depressed 100% Lonely 100% Despair 90%	Although I am on my own now, I am seeing friends tomorrow, and they want to be with me. 10% Just because I am not in a relationship at the moment, does not mean I never will be. 15%	Depressed 85% Lonely 90% Despair 85%

Table 3.1 Example of a Daily Thought Record

The objective of this study was to compare the efficacy in moderate to severe depression of antidepressant medications with cognitive therapy in a placebo-controlled trial.

Clients diagnosed with moderate to severe depression were randomly assigned to one of the following interventions:

➡ 16 weeks of medications (n = 120);
➡ 16 weeks of cognitive therapy (n = 60); or
➡ 8 weeks of pill placebo (n = 60).

Participants: 240 outpatients, aged 18 to 70 years, with moderate to severe major depressive disorder.

Interventions: The medication group received paroxetine, up to 50 mg daily, supplemented with lithium carbonate or desipramine hydrochloride if necessary. The therapy group received individual cognitive therapy.

Main outcome measure: The Hamilton Depression Rating Scale, which is a self-complete questionnaire, provided continuous severity scores and allowed for patients to be designated in terms of response and remission.

Results: At 8 weeks, response rates in medications (50%) and cognitive therapy (43%) groups were both superior to the placebo (25%) group.

Analysis based on continuous scores at 8 weeks indicated an advantage for each of the active treatments over placebo, each with a medium effect size. The advantage was slightly greater for medication relative to placebo, compared with cognitive therapy relative to placebo.

At 16 weeks, response rates were 58% in each of the active conditions; remission rates were 46% for medication, 40% for cognitive therapy.

Conclusion: Cognitive therapy can be as effective as medications for the initial treatment of moderate to severe major depression.

EVALUATION OF OUTCOMES

Some of the earliest outcome studies of counselling and psychotherapy were carried out by Carl Rogers in the 1940s (Cartwright 1957) These early studies provided evidence for the effectiveness of client-centred therapy in bringing about change in the client.

A number of outcome studies of person-centred counselling have been carried out more recently. In a review, Greenberg, Elliot and Lietaer (1994) found studies published between 1978 and 1992, involving 1272 clients. Of these studies, 15 were comparisons with no-treatment or waiting-list groups, and 26 studies compared person-centred counselling with another therapeutic approach. The results of these studies show a general efficacy of person-centred counselling, but no more or no less effective than any other approach.

Cognitive behavioural therapy has been used to treat most psychological disorders and has been found to be more effective in the treatment of some than in others. Butler and Beck (2000) have reviewed 325 studies of 15 disorders or client groups. They also compared CBT with alternative treatments. A comparison of CBT with antidepressants in the treatment of depression showed CBT to be slightly more effective. However, one year after treatment stopped, depressed clients who had received CBT had half the relapse rate of clients who had been treated with antidepressants.

The results of research into systemic therapy tend to support this approach for a range of psychological problems (Shadish et al. 1995). However, when families who had received systemic therapy were followed up, the results were disappointing. The patterns of interaction that had caused the initial difficulties had re-emerged and when the families were asked about the therapy they confessed that they had often colluded in hiding important family secrets from the therapists (Selvini-Palazolli et al. 1989).

CURRENT DIRECTIONS

The demand for psychological therapy in Britain is rapidly increasing (Department of Health 1999), however the issue of resourcing this increasing need is a contentious one. While on the one hand there is the demand for increased access to psychological therapies, there is, on the other hand, as we have seen, a lack of evidence on the efficacy and cost effectiveness of the different psychotherapies available. Randomised trials cover only a limited number of treatments, and many treatments remain unevaluated in relation to many conditions (Roth and Fonagy 2004). There are real difficulties in providing meaningful evidence on all psychotherapies, more so with the analytic ones than the cognitive behavioural therapies. Beutler, Machado and Neufeldt (2004) suggest that factors related to the therapist and the client are likely to be as key to the success of the therapy as the type of therapy on offer. For example, self-reflective and introspective individuals seem to benefit more from insight-oriented therapies (such as psychodynamic therapy), whereas impulsive and aggressive clients respond better to symptom-focused procedures (such as CBT) (Ibid. 2004). Furthermore, research suggests that a skilled therapist achieves successful outcomes with the right client, irrespective of the type of therapy they provide.

There is a considerable body of evidence from randomised controlled trials for the efficacy of psychotherapy in depression, panic, generalised anxiety disorder, eating disorder and personality disorder. Cognitive behaviour therapy, family therapy, person-centred therapy and some psychodynamic therapy have been shown to significantly reduce psychological and behavioural symptoms that impair peoples' lives (Roth and Fonagy 2004). However, sadly, many clients are left with residual symptoms and often seek further treatment (Ibid. 2004).

Clients with the least complex and shorter duration of psychological problems respond best to treatment. The theoretically-based therapies with a coherent theoretical means of action, such as those provided by counselling psychologists, produce better results than those that do not have a theoretical model informing the practice (Wampold et al. 2002).

Recently, differences between individual therapies in relation to specific disorders have begun to emerge. The efficacy of cognitive behaviour therapy for anxiety disorders is firmly established. Psychodynamic therapy has been shown to be effective in severe personality disorders (Leichsenring and Leibing 2003) which do not respond well to cognitive behaviour therapy (Dare et al. 2001), and family therapy is effective in anorexia nervosa (Dare et al. 2001).

From the days of Freud's first analyses of the Viennese bourgeoisie, psychotherapy has established itself outside the state sector. In Britain today, there is still more private than state provision of psychotherapy. The profession of counselling psychology is in a strong position to allow evidence-based therapy to become more accessible to more people, not just those who can afford it, and enable the NHS to respond to the growing demand for mental health services.

USEFUL WEBSITES

The British Psychological Society's Division of Counselling Psychology: www.bps.org.uk/careers/areas/counselling

The British Association for Counselling and Psychotherapy (BACP). The umbrella organisation for counselling in the UK: www.bacp.co.uk

The United Kingdom Council for Psychotherapy (UKCP). The umbrella organisation for psychotherapy in the UK: www.psychotherapy.org.uk

Exercises

Exercise 1

Have another look at the case of Christine that is described on p. 64. Christine's problems were looked at from the systemic perspective.

➧ How would you understand and explain Christine's difficulties from a cognitive behavioural perspective? What might have caused her to feel the way she does?

➧ If you were working as a cognitive behavioural therapist, how would you help Christine overcome her difficulties? What would her treatment involve?

Exercise 2

Construct a genogram of your family. Include at least three generations providing relevant information for each member, e.g. sex, age, marriages, deaths etc. Also indicate emotional relationships between members.

Exercise 3 – Counselling skills

The skill of listening to clients is just one of the counselling skills used by counselling psychologists in their work. Below are some exercises demonstrating a number of factors which help clients feel they are being listened to. They should be carried out in pairs:

Exercise 3a: Effect of distance

➧ Place two chairs, ten feet apart, each of you take a seat. One starts telling the other about a minor problem they are having. Swap roles. How does the distance affect the conversation?

➧ Move the chairs to a comfortable distance then measure that distance – knee to knee. Is it about 18 inches, an average social distance? Does this seem too close, or too far away?

Exercise 3b: Body position

➧ **Posture**: In pairs, both seated, one talks for five minutes and the other listens while:
  (a) Sitting with arms and legs tightly crossed.
  (b) Sitting sprawled loosely in your chair.
  (c) Adopting a relaxed and attentive body posture.

➧ **Trunk lean**: In pairs, both seated, one talks for Five minutes and the other listens while:
  (a) Leaning right back.
  (b) Leaning far forward.
  (c) Leaning slightly forward.

➧ **Eye contact:** In pairs, both seated, one talks for five minutes and the other listens while:
  (a) Avoiding partner's gaze.
  (b) Staring at partner.
  (c) Maintaining good eye contact, yet looking away every now and then.

Exercise 3c: Eyes closed

➧ In pairs sit facing each other with your eyes closed. Discuss how you spent Christmas for five minutes, then swap. Discuss your reactions to the experience. What non-verbal behaviours did you find most difficult to do without?

Exercise 3d: Silence

➧ In pairs, both seated, one talks for five minutes about a minor problem they are having, while the other listens but does not speak.

Adapted from *Practical Counselling and Helping Skills* by Richard Nelson-Jones (1993).

Educational Psychology

EDUCATIONAL PSYCHOLOGY IN THE BRITISH PSYCHOLOGICAL SOCIETY (BPS)

Educational psychologists are encouraged to become Chartered Educational Psychologists within the BPS, the organisation responsible for training and ethical standards within the profession. Regulation is voluntary, though there are proceedings in place to make regulation mandatory, to ensure that only appropriately qualified individuals can practise as 'psychologists'. Within the BPS, appropriately qualified educational psychologists can become members of the Division of Educational and Child Psychology (DECP) and practise as Chartered Educational Psychologists. The DECP keeps members up to date with research and other developments in the field through newsletters, publishing the *Journal of Educational and Child Psychology*, and through organising conferences.

PRINCIPLES OF EDUCATIONAL PSYCHOLOGY

Educational psychology is an exciting area of applied psychology, linking knowledge about the development of children and young people to education. It is concerned with how children feel, interact, learn and behave. It involves the application to education of psychological theories, research and techniques, with the aim of establishing a body of knowledge about the psychological and educational development of children within the context of home, school and the community.

This body of knowledge comes from a number of areas of study within psychology; traditionally these are:

➡ studies of child development;
➡ the development of learning and understanding in children (cognitive processes);

➡ studies of emotional and behavioural difficulties in children and young people;

➡ testing and assessment in areas such as intelligence and personality.

Increasingly, however, studies of the way in which systems and organisations operate and what makes them effective have become influential within educational psychology. There has also been increased recognition that education takes place in a social context and that a child's development can be influenced by factors at various levels, such as parent–child, family and peer relationships, and socio-economic, social and political factors – that is, a recognition of *ecological* influences on development.

Educational psychologists seek to apply this knowledge for the benefit of children, young people and their families.

WHAT AN EDUCATIONAL PSYCHOLOGIST DOES

Most educational psychologists work for local authorities where the educational psychology service is one of a number of support services for children and young people. Educational psychologists work in schools, colleges, nurseries and special schools and units. They may work directly with children and young people, either through observation and assessment, or perhaps with a group of children in relation to learning, behaviour or emotional difficulties.

Educational psychologists work in consultation with parents, teachers and other education staff, such as advisory teachers. They may carry out joint school and family work and provide training and workshops for teachers and other professionals, for example a whole-school approach to combat bullying. Educational psychologists may be engaged in action research (see Chapter 11) and school projects.

Traditionally, educational psychologists have played a key role in the assessment of children with complex difficulties (special educational needs). For example, these might be learning or behavioural difficulties, or a hearing or visual impairment. Some children with very complex needs may require additional support in school or a placement in a special school or unit. These children may have a statement of special educational needs which is a legal document outlining the special provision the local authority must make for that child. The educational psychologist will write a report contributing to that statement, outlining what they feel are the child's educational needs.

Increasingly, educational psychologists are becoming part of multi-professional teams. For example, behaviour and education support teams (BESTs) may contain an educational psychologist specialising in emotional and behavioural problems, an advisory teacher for behaviour, a family support worker who may have a social services background, and a mental health worker attached to the local Children and Adolescent Mental Health Service (CAMHS). Educational psychologists work closely with a number of other agencies, such as social workers, community services for young offenders and health services, such as speech and language therapists.

Many educational psychology services have a critical incident support team of specially trained educational psychologists who respond to a crisis or traumatic incident involving or likely to affect children at school, such as the death of a child.

In 2006 the Department for Education and Science (Farrell et al. 2006) undertook a review of the functions and contribution of educational psychologists. The review found that educational psychologists are highly valued for their application of psychological knowledge to school problems and the work they do with children with complex special educational needs.

Reorganisation of educational psychology services, as part of a local authority's Children's Services, began in the light of new legislation, primarily the Children's Act 2004, which gave legal force to the Green Paper *Every Child Matters* (DfES 2003). This followed consultation with services and young people themselves on what were considered to be key areas contributing to well-being in childhood and later life. The five key outcomes appear in the left-hand column of Table 4.1. Children's Services will be evaluated in the light of their contribution to these five outcomes. The review found that educational psychologists contributed to all five outcomes. Examples are shown in the right-hand column of Table 4.1.

The Children's Act also puts a legal obligation on local authorities to extend multi-agency working. The review found that educational psychologists were working effectively in multi-agency contexts in all aspects of their work. The distinctive contribution of educational psychologists to working with children was seen to be related to their academic background, specialist knowledge and training. Interestingly, training for educational psychologists has undergone radical restructuring (see 'How would I become an educational psychologist?'). It is anticipated that the changes to Children's Services will provide new opportunities for educational psychologists in community work and mean a possible reduction in school-based work.

Key outcomes	Contribution of educational psychologists
Being healthy	Helping children's emotional development
Staying safe	Preventing bullying and discrimination
Enjoying and achieving	Helping children in their personal, social and educational achievement
Making a positive contribution	Helping children to develop appropriate behaviour in and out of school
Achieving economic well-being	Helping pupils to progress to further education, employment or training on leaving school

Table 4.1 Examples of educational psychologists' contributions to the five key outcomes of Every Child Matters (DfES 2003)

How would I become an educational psychologist?

The training of educational psychologists has undergone radical changes in the early twenty-first century. Traditionally, there was a requirement for an honours degree in psychology recognised by the British Psychological Society (BPS), teacher training, at least two years' teaching experience and professional postgraduate training as an educational psychologist (EP) – usually a one- or two-year Masters degree course.

From September 2006, however, all postgraduate training courses in educational psychology became three-year professional doctorates (see below). Upon successful completion, candidates are eligible for chartered status with the BPS as a Chartered Educational Psychologist. The requirement of a teaching qualification and teaching experience no longer applies, although evaluation of the role of the EP often cites knowledge of education as one of the unique contributions the EP makes in working with schools. The implications of these changes in training can only be assessed over time.

Educational psychologists are regarded as having detailed knowledge of different educational and community contexts and of the different demands of such contexts. They are also seen to be ideally placed to form a 'bridge' between education and other agencies (Farrell et al. 2006).

New training route for educational psychologists

1 Eligibility for Graduate Basis for Registration (GBR) in the BPS – recognised honours psychology degree.
2 Ability to demonstrate relevant experience of working with children within educational, childcare or community settings.

There has been considerable debate about the definition of 'relevant' experience. Examples given by the BPS include work as a teacher, graduate assistant in an educational psychology service, learning support assistant, educational social worker, learning mentor, speech and language therapist, care worker, worker in an early years setting. 'Voluntary experience of various kinds may assist applicants in demonstrating a breadth of relevant experience' (BPS website 2006). Applicants will need to show how they have been able to apply the knowledge of psychology gained in their degrees. (Further information can be obtained from the BPS website: www.bps.org.uk)

New course content

MSc courses in educational psychology aim to develop academic knowledge, research ability and professional competence. Trainees will undertake:

- a range of learning activities at the university;
- at least 300 days of professional placement work under supervision;
- a substantial empirical research project.

University fees will be paid by Local Government Employers (LGE).

Employment and placement

Year 1 applicants will be employed as trainee educational psychologists by a local authority and will be supervised directly by course tutors. Years 2 and 3 trainees will need to be employed as assistant educational psychologists, on a salary agreed with the local authority. They will be supervised by an educational psychologist employed by the local authority and supported by the university. Work on placement is expected to reflect the 'generic role' of the educational psychologist. Precise arrangements will be determined by course centres in consultation with local services. (Further information can be obtained from BPS website: www.bps.org.uk)

Box 1 Post-professional training

There is now a requirement by the BPS for all Chartered Educational Psychologists to provide evidence of continued professional development (CPD), with a minimum requirement each year. The BPS has developed a National Occupational Standards (NOS) framework, in relation to which applied psychologists set targets and produce evidence of CPD towards achieving those targets. Generic key roles of the NOS framework are outlined below:

- *Ethics*: to develop personal-professional standards.
- *Practice*: to apply psychological methods, theory and knowledge.
- *Research*: to research and develop new and existing psychological methods, models, theories and instruments in psychology.
- *Communication*: to communicate psychological knowledge, methods, needs and policy requirements.
- *Training:* to develop and train in the application of psychological skills, knowledge and practices.
- *Management*: to manage the provision of psychological systems, services and resources.

Box 2 Professional journals

Both the British Psychological Society (BPS) and the Association of Educational Psychologists (AEP) produce journals relevant to educational psychologists. These include:

- *British Journal of Educational Psychology* (BPS)
- *British Journal of Developmental Psychology* (BPS)
- *Educational Psychology in Practice* (AEP).

Box 3 Career opportunities for educational psychologists

1 Local authorities

Most educational psychologists work for local authorities. In many authorities, following legislation affecting Children's Services (see above, p. 74), educational psychology services (EPS) have become part of a combined Children, Schools and Families service, with social services, but also incorporating other agencies, such as specialist teachers and education welfare officers.

The career structure within the EPS is normally basic grade, senior and principal posts. Some larger authorities may also have deputy principal posts.

➠ *Basic grade educational psychologists* will normally be responsible for an area of mainstream and special schools or units to which they pay regular visits. Most educational psychology services have a time allocation model of service delivery to schools, that is, an agreed number of sessions per year. However (as mentioned above), changes in the delivery of Children's Services are likely to mean increased opportunities for educational psychologists to develop more community- and non-school-based work.

➠ *Senior educational psychologists* may be in management posts, such as managing the local area team of EPs, or may have 'specialist' posts, for example responsibility for a specific area such as speech and language or physical and neurological impairment.

➠ *Principal educational psychologists* traditionally have been responsible for organising and managing the educational psychology service within the local authority. However, changes to Children's Services and the implementation of multidisciplinary work have meant more local authorities are looking at new and different ways of managing and organising their educational psychology services (AEP newsletter, 9 August 2006). This has led some authorities to consider the removal of direct management of educational psychology teams by a principal educational psychologist.

2 Assessment units

Some educational psychologists work for health authorities in assessment units, which may be multidisciplinary or hospital-based paediatric assessment units, or child psychiatric units.

3 Teaching, training and research

Some educational psychologists teach in university departments and may be involved in training courses for educational psychologists. Some such tutors often work part-time as practising senior educational psychologists. Others may be involved in research. Educational psychologists may also be concerned with teacher training.

4 Private practice

An increasing number of educational psychologists work in private practice, as consultants or expert witnesses to the courts.

DEVELOPMENT OF EDUCATIONAL PSYCHOLOGY

In England the educational needs of the blind and deaf were recognised by legislation in 1839. From the 1880s onwards several developments in psychology and educational philosophy combined to contribute to the development of educational psychology and, subsequently, 'school psychologists'. In 1889 the Elementary Education (Defective and Epileptic Children) Act created a new category of handicap, that is, 'educable mental defectives' (see Gillham 1978). Education authorities were then expected to ascertain the number of 'defective' children in their area and provide for them. Identification and selection fell to the medical profession initially, though eventually such decisions became the responsibility of people more directly involved in education.

Such developments necessitated more objective methods for the assessment of children. At around the same period, the beginnings of psychometric testing, or 'mental measurement', were taking root, for example Alfred Binet's work in Paris, identifying children who would not benefit from state school education. The outbreak of the First World War led to the development of tests of specific skill in order to allocate conscripts to different tasks.

Educational psychology was influenced by the behaviourists, in particular William James at Harvard, who started a laboratory for the scientific study of psychology and in 1889 published his classic book, *Talks to Teachers*. In 1903, Thorndike published the first book with the title *Educational Psychology*, emphasising scientific approaches to the study of educational programmes. In 1910, a journal of educational psychology was founded and the first article was written by Thorndike (see Pettibone and Jernigan (1989) for a summary).

Sir Cyril Burt became the first school psychologist in the UK in 1913, when he was appointed to the London County Council. His work on identical twins was influential in the nature–nurture debate on intelligence, although his results in this area are now considered to be unreliable. In addition, Burt influenced the role of the psychologist in education, a role he saw primarily as one of 'scientific researcher'.

The second 'school psychologist' in the UK was not appointed until 1931, in the city of Leicester (see Dessent 1978: 28). At about this time, the Child Guidance Movement was growing, with its emphasis on a multidisciplinary approach to the guidance of children with problems. By 1944 there were 70 child guidance clinics in the UK. Teams usually had a medical director (psychiatrist), who performed the major diagnostic role. Educational psychologists worked mainly with children in schools or administered tests to aid the psychiatrist's diagnosis. Psychiatric social workers interviewed parents. In this way psychologists were identified with what became known as the 'traditional' or even 'medical' model. The causes of problems were seen to be primarily within the individual, and the educational psychologist was heavily involved in psychometric assessment and the allocation of children to special education. This led to expectations by schools and other professionals of what the educational psychologist's role involved (Dessent 1978), a role to some extent reinforced by legislation.

The Education Act 1944 created the concept *educationally sub-normal* (ESN), and confirmed educational psychologists in a central role advising local authorities in relation to special educational needs. Circular 2/75 (DES 1975) ended school placement decision-making by the medical profession. It was considered more appropriate for the educational psychologist or adviser in special needs to be involved in this.

The Summerfield Report (1968) investigated the work of educational psychologists, their numbers and their training. At that time there were 368 educational psychologists in local authorities. Over half of these authorities had only one educational psychologist, and only 15 per cent had more than four (Summerfield 1968, quoted by Dessent 1978). The report emphasised the diagnostic and therapeutic work of the educational psychologist. There was little evidence of the 'scientific researcher' role considered by Burt to be central to the role of the school psychologist. Summerfield also challenged the usefulness of teaching experience for educational psychologists.

The economic boom of the 1960s contributed to the growth of support services in the late 1970s and the 1980s. Expansion led to the development of school psychological services, at first closely linked with child guidance clinics, with some educational psychologists working for both. However, a number of influences served to separate the services, and in the early twenty-first century most educational psychology services operate completely separately. These influences coincided with a continued and growing 'unease' within the profession in relation to the traditional model, together with moves to develop strategies for intervention for children rather than diagnostic work. In addition, there were developments in understanding the context in which a child was learning (social-ecological factors).

New directions were urged by the *reconstructionists* (see Gillham 1978). This was a movement away from individual casework towards 'systems' approaches. These involved looking at organisations like schools *as a whole* in order to be *proactive* (i.e. to *prevent* learning or behavioural difficulties) rather than *reactive* (i.e. to come in with the 'treatment' after the problem had been identified). The new directions were to include an emphasis on in-service training, particularly for teachers and schools, and on developing consultation models of working.

These approaches did not stem the flood of individual referrals to educational psychologists, however, nor were they particularly effective in directing change, that is, the 'reconstructing' was not as successful as had been hoped (see Dessent 1992). One of the reasons for this was new legislation again, particularly the Education Act 1981 and the Education Act 1993, which clarified the concept of *special educational need* and confirmed the central role of the educational psychologist in the identification and assessment of the special educational needs of individual children. As far as possible, children with special educational needs were to be educated in their local mainstream schools. Children were to undergo a staged process of needs assessment. If necessary, children with exceptional needs would require a *statement*. Once such a statement of special educational needs had been made by a local education authority (LEA), that authority was bound by law to make provision for those needs. The educational psychologist's role is to assess the child and advise the LEA on the child's special educational needs (i.e. give psychological advice).

The Disability Act 1995, amended by the Special Educational Needs and Disability Act 2001, made it unlawful for schools and LEAs to discriminate against disabled pupils. This was further strengthened by the Disability Discrimination Act 2005, which required schools and LEAs to promote equality of opportunity for disabled people. It required schools to make themselves accessible to disabled pupils, in terms of both curriculum and physical access. This was helped by funding, such as the Schools Access Initiative for the installation of lifts and ramps for physically impaired pupils, or acoustic work for children with hearing impairments.

In 2000 a government working party published an update on the work of educational psychologists (DfES 2000). This concluded that EPs were involved in four levels of work:

1 Individual child
2 Groups of children
3 Whole-school work
4 Work at local authority level, such as how best to deliver a service, and in the development of local authority policy and provision (e.g. for children with special educational needs).

There was an increased emphasis on working with other agencies, such as social services, and the report made some recommendations about service delivery.

In 2003 the government published a Green Paper entitled *Every Child Matters*, outlining improvements to the ways organisations work with children and young people. This followed outcry over the tragic death of eight-year-old Victoria Climbié from extreme abuse, which had not been recognised by the local services involved. Following consultation with young people themselves, the Green Paper concluded that there were five outcomes directly related to the health and well-being of young people (see Table 4.1 on p. 75). These outcomes became the measure by which Children's Services would be judged following the Children's Act 2004.

This Children's Act provides a national framework for change in the 150 local authorities in England, including statutory, voluntary and community sectors. Services are to be reconfigured around the child and family in one place, for example children's centres and extended schools. It puts a duty on local authorities to promote cooperation between agencies to improve children's well-being as defined by the five Every Child Matters (ECM) outcomes. Databases are to be developed with information on all children, each of whom will have a unique identifying number. Complex special educational needs cases are to be coordinated through a lead professional. Plans have been proposed for 'extended schools' to provide childcare and other activities, and to support children and parents, including access to specialist services on school sites. It is suggested that schools may wish to combine resources and group together, making 'cluster' arrangements to develop their role in delivering services (see below).

These new developments in the structure and organisation of Children's Services are likely to offer opportunities for educational psychologists to extend their involvement in multi-agency working.

What are special educational needs?

Under the 1981 and 1993 Education Acts, a child is considered to have special educational needs (SEN) if he or she has a 'learning difficulty' which requires 'special educational provision'. Such provision is in addition to, or different from, that which is normally available. This might be additional teaching support within the child's mainstream school, for example. Definition of learning difficulty under the Acts is that the child has either:

1 a significantly greater difficulty in learning than the majority of children of the same age; and/or
2 a 'disability' which prevents the child from making effective use of the facilities of the local school. (Education Act 1993)

It was originally estimated that about 2 per cent of children will have difficulties severe enough to warrant statementing, while a further 18 per cent are likely to experience difficulties at school at some stage in their educational careers (Warnock Report 1978). In practice, on average across all local authorities, 3 per cent of all pupils in schools have statements of SEN, though there are regional variations, for example 2.05 per cent across the eastern region (East Region SEN Benchmarking 2004).

Educational psychologists have promoted and supported the inclusion of pupils with SEN in mainstream schools. In 2000, 60 per cent of pupils with statements were placed in mainstream schools (nursery, primary and secondary). This represented an increase from 54 per cent in 1995, and from 59 per cent in 1999. In the same year, 37 per cent of statemented pupils were in special schools or pupil referral units (for pupils who have been excluded), and 3 per cent were in independent schools. This represented a reduction in statemented pupils in special schools, from 44 per cent in 1995, and from 38 per cent in 1999 (DfES 2000).

Within the group of children identified as having SEN will be a range of difficulties and impairments. The educational psychologist will need to have some understanding of how to assess difficulties in these areas, how such difficulties are likely to affect a child's ability to cope with his or her learning environment, and how to adapt or modify the learning environment to facilitate the child's difficulties.

Categories of special educational need

Sensory impairment

Visual impairment

The effects of visual problems on a child's development depends on the severity, type of loss, age at which the condition appears and overall functioning level of the child. Many children who have multiple disabilities also have visual impairments (NICHCY 2006). One in 1000 children suffers from visual handicap severe enough to affect educational progress, on a continuum from not seeing well enough to recognise things in a picture book, for example, to blindness. The incidence of severe visual impairment or blindness in children under 16 years of age is 6 per 10,000. Major causes are damage to the cerebral/visual pathways and hereditary disease (*Archives of Disease in Childhood* 2004).

Hearing impairment

Hearing loss interferes with the reception and production of language, and consequently can be crucial to a child's educational development. Hearing losses can be categorised as slight, moderate, severe or profound. The loss can be prelingual (before spoken language has developed) or post lingual. It can be conductive in nature

Figure 4.1 Adapting the learning environment can present new challenges to teachers

(i.e. there is a reduction in the intensity of the sound reaching the inner ear) or sensori-neural (i.e. a defect of the inner ear or auditory nerve). Each year 840 babies are born with significant deafness. One in 1000 children are deaf at three years old. In 2006 there are about 12,000 children aged 0 to 15 years who were born deaf, and a total of about 20,000 aged 0 to 15 years who are moderately to profoundly deaf (www.rnid.org.uk).

There has long been a debate within education as to the most appropriate method of teaching children with hearing difficulties to communicate. Traditionally, these methods have been the auditory-oral versus manual (signing) approaches, though 'total communication' approaches have combined elements of both. Evaluation of the success of methods is difficult, since such evaluations need to take into account both educational achievement and the social/emotional adjustment of the child. There are an estimated 50,000 British Sign Language users (www.rnid.org.uk). Some children are able to receive cochlear implants to help them receive and begin to interpret sound.

Dual sensory impairment (deafblindness)

Some children have a dual sensory impairment. Many authorities will have a specialist advisory teacher to help schools work with these pupils. There are an estimated 23,000 deafblind people in the UK (www.rnid.org.uk).

Physical/medical difficulties

Physical impairment can result from cerebral palsy or spinal cord injury. Cerebral palsy occurs in about 1 in 400 births in the UK, causing varying degrees of gross and fine motor difficulties and affecting muscle tone, though there is not necessarily any cognitive impairment. Children with cerebral palsy often have other associated needs, for example 25–30 per cent have epilepsy, 25–35 per cent have visual difficulties, 25 per cent have a hearing impairment and 20 per cent have no speech. Developments in neonatal care have resulted in an increase in survivors with additional profound and multiple disabilities (Scope, http://www.scope.org.uk/).

There is a range of other conditions in which impairment of motor function may be implicated (e.g. dyspraxia) and a wide variety of low-incidence rare conditions that can affect both physical and cognitive development (see Contact a Family 2004).

Specific syndromes

A 'syndrome' is a set of symptoms that together indicate an abnormal condition. Sometimes a genetic link is known, such as with Down's syndrome. In others, such as Tourette's syndrome (characterised by motor and vocal habits, or tics), aetiology is less clear. Down's syndrome occurs in 1 in 650 births and is associated with varying degrees of learning difficulties, sensory impairment and medical complications, particularly heart defects.

Speech and language disorders

There is a wide range of speech and language disorders. A child can have difficulties with the physical processes required to produced sounds (e.g. articulation, resonation) or difficulties in one or more of the language dimensions:

➡ phonology (sound);
➡ morphology (word structure);
➡ syntax (sentence structure);
➡ semantics (word meaning);
➡ pragmatics (language function).

Educational psychologists are concerned with the assessment and identification of disordered and delayed speech, and the effects on children with difficulties such as verbal dyspraxia (difficulties in the production of speech sounds).

Learning difficulties

The definition of learning difficulties under the 1981 and 1993 Education Acts is provided above (see p. 79). In practice, learning difficulties identified by schools range across a whole continuum, through those that schools can cope with (e.g. by adapting or differentiating the curriculum) to those requiring additional support in mainstream classes (*moderate learning difficulties*). In addition, there are groups of children who require an extremely modified and differentiated curriculum (*severe and profound learning difficulties*).

Although the 1981 and 1993 Education Acts emphasise inclusion as far as possible (mainstream schools are expected to provide an appropriate curriculum and have resources to cater for the needs of all children, whether they have learning difficulties or other special needs), some LEAs still segregate children with moderate learning difficulties, either for part of the time (e.g. special units attached to a mainstream school) or all the time (a separate system of segregated special schools). The aetiology of moderate learning difficulties is often unknown. Many children in this category will have post-16 educational provision or join appropriate college link courses. Most will be fully independent as adults.

The aetiology of severe/profound learning difficulties may include genetic disorders, infectious diseases or brain damage at any stage of development. These children will require post-16 educational provision and are unlikely to be able to lead independent lives as adults.

Specific learning difficulties

There is also considerable debate within education concerning a further group of children who may be identified as having *specific learning difficulties*. This term has generally replaced the umbrella label of 'dyslexia'. Typically, a child appears of at least average cognitive ability, but has specific difficulty in one or more areas of attainment, such as reading or spelling, and/or a particular difficulty in expressing himself/herself in writing (dysgraphia). A child may also have a specific number problem (dyscalculia). There has been considerable debate

about whether 'dyslexia' exists as a separate type of learning difficulty (see the dyslexia debate at http://www.literacytrust.org.uk/Database/dysresearch.html).

Emotional, behavioural and social difficulties (EBSD)

Children in this category show age-inappropriate behaviour over a period of time that results in difficulty with peer relationships or confrontations and failure to conform to school discipline. Such behaviour is often linked to poor self-esteem and low achievement (Hardman, Drew and Egan 2005).

The category of EBSD can include children with phobias, neurotic children, autistic children and those with oppositional defiance disorder (ODD). Assessment in this area is difficult and requires a wide range of approaches, such as observations, ratings and standardised tests. Looked-after children (i.e. those children in care) are particularly vulnerable, both academically and socially/emotionally. They may have emotional difficulties related to a history of abuse and/or disrupted peer relationships because of a number of school moves.

Educational psychologists may be involved in therapeutic approaches such as *cognitive behavioural therapy* (CBT) for pupils with social or emotional difficulties (see Chapter 2). These approaches are designed to change how an individual thinks (cognition) and what they do (behaviour). There are a number of approaches exploring core beliefs and dysfunctional assumptions (see Wilson and Branch 2006).

Brief therapies or *solution-focused therapies* concentrate on the current situation and how to move on from it, rather than in-depth analysis of causes. At its simplest, a pupil might be asked to rate themselves on a 10-point rating scale in relation to a perceived problem, such as peer relationships or self-image. They are asked how far along the scale they would like to be in six months or a year, for example. Pupils are asked what they would need to do to get to that point. A programme is worked out with specific targets to help the pupil move along the scale.

Figure 4.2 Advances in technology have helped many children to improve their access to the curriculum

A pupil with peer relationship difficulties may also be helped by strategies such as *circle of friends* (e.g. Newton, Taylor and Wilson 1996). This approach is intended to enhance the inclusion of pupils experiencing difficulties because of a disability or crisis, or who exhibit challenging behaviour towards others. It mobilises support from the pupil's peers to provide a support network for the pupil and help solve the pupil's problems.

Group or *whole-school approaches* might involve providing training to staff on developing *emotional literacy*, that is, the ability to express and understand one's feelings. The aim of emotional literacy programmes is to develop people's emotional intelligence, so that they can identify and communicate their feelings. This, in turn, helps them to fulfil their emotional needs and communicate these in order to obtain the emotional support and understanding they need from others and to be able to give emotional support and understanding to others (e.g. Sharp 2001).

In growing awareness of the effects of children's emotional states and their understanding of social situations on learning and behaviour, the DfES has recently developed materials to be used in schools on the *social and emotional aspects of learning* (SEAL). These materials cover personal development (e.g. self-awareness and managing feelings) and interpersonal/social skills. Educational psychologists may be involved in training interventions in schools to promote social skills and social inclusion (e.g. Denham et al. 2006).

Attention deficit (hyperactivity) disorder (ADD and ADHD)

ADD is gaining recognition as a particularly difficult category and is characterised by high distractibility, fleeting attention and an inability to focus attention on relevant detail at an age when such control is expected.

ADHD includes children who cannot maintain attention because they cannot remain still for long enough. Clearly, inability to maintain attention creates a significant barrier to learning. In addition, such a disorder creates considerable difficulty in assessing a child's underlying cognitive ability.

The incidence of attention disorders is about 3–5 per cent of the school population, with more boys than girls in a ratio of about 3:1 (UK Healthcare, http://ukhealthcare.uky.edu/content/content.asp?pageid=P00973). Most schools, therefore, will have a number of pupils with ADD or ADHD. Educational psychologists may be involved in advising individual teachers or giving whole-school INSET on the management of behaviours related to these disorders. Some educational psychologists may be involved in *anger management* for pupils with behaviour difficulties and they are also likely to be working with the local *behaviour support team* (BST), helping schools to manage pupils with ADD and ADHD – many of whom may be on medication for the condition.

Information from other disciplines, such as neuropsychology, is beginning to inform these disorders. Advances in brain scanning techniques have shown that areas of the brain related to impulse control in children with attention disorders are different in size and activity from the brains of children without these disorders (Peterson 2003).

Multi-handicapping conditions

Naturally, the categories above are not mutually exclusive and children may have combinations of difficulties. Many children with cerebral palsy also have epilepsy. Conditions such as autism may involve severe learning difficulties with severe behaviour problems. Some children with severe learning difficulties may have hearing impairments. For children with severe or profound learning difficulties, teaching strategies are often based on breaking tasks into smaller target behaviours with a highly differentiated curriculum.

Autistic spectrum disorders/communication disorders

Autism is a biological disorder of the brain that impairs communication and social skills. It occurs in about 1 in 500 children and can range from mild to severe (National Autistic Society online). *Asperger's syndrome* is a less severe disorder of verbal and non-verbal communication skills, with a restricted range of interests. There have been concerns that the overall incidence of autistic spectrum disorders (ASDs) has been rising, and a recent study indicates more than 1 in 100 children may be affected by ASDs (Burns 2006).

Educational psychologists may be involved with the local autism team in helping autistic pupils to be included in mainstream schools, for example through individual assessment of strengths and weaknesses and/or through INSET to school staff. 'Social stories' might be used to prepare pupils for life experiences, that is, personalised stories written to explain what happens in challenging and confusing social situations (e.g. Gray 2000).

Again, advances in neuropsychology are providing insight into areas of SEN such as autism. A brain scan study by neuroscientists in California, led by Mirella Dapretto, indicated an absence of 'mirror neurons' in autistic children, relating to their inability to recognise and respond to emotions in others. Mirror neurons are thought to help us understand how others are feeling, for example by mirroring in ourselves feelings of sadness if we see someone looking miserable (Dapretto et al. 2006).

Gifted and talented children

There has long been a debate about the extent to which gifted children have 'special educational needs'. Traditionally, gifted children have been recognised by high scores on intelligence tests, but now broader concepts are used, such as creativity, specific academic ability and music (Davis and Rimm 2004 in Eggen and Kauchak 2007).

The challenge for schools is to provide an educational environment that can maximise the child's academic as well as social-emotional development. The educational psychologist may well be faced with having to give advice in relation to a gifted child. Approaches tend to involve moving a child up a year at school (acceleration) or helping to provide a specialised curriculum.

In the UK a national programme (NPGATE) for gifted and talented children is being developed at the time of writing (SENCO Week 2006). A longitudinal study in the USA of gifted and talented pupils found that in addition to being high academic achievers, these students were better adjusted as children and adults, had more hobbies, read more and were healthier than their peers (Steiner and Carr 2003).

The main categories of special educational needs have been outlined here. Local authorities have access to a variety of data sets and indicators of special educational needs via the National Performance Framework, which allows them to monitor and develop support for SEN.

The educational psychology service is an essential part of this process, assessing special educational needs and working with schools and families to provide appropriate interventions to remove pupil's barriers to progress and increase pupil performance.

Example of an intervention in educational psychology: The effect of social skills interventions in the primary school (Denham et al. 2006)

Brent is an area of London with a diverse socio-economic and cultural community. Between 2000 and 2003, the local Educational Psychology Service implemented two social skills interventions to promote social inclusion in six primary schools. Following this, an evaluation of these interventions was carried out by educational psychologists in training.

Aim: Social skills training aims to develop socially acceptable learned behaviours in children who appear to lack these social skills.

Method: In total, 45 boys and 23 girls between the ages of 7 and 11 were selected (roughly equal numbers in each age group) who were at risk of permanent exclusion from school because of their behaviour.

Pupils were withdrawn from class for 30 minutes per week for a 12-week intervention.

They were assigned to one of two groups (*peer mentoring* or a *skills training* group), based on their teachers' judgement about which approach would be more beneficial to their particular needs.

The *peer mentoring* group included those with the most challenging behaviour and involved small-group problem-solving exercises (e.g. to resist inappropriate peer pressure, understand the perspective of others and communicate feelings more effectively). Exercises involved a lot of role-play and discussion.

The *skills training* group involved an adult facilitator 'coaching' children lacking in social skills and confidence. This involved a lot of turn-taking exercises and managing emotions through play-based activities.

Pupils, teachers and parents were given pre- and post-intervention questionnaires, followed up by structured pupil and teacher interviews. The social skills questionnaires were designed to see:

➠ if the child perceived him or herself as having difficulties in social situations;
➠ teachers' perceptions of the level of the child's social difficulties; and
➠ parents' perceptions of their child's social difficulties.

These questionnaires were from a Social Skills Training Package developed by Spence (1995 – details in Denham et al. 2006).

The interview proformas were designed by the educational psychologists in training.

Results: No significant differences were found between the peer mentoring and skills training groups. Pupils in both groups, however, rated themselves significantly higher in social skills after the intervention, compared with before, and their teachers also rated both groups higher.

No significant differences were found between pre- and post-intervention parents' ratings. Those involved in the study felt that perhaps the newly acquired skills of these pupils did not generalise to the home, or that parents had not felt their children were particularly lacking in social skills prior to the intervention. Parents' perceptions of their children's behaviour may have been different from the perceptions of the school, or indeed behaviour at home could have been different.

Interviews six months later also showed that pupils and teachers still felt the interventions had made a positive difference to their social skills and social inclusion. Pupils felt better able to control their behaviour and solve problems.

Conclusion: The authors felt that social skills training was a valuable tool in helping to include pupils with social and emotional difficulties in the mainstream school environment.

RESEARCH, THEORY AND APPLICATIONS

Assessment and testing

The evaluation of learning has long been an issue in psychology and education. In the course of their school careers, children will undergo a number of formal and informal assessments. The Education Reform Act (ERA) 1988 introduced new procedures for testing children at ages 7, 11, 14 and 16. Records of achievement are used to record progress and attainment within the national curriculum assessment system. In addition, 'p' scales have been developed to describe attainment for pupils who are working below level 1 in the national curriculum. This type of assessment indicates a shift on the part of educators and psychologists away from standardised tests, towards more flexible types of assessment in an educational context.

Tests can be divided into *norm-referenced* or *criterion-referenced* tests:

➠ Norm-referenced tests are standardised on a given population, and measures are taken of their *reliability* and *validity* (see Chapter 11). The psychologist, therefore, is able to compare a child's score with the typical score of a child of that age from a large sample of the population. A typical example of a norm-referenced test is the traditional intelligence test or IQ test (see below).
➠ Criterion-referenced tests indicate whether a child has successfully achieved a given objective, irrespective of whether this is appropriate for his or her age, that is, a pupil passes or fails regardless of the percentage of individuals of the same age who perform at that level. An example might be the ability to recognise individual letter sounds. This could be broken down into a number of sub-units, so that the number of these a child has achieved gives an idea of progress towards the overall objective.

Assessment under the national curriculum is criterion-referenced. Standard assessment tasks (SATs) are carried out by the child's individual class teacher. Educational psychologists may need to carry out further assessment, and they employ a wide variety of assessment techniques to do so (some of these are shown below). Of the many tests available, some are 'open' and can be used by any individual (e.g. most reading tests); others are 'closed' and available only to those who have particular qualifications and/or training (e.g. intelligence tests). Given the sheer volume and variety of tests available, those outlined below are only a small sample to illustrate areas in which tests might aid the assessment of children by educational psychologists:

➧ rating scales;
➧ direct observation;
➧ interviews (structured, semi-structured or informal), with pupils, staff and parents;
➧ dynamic assessment;
➧ tests of ability;
➧ tests of attainment;
➧ questionnaires.

The assessment of school-based learning difficulties

In assessing learning difficulties, the first step is some definition of what constitutes a learning difficulty. Criteria in terms of the 1993 Education Act have already been mentioned (see above, p. 79). In addition, there will be a further group of children with some degree of learning difficulty which has been recognised by the school. The educational psychologist would usually become involved in individual work with the child at the stage where the school has used its resources (e.g. additional small-group teaching), but feels the child has failed to make sufficient progress. The educational psychologist would begin with the teacher's assessment, but also view the child's work relative to his or her peers, and then make decisions about the need for further assessment.

Tests of attainment

Both educational psychologists and school staff may be concerned with a child's level of attainment in reading, spelling and numeracy, as well as handwriting skills. Such assessments can range from informal assessment (e.g. a noticeable improvement in the number of words spelt correctly in a weekly test) to standardised tests. A large number of 'open' reading tests are available to measure word recognition skills or ability to read and understand text. Similarly, there is a range of spelling and numeracy tests readily available for school use.

If a test of attainment is needed, educational psychologists are likely to use a test such as the Wechsler Objective Reading Dimensions (WORD) (Wechsler 1993), which covers reading, comprehension and spelling skills, and is designed to partner the Wechsler Intelligence Scale for Children (WISC) (Wechsler 2003) to see to what extent a child's actual score differs from a score predicted from the child's IQ. In the same way, the Wechsler Objective Language Dimensions (WOLD) (Wechsler 1996) is designed to relate attainment scores to ability scores on the WISC, to look at differences between expected and actual scores as indicators of underachievement, for example. The British Ability Scales (see below) similarly contain tests of attainment.

Tests of ability

Tests of ability have been developed to measure underlying constructs which are not a direct result of training, such as intelligence and personality. Intelligence is clearly an important construct in education, and intelligence tests have been used to make predictions about future academic achievement (see Davenport's 1994 summary).

Modern intelligence tests tend to sample a wide range of verbal and non-verbal abilities, such as general knowledge, vocabulary and visual spatial ability. The Wechsler tests, developed by David Wechsler and widely used, relate a child's score to the distribution of scores of other children of the same age. The Wechsler Intelligence Scale for Children was initially standardised on American populations and then re-standardised on British populations. The test has been through several revisions, the latest of which is the WISC-IV UK (Wechsler 2003), standardised on the UK population.

The British Ability Scales (BAS) (Elliott, Smith and McCullock 1996, first published 1979) also include a battery of verbal and non-verbal tests, some visual/perceptual tests and also cognitive tests based on aspects of Piaget's theory of cognitive development (see below, p. 91). The BAS introduced a statistical procedure which meant that the test could be used either as criterion-referenced assessment, using pass/fail criteria on individual items, or as norm-referenced assessment in relation to an age-stratified UK population.

In the past, intelligence testing was often a standard part of assessment of a child by an educational psychologist. This is not generally the case today, with many educational psychologists and educational psychology services preferring to work with a consultation model approach to helping schools handle children's difficulties (see below, p. 91). Rather than assessment for a specific IQ score, the educational psychologist is likely to use the verbal and non-verbal tests in a diagnostic way to obtain a profile of the child's strengths and weaknesses. For example, this may indicate perceptual difficulties that are affecting a child's ability to learn to read.

Assessment of speech and language difficulties

Speech and language difficulties can not only affect a child's access to the curriculum but may also have significant effects on a child's ability to interact with their peers and, therefore, on their social-emotional development. The educational psychologist would generally work closely with the local speech and language therapist to assess the child's ability to communicate (*expressive language*) and to understand what is said (*receptive language*). Assessment would involve information from those who know and work with the child (parents, teachers, speech therapists) and direct observation and assessment. Educational psychologists gain experience of a number of tests of language development through their training.

Assessment and interventions with emotional, social and behavioural difficulties (ESBD)

The terms EBD and ESBD lack a clear definition, but are used with pupils experiencing difficulties related to their emotions and behaviour, and can cover an extensive range of human behaviour. For the practising psychologist, assessment is likely to begin with teacher reports of the frequency and intensity of the behaviour of concern, for example, temper tantrums, fights and victimisation. The extent to which the child's behaviour and/or self-perceptions were maladaptive to his or her educational environment would need to be ascertained. Observation would often be a further step, followed by an individual interview with the child. Rating scales might be used to establish the child's self-perception. Some tests attempt to measure the emotional adjustment of children and young adults. Others may be used to assess the level of autistic behaviour shown by a child. Sometimes

behavioural problems result from frustration in the learning situation, in which case some additional assessment of possible learning difficulties might be undertaken.

A number of studies have highlighted the difficulties of assessment in this area. McCall and Farrell (1993) investigated how 57 educational psychologists would assess a particular emotional and behavioural difficulty and found that 44 per cent used some tests, while over half used no tests. Of those using tests, 22 different personality tests and procedures were mentioned. In a more recent study, Rees, Farrell and Rees (2003) asked 107 educational psychologists in 16 different local authorities to provide information about one of their most recent EBD referrals, how they had assessed the pupil and what interventions they had recommended, if any. Analysis showed that 73 per cent actually observed the pupil as part of the assessment, while 89 per cent interviewed their pupil. In 41 per cent of cases, a cognitive test such as the WISC or BAS was used. Personality tests and measures of self-esteem were used in just 24 per cent of cases, whereas a reading test was administered in 51 per cent of cases and a numeracy test in 27 per cent. This may be a reflection of the fact that there is evidence of a link between emotional and behavioural difficulties and learning difficulties (Farrell, Crutchley and Mills 1999). Rees, Farrell and Rees (2003) also point out some interesting differences between the two studies. In their study, 28 per cent of referrals went on to receive a statement of special needs, while 11 per cent of the EBD pupils referred were then placed in a special unit or special school. In the McCall and Farrell study (1993), 72 per cent received statements and 61 per cent were placed in special units or schools following assessment. This may reflect the increased emphasis on including pupils with SEN in mainstream schools, as well as the increased delegation of funds from local authorities to mainstream schools to provide resources for SEN pupils.

Assessment and interventions with early developmental delay

Educational psychologists are not only concerned with school-based assessment. They will often be involved with the assessment of preschool children, and especially in the assessment of early developmental difficulties which are likely to affect educational progress and future school placement. Such difficulties might include *sensory impairment, motor* (movement*) difficulties* and *general cognitive delay*.

There are a number of developmental scales that can be used in preschool assessment, covering physical, social, speech and language and cognitive development. Some educational psychology services have helped local authorities to develop their own early assessment preschool tests, in addition to the new national assessment procedures for the Foundation Stage.

Educational psychologists may also be involved in local *portage systems*, an intervention approach involving parents and professionals working with young children with special needs. This provides a step-by-step approach to developing areas such as speech and language, motor development and cognitive skills.

Dynamic assessment

There are a number of difficulties with one-off assessments of a child's potential, both theoretically and practically (e.g. Fuerstein et al. 1980; and see below). Approaches have therefore been developed to look at a child's ability to learn from an intervention. These *dynamic assessment* approaches typically involve a pre-test–intervention–post-test model of assessment. Fundamental to dynamic measures is the 'mediated learning experience', an interaction between the child and a 'mediator', whose role is to observe how the child approaches the problem. The mediator is in a position to observe the learner's thinking process, that is, to interpret what the learner has accomplished and how they arrived there. The process of how the solution was arrived at informs further learning and may be discussed with the learner. This approach can be linked to *mediated learning*, or Vygotsky's *zone of proximal development* (see below).

Working with schools

The educational psychologist as expert

The local educational psychology service will offer a particular service to schools, which may involve an agreed number of visits to the school. The nature of

work with schools has been the subject of much debate within the profession. Traditionally, educational psychologists have focused on the individual child to provide solutions to problems. The teacher refers the child to the psychologist, who then assesses the child to find the 'problem'. Within this model, the psychologist may well consult with others, such as parents and teachers, but is still essentially seen as the 'expert'. As discussed above, this has come about in part because of legislation defining the role of the psychologist in the assessment of and provision for children with special educational needs. Gradually however, there have been moves towards more consultative approaches, at both a school and service level (Larney 2003).

The educational psychologist as consultant

One simple extension of the child-focused approach was what Labram (1992) terms 'technical involvement'. This represents a simplified 'consultancy model', where the consultant draws on expert knowledge and skills to resolve clearly defined problems.

The consultant (e.g. educational psychologist) provides services to the consultee (e.g. the teacher) about the presenting problems of the client (e.g. the child). The consultant's aim is to improve the skills of the consultee so they can prevent, or respond more effectively to, similar problems in the future. The whole is a collaborative process, which aims to *remediate* and *prevent* (Gutkin and Curtis 1999 in Larney 2003).

A number of consultation models can be identified, principally:

➡ mental health consultation;
➡ behavioural consultation;
➡ process and organisational/systems consultation.

Mental health consultation is a psychiatric model developed in the 1960s by Caplan. It focuses on why the consultee is having difficulties and is designed to help overcome these from a psychoanalytic theory background. It is not widely used in working with schools, partly because of its theoretical roots, but also due to a lack of supporting empirical evidence for its effectiveness (Gutkin and Curtis 1999 in Larney 2003).

Behavioural consultation is more widely used and is rooted in social learning theory (see below). The consultant leads the consultee through a structured problem-solving process. This typically involves:

➠ problem identification;
➠ problem analysis;
➠ implementing a plan;
➠ evaluating success.

A criticism of this approach has been its lack of focus on the consultant–consultee relationship, and further research is needed (Larney 2003).

Process and organisational/systems consultation models developed from the psychology of groups and organisations. Typically, the client is a group within an organisation or is the entire organisation itself (Gutkin and Curtis 1999 in Larney 2003; Wagner 2000). In process consultancy the aim is to make people more aware of the events and processes in their environment which affect their work. In systems consultancy the aim is to change, for example schools at an organisational level.

Evaluation of consultation approaches

The practice of consultation as a model of service delivery is gradually becoming more popular (Larney 2003). A number of studies have attempted to evaluate the effectiveness of consultation. Researchers make a distinction between assessing the *outcome* of consultation (i.e. the gains for the consultee) and the *process* of consultation. Outcomes have generally been assessed using qualitative techniques, such as pre- and post-test questionnaires and semi-structured interviews. Process evaluation techniques tend to involve more quantitative data, such as a systematic analysis of verbal interaction between consultant and consultee, or the drop-in referral rates to the educational psychology service.

Larney (2003) summarises the evaluation of three educational psychology services in the UK. Typical teacher perceptions of consultation were that they felt:

➠ better skilled at problem analysis;
➠ better able to handle similar problems in the future;
➠ more confident; and
➠ more supported by the educational psychologist.

One study reported positive feelings from schools about the increased involvement of educational psychologists in the classroom. Educational psychologists enjoyed greater satisfaction in doing more preventative work in schools.

A general criticism of these evaluations, however, has been that they focus on the benefits for the consultee, but not on those for the client. A further criticism has been the reliance on qualitative rather than quantitative data (Larney 2003).

The evaluation of the process of consultation has generally been from studies in the USA. Key factors (reviewed by Larney 2003) are:

➠ the nature of the interaction between consultant and consultee;
➠ the attitude of the consultee (i.e. the extent to which the consultee is motivated and willing to participate in consultation);
➠ the skills of the consultant in terms of what they know about the problem (content) and their consultation (process) skills.

As with outcome evaluation, there have been criticisms of process evaluations in terms of methodological weaknesses, such as lack of control or comparison groups. A number of other difficulties with consultation are also outlined (Larney 2003):

➠ The need for adequate preparation – school staff need to understand the process and accept new ways of working. A small-scale study in Birmingham schools by Ashton and Roberts (2006) found that special educational needs coordinators (SENCOs, i.e. teachers with a special role in the inclusion of children with special needs) valued the traditional educational psychologist role, while the educational psychologists saw themselves as offering a much wider range of services of value to the schools.
➠ Potential consultees need to get to know the consultant.
➠ The consultant needs to get to know the school, its staff and its ethos.
➠ A continued need via legislation for educational psychologists to be involved in individual assessment of children.
➠ The lack of evidence that consultation is more effective in relation to client outcomes.
➠ A reluctance on the part of some educational psychologists to abandon the traditional model.

Despite this, many educational psychology services now operate within a 'consultation model' of service delivery, even though definitions of this term and what practices are included within it continue to be vague (Leadbetter 2006).

In practice, most educational psychologists will make decisions about the level of intervention necessary in consultation with school staff and parents. The aims of consultation, whether at individual, group or organisational level, are to find solutions to school-based problems and make sense of pupils' difficulties within the classroom or wider school context.

A day in the life of an educational psychologist

- ➤ 9.15: Arrive at school – short meeting with head teacher to discuss Joseph's inclusion. Joseph is Year 2 in mainstream school. He has four-limb cerebral palsy, uses a communication aid and has significant learning difficulties. Head teacher not happy about the level of support from his statement.
- ➤ 9.30: Observe Joseph in class – he is very segregated with his teaching assistant. Joseph did not join in any activities.
- ➤ 10.30: Talk to class teacher and teaching assistant (TA) about involving Joseph more, e.g. using pre-programmed messages on his communication aid related to the story the class are reading.
- ➤ 11.00: Take Joseph out with the TA for update on his progress – try some individual assessment using eye pointing – Joseph won't work with me.
- ➤ 11.45: Meeting with Joseph's mother – some issues for annual review.
- ➤ 12.30: Feedback to head teacher.
- ➤ Lunchtime: no time for lunch (again!) except quick sandwich and drink in the car and off to next appointment.
- ➤ 1.30–3.30: Discussion with special educational needs coordinator (SENCO), then observation of George (4 years) who is experiencing anxiety about coming to school. Meeting with class teacher, SENCO and mother to discuss strategies. Just time to get to whole educational psychology service (EPS) meeting (continuous professional development).
- ➤ 4.00–5.00: Meeting for whole EPS on SEN inclusion strategy. Phew! Now just two reports to write!

Applications of theories of learning and behaviour to educational practice

The discipline of educational psychology borrows from a number of theoretical backgrounds, including those dealing with the more 'observable' aspects of changes in children's *behaviour* (behaviourist theories) and others more related to *thinking processes* and *memory* (cognitive theories). Others have been concerned with 'thinking about thinking', or understanding *mental constructs* (constructivist theories).

Behaviourist theories

Behaviourist theories, particularly influenced by the work of Skinner in the 1950s, explain learning in terms of observable behaviours based on the influence of environmental stimuli. Learning is seen as a relatively enduring change in observable behaviour that occurs as a result of experience, as distinct from genetic/biological factors or illness or injury (Schunk 2004).

Detailed accounts of behaviourist theories are given elsewhere (Chapter 10), but the principles underlying behaviourism can be seen in many aspects of learning and education. For example, the principle of *reinforcement* is used widely. In the classroom teachers may use it to encourage and motivate learning, or to increase attention and time on task. Reinforcers can range from simple praise to star charts or letters home to parents. Having developed the appropriate behaviour in a child, the teacher may use a *schedule of reinforcement*, for example not rewarding every time, but gradually removing the reinforcement until the behaviour becomes self-sustaining or the child is motivated from within (intrinsic motivation). Teachers would want to ignore attention-seeking behaviour, that is, a programme of *extinction*. Teachers may withdraw children to a safe place if their behaviour becomes unacceptable – 'time-out' procedures. Another example would be pupils experiencing anxiety following poor performance in a science test (*test anxiety*), which may become a *conditioned response* to other science tests and could even *generalise* to other test situations. However, this anxiety may not show itself in an English test; that is, the pupil may *discriminate* (give different responses to different stimuli). Teachers may take advantage of the Premack principle, where a more desired activity serves as a reinforcer for a less desired activity, for example. Behaviourism is widely used in applied behaviour analysis, systematically applying behaviourist principles to change student behaviour.

As will be explained in Chapter 10, in general, stimulus-response, behavioural approaches were not able to deal effectively with 'thinking', since, in the original versions, mental concepts were ruled out as objects of scientific study. In particular, they dealt poorly with the way language develops in children. Behaviourist approaches, therefore, have been confined generally to the more 'observable' aspects of behaviour, and hence are more relevant to classroom behaviour and its management than to the internal processes involved in the retention of information and how that information may be subsequently used.

Cognitive theories of learning

Social learning theory (Bandura 2001) is interested in the extent to which learning is affected through observation, and provides a bridge between classic behaviourism and cognitive approaches within psychology. Social learning theorists view learning as a change in mental processes that creates the capacity to demonstrate different behaviours. (Hill 2002 in Eggen and Kauchak 2007).

Bandura considers that four factors are central in observational learning:

1 *attention* – looking at the relevant aspects of the behaviour of others ('models');
2 *retaining* information;
3 *reproducing* information or behaviour;
4 being *motivated* to reproduce information or behaviour (see below).

Clearly teachers can *model* desired behaviour and reinforce those learners who display desired behaviour, ensuring that other students' attention is drawn to these outcomes.

Bandura's later theories include the processes of *self-regulation*, or *self-management*, and *self-efficacy*. Self-regulation involves setting one's own standards and being able to observe one's own behaviour reflectively. Self-management includes training and encouraging students to set their own goals, self-evaluate their progress and reinforce themselves for work successfully completed. Self-efficacy is a belief in one's abilities to organise actions to meet objectives, solve problems, and so on. However, as with all theories of human behaviour, social learning theory has strengths and weaknesses. In particular, it is not able to explain why learners imitated some models and not others, nor to explain the role of context and social interaction in complex learning (Eggen and Kauchak 2007).

Purely cognitive theories are concerned with the internal processes involved in thinking and remembering. These theories explain learning by focusing on changes in mental processes and constructs that occur as a result of people's efforts to make sense of the world.

Piaget's theory of cognitive development

A particularly influential theory has been that of Jean Piaget (1954, 1963), who was concerned with the way children's thinking developed over time. He was interested in the *processes* involved (how a child arrived at a conclusion) rather than *content* (what the child knew). Piaget believed that children's thinking goes through distinct stages where thought is radically *restructured*. Thinking is based on internal representations of the world called *schemas* or *schemata*. For example, when a child consistently and accurately reaches out for a favourite toy placed in different positions, the child may be said to have a schema of how to obtain the toy; recognising any dog is evidence of a general schema for dogs.

Piaget considered that schemata change with new information in order to maintain a state of *equilibration*, or balance, whereby problems encountered in the environment are solved at the current stage of development, sometimes creating odd 'solutions' from an adult's point of view. Piaget (1963) considered that children go through four stages of development:

➡ A *sensori-motor* stage (0 to 2 years), when children use their senses and motor (movement) skills to make sense of their world. They acquire object permanence (the idea that things stay as and where they are) and learn to imitate others.
➡ This is followed by the *pre-operational* stage (2 to 7 years), when children make huge progress in language development, learn a large number of concepts, and perception plays a significant part in how they interpret events. Children go through a period of *egocentrism*, that is, they have difficulty seeing the world from any perspective but their own.

At the *concrete operations* stage (7 to 11 years) children are able to think more logically, develop understanding of conservation (e.g. of weight, volume) and become less egocentric.

Finally, in the *formal operations* stage (11 to adult), children develop the ability for truly abstract reasoning, e.g. dealing with concepts such as justice and equality.

Piaget's theory was influential in that it offered a possible explanation of how and when a child is ready to learn or develop a specific level of understanding (Wood 1998). Despite criticisms, and a general lack of recommendations for educators, Piaget's theory has had a strong influence in education, particularly in relation to preschool development, nursery and early school years. Piaget's theory emphasises the need for:

developmentally appropriate education, with material and approaches at different ages linked to a child's stage of cognitive development; material should be pitched just at and slightly beyond the child's current level of understanding; the teacher may gently introduce *dis*-equilibrium in order to promote further exploration;

an emphasis on the importance of a child's own *active involvement* in learning situations; children should be encouraged to discover for themselves; teachers should tap their *intrinsic motivation* to learn; teachers need to provide a variety of activities that allow the child to interact with its environment;

recognition of individual differences in going through the stages of development; with this recognition comes the need to teach to individual needs in small groups rather than the whole class.

Piaget's ideas, together with those of Bruner (1966), were influential in the development of *discovery learning* approaches. These approaches emphasised the need:

for students to learn from their own active explorations;

to start with 'real' problems and to help students develop appropriate problem-solving techniques in order to break down the problems, using the teacher as a resource;

for *cooperative learning*, with children working in pairs or groups (see below, p. 96).

The aim is to arouse curiosity, increase *intrinsic motivation* and help children to become more independent learners. Teachers provide resources with which children explore relationships (e.g. scales and weights). Difficulties may arise if the information is too far beyond a child's cognitive level. In addition, it may not be easy for children to generalise from a specific real-life incident to other similar situations. However, there have been criticisms of discovery approaches and of group learning (see below).

Information-processing theories

Further advances in attention and memory processes produced more implications for educational practice. *Information-processing* models attempt to explain how information is selected to be stored and how it is retrieved from memory. The emphasis is on a model of humans as processors of incoming information which requires identification, categorisation and analysis. This involves *memory stores*, *cognitive processes* and *metacognition* – knowing about how we know.

Memory stores hold information and are considered to include *sensory memory*, *working memory* and *long-term memory*. Sensory memory is considered to hold information from the environment for a brief time, that is, for about one second for visual information and two to four seconds for auditory information (hearing) (Leahy and Harris 2001). Sensory memory is considered to hold information until you attach some meaning to it and it is transferred to working memory. Working memory is the conscious part of the process and includes deliberate thought (Paas, Renkl and Sweller 2004 in Eggen and Kauchak 2007). Working memory has limitations and is generally considered to be able to hold about seven items of information at a time, though items of information that have common characteristics may be grouped or 'chunked' to effectively become one unit rather than several. These ideas were developed by Miller in the 1950s and are still influential (Miller 1956 in Eggen and Kauchak 2007). Some researchers consider that working memory has a visual component (processing visual information) and an auditory (hearing) component that work together, so that learning should be increased if information is both visual and auditory (Clark and Mayer 2003 in Eggen and Kauchak 2007). Information may then be passed to long-term memory (LTM), which is apparently limitless.

Within LTM a distinction can be made between *declarative knowledge* (knowledge of facts, definitions and rules) and *procedural knowledge* (knowledge of how to perform tasks). Declarative knowledge can be judged by what people say, whereas procedural knowledge is shown by what people can do. Cognitive constructs (schemas) organise information into meaningful systems (Andersen 2005). Information is more easily retrieved if schemas are interconnected, if they have something in common. Remembering a list containing the names of animals and flowers that can be grouped is easier than remembering a list of nonsense (made-up) words. Meaningfulness facilitates recall (Gagne, Yekovich and Yekovich 1997 in Eggen and Kauchak 2007).

Cognitive processes, such as attention and perception, as well as opportunities to relearn and rehearse information, affect long-term memory. An understanding of these factors, that is, of knowing how to learn and remember, is *metacognition*. Advances in knowing more about the development of thinking about thinking led to further developments in theoretical approaches to learning.

Constructivist theories

Some approaches to learning have taken a dynamic view of learning and behaviour, that is, that feeling, cognition and behaviour need to be considered together, along with social aspects, for a fuller understanding of human behaviour. Constructivists believe that learners construct their own reality, based on their perceptions of prior experiences and beliefs, and that they interpret objects and events through their own view of reality (Jonasson 1991).

In this view, knowledge is constructed from experience and learning is a personal interpretation of the world. The extent to which social interaction is relevant to internal representations has been a matter of some debate. Piaget's theory emphasises the development of individual (psychological) constructivism, where social interaction may influence the learning process, but as a catalyst for reconstruction. For example, if a child expresses an idea that causes disequilibrium in another, this may be resolved by the child reconstructing their

understanding. However, Vygotsky's work (see below, p. 94) emphasises the influence of social factors on the development of internal representations (*social constructivism*); that is, interactions with adults, more capable peers and cognitive tools are internalised to form mental constructs.

The key message of *personal construct* theory (e.g. Kelly 1955) is that the world is 'perceived' by a person in terms of whatever meaning that person applies to it. The individual is not a prisoner of past events, but is capable of applying alternative constructions (meanings) to any events in the past, present or future. The individual creates his or her own way of seeing the world.

Other approaches involve an understanding of the constructs (*theories of mind*) of others (e.g. Carruthers and Smith 1996). Human minds develop understanding that others also have minds with different and separate beliefs, desires, intentions and mental states. We become able to form ideas, hypotheses or mental models as to what these beliefs, desires and intentions are. Theory of mind (TOM) involves the cognitive ability to understand others as intentional beings.

A body of knowledge from developmental psychology using 'false belief' tasks (see Box 4, below) indicates a change between the ages of three and five years in a child's ability to distinguish what is the case and what people believe is the case. Second-order beliefs (e.g. John thinks that Susan thinks...) develop later (Perner and Wimmer 1985).

Autistic children typically have difficulty in these tasks (Baron-Cohen 2000). Neurological evidence would suggest that this is not just a reflection of the language and communication difficulties associated with autism, as described earlier (see p. 83). Language is, of course, a way of expressing meanings and thoughts, and a key to understanding intentionality.

This emphasis on the relationship between language, social interaction and higher-order thinking can be seen in Vygotsky's work on language and social interaction (1978, 1986). Piaget believed that children's habit of talking out loud when no one is there to hear what they say demonstrated further evidence of 'egocentrism' and served little purpose. However, Vygotsky believed that such speech served a central and powerful role in the development of thinking. He believed that thought was very much dependent on the existence of social speech and that social interactions themselves are the root of our higher thinking processes.

There is now considerable literature documenting associations between social factors (such as parenting styles – see below, p. 99) and children's understanding of mind. De Rosnay and Hughes (2006) present a substantial review of findings that suggest that conversational interactions are also fundamental to children's socio-cognitive development, and that more opportunities for conversation (e.g. parental conversation with children) lead to a broader and deeper understanding of the minds of others, and perhaps speed up the child's progress *towards* understanding other people's minds.

The theoretical approaches discussed above are not mutually exclusive and overlap to some extent. They show a progression of development of ideas, as knowledge of development and learning increased. Classroom practice is likely to involve strategies based on all three, for example a reward system for good work or behaviour, 'chunking' of information to prevent overload, opportunities for rehearsal and activities and interactions to mediate learning.

Applications of mediated learning approaches

A strong implication from Vygotsky's view is that simply providing children with materials, then leaving them to discover, as promoted by Piagetians, will not be successful. The child needs this, *plus* support. Vygotsky's *zone of proximal development* (ZPD) is the area in which a child can solve problems, but not unaided, in other words, the area in which they are ripe for learning and discovery. This explains why another learner who has not long ago gone through the same learning experience is often a good tutor – still in a similar ZPD, they understand the difficulties.

The teacher needs to identify problems in the child's ZPD and provide a *scaffold* of the useful speech, nudges, demonstrations and explanations that will help the child move on. As this produces greater competence in the child, so the teacher withdraws the scaffolding until the learner can comfortably solve this level of problem on their own. The term *scaffolding* has become commonly used for this approach to the design of classroom learning (see Wood 1998).

An emphasis on looking at 'mediated' learning has led theorists to consider how learners 'learn how to learn' – the processes of *metacognition*. The emphasis here is on how learners *monitor* their progress (Flavell 1985) and think about their thinking.

Box 4 Examples of testing children's understanding of the mental states of others using 'false belief' paradigms

1 Bobby puts his teddy bear in his bedroom cupboard. After he has gone out to play his mother comes to tidy his room. As she opens the cupboard the teddy bear falls out, so she puts the teddy bear in the toy box under Bobby's bed. Later, Bobby comes in to get his teddy bear to play with. Where does Bobby look for his teddy bear? Where is the teddy bear?

Young children (3 to 5) are likely to think Bobby will look where *they* know it is and not where he left it. (Adapted from Wellman and Bartsch 1988.)

2 Alice does not like her dinner, but her mother says she has to eat it. Her mother has to leave the room to answer the telephone. While she is out, Alice scrapes her dinner into the dog's bowl and the dog starts to eat it. When her mother comes back she sees that Alice's plate is empty. What does Alice's mother think? Did Alice eat the food? Then Alice's mother notices some of the dinner that is still in the dog's bowl. What does Alice's mother think now? Did the dog eat the dinner? (Adapted from Perner and Wimmer 1985.)

Fuerstein's work (e.g. Fuerstein et al. 1980) has looked at the effect of 'mediated learning experience' to help a child adapt to new learning experiences, that is, a 'learning how to learn' approach. Techniques such as dynamic assessment have been developed from this approach, typically involving a pre-test, intervention and post-test model of support for the child. Learners need to recognise what is important, plan their next moves in problem-solving, balance their time, predict outcomes and evaluate their progress by checking the results of strategies used, discarding them if unsuccessful. Learners who *use* information given, *and* attempt to understand *why* the information is given, tend to do better in learning.

Motivation

Behaviourist approaches

Since reinforcers increase learning, they act as motivators. However, these theoretical approaches do not explain *intrinsic* motivation – new learning without any observable reinforcer. In addition, some evidence suggests that the use of reinforcement can reduce interest in intrinsically motivated tasks – children may begin to *expect* rewards as a condition of learning (Sansone and Harackiewicz 2000 in Eggen and Kauchak 2007).

Cognitive approaches

Cognitive theories consider that the basis of motivation is the need to understand; that is, children are naturally motivated to learn when an experience is not consistent with their current level of understanding. Within the general term 'cognitive theories' there are at least five approaches to explain motivation, outlined below. (The interested reader is referred to Eggen and Kauchak 2007, Chapter 10, for a more detailed account.)

- *Expectancy x value* theory suggests that people are motivated to engage in an activity to the extent that they expect to succeed multiplied by the value they place on success, so that if a pupil's expectancy of success is at or near zero, or the value placed on a task is zero, then motivation will be zero (Tollefson 2000).
- *Self-efficacy* is the extent to which an individual believes in their ability to be successful. This may vary between subjects and tasks. Self-efficacy is influenced by past performance, history of

success and observing good models. It can be increased by encouraging pupils to set challenging but achievable goals (Brophy 2004).
- *Goal setting* can have a strong impact on motivation to learn (Elliot and Thrash 2001). Research has distinguished *learning goals* from *performance goals*. A learning goal focuses on mastery of a task or increasing understanding. A performance goal is concerned with competence and how it compares with the competence of others. Learning goals are most effective and lead to sustained interest. Pupils who adopt a learning goals approach attribute success to internal, controllable causes (Eggen and Kauchak 2007). Goal theory has been related to personal feelings about the nature of intelligence. Some research indicates that individuals may have either an entity view of intelligence or an incremental view. An entity view is the belief that ability is fixed and stable, and therefore not within one's control. Such people are likely to adopt performance goals. The incremental view is that ability can be improved with effort. People with these beliefs are likely to adopt learning goals (Quihuis et al. 2002 in Eggen and Kauchak 2007).
- *Attribution theory* attempts to describe how learners explain their successes and failures, that is, what they *attribute* these successes and failures to. Attributions can be described on three dimensions. The first is the location of the cause (*locus*), which can be within the learner (such as ability and effort) or outside the learner (such as luck and task difficulty). The second is *stability* the extent to which the cause can change. Effort is considered unstable since it can change, whereas ability is considered stable. The third is the extent to which the learner is in *control* of the learning situation or accepts responsibility for their performance – they may be in control of effort invested, but not in control of the task difficulty (Weiner 2000).
- *Self-determination theory* considers how learners decide to act on their environment, how they make choices and decisions. It is concerned with what are perceived to be innate psychological needs – competence, autonomy and relatedness. The need to master one's environment (develop *competence*) is considered intrinsic (internally driven) and has its roots in basic survival. *Autonomy* relates to one's ability to be independent and alter one's environment.

Relatedness is the need to feel accepted by others in one's social environment, and is concerned with feelings of worth and respect (Levesque et al. 2004).

The following section looks at a number of other factors that can affect children's learning and behaviour.

TEACHER BEHAVIOUR

One major area of research has been into those factors and qualities which make for effective teaching and happy classrooms. Interest is in the factors which influence the way in which teachers generally affect the social and academic development of their pupils. Some studies have focused on teacher characteristics and expectations.

Teacher characteristics

We have seen that self-efficacy is a child's beliefs about their own capabilities. An extension of this concept is *personal teaching efficacy* (Bruning et al. 2004). Teachers with high personal teaching efficacy take responsibility for the success or failure of their own instruction. They praise competence and avoid the use of rewards to control behaviour. Low personal efficacy teachers are more likely to blame other factors for low achievement, for example low intelligence or home factors. They also have lower expectations. Low efficacy also contributes to teacher stress and teacher burnout (Brouwers and Tomic 2001).

Considerable research has identified a number of essential teaching skills, including attitudes, organisation and communication skills (Good and Brophy 2003). Positive teacher attitudes are fundamental to effective teaching, and teacher characteristics such as efficiency, enthusiasm, caring and high expectations promote motivation in pupils and lead to higher achievement (Brophy 2004). Effective communication is an important factor in student achievement and student satisfaction with instruction/ratings of teachers (Good and Brophy 2003). There are four aspects of effective communication:

➡ using *precise language*;
➡ keeping instruction thematic and to the point (*connected discourse*);
➡ giving clear *transition signals* in moving from one idea to the next;
➡ alerting students to important information (*emphasis*). (Eggen and Kauchak 2007)

Teacher's use of praise is an interesting area. Young children seem to accept praise even when overdone, while older children assess the validity of the praise and what they believe it communicates about their ability. Young children love to be praised openly in front of the class, while with adolescents praise is best given quietly and individually (Good and Brophy 2003). Highly anxious students and those from low socio-economic backgrounds tend to react more positively to praise than pupils who are more confident or from more advantaged backgrounds (Good and Brophy 2003). Harrop and Swinson (2000) looked at the rates of approval and disapproval in British schools. In the 1970s teachers gave more disapproval than approval. By the 1980s this trend was reversed. A quarter of a century later, Harrop and Swinson found that approval was given predominantly to pupils working individually rather than in groups, and that redirection by the teacher following disapproval (i.e. telling the child what they should be doing) was much lower in secondary than in infant or junior schools.

Teacher expectations

Teachers treat pupils they perceive to be high achievers differently from those they perceive to be low achievers (Weinstein 2002). They provide more *emotional support* by interacting more often and more positively. They give more eye contact and even stand closer. Teachers make more *effort* for those they perceive as high achievers, for example giving more full explanations, being more enthusiastic and expecting more. They ask their perceived high achievers more *questions*, give more praise and longer feedback (Good and Brophy 2003). Differential treatment may influence the learner's beliefs and expectations. Children of all ages are aware of the different expectations teachers have of them (Stipek 2002).

PUPIL BEHAVIOUR

Pupil interactions and cooperative learning

The emphasis on learning-through-discovery approaches has led to many classrooms being organised with children sitting in groups. This naturally encourages pupil interactions. Cooperative learning is grounded in social constructivism in that it relies on cooperative social interaction to facilitate knowledge construction. It is a very popular instructional model in schools in the early twenty-first century, though many teachers equate any form of getting pupils into groups with cooperative learning (Johnson and Johnson 2006). Truly cooperative learning involves pupils working in groups small enough (typically two to five) that they can participate in a clearly assigned task with clear learning objectives, and where learners depend on one another to reach objectives – *positive interdependence* (Johnson and Johnson 2006). Examples are pairs working together to ask and answer questions about a lesson (*reciprocal questioning*) or to elaborate on each other's thinking about a maths problem (*scripted cooperation*). A further example is the *jigsaw* approach (Arouson et al. 1978). The basis of this method is for students to work in a group, with each being given responsibility for a piece of work, but where all the pieces are needed to complete the work. There is evidence that working in groups helps develop social skills and may have positive implications for the acceptance and social integration of pupils from minority ethnic groups (Johnson and Johnson 2006).

Working in groups may not suit all learning situations. For example, Klahr and Nigram (2004) looked at relative effectiveness of discovery learning versus direct instruction in children of junior school age. The task involved designing and interpreting unconfounded experiments in science. More children learned from direct instruction than from discovery learning, and were better able to transfer their knowledge. Different types of learning skills, social skills and attention control may be necessary for a successful group work situation, or it may be better suited to particular tasks or areas of the curriculum.

Fawcett and Garton (2005) looked at the effect of peer collaboration on children's problem-solving ability. In terms of Vygotsky's theory, cognitive change is linked to collaborative interaction with a more competent partner, whereas Piaget's theory would say that cognitive change occurs from cognitive conflict arising from peer interaction. Six-and seven-year-olds carried out a pre- and post-test task of block sorting. They then worked either individually or in pairs of the same ability or different ability (as determined by the pre-test), under either 'talk' or 'no-talk' conditions. The experimental task was to complete a card-sorting activity. The researchers found that children who worked collectively obtained significantly higher correct sorts than those working individually. However, in the post-test task it was found that only those paired with a higher ability peer and who were in the 'talk' situation showed a significant improvement from pre-test scores. It was concluded that simply assigning pupils to groups and telling them to work together will not necessarily promote real cooperation or help children achieve more. Influential factors were a child's zone of proximal development as well as interactive skills, that is, the child's ability to provide explanations and their sensitivity to the other pupil's needs.

Peer influences

Peers influence children's development in two ways: by communicating attitudes and values, and by forming friendships or excluding children from friendships (Betts, Zau and Rice 2003 in Eggen and Kauchak 2007). Peer influences can be positive or negative. For example, researchers have found that a pupil's choice of friends can predict his or her grades, level of disruptive behaviour and teachers' ratings of involvement in school (Berk 2006).

PROBLEM BEHAVIOUR IN SCHOOLS

Educational psychologists will be involved in a range of behaviour problems in school. These are likely to include:

➡ Distracting, attention-seeking behaviour (e.g. calling out, wandering round the class). This kind of behaviour lends itself to behaviour management programmes, such as token systems and raising awareness through pupils charting their own behaviour.
➡ Withdrawn, anxious behaviour – this may be related to a number of factors, such as domestic

difficulties, abuse or bullying (see below). Educational psychologists may be involved in approaches such as cognitive behaviour therapy (see above), or in working closely with the local Children and Adolescent Mental Health Service.

➠ Anti-social behaviour, on a continuum from verbal insults to extreme physical aggression. Educational psychologists may be involved in direct working on anger management, or referring to agencies such as pupil referral units to carry out this work in the school.

➠ Bullying – this may be directed towards one or two individuals for a variety of reasons, or may be pervasive within a given school culture. Bullies typically come from homes where parents are authoritarian, hostile and rejecting (see below). Their parents frequently have poor problem-solving skills and often advocate fighting as the solution to conflicts (Ma 2001). Pupil factors in aggression have been linked to deficits in pupils' ability to understand the perspective of others, moral development and self-regulation (Crick, Grotpeter and Bigbee 2002). Boys tend to bully physically while girls bully more verbally. Boys bully more than girls by a ratio of 3:1, which may reflect a greater tendency to be aware of and report physical bullying (Ma 2001). Large-scale studies have found that about 20 per cent of children of primary school age report bullying at some stage, with about 10 per cent at secondary schools (see Smith and Sharp 1994; Olweus 1993). Risk factors for victims include rejection by peers and overprotective families. Risk factors for bullies include inconsistent home discipline and aggressive fathers. Children who are both bullies and victims may come from particularly disturbed family backgrounds (National Children's Bureau 2000). Bullying is now of such concern in the UK that a House of Commons Select Committee (Education and Skills) is about to undertake an inquiry into bullying (AEP newsletter, 20 September 2006).

➠ Some children show patterns of violent and aggressive behaviour towards peers and adults which are not necessarily related to individual victimisation or bullying. Some of these children may be identified as having social and emotional problems requiring special help or even a special school. Again, more boys than girls are referred as having such problems (McCall and Farrell 1993), although assessment in this area is a difficult issue.

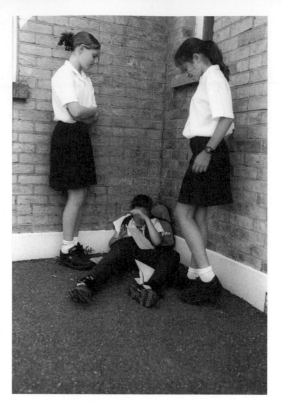

Figure 4.3 For too many young people, bullying is a fact of life

The school as an organisation

Systems approaches developed out of work in the 1950s and 1960s on language teaching, programmed instruction and computer-assisted learning. They typically involve a flow chart of objectives, strategies and evaluation. Systems approaches can be applied to teaching and designing a course or curriculum, and are being applied increasingly to looking at organisations such as schools and service delivery within a local authority.

A number of studies have attempted to investigate the effects that schools have on pupils' success, that is, how effective schools are and what makes some schools more effective than others. It is possible to view the school as an organisation or 'system', and to look at factors within that system which facilitate or inhibit learning and achievement, as well as affecting pupil behaviour. Factors such as the previous success rate of the school, expectations of success, type of leadership, channels of communication within the school and parental involvement have all been indicated as important factors.

The role of the school as an organisation within the wider community is changing too. As a way of delivering Every Child Matters (DfES 2003), the development of *extended schools* is being promoted. With additional funding, schools are being encouraged to provide:

➡ 'wrap-around' childcare, from 8 a.m. to 6 p.m. all year round;
➡ parenting and family support (e.g. a member of staff who speaks a minority ethnic language predominant in the community and who can provide a pastoral role as well as English-language classes);
➡ varied activities, such as study support, sport and music clubs;
➡ swift and early referral to specialist support services – in some cases, representatives from these services, such as a social worker, community nurse or parent partnership support worker, may have an office base in a local school;
➡ community use of facilities, including adult and family learning courses.

By 2010, all children and their families should have access to extended services through their schools. In some areas schools are grouped into 'locality groups', with representatives from all support agencies, in order to bring about closer integration of Children's Services. As part of these groups, educational psychologists will gradually extend their work into the community.

FAMILY, SCHOOL AND COMMUNITY

Previous sections have dealt with the areas of knowledge relevant to assessment and intervention in working with children in schools. The educational psychologist's brief extends beyond the school to the family and the wider community. It is important to look at how the home situation, family attitudes, values and culture can influence the child's academic and social progress at school.

Home, early learning and school

The importance of parents in children's attainments has long been recognised. An early study by Douglas (1964) found that parental attitude to education was the single most important factor in predicting success. More recent evidence suggests this is still the case. Feinstein and Symons (1999) used data from the National Child Development Study, which followed the development of all children born in England, Scotland and Wales in a particular week in March 1958. They found that parental interest in their child's education was the major influence on attainment. Using data from the same study, Wedge and Essen (1982) recorded the link between poverty and poor attainment. This link is still in evidence a quarter of a century later. A number of studies (Flouri 2006; Schoon et al. 2002) have shown a continued link between socio-economic disadvantage in childhood and attainment. Interestingly, they also found that the educational attainment of the mother is a significant factor.

Parents naturally exert an important influence on their children's development. Research indicates that certain parenting styles promote more healthy personal development than others (Baumrind 1991), and the effects of these styles can last into adulthood, affecting motivation and achievement in further education (Collins et al. 2000). These differences in style relate to parents' *expectations* and their *responsiveness*. Using expectations and responsiveness as a framework, researchers have identified four patterns of parenting and the child characteristics associated with them.

➡ *Authoritative* parents are consistent, firm but caring. They explain reasons for rules and have high expectations. Their children are confident, have high self-esteem and are successful in school.
➡ *Authoritarian* parents stress conformity and are detached. Their children are withdrawn, lack social skills and may be defiant.
➡ *Permissive* parents have limited expectations, set few boundaries and make few demands. Their children are immature, poorly motivated and lack self-control.
➡ *Uninvolved* parents show little interest in their children, with few expectations. Their children lack self-control and long-term goals. (Summarised in Eggen and Kauchak 2007: 63; see also Maughan and Ciccetti 2002.)

Early intervention

The links between poverty, parenting and lack of early stimulation led to the Headstart project in the USA in the 1960s. In targeted regions, children received extensive intellectual and social stimulation, as well as dietary supplements, a year before entry to kindergarten. These children initially showed gains in IQ points over age peers not in the project, though these gains disappeared early in primary school. However, longitudinal studies of children did indicate gains for those who had received preschool input. Gorey (2001 in Jarvis 2005) reviewed 35 studies and found large effects maintained over a long period. About 70 to 80 per cent of the children in preschool programmes did better at school than those in control groups, and those who attended preschool had lower rates of unemployment, poverty and crime as adults.

Following recognition of the importance of preschool education and the influence of deprivation, a programme to provide free early education for three- and four-year-olds (the Sure Start programme) was developed in the UK. This provides quality childcare and after-school activities in close collaboration with children's centres, to provide health and family support, particularly in disadvantaged areas. In addition, initiatives such as the development of Education Action Zones (introduced through the Schools Standards and Framework Act 1998) were introduced to raise standards in some of the most deprived regions through additional funding. Initiatives through the Children's Act 2004 are intended to extend the role of the school in all communities and encourage links between families, schools and support services for children.

Community and culture

A growing trend in educational achievement has been for girls to do better than boys in GCSE examinations, with 61.4 per cent obtaining five or more at grades A* to C, compared with 51.4 per cent for boys (DfES 2006). A number of studies have also looked at the achievement of minority ethnic groups within the education system. Figures from the 2001 National Census show that students from African Caribbean, Pakistani and Bangladeshi ethnic minority groups do least well, and that pupils from these groups, particularly Afro-Caribbean boys, were more likely to be excluded from school. Preschool experience, especially for those with English as an additional language, had noticeable effects on starting primary school. Across all ethnic groups, girls out-achieved boys, and this was most noticeable among Black Caribbean and African girls and boys. Interestingly, African Caribbean pupils who do not perform well at GCSE, had been higher achievers at earlier stages of schooling. Indian and Chinese groups outperform other groups in all assessments. Students from Black Caribbean, Indian and Pakistani backgrounds perform better in predominantly white schools in GCSE examinations (Johnston, Wilson and Burgess 2006).

The reasons for different educational outcomes are complex, involving language, cultural and socio-economic factors and length of time in the education system, but research indicates that economic disadvantage has a significant effect on educational attainment (see above; also Gillborn and Mirza 2000, quoted in http://www.cre.gov.uk/duty/reia/statistics_education.html).

In working with children from minority ethnic groups and their families, the educational psychologist will need to work at both the individual, school and family level. The psychologist will need to ensure:

- effective communication with parents if the primary home language is not English;
- that developmental and learning difficulties can be distinguished from English as a second language difficulties in some families;
- there is awareness of factors likely to be affecting the child's motivation and achievement at school.

The psychologist may be involved in the development of a *whole-school policy* in relation to equal opportunities and cultural difference. Ethnic minority pupils do better in schools where there is:

- strong leadership;
- high expectations;
- effective teaching and learning strategies;
- parental involvement;
- an ethos of respect;
- a clear approach to racism and poor behaviour (DfES 2003).

Figure 4.4 Learning together to create equal opportunities and cultural understanding

Cowie and Rudduck (1991) found evidence that cooperative learning strategies can help to create equal opportunities for all pupils and foster a social climate more conducive to learning. Singh (1991), using Aronson's *jigsaw method* in Sunderland, increased cross-race friendships equally for students of different ethnic backgrounds, sex and achievement levels.

Again, the influence of the Childrens' Act 2004 is likely to lead to changes affecting the school's role in the community, such as through encouraging 'clustering' of schools to share good practice. The combination of Education Action Zones, Sure Start, extended schools, parenting programmes and neighbourhood renewal programmes is helping to put into practice government policy on developing 'learning communities', and providing children and families with the necessary life experiences to enable lifelong learning and the development of skills for life.

CURRENT DIRECTIONS IN EDUCATIONAL PSYCHOLOGY

The changes in the provision of services for children, together with changes in the training of educational psychologists, make for an exciting and challenging time for educational psychology. The challenges include the need to:

- maintain relevance to those working directly with children;

- develop further understanding of the complex interactions between the child and their environment;
- maintain scientific rigour in collecting information, developing and evaluating interventions;
- continue to ensure that what educational psychologists do contributes to the development and well-being of young people.

The 2006 review of the role and functions of educational psychologists found an 'almost universally held view' among schools, other professionals, managers and local authority officers that educational psychologists had been too heavily involved in statutory assessments, which had prevented them from expanding their work into other areas where they could maximise the impact of their psychological skills and knowledge (Farrell et al. 2006).

The review recommends that educational psychologists take advantage of the trend to a reduction in statutory work to expand into areas that will enable them to use their knowledge and expertise more fully, such as individual and group therapy, staff training and systems work. However, all respondents identified an important role for educational psychologists in working with individual children who have complex and challenging needs. Parents in particular appreciated individual assessments of their children and the knowledge they gained from these. The review considers that there will always be a role for educational psychologists in this area and recommends that they should continue to play a key part in the statutory assessment of children with complex needs. The review considers that educational psychology services should look at how their work can link more closely with other professions, particularly the work of clinical psychologists.

The field of educational psychology is undergoing fundamental changes in the early years of the twenty-first century, with a combination of radical new training programmes and changes in service delivery related to the Children's Act 2004 and the Every Child Matters agenda. This makes it an exciting time, with opportunities for educational psychologists to widen the context in which they work. Research-orientated training may also increase educational psychologists' ability to contribute to systems work within the local authority.

> This new context provides EPs with many challenges and opportunities and is one in which they can make a major contribution to meeting the needs of all children in line with the requirements of the ECM (Every Child Matters) agenda.
>
> (Farrell et al. 2006: 12)

Educational psychology remains an exciting and challenging field of applied theory and practice. Its knowledge base is continuing to grow, through national and international research, and through further developments in practice.

RECOMMENDED FURTHER READING

Eggen, P. and Kauchak, D. (2007) *Educational Psychology: Windows on Classrooms*, seventh edition. Upper Saddle River, NJ: Pearson Education. (A very readable and comprehensive textbook.)

Jarvis, M. (2005) *The Psychology of Effective Learning and Teaching*. Cheltenham: Nelson Thornes.

Wood, D. (1998) *How Children Think and Learn*, second edition. Oxford: Blackwell.

USEFUL WEBSITES

AbilityNet: http://www.abilitynet.org.uk

Association of Educational Psychologists (AEP): http://www.aep.org.uk

British Psychological Society (BPS): http://www.bps.org.uk

Cognitive behavioural therapy: http://counselling resource.com/types/cognitive-therapy/

National Autistic Society: http://www.nas.org.uk

Office of National Statistics: http://www.statistics.gov.uk

Special Education Needs and Disability (Teachernet): http://www.teachernet.gov.uk/wholeschool/sen/

Exercises

1 Arrange a visit to talk to an educational psychologist from your local educational psychology service about their views on the relevance of teacher training and teaching experience to the work of the educational psychologist.

2 Define 'norm-referenced' and 'criterion-referenced' in relation to testing. List the ways in which you think tests might not give an accurate picture of a child's current ability. Try to get hold of an actual test in order to make this assessment. How might 'dynamic assessment' add to a child's learning profile?

3 Sarah is a newly qualified teacher (NQT) in her first year of teaching. She has a class of Year 4 pupils (eight- to nine-years-olds) and has identified a small group of children who are poorly motivated. Sarah has the opportunity to discuss the situation with the school's educational psychologist. With a colleague, role-play the consultation meeting between Sarah and the educational psychologist. A second colleague might like to listen or tape-record the conversation and then you should all analyse it in terms of the content (subject-related) and the process (e.g. skills and attitude of Sarah and the educational psychologist).

4 Consider the five outcomes of Every Child Matters (see p. 75) and discuss ways (in addition to the examples given) in which educational psychologists could contribute to these. To what extent do other Children's Services, such as social workers and those working with young offenders, contribute to these outcomes?

5 In what ways might closer community links between schools, families and Children's Services reduce the incidence of bullying in schools?

Environmental Psychology

The news continues to be dominated by stories of traffic jams on roads and public transport delays adding to the stress of our busy lives. Such negative effects of the environment are the subject matter of environmental psychology. However, the picture is not all bad. I read recently of the development of a garden at a children's hospital as a way of improving the environment for the sick children. This provides an example of environmental psychology in action and the way in which the environment affects our behaviour.

Box 1 How does the environment affect you?

Think about a day in your own life. List the ways in which the environment has influenced your behaviour. How often have you ended up doing something that you did not plan because of events unrelated to yourself? How often have physical and social events caused you to be angry, irritated, sad, excited or happy? For instance, has noise really irritated you? It is likely that your list will contain many of the areas researched by environmental psychologists and discussed in this chapter.

WHAT IS ENVIRONMENTAL PSYCHOLOGY?

Problems with definitions

Definitions are always a useful starting point, as long as we recognise that definitions are oversimplified summaries. This can pose a problem in a diverse area like environmental psychology, leading to the imposition of limitations on subject matter by setting rigid boundaries of the field. One of the lessons that applied psychologists have learned is that a narrow focus which draws only on knowledge and method in one field of psychology is likely to be ineffective. As a result, approaches have developed which combine several fields, such as the area of occupational health psychology, an amalgam of occupational psychology and health psychology. A second problem with definitions is that psychology is a living discipline which is continuously growing and changing as new research is produced. It follows, therefore, that definitions are likely to become outdated and need to be changed to reflect new developments. This is indeed the case with environmental psychology.

Towards a definition

Burroughs (1989: 4) provides the following definition of environmental psychology, as 'the study of the interrelationships between the physical environment and human behaviour'. Gifford (1987: 9) provides a similar definition: 'environmental psychology is the study of transactions between individuals and their physical settings'. An important aspect of both definitions is that they define the process as *reciprocal between the person and the environment*. In other words, not only does the environment influence the individual, but the individual also impacts on the environment. Both definitions are based on Lewin's (1951) famous equation: B=f (PE), where B is behaviour, P is the person and E is environment. The equation states that *behaviour is a function of the person, the environment and the interaction between the two*, and is referred to as a *person-in-context* approach to understanding behaviour. The basic perspectives in psychology tend to focus on one or other side of this equation in seeking causes for behaviour either in the person or the environment. It is important to recognise that for Lewin it was not simply a matter of combining these perspectives. He argued that research should take account of the *interaction*, something that was advocated by many psychologists in the 1970s, but which was often ignored in practice. An *interactional* perspective is a central principle of environmental psychology.

Both definitions above limit the area of environmental psychology to the *physical* environment, and this reflects the evolution of the field from what was called *architectural psychology* in the early 1960s. It is a good example of the way in which a definition can be limiting and misleading. First, it is perfectly clear from a brief glance at the areas listed as falling within the domain of environmental psychology that the definition is actually contradicted by the subject area. Research into *crowding*, *personal space*, *territoriality* and *urbanisation* clearly includes both the *social* and *physical* environment.

In addition (as we shall see later), understanding the influence of *physical* settings on behaviour is inextricably bound up with *social* aspects of the setting. In many cases, the main effect of a physical setting on behaviour is through the meaning it has acquired from social interaction. A lecture theatre is just another room in physical terms. However, people tend to behave in a particular way in a lecture theatre because its function has been defined in social terms. In the introduction to a text on environmental psychology (Proshansky, Ittelson and Rivlin 1976), one of the most prominent American environmental psychologists, Harold Proshansky, concludes: 'The physical environment that we construct is as much a social phenomenon as it is a physical one'. The French psychologist Claude Levy-Leboyer (1982) echoes this: 'The physical environment simultaneously symbolises, makes concrete, and conditions the social environment'. It would therefore seem appropriate to suggest that environmental psychology is also concerned with the *social* environment, and while it may not be the major focus, it is unavoidably part of its subject matter. If we were to summarise the discussion so far we could postulate a definition of environmental psychology as: 'the study of the transactions between individuals and their physical and social environments' (Cassidy 1997: 4).

WHAT AN ENVIRONMENTAL PSYCHOLOGIST DOES

The critical mass of environmental psychologists tend to be academics – teaching, carrying out research and building a knowledge base. This is because (at the time of writing, 2006) there is no recognised profession of environmental psychologist in the way that there is for other fields, such as clinical or occupational psychology. There are postgraduate courses in environmental psychology, leading to both masters and doctoral qualifications, but these are relatively few in comparison with some other fields. The most common route to a career in environmental psychology is through a postgraduate research degree (PhD or DPhil). On completion, individuals go into teaching, research or consultancy, or a combination of these.

Applied environmental psychologists tend to concentrate on consultancy regarding the behavioural aspects of building and other physical environmental structure design. Thus they might be consulted on any aspect of the process, beginning with working out what the building is supposed to do (e.g. enhancing interaction in a home for the elderly) and how the building might be designed to meet its aims, and then assessing how effectively it does its job once it has been built and occupied. The opportunities for consultancy would appear to be increasing with the development of community psychology and the recognition of the social or people element in environmental psychology.

A day in the life of an environmental psychologist

Most environmental psychologists are academics, working in universities, and combining teaching, research and consultancy in their normal working life. The balance of activities will vary from day to day, and more often than not each day will be devoted to one or other of the above. For example, Monday and Tuesday might be mainly teaching days, Wednesday may be divided between meetings and research seminars, and Thursday and Friday devoted to research and/or consultancy. Days on which activities are mixed might be organised as follows:

- 8.00–9.00: Dealing with mail and student queries.
- 9.00–11.00: Teaching undergraduate students.
- 11.00–11.30: Dealing with follow-up student issues.
- 11.30–1.30: Doing a literature search for a research paper.
- 1.30–2.00: Lunch.
- 2.00–3.00: Supervision session with PhD student.
- 3.00–5.00: Preparing a research funding bid.
- 5.00–6.30: Working on data analysis for research paper.

Box 2 Focus on practice – evaluating the impact of building design on quality of life in nursing homes for older citizens

The Design in Caring Environments (DICE) study (Parker et al. 2004) looked at building design and quality of life in 38 care homes around Sheffield in the UK. Part of the study involved the development of a tool to measure physical environment, the Sheffield Care Environment Assessment Matrix (SCEAM).

The study found that many aspects of the building design (physical environment) were related to quality of life. Perhaps most interesting in this study was the finding that a focus on health and safety requirements, and modifications forced on the homes by law in this area, actually had a damaging effect on the quality of life for more physically able residents.

Interestingly, the level of staff morale was better predicted by non-institutionalised environments for the residents, than by the facilities provided for staff.

Environmental psychologists carry out studies like this as the basis for recommendations about future building design.

How would I become an environmental psychologist?

Becoming an environmental psychologist involves either completing one of the few MSc courses in environmental psychology offered at universities in the UK, or completing a research degree (PhD/DPhil) in an area of environmental research. It is then usual to go into teaching or full-time research and to become involved in consultancy on a part-time basis. Many of those with a background in environmental psychology use it in other areas, such as community psychology or criminological psychology. The most famous example is David Canter, who has moved from being one of the leading British environmental psychologists to his current position, in the early twenty-first century, as a leading British criminological or investigative psychologist.

DEVELOPMENT OF ENVIRONMENTAL PSYCHOLOGY

Psychologists have always been interested in the ways in which the environment influences behaviour and, in this sense, the history of environmental psychology is as long as the history of psychology itself. For a variety of reasons, however, there has been a tendency to acknowledge that environmental factors play a causal role in behaviour, but not to follow this acknowledgement with serious research. It is generally accepted that a turning point occurred with the ideas of Kurt Lewin (1890–1947), who developed some of the main principles on which environmental psychology is based. Lewin's work is generally acclaimed within the field of social psychology, and it is within this field that we find the first serious stirrings of what was to become the separate field of environmental psychology. It is from the work of social psychologists in the 1940s and 1950s that the knowledge base of environmental psychology has developed. Lewin introduced the term *psychological ecology* to describe his field of study. This was later changed to *ecological psychology* by Roger Barker and Herbert Wright. The term *architectural psychology* was used for two conferences in 1961 and 1966, and it would appear that it was only around 1969 that the field began to be called *environmental psychology*. During the 1970s the zeitgeist favoured environmental psychology and it flourished. Traditionally taught as part of courses on social psychology, environmental psychology now began to appear as a separate course within undergraduate psychology programmes.

This potted history of environmental psychology largely reflects what happened in the USA. It would appear that changes in political attitudes during the 1980s were not so favourable to the field, and growth slowed down somewhat in the last decades of the twentieth century. The vast bulk of research in environmental psychology has taken place in the USA, encouraged by political attitudes during the 1960s and 1970s. However, one must acknowledge the European influence on the field made by psychologists such as Lewin, who moved to the USA in advance of the First World War. It is arguably the integration of these European ideas with American pragmatism that has produced the most radical developments in applied psychology. In Britain, many undergraduate degree courses in psychology in the 1970s offered environmental psychology as an optional course, but this practice seems to have diminished. This does not mean that environmental psychology has disappeared, however, with many of its areas presented instead within courses on social psychology.

The development of any discipline is brought about by a combination of many influences; the current knowledge base is only one of these factors, and perhaps one of the least influential. More important are social and political attitudes, which determine the popularity of the discipline and, as a consequence, the human effort that will be exerted in its advancement. Part of this process is the funding of research and the employment of practitioners in the area. At the moment it would appear that funding for environmental research is not a priority. In the USA the principles and methods of environmental psychology have been utilised in the development of *community psychology*, an area of practice that has been around since the mid 1960s, but which only began to take off in Britain in the first decade of the twenty-first century. It may be that environmental psychology as a field will be subsumed by this new field. Whatever happens, there is no doubt that the work of environmental psychologists over the relatively short history of the field has made a major contribution to knowledge and practice in applied psychology.

RESEARCH, THEORY AND APPLICATION

Research, theory and application in environmental psychology are inextricably bound together, since research always has an applied focus and theory is the result of research. In this section we will look at a representative sample of the areas covered by environmental psychology. Given the limited amount of research and practice in environmental psychology in Europe, the bulk of what follows relies heavily on the American literature. Some very good work has been done by researchers such as David Canter and Terence Lee in the UK, and Claude Levy-Leboyer in France. Given the space, it would be possible to devote a separate chapter to all the topic areas covered by environmental psychology. Within the constraints of a single chapter, however, we can only sample these areas, and it must be stated at the outset that there are a variety of ways in which the subject matter could be categorised. I have chosen to use three categories:

1 *Interpreting the environment* (or environmental perception), which includes the model of the person in environmental psychology.
2 *The impact of the environment*, which covers environmental stress and the environment as a setting for behaviour.
3 *Living in the environment*, which covers the areas of *proxemics* and *using the environment*.

Interpreting the environment (or environmental perception)

Given that a person-in-context model is fundamental to environmental psychology, a good place to start a discussion of theory and practice is by looking at how the person sees their context (i.e. their environment). Through this we can build up a model of the person in environmental psychology. This is important because the basic assumptions that psychologists hold regarding the person in any field of psychology will set the boundaries for their theoretical perspectives and the research method they use. In turn, these will determine how the knowledge is applied.

How the person comes to understand and deal with the environment can be understood in terms of perception. The study of perception in cognitive psychology attempts to explain how we become aware of information in our environment, how we process that information and how we give meaning to that information, which eventually leads us to respond to it in one way or another. A vast amount of research has been carried out and a number of influential theories have been developed, for example by J. J. Gibson (1979), R. L. Gregory (1966) and U. Neisser (1976). Initially, theories tended to be one of two types:

➠ *bottom-up theories*, which focus on how the information itself, and ultimately the environment, determines our interpretation;
➠ *top-down theories*, which focus on how our stored previous experiences influence our interpretation of new information.

It is generally accepted these days that any universal theory of perception must include *both* bottom-up and top-down processes (see Figure 5.1 for an illustration). It is difficult to conceive of a situation where the information itself and its context (the external or bottom-up aspects) will not be important in providing cues to aid our interpretation. For example, let us look at the most under-researched sense modality – smell. If we were to become aware of a mix of exotic aromas while standing outside a Thai restaurant, we would know the source was the Thai food being cooked inside.

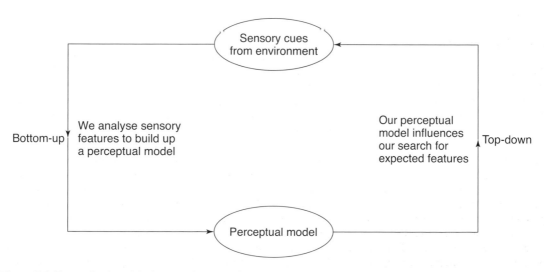

Figure 5.1 The cyclical model of perception, showing top-down and bottom-up processing
Source: Neisser (1976)

However, we might be confused to pick up the same smell in the middle of a deserted island. We required both the aroma and the context (the restaurant) in order to begin to give some meaning to the smell. But that is not the complete story. If we had never previously encountered this particular aroma, we would be unable to give meaning to it. The memory of this aroma from the past is located internally and its use in helping to give meaning to the smell is the top-down aspect. Thus we can see both bottom-up and top-down processes interacting to give some sense of meaning to the experience. Previous experience will also be important in determining our emotional reaction to the smell. The area of smell has not been researched extensively, though it is recognised as a potential ambient stressor (more on this later) and as a source of pollution. In 1996 one American organisation introduced rules governing body odour in the workplace. They have made it a disciplinary offence both to exude excessive natural body odour and to use too much artificial perfume!

Another example of the interaction of bottom-up and top-down processing can be seen in the area of vision. Although the light reflections that hit our retina are essential to seeing, it is true that ultimately we see with the mind. We can demonstrate this very simply by the visual illusion shown in Figure 5.2. Here we see an overlaid triangle which is not actually there; we add the information from our experience, which leads us to expect a complete picture. This principle of *closure* (completing the picture) is central to gestalt approaches to psychology. The gestalt approach (discussed later in relation to the environmental psychology position on reductionism) is based on the assumption that *the whole is greater than the sum of its parts.* What makes the whole greater than the sum of its parts in psychology is generally the *meaning* given to the experience by the individual. From the vast store of research on the area, it can be concluded generally that as we grow and develop, we encounter a wide range of information, which increases in complexity with the complexity of encountered environments. We develop *cognitive schemata*, blueprints or cognitive maps of our world, which guide our perceptual processes. The essential aspects of this guidance are *filtering of* and *giving meaning to* incoming information from the environment. Filtering occurs at all stages in the process and determines what aspects we attend to, what aspects we store in memory and, ultimately, the aspects to which we respond. Bottom-up aspects are also active in this filtering process; for example, attention will be influenced by aspects of the stimulus such as novelty, intensity and movement. Any consistency over time within an individual's behaviour can be explained partly in terms of similarity or continuity between situations (the *environment* factor), and partly in terms of the development of particular cognitive styles reflecting stability in cognitive schemata – in other words, an enduring cognitive map of the world (the *individual* factor).

Environmental perception

The process of research in cognitive psychology tends to be experimental, reductionist and focused on explanations at the individual level. Environmental perception (a central area of environmental psychology), on the other hand, adopts a holistic approach which focuses on perception as a total process in the natural environment. The aim is to bring together the pieces gleaned from the reductionist, laboratory-based research in order to understand how we perceive the real world, and from this understanding to devise ways in which we can improve it. It uses a multi-method approach, with the ideal being the *full-cycle model* proposed by Cialdini (1980), where research begins with an

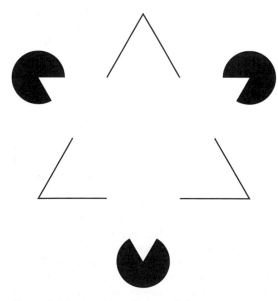

Figure 5.2 Seeing things that aren't there

initial analysis of the behaviour in its natural setting. The model devised from this initial analysis is then tested experimentally, and the results from the experimentation are tested again in the natural setting. Modification of the model occurs at all stages, as appropriate, particularly in adapting experimental explanations to the real world. Since the meaning given by the individual to experiences is central to the process of perception, any analysis must pay particular attention to personal meaning. All too often research ignores the very simple principle embodied in the statement by George Kelly (1955): 'If you really want to find out what is wrong with a client, ask them, they may tell you'.

The carpentered world hypothesis

Environmental perception has tended to focus on how the physical environment shapes our cognitive schemata. A proposed explanation of how different environmental experiences can lead to differences in perception between cultures is the carpentered world hypothesis demonstrated by Turnbull (1961). Turnbull was a social anthropologist who worked with the Pygmies who inhabit the rainforest of central Africa. These people live most (if not all) of their life in a forest environment, and hence never develop *distance perception* (i.e. the ability to relate size to distance over longer distances and to understand that objects appear smaller the further away they are in the natural environment). Our reliance on a variety of learned cues in distance perception is demonstrated by a television advertisement for a particular beer. In the advertisement a man appears to walk off into the distance across a desert, leaving a beer bottle in the foreground. However, after walking for some time, the man turns to his left and walks into a giant beer bottle. The illusion is based on our expectations about the relationship between distance and size. Meanwhile, back in Africa, Turnbull took his Pygmy guide onto the plains and showed him the plains buffalo. As they walked towards the buffalo, the guide grew fearful and wanted to run away in terror. He could not understand how an object (the buffalo), which appeared like a tiny insect at a distance, grew larger as they approached it. The phenomenon is explained in terms of our cognitive schemata (view of the world) becoming shaped to fit the physical environment within which we live – for most westerners, this view of the world is a 'carpentered' one, with very many cues to distance (corners of buildings, telephone wires disappearing

into the distance, and so on). We not only live within a physical environment, but also a social environment. Thus our cognitive styles are also shaped by our social and interpersonal experiences.

Each of us will see the environment we look at in different ways. For example, a developer, a farmer and a tourist looking at the same piece of countryside will have quite different perceptions of it. Though they receive much the same *physical* stimuli, the tourist might have an overall view (a gestalt) of 'a pretty scene', the farmer may see the fields in terms of current crops, who they belong to and so on, whereas the developer may superimpose a new bypass or superstore complex.

Social influence and attitude

The social equivalent of the carpentered world hypothesis is the area of social influence, and the social psychological cognitive schemata, or cognitive style, is our system of attitudes. We develop complex systems of interrelated attitudes which help us to simplify, categorise and react to the social world. These attitudes will vary in terms of their importance (central or peripheral) and the functions they fulfil. They lead to stereotypes and expectations about the social world which determine our reactions to it. A good example of this is the way in which prejudice affects our memory of events, something that is important in terms of *eyewitness testimony* (see Chapter 6). As with the physical environment, attitudes will be influenced by forces ranging from interpersonal up to the level of culture, and such influences will be reflected in individual and cultural differences.

The interrelated nature of social and physical environments

This very simplistic summary of the social psychology of attitudes highlights the fact that in psychology, traditionally, it has been the accepted procedure to treat the physical and social environments as two separate areas of influence and study. This is evidenced by the two separate literatures, one located mainly within *cognitive psychology* and the other within *social psychology*. The integration of the two is essential, since it is clear that our understanding of behaviour in the physical environment cannot be divorced from interaction with the people who occupy it, while social interaction always has a physical context. For example, how we feel about and react to an empty physical place is very often influenced by its association with people who have previously and may in the future occupy it. The farmer, above, has a view of the fields which is influenced by his or her attitude to the tourists or developer, either of whom may ruin the farmer. Barker's (1968) *Ecological Psychology* demonstrates clearly how social behaviour is shaped by its physical context. A very good example of the importance of attitudes in environmental psychology is in the area of environmental appreciation or preference. The work of Kaplan and Kaplan (1982) is the most prolific in the area; the authors have conducted a great deal of research into the factors that influence our likes and dislikes, and hence preferences, for different types of environment. Some good British work on environmental evaluation and meaning was carried out by David Canter (1968, 1969, 1983), and demonstrates the ways in which our evaluation of the environment and the meaning we give to it influence our behaviour in that environment; this can be applied usefully in the planning of physical environments such as new housing projects (Canter and Thorne 1972).

Just as our perceptual processes can be demonstrated to be vulnerable to deception in the form of visual illusions in the laboratory, so can we (like Turnbull's Pygmy) be deceived by the physical environment. An example of this is the *terrestrial saucer effect* discussed by Gifford (1987). This is an illusion created by the juxtaposition of mountains in a natural landscape, which can lead to rivers appearing to run uphill, or to roads which actually incline upwards, appearing to be sloped downwards. I know of a road (in Northern Ireland) where, if you stop your car with the handbrake off, it will appear to roll uphill. You may have experienced the phenomenon when driving: your car engine indicates that you are travelling uphill, while what you see appears to be a level or downward-sloping road. If you are a cyclist you might have experienced this even more closely (and more emotionally!).

The empirical evidence from perception and social cognition research raises important questions about our definition of reality. It would appear that the real world of our experience is more a subjective than an objective reality – the notion that beauty really does lie, at least partially, in the eye of the beholder.

Environmental personality

Before leaving this section we will take a brief look at a personality approach to understanding the person aspect of the *person-in-context model*. In essence, this involves categorising people in terms of their typical reaction to the environment. In a broad sense we are probably all aware of individual differences in this area. For example, some people like cities, while others prefer rural life. Some people enjoy sandy beaches, while others like rugged mountain terrain. In considering these examples we have identified one of the problems with personality approaches, that is, they provide a *description* of behaviour or experience, not an *explanation*. We describe a person as being a 'city lover' as opposed to a 'country lover', but doing this does not provide us with an explanation as to *why* this is the case. In order to explain their preference we would need to consider their life experiences, or their particular biological or psychological needs and motivations. On the other hand, it can be argued that any scientific approach begins with some sort of classification or description of subject matter. There is a strong case to be made that personality theory has always been based on the environment, since the traits that have been produced are based on the person's reaction to their environment. From observing how people behave, we infer a level of need for stimulation from the environment which is the basis of Jung's *extraversion–introversion* concept – extroverts need more external stimulation than introverts do, and they are oriented more towards material things. Indeed many of the early personality theorists did adopt a person-in-context model. Henry Murray's *needs-press* theory of personality explained behaviour in terms of the interaction between the needs of the person and the influence of the environment, which he called 'press' (Murray 1938). A number of environmental psychologists have attempted to describe the environmental personality using traditional questionnaire methods. An example is the work of McKechnie (1974), who developed the Environmental Response Inventory (ERI). This 184-item questionnaire measures eight dispositions towards the environment, as outlined in Box 3.

Box 3 The eight environmental personality traits from the ERI

Pastoralism: The tendency to oppose land development, preserve open space, accept natural forces as influences and prefer self-sufficiency.

Urbanism: The tendency to enjoy high density living, and appreciate the varied interpersonal and cultural stimulation found in city life.

Environmental adaptation: The tendency to favour the alteration of the environment to suit human needs and desires, oppose developmental controls, and prefer highly refined settings and objects.

Stimulus seeking: The tendency to be interested in travel and exploration, enjoy complex or intense physical sensations, and have very broad interests.

Environmental trust: The tendency to be secure in the environment, be competent in finding your way around, and be unafraid of new places or of being alone.

Antiquarianism: The tendency to enjoy historical places and things, prefer traditional designs, collect more treasured possessions than most other people, and appreciate the products of earlier eras.

Need for privacy: The tendency to need isolation, not appreciate neighbours, avoid distraction and seek solitude.

Mechanical orientation: The tendency to enjoy technological and mechanical processes, to enjoy working with your hands, and to care about how things work.

(Source: Cassidy 1997: 29)

The personality approach has obvious utility in environmental design and trying to fit people to places, for example in designing rehousing projects where people are being moved from their original homes for some reason (Lee 1976). The limitations of traditional personality perspectives which assume stable traits is questionable, however, in the light of work showing that *situations* produce similar behaviour patterns, irrespective of any individual personality differences (see Chapter 10; also Barker and Wright's (1955) work on behaviour settings).

The impact of the environment

With some basic ideas about the person in the environment in mind, we now turn to the other half of the equation, that is, the environment, to see if we can find some general conclusions from the research and practice of environmental psychology.

In very basic terms, our encounters with both physical and social aspects of the environment will impact on us in a number of ways. This may be in terms of restricting or facilitating our behaviour, providing resources which improve the quality of our life, or making demands which overstretch our coping resources and lead to negative health consequences. In other words, the environment is a source of either reward or punishment. In many cases, in fact for the greater part of our lives, our encounters with the environment will appear to be neutral, but appearances are deceptive. It will be the case that strength of reward or punishment is low, or that some aspects are rewarding and some punishing. In any situation, the variety of stimuli affecting us is numerically great, interrelated and complex. However, as we know from perception research, only some of these stimuli will actually be attended to or come to have any significant meaning for us. It will be those with greater reward or punishment strength that become most significant. Research on how the environment impacts on the person has focused on a number of areas, explored below.

Emotion and motivation – environmental stress

How the environment impacts on our emotional life is generally subsumed under the area of stress research. Stress is covered in more detail in Chapter 7, and for a more detailed review see Cassidy (1999). In this chapter we shall focus more on the effects of the environment, which tend to be contained under the stimulus approach to stress.

The focus of the *stimulus* approach has been to identify potential sources of stress for the individual in the physical and social environment. A vast literature has accumulated, providing evidence of the stressful effects of a vast range of stimuli, which at first seems to provide the reader with an impossible task when trying to produce any general conclusions. However, some general statements can be made. First, a system which allows categorisation is useful, and the one used by Rotton (1990) seems to be appropriate. This gives us four categories:

➠ ambient stressors;
➠ cataclysmic stressors;
➠ life stressors;
➠ microstressors.

It is important to be aware from the outset that any categorisation such as this is a working tool, which does not preclude alternative categorisations, and acknowledges the overlap and interaction between categories and the coexistence of events in the life experience of the individual which appear under different categories. In order to place events in particular categories, one must have dimension, which allows evaluation of events; for this system the dimensions are: *severity*, *scope* and *duration*.

The *severity* of an event is assessed on a dimension from high to low; the *scope* in terms of the number of people affected, ranging from individual to community; and the *duration* in terms of how long it lasts, which can range from *acute* (of temporary duration) to *chronic* (always present).

Ambient stressors, such as noise, temperature, climate, pollution and crowding, are: of low to moderate severity; affect individuals, groups and whole communities in scope; and are chronic in duration.

Cataclysmic stressors, such as war and major disasters, are high in severity, affect whole communities and are generally acute in duration. It is important to point out that stressful events are developmental and change over time. The immediate impact of war or disaster is severe, widespread and acute, but the effects of disaster or war for survivors and families become less severe, more individual and chronic in the long term. Thus the immediate impact fits the cataclysmic label, but the long-term effect fits the life stressor category.

Life stressors are those generally listed under the label 'major life events', such as bereavement, divorce, unemployment and moving house. They tend to be high in severity, individually focused and towards the acute end on the duration dimension. The classic studies of life events are those of Holmes and Rahe (1967), which produced the well-known Social Readjustment Scale, listing 43 major life events with their stress weightings, and Brown and Harris (1978), which produced the Life Events Directory, a structured interview technique for assessing life events.

It is not always the major events which cause most stress, however, and it is often said that the accumulation of little irritations can be much more stressful. These *microstressors* – such as losing your keys, sleeping in and being late for work, dealing with an awkward or pushy salesperson and concerns about weight – are everyday events which have a cumulative effect. While writing this chapter there was a brief power cut which resulted in the loss of about three pages of text which I had not saved. I was also expecting something in the post which did not arrive. Neither of these were major life events, but together they did have an emotional effect. These types of events tend to be low in severity, mainly affecting the individual, but chronic in that they are always around. Kanner et al. (1981) label these 'daily hassles', and their alternative 'daily uplifts' (see Chapter 7). It is the accumulation of daily hassles and the lack of daily uplifts which can have a detrimental effect.

Stress or challenge? Warr's Vitamin model

These four categories of stressors, each covering a very large number of events, give us some idea of the vast number of events that have been empirically linked with the experience of stress. In fact, research supports the conclusion that any event in the physical or social environment has the potential to be a stressor. Alternatively, the same events have the potential to be *challenges*, which stimulate individuals to greater efforts in problem-solving and coping, and ultimately produce a sense of growth and development as a person. Even the most distressing events can have a positive side if dealt with successfully. Peter Warr's (1987) Vitamin model of the relationship between the work environment and mental health can help in understanding the notion of threat and challenge. Warr's model was derived from research on the positive and negative effects of work and unemployment. Warr suggests that the analogy of the effect of vitamins on physical health can be applied. The lack of some vitamins, such as C and E, is detrimental, but more than the required amount has no ill effect. This type of influence Warr calls *cumulative effect*. On the other hand, vitamins such as A and D have a negative effect if we have too little or too much, and need to be sustained at an optimal level for good health. This effect is referred to as *additional decrement*. Events which are positive, such as good health, or daily uplifts, tend to operate in terms of cumulative effect; in other words, we cannot really have too much good health. However, events that have the potential to be stressful operate within the additional decrement model, in that an optimal level of stress acts as a motivator, while too much becomes detrimental. Stress that motivates is a challenge, while stress which has negative consequences is a threat.

Characteristics of stressful events

In trying to understand the role of the environment in the stress process, one useful approach is to try to identify aspects or characteristics of events or stimuli which increase their probability of being perceived as stressful. We know that any event has the potential to be stressful, but what are the distinguishing features of the event where stress occurs? Four dimensions have been identified in the literature:

➡ controllability;
➡ predictability;
➡ threat;
➡ loss.

Controllability is a central dimension. It is both an aspect of the environment and part of the person's appraisal process. The classic studies are the *learned helplessness* studies of Seligman and his colleagues, carried out in 1966–67 and reported in Seligman (1975). Using animals, they demonstrated the stressful consequences of being in an environment where escape was blocked while being given electric shocks. The animals became apathetic and did not attempt to escape when their escape route was unblocked. They had learned to be helpless. These studies were later modified to demonstrate that when the animals were given an escape route, and therefore some control over the environment, the stressful consequences were modified. The evidence for the central role of controllability in the stress process is very strong.

If an event is unpredictable, it will also present problems of control, in that we can never be totally sure of our effectiveness in coping with the unpredictable. On the other hand, events that are totally predictable may also be stressful – for example, a very boring job. It is not surprising that studies have shown that stressful events tend to load on one or other of the extremes of *predictability*.

The literature shows that stressful events contain elements of *threat* or *loss*. For example, being told one is to become unemployed involves both loss of a job and a threat to social identity (Branthwaite and Trueman 1989).

In essence, if one looks at the range of events that have been shown to be stressful, one can see elements of threat and loss and of predictability. Threat, loss and predictability influence control, and it is likely that it is through their effect on control that they determine *appraisal* – the assessment of the event – by the individual, as stressful. What is suggested is that where an event removes or reduces the opportunity for control, it is more likely to be perceived and experienced as stressful.

In summary, we can say that any event has the potential to be stressful, but will only be experienced as stressful if so perceived by the person. Events are more likely to be perceived as stressful if they involve threat or loss, or are unpredictable, therefore reducing or removing opportunities to exercise power or control over them.

Social support

Another aspect of the social environment which has been identified clearly as important in the stress process and in the development of problems is the quantity and quality of *social support* available. One way to conceptualise the environmental influence is to see the environment as the base of resources for the person in dealing with life. Where resources are lacking or inadequate, problems are more likely to develop. The major resources suggested are provision of social support (e.g. friends, colleagues, family) and opportunities for power and control.

In the following sections we will focus on ambient stressors and cataclysmic events in terms of disasters, since life events and daily hassles and uplifts are covered in detail in Chapter 7.

Ambient stressors

As described above, ambient stressors are sources of stress that are a constant part of our environment and tend to have low severity, affect large numbers of people and are chronic in duration. There are many examples: noise, temperature, chemical pollution, wind, humidity and also things like crowding, queuing and traffic jams, which are becoming increasingly part of the daily life of those who live in cities and large towns. We will focus on two categories here: noise and weather/climate.

1 Noise

Our environment is subject to permanent and continuous noise pollution. It is impossible to find places, even in the most isolated rural areas of Britain, where our peace is not broken by the distant hum of traffic, the sound of passing aeroplanes or the sound of farm or building machinery. We are often unaware of the noise that fills our world and we do habituate to it to some extent. Have you ever been to a dance club where the music has been so loud that you are unable to talk over it? Have you ever been disturbed by the sound of a low-flying aircraft, or next-door's lawnmower early on a Saturday morning? What is common to both these situations is the high level of sound. In fact, the level of sound in the dance club is probably by far the highest. However, while you might have enjoyed the sound in the nightclub, the other noises caused some annoyance as you tried to roll over and go back to sleep. In fact, the latter was unwanted sound, which provides us with a useful and simple definition of noise.

Sound is generally described in three dimensions, the most obvious of which is *loudness*. This is technically defined in terms of the amplitude of the sound waves. In addition, there is *timbre*, or *tonal quality*, and *pitch*, which describes the frequency of wavelengths but is experienced as 'high' or 'low' sound, as in musical scales. The human ear can only detect sounds within a range of pitch and above a minimum level of loudness. In addition, the combined effect of loudness, timbre and pitch varies in the way they are perceived.

Sound may be unwanted for two main reasons: it may be of a loudness, timbre or pitch which causes us *physical discomfort*, or it may be unwanted because of the *situation*. For example, a lawnmower is not normally uncomfortable, but it is unwanted outside the window while you are in the middle of an examination!

The physical damage to hearing caused by noise in the workplace has attracted extensive research and legislation. Research has shown that large numbers of workers develop hearing problems because of noise. One estimate suggests that three million Americans suffered noise-induced hearing loss in 1972, and that this figure had grown to nearly ten million by 1991 (Veitch and Arkkelin 1995). This is despite extensive health and safety legislation which both controls noise levels at work and makes it a legal necessity to wear protective ear devices.

In addition to physical damage, it is also clear that, as a stressor, noise contributes to many mental health effects, and to both acute and chronic physical illness (Evans and Stecker 2004). Humans adapt to sound, a process known as habituation (see Box 4).

Box 4 Things that go bump in the night

In a residential area of New York during the early 1970s, the overhead tram system, which had been part of the environment for many years, was removed. When it was running it had passed quite close to many blocks of flats at periodic intervals throughout the day and night. After it ceased to run there was a massive increase in the number of residents reporting to their local medical centres complaining of sleep disturbances. It took the medics some time to make the connection, but eventually the only plausible explanation was in terms of habituation. The residents had habituated to the sound of the trams over the years and now that they were no longer there, they were aware of something missing. They were being disturbed by the sound of silence (to quote the Simon and Garfunkel song).

While the potential to habituate to ambient stressors such as noise means that people may not be aware of these stressors, the question that psychologists need to address is whether habituation removes the harmful effects. The correlational evidence would suggest that whether or not we are aware of noise, over long periods it is still a chronic stressor (Evans and Stecker 2004; Levy-Leboyer 1982). Noise is part of our general environment and has effects other than those observed at work. For example, noise in the home has been shown to have a detrimental effect on child development in areas such as language acquisition, attention and reading ability (Stansfield et al. 2005). Given the evidence for massive increases in noise levels in all areas of life in the early twenty-first century, this developmental effect is rather worrying.

Noise has also been linked with miscarriages and birth defects (Veitch and Arkkelin 1995). It is important to recognise the wide range of environmental variables which may contribute to these sorts of problems and the difficulty in isolating the effect of any one variable. Hence the best that can be said is that noise is one of the possible contributory factors.

In summary, research supports the conclusion that noise in the environment is associated with negative consequences in terms of both physical and mental health. However, not everyone suffers these negative consequences. On the other hand, the evidence has been sufficient to lead to legislation. It would seem appropriate that environmental psychologists should be involved in preventing these negative consequences. The question is: What can be suggested from the evidence? One problem with this area is that much of the noise in our environment has been produced by developments in industry and technology. With the major economic contribution involved, it is not surprising that the attempt to reduce noise levels is a somewhat uphill struggle. The most obvious intervention must be through changing attitudes of governments and those who wield the reins of power, although one alternative is to utilise the potential positive side of sound (see Box 5).

Box 5 If music be the food of love...

While unwanted sound in the form of noise can be both physically and psychologically damaging, sound that is desired (e.g. music) can have a healing effect. It is widely recognised that music, and other sounds such as the sound of the sea, birdsong or whale communication, can be relaxing and can be used effectively in stress reduction. Research on memory and recall in cognitive psychology has shown that noise interferes with the ability to recall in serial recall tasks (Salame and Baddeley 1989). Initially it was thought that any type of noise had a disruptive effect on attention and recall. However, recent research has begun to distinguish between background music and other forms of noise, and there is some evidence that background music can enhance performance on some types of tasks (Davies, Lang and Shackleton 1973).

A study by Arnon et al. (2006) suggests that live music can have a beneficial effect on premature babies in neonatal intensive care. The babies had a slower heartbeat and deeper sleep patterns as a result of the music therapy. Given the potential positive effects of some forms of sound on both emotions and performance, it may be worth looking at the possibility of modifying noise in situations where it cannot be eliminated. No doubt the idea of ten-ton trucks with exhausts blasting out the 1812 overture, the current number 1 or sounding like a nightingale singing in Berkeley Square are pipe dreams. However, a basis for future research might be the notion that if we cannot eliminate noise, we could make it more pleasant.

2 Weather and climate

Weather is somewhat of a preoccupation for many people in our society and is often used as a non-controversial topic when making polite conversation. When I was growing up in a farming community I remember how boring it was to listen to the many predictions and speculations about current and future weather. Of course, weather is of particular concern for the farming community, since their livelihood depends on the predictability of seasons. Weather and climate cover a wide range of atmospheric conditions, including wind, rainfall, sunshine, heat, humidity and storms. Like it or not, much of our behaviour is controlled by these aspects of our environment, determining things like the clothes we wear, whether we can go outside or are confined indoors, the types of leisure activities we can pursue and how comfortable or uncomfortable we feel physically. These are the obvious effects. Research in psychology has shown that there are many more subtle and far-reaching effects of weather and climate. As with many other areas of real-life research, there are many difficulties involved. One major problem is that weather and climate coexist with a wide range of other environmental factors, and hence it is difficult to distinguish between the direct causal effects of weather and the effects of *confounding variables*. An example will illustrate this.

One effect of weather and climate that has been widely researched is the effect of heat on aggression. The best-known work on this is that of Robert Baron (1972, 1978). Baron used his theory of the causal relationship between heat and aggression to explain the American university campus riots of 1966. He suggested that the most intense rioting took place after the hottest periods. However, there are a lot of other possible confounding variables. For example, a range of student issues were being opposed at the time. There is also the fact that the warm dry weather facilitated large open-air meetings. Consumption of beer and lager tend to increase during periods of hot weather, in an obvious response to heat-induced thirst. These are only three from a range of possible factors which could have contributed to the violence. You can begin to see the difficulty in identifying which factor was most influential. In fact, some would argue that this type of thinking is essentially the problem because it leads to attempts to establish simple explanations based on *single* variables. Real life does not operate like this and perhaps a more fruitful approach would be to try to identify the *combination* of factors which contribute to behaviours such as aggression. This *multivariate* approach reflects many of the principles of environmental psychology.

Another effect of weather and climate which has attracted attention is the relationship between sunlight and health. Recently, with the recognition of the deterioration of our upper atmosphere as a result of pollution, and the fact that this has led to people being exposed to more harmful rays, there

has been an increase in concern about a number of environmental issues. It is recognised that while sunlight is necessary for the survival of our planet, direct exposure to some forms of ultraviolet radiation can cause illnesses such as skin cancer. This has impinged on the field of environmental psychology in terms of attempting to understand environmental behaviour and how it might be changed to reduce pollution. (This is discussed later in this chapter.)

It has also been recognised that the absence of sunlight may have a negative effect on mental health. This has led to the recognition of a form of depression called seasonal affective disorder (SAD) (see Box 6).

Box 6 Do you feel SAD in the winter?

A small number of individuals exhibit behaviours such as social withdrawal, loss of motivation and general unhappiness during winter months, some of them to such a degree that they are considered clinically depressed. In the summer they tend to move to the other extreme and appear almost manic. This effect has been linked to the amount of sunlight available and is recognised as a clinical disorder called *seasonal affective disorder* (SAD). The use of 'light therapy', exposure to bright light for about two hours per day, appears to alleviate SAD (Byerley et al. 1987). This has led to the postulation of a direct link between sunlight and physiological processes underpinning emotions. Most people, however, experience *some* depression of mood during winter and some elevation of mood during summer, which raises questions about the best explanation. While biological processes are undoubtedly involved, there are alternative possibilities. One such alternative explanation is based on the observation that there are more positive experiences associated with summer in most people's lives. Summer is associated with holidays, more freedom to engage in outdoor leisure activities and the opportunity to wear a greater variety of bright, comfortable and attractive clothing. Again, this identifies the difficulties and dangers of single and simple explanations for real-life behaviour.

There is clear evidence that weather and climate are implicated in a wide range of effects. For example,

Rosen (1985) suggests that there are correlations between weather factors and 44 conditions, including blood pressure, migraine headaches and mood shifts. Deisenhammer (2003) and Deisenhammer, Kemmler and Parson (2003) suggest a link between weather, climate and suicide, with more suicide occurring during storms than at other times. Attempts to explain the effects of these variables on the psychology and physiology of humans have drawn on biological factors in the main. The research so far is inconclusive.

Box 7 Warm weather and eating disorders

A study by Sloan (2002) looked at symptoms of eating disorders among college females in the south-east and north-east of the USA. She found that those in the south-east engaged in more bulimic behaviours (binge eating followed by vomiting) than those in the north-east. The south-easterners were also more concerned with their body shape than were their north-eastern peers. There is much to be said for cold climates and baggy jumpers!

In essence, research on the effects of weather and climate has identified a range of variables as being implicated in the development of both physical and psychological disorders. However, because of the complexity of the relationships involved, the conclusions are still rather general. In fact, there is room for a great deal of development of research in this area. In addition, the ever-changing nature of our weather and climate as a process of both the natural evolution of the planet and the damage being done by pollution has hardly been recognised. It would appear that there may be support, born out of necessity, for taking this issue more seriously in the future. In the meantime it is a worthwhile area for research.

Cataclysmic events

We have considered some aspects of ambient stressors and we now turn to the area of cataclysmic events, which are described as high-severity events, affecting large numbers of people and generally of limited duration. These types of events are generally divided into two categories: *war* and *disasters*. We will consider the latter. Disasters are defined as: 'any event that stresses a society, a portion of that society, or even an individual family, beyond the limits of daily living' (Gist and Lubin 1989).

The history of the world we live in contains many reports of large-scale natural disasters, perhaps the first of which was the (biblical) flood. Volcanic eruptions, earthquakes, floods and wind storms have claimed thousands of lives and are evidenced on the physical canvas of our world. One such example is the Giant's Causeway in Northern Ireland, which is the result of a volcanic eruption. North-western Europe has not experienced the *natural* disasters which have hit other parts of the world in the recent past. However, it has not escaped the tragedy of *artificially created* disasters (see Box 8).

Box 8 Disasters (natural and otherwise)

I am sure no one is unaware of 9/11 in the USA or 7/7 in London. Both were deliberately engineered events which led to extensive injury and loss of life. Equally, people will have been awed by the tsunami which devastated many areas around the Indian Ocean in December 2004, and the destruction that visited New Orleans as a consequence of Hurricane Katrina in August 2005. Such cataclysmic events have consequences for a wide range of people, from the survivors to the bereaved and those workers who are involved directly and indirectly in rescue services. While the psychology of disasters has become more the domain of *community psychology*, it is relevant here for two main reasons. First, environmental psychology has provided the inspiration and much of the knowledge base for community psychology; and second, environmental psychology has a lot to contribute both in determining how and why these disasters occur and in dealing with the consequences. It is one of those areas where the boundaries of fields become blurred in practice.

A special mention should be made of the children who experience these cataclysmic, and indeed other traumatic events (Williams 2006; Gaffney 2006). In 2004 I was involved with a group of other psychologists and psychiatrists in setting up the Centre for Psychosocial Health in Iraq. The focus

---

of the centre is on the psychosocial consequences for the children in this particular war zone. What is most noticeable is the amazing resilience of children in such situations, but we still do not really know much about the longer-term consequences.

Traditionally, the psychological consequences of such events have been seen in terms of trauma and, at the extreme, post-traumatic stress disorder (PTSD). However, as with the children, many adults who experience disasters do *not* develop PTSD – typically this is true of more than 50 per cent. This has led to a new focus on what is described as 'post-traumatic growth' (Linley and Joseph 2003).

This brief look at how the environment impinges on the individual gives a flavour of the rich source of information – and the complexity of that information – which is available to the environmental psychologist. It is clear that if we are to live in harmony with our environment we need to understand the consequences of the many aspects of it that we take for granted so often. While environmental psychology has gone some way towards trying to improve our understanding, there is a lot still to be done.

Living in the environment

Proxemics

Proxemics refers to the relationship between people and space in the environment and covers the topic areas of *personal space, territoriality, crowding* and *privacy*. The field was founded by E. T. Hall (1966).

1 Personal space

Personal space refers to that invisible bubble we all carry around with us, which defines how close we will get when approaching other people and how closely we will allow other people to approach us. To a very large extent it is a function of our relationship with the people involved and the society or culture to which we are accustomed. To some extent the terminology is misleading, since in fact what we are considering is *interpersonal* space – it only becomes important when we interact with others. In addition, we need to be aware that the bubble can expand or shrink. Hall (1966) identified four categories of personal space, each of which can be divided in two, near and far:

- Intimate distance, 0–45cm: this closest distance is generally the domain of those who have an intimate relationship with each other, but also includes situations where the social rules allow contact, for example in a wrestling match. Hall distinguishes between near situations requiring body contact (love-making) and those which require being very close but not in contact (whispering). It is quite clear that the distinction is rather artificial, since whether or not contact occurs will depend on a variety of things, such as the social setting.
- Personal space, 45–120cm: this is the zone generally reserved for good friends or intimate partners in a social setting. Again, Hall defines two aspects of this, based on the level of friendship. The near aspect is reserved for couples or very close friends, while the far phase is used by acquaintances or friends.
- Social distance, 120–350cm: this is the zone where those who are not acquainted interact or where business transactions occur. The near distance would be used by those being introduced or for informal business transactions, whereas the far phase would be reserved for formal business processes.
- Public distance, 350cm or more: this is subdivided into a near phase, such as the distance between a speaker and an audience, and a far phase, such as the distance between the public and an important public figure.

These categories help to illustrate the different functions of personal space, but on the face of it appear to be rather artificial. In fact, it is likely that personal space spans a vast continuum which is determined by a number of factors, including relationship with the person, cultural or societal norms and the immediate environment. The important contribution of these categories lies in identifying the ways in which they influence behaviour and experience. We do tend to maintain distances between ourselves and others and to reserve various distances for different people. If a stranger invades our intimate distance we feel angry or frightened. A serious aspect of this is the invasion of intimate space in the workplace. Different cultures tend to have different sizes of personal space bubbles. For example, Middle Eastern peoples tend to tolerate closer distances than people from Britain. The caricature is the British person and the Middle Eastern person who meet for the first time and end up going round and round the room, as the British person keeps moving backwards to avoid what is seen as an invasion of personal space.

Research also suggests that the personal space bubble is not circular, but elliptical, in that it is bigger in front and behind us than at the sides. This means that we will tolerate people coming closer to us at the side than in front or behind. It is perhaps not surprising that violent criminals tend to prefer very large areas of personal space behind them!

2 Territoriality

Related to personal space is the concept of *territoriality*, which originated in work on animals. The acquisition, marking and defence of territory is essential to the survival of animals in the wild, in terms of both provision of food and drink and in enabling the continuity of the species through mating. Very often, animal territoriality involves *group* territory rather than *individual* territory, and watching any of the wide range of nature programmes on television will give you an idea of the processes involved. Territoriality can be observed in domesticated animals as well. A cat will mark out the boundaries of its territory by urinating around the borders and will defend that territory against invasion by other cats. In human societies territorial behaviour can be observed at its most horrific in wars. However, it occurs on many less obvious levels as well. We build houses, erect fences or other markers and defend this claimed territory against invasion. A great deal of anger is frequently generated over parking places in a street. People tend to regard the space outside their house as theirs and will resent another driver parking there. The strength of resentment will vary from person to person. People leave towels on sunbeds at the beach to mark their territory, and in libraries students place books and other belongings on desks to mark the spot which they intend to occupy. Territoriality on this level is closely related to personal space in that markers serve to indicate territory and to reduce the likelihood of an invasion of personal space. It is likely that all of us have experienced irritation when someone takes our seat,

and observed others being irritated when we have encroached on their territory.

Again, psychologists have tried to measure and define territoriality; the most commonly used categorisation is that produced by Altman and Chemers (1980), which identifies three types: *primary*, *secondary* and *public territory*.

➡ *Primary territories* are spaces which are felt to be owned by an individual or an interdependent group on a relatively permanent basis, and which are central to their daily lives. One's home is a primary territory and so also could be one's nation. It is not the size that matters, but the psychological importance, which will be indicated by the strength of feeling aroused when the territory is encroached upon, and the strength of the defence response.

➡ *Secondary territories* are generally less important to the person and are likely to be owned only on a temporary basis, for example a locker in a changing room. The distinction between a primary and a secondary territory is not an objective one, but rather depends on the individual's perception of its importance to them. Hence to distinguish between what is primary and secondary territory for a particular person we would need to know how that person felt about it.

➡ *Public territories* are more distinct in that they do not belong to any one person and are generally accessible to anyone, for example a beach.

Objects and ideas also come into the arena of territoriality. We mark objects and go to great lengths to ensure that they remain with us. Similarly, we defend our ideas through copyright, patents and rules about plagiarism. The latter raises the issue of the legal system, and indeed many aspects of territoriality are subject to laws in many societies. Invasion of another's home is burglary, for example.

There is some debate about why we behave in territorial ways and part of this debate hinges on the nature–nurture controversy (see Chapter 10). Some theorists from the sociobiological perspective argue that territorial behaviour is *inherited* and is a carry-over from our evolutionary past. Others argue that it serves an organising function and is *learned*. The second explanation is founded on the basic notion from cognitive psychology that our cognitive processes operate to simplify the world and do this through categorising information. These cognitive processes are based on the biological processes in the brain and central nervous system, which provide the 'hardware' for psychological functioning. In this explanation, what is inherited is a brain which is physically designed to categorise. The types of categories, hence the types of territorial behaviour, are a function of our experience in the world – that

is, the content is not programmed at birth. Territorial behaviour is very much dependent on social and cultural factors.

What benefit can we derive from a knowledge of territoriality in humans? Again, since it impinges on the emotions and behaviours of people, it helps in environmental design. However, a more specific application is suggested in the area of crime reduction in Box 9.

Box 9 Using territoriality to fight crime

A concept that has attracted a lot of attention with regard to crime prevention is the notion of *defensible space*. The idea is that space which was originally public space is organised so that residents feel some sense of ownership of it. It is based on the observation that much crime in the community is centred around public space. While offenders are unlikely to congregate in someone's front garden, they are likely to occupy public spaces such as street corners or pathways. Newman (1972) studied crime rates in two housing projects in New York. While both projects housed the same number of people, one (Brownsville) was organised in smaller blocks, each catering for five or six families, while the other (Van Dyke) was high-rise. In Brownsville the buildings were built around courtyards, while the large Van Dyke blocks were separated by large parks. In essence, the area around the Brownsville blocks was defensible, while the Van Dyke parks were public and became a base for juvenile gangs. In Brownsville people knew their neighbours and a sense of community developed, whereas families in Van Dyke kept to themselves. The difference in crime rate was marked, with the rate in Van Dyke 50 per cent greater than that in Brownsville. While it is difficult to be exact about the causes for such a difference in the natural environment because of the number of possible variables, it has been suggested that four factors are important (Newman 1972):

➠ *Zone of territorial influence:* this refers to markers which indicate to outsiders that an area is private rather than public.
➠ *Opportunities for surveillance:* this involves two

aspects. First, a physical arrangement of the environment so that intruders can be spotted easily; and second, knowing who is and who is not an intruder. The latter is enhanced by smaller groupings and a sense of community.
➠ *Image:* this refers to the identity portrayed by the design of the building. High-rise blocks tend to be similar wherever they appear and do not portray a sense of individuality. In fact, there is often little difference externally between a high-rise and a multi-storey car park! Individuality also suggests privacy and is linked to the zone of territorial influence.
➠ *Milieu:* this refers to the surroundings of the buildings, or the setting. Buildings that are set in the middle of open public space are more likely to attract vandalism than those organised around more personalised space, such as the courtyards in Brownsville.

Central to the effect of the environment on crime is the facilitative effect of the environment in generating a sense of community in inhabitants (Halpern 1995). People must be able to feel some sense of ownership of the environment and hence a sense of responsibility for it. Robinson (2000) concludes that characteristics of the environment do influence crime. A very successful programme of crime prevention using environmental design has been running in Scandinavian countries since the 1970s (Midveit 2005). The programme, called Crime Prevention through Environmental Design (CPTED), shows that symbolic measures (such as music playing) are as effective as walls in deterring criminal behaviour; symbols that indicate that a building is occupied act as deterrents to crime.

---

3 Crowding

Crowding is closely related to the first two points, since it is suggested that the effect of crowding on

behaviour and experience is occasioned largely by its effect on personal space and territoriality. In other words, people feel crowded because their territory or personal space is being invaded by others. Crowding is at once a fairly simplistic concept, in that we all have some experience and personal view of crowding, and a complex concept when we come to consider its impact on us. Imagine the following situations, for example: an airport lounge when several flights have been delayed, a London underground train or a Greek bus in the rush hour, an office party, a discotheque and a live concert. We could envisage all these situations having significant similarities from the outside observer's point of view, yet differing greatly in terms of the experience of an individual in the middle of it all. We can imagine a lot of anger and distress being experienced in the airport, the bus and on the underground, but a great deal of enjoyment and pleasant experiences occurring at the party, the discotheque or the concert.

The difference just outlined leads to a major distinction, which has been drawn by environmental psychologists between *crowding* and *density,* as a result of their research findings (Stokols 1972). *Density* refers to the number of people in a prescribed space (e.g. the number of people per square kilometre in a city) and is an objective measure. *Crowding* refers to our experience of the number of people in a given setting and is a subjective, psychological concept. The importance of the distinction lies in how useful each concept is in predicting behaviour and experience. From the example outlined, a measure of density would predict a similar experience in all six situations and would therefore be of very limited use. To measure crowding we would need to ask people about their experience. There are a great many variables that will influence our experience of crowding. These will include our relationship with the people involved, the duration of the experience, the physical context of the experience and the meaning of the experience. We are likely to feel less crowded in a group of friends than a group of strangers if we have chosen to be there. However, there may also be situations where the opposite is true. For example, it may feel more uncomfortable to be crowded by a work colleague whom we know, but with whom we are not intimate, than by a total stranger on a train. Again, we tend to be more tolerant of crowding if we know it is short term and will end soon.

Box 10 The behavioural sink

While there are many problems with animal studies in terms of both the ethics involved and the generalisation of findings to humans, a series of studies by Calhoun (1962) is pertinent to the effects of crowding on behaviour and experience. Calhoun built an environment for rats where they were provided with abundant food, water and nesting material and allowed to live and breed freely. As the population of rats grew in size, Calhoun was able to observe the effects of increased crowding. In fact, the behaviour of the rats under crowded conditions deteriorated so much that Calhoun coined the phrase *behavioural sink* to describe the effect. Despite a quarter of an acre of space, with no predators, the population levelled off at 150, while such a space might have been predicted to accommodate several thousand. The reason for this was the very high level of infant mortality caused by the aggressive attacks from adult males on pregnant females, and often cannibalism in eating the newborn. The females lost their maternal instinct and often abandoned their young. In general, there appeared to be a vast increase in psychopathology. Aggression was rampant, and aberrant sexual behaviour was common. Some animals became hyperactive, while others became withdrawn and appeared depressed. There have been many criticisms of Calhoun's research, not least because of the distress caused to the animals. Critics have suggested that the environment was not natural even for rats, and ultimately findings from animal studies may not be generalised to humans. However, this study inspired much of the work on crowding in humans that followed and there is nothing to contradict the suggested relationship between extreme crowding and psychopathology. One would expect that a human replication of such extreme conditions would not be allowed to occur. Evidence from human studies suggests that crowding is implicated in socio-emotional and cognitive difficulties in child development (Evans 2006) and may even be related to prenatal effects of crowding experienced by the mother during pregnancy (Kimhy et al. 2006).

4 Privacy

Privacy is something we are very much aware of these days as we observe the ongoing debate about invasion of privacy by the media. The concept of privacy is something that impinges on each of us daily. People talk about being given 'space' to grow and develop. In research on relationships it is recognised that even intimate partners need time away from each other. In essence, privacy is about seeking respite from the direct influence of others. Altman (1975: 18) defines privacy as: 'selective control of access to the self or to one's group'.

As with most areas of psychology, the concept of control is important and identifies the psychological aspect of privacy. It is not necessarily the case that the person desires to isolate themselves; simply having the option to do so may be sufficient. It is when this option is removed that psychological distress ensues. As with crowding, therefore, we need to be aware that measurement is not an objective estimate, but involves how it is appraised by the person. This includes the level of privacy preferred by the person. The flow model shown in Figure 5.3 illustrates this interactional perspective on privacy and also provides a model of the relationship between personal space, territoriality, crowding and privacy.

The discrepancy between *achieved privacy* and *desired privacy* will be a good predictor of the emotion experienced by the individual. This discrepancy will be a function of the individual's experience and personality in interaction with the environmental constraints imposed. In terms of desired levels of privacy, it is easy to observe how individuals differ. Some students study better alone and isolated, while others prefer more open space in a library. Some people work better in their own individual office; some quite like sharing office space. It should be fairly clear that this will relate to the strength of the territorial motive and the size of the personal space bubble.

We live in an age where electronic surveillance is all around us and, rather frighteningly, it is now beginning to invade the workplace. D'Urso (2006) estimates that in the USA nearly 80 per cent of organisations use some form of employee surveillance. While attitudes towards this invasion of privacy are generally negative, little is known about the psychological consequences of being continually monitored.

What can we learn from research on privacy in terms of applying environmental psychology? Again, it can contribute to environmental design (see Box 11).

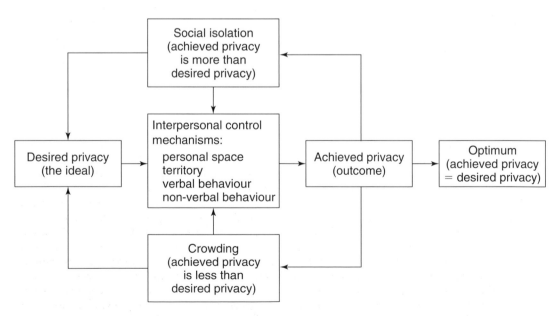

Figure 5.3 Privacy as the central process in the regulation of space
Source: Altman (1975)

Box 11 Open-plan or secluded offices?

We spend up to a third of our life at work, and the work environment is perhaps the one over which individuals have least control in terms of its design or layout. For those who are involved in designing work buildings, all the factors relating to proxemics, and many more, are important. One question that is often addressed is whether it is better to create one large open office for staff in a department or to provide everyone with their own individual office. These questions are generally driven by considerations of the effects of different types of office design on performance and productivity. However, these days it is widely recognised that performance is only one part of a dynamic system of human behaviours and experiences. In other words, performance is related to levels of motivation, job satisfaction, absenteeism, job turnover, stress levels and even physical healthiness. Hence factors that influence one will influence others as well. Early reviews of open-plan offices showed an increase in levels of symptoms of illness, absenteeism and in turn a general reduction in motivation and performance. The conclusion drawn from the experience was that the building itself was the source of the problems – something that has been labelled *sick building syndrome*. This phenomenon, which recognises that the design of particular buildings can cause physical illness in workers, was identified in the 1980s. At the time of writing (2006), a debate is in progress as to what factors are most important. Some theorists focus on psychological factors (Mendelson, Catano and Kelloway 2000), others explore the physical aspects (Magnivita 2001), and other studies indicate interactions between job-related factors and personality (Runeson and Norback 2005). It is unlikely that any one factor will emerge triumphant, and more likely that a number of interdependent factors are involved. However, the identification of sick building syndrome provides strong support for the need when planning work environments to keep in mind the range of possible influences on people.

Sick building syndrome is not necessarily associated with open-plan offices. The example above just serves to show how a change of office design can have a major effect on people at work and that the effects of work environments on behaviour are not likely to be in terms of any *single* dimension or aspect of the design. In terms of the debate about open-plan or individual offices, research seems to point to privacy as a major factor in satisfaction with work environments (Lee 2005; Maher and von Hippel 2005). These researchers found that regardless of job type, workers generally preferred individual offices and identified privacy as a major concern. In fact, privacy correlated positively with job satisfaction, satisfaction with the workplace and job performance. While correlational studies do not allow any definitive conclusions about causality, they do indicate factors that planners need to consider in their work. The evidence is that open-plan offices have more disadvantages than advantages, mainly because they impinge on workers' need for privacy.

Using the environment

Planes, trains and automobiles

The growth in transportation and travel has made our world very small, but the side effects of transportation could make it disappear altogether in time. In 2006 the owner of Virgin (Richard Branson), one of the biggest air and train companies in the world, pledged the profit from his transport business for the next ten years to research and interventions to reduce air pollution. That the transport industry itself recognises the damage being done should convince us that this is a serious problem.

In the early twenty-first century, attention has focused on the school run for various reasons, with a massive drop in the number of children walking to school. Fear of crime has been one cause. At the same time, reduction in school bus services and increased car ownership means that many parents drive their children to school even when the school is within walking distance. This has contributed to increased congestion and increased emission of damaging carbon monoxide and other gases, and has become a source of stress and conflict in cities. Alongside this there is a growing concern for childhood obesity, attributed to poor eating habits and lack of exercise. Evidence suggests that the decision to drive rather than walk is based on perceived danger such as lack of traffic lights and pedestrian crossings (Timperio et al. 2006). Not only does being driven to school remove an opportunity for exercise, but it also seems to be related to a general reduction in active behaviour (Cohen et al. 2006). This appears to be an area for the future in environmental psychology.

We have now sampled some areas of environmental psychology and got a flavour of the vast area which has been and needs to be researched. As with any area, the initial exploratory research needs to be improved upon and there is a need to learn from past experience. Research in psychology often tends to generate more questions than it answers, which is not necessarily a bad thing. Environmental psychology attempts to provide some understanding of the transaction between humans and their environment, and provides us with suggestions which may be used to improve the human condition. We now turn to the basic principles of the approach, which help us to understand how it differs from other applied fields.

PRINCIPLES OF ENVIRONMENTAL PSYCHOLOGY

An alternative way in which we might define environmental psychology is to list its basic principles and provide a list of topics or issues to which it has directed attention. We have sampled a selection of topics and now turn to the principles. The basic principles of a field outline the *basic assumptions* or *philosophy of behaviour* of psychologists who work in the field and determine the way in which they operate.

An interactional perspective

The interactional or person-in-context perspective is discussed above (p. 107); it reflects a very basic assumption in environmental psychology that reciprocal relations of causality exist between the person and the environment.

Application and research – a reciprocal relationship

The applied orientation is also based on the philosophy of Kurt Lewin, that academic and applied psychology should go hand-in-hand and that the best approach is that of *action research* (see also Chapter 11), whereby research is a problem-solving exercise, focusing on real-world problems, and where results inform both knowledge and practice. Lewin was particularly concerned by the separation that existed between academic psychology, which took place in the universities, and the practice of psychology, which took place in the real world. The following quotation (Lewin 1951: 169) exemplifies his position:

> The greatest handicap of applied psychology has been the fact that, without proper theoretical help, it had to follow the costly, inefficient, and limited method of trial and error. Many psychologists working today in an applied field are keenly aware of the need for close co-operation between theoretical and applied psychology. This can be accomplished in psychology, as it has been accomplished in physics, if the theorist does not look toward applied problems with highbrow aversion or with a fear of social problems, and if the applied psychologist realises that there is nothing so practical as a good theory.

Environmental psychology adopts the approach that theory and practice are necessarily interrelated. Psychology traditionally has sought individual-level explanations for behaviour and tended to ignore the larger-scale environment. For example, the five traditional perspectives in psychology – *behaviourism*, *cognitive psychology*, *humanistic psychology*, *biological psychology* and *psychodynamics* – all focus on the individual in seeking causes for behaviour. Thus studies generally have involved oversimplified environments and used a *micro*-level analysis. While these perspectives all contribute to an understanding of behaviour and experience, it is clear that no one perspective provides a complete explanation. In addition, they tend to ignore factors at a more *molar* level, such as the influence of groups and social and cultural factors. Environmental psychology moves towards a *molar*-level analysis by trying to understand the individual in his or her natural habitat. It is clear, for example, that an analysis of the experience of commuting must include consideration of economic and political factors that influence current transport policy and systems, especially at the level of trying to improve those systems.

This problem of *ecological validity* (see Chapter 11) has led environmental psychologists to locate their research in real-world settings. However, because of the difficulties in controlling variables in the field, environmental psychology research sometimes does not reach an ideal level of ecological validity. This can be overcome to some extent by the use of a *multi-method* approach or a *full-cycle model* of research, as discussed below.

Box 12 Spotlight on research methods in environmental psychology

Methodological issues are central to applied psychology because it is through the choice of method that the range of application will be limited or enhanced. In environmental psychology a *multi-method* approach is used. In essence, this reflects a philosophy of problem-centred research, where the problem being investigated determines the method rather than the other way round. In experimental psychology it is often the case that topics which are not accessible by experimental methods are ignored. For example, the study of mental processes was rejected by early behaviourists. There is a wide range of methods available and these are covered in introductory texts on research methods in psychology (e.g. Coolican 2004). For the purposes of introducing students to the different methods, they tend to be presented separately in introductory texts. However, in applied psychology, methods often have to be combined or modified. It is useful to think of the methods as a set of tools; just like any other tools, they can be used in combination with each other and often for purposes other than that for which they were designed. As long as we all know and follow ethical guidelines and are aware of the reliability and validity of our methods, we can be inventive in their application to applied problems. In this brief introduction to environmental psychology we have encountered a range of different methods which are covered in more detail in Chapter 11.

The ideal model of research in environmental psychology is one which employs *multiple methods* and allows analysis at *multiple levels*. However, this is not often the case in practice, and frequently knowledge in an area is accumulated by integrating research carried out by different researchers, each using a single method. For example, in this chapter, in the section on environmental perception, we drew on experimental work (Gibson 1979), participant observations (Turnbull 1961), and attitude research using questionnaire and survey methods. It should be fairly obvious why many researchers don't actually use a multi-method approach. It is mainly because of the time and expense of such a large-scale project. At the same time, it is possible to see that a more complete understanding is achieved when data from all sorts of sources and methods are collated.

A good example of multiple methods used, albeit not by the same researchers, is in the area of crowding. Box 10 provides a description of a study by Calhoun (1962) which used rats in an investigation of crowding. A study by Galle, Gove and McPherson (1972) used a survey method to investigate the correlation between crowding and social pathology in Chicago.

An interdisciplinary approach

Related to the issue of levels of analysis and the advocacy of research and practice based in the real world is the need for an interdisciplinary approach. The traditional compartmentalising of disciplines in the academic world often leads to situations where several disciplines are covering some common areas. The most obvious examples are psychology and sociology. In understanding and modifying behaviour in the environment, several disciplines make a contribution. For example, those with backgrounds in architecture, environmental studies, social geography, urban studies and anthropology will all have a contribution to make. In addition, to be effective in practice, environmental psychologists will need to take account of factors that fall within the domains of the other specialists just listed – and more, since this is not an exhaustive list. This may be done through working with other specialists; or in some cases the environmental psychologist may have had training in some of the other disciplines. Interdisciplinary work is necessary in all areas of applied psychology, and how well the interdisciplinary principle is put into practice is a determinant of the effectiveness of the approach.

A holistic approach

Environmental psychology reflects a holistic rather than a reductionist philosophy, in which it is recognised that reductionism is often necessary because of the complexity of the subject matter, but where it can only be useful within a holistic framework (see reductionism and levels of analysis in Chapter 10). However, since the issue is an important one in both research and practice, and has far-reaching implications for the philosophy of science applied to psychology, it is important to highlight it. Science has assumed traditionally that anything can be understood by breaking it down to its basic components (see Chapter 10). The objection to this comes from those who argue that 'the whole is more than the sum of its parts', and in psychology is represented by the *gestalt* theorists (Wertheimer 1944). The ultimate in reductionism is the assumption that everything in the universe will eventually be explained in terms of physics. However, even in physics, reductionism is being challenged as a sound basis for science. As Stephen Hawking says in his book *A Brief History of Time* (1992: 11): 'If everything in the universe depends on everything else in a fundamental way, it might be impossible to get close to a full solution by investigating parts of the problem in isolation'.

Certainly in psychology it is widely accepted that events and experiences are interrelated in fundamental ways which should make us wary of what can be gleaned from partial analysis. In environmental psychology, reductionist approaches are seen as limited and would only be used in the context of a holistic model.

Multivariate methods

To meet the requirements of a holistic approach, methods used need to be *multivariate* (i.e. using a large number of independent and dependent variables – see Chapter 11) rather than the more limited traditional *univariate* approach (one independent variable, one dependent variable).

Systems models

Finally, a principle which is becoming more a part of applied psychology is the adoption of a systems model of the person and their world. The concept originated in biology, where it describes not only the interrelatedness, but also the interdependence of biological processes. In environmental psychology it is recognised that the person and their world operate in a similar fashion. The importance of a model like this becomes most obvious in applications where change is being made in some aspect of the person–environment relationship. Instigating change in this way without recognising the possible unintended consequences can be disastrous. For instance, at the time of writing (2006) there is a new debate in the press and in government about the ill effects of high-rise housing. Now even government ministers are recognising that deteriorating mental health, family breakdown and serious crimes are all likely results of not clearly considering the whole system in making a person- or environment-oriented intervention. Adopting a systems model allows the practitioner or the researcher to recognise important links and to avoid, as far as possible, the negative consequences of an intervention. The concept is bound up inextricably with the issues of reductionism and levels of analysis. Using a reductionist approach or a micro-level of analysis is likely to ignore the interdependence of parts.

These basic principles reflect the ways in which environmental psychologists approach research and practice in the first decade of the twenty-first century. They are all logically interrelated. Not all textbooks will present the principles in the same format, but the basic ideas covered will generally be the same. An understanding of the principles enables us to better understand how environmental psychology relates to psychology in general and gives an insight into the approach adopted by the environmental psychologist.

A major issue of concern in Western Europe and the USA is childhood obesity. Environmental psychology can play a role here in areas such as walking to school and promoting lower-fat food choices. A study by French et al. (2004) involved an environmental intervention to promote better food choices through Trying Alternative Cafeteria Options in Schools (the TACOS study). Twenty secondary schools were targeted and randomly assigned either to an environmental intervention group or to a control group over a two-year period. The intervention had two aspects:

⇒ increasing the number of low-fat products available in the dining area;
⇒ involving students in a range of promotional activities for which they were paid.

The promotional activities included arranging taste tests, media advertising campaigns (using posters and videos) and carrying out surveys of student food choices.

The outcome of the intervention was assessed in two ways:

⇒ the percentage of lower-fat foods sold after, compared to before, the intervention;
⇒ the students' self-reported food choices before and after the intervention.

There were significant increases on both measures, indicating that the intervention affected students' attitude towards lower-fat food and their actual behaviour in buying more lower-fat foods.

CURRENT DIRECTIONS IN ENVIRONMENTAL PSYCHOLOGY

The boundaries of the different areas of applied psychology are less rigid in the real world than it might appear from academic texts. Any intervention that aims to change the environment in order to change behaviour is technically environmental psychology, though in the real world it may appear under a different applied title. For example, the work described in the 'Example of an environmental psychology intervention' above could also be described as health psychology. In the USA, much of the work on changing the design of neighbourhoods to enhance well-being comes under the rubric of community psychology.

There is much work to be done by environmental psychologists, whether that work is described as environmental psychology or as something else. One such area for the future lies in changing attitudes and behaviours in regard to preserving the planet. There are national and international agreements on reducing carbon emissions, and other strategies aimed at prolonging the life of our planet, but the difficulty remains in persuading people to comply with them. Our individual impact in terms of carbon emissions is described as our 'carbon footprint' and there are many ways in which we can reduce it, from just turning down the temperature control on our washing machine to reducing our use of air travel.

Recent research suggests that choosing environmentally friendly behaviour is part of a general positive stance on environmental issues (Thogersen and Olander 2006). In fact, Milfont and Duckitt (2006) suggest that attitudes towards the environment can be categorised under three concerns: altruistic, biospheric and egoistic. Reducing egoistic concerns and increasing altruistic and biospheric concerns may be a way of getting people to behave more positively towards their environment. Environmental psychologists can utilise the many behaviour change strategies available to begin the process of attitude change and make a valuable contribution to this important issue. At a more specific level, the provision of information and support can be effective. Bamberg (2006) shows that providing a free public transport ticket and schedule information to people who had just moved into an area significantly increased their likelihood of using public transport and reducing their carbon footprint.

CONCLUSION

With this brief look at environmental psychology it is hoped you will have gained some sense of the immediate relevance of psychology to understanding and improving the quality of everyday life. In addition, you may have recognised the living quality of psychology in the fact that as a discipline it is developing continuously. Much has been achieved, but there is yet much to do. A simple definition of the field would be: *the application of psychological knowledge and method to understanding the process and implications of the human–environment transaction and applying the insight attained to improving the quality of the experience.* All behaviour and experience occurs within the environment, which suggests that the subject matter of environmental psychology is very broad indeed. In many ways it has generated a wealth of data about the effects of the environment on behaviour, yet much of this only provides us with a broad general knowledge of the process. Just as relationships with people begin at a very general level but must proceed to much greater depths before we really know them, so too must we move from this broad acquaintanceship with our environment to deeper levels of friendship.

RECOMMENDED FURTHER READING

Bonnes, M. and Secchiaroli, G. (1995) *Environmental Psychology: A Psycho-social Introduction.* London: Sage.

Cassidy, T. (1997) *Environmental Psychology: Behaviour and Experience in Context.* Hove: Psychology Press.

Veitch, R. and Arrkelin, D. (1995) *Environmental Psychology: An Interdisciplinary Perspective.* Englewood Cliffs, NJ: Prentice Hall.

Exercises

The following exercises are designed to give you a more practical understanding of environmental psychology and to encourage you to engage with some of the issues involved. They attempt to give you some insight into the use of multiple methods and the use of multiple levels of analysis in environmental psychology. In addition, they may be useful in raising your awareness of your own relationship with the environment.

1 Evaluation of the physical environment. This exercise can be carried out in a small group or on your own. It can be considered as one large exercise or you may want to take just one or two of the stages. The aim will be to consider the building in which you study in terms of how effectively it fulfils its functions. You might want to focus on just one room (such as your classroom, sports hall or refectory), or on several rooms or even the total building.

➠ Stage 1: Start by rating the overall response to the place for yourself and a sample of your peers. You can use the dimensions below and add your own dimensions if you wish.
When I am in this building/room I generally feel:
Pleasant/Unpleasant
Happy/Sad
Comfortable/Uncomfortable
Relaxed/Tense
Motivated/Unmotivated
Angry/Calm
Frustrated/Encouraged

➠ Stage 2: Now consider how the physical environment might influence these responses. You could take a sub-sample from those who carried out stage 1 and interview them. Focus on what aspects of the environment contributed to their ratings of the place. Distinguish between physical aspects and social (people) aspects.

➠ Stage 3: This stage involves an observational method. Start by carrying out a general observation of how people interact with their environment in selected parts of the building. Try to identify negative and positive aspects. Are there particular aspects of the physical environment that seem to cause problems, to frustrate people? Are there aspects which seem to be conducive to effective functioning?

➠ Stage 4: Drawing on the information you have gathered from the above, and your knowledge of environmental psychology, make recommendations about changes which could improve the effectiveness of the building. Remember to consider all aspects of the environment, including things like noise levels, temperature and lighting, as well as positioning of entrances and exits, furniture, and so on.

2 Design and carry out a simple survey among your peers to assess their environmental personality. Use the dimensions outlined in Box 3 (p. 111) to guide your work. Is there a common profile?

3 Keep a diary for two weeks recording your relationship with the environment. At the end of each day record significant events of the day in terms of how your environment has provided positive or negative experiences for you. Distinguish between physical and social aspects of the environment. At the end of the two weeks consider how the information from your diary relates to what you know about environmental psychology. Has the exercise made you more aware of your environment?

Forensic Psychology

INTRODUCTION

Forensic psychology is a branch of applied psychology which applies psychological principles to an important real-life setting: the criminal and civil justice system. It is very much rooted in empirical research, theory and practice, and is one of the fastest-growing areas of applied psychology, following a funded expansion of psychologists working with offenders in prison in 1996. This aspect of forensic psychology tends to be overshadowed by media focus on the work of investigative psychologists assisting the police, but it is fair to say that the field of forensic psychology has broadened considerably and certainly seems to have captured the interest of the public, and the increasing number of students who wish to join the profession. As Thomas-Peter (2006: 24) observes, 'These are rare times for psychology and applied psychologists within corrections. Never has psychology been more influential'.

Forensic psychologists work mainly in the prison and probation service, developing one-to-one or group intervention techniques and treatment programmes for use with offenders, those on community orders and others under supervision. They work to address their offending behaviour and/or to address their psychological needs, for example to manage depression, anger or anxiety. Using expertise based on psychological theory and research, forensic psychologists work closely with other professionals and agencies, both in the assessment, treatment and management of individuals, and in the development of institutional policy and working practices.

FORENSIC PSYCHOLOGY IN THE BRITISH PSYCHOLOGICAL SOCIETY (BPS)

The Division of Forensic Psychology (DFP) was founded in 1999, having formerly been established as the Division of Criminological and Legal Psychology in 1977. The DFP serves to represent the interests of the increasing number of psychologists who work in the criminal and civil justice systems, drawing its membership from forensic psychologists employed in universities, prisons, health, education, police and social services. In 2006 the Division had over 1700 members (see http://www.bps.org.uk/dfp/dfp_home.cfm).

The DFP arranges scientific meetings and symposia for its members, and is actively involved in the publication of research and policy documents in forensic psychology, but one of its primary aims is to ensure high quality training is completed before registration as a Chartered Forensic Psychologist is possible. Responsibility for assessing courses in forensic psychology for BPS accreditation, and approving the supervised practice requirements for training to become a Chartered Forensic Psychologist, lies with the DFP, in terms of ensuring professional accountability.

PRINCIPLES OF FORENSIC PSYCHOLOGY

Forensic psychology is essentially the application of psychological principles and methods to the study of criminal behaviour and legal processes. It draws on many different theoretical areas of psychology, such as developmental psychology to explore the origins of aggressive behaviour, cognitive psychology to inform best practice in interviewing witnesses, and social psychology to evaluate how small group dynamics may affect juror decision-making. While the term 'forensic psychology' literally means psychology applied to courts of law, it now encompasses a vast area of applications representing the diverse fields of practice. Thus forensic psychologists may be involved in the treatment of mentally disordered offenders, assessing the likelihood of reoffending, providing expert testimony or advising on commercial litigation cases. It is important, however, to recognise the role of the forensic psychologist as a research-practitioner, someone whose practice is informed by research evidence. The development of evidence-based practice within the prison service is clear evidence of the increasing collaboration between researchers and practitioners, such that 'practitioners' work is increasingly grounded in scientific research and, reciprocally, practice concerns have a greater influence on research' (Crighton 2006: 7).

WHAT A FORENSIC PSYCHOLOGIST DOES

Most forensic psychologists are employed by HM Prison Service – around 40 per cent according to a recent survey of DFP members (Davies 2005). A further 22 per cent work in NHS forensic settings, and 12 per cent in universities, while the remainder are employed in rehabilitation units, young offender teams, the probation or police service, the courts or private consultancies. Forensic psychologists are likely to be involved in both research and practice, for example delivering programmes in anger management, social and cognitive skills, or sex offender rehabilitation, while also evaluating the effectiveness of such programmes and conducting follow-up studies. Other key tasks undertaken by forensic psychologists include giving evidence in court, mediating between parties to resolve legal disputes, advising parole boards and mental health tribunals, crime analysis, risk assessment, developing programmes to address stress, bullying or addiction, and drawing up strategies to deal with critical incidents such as hostage negotiation.

A day in the life of a forensic psychologist

Not only are all days different, but a day in the life of a forensic psychologist will vary according to the setting in which they work. If they are working in a prison they may well attend a team meeting in the morning; visit prisoners on the wings; interview individuals who are due for release, or who may have become eligible for parole, in order to produce risk assessment reports; participate in the running of a specific rehabilitation programme, such as 'Enhanced Thinking Skills', and undertake research projects to evaluate the effectiveness of these programmes. Those psychologists working with specific offender groups, such as juveniles, lifers, women or vulnerable prisoners (such as sex offenders or self-harmers), will be offering specialist advice and intervention strategies, reflecting current practice informed by research. It should be clear that working in such an environment requires maturity, confidence, the ability to work productively with other professionals and, above all, a grounded body of knowledge and expertise based on empirical findings.

DEVELOPMENT OF FORENSIC PSYCHOLOGY

Garland (1994: 27) states that 'as with most "human sciences", criminology has a long past but a short history', and the same is true of forensic psychology. Discourse about the causes of crime and the link with human nature has existed for centuries. For instance, Lombroso (1911) argued on the basis of post-mortem investigation that criminals had different physical features to non-offenders, and that this demonstrated how criminals therefore represented an earlier and more primitive evolutionary stage of development. Half a century later, Eysenck (1964) argued that criminals inherit a particular kind of nervous system, which means they are also likely to develop a crime-prone personality, and in 2006 Prime Minister Tony Blair argued that state intervention to prevent the development of anti-social and criminal behaviour should begin before birth. These views represent somewhat extreme views of the origins of criminal behaviour and possible (albeit controversial) remedies, and the debate will no doubt continue.

It was only during the 1980s, however, that the discipline of forensic psychology emerged in its own right, rapidly developing an established and acknowledged body of knowledge based on empirical research and practice. Its roots lay in classic developments within the wider discipline of psychology, such as memory, group dynamics and

Figure 6.1 Lombroso's 'criminal face'

psychometric assessment, but there were also important contributions from psychiatry, law, criminology and social policy in relation to mental illness, the capacity to stand trial and the need to rehabilitate offenders. Key areas for research were eyewitness testimony, the evaluation of treatment programmes and challenging the difficulties associated with progressing particular types of crime investigation, such as child sexual abuse, rape and domestic violence.

Increasing concern about the need to treat and prevent crime, particularly in offenders already imprisoned, prompted the next wave of research. As a result, there was a dramatic increase in the application of psychological principles to crime issues, and the positive potential of forensic psychologists within a range of settings was increasingly recognised, with the establishment of the Home Office Research and Statistics Directorate and the development of formal training programmes for forensic psychologists in the 1990s. Forensic psychology is still an evolving discipline and the contributions of academics and practitioners will continue to shape its development, reflecting renewed interest in risk assessment and risk management, crime reduction, crime prevention and early intervention with families likely to experience difficulties associated with future offending.

RESEARCH, THEORY AND APPLICATIONS

Attitudes to crime and its victims

How we learn about crime will depend on the sources we access, and the credibility of those sources, but the impact of this information can critically influence our attitudes to offenders, victims, social policy and, most crucially, our assessment of our own risk of becoming victims. If we think (possibly mistakenly) that we are very likely to become crime victims, we may alter our behaviour and lifestyle needlessly. Equally, if we consider ourselves not to be likely crime victims, we may take risks which are avoidable.

There is a significant mismatch between crime rates as measured by the British Crime Survey (BCS), official recorded crime statistics, media reporting of crime and government interpretations in policy documents. There is both over-reporting (of violent crime) and under-reporting (of domestic violence and white-collar crime). Surveys suggest that as a nation we are now more afraid of being the victims of crime, despite the fact that crime rates are falling. Why? According to the 2006 BCS, many people, particularly women and older people, still feel that crime has risen, despite a 17 per cent fall since 1999. It was also reported that 39 per cent of tabloid readers believed that crime had increased, compared with 19 per cent of broadsheet readers (Walker, Kershaw and Nicholas 2006). This confirms a large gap between the fear of crime and the actual crime rate, with suggestions that while the biggest falls have taken place in crimes such as burglary and car crime, this receives little publicity, while in contrast, violent crime, which is much rarer, attracts more media coverage and thus impacts on people's overall fear of crime.

Most of us get our information about crime from the popular media – television and radio news, and the newspapers. Felson (2002) suggests that much of this information is misleading, and that the public may consequently view crime as dramatic, exciting, action-packed, planned and usually successful in terms of profits. The way the media represents crime is quite specific, and is entirely reliant on selling newspapers and reaching the biggest audiences. Since sensational stories attract the most people, these are the ones that feature most. They involve the most shocking crimes (murder, rape and any crime against children), or the most prolific or exceptional offenders, despite the fact that these represent only a small minority of crimes (Peelo et al. 2004).

Media representations are often responsible for generating an inaccurate view, for instance that violence is endemic, and that most offences are committed by wicked individuals who have been badly brought up. However, the reality is somewhat different: most crime is ordinary, unplanned and low-key; most crime is committed by young men, who are also more likely to be victims of violence; some serious crime is committed by large organisations; victims of vandalism and common assault tend to suffer repeat victimisation; drugs and alcohol are significantly associated with crime; motivation is diverse; and 5–10 per cent of offenders commit 50–60 per cent of all crime (Dixon et al. 2006).

How do we measure crime?

Each year in July a report is published by the Home Office which outlines the latest levels and trends in crimes in England and Wales. Since 2002 the report has been based on two sources of data – the British Crime Survey (BCS), and police recorded crime statistics (sometimes referred to in the literature as the 'official' crime statistics).

The BCS is a victim survey in which adults are asked about their experiences of crime in the previous 12 months. It includes property crimes and some personal crimes, and is believed by some to provide a better reflection of the true extent of crime because it includes crimes that are not reported to the police and therefore not recorded by them. The BCS figures are also not affected by changes in police recording practices. The methodology of the BCS has remained the same since the survey began in 1981, and it is therefore considered to be a good guide to long-term trends. Some of the crimes not covered by the BCS, however, include thefts from businesses and shops, fraud, crimes against children, murder and 'victimless' crimes such as illegal drug use.

Police recorded crime statistics provide a good measure of trends in well-reported crimes, and can be useful for local crime pattern analysis. However, they do not include crimes that have not been reported to the police, and this may include a range of offences, such as violence against the person, where the victim chooses not to report or decides to take their own retaliatory action. Similarly, some crimes are not reported to the police because members of the public feel the police are too busy or may not investigate the reported crime sufficiently thoroughly.

The official crime figures for 2005–6 suggest that overall crime levels have remained stable over the last two years, notwithstanding a small increase in violent crime. Moreover, it is claimed that, following a peak in 1995, crime has fallen by 44 per cent in the last ten years. However, an analysis of Home Office figures by Rose (2006) reveals that there is little mention in the official report of the alarming drop in conviction rates. For example, only 9.7 per cent of all 'serious woundings' reported to the police result in a conviction; for robberies the figure falls to 8.9 per cent; and for rape it is 5.5 per cent. While the number of recorded rapes rose from 6281 in 1997 to 12,867 in 2004–5, the conviction rate dropped from 9.2 per cent to 5.5 per cent. These alarming figures tend to be masked by media reports of rising numbers of people in prison, but this reflects the longer sentences being passed rather than successful prosecutions.

Mirrlees-Black and Budd (1997) suggest that only 36–49 per cent of crimes committed on a daily basis are reported to the police, and that between half and two-thirds of all crimes committed never reach the attention of the police as gatekeepers of the official statistics. The Crime and Society Foundation published a report in 2004 (http://crimeandsociety.org.uk/publications.html) claiming that official crime statistics (police figures and the British Crime Survey) are not a reliable measure of the true level of offences. However, they can serve a significant purpose in providing governments with a false means of claiming success in reducing crime. Subsequently, the Statistics Commission (2006) published a report recommending greater distance between the production of crime statistics and official bodies such as the Home Office and the police, in order to reduce public doubts about the reliability of crime data.

What is the extent of criminality?

This very much depends on definitions of crime, and traditionally many offences go unnoticed or unlabelled as 'real' crime and are therefore not recorded (e.g. thefts of stationery from the office, using the work phone for personal calls, fiddling expenses, organised crime, corporate crime, tax evasion). Generally speaking, white-collar or middle-class crime tends not to 'count'. Within traditional definitions though, the extent of criminality is quite broad and is much more 'normal' than most people think. Prime et al. (2001) revealed that 33 per cent of males and 9 per cent of females born in 1953 had been convicted of at least one offence before the age of 46, and that 7 per cent of males and 1 per cent of females born in 1953 had received a custodial sentence before the age of 46, with 55 per cent of convicted males and 80 per cent of convicted females having criminal careers of less than one year. Similarly, Flood-Page et al. (2000) showed that 50 per cent of 12- to 30-year-olds admitted at least 1 of 27 offences at some point in their lives, and that the most prolific 10 per cent of offenders were responsible for nearly half of all the crimes admitted by the sample.

Fear of crime

As outlined above, the 2006 BCS revealed that despite crime rates falling, 63 per cent of people thought that crime had risen in the last two years, and 30 per cent believed that crime had risen 'a lot' (Walker, Kershaw and Nicholas 2006). Women were more likely to believe this than men, and older people were more likely than younger age groups to think that crime had increased. This often translated into a fear of becoming a crime victim, and 17 per cent of people expressed high levels of worry about becoming a victim of violence. Women were generally more fearful than men, while younger people were more afraid of becoming victims of violence or burglary than were older age groups. This reflects the actual risk of becoming a victim of violence – men aged 16–24 have a 12.6 per cent risk compared to men aged 25–34 (5.5 per cent); while women aged 16–24 have a 7 per cent risk compared to women aged 25–34 (2.8 per cent), and women aged 75+ (0.2 per cent). The factors most strongly associated with worry about becoming a crime victim were being female, being from an ethnic minority group, believing there was a danger of an unprovoked attack from a stranger and perceiving disorder in their local area. However, Farrall and Gadd (2004) caution against assumptions that large numbers of people are continuously fearful of crime. When they surveyed people about the frequency and intensity of their fearfulness, they found that of the 30 per cent of respondents who said they had felt fearful, 49 per cent said they had only felt fearful one to four times over the last 12 months.

This is not to minimise fear of crime in any way, and it is clear that experience of being a victim or knowing victims of crime can influence levels of fear significantly. Dixon et al. (2006) suggest that the impact of crime in terms of having been a victim or fearing becoming a victim goes beyond the immediate loss or pain, and may be long term. It can threaten people's identity, reducing their social mobility and sense of well-being, affecting their life choices and undermining their trust levels. Moreover, the harm of crime is unevenly distributed, and is amplified by poverty and disadvantage, with repeat victimisation common. Farrell and Pease (1993) showed from BCS findings that 4 per cent of all victims disproportionately experience 43 per cent of crime – thus, being victimised once, for some individuals, significantly increases the chance of being a victim again. Some of the characteristics of those likely to suffer repeat victimisation were: living in a 'bad' area, having a 'chaotic' lifestyle and being in an abusive or volatile relationship. Dixon et al. (2006) demonstrate that people in low-income households are almost twice as likely to be mugged or burgled as those living in households with incomes of £30,000 or more – affluence seems to buy protection from crime.

Our view of victims

We are not always very sympathetic towards victims of crime though. The concept of a 'belief in a just world' locates the degree of sympathy felt towards a victim in the psychological attitudes of the observer, and can help us to understand why some often very deserving victims appear to receive very little sympathy. It is an unusual concept because it is almost counter-intuitive – surely seeing a suffering victim will arouse nothing but sympathy and a desire to help? – but very often this is followed by a cognitive process which determines that we differentiate ourselves from the victim in a significant way. We would all like to believe that the world is a fair place, and that people by and

large get what they deserve. If this were not true it would increase our sense of vulnerability, and make our attempts to introduce order and predictability rather pointless. When we see someone suffer who has not done anything to deserve that suffering, it calls into question our belief in a just world. In order to make sense of the suffering we may convince ourselves that the victim in some way did deserve their fate. This attributional process was originally described by Lerner (1965) as the *just world hypothesis*. In its simplest form, it states that 'individuals have a need to believe that they live in a world where people generally get what they deserve and deserve what they get' (Lerner and Simmons 1966: 204). There seems to be a need to consider victims as in some way different from the rest of us in order to protect our own fragile hold on a view that the world is a safe place, and research in this area is ongoing (see Furnham 2003).

Victim derogation seems to be particularly likely in relation to specific crimes, such as rape (Murray, Spadafore and McIntosh 2005). A random attack on an innocent victim challenges a strong belief in a just world, and in order to restore balance the victim is blamed as in some way having deserved their fate. For example, a female victim of rape may be blamed for having dressed or behaved provocatively, or for having risked her own safety by drinking heavily or walking home alone at night. There may be a gender difference though. For instance, Lerner and Miller (1978) suggest that women, regardless of their level of belief in a just world, tend not to blame or derogate rape victims as much as men do because they empathise with the victims.

The way we view victims, particularly the vulnerable, the disadvantaged, and those who suffer repeat victimisation, is important within a concept of social and restorative justice, and we should not forget that offenders and their families are often victims too. Many offenders have been failed by their parents and by public services, or they may have mental health or addiction problems which have not been adequately treated. Thus it will always be the case that there are inevitable tensions between the needs and interests of victims and offenders. However, a recent report suggests that the vast majority of crime victims do not believe that prison reduces levels of offending, and that the government needs to invest more in tackling the causes of crime and providing treatment programmes for offenders (Smart Justice 2006). In a climate where the prison population topped 79,000 for the first time (2006), with the Home Office planning to build more prisons and a 67 per cent reconviction rate within two years of release, it seems the time is right to focus more on prevention and treatment than on punishment.

Assisting the police in crime investigation and crime analysis

Many people believe that all forensic psychologists are offender profilers. Although this view is erroneous, it is fair to say that the media portrayal of such individuals has done much to raise the profile of the discipline, endowing forensic psychology with what Canter and Youngs (2003) describe as the 'Hollywood effect'. Offender profilers have been portrayed as assisting the police with their investigations in a significant way, by contributing psychological insight into inquiries to such an extent that it is possible to identify a prime suspect. This is not an accurate portrayal, and while forensic psychologists do assist the police, either as private consultants, crime scene analysts or as behavioural investigative advisors employed within the police service, their contribution is only one alongside that of forensic anthropologists, forensic dentists, pathologists, forensic accountants, and so on. The drivers of the investigation are always experienced police officers.

According to Canter (2004), offender profiling dates back to the nineteenth century, when contributions were based largely on clinical expertise, while more contemporary developments have occurred in America, Canada, Holland, Australia and the UK, and include more research-based approaches, such as geographical profiling or statistical profiling (described later in this section). There have been attempts to move the potential contribution of profiling beyond serious crime such as serial murder and rape, but the focus remains on homicide, even though the vast majority of these crimes are resolved quickly since most of them are committed by people known to the victim, and there are often witnesses or forensic evidence linking the offender to the crime. There remains, however, a very small number of serious and unresolved violent offences where the police experience difficulty identifying the perpetrator or perpetrators, and in these cases they may call on the advice of forensic psychologists, among others. The provision of behavioural investigative advice to the police is now some steps ahead of the traditional approach to offender profiling, more systematic and evidence-based, reliant less on intuition and more on rigorous analysis which can be justified.

What is offender profiling?

Jackson and Bekerian (1997: 2) suggest that offender profiling occurs when 'behaviour is exhibited at a crime, or a series of similar crimes, and studying this behaviour allows inferences to be made about the likely offender', while for Ainsworth (2001: 7), 'at the heart of most profiling is the belief that characteristics of an *offender* can be deduced by a careful and considered examination of the characteristics of the *offence*'. Although the production of offender profiles has been widely regarded as helpful by the public, doubts remain as to its efficacy, with Canter and Alison (1999: 6) describing profiles as 'often little more than at best, subjective opinion, common sense or ignorance, or at worst deliberate deception'.

The FBI approach to profiling

Offender profiling is commonly regarded as having its contemporary origins in the Behavioral Science Unit of the American FBI, where it was suggested that crime scenes revealed clear evidence of whether offences had been committed by 'organised' or 'disorganised' offenders (Douglas et al. 1992). Muller (2000) suggests that an organised offender is an intelligent underachiever with good social relationships, but with an underlying anti-social personality. The crime scene of such an offender will show signs of control and planning, a weapon and restraints having been brought to the scene, and the victim being a targeted stranger. In contrast, the disorganised offender will be of low intelligence, socially inept and with a poor employment record. This crime scene will show no premeditation, with whatever is at hand used as a weapon. The victim will have been selected at random, and the attack will be brutal but quick.

This approach to profiling is based on experience and intuition informed by information gleaned from previous crime scenes and incarcerated offenders, and there are four main stages in the construction of a profile:

1 *Data assimilation*: the collection of a variety of information (e.g. police reports, crime scene photographs, pathologist's reports, witness reports).

2 *Crime scene classification*: deciding whether the crime scene falls into the organised or disorganised typology.

3 *Crime scene reconstruction*: generating hypotheses about what occurred between the offender and the victim, the sequence of events and the offender's modus operandi.

4 *Profile generation*: hypotheses about the offender are drawn together (demographic features, such as social class, type of work, age, lifestyle; behavioural habits; and personality dynamics).

Although the FBI's approach to offender profiling has captured the public imagination and that of media moguls, it has been consistently criticised because it has had little formal scientific evaluation and there is an over-reliance on subjective intuition, making it more of an art than a science. Moreover, Alison and Barrett (2004: 59) suggest that this approach, whereby typologies of offenders are derived from crime scene investigations, is not sustainable because it contains 'many erroneous lay beliefs about the consistency of human behaviour and the ability to classify individuals into discrete types', alongside an over-reliance on dated personality theory.

Investigative psychology and statistical profiling

In the UK offender profiling is more significantly associated with investigative psychology and the work of David Canter, who draws on his own expertise in environmental and social psychology within a robust and accountable methodological framework. The focus is still on the crime scene, but the aim is to identify a pattern of co-occurring characteristics through the use of specific statistical techniques, such as smallest space analysis or facet theory. These are used to identify how likely certain features of a crime scene are to exist and coexist with other features at other crime scenes, and to construct base lines. For instance, some features of sexual assault are likely to occur together in most cases, while other patterns may be quite rare. An apology is unlikely to occur during a rape, for example, so if a series of rape cases highlights a particular pattern where the offender always apologises to the victim, it is likely that the offender

may be the same in all these cases. Data analysis can identify the statistical chances of this occurring, and may also identify other key features specific to a particular offender. Canter believes that the value of offender profiling can only be in terms of its practical use to police investigators, so speculation about offender motivation is meaningless unless it impacts directly on prevention and detention. Details of these statistical approaches to profiling have been placed in the public domain for other researchers to evaluate and develop, in marked contrast to the work of the FBI.

Crime scene assessment involves identifying what behaviour was exhibited by the offender and the victim at the crime scene, analysing what occurred as part of an ongoing social interaction. Canter (1994) suggests that psychological principles can inform profiling in the following ways:

➡ *Interpersonal coherence*: actions performed by offenders will make sense within the offender's own psychology, for example the choice of victim will be significant, while interaction with the victim may reveal a level of social competence.

➡ *Significance of time and place*: the location the offender chooses to commit offences will be important because the offender needs to feel in control.

➡ *Criminal characteristics*: analysing crimes and offenders in order to classify them in terms of categories or subcategories and identify patterns.

➡ *Criminal career*: this will influence the offender's behaviour in terms of consistency and repetition, though there may also be escalation as the offender's confidence grows.

➡ *Forensic awareness*: offenders who have had previous contact with police investigations are likely to take steps to cover their tracks and mislead investigators. For instance, Davies (1997) found in a study of rapists that if precautions had been taken to conceal fingerprints it was highly likely that the offender had a previous record for burglary.

Canter's approach to crime investigation has achieved considerable success, most notably in the successful prosecution of John Duffy (see Figure 6.2), the 'Railway Rapist', in 1988; and Canter is responsible for raising the scientific status of profiling as a means to assist the police.

Forensic Psychology

Box 1 The case of the Railway Rapist

During the period 1982–86, 24 serious sexual assaults took place in north London, near to railways. It was believed that one man was involved, although on some occasions he had an accomplice. Between 1985 and 1986, three murders occurred, and forensic evidence indicated links between the rapes and the murders. Surrey Police asked Professor David Canter to work with them on this case, and together they compiled a table of all the offence details in order to identify a pattern. A profile was drawn up and included the following description of the perpetrator:

➠ lives in the area circumscribed by the first three cases;
➠ probably lives with a partner, possibly without children;
➠ is mid to late twenties, right-handed, an 'A' secretor (i.e. secretes a particular blood group into other bodily fluids);

➠ holds a semi-skilled or skilled job, with weekend work;
➠ has knowledge of the railway system;
➠ has a criminal record, probably involving violence.

When John Duffy was arrested in November 1986, it turned out that he lived in Kilburn, was separated from his wife, in his late twenties, right-handed, an 'A' secretor, a travelling carpenter for British Rail, and was known to the police for violence against his wife, including rape. Duffy was initially 1505th in a list of 2000 suspects, and Canter's profile enabled prompt action to be taken to investigate his alibis. In 1988 Duffy was convicted for two murders and five rapes, but it was only in 2001 that DNA evidence was sufficiently robust to convict Duffy's accomplice, David Mulcahy. Duffy had offered up Mulcahy's name after counselling interviews with a forensic psychologist.

Figure 6.2 John Duffy

Kocsis, Cooksey and Irwin (2002) also used a statistical approach to profiling in their investigation of 85 Australian sexual murders. Adopting multidimensional scaling, they produced a five-cluster model of sexual murder behaviour – a central cluster representing behaviours common to all the murders, and four distinct additional patterns (predator, fury, perversion and rape). The key themes in the central cluster are intercourse, violence and premeditation. Predators fall into the same mould as organised and sadistic offenders, and were characterised by being typically older, living with a partner, well groomed, collectors of pornography and likely to reoffend, possibly with an accomplice. The fury pattern features souvenir collection and an indication of deep-seated hatred expressed as violent sexual assault. The perversion offender type is likely to choose young victims, and there is an element of paedophilia with attempts at reassurance during the assault, while the rape pattern represents an offender who intends to rape but not murder, possibly within the context of another offence, such as burglary.

Geographic profiling

This approach to crime detection draws on theories of mental maps and home range to study offenders' spatial behaviour. The concept of *home range* is based on the notion that there is a geographical area around our homes in which we travel comfortably – a cognitive map, which provides reassurance. Geographic profilers focus on the area where the victims of crime are targeted rather than details of the crime scene, identifying the patterns exhibited by serial offenders and using this to target the offender's 'buffer zone' around their own home where they are unlikely to commit a crime for fear of recognition (Godwin 2000). Police resources can then be used effectively, for instance dropping e-fits of a likely offender in the buffer zone, in the hope that they can be identified.

Does profiling work?

Campbell (1976: 119) ominously suggested that 'there is no clear evidence that psychologists are any better than bartenders at the remote diagnosis of killers'. Interestingly, the police tend to regard profiling favourably, though this does not necessarily relate to the likelihood of arrest (Gudjonsson and Copson 1997). When Alison, West and Morgan (2003) offered two very different profiles to police officers and asked them to evaluate the accuracy of the profile against the known facts of the convicted offender, both groups felt the profile they had seen was useful, regardless of the fact that they were very different. In other words, police officers seemed to select those features of the profile which most closely fitted the facts and were happy to ignore the rest, perhaps content that the profile appeared to confirm the accuracy of the investigation outcome.

Alison and Barrett (2004: 72) argue that when investigators are faced with complex cases and pressure to secure an outcome, they may begin to generate narratives relying on very general and simplified psychological theory in order to make sense of the data, and in so doing produce plausible explanations which are simply not warranted by the evidence. This is not dissimilar to the *Barnum Effect*, whereby ambiguous data, for example in psychometric assessment, is seen to come from an authoritative source, and is then imbued with undeserved credibility and accuracy, when in reality the bland statements could apply to a wide range of personnel and situations. Alison and Barrett urge caution, concluding that 'ambiguous and unverifiable information is particularly dangerous when it masquerades as scientific fact', and does no favours to the development of a robust system of profiling.

It is clear that all types of profiling must be subject to rigorous evaluation, though it is equally clear that applying psychological knowledge and methodology to the investigation of crime has obvious potential in terms of resource deployment and operational strategy. If this potential is to be fully realised then the further development of a productive and realistic working relationship between the police and forensic psychologists is essential.

Eyewitness testimony

Psychologists have made more contributions to the literature on eyewitness testimony than in any other area. The accuracy of memory is important in many situations, but absolutely critical in one – the courtroom. Justice crucially relies on reliable testimony, from eyewitnesses and expert witnesses, and from scientific evidence. If this testimony is not reliable, the innocent may be wrongfully imprisoned and the guilty may go free. Jurors and police officers attach considerable importance to the evidence of eyewitnesses, despite generally accepted knowledge that there have been many cases of mistaken identification. They want to hear hard evidence, and who is likely to know better than a witness whose evidence is compelling? Unfortunately, as Cutler and Penrod (1995) point out, eyewitnesses can be '100% confident and still be 100% wrong'.

With rapid developments in DNA technology it has become easier to identify genuine perpetrators, and the American Innocence Project, set up in 1992, deals with cases where post-conviction DNA testing can provide conclusive proof of innocence where eyewitness misidentification has led to injustice. So far the project has secured the release of 183 prisoners wrongfully imprisoned, and Scheck, Neufeld and Dwyer (2000) estimate that 75 per cent of these cases involved misidentification by eyewitnesses.

One example of the cases the Innocence Project manages was Herman Atkins, who was convicted in 1988 for robbery and rape, and sentenced to 45 years' imprisonment. In 1986 the victim was at work in a store when she was raped and robbed at gunpoint. She was taken to the police station where her clothing was sent for DNA analysis, and while there she saw a wanted poster for Atkins. She was then shown a set of photographs and identified Atkins as her attacker. A witness who worked near the victim's store was also shown the wanted poster, and subsequently identified him as a man who had been in her store on the day of the assault.

At the trial these two identifications were presented as strong evidence, as was the testimony of the scientist who had carried out analysis of stains on the victim's clothing. He concluded that statistically Atkins was in a population of 4.4 per cent of people who could have committed the rape. Atkins provided an alibi witness in his own defence but was found guilty. In 1999 the Innocence Project requested the victim's clothing for DNA testing and was able to demonstrate that the semen found there did not belong to Atkins. After spending 12 years in prison for a crime he did not commit, Atkins was released in 2000 (see http://www.innocenceproject.org for details of more cases).

In spite of misidentifications, eyewitness testimony can play a very important part in the apprehension of criminals, and is probably the most common form of evidence offered by the prosecution (Penrod et al. 1995). However, it may be that the police and the public – in the form of jurors – place too much faith in eyewitness reports. Kebbell and Milne (1998) found that the police believe eyewitnesses are reliable and accurate most of the time, with 75 per cent of them thinking that eyewitnesses were never or rarely incorrect. Loftus (1979) demonstrated this vividly when she gave mock jurors three versions of a crime. Eighteen per cent of the jurors convicted when there was only circumstantial evidence, 72 per cent convicted when there was an eyewitness, and this second figure still only dropped to 68 per cent when the eyewitness testimony was significantly discredited.

The study of memory in relation to eyewitness testimony

Human memory has often been described as if it were a combination of a camera and a video recorder producing an accurate representation of what has been seen, but psychological research has demonstrated that memory processes are extremely susceptible to influence and, according to Loftus (2003: 231), are more likely to produce a 'synthesis of experiences rather than a replay of a videotape'. Developments in cognitive psychology since the 1980s suggest that perception and memory are active, constructive processes, and that people's perception of the world around them is crucially related to their understanding of that world. These findings go back to Bartlett (1932) and his early demonstration that when asked to remember a story, we try to 'make sense' of it. Who we are will determine how we make sense of what we perceive,

and thus factors such as age, cultural background, emotions, specialist knowledge and expectations will all play a part.

In spite of a wealth of research into the reliability of eyewitness testimony, there is considerable dispute over the real-world applicability of such research, especially as much of it is conducted in the laboratory using volunteer participants. In real life, eyewitnesses have no choice about giving testimony and may not only have been affected emotionally by what they saw, but may also have been victims themselves. It is essential, therefore, that laboratory research findings are validated in real-world settings.

Kapardis (2003: 35) suggests that variables which can influence the reliability of eyewitness testimony may be classified into four possible categories in the literature: event characteristics, witness characteristics, perpetrator variables and interrogational variables.

Event characteristics

⇒ *Passage of time*: children and adults tend to forget things over time. Van Koppen and Lochun (1997) used archived police records to examine witness descriptions of robbers. More complete descriptions were likely when there was a shorter delay between the crime and the report. Recall is subject to deterioration over time, though there can be remarkable exceptions.

⇒ *Frequency*: the more times an event occurs, the more likely it is that people will remember it (for example, a bank robber visiting a bank to do a dry run before a robbery), but if people are asked to remember a specific occasion from a series of recurring events, recall accuracy decreases the more frequently the events have occurred.

⇒ *Duration*: committing a crime can take a few seconds, several minutes or longer. The longer a witness has to view a crime, the more accurate their testimony is likely to be (Van Koppen and Lochun 1997), though stress may lead to an overestimate of duration (Sarason and Stroops 1978).

⇒ *Illumination*: the amount of light available at the crime scene is important. Yarmey (1986) found that witness accuracy in terms of the incident and the perpetrator was better during daytime than towards the end of daylight and at night.

Weapon: the presence of a weapon is stressful for victims and witnesses, and increases physiological arousal. In real life, witnesses can fear abduction, injury or even death. Cognitive efficiency is said to decline if the arousal level increases beyond an optimal level, simply because the witness cannot attend to all cues or determine which are relevant. Eysenck's personality theory also predicts that when we are highly aroused we cannot attend to cues in the environment efficiently because our energies are being used on anxiety. However, not all psychologists agree with this view of a simple relationship between arousal and recall (Christianson 1992), and the literature is not consistent. For example, Loftus (1979) suggests that high stress levels affect memory negatively, while Yuille and Cutshall (1989) report 88 per cent accuracy in the recall of witnesses to a homicide five months after the event. These studies tend to reveal the chasm between laboratory studies and real-life events, since laboratory studies can never reproduce the trauma of real crime.

Weapon focus: studies have shown that when witnesses are faced with someone armed with a weapon they will tend to focus attention on the weapon, thereby reducing their ability to identify the perpetrator (Loftus, Loftus and Messo 1987). These findings were replicated when Maass and Kohnken (1989) simulated the weapon effect in a study where students were approached by an experimenter holding either a syringe or a pen and who either did or did not threaten to administer an injection. Exposure to the syringe decreased identification of the suspect, but enhanced recall of hand movements. Steblay's (1992) meta-analysis of weapon-focus studies revealed that six supported unhelpful focus on weapons, while 13 showed no significant difference in accurate recall between weapons-present and weapons-absent events.

Flashbulb memory: Brown and Kulik (1977) suggested that we remember significant and unexpected events, such as the assassination of President Kennedy in 1963, vividly and in some detail, for instance where we were when we heard of the event. Others (e.g. Christianson 1992) suggest that flashbulb memories may not always be so accurate. For instance, when Neisser and Harsch (1992) questioned eyewitnesses to the space shuttle *Challenger* explosion 32 months after the event, they found that witnesses' recollections of place, activity and time contained only 30 per cent accurate answers and 42 per cent totally inaccurate answers. However, when Wright (1993) questioned people who had been at the Sheffield football stadium when 95 supporters died, their recall was influenced by their emotional investment in the event. This suggests we may reconstruct our memories of important events to support a particular viewpoint, and this strengthens our recall of specific features. The defining feature of flashbulb memories is nonetheless 'the undue confidence with which these memories are held' (Weaver 1993: 39). Witnessing a traumatic event can increase recall assurance, but not necessarily accuracy.

Witness characteristics

Personality factors: neuroticism seems to affect witness identification, with individuals low in neuroticism demonstrating increased accuracy as arousal levels increase (Bothwell, Brigham and Pigot 1987), while witnesses high in impulsivity take less time to decide whether an offender is in a line-up than more reflective individuals (Stern and Dunning 1994). Similarly, individuals with a high need for approval performed better in identification tasks (Schill 1966), and the time at which an incident occurred affected the accuracy of recall, dependent on whether the witness was a 'morning' person or an 'evening' person (e.g. they were more likely to remember details of an event occurring early in the day if they were someone who felt more lively in the mornings) (Diges, Rubio and Rodriguez 1992).

Mood/emotion: people find it easier to recognise something than to recall it, so context and cues which might aid retrieval, such as the evocation of a particular mood or feeling, are important. Gudjonsson (1992) suggests that returning a witness to the crime scene improves recall by making the most of retrieval cues through the process of almost reliving the original context. This is an important aspect of the cognitive interview technique, where psychological retrieval strategies are used to improve recall. The *cognitive interview* is a forensic tool that employs a series of memory retrieval techniques designed to increase the amount of information that can be obtained from a witness. It was developed by psychologists (Gieselman et al. 1984) and is used by police officers to obtain accurate reports from witnesses, resulting in 40 per cent more valid information being produced than standard interview techniques (Memon and Higham 2000). The techniques of the cognitive interview are based on psychological theory and include reinstating the original encoding context in order to access stored information, by asking the witness to 'go back' to the original event and imagine themselves there – what they heard, saw and smelled. Another technique is accessing information from a variety of starting points, rather than a chronological recall (from start to finish). The cognitive interview can become even more effective if social components are added, for instance establishing rapport, transferring control from the interviewer to the witness, using open questions which require elaborate responses, not interrupting, and being responsive to the witness's individual style.

➡ *Drugs*: alcohol impairs cognitive performance, specifically interfering with the acquisition and encoding of information, and also the accuracy of recall (Steele and Josephs 1990). The use of cannabis has similar effects (Thompson 1995).

➡ *Age*: the very young and the very old are often viewed as less reliable witnesses, and there is evidence to suggest that 'cognitive slowing' does occur with ageing (Light 1991), specifically in relation to short-term memory retention (Craik 1977). However, Bornstein (1995) suggests that adult witness testimony can be improved by using the following strategies: ask precise questions, avoid leading questions and use the cognitive interview technique.

➡ *Gender*: female witnesses may be preferred to male witnesses by the police (Levine and Tapp 1971), but women tend to overestimate the duration of an event more than men (Loftus, Loftus and Messo 1987). However, men are more likely to suffer colour vision deficits and hearing loss, which can adversely affect their accuracy as witnesses.

➡ *Stereotypes*: we all tend to see what we expect to see, and as Buckhout (1974: 26) pointed out, 'expectancy is seen in its least attractive form in the case of biases or prejudices'. Stereotypes enable us to use a form of shorthand to speed up our impression-formation processes, but unfortunately they are not always accurate. Crime lends itself to the reinforcement of popular stereotypes (with the directors of films and pantomimes acutely aware of this coding), and psychological research has provided evidence for the existence of stereotypes about what criminals look like (e.g. Bull and Green 1980; MacLeod, Frowley and Shepherd 1994). This can then influence the way witnesses recall details of a glimpsed event, particularly in the area of race (e.g. Allport and Postman 1947). Physical attractiveness is a powerful stereotype, for instance the belief that 'what is beautiful is good' (Dion, Berscheid and Walster 1972). Attractive people are rated as more socially competent, sexual, happy, assertive and popular than less attractive individuals (Feingold 1992). It is likely that attractive faces will be remembered more than unattractive faces.

➡ *Confidence*: if a witness is to be believed they must be credible, and their confidence in their own testimony is seen by Wells (1993: 58) as 'the most powerful single determinant' of their perceived credibility. Unfortunately, the relationship between witness confidence and witness accuracy is not significant (Leippe 1994). Williams, Loftus and Deffenbacher (1992) explain this in terms of cognitive dissonance – the more times a witness repeats the same account, the more their own confidence will increase in terms of its perceived accuracy, and the more need there will be to appear consistent. It might be assumed that the testimony of police officers would be seen as more accurate than that of non-police personnel, and would be presented more confidently, but Ainsworth (1981) found no differences between groups of experienced police officers, novice police officers and a control group of ordinary people in their recall of a staged crime event.

Perpetrator variables

Most research on our identification of others has tended to focus on facial features, but body shape and movement can also be influential factors. Barclay, Cutting and Kozlowski (1978) showed how gender could be ascertained by witnesses on the basis of body movement indicated by a light attached to each ankle. The hips of males and females are fundamentally different and this shows in the way they walk. However, estimates of height were influenced either by the height of the witness (Flin and Shepherd 1986), or post-event information about the occupation of the person witnessed (Christiansen, Sweeney and Ochalek

1983). In other words, if witnesses were small themselves they overestimated the height of others, and if others' occupations were presented as high-status, this resulted in taller estimates.

Identification across races is less accurate than own-race identification by adult witnesses, whether they are black or white (Bothwell, Brigham and Pigot 1987), though frequency of contact can reduce this bias. For instance, Dunning, Li and Malpass (1998) found that basketball fans were able to identify African American faces as easily as European ones, in contrast to non-basketball enthusiasts. There is also a higher rate of false identifications in cross-racial cases (Thomson 1995).

Interrogational variables

Post-event information presented to witnesses can contaminate their evidence and render it unreliable. Psychological studies where 'misinformation' has been planted show how witness recall can be significantly influenced to produce errors (Williams, Loftus and Deffenbacher 1992). Similarly, the use of leading questions which contain misinformation can have the same effect, as Loftus and Palmer (1974) demonstrated vividly:

> Participants viewed a film of a car accident and were asked to estimate the car's speed. Estimates varied depending on which verb was used to describe the accident. When participants were asked how fast cars were going when they 'contacted' each other the estimate was 31.8 mph, but when the verb 'smashed' was used instead, the estimate was 40.8 mph. This latter group were also more likely to report having seen broken glass at the scene even though there wasn't any.

When we see something we process certain details, which are then held together by our existing mental schemata which can introduce bias. Subsequent misinformation can become part of the recall and trick us into reconstructing our memory of the event we witnessed. Loftus (1993: 530) says: 'The new information invades us, like a Trojan horse, precisely because we do not detect its influence'. Once misinformation has been presented, the person may come to believe in its accuracy and be unable to change their view. One reason for this is that people believe the misinformation, but do not recall where or when they heard it – this is called *source monitoring error* and can occur when we confuse what is real and what is fantasy or imagined. This happened in a study carried out by Crombag,

Wagenaar and Van Koppen (1996), when they asked participants what they had seen of the real-life crash of a Boeing 747 in Amsterdam. Sixty per cent of participants said they had seen the incident on television, even though no footage had been shot or aired. The conclusion was that participants had confused the information they already had about previous air crashes with the suggestion that they must have seen this one on television.

Source monitoring errors can affect eyewitness identification by *unconscious transference* too – remembering something seen in one context even though it was encoded in another. Memon and Wright (1999) tell how a witness described Timothy McVeigh, who was subsequently convicted of the Oklahoma bombing, coming into his shop to rent a truck. This description led to McVeigh's arrest. The witness also described another person being with McVeigh, and eventually this man was traced too. It emerged, however, that although this second man had been into the shop, he had not been with McVeigh and was not associated with the bombing. The witness had remembered the second man, but mistakenly remembered him as being with McVeigh.

Line-ups or identity parades

Witnesses may be asked to select a suspect from an identity parade or line-up, where the suspect is presented live alongside a number of innocent people, or foils. In the UK the Devlin Report in the 1970s highlighted a number of cases where wrongful convictions had been made on the basis of misidentification, and as a consequence the procedures involved in line-ups were improved. However, Wright and McDaid (1996) show how, in a survey of London identification parades, an innocent foil was chosen by the eyewitness in 20 per cent of cases. In other countries it has been argued that even where the guilty party *has* been identified by a witness, 20 per cent of these are lucky guesses, and that as many as 50 per cent of witnesses are guessing (Penrod 2003).

Wells et al. (1998: 17–24) proposed four general principles to protect innocent suspects, and these are now used to guide procedures for line-ups and for photo-spreads:

➡ use of the blind technique, that is, the person who conducts the line-up should not be aware which member of the line-up or photo-spread is the suspect;

➟ the eyewitness should be told explicitly that the person organising the line-up or photo-spread does not know which person is the suspect, in order to ensure neutrality and reduce expectations;

➟ the suspect should not stand out in the line-up or photo-spread as being different from the others, based on the witness's description or other factors which might draw attention to the suspect, as this clearly presents evidence for an appeal on the grounds of bias;

➟ a clear statement should be taken from the eyewitness at the time of the identification as to their level of confidence about their selection.

These principles are based on what distinguishes a good psychology experiment from a bad one, namely experimenter bias, social desirability, demand characteristics, neutrality of stimuli, and so on. Kassin (1998) goes further and suggests that line-ups should be recorded on camera, just as police interviews with suspects are recorded on tape to prevent bad practice.

Eyewitnesses do tend to assume that a line-up would not be being offered unless the suspect is present, so may be more inclined towards selection on the basis that someone close in appearance to the suspect must be the culprit. This is called 'relative judgement theory', and may occur because witnesses are often unwilling to say that they recognise no one in the line-up as it will be seen as wasting everyone's time. When Wells (1993) investigated this by telling all witnesses that the suspect might not be present, but then showed some of them a line-up with the suspect, and others a line-up without the suspect, he found that 54 per cent of those who identified the suspect correctly said they definitely would have identified someone else even if the suspect had not been there. In line-ups where the suspect is not present, there is thus a strong chance that innocent people will be selected.

In the USA an alternative of the line-up is the *show-up*, where the police present a single individual to the witness. This ought to reduce the possibility of relative judgement, but the fact that the police feel confident enough to show the witness one suspect might indicate their confidence in his or her guilt.

When Steblay et al. (2003) carried out a meta-analysis comparing show-ups with line-ups, they found that line-ups were more likely to result in a witness choice than show-ups, whether the suspect was present or not. False identification of an innocent foil is more common in show-ups than in line-ups.

Although the US Supreme Court decided in 1972 that witness confidence was an indicator of accuracy, research indicates that confidence is a rather poor predictor of accuracy. For instance, Cutler and Penrod (1988) compared statements of confidence made prior to identity parades/line-ups and subsequent to correct identification of the offender – the overall correlation was 0.2 or less, on a scale of −1 to +1. Kebbell, Wagstaff and Covey (1996) found that witnesses may be confident and also accurate about easy details for recall (e.g. gender), but if they are asked hard questions, such as 'eye colour', there is a low correlation between confidence and accuracy.

A possible way of distinguishing between good eyewitnesses and poor eyewitnesses is the 10- to 12-second rule (Dunning and Perretta 2002). Eyewitnesses who identify someone from a line-up quickly tend to be more accurate than an eyewitness who takes longer. A possible explanation for this is that the eyewitness who identifies the offender correctly needs to match the characteristics of each member of the line-up against the characteristics of the offender the witness is holding in their memory. This takes a certain amount of time, but is relatively speedy because the major characteristics can be identified quickly. Where the offender is not in the line-up or the memory of major characteristics is weak, the process will take longer.

When Wogalter, Malpass and McQuiston (2004) examined actual procedures used by US police they found some examples of good practice:

➟ officers tended to choose line-up foils on the basis of ethnicity, hair and face shape, which reflects research evidence suggesting that witnesses recall upper facial features more readily than lower facial features;

➟ officers reported that they gave witnesses the option not to choose anyone, but failed to warn witnesses that facial features can change.

There were also examples of bad practice:

➡ the majority of officers chose foils on the basis of their similarity to the suspect, rather than the descriptions offered by witnesses. However, this can cause confusion because the suspect may consequently stand out because they share characteristics with the foils, but the foils may not actually look much like each other. This can then encourage selection of the suspect;

➡ most assessments of the fairness of the procedures are provided by fellow officers (94 per cent), with the advice of defence lawyers rarely requested (15 per cent).

Conclusions

In spite of the considerable amount of research into eyewitness testimony, there are some criticisms of its value. Konecni, Ebbeson and Nehrer (2000) suggest that psychologists acting as expert witnesses have misled courts about the validity of research findings on eyewitness testimony, overemphasising academic agreement about models of memory. The main critique is the lack of generalisability of laboratory research to real life, but specifically they suggest that:

➡ studies of eyewitness testimony are not consistent in their outcomes;

➡ participants in eyewitness testimony research are usually students;

➡ the length of exposure in laboratory studies is usually very short by comparison to real-life crime events;

➡ researchers cannot draw conclusions about accuracy levels based on their studies (e.g. increasing exposure time is often said to be associated with increased accuracy of identification, but it also increases risk);

➡ expert witnesses rarely comment on the controversies or inconsistencies in the field of eyewitness testimony research.

They conclude that because of the difficulties in translating research findings to particular decisions in particular cases, expert witness testimony on eyewitness testimony should not be allowed in courts.

Child witnesses

Children form a specific category of eyewitness, particularly in cases of alleged sexual abuse where a child may be the only witness to offences which could have occurred some time ago. Concerns have been expressed about children's ability to give evidence in court, the likely credibility of such testimony, and the need to preserve defendants' right to a fair trial. In the last quarter of the twentieth century and the early years of the twenty-first, there has been something of a sea change in the way child witnesses are viewed. Children's evidence has traditionally been seen as unreliable by the courts, with concerns about their suggestibility, their poor memory and, in the case of very young children, their inability to recognise the difference between right and wrong. This very negative view of children's ability to provide evidence about what might have happened to them led to many miscarriages of justice, one of the most notable of which was the acquittal of the actor Peter Adamson, who played Len Fairclough in *Coronation Street*, reported by Westcott and Davies (2002). In 1983 he had been accused of the indecent assault of two eight-year-old girls to whom he was giving swimming lessons, and although one of the girls gave a reasonable account, she broke down under cross-examination, and subsequently tried to commit suicide. The other victim then refused to give evidence, and the case collapsed. Subsequently, the actor admitted to a reporter that he had probably committed the offences.

Other miscarriages of justice and a growing awareness of the extent of child sexual abuse led to the development of a different view of potential child witnesses, and the Hedderman Report (1988) concluded that, with appropriate support and a different approach to interviewing, children could be credible witnesses in court. Some of the subsequent significant developments in legislation and research in this area include the introduction of live links, videotaped interviews, the Memorandum of Good Practice (1992), research in the area of suggestibility and Achieving Best Evidence (2002).

The 'live link'

Monitors were introduced in court buildings to enable child witnesses to give their evidence away from the courtroom and protect them from having to face the accused. It was clear that children found the unfamiliarity and formality of courtrooms very intimidating (Davies and Noon 1991), and that sitting away from this site, with a supporter, enabled them to provide their evidence more clearly. This also satisfied those lawyers who still wanted to cross-examine child witnesses, but they were advised not to use jargon and to avoid intimidation strategies. There were some concerns that jurors would not be able to detect deception via live-link cross-examinations, but Orcutt et al. (2001) showed that the use of CCTV had no impact on accuracy, when they compared truthful and deceptive accounts provided live and via monitors. The development of live links seemed to help children to provide evidence, but it also introduced a 'distance' between them and the jurors. Rapport is difficult to achieve via a live link, and children's distress was sometimes too 'contained', which might have left some jurors unconvinced. When Golding et al. (2003) evaluated jurors' reactions to child witnesses who were calm and those who cried, they found that the 'teary' condition resulted in more guilty verdicts.

Videotaped interviews

The 1989 Pigot Report identified the necessity of prioritising the needs of child witnesses in cases of alleged sexual abuse, in order to ensure that their distress was reduced while also meeting the needs of justice and fairness. It recommended the replacement of live testimony from children by videotaped interviews conducted early and by skilled interviewers, but this was vigorously opposed by lawyers, and a compromise was achieved whereby early interview evidence on videotape could be presented, but should be accompanied by the use of cross-examination via live link at trial. By 1998 both live-link and videotaped evidence were being used widely, but with little impact on conviction rates, so attention shifted to improving the quality of interview evidence provided on tape in order to address criticisms of children's suggestibility and the inappropriate use of leading questions which undermined the credibility of children's evidence.

The Memorandum of Good Practice

This was introduced in 1992 and provided a code of practice to be followed when interviewing children. It was proposed that interviews should have four distinct phases:

1 Setting rapport and establishing ground rules, so that the interviewer can make a connection with the child and reduce uncertainty, while also establishing 'rules' such as the difference between the truth and a lie.

2 A free narrative phase, when the child is given the opportunity to describe what happened in their own words and without interruption.
3 A questioning phase, when the interviewer can prompt the child to provide more detail in relation to what they have already said.
4 Marking closure, when the interviewer summarises what the child has said in their own words and draws the session to a close.

The type of questions used in the questioning phase is very important. These should be open-ended, allowing the child to provide detail. They can be specific, but must not be leading questions.

Research on children's suggestibility

Increased concern about child abuse and the need to secure prosecutions has led to considerable research in the area of child witness testimony and its reliability. A particular focus has been the vulnerability of children in interview situations and their potential suggestibility. Research in this area clearly has to be conducted sensitively in order to avoid distress, and so is almost invariably limited in its application to real-life cases. However, Loftus and Guyer (2002) provide a fascinating account of a real-life case where so-called 'recovered memory' of child sexual abuse occurred, and then go on to demonstrate how this was almost entirely the result of leading questions and selective interview strategies on the part of the therapist, resulting in the child's increased suggestibility (see http://faculty.washington.edu/eloftus/Articles/Jane Doe.htm).

Leichtman and Ceci (1995) examined the effects of repeated interviews under varying conditions with children aged three to six years. Following the visit of a stranger (Sam Stone) to their nursery, some children were interviewed, with suggestive questions about the event, once a week for the four weeks following the visit. All the children were interviewed ten weeks after the event by a new interviewer who had not been present when Sam Stone visited, and who simply asked the children to recall what had happened. Prior repeated suggestions increased false reporting, and the children tended to embellish their statements after repeated interviewing. This study showed that free recall performance can be affected by suggestions, and the inaccuracies will be maintained during questioning, whereas the previously held view was that free recall can produce an uncontaminated account.

Bruck and Ceci (1999) suggest that the reliability of a child's report has more to do with the skills of the interviewer than any natural limitations on memory. They found that interviewers tended to develop questions based on their own beliefs and then asked them in a way which would sway the child's account. Techniques such as the use of anatomically detailed dolls and guided imagery also increase suggestibility, as does repetitious questioning which implies non-belief in the first responses. They also argue that children display social compliance because they want to please adults, and that the onus of responsibility must lie with interviewers to ensure that the risk of suggestibility is reduced. The Memorandum of Good Practice has tried to anticipate these problems by advising that interviews be conducted as soon as possible after a charge has been made, minimising the number of interviews conducted, and recording what questions were asked. Despite this, Sternberg et al. (2001) found that when interviews with children were analysed there were low rates of leading questions, but there were also high rates of use of specific and closed questions, and not much use of open-ended questions.

Achievement of Best Evidence in Criminal Proceedings: guidance for vulnerable and intimidated witnesses, including children (2002)

This is a revision of the Memorandum of Good Practice which covers all vulnerable and intimidated witnesses. It advises prior preparation of witnesses in relation to what they can expect when they go to court, and aims at different agencies working together to develop good practice. Critics of the Memorandum of Good Practice had said that the restriction of interviews to one hour created problems, and that there had been insufficient guidance on how to interview very young children, ethnic minorities or individuals with special needs. A significant criticism was that the emphasis on securing strong and convincing evidence was at the expense of providing therapeutic support for the child.

The revised guidance acknowledges these criticisms and leaves the length of interviews to the professional judgement of interviewers. It also provides specific guidance on interviewing the very young, and those with special needs. There is more detail on the planning phase of interviews, and the provision of a set of words to describe the ground rules. Guidance is also given on how to probe inconsistencies in accounts given. There is an emphasis on the use of open-ended questions, and more recognition that children, like adults, do sometimes lie or make errors when giving testimony.

Conclusion

There have been considerable advances in the way child witnesses are viewed, and genuine attempts have been made to ensure their voice is heard. Legislative changes which reflect research and professional advice have brought about considerable improvements. However, areas for concern remain. Lawyers are still doubtful about the balance achieved between believing children's testimony and ensuring defendant's rights to a fair hearing. A particular concern expressed by lawyers is the possible use of coaching, particularly in the pre-interview phase and while children are cross-examined via live link. There is also insufficient training of interviewers, no nationally approved system of accrediting interviewers, and no cohesive national system for the effective preparation of child witnesses through the court process (Westcott and Kynan 2006). Children who have suffered abuse are still expected to deal maturely with an inquisitorial criminal justice system, revealing embarrassing details to complete strangers, and often with insufficient support through a traumatic period of their lives.

Juries

While the jury is held to be the cornerstone of the English legal system, only a small percentage of criminal cases are actually considered by a jury (most cases being considered by the lower magistrates' courts), and there are moves afoot to remove the jury altogether from cases involving complex fraud or scientific evidence, though this government proposal is meeting resistance. Nonetheless, the concept of a jury and the opportunity of trial by one's peers continue to hold not only great dramatic value, but also the principle of equity. Kapardis (2003: 134) argues that the jury's symbolic importance far outweighs its practical significance, particularly in view of reduced judicial discretion in sentencing and the practice of plea-bargaining.

There exists an extensive body of research on juries, including topics such as juror selection, jury decision-making processes, the effects of pre-trial publicity and the influence of expert witnesses, but much of this is from the United States because of restrictions on the interviewing of English jurors about real cases. The best-known study of real juries was undertaken by Kalven and Zeisel (1966), who, in *The American Jury*, collected data from 555 judges and 225 jurors. They reported that most jurors decide on their verdict before they retire to deliberate, and the majority view generally prevails. Moreover, the judge agreed with the jury in 75 per cent of the cases, though as Stephenson (1992) subsequently pointed out in a re-analysis of these data, while the judges and jurors might have agreed that a majority of defendants was guilty, there was low agreement on whom to find not guilty – quite a critical area.

Tinsley (2001) undertook research in New Zealand, which has a similar criminal justice system to England, and found from her study of 48 trials, and interviews with over 300 real jurors, that there was a 50 per cent agreement rate between juries and judges about verdicts, less than that found by Kalven and Zeisel (1966). She found that jurors took their role seriously and felt they were carrying out an important civic duty, but would have appreciated more explanations of the legal framework and a presentation of the facts of the case in order to reach an understanding of the crucial issues and areas of disagreement. Jurors did not wait until the end of the trial to reach a decision; they were actively constructing a story to explain events as the trial progressed. While they were prepared to change the story as new evidence emerged, inevitably their judgement was affected by the approach they had already adopted.

The majority of jury research is conducted with mock jurors and simulated trials, though these have been criticised for their lack of parity with reality, for instance the difficulty in reproducing a court atmosphere and what may be complex legal issues. Moreover, the reality of a juror's responsibility in determining the fate of a defendant is difficult to simulate, especially when participation in a mock jury forms part of an undergraduate's course requirements. The outcomes of mock jury research are interesting, but it would be unwise to make too much of their findings.

Who sits on juries?

While no qualifications are required to sit on a jury (other than age and the right to vote), and one might therefore assume that the first 12 people selected would form the jury, there are procedures by which objections may be made to a limited number of potential individual jurors. Objections can be made by both the prosecution and the defence teams, and are often based on assumptions about the personalities, attitudes and beliefs of potential jurors which, it is believed, may influence their judgement. American lawyers routinely call upon the services of psychologists during what is called a voir dire hearing to select jurors who they believe will be sympathetic to their client. Factors which could influence juror selection by defence lawyers might include the importance of choosing jurors with similar backgrounds to the client on the assumption that similarity increases identification, empathy and understanding, along with body language and physical appearance, which might indicate character 'strength' or 'weakness' on the basis of their likelihood to be influenced (Mauet and McCrimmon 1993).

Jury deliberation

When a trial reaches its conclusion, the judge normally reminds jurors of their duties and may sum up the key points of the case. The jury then retires to discuss the case and reach a verdict. Kalven and Zeisel (1966) reported that in nine out of ten juries, the deliberation task is to convince a minority of jurors to change their minds and go with the majority view. However, this has been disputed by Pennington and Hastie (1990), who suggest that the relationship between initial views and final jury verdicts is more complex and can be influenced significantly by how views are expressed and how discussions are managed. For instance, 'verdict-driven' deliberations involve jurors announcing their verdict preferences before discussion begins, while 'evidence-driven' deliberations are characterised by jurors announcing their views after preliminary discussions have taken place. This can make a crucial difference, as can instructions about the need to reach a unanimous decision or being able to report a majority verdict. For instance, when jurors are told a majority verdict is acceptable, minority jurors play a lesser part in the discussions; and jury deliberation will take longer if the jury is evidence-driven rather than verdict-driven (Hastie, Penrod and Pennington 1983). These factors may not have been taken into consideration in the early research, and when Sandys and Dillehay (1995) asked real jurors about deliberation, they reported that they had spent an average of 45 minutes discussing cases before having a first ballot, confirming the view that discussion has a greater impact on reaching a verdict than Kalven and Zeisel maintained. Tinsley's study (2001) highlights how the most important factor in effective jury decision-making is not whether or when ballots are held, but the systematic nature of assessing the evidence and applying the law. This is where the role of the foreperson becomes paramount. The foreperson must be able to facilitate discussion, provide direction and keep the discussion focused, yet is often untrained in this role and receives little guidance.

Hastie (1993) proposes four models of jury decision-making, three of which are mathematical and draw on information-processing theory, while the fourth is a cognitive story model. In this latter model jurors are said to actively construct a narrative to make sense of the evidence presented to them, and to use this to reach a verdict. It is possible within this model for different jurors to reach different decisions, even though they have heard the same evidence, because of their subjective interpretation of that evidence. This model echoes media constructions of celebrity trials.

Extra-legal factors influencing juror decisions

Other factors play a part in the social process of jury deliberation too. For instance, socially 'successful' jurors talk more than less successful ones, men talk more than women, and the foreperson talks a lot more than anyone (Ellsworth 1993). Although jurors are expected to be impartial, it is clear that their views can be influenced by a number of extra-legal factors, such as defendant attractiveness, ethnicity, empathy and exposure to pre-trial publicity.

A significant relationship appears to exist between perceived beauty and positive qualities. For example, being viewed as more sociable, dominant, sexually warm, mentally healthy and intelligent seems to coexist with being seen as attractive (Langlois et al. 2000). Early findings suggested that physically attractive defendants would be treated more leniently because of the 'what is beautiful is also good' hypothesis (Dion, Berscheid and Walster 1972), and Ellsworth and Mauro (1998) provided support for the attractiveness-leniency effect. Due to the assumption that physical appearance might influence judgements, lawyers routinely try to improve their clients' appearance (DeSantis and Kayson 1997: 679). This demonstrates awareness of impression formation being very dependent on physical appearance, and agreement on what type of face is classified as 'attractive' in western culture (Hogg and Vaughn 2002). Faces with a youthful appearance are considered more appealing, as is facial symmetry, smiling, high cheekbones, dilated pupils, arched eyebrows and full red lips (Rhodes and Zebrowitz 2002). These views tend to be reinforced in the media, where heroes and heroines are portrayed as attractive, while villains are not (Feingold 1992). A 2006 American case involved Debra Lafave, a teacher accused of having sex with one of her 14-year-old pupils. Her lawyer argued that his client was 'too pretty for prison', the media took up her case and the alleged victim's mother decided not to put her son through the ordeal of a trial.

Research into the effect a defendant's appearance can have on jurors' decision-making supports the view that there is a favourable bias towards attractive defendants. DeSantis and Kayson (1997) asked mock jurors to read a fictitious burglary case and asked them to recommend a suitable sentence, with some of them seeing a picture of an attractive defendant and others seeing a picture of an unattractive defendant – the unattractive defendant received harsher sentences. Abwender and Hough (2001) introduced dimensions of ethnicity and gender as well as attractiveness, and found, in addition to a favourable bias towards attractive defendants, that black participants were more lenient towards black defendants; and while female participants treated unattractive female defendants more harshly, the opposite was true of male participants, who were more favourable towards unattractive defendants. However, Abwender and Hough (2001) also found that if participants were informed that defendants had used their attractiveness, for instance in fraud crime, the tendency towards favourable bias disappeared.

Haegerich and Bottoms (2000) demonstrated how mock jurors' estimates of guilt in cases where defendants were accused of murdering their parents, but who claimed a defence of sexual abuse, were influenced by lawyers' attempts to promote empathy for the defendants. This led to fewer findings of guilt, though the lawyers' strategy was more successful in female jurors than in male.

Finch and Munro (2005) investigated mock jurors' attitudes in rape cases involving alcohol or drugs, and found that in reaching a decision jurors relied on numerous extra-legal factors, such as rape myths, misconceptions about the effect of intoxicants and factors such as the motivation of the defendant in administering the intoxicant. They point to widely held misconceptions about the effects of 'date-rape drugs' automatically leading to unconsciousness, rather than the reality, which is a disassociation between mind and body and a subsequent amnesia. This significantly impacted on jurors' views of consent and responsibility, leading to a position where if the defendant and victim were seen to be equally intoxicated (as a result of drugs or alcohol), it was considered unfair to hold the defendant criminally liable for intercourse, even when the victim's intoxication had rendered her incapable of giving meaningful consent to intercourse. Finch and Munro point out that this view is in direct contrast with the legal position under the Sexual Offences Act 2003.

The influence of pre-trial publicity on juror decisions

A large number of studies, including Fein et al. (1997) and Devonport, Studebaker and Penrod (1999), suggest that exposure to pre-trial publicity negatively affects jurors and increases their support for the prosecution, as well as their tendency to find the defendant guilty. These concerns are not new. In 1954 Dr Sam Sheppard was convicted of murdering his wife Marilyn, but at a retrial this verdict was overturned when the Supreme Court cited excessive and damaging media coverage of his first trial (see http://www.samreesesheppard.org/shepvsmax.html).

There have been notable 'celebrity' trials since this case which have attracted considerable media attention and have been the focus of considerable pre- and post-trial publicity. One of these, Louise Woodward, appears to support the findings of Devonport, Studebaker and Penrod (1999), while the other, O. J. Simpson, does not. Interestingly, the same lawyer, Barry Scheck, played a part in both cases, and is one of the founders of the Innocence Project.

Louise Woodward was an English au pair accused in 1997 of murdering the 18-month-old infant in her care by shaking him. She was found guilty of second-degree murder and sentenced to life in prison, but a month later the judge reduced the finding to involuntary manslaughter, sentenced her to time already served, and she was freed. Media coverage of the case was intense, and much of the pre-trial publicity focused on Louise, notably her apparent lack of emotion, poor character and her allegedly 'wild' partying. The jurors claimed not to have been influenced by publicity about Louise or the baby's parents, but they would not have been able to avoid it. Other issues may have also played a part in the furore about the verdict and its subsequent overturning, including conflicting expert witness testimony, complex medical evidence, differing cultural expectations of appropriate displays of emotion and aggressive lawyers (see http://www.courttv.com/archive/casefiles/nanny/nanny.html).

Figure 6.3 Louise Woodward

In 1994 O. J. Simpson, a famous American footballer and sports commentator, was accused of the brutal murder of two people, one of whom was his ex-wife. His trial was televised and he was found not guilty in 1995, though he was later found responsible for their deaths by the civil courts in 1997. Prior to his arrest, O. J. Simpson had agreed to hand himself in to the police, but was later reported to be driving erratically on the interstate highway after leaving what appeared to be a suicide note. Live helicopter coverage of the police chase featured on all TV stations, and after his arrest Simpson's mugshot and articles about his case appeared in newspapers nationwide. Despite the overwhelming evidence against him, Simpson was found not guilty mainly because the testimony of the police investigators was undermined by the formidable legal team acting for Simpson. The trial was inevitably affected by the media frenzy surrounding it, and speculation about the outcome continued for a long time afterwards. For instance, an NBC poll in 2004 found that 77 per cent of those polled thought that Simpson was guilty, but within this figure there was a sharp racial divide, with only 27 per cent of the black people polled believing in his guilt, compared to 87 per cent of white people polled (see http://www.courttv.com/casefiles/simpson/index.html).

A third case which vividly illustrates the effect of negative pre-trial publicity concerned the murder of two English schoolgirls, Jessica Chapman and Holly Wells, in 2002. An iconic photograph of the two girls in bright red Manchester United football shirts, taken on the afternoon they went missing, epitomised their innocence and the futility of their deaths. Ian Huntley, a caretaker at the girls' school in Soham, Cambridgeshire, was accused of their murder, while his girlfriend, Maxine Carr, not present during the weekend the girls disappeared, was accused of perverting the course of justice by not telling the police what she knew about Huntley seeing the girls on the day of their disappearance. Negative pre-trial publicity about Huntley and Carr was intense, and after Huntley was sentenced to life for murder Carr became one of only four people, and the only non-murderer, to be granted indefinite anonymity because of the threats to her life. In many ways the public vilification of Carr was more severe than that of Huntley, and this can be accounted for by the highly negative publicity she received, alongside other factors such as her gender and perceived unattractiveness (see http://news.bbc.co.uk/1/hi/in_depth/uk/2003/soham_trial/default.stm).

Hope, Memon and McGeorge (2004) suggest that the effects of negative pre-trial publicity can best be

Figure 6.4 O. J. Simpson

Figure 6.5 Jessica Chapman and Holly Wells

understood within Hastie's (1993) proposed framework that jurors construct narratives to help them understand the evidence presented to them, with pre-trial publicity acting as a filter to enable jurors to select one 'story' rather than another. Cognitive dissonance (Festinger 1957) can then act to reduce the likelihood of another story, for instance the one presented by the defence, taking the place of the original story adopted. Hope, Memon and McGeorge (2004) argue that exposure to negative pre-trial publicity predisposes jurors to view the prosecution as a source of authority and to devalue alternative 'stories' of what occurred accordingly. This finding supports Kovera (2002), who demonstrated that exposure to brief but different types of media coverage of acquaintance rape altered mock jurors' weighting of types of evidence and their views of the defendant.

Expert testimony

Forensic psychologists may be asked to appear as expert witnesses in court and, as is the case with any expert testimony, their contribution can make a significant impression on the jury. English courts are wary of this potential influence, especially in view of recent miscarriages of justice, such as the cases of Sally Clark (2003) and Angela Cannings (2004), where the juries were presented with seemingly irrefutable odds of 73 million to 1 against natural successive sudden infant deaths by Professor Roy Meadow, an eminent paediatrician, but clearly not an expert in statistics. The Royal Society of Statisticians criticised Meadow's statement as misleading (see http://pass.maths.org.uk/issue21/features/clark/ for a full analysis). Both convictions were quashed by the Court of Appeal as unsafe.

In America stringent rules on admissibility of expert testimony are applied, and these may be introduced in England in the future. What this will mean, for example, is that if profilers are called to give evidence in court they will have to demonstrate that their area of expertise is one which has general acceptance in the scientific community – it is doubtful whether this could be satisfactorily evidenced at the time of writing (2006).

The experience of being a juror

Undertaking jury service can involve a lengthy period of concentration, exposure to legal jargon and an enormous responsibility in relation to defendants. Participation in trials involving allegations of extreme violence can also induce considerable stress in jurors. However, when Matthews, Hancock and Briggs (2004) interviewed 361 people who had recently completed jury service, they found that 50 per cent of them were enthusiastic about having served as jurors, regarding it as a 'moral duty', but one that had also provided an opportunity for personal fulfilment, and 55 per cent said they would be happy to repeat the experience. Two-thirds of respondents had a very positive view of their experience as a result of the professionalism of court staff, though they were critical of delays, the trivial nature of some cases and the standard of court facilities. They also felt that they would have benefited from more explanations of jargon and the nature of the evidence, and would have liked to have been able to take notes or ask questions during the cases. However, only 19 per cent said they were worried about reaching the 'wrong' verdict.

Conclusion

Much of the research on juries is contradictory, and the difficulties associated with research involving jurors do not further our understanding. If the jury system is going to continue it will need reform and evaluation of those measures. Levine (1992) proposes allowing jurors to take notes and question witnesses where appropriate, view videotapes of the trial and take a more active role in sentencing. Kapardis (2003) goes further and suggests that jurors should be given the opportunity to attend short courses, preparing them for their role and introducing them to basic principles of law and the dynamics of decision-making. He points out that forensic psychologists are well placed to provide tuition on such courses.

Example of a forensic psychology intervention

One area where forensic psychologists have made significant interventions is *risk assessment*. Appraising risk is a constant in human decision-making and features in many aspects of personal and business lives. Insurers, bankers, politicians and engineers all need to make very accurate risk assessments to guide their decisions, but we all do something similar when we consider buying a house, for example. In forensic settings, risk assessment means estimating the chance of an adverse outcome, for instance the chances of a released offender committing further crimes.

In the early years of the twenty-first century, controversies surrounding the early release of particular offenders, and further crimes being committed while offenders are under supervision, have revealed the extent of public and media interest in this area, and demonstrated their intolerance of risk assessment/management failings. Risk assessment and risk management have been important elements of forensic psychology practice for many years, but developments and enhancements in forensic practice in this area, policy and legislative changes, and the move towards an increasingly risk-aversive society have all meant that risk assessment has become central to the criminal justice system, and hence to forensic psychology practice. The completion of risk assessments is now commonplace in all stages/elements of the criminal justice system and they also play a crucial role in the civil justice system, particularly in family courts.

Traditionally there have been two approaches to risk assessment: the clinical approach and the actuarial approach. The clinical approach relies on the experience and judgement of practitioners, including psychiatrists and clinical psychologists, who will also use psychometric measures to assess the likelihood of future violent or inappropriate sexually motivated behaviour. However, this approach has been criticised because many of the categories used are too broad, not all clinicians are equally experienced in specialist areas, and the subjective nature of this type of assessment is too error-prone (Dernevik et al. 2000).

The actuarial approach relies on statistics and predictions of risk on the basis of data indicating the relationship between a number of predictor variables and reoffending variables in a large group of offenders. A strong relationship between these variables is likely to predict higher recidivism rates in similar groups of offenders. Unlike the clinical approach, it does not give any importance to individual factors.

Neither system is foolproof, and simple approaches can be impressive, albeit bordering on the 'common-sense'. For instance, Gretenkord (2000) studied men hospitalised in a forensic unit and focused on four predictors of recidivism: presence of personality disorder; previous offences of violence; two or more aggressive incidents in the hospital; and age at discharge. The highest risk group were younger inmates who had a personality disorder, previous convictions for violence and a record of violence in the hospital. Of this group, 65 per cent committed further violent offences on release, and although this is impressive, not everyone in the group could have been kept incarcerated indefinitely, so risk management becomes a key issue. Kemshall (2001) concludes that the strength of the clinical method is in its individualistic approach, which, although it is considered less reliable than the actuarial approach, can result in overly simplistic outcomes in not sufficiently taking into account the complexity of the processes involved. She proposes a more holistic approach to risk assessment, combining the strengths of both approaches.

Blackburn (2000) identifies specific risk factors for violence:

- historical factors – previous violence, adverse family conditions, social maladjustment, being male and being young at first offence;
- dispositional variables – deviant cognitive, emotional and social tendencies, such as deficient problem-solving skills and anti-social beliefs;
- clinical factors – psychopathy, anti-social personality disorder, substance abuse;
- situational factors – the behaviour of others, support systems, stress, work problems, family disharmony, relationship issues.

These appear to have informed the development of OASys (the Offender Assessment System) – a new national system in the UK for assessing the risks and needs of an offender (see Howard 2006). The system has been jointly designed by the prison and probation services, and at its heart is comprehensive assessment and electronic sharing of the information obtained between the police, probation and prison services. It is basically a risk and needs assessment tool, which helps to ensure that managers in the prison and probation services have a proper assessment of the offenders in their care. It includes structured, evidence-based, best-practice analysis techniques to help them in their decision-making, resource planning and management, performance evaluations and assessment monitoring. OASys can supply the information needed for appropriate supervision measures when moving offenders within and between communities and prisons.

OASys also helps to assess the likelihood of an offender being reconvicted and the risk of harm he presents both to himself and others, examining factors such as offending history, financial management, relationships, lifestyle and drug abuse. If an offender's assessment identifies any

risk factors, such as violence and substance misuse, or education needs which attract particular attention, where appropriate OASys will trigger the use of further specialist assessments. The OASys programme is designed to reduce reconviction rates and the risk of harm to the public, staff and offenders themselves. This approach to sharing data will ultimately help the police and prison services make better-informed, defensible decisions in managing offenders. It will also help in identifying need for particular interventions in specific areas, and should provide research data in order to produce statistical reports, highlight trends in offending and evaluate the effectiveness of interventions, regimes and work programmes.

CURRENT DIRECTIONS IN FORENSIC PSYCHOLOGY

It seems likely that as the evidence base in forensic psychology practice and research grows, so forensic psychologists will be asked increasingly to provide contributions to criminal and civil justice policy developments. One of these is in the vexed area of falling rape convictions. Although the number of rapes reported to the police has increased steadily, from 6281 in 1997 to 14,449 in 2005–6, the conviction rate has dropped from 9.2 per cent to 5.2 per cent (and was 33 per cent in 1977). Women are already seen as less than credible witnesses in rape cases, with rape trials characterised by attempts to suggest unreliability or poor character. Kelly, Temkin and Griffiths (2006) report how legislation designed to limit evidence about a victim's prior sexual history being presented in court is not working, with almost half of the judges they interviewed not being aware of the legislation, and sexual history material being included in over 75 per cent of cases studied. Among a range of strategies designed to improve the conviction rate is the proposal that expert witnesses, such as forensic psychologists, might be asked to provide evidence for the prosecution (Office for Criminal Justice Reform Consultation Paper 2006).

If these proposals are accepted, forensic psychologists' expert testimony would take the form of dispelling myths and stereotypes concerning how a victim ought to behave, and help a judge and jurors to understand the normal and varied reactions of rape victims. In 2006, any omission, discrepancy or delay in reporting the

offence, or any unbecoming or puzzling behaviour on the part of the victim, is likely to be used by the defence to make him or her appear unreliable or untruthful. However, a forensic psychologist acting as an expert witness will draw on research evidence illustrating how such discrepancies or unpredictable behaviour are part of a pattern of common psychological reactions known as 'rape trauma syndrome', a type of post-traumatic stress disorder which occurs if someone has experienced sexual assault. Examples of such evidence include Garrison (2000), Lonsway (2005) and Temkin (2000).

Forensic psychology is still developing, and its empirical and evidence-based body of knowledge can shed valuable light on a range of psycho-legal issues, but in order to bolster public and political estimates of the value of forensic psychology, academics and practitioners need to work together to demonstrate rigour, reliability and groundedness. Thomas-Peter (2006) warns that forensic psychologists need to ensure that they do not fall prey to an increasingly reactionary and managerialist correctional system, whereby the individual needs of offenders are ignored in a swathe of blanket implementation of treatment programmes and unnecessarily rising numbers of offenders being sent to prison. Instead they should retain their critical and reflective skills and consider the 'bigger picture' – the socio-political context of crime – and the application of theoretically and research-driven psychology within it, namely identifying how and which offenders are best enabled to change within a holistic framework, and then engaging those who are 'ready' in credible intervention.

RECOMMENDED FURTHER READING

Forensic psychology

Adler, J. (ed.) (2004) *Forensic Psychology: Concepts, debates and practice*. Cullompton: Willan Publishing.

Harrower, J. (2001) *Psychology in Practice: Crime*. London: Hodder & Stoughton.

Kapardis, A. (2003) *Psychology and the Law: A critical introduction*. Cambridge: Cambridge University Press.

Towl, G. (ed.) (2006) *Psychological Research in Prisons*. Oxford: Blackwell.

Attitudes to crime and victims

Ainsworth, P. B. (2000) *Psychology and Crime: Myths and reality*. Harlow: Longman.

Offender profiling

Ainsworth, P. B. (2001) *Offender Profiling and Crime Analysis*. Cullompton: Willan Publishing.

Alison, L. J. (2005) *The Forensic Psychologist's Casebook: Psychological profiling and criminal investigation*. Cullompton: Willan Publishing.

Eyewitness testimony

Ainsworth, P. B. (1998) *Psychology, Law and Eyewitness Testimony*. Chichester: Wiley.

Juries

Carson, D. and Bull, R. (eds) (2003) *Handbook of Psychology in Legal Contexts*. Chichester: Wiley.

USEFUL WEBSITES

Centre for Crime and Justice Studies: www.kcl.ac.uk/ccjs

Crime Information Website: www.crimeinfo.org.uk/index.jsp

Home Office (search for the Research and Statistics Directorate to gain access to latest reports and crime figures): www.homeoffice.gov.uk

Smart Justice – unlocking the solutions to crime: www.smartjustice.org/

Exercises

Crime – fact or fiction?

Read the following statements and decide whether each one is true or false:

1. Crime rates have risen in the last ten years.
2. Only 10 per cent of crimes involve violence.
3. The UK murder rate is falling.
4. Fewer offenders are imprisoned compared to five years ago.
5. The rate of child abduction and murder is going up.
6. Women are more likely to be attacked than men.
7. Old people are right to be afraid of crime.
8. Eighteen per cent of men in the UK have a criminal record by the age of 40.
9. Those in the age group 16–24 years are most at risk of becoming murder victims.
10. Women are more likely than men to be convicted of shoplifting.

Answers

1. **False**
   Crime rates have fallen. From 1918 there was an annual rise in crime of about 5 per cent, but in the 1990s the figure started to go down, with a 44 per cent fall between 1995 and 2006. However, although crime rates are said to have fallen (e.g. in 2005–6 both official police data and the British Crime Survey reported a 1 per cent drop in overall crime), these two sources also report big differences in crime, with the police recording 5.6 million crimes per year and the BCS about 11 million. Moreover, the overall figures mask a rise in personal violence and very low conviction rates.

2. **False**
   Only 6 per cent of recorded crimes involve violence, and only 0.01 per cent of these are homicides. Property crime amounts to 78 per cent of crime, according to the BCS and official police data.

3. **True**
   This figure does tend to fluctuate though. For instance, in 1991 there were 725 homicides; in 1999–2000, 766; then in 2002–3 there were 1043, though the main reason for this was Harold Shipman. In 2003–4 there were 853 homicides; in 2004–5, 859; and in 2005–6, a reduction to 765.

4. **False**
   In spite of numerous attempts to persuade magistrates and judges not to send people to prison, between 1980 and 1998 there was a 94 per cent increase in the number of people sent to prison. In 2006 there were 79,094 people in prison in the UK, just short of capacity, with the government planning early release schemes to free up places, and plans to build eight new prisons.

5. **True**
   The figures are rising – child abductions were 196 in 1991; 921 in 2003–4; and 1028 in 2004–5; BUT the rise is mostly due to disputed custody cases rather than stranger abduction. Child murder rates have been stable for some time. About 7 children are murdered each year by strangers, while 60–70 children are killed each year by their parents.

6. **False**
   Men aged 16–24 have a 12.6 per cent risk of becoming the victims of violent crime, by comparison with a 7 per cent risk rate for women of the same age. However, a recent report suggests that young women are particularly vulnerable when they have been drinking – they were found to be more likely to have been involved in an argument (59 per cent, compared to 45 per cent of men) or a fight (11 per cent compared to 9 per cent), and to have been arrested or cautioned by the police (27 per cent compared to 16 per cent) (Report from the Portman Group 2005). Men are more likely to be victims of violence committed by strangers, while women who are attacked are more likely to know their attacker, for instance in cases of domestic violence.

7. **False**
   In spite of what they read in the press or see on TV, older people do not need to be afraid. People under 29 are 13 times more likely to be victims of crime, and women aged 75 and over have only a 0.4 per cent risk of becoming the victims of violence.

8. **False**
   The figure is actually higher – almost 32 per cent of British men have a criminal record for a non-motoring offence by the time they reach the age of 40. One in 60 men will have been convicted of a sex crime by the time they are 40, and 1 in 90 will have been convicted of a serious sex crime. (See Prime et al. 2001).

9. **False**
   Children under the age of 12 months (57 in every million) are four times more likely to be killed than any other age group.

10. **False**
    In spite of the stereotype, more men than

Applied Psychology

women are jailed for shoplifting, and they are older, more organised and steal higher-value goods to order. Women were most likely to steal cosmetics, perfume, clothes, baby-wear and groceries, while men took hairdryers, electric toothbrushes and power tools (Bamfield 2005).

Quizzes from the Crime Information website

Go to each of these sites and you will be presented with the opportunity to test your knowledge of the following crime-related areas, and how you might reach a judgement in two criminal cases:

Crime statistics:
http://www.crimeinfo.org.uk/quiz/quiz.jsp?id=3&reset=
There are quizzes here on data relating to anti-social behaviour, knife crime, terrorism, gun crime, alternatives to custody, the police, serious and organised crime and children in custody.

Crime information:
http://www.crimeinfo.org.uk/quiz/quiz.jsp?id=3&reset=

Judge for yourself:
http://www.crimeinfo.org.uk/servlet/sentencing exerciseservlet?command=visitexercises

➠ A racial assault on a bus driver – you must decide the appropriate sentence.
➠ Parole exercise – you must decide whether John Blank can be released on parole.

Eyewitness testimony

Read the following statements and decide whether each one is true or false:
1 Police officers are more accurate witnesses than ordinary people.
2 Women are more reliable witnesses than men.
3 Reflective individuals will make more accurate identifications than impulsive individuals.
4 Confident witnesses are more likely to be believed.
5 Adults are more reliable witnesses than children.
6 When we see a very dramatic event, such as a violent assault or a road accident, we are more likely to remember what we have seen.

Answers
1 True or false, depending on which research paper you cite.
The jury is out on this one. Ainsworth (1981) found no differences between groups of experienced police officers, novice police officers and a control group of ordinary people in their recall of a staged crime event, but Christianson, Karlsson and Persson (1998) found that experienced police officers were superior in recall and identification of suspects by comparison with students and teachers.
2 True, but…
The police seem to prefer female witnesses, but each gender has potential flaws in recall. Women tend to overestimate the duration of an event, while men are more likely to suffer colour vision deficits and hearing loss. Men and women are more likely to remember details stereotypically associated with their gender.
3 False
In fact, people high on impulsivity make quicker and more accurate identifications in line-ups.
4 True, but…
Unfortunately this does not mean their testimony is likely to be more accurate.
5 True, but…
The very young and the very old are often viewed as less reliable witnesses, and there is evidence to suggest 'cognitive slowing' does occur with ageing, specifically in relation to short-term memory retention. Using the appropriate questioning strategy (e.g. the cognitive interview) with children and older adults, however, can produce more accurate testimony.
6 True, but…
Witnessing a traumatic event can increase recall assurance, but not necessarily accuracy.

Health
Psychology

Health psychology applies psychology to the study of health and illness. Areas that health psychology concerns itself with include the study of how our behaviour makes us ill; how to encourage us to behave in ways that keep us healthy and prevent illness; the impact of hospitals and the health care system on us; and how to cope with stress in our lives. In fact, wherever people interact with the health care system, are affected by their health or affect their health, you will find health psychology. For example, a health psychologist might be interested in:

- how to encourage people to be safe in the sun and to minimise their risk of skin cancer;
- how to help someone adjust to receiving a diagnosis of a terminal illness;
- how best to help and support someone who wants to give up smoking;
- what type of information to give someone to prepare them for heart bypass surgery.

Although physical health and mental health are closely related, health psychology focuses on people who do not primarily have specific mental health problems (such as schizophrenia or depression) or learning difficulties (such as Down's syndrome or brain injury) – these areas are more within the remit of clinical psychology, as discussed in Chapter 2 of this book.

HEALTH PSYCHOLOGY IN THE BRITISH PSYCHOLOGICAL SOCIETY (BPS)

Health psychology within the BPS has grown quickly since its establishment as a Special Group in 1986 and, subsequently, as a Division in 1997. As health psychology within the BPS celebrated its 20th birthday in 2006, there were over 1200 members. The Division has three grades of membership: Full membership for Chartered Health Psychologists; In-training membership for students on accredited postgraduate health psychology courses; and General membership, which is open to those not falling into the other two grades. To be a member of the Division of Health Psychology, you must also be a member of the British Psychological Society.

The Division of Health Psychology has a website which offers more information on its activities (www.health-psychology.org.uk). The Division of Health Psychology liaises closely with the British Psychological Society on key committees, such as the Board of Examiners in Health Psychology, to review and regulate accredited training in health psychology within the UK. It lobbies for the provision of a Department of Health funded training scheme and further development of the professional role of health psychologists. The Division of Health Psychology liaises with the Department of Health and other relevant policymaking bodies which call for consultation and input in relevant areas. All members of the Division of Health Psychology receive a quarterly journal, *Health Psychology Update*. This publishes scientific research within the area of health psychology and topical articles on professional issues. An annual conference is organised each year, which provides a forum for health psychologists to meet and present the latest research and practice.

WHAT DO HEALTH PSYCHOLOGISTS DO?

Health psychologists work in a number of areas. A survey conducted at the end of 2004 by the Division of Health Psychology investigated the diversity of employment of health psychologists within the UK (DHP 2006). Health psychologists were found to work mainly in universities (54 per cent) or NHS settings (39 per cent), with approximately 6 per cent working in other areas, such as the prison service, civil service, charities and research councils.

About half the health psychologists in universities are employed as lecturers and half in a primary research capacity. Health psychology is taught at undergraduate and postgraduate level in universities. All accredited Masters degrees in health psychology and the BPS Stage One qualification in health psychology cover the same

core curriculum, as shown in Box 1. Undergraduate modules in health psychology will usually cover some of these areas. Lecturers tend to take the main responsibility for teaching health psychology, although research staff often contribute specialist lectures. Lecturers are also generally involved in research which may complement and link to their teaching.

Box 1 Core curriculum for Stage One training in health psychology

➡ Context and perspectives in health psychology
➡ Epidemiology of health and illness
➡ Biological mechanisms of health and disease
➡ Health-related behaviour (e.g. theoretical models and behavioural risk factors)
➡ Health-related cognitions (e.g. risk-taking and decision-making)
➡ Individual differences in health and illness (e.g. personality factors)
➡ Stress, health and illness
➡ Long-term conditions/disability
➡ Lifespan, gender and cross-cultural perspectives in health psychology
➡ Health care in professional settings
➡ Applications of health psychology
➡ Research methods
➡ Measurement issues
➡ Professional issues.

Within the NHS, health psychologists are most frequently found in either chronic illness management settings or primary health promotion areas. Chronic illness management settings can include pain clinics and cardiovascular rehabilitation clinics. Health psychologists can be found in any of the areas of health promotion where there are attempts to help people adopt healthier lifestyles, some examples being smoking cessation clinics or healthy eating courses. Within a prison, a health psychologist might organise education courses on healthy lifestyles or work with prisoners on a one-to-one basis. Health psychologists will often be involved in the design and evaluation of health promotion interventions, linking the design to what is known about the best way to motivate people to change their behaviour and teach new skills.

Health psychologists might work with staff in various settings on how best to communicate with their patients or clients on health issues. Health psychologists working in areas of occupational health can help to make the workplace a healthier environment, and help people to deal with the stress of their working lives. This type of work is not limited to health care settings. At a policy level, some health psychologists are involved in planning service provision and making strategy decisions on how best to improve public health, such as how to implement health initiatives. This type of work may be conducted within the NHS, the government, charities or research councils.

A health psychologist might be involved with research based in various settings, including the NHS, universities, private companies and the public sector. Research involves designing studies to investigate theory or issues, collecting and analysing data and usually the dissemination of findings via conferences, published papers or reports. Research can be conducted in any area and will usually fall under one of the core areas listed in Box 1. Research is usually designed to address broad areas of interest determined by those funding the research. Consultancy is similar to research and will often use some of the same techniques for data collection, but often *applies* theory rather than develops it, and will tend to be very focused on the needs of the funder. Examples of consultancy projects might include the evaluation of local initiatives or the design of a health promotion programme. Health psychologists are in demand to conduct this type of work due to their expertise in research methodology and knowledge of relevant techniques and theories. Consultancy projects tend to be designed to answer very specific questions posed by those paying for the research from the public or private sector, such as research councils, charities, drug companies and local primary care trusts.

A day in the life of a health psychologist – smoking cessation advisor

➠ 8.30: Arrive at work in the public health department.

➠ 9.00–10.00: Run a smoking cessation workshop in a nearby clinic. This is the first session of the seven we normally offer and lasts about an hour. In the first session, using a brief questionnaire, we assess people's motivation to quit. If scores indicate that they are not very motivated to quit, we advise them to consider whether they should attend a course at another time when they are more ready to give up smoking. People are less likely to be successful at quitting if they are not ready to quit, for example if they have only come to the course because family members have nagged them, rather than because they want to.

One of the main things to discuss with people early on is the types of withdrawal effects they might expect and how they can deal with them. We discuss if people want to use medication to help them, and, if so, whether they want to use nicotine replacement or Zyban. Zyban is a drug which blocks the action of nicotine in the body, whereas nicotine replacement, as the name suggests, replaces the nicotine that people would get from smoking from a source such as patches or gum. The two would work against each other, so they cannot be used in conjunction with each other. Once people have made their decision, if necessary we will write to their GP stating what is advised and asking the GP to prescribe the medication as the person is attending the smoking cessation service.

Another activity we may do in the first session is to test people's carbon monoxide levels using equipment like a breathalyser. Carbon monoxide is a toxic gas and levels are typically higher in smokers, but quickly decline once they give up. Measuring carbon monoxide levels highlights the reality of the damage caused by smoking and can be very thought-provoking. Ongoing measurements can also provide an excellent means to track progress and keep up people's motivation during the process of quitting.

➠ 10.30: Speak to a practice nurse about a training session I am doing based at their surgery for practice nurses who need to deliver smoking cessation advice. As well as delivering sessions, a smoking cessation advisor may provide supervision and run training sessions for other health professionals who need to run smoking cessation workshops or provide advice. This is a regular part of my job, as all health professionals who deliver smoking cessation advice are required to have training.

➠ 11.30–12.00: One-to-one appointment with someone four weeks into the process of becoming a non-smoker. We offer people the option to attend either one-to-one or group sessions. Individual appointments are usually 20–30 minutes long. At this stage in the process of giving up, we tend to explore specific problems people have encountered, such as weight gain and dealing with difficult situations, such as being out socially and drinking alcohol but not smoking.

➠ 12.00–1.00: Lunch.

➠ 1.00–4.00: Work on updating our smoking cessation leaflets. On a less regular basis there is work to do to promote the service as widely as possible. This may include designing promotional literature and ensuring it is current, and running information days.

➠ 4.00: Put in an application to attend a conference. A health psychologist will attend relevant conferences to ensure they remain up to date with best practice in the field.

➠ 4.30: Telephone call with personnel manager in a local business who is planning a smoking cessation information event for employees. Our smoking cessation courses usually take place in a clinical setting, although we may travel to other settings to run sessions (e.g. in a workplace).

➠ 5.00: Home! Often I run a smoking cessation clinic in the evening or at the weekend, as this is a good time for people who work full-time to attend, but today I am finishing early.

How would I become a health psychologist?

Common to most specialist careers in psychology, the foundation for training is an undergraduate degree or conversion diploma which provides graduate basis for registration (GBR) with the British Psychological Society. This qualification provides general knowledge of psychology on which subsequent, more specialist study will build.

Specialist postgraduate study in health psychology is currently divided into what is known as Stage One and Stage Two training. Both levels of training are required before someone can call themselves a Chartered Health Psychologist. A Chartered Health Psychologist is considered competent to practise independently of supervision.

Stage One training provides in-depth coverage of the theoretical foundation of health psychology. This training is usually provided by an accredited Masters degree in health psychology, although students can also register directly with the British Psychological Society to take the qualifying exams and present a dissertation. A list of courses accredited for providing Stage One training in health psychology can be found on the British Psychological Society website; applicants apply directly to courses they are interested in. In 2006 there were 22 accredited Stage One courses within the UK. A Masters course in health psychology can usually be completed in one year full-time or two years part-time. During this time, students study a range of modules and complete coursework and exams to demonstrate their understanding of the core curriculum (see Box 1),

as well as producing a research dissertation, which is a major project in an area related to health psychology.

Stage Two training in health psychology focuses on more practical skills. Trainees are required to demonstrate their competency in relation to four core areas: professional development, teaching, research and consultancy; and then two other areas which they can select from a range of options. Optional competencies include providing psychological advice to aid policy decision-making for the implementation of psychological services; direction of the implementation of interventions; or contributing to the evolution of legal, ethical and professional standards in health and applied psychology.

Stage Two university courses are composed of modules which relate to the competencies just described; trainees complete assessments for these modules, which enable them to demonstrate their competencies. These normally lead to a qualification at doctorate level.

In 2006 there were six Stage Two university courses within the UK. A list of all accredited Stage Two courses can be found on the BPS website. A Stage Two university course usually lasts for two years full-time or can be completed part-time in up to five years.

Alternatively, trainees can register for the independent route of Stage Two training with a single supervisor. In conjunction with their supervisor, the student must submit a detailed plan as to how they will collate evidence of their Stage Two competencies. The supervisor must be a Chartered Health Psychologist and must also be registered as a trained supervisor. Over the two or so years of Stage Two training, the trainee and supervisor meet so that the trainee receives ongoing advice and support. During this time, the trainee will normally be employed within one or more settings which enable them to practise health psychology, such as a research setting or direct clinical care. The trainee is required to demonstrate that they have met the competencies by providing evidence such as lesson plans, consultancy contracts, a practice and supervision log, funding applications and publishable papers, as appropriate. Trainees also have a viva voce examination where they are asked questions about their evidence and supervised practice. Stage Two trainees are registered for a minimum of two years and must normally complete within five years.

DEVELOPMENT OF HEALTH PSYCHOLOGY

Health psychology first came into use as a term in the late 1970s. One of the earliest and best regarded definitions of the scope of health psychology was that given by J. D. Matarazzo in 1982. Many regard him as the grandfather of health psychology. Matarazzo (1982: 4) defined health psychology as follows:

> Health psychology is the aggregate of the specific educational, scientific and professional contributions of the discipline of psychology to the promotion and maintenance of health, the prevention and treatment of illness, the identification of aetiological and diagnostic correlates of health, illness and related dysfunction and to the analysis of improvement of the health care system and health policy formation.

Although this definition has been criticised as being too all-encompassing, it has been adopted by the professional associations of Health Psychology in both the UK and the USA.

As we have seen here, health psychologists are interested in almost all areas of life that are related to health, but defining health itself is more tricky! One commonly cited definition of health is that given by the World Health Organization (WHO) in 1948: 'the state of complete physical, social and spiritual well-being, not simply the absence of illness'. This definition emphasises that health should not be considered the opposite of illness, and highlights the multidimensional nature of health. Some people feel that this wide definition of health makes it unattainable for many people.

Box 2 Defining 'health'

How do you define the terms 'healthy', 'ill', 'disabled' and 'injured'? Which of the following people do you consider to be ill?

➡ A person currently suffering with a cold.
➡ A person with depression.
➡ Someone who is unhappy.
➡ A person with cancer in remission.
➡ An elderly person with Alzheimer's disease.
➡ Someone who has just been injured in a car crash.
➡ A person who is paralysed from the waist down.

Do your conclusions agree with the WHO definition of health?

To understand the development of health psychology, it is important to appreciate the history of how the causes of ill health have been understood (and how this understanding has changed) over time. Some of the earliest and most dominant theories of health and illness were those of the Greek scholars, the most famous of whom were Galen and Hippocrates. Their theories suggested that health and personality were dependent on the balance of four types of fluids within the body, called 'humours'. Disease occurred when something caused an imbalance in the fluid levels, such as extremes of heat or cold, the type of food consumed or exhaustion. Treatments to restore your bodily balance concentrated on redressing any imbalance, perhaps through bloodletting or using poultices to draw out poisons, or purges to induce vomiting. The humoral theory remained dominant until the fall of the Roman Empire, when Europe entered the era referred to as the Dark Ages (*c.* AD 500–1100). At this time, the Church was the dominant power, and religious explanations for health and illness, such as demons and malign spirits or curses, were blamed as the cause of illness. Treatments were often designed to drive the 'evil' out of the body.

It was not until the time of the Renaissance (fourteenth to sixteenth centuries) that medical understanding began to advance towards what seems familiar to us today. With the development of the microscope in the seventeenth century, came the ability to see some of the previously unknown disease organisms. Being able to isolate and see disease organisms for the first time revolutionised thinking on disease causation and led to the widespread rejection of previous theories based on the humours or on religion. Much of this was formalised in 1864, when Pasteur developed his germ theory which established how micro-organisms cause illness. Once germ theory was established, it was clear why hygienic practices such as washing hands and surgical instruments were so important in health care settings, and once hygienic practices were put in place, deaths from surgery and childbirth declined dramatically. The understanding of how germs cause illnesses was also applied in many public health initiatives to provide clean water, sanitation and improvements to diet. The development of successful vaccination programmes and antibiotics in the early twentieth century also made a massive difference to public health and led to a reduction in rates of infectious illness.

On the wave of this increased understanding of the causes of illness and subsequent medical and public health initiatives, came a dramatic increase in life expectancy. If we look back to the start of the twentieth century, one in three babies born in the UK could expect to die before the age of 5 years and only a quarter of the population lived to 65 years. This can be compared to the end of the twentieth century, when less than 1 per cent of the UK population would die before age 5, and almost 85 per cent of people lived past the age of 65. The main causes of death and illness at the start of the twentieth century were infectious and respiratory conditions, such as tuberculosis, influenza and food poisoning. By the mid twentieth century, the proportion of deaths due to infectious and respiratory conditions had declined dramatically and it seemed as if infectious disease would soon be wiped out. In fact, in the United States in 1969, the surgeon general commented that we could soon expect to 'close the book on infectious disease'. These advances in medical understanding, coupled with the huge improvements in life expectancy and the decrease in infectious illness rates, led to the general acceptance of what is termed the *biomedical model*, by which disease is attributed to physical disorders. It was an age of great optimism regarding the power of biomedicine and, by extension, the biomedical model. However, while deaths from infectious illnesses were on the decline, new killers were stepping into the limelight.

The diseases that took over as a cause of death and ill health were chronic conditions. For example, in 1950, half of all deaths were due to circulatory conditions, and the proportion of deaths from cancer had also increased. Initially it was thought that these chronic conditions were purely the result of the body breaking down in old age. Lester Breslow (1998: 2), a leading public health specialist, commented that at the time the prevailing view was that 'the population was aging and older people's health simply "degenerated"; thus they would inevitably suffer "degenerative diseases"'. Despite the feeling that these conditions were inevitable, a number of large-scale epidemiological studies were set up to investigate more fully factors associated with the development of chronic conditions. These studies often followed thousands of individuals over many decades, and involved repeated waves of data collection to see how biological and lifestyle factors impacted on life expectancy and health status.

The results of these studies began to be published in the late 1970s and it was at this time that the field of health psychology was born, as it became apparent that the causes of ill health were more complicated than the biomedical model suggested. One of the key findings was the recognition that many of the risk factors for these conditions were related to people's behaviour and social conditions. Disease was not inevitable and lifestyle had a large part to play in who stayed well and who became ill. For example, before the landmark study of Doll and Hill was published in 1950, it was not clear that there was any link between smoking and the development of lung cancer. Today we know that approximately 90 per cent of all lung cancer cases are related to smoking, and the thought that we were previously unaware of this risk is almost unbelievable.

Another classic study highlighting the link between lifestyle and health was that of Belloc and Breslow (1972). They examined the impact of seven different health behaviours on the risk of death in a sample of more than 7000 people living in Alameda County in California, in the USA. They found that over the course of their study, people following six or seven of the health behaviours had half the risk of dying early compared to those following three or fewer health behaviours.

Box 3 Belloc and Breslow's seven health behaviours – what's your score?

How many of the following health behaviours do you practise?

➡ Remain at a healthy weight for your height.
➡ Do not smoke.
➡ Moderate or no use of alcohol.
➡ Get regular exercise.
➡ Eat breakfast on a regular basis.
➡ Get a good night's sleep.
➡ Do not eat between meals.

Would you be prepared to change your behaviour if it might increase your lifespan?

The recognition that behavioural factors influence the likelihood of developing an illness led to the development of a field of study called *behavioural medicine*, which studies the impact of behaviour on health. This recognition was also important for the development of health psychology. Whereas risk factors such as age, gender or genes cannot be changed, there is potential scope for changing people's behaviour, and therefore their risk of ill health, if the best ways to motivate people to change can be understood.

An initial approach within behavioural medicine, inherited by health psychology, was very much to take the view that individuals are primarily responsible for the choices they make in their behaviour. Knowles (1977: 58) stated that 'over 99 percent of us are born healthy and made sick as a result of personal misbehaviour and environmental conditions'. He went on to add: 'the solution to the problems of ill health … involves individual responsibility, in the first instance, and social responsibility through public legislature and private volunteer efforts, in the second instance'. These harsh words emphasise the victim-blaming approach which characterised some of the early health psychology research. Health psychology has flourished particularly within countries with an individualist rather than a collectivist approach. An individualist society values concepts such as individual responsibility and doing things for oneself, whereas a collectivist society tends to value and encourage social responsibility and, especially, duty to family. As health psychology has developed as a discipline, it has moved away from its behavioural medicine roots; it has recognised increasingly that people do not always have complete freewill to make decisions about their health behaviour, and has also focused on the influence of the environment on health – both directly and by constraining behavioural choices.

In addition to behavioural factors, the social environment was recognised as influencing our health. Berkman and Syme (1979) used the same Alameda sample as in Belloc and Breslow's health behaviours study described above. At the start of the study, the research participants were surveyed to establish their social network characteristics. The types of relationships Berkman and Syme recorded were: marriage, contact with close friends or relatives, church membership, and membership of formal or informal groups such as recreational or social clubs. After taking into account other important influences on health, such as existing illnesses and health behaviours, there was a clear pattern that those who had more developed social networks were much more likely to be alive at follow-up.

The link between psychological factors and health came to prominence in the early twentieth century with the development of psychosomatic medicine. Freud was one of the key thinkers in this area and popularised the notion that mental distress could itself result in physical disorders without the involvement of bacteria or viruses. Although controversial, the work of Freud and others also changed thinking on the causes of illness.

Much of the thinking on the wider determinants of health was crystallised in an article by Engel (1977). Engel's article strongly challenged the dominance of the biomedical model in terms of explaining health and illness. Engel argued that the biomedical model was too limited in considering only the biological causes of illness. Engel proposed that health could best be understood using a *biopsychosocial* model of health, where explanations took account of biological, psychological *and* social factors. This appreciation of a wider range of determinants of health is at the foundation of health psychology.

The continued growth of health psychology as a discipline can be attributed in part to ongoing developments in medical technology. These developments mean that new medical procedures become available, some of which are so novel that there are many unanswered questions surrounding how best to treat patients. For example, health psychologists have been asked to advise on the issue of face transplant surgery – how best to prepare the patient for this procedure; and how to encourage potential patients to persist with what may be lifesaving but uncomfortable treatments.

Scientists have also made great advances in their ability to read the genetic code and, for a limited number of conditions, can now provide genetic tests which can, with varying degrees of certainty, enable people to predict their likely future health and their susceptibility to certain conditions. Health psychologists can assist in the presentation of this information and help people to manage the knowledge.

The cost of health care also provides great impetus to the work of health psychologists. The UK National Health Service was established in 1948. It was designed to be able to provide care free at the point of delivery from cradle to grave. However, spending on the NHS has mushroomed over the years. Sidestepping the debates surrounding what should or should not be funded, one thing is clear: the NHS will never receive sufficient funding to be able to provide all requested treatments. These demands on funding mean that there is a strong pressure to ensure that people use the NHS in the most efficient manner, and that use of the health service is avoided through preventative means wherever possible. How you motivate people to curb their unhealthy behaviour and follow a more healthy lifestyle is still the subject of much research within health psychology.

Another consequence of the change in patterns of health is a massive increase in the number of people who live many years of their lives with chronic health conditions, such as diabetes or HIV, or disabilities, such as an amputation or deafness. Providing care for people with chronic conditions and disabilities accounts for a large percentage of the costs of the health service, and living with such a condition can impact significantly on a person's quality of life. Health psychologists play a key role in the study of how people cope with chronic illness or disability, and how best they can be helped to live fulfilling lives and minimise their reliance on the health service.

Finally, our role as patients has also changed. The model of health care suggested by the biomedical model was very much one in which the doctor is in control. Since 1998, in the UK, people have had the right to see their medical records, although some parts can be withheld if a health care professional feels the information may cause serious harm. Whereas 'doctor's orders' used to mean just that, paternalistic models of health care are now out of favour, and today's health care consumer expects a more balanced and equal partnership with their health care provider. We know that people do not always take medicines as prescribed and may deliberately vary their treatment, even though this causes a great deal of waste to the health service and the loss of therapeutic benefit for patients. Our expectations of when and how to access health care have also changed – sometimes in ways that mean increased cost. Government policy emphasises the role of choice within the health care system. Health psychologists research the impact of the health service on us as patients and how the health service can best provide an efficient service.

PRINCIPLES OF HEALTH PSYCHOLOGY

Health psychology takes a biopsychosocial approach to the study of health and illness. A biopsychosocial approach acknowledges that there are wider influences on health than merely biological ones, with behavioural, psychological and social factors all being important. This contrasts with a pure biomedical model, which only takes into account the most direct biological causes, such as disturbed physical functioning or infection. For example, if a person develops lung cancer, within the biomedical model the cause of this would be identified as the genetic mutation which causes the cell reproduction to become cancerous in nature. A biopsychosocial approach, however, would also consider as causal factors of the disease such behaviour as heavy, lifelong smoking, a social background in which smoking is the norm, low self-confidence in ability to give up and a coping strategy of using cigarettes to relax. Thus a biopsychosocial model takes a broader perspective on causal factors of disease.

In contrast to biological and genetic factors, which we cannot control, another principle of health psychology is that behavioural, psychological and social factors can be modified, and are therefore worthy of study in an effort to increase health and reduce experience of illness. To a certain extent, this recognises the role of the individual as having some responsibility for their own actions and lifestyle, although, as noted above, it can be argued that some circumstances beyond our control often limit behavioural choices.

Kurt Lewin (1951: 169) famously stated: 'there is nothing so practical as a good theory'. Health psychology, at its roots, is a theory-based discipline. Health psychology takes an evidence-based research stance to the investigation of problems. This involves the development of testable hypotheses, collection of data and theory development.

RESEARCH, THEORY AND APPLICATIONS

With all the interesting questions that are raised, it is not surprising that health psychology is an area heavily underpinned by research. The next section considers applications of health psychology research and theory to: understanding and changing health behaviours; stress and its relationship to health; our interaction with the health care system; and the care and support of people with long-term conditions or disabilities.

Understanding and changing health behaviour

Health behaviours

A number of health behaviours are known to have a negative impact on health. Some of the key health risk behaviours in the UK are: smoking, excessive alcohol consumption, poor diet, lack of exercise and risky sexual practices. Smoking is currently the most influential behaviour on health. It is estimated that half of all lifetime smokers will die prematurely because of their habit, although the risks do decline if smoking is given up (Doll et al. 2004). Following the health risks of smoking in magnitude are the risks of being obese: cardiovascular disease, cancer and arthritis, to name but a few. Obesity is related to poor diet and excessive consumption of calories relative to levels of physical activity. In the UK, our relationship with alcohol is also becoming more problematic as time goes on. Excessive alcohol consumption can have immediate health effects. For example, one in six deaths on UK roads is alcohol related, and one in six people attending Accident and Emergency departments has alcohol-related injuries or problems. Over the longer term, alcohol is related to liver disease, cancers within the digestive system and cardiovascular disease. The UK record with regard to sexual health is no better! We have the unenviable position of having the highest teenage pregnancy rates in Europe (in 2006); and the rates of sexually transmitted infections doubled between 1991 and 2001.

Despite these obvious risks, many people continue to engage in unhealthy behaviours. Much of the information we have on health status and health behaviours comes from large-scale surveys undertaken by the Office for National Statistics (ONS). You can see more information on health statistics on the ONS website (www.statistics.gov.uk). From ONS surveys, we know that approximately 25 per cent of the UK population smokes. Among the younger age groups (up to 19 years) more females than males smoke, but in older age groups the pattern is reversed. Government surveys show that almost three-quarters of smokers say that they would like to be able to give up, and each year over half a million people access NHS stop smoking services. The percentage of obese people within the UK increased dramatically over the latter part of the twentieth century, with 23 per cent of the adult population and 17 per cent of children categorised as obese in 2004. Analysis of lifestyle changes over the same time period suggests that this increase is primarily due to more people having a sedentary lifestyle. ONS surveys document that almost one in three UK adults exceeds the recommended safe daily drinking guidelines each week. Rates of binge drinking are highest in the younger age groups, and rates for girls are approaching rates for boys. High and increasing rates of sexually transmitted infections and unplanned pregnancies are a direct result of the significant number of people who engage in risky sexual behaviour. In the UK, the average age of first sexual intercourse is 16 years. Approximately 40 per cent of young people aged 15–16 years, 29 per cent of those aged14–15 years and 14 per cent of those aged 13–14 years are sexually active, and approximately half report risk behaviours of not using condoms or other forms of contraception at every intercourse (Wallace et al. 2007).

One key area of health psychology research is the study of what motivates us to engage in healthy and unhealthy behaviour, and how we can be motivated to behave in a manner more likely to keep us healthy. Health psychologists are in demand to help people adopt healthier behaviours in many different ways, including motivating people to give up smoking, drink alcohol sensibly, take more exercise, eat a healthier diet and engage in safer sexual behaviours.

Box 4 Obesity – a problem even after death

In October 2006, the National Society of Allied and Independent Funeral Directors reported that the increasing number of obese clients was leading to a decline in the number of funerals where pall-bearers were able to carry the coffin.

Health behaviours are, to some extent, like any other behaviours, and it should be no surprise that health psychology has drawn heavily on general theories of behaviour to understand health behaviour. The major theoretical approaches in psychology are described more fully in Chapter 10. It may be useful to review that material in order to provide a background to the approaches taken in health psychology to understanding and changing health behaviour.

Behaviourist approach

Classical conditioning

Classical conditioning can be used to explain some of our health behaviour. For example, classical conditioning explains how someone might develop a phobia of going for health checks from a single bad experience in childhood at the doctor's. This may have serious implications for their future health if it makes them reluctant to seek help when they need it. Classical conditioning can also explain how people develop conditioned responses when one event comes to reliably predict another. Often people turn to eating to act as a comfort. In these cases, food that has repeatedly been paired with affection in the past, comes to trigger the same feelings of comfort. Classical conditioning processes explain why it can be difficult to change health behaviours, as our environment may cue our unhealthy behaviours. For example, the pleasures of smoking become paired with many other daily activities. Repeated reminders of the circumstances in which they used to have a cigarette (e.g. on a coffee break, when walking to work, after a meal or after a row at home) might explain why so many people find it hard to break bad health habits.

Health psychologists use the understanding of how classical conditioning affects behaviour to design interventions to help people change their behaviour. Two commonly used interventions which rely on classical conditioning to break bad health habits are *stimulus control* and *response substitution*. People who are trying to change health behaviours are often recommended to avoid situations in which the problem behaviours usually occur. Smokers might be advised to avoid the situations which they associate with smoking (e.g. coffee at break-times, relaxing after a meal, socialising in the pub). People who overeat are advised to remove snack foods from their home, and to avoid eating out or spending too long shopping for food. This technique is called *stimulus control*, as you are controlling the environmental stimuli which cue the behaviour. *Response substitution* involves finding more suitable alternatives for problem behaviours that are automatically cued. People who smoke because they were cued by needing to do something with their hands can be encouraged to carry dummy cigarettes; those who seek oral gratification can be encouraged to carry chewing gum or sweets. Overeaters can be encouraged to keep a stock of healthy, low-calorie snacks.

Operant conditioning

Operant conditioning describes a process of learning which occurs by trial and error and is dependent on the environmental response to the behaviour, rather than the environmental cues in classical conditioning. Operant conditioning processes explain how our environment rewards and punishes us for our behaviour. For example, a teenager who starts to smoke may gain social approval from their peers; they may also avoid being teased (i.e. punishment) for refusing a cigarette. This combination of positive reinforcement for the smoking behaviour and punishment for not smoking leads to the establishment of the behaviour.

Health psychologists can also use operant conditioning principles to help change behaviour. Charges levied by health care providers for missed appointments, for example, can be seen as an intervention using the operant conditioning principles of punishment. Contingency contracting is another technique, where people are encouraged to set themselves goals and agree to pay a 'fine' if they do not stick to the desired behaviour. Generally, however, punishments and negative consequences are not as powerful as rewards and positive outcomes in changing behaviour. Rewards can be used to positively reinforce healthful behaviours. For example, patients may be given monetary incentives to increase adherence to treatment regimes or attendance at clinics.

Social learning theory

Social learning theory is also important in explaining various health behaviours. For example, young adults who see adults smoking are far more likely to smoke themselves, especially if they see the behaviour associated with other desirable features, such as being grown up, rebellious or desirable to sexual partners. Likewise we can provide good examples to children that may encourage them to act in a healthy manner. Provision of a positive example of a person coping successfully with a medical procedure can be useful in helping people to prepare themselves for the same medical procedure, and in reducing anxiety. Again, these techniques are particularly useful for children

(Justus et al. 2006). The involvement of celebrities endorsing health behaviours works on the social learning principle that people will take more notice of the message if they admire the person giving it and aspire to be like them. For example, Robbie Williams has been involved in a campaign endorsing testicular self-examination and many celebrities have been seen in adverts highlighting the value of blood donation.

Cognitive theories of health behaviour

Another way in which health psychologists can understand factors which might determine health behaviours is to describe the thought processes which might be going on in someone's mind as they think about health behaviours. Some commonly used cognitive models of health behaviour are described below: the *health belief model*, the *theory of planned behaviour* and the *transtheoretical model*.

Health belief model

The *health belief model* was originally developed to explain attendance at tuberculosis x-ray screening sessions (Hochbaum 1958). Those who believed that tuberculosis was very severe, that they were susceptible to developing the condition, that x-ray screening was beneficial in early detection and who perceived few barriers to attending the screening session were most likely to attend. Formalising the health belief model, Becker (1974) suggested that our likelihood of engaging in a health behaviour is determined by our perceptions of the threat to our health related to the behaviour and a costs-benefits analysis. Our perceptions of threat are determined by how susceptible we feel we are to the consequences of not taking action and how severe these consequences are seen to be. Our costs-benefits analysis takes into account the barriers to action and whether the effort and other costs of taking action outweigh our perception of its benefits. Health behaviours can also be cued by external factors, such as a reminder from the dentist that our check-up is due, or from internal factors, such as a pain or loss of physical function. A later formulation of the model also included health motivation (i.e. how concerned we are about health) as a factor determining likelihood to engage in health behaviour.

The health belief model has since been applied to a variety of health behaviours (Abraham and

Sheeran 2005). It has had its greatest success in predicting behaviours which occur once or over a short period of time (e.g. immunisation or attending screening), and has been less successful in predicting longer-term behaviours, such as successfully dieting and establishing an exercise routine, or behaviours with strong social influences, such as consistent use of condoms. The most important predictor of the likelihood of health behaviour seems to be perceived barriers, followed by susceptibility, benefits and severity. Relatively little research has been conducted on the effects of cues to action or health motivation.

Box 5 The health belief model

Dear Parent (as addressed)
Council records indicate that _____ is overdue for the following vaccination:
TRIPLE ANTIGEN 1st 2nd 3rd CDT
POLIOMYELITIS 1st 2nd 3rd 4th
MEASLES TRIPLE ANTIGEN BOOSTER
Please present your child with this card for vaccination at the Lower Civic Hall at ___ p.m. on _____.

If you are unable to attend or wish to change the appointment date, or you do not wish to continue, are continuing elsewhere or changing address, please contact the HEALTH DEPARTMENT, TOWN HALL, STURT STREET, BALLARAT. PHONE: 313 277

Dear Mrs Quinn
MEASLES is still a problem in Ballarat, particularly for children under the age of 2 years. Some children suffer severe complications. The children who are most likely to catch measles are those who have not been immunised. Immunisation is very effective. There is almost no chance of side effects. Clinics are held at the Lower Civic Hall in Mair Street from 2 to 3.40 p.m. EVERY SECOND WEDNESDAY. Immunisations are given by a doctor. Of course, immunisation is free!
The next clinic is on Wednesday 14 December. If GEORGIA is not yet immunised against measles, you should bring her along.
Regards
Bob Scurry
Health Department
Enquiries ph 313 277

The standard reminder card is shown first, followed by the reworded card. Can you see how elements of the health belief model were incorporated?
(Adapted from Hawe, McKenzie and Scurry 1998).

The health belief model has also been used to design interventions aimed at promoting healthier behaviour. A study by Hawe, McKenzie and Scurry (1998) investigated the impact of using the health belief model to inform the design of reminder cards to prompt parents about the need for measles vaccinations for their children. The study was based in the Australian city of Ballarat. Parents whose child was due for their first measles vaccination were sent either a standard postal reminder card or one based on the health belief model (see Box 5). Of those parents who got the standard reminder, 67 per cent took their child to be vaccinated. This was significantly less than the 79 per cent of parents who received the reminder card based on the health belief model.

The health belief model suggests that those with a greater belief in their susceptibility are more likely to take protective health actions. However, it has been recognised that, in general, people are not always rational and tend to underestimate their actual susceptibility to illness – the 'I never thought it would happen to me' factor. Weinstein (1984) has carried out research which highlights how people are unrealistically optimistic about their susceptibility to various health problems. This may be due to:

➧ lack of experience with the problem;
➧ belief in their ability to control or offset the risk;
➧ belief that if it hasn't happened, it won't happen;
➧ belief that the problem is infrequent.

Personal contact with someone who has experienced the same health problem may counteract some of these non-rational beliefs.

Behaviour will not always be rational and considered if people do not have or take time to think clearly. It is likely that some behaviours happen automatically or with little thought – such as habitual behaviours which are carried out with little conscious deliberation. In addition, people may not always be able to think logically. For example, people under the influence of alcohol or other drugs may have impaired judgement.

One application of the health belief model to health promotion is in the design of campaigns to induce fear of the consequences of health behaviours that are to be changed. The application of this can be seen in increasingly hard-hitting health promotion campaigns, such as the campaign launched in November 2006 about the dangers of binge drinking, featuring a woman lying naked and drunk in a road having been raped, and a man falling from scaffolding having tried to act like a superhero while drunk. According to the health belief model, increasing someone's perception of threat should have the effect of increasing their likelihood of performing health-protective behaviours. This has been dubbed the 'deterrence-by-horrible-example' theory (Stuteville 1970: 39). Original analyses suggested that the effects of fear in motivating behaviour could be relatively short-lived, and that fear may produce feelings of helplessness where even low levels of protective behaviour are abandoned or cause people to avoid seeking information about the health risk (ibid.). More recent synthesis of a wider body of research suggests that in general there is *not* a point at which increased fear tips into inaction (Witte and Allen 2000). However, it is critical when using fear to motivate behaviour change to also encourage self-confidence that the person can do something effective to reduce the threat.

Theory of planned behaviour

A second model, the *theory of planned behaviour* developed by Ajzen (1991), is one of the most commonly used models of health behaviour, although it has its origins in more general social psychology models. It is derived from an earlier formulation called the *theory of reasoned action*. It has certain advantages over the health belief model in that the social environment is given prominence in its ability to influence our behaviour. It still shares some of the same disadvantages of all cognitive models, however, in that it also assumes that people make rational and considered decisions about their health.

The theory of planned behaviour focuses on the thought processes which lead to a person intending to behave in a certain way. The model suggests that our intention to act is informed by three key factors:

➠ *Attitudes*: how we feel about engaging in the behaviour – do we think that to do so would be good or bad, worthwhile or a waste of time, and so on?
➠ *Social norms*: the social pressure on us to behave in a certain manner from our family, peers and other people whose opinion we value.
➠ *Perceived behavioural control*: whether we feel confident that our current skills and resources will enable us to complete the behaviour or whether external barriers may intervene.

The theory of planned behaviour has been particularly successful in predicting behaviours such as smoking, alcohol consumption and exercise. The perceived behavioural control – and a related concept of self-efficacy, which refers to our feeling of being able to take effective action – has been particularly useful in the prediction of health behaviours. Considering many studies, the factors within the theory of planned behaviour can explain about 60 per cent of the variability in our intentions (Armitage and Conner 2001).

There are problems with the theory of planned behaviour though. As this model was developed as a general model of behaviour, it does not have any specific references to health values, as the health belief model does. A number of commentators have suggested additional factors that may need to be taken into account. In particular, the model considers only cognitive determinants of attitudes and beliefs. One of the most promising 'extra' variables is that of 'anticipated regret', which relates to the strength of emotional disappointment which may occur if the intended behaviour is not completed (Richard, Van der Pligt and de Vries 1995).

The theory of planned behaviour and the health belief model also only relate to the motivational stage, or intention-formation stage, and do not address what can be termed the action stage, which relates to the translation of intention into behaviour. Research has revealed that even when intention is high, people do not always follow through with the intended behaviour (Conner and Sparkes 2005). Further analysis by Webb and Sheeran (2006) demonstrates that in various studies which have successfully increased intention, the impact on behaviour has been more modest. It is said that 'the road to hell is paved with good intentions', and good intentions, unfortunately, are not enough to ensure good behaviours!

Much research has investigated what is known as the intention–behaviour gap. One of the most promising strands appears to be that of *implementation intentions* (Gollwitzer and Schaal 1998). Asking someone to make an implementation intention requires them to make a specific plan as to when and where they will carry out the behaviour. The theory is that when in that situation, the person will be cued to carry out the behaviour. For example, Kellar and Abraham (2005) found that psychology undergraduates who had been asked to plan specifically where and when they would buy fruit and vegetables, and plan meals that included fruit and vegetables for their lunch and evening meals, ate significantly more fruit and vegetables in the week following the plan making than students who did not make these specific plans. Similar effects have been found for a range of other health behaviours, including increasing levels of exercise, breast self-examination and consumption of vitamins (Sheeran et al. 2005).

Transtheoretical model

Another very popular model of health behaviour change combines the motivational and action stages within the one model. The *transtheoretical model*, or *stages of change model*, as it is also known, was developed by psychologists James Prochaska and Carlo DiClemente in the early 1980s. It proposes five stages through which people move in the process of engaging in a health behaviour:

- *Pre-contemplation*: At this stage of the change process, the person is not thinking about the behaviour change and typically states they would not be likely to make any change in the behaviour for at least six months.
- *Contemplation*: By this stage, the person has developed some attitudes and beliefs concerning the behaviour, although they are not committed to taking any action. At this stage, people may weigh up the pros and cons of changing their behaviour.
- *Preparation*: People in the preparation stage may intend to change their behaviour in the next few months. They have already made some small changes (e.g. changing to a lower tar brand of cigarettes, although you would not classify them as having given up).
- *Action*: At this stage, people obviously modify their behaviour to an extent which has a significant impact on their health risks (e.g. give up cigarettes, abstain from alcohol or commence an exercise programme).

- *Maintenance*: Maintenance can be seen as an active stage where the individual has sustained their action over the long-term (usually longer than six months).

Progression through the stages is not necessarily linear, and people may relapse from one stage to an earlier one. For example, research by Prochaska, DeClemente and Norcross (1992) on smoking found that, when trying to give up, smokers need three to four action attempts to become non-smokers, with about 15 per cent of those who relapse going back to the pre-contemplation stage, and 85 per cent to the contemplation or preparation stages.

The model is also known as the transtheoretical model because it was an attempt to integrate understanding of the factors which motivate the process of change from a number of theoretical perspectives, such as cognitive and behavioural approaches. Prochaska and his colleagues determined that there are ten processes which can help to move people from stage to stage of the model. These were subdivided into what are called the experiential processes, which help a person to progress through the early stages of change to make a decision to change; and behavioural processes, which are used in the later stages of change to maintain new behaviour. For example, to help move people from the pre-contemplation to the contemplation stage, it is suggested that consciousness-raising be used. This process helps the person to recognise the need to change their behaviour through consideration of the pros and cons. This tactic is not so useful to people who have already changed their behaviour, but once someone has made a commitment to change, learning tactics to help avoid situations where you might encounter temptation to engage in the bad behaviour will help people to maintain their new behaviour.

According to the transtheoretical model, a person will be most likely to be successful in their health action when they:
1 have reached the preparation stage, having weighed up the pros and cons of their current behaviour;
2 believe in their own ability to make a change;
3 change with the support of family and friends;
4 are able to avoid cues to the previous unhealthy behaviours;

5 are able to find rewarding alternative behaviours;
6 are rewarded by themselves and others for maintaining the change.

The model was originally devised to account for behaviour in terminating behavioural addictions, such as smoking, drug abuse and alcoholism, and it traces it roots back to clinical psychology. It has been applied to a wide variety of behaviours, however, including contraceptive use, breastfeeding and mammography screening. Understanding the stages of change can help to target health promotion campaigns at people who are ready to make a change. Taking a transtheoretical approach to changing health behaviour suggests that different interventions may be useful for people at different stages of change. This model also has advantages over the health belief model and the theory of planned behaviour, in that the processes which motivate change are clearly specified. Critics (e.g. Sutton 2005), however, have argued that the stages described do not actually represent clear-cut, distinct stages with their own characteristics, but rather vary only in the degree to which the processes are used.

Figure 7.1 Food Standards Agency advertisement – Sid the slug

Figure 7.2 Food Standards Agency website
Source: http://www.salt.gov.uk/tv_ads.shtml

Box 6 Sid the slug health promotion campaign

In September 2004, the UK Food Standards Agency launched a health promotion campaign to increase understanding of the health risks of excess salt in the diet. At the time the campaign was introduced, the health risks of excessive salt intake were not widely known by the general public. The advert where Sid is complaining how bad salt is for his heart is a good example of an advert just designed to raise awareness about an issue, but it does not really encourage any particular health action. This type of advertisement would be most useful to people in the pre-contemplation stage. It can be seen as consciousness-raising as it highlights the dangers of salt. There are no specific recommendations for action; the goal is just to get people thinking about the behaviour – in this case, salt consumption. A second wave of advertisements was introduced in October 2005. These depicted food packets comparing their labels and salt content with each other. They were aimed at encouraging a specific change in behaviour, that of people becoming more aware of labels and how to interpret labels regarding the salt content of foods.

Some of the problems with the transtheoretical model may account for the less than consistent success rates of health promotion programmes based on it. For example, computer programs can be used to determine which stage of change a person is currently in and, therefore, which processes of change they might be receptive to. Information can then be given which matches the stage of change. Analysis of research evidence, however, suggests that health promotion programmes that are matched to the recipient's stage of change are no more successful than those which do not vary their approach (e.g. Bridle et al. 2005).

At an individual level, a one-to-one counselling method called *motivational interviewing* (Miller and Rollnick 2002) can be used to understand someone's current position with regard to changing their behaviour. This is a counselling technique which helps clients to explore their feelings towards their behaviours and, through this process, to find their own intrinsic motivation to change. Motivational interviewing has been widely used within clinical and counselling psychology, and has a strong history of use within the field of substance misuse and addiction. More recently, however, there appears to be some promising evidence of the usefulness of motivational interviewing within physical health settings, such as helping patients to stick with hypertensive medication, or assisting people waiting for coronary artery bypass surgery to make lifestyle changes (Knight et al. 2006).

With their knowledge of methods and theories of behaviour change, health psychologists are well placed to contribute to the design of health promotion interventions. Many health promotion interventions are designed with only tenuous links or no explicit links to theory (Michie and Abraham 2004). An explicit theory is important as it allows the designer to identify how and why their intervention should change the factors they are interested in. For example, a change in behaviour might be hypothesised to occur because of a change in attitudes or self-confidence. The most appropriate methods to change these intermediate factors can then be selected and their success monitored. All too often, health promotion interventions are designed without clearly explaining or understanding the factors which need to be changed, and without specifying which aspects of the intervention are to address each factor. In these cases, if the intervention is successful, it is not clear why it has worked and, therefore, which aspects should be repeated. Alternatively, if it is not successful, it is not clear why not and, therefore, what should be changed.

Intervention mapping is a structured process consisting of six steps for designing health promotion campaigns (Bartholomew et al. 2006). The first step is to fully understand the health issue and the factors that contribute to the problem behaviour which is to be changed. This understanding can be gained by working with people who may be the targets of the health promotion, with other experts or by reviewing the literature. Once the problem has been fully understood, clear goals are set – not only to change the end-point behaviour, but also to change the

intermediate factors which contribute to the behaviour. At the third stage, tried and tested methods to change the intermediate factors can be selected. These methods should be pilot-tested at the fourth stage, when the actual intervention is designed. The fifth stage of intervention mapping requires consideration of the factors which need to be in place for the intervention to be widely adopted by organisations. A final stage concentrates on designing an evaluation plan for the campaign. It is not only the final goal that should be monitored (e.g. to see if people do give up smoking), but also the intermediate factors that were considered necessary for the change, for example increases in self-confidence. The intervention should also be evaluated for how consistently it can be delivered and how enjoyable it was for those taking part.

Stress and its relationship to health

We use the word stress day in, day out. So what is stress? The extract from a newspaper article in Box 7 suggests that commuters might experience more stress than fighter pilots. Do you think this is true? Is this a reasonable conclusion given what the researchers say about their results? By what standards should we judge stress?

Box 7 Want to feel less stress? Become a fighter pilot, not a commuter (Andrew Clark in *The Guardian*, 30 November 2004)

Combat pilots flying over hostile territory should thank their lucky stars that their journey home does not involve catching the 5.15pm from Waterloo. The experience might just make them stressed.

Commuters on Britain's rush-hour roads and railways suffer greater anxiety than fighter pilots or riot police facing angry mobs of protesters, according to research published today which suggests that many travellers retreat into a 'light hypnotic trance' as a defence mechanism.

Psychologists found that travellers tackling peak-hour congestion experienced heart rates as high as 145 beats per minute, compared to an 'at rest' rate of 65 for a healthy young adult.

Dr Lewis, who conducted the research, said the symptoms of stress were equivalent to those measured in his past studies using combat pilots and police officers.

Psychologists quantify stress in a number of ways. One of the first approaches to stress concentrated on the physiological changes which occur when we are stressed. Taking this *response approach*, the extent of the stress we experience can be measured by the strength of our physiological changes. These changes are generally produced by activation of the sympathetic nervous system and the secretion of a number of hormones, primarily epinephrine (adrenaline) and cortisol. A number of physiological changes can be measured, such as increases in heart rate and blood pressure, levels of sweating or (by taking samples of blood or saliva) changes in immunological factors or hormonal activity.

A different approach to the measurement of stress is to assess the number of times someone experiences events or situations that most people report as being stressful. These can be major events, such as experiencing a natural disaster, the death of a loved one or being made redundant, or more minor, everyday irritations, such as losing your keys or having an argument. Lists of such events can be included on questionnaires to provide a score representing the experience of stressful events over a certain timeframe, although producing a list comprehensive enough to cover all relevant sources of stress for all people, while still being reasonably short, can be difficult.

Another difficulty with the *life events approach* just described is that it assumes that an event causes as much stress to one person as it does to another, but people differ widely in the meaning they attach to an event. For one person, Christmas may be seen as a happy, fun-filled, festive occasion, whereas for another person it may be a time of intense worry, as they try to budget for presents they feel they cannot afford and dread the family get-together. In addition, any generic list for all people will miss important sources of stress for some.

The final approach to understanding stress is to take an approach to stress which recognises individual differences in how we respond to situations. The *transactional model* of stress proposed by Lazarus and Folkman (1984) takes an approach that stress is 'in the eye of the beholder'. Taking this approach to stress, no event would be seen as stressful in and of itself; instead, any event can be appraised as stressful depending on how it is interpreted and how well the person feels they can cope. Lazarus and Folkman (1984) theorised that the interpretation of an event as stressful is dependent on two appraisals. Our first appraisal relates to the meaning attached to an event – is it seen as benign, a threat, harmful or as representing a challenge? The second appraisal concerns our perception of our ability to cope and the resources we have to meet the requirements of the event. Stress results when a person's perceived or real ability to cope is exceeded by the perceived or real demands of the event. Different people and different types of personality will vary in their perception of events and in their perceived ability to cope with events. However, the transactional approach has been criticised for the circularity of its definitions. Within this approach, stressors and coping resources are only defined in terms of each other, that is, a stressor is anything that elicits coping, and a coping resource is anything that mitigates the impact of the stressor.

The transactional approach requires a subjective measurement of stress – asking someone how stressful they find life in general or a specific event, or what events they find most stressful. Subjective stress questionnaires have been developed (e.g. Perceived Stress Scale, Cohen, Kamarck and Mermelstein 1983), and researchers have also been able to use a structured interview to explore relevant sources of stress (Brown and Harris 1978). Coping checklists have also been developed, such as the COPE scale (Carver, Scheier and Weintraub 1989), which covers 14 different styles of coping including planning, turning to religion and denial.

Box 8 The individual experience of stress

How would you appraise the event depicted in Figure 7.3?

Figure 7.3 Paragliding – a stressful experience?

Some people find flying a paraglider and navigating the air currents a challenging but serene pursuit, while for others, the thought of being 'dangled at height by some flimsy lengths of string under an air-filled bag' signals a threat which would exceed their ability to cope. This highlights how appraisals, and therefore experience of stress, can be very individualistic.

Stress and health

Our interest in stress is due primarily to the proposed links between stress and ill health. The short-term physiological changes which occur in the stress response help to prepare the body for sudden energy expenditure. Cannon (1932) coined the term the *fight or flight* response to describe this physical response of the body. Early studies, however, particularly Selye (1956), demonstrated that sustained periods of stress were accompanied by an increased susceptibility to illness.

In the late twentieth century, the term *allostatic load* was used to describe the wear and tear caused to the body by the stress response and the impact of lifestyle habits such as smoking and poor diet (McEwen 1998). Although the short-term physical changes we experience during the stress response have a number of benefits in terms of mobilising the body for action, each stress response causes a degree of allostatic load, as it places the body in a

higher level of functioning. If your reaction to stress is excessive, this creates additional allostatic load and damage. Allostatic load is also produced if the body does not quickly revert back to normal once the stressful event has passed, or if recovery of physical systems is not synchronised appropriately. In particular, cortisol has been implicated in helping the body to 'switch off' the stress response. However, if this is not in proportion to levels of activation, then some systems of the body, such as the immune system, can be pushed to levels that are below optimum functioning. It is recognised that experience of stress may also lead to illness due to a reduction in care behaviours and an increase in riskier behaviours, such as smoking, eating habits, alcohol consumption and drug abuse in people reporting high stress levels (e.g. Ogden and Mtandabari 1997).

Some of the earliest research linking stress and illness was published by Rahe, Mahan and Arthur (1970), who used questionnaires to measure recent experience of stressful events among sailors in the Royal Navy. They found that those sailors who reported the higher levels of stress also had higher levels of illness. Any research which asks people to think back is vulnerable to errors in memory. Schroeder and Costa (1984) highlighted a number of less obvious problems with this type of research. First, some items can be seen as both a source of stress and a possible consequence of stress, such as experiencing illness. If the same items are on both scales, this will artificially make scores more similar. Second, people will be biased in what they remember, depending on what type of health state or mood they are in when questioned – if we are feeling grumpy or unwell, we tend to recall more negative events than when we are feeling healthy and happy. This also holds for general disposition – people who have personalities with higher levels of neuroticism tend to recall more experiences of stress and of illness.

Despite concerns about findings based on life events questionnaires, evidence from people in objectively stressful situations certainly links experience of stressful events to adverse health outcomes. The cardiovascular system is very noticeably affected by the stress response, and researchers have found higher levels of heart attack, stroke and sudden cardiac death in populations exposed to major and severe stressors, such as natural disasters, war or industrial accidents. For example, Ruidavets et al. (2006) found that acute cardiac death rates in a population living near the site of an industrial explosion in France were approximately 3.5 times higher than usual for the first few days afterwards. Even such everyday events as getting angry, emotional or overexcited have been linked to increases in heart attack rates in those with predisposing risk factors (Strike and Steptoe 2005). For example, Carroll et al. (2002) analysed rates of hospital admissions around the time that England was playing in the 1998 World Cup. They found that on the day England was involved in a penalty shootout and subsequently lost to Argentina, rates of heart attack were up by 25 per cent. A similar increase in risk is seen with so-called birthday-related stress: researchers have found a 27 per cent increased risk of developing a stroke or having a heart attack on your birthday compared to three days either side (Saposnik et al. 2006).

Within the brain, subtle changes are caused by repeated or prolonged stress responses which make people more likely to develop depression (Checkley 1996). The longer-term effects of stress on the immune system lead to increased levels of coughs, colds and other infections (Cohen, Tyrrell and Smith 1991), as well as delays in wound healing (Glaser 2005). For example, Kiecolt-Glaser et al. (1995) found that wound healing took about 24 per cent longer in women caring for a husband with Alzheimer's disease compared to similar women not experiencing such a chronic stressor. Effects of stress can also be seen more widely in those with increased susceptibility to type two diabetes, obesity and autoimmune disorders (Sapolsky 2004).

So what is it about some events that makes them so stressful, and what can we do to make life less stressful? Researchers in this area have isolated a number of variables which seem to be able to moderate our experience of stress. If you place a human or animal in a situation where they have some form of control over a stressor, then stress responses are not as strong. A sense of predictability also reduces stress levels. Much of this research has been conducted in a laboratory, where sources of stress can be as minor as a small electric shock, and the sense of control provided by having a lever to press, or predictability signalled by a buzzer to

announce forthcoming shocks. However, parallels can be seen in real life. It has long been recognised that people in jobs with high levels of demands and low levels of control suffer the highest levels of illness, and also have reduced life spans in comparison to those with greater levels of control.

The relationship between job demands, control and stress was first demonstrated by Karasek (1979). Karasek found that employees with the highest levels of job demands, but low levels of control in terms of decision-making, had higher levels of various symptoms of stress, such as disturbed sleep, anxiety and exhaustion. Based on this research, Karasek proposed a model of job stress which suggests that there is an optimum level of demands, with both very low levels and very high levels causing stress. Later models also integrated the stress-buffering effects of social support. A systematic review of the evidence collected since Karasek's model was proposed has tended to support the association of these three factors – extreme demands, low control and low support – with rates of illness and staff absence (Michie and Williams 2003).

Understanding the factors that make situations stressful has important implications for reducing stress levels. Health psychology is also particularly concerned with stress experienced by those who work within health care settings. Research suggests that levels of stress among health care professionals are higher than for other occupational groups (Michie and Williams 2003), so a great deal of work has been conducted on the issue of staff burnout within medical professions and settings.

Within the workplace, occupational health psychologists have been able to work successfully to reduce the stressful nature of the work environment. In part, this may be achieved by reducing the demands of the physical environment – ensuring that noise levels are reasonable, ambient temperature is comfortable and lighting is appropriate. Providing workers with some sense of control over their working environment, such as allowing them to decide the order in which they complete their tasks, can help to reduce stress levels. Rotating staff between tasks can also help to keep interest levels high, and avoid the problem of too low a level of demand and boredom. Increasing opportunities for workers to interact with each other and take advantage of social support can also help to reduce stress. A study by Michie, Wren and Williams (2004) found that making changes in the work environment of hospital cleaners to increase control and increase support from other workers resulted in lower sickness rates.

Health psychologists also work more generally to enable people to manage the stresses within their lives. One of the first aspects of a stress management programme is often to get the person to keep a diary of what aspects of their life they find stressful. Analysis of a stress diary may identify events or circumstances which it might be possible to avoid. Alternatively, people can be provided with skills to prevent some sources of stress in certain situations. For example, if a student finds doing assignments extremely stressful due to not having enough time to meet the deadline, time management techniques may help to reduce stress. If certain relationships seem to cause stress, communication skills may be useful.

Another tactic is to try to change how people appraise events and their coping skills. The transactional model would suggest that our experience of stress is determined in part by what we perceive as stressful. Certain cognitive styles, such as always looking on the negative side, can mean that more of your life is perceived as stressful, whereas a more optimistic style is associated with reduced experience of stress. If you can change the perception of the event, you can potentially reduce stress: this is a cognitive approach to stress management.

Other approaches try to help people to reduce the physical response to stress, such as increased heart rate, blood pressure and breathing rates. This may be achieved by relaxation training, progressive muscle relaxation, meditation or biofeedback. For example, in relaxation training, participants are taught how to breathe deeply, and these techniques are practised so that when the person starts to feel stressed they can counteract this with their deep breathing.

Health psychology research on stress continues to explore the links between stress and illness, and, more importantly, to investigate methods of reducing stress in daily life and helping people to cope better with the stress they experience.

Interaction with the health care system

In the UK, where the majority of health care is free at the point of delivery, health psychologists have been called on to address challenges of how to encourage people to make the most appropriate use of health care services.

An important factor determining the use of resources is not just the level of illness in the population, but also when and how we decide to make use of the health care system. Both under- and over-utilisation of health care services can cause problems. Under-utilisation might at first glance appear to cause fewer problems to society, in that if a person is not interacting with the health care system, they will not be using any resources. Delay in seeking treatment, however, can mean that resulting conditions are more expensive to treat and the person may take longer to recover and get back to work than if they had sought help earlier. At a personal level, delay in seeking treatment can result in a more serious condition, with a greater impact on quality of life – it might even mean the difference between a survivable condition and a fatal one. Thus the study of the factors which influence why people delay seeking medical care is of great importance.

To understand some of the reasons why people make use of health care services, it is necessary to understand how people recognise that they are ill and then make a decision to make use of the health care system. People do not always recognise when they are ill. This can be the case especially when symptoms are vague. Leventhal, Meyer and Nerenz (1980) have pioneered research into what are known as common-sense models of *illness representations*. Illness representations are the mental models that people have about illness. If illness representations are not correct, there is a risk that people will not access services when they need them. Illness representations are based on information we get from informal sources such as friends and family, formal sources such as health care professionals and our own experience with illness. From these sources we build up a picture of illnesses in terms of their causes, consequences, labels and symptoms, likely duration and controllability.

Illness representations of identity are important as they determine how we label the symptoms we experience. This can have an impact on whether we recognise symptoms accurately as being an illness. Illness representations of controllability also influence how we cope with illness and how likely we are to recover. For example, people who see their illnesses as uncontrollable are less likely to take active steps to cope (Hagger and Orbell 2003). Interventions which aim to change maladaptive illness representations have been shown to increase the number of people who return to work after a heart attack, for example (Petrie et al. 2002).

Box 9 Delays accessing health care for stroke patients

The medical condition of a stroke is caused by a clot or bleed within the brain, and can lead to death or disability due to resulting brain damage. The seriousness of the consequences of a stroke can be limited if the person experiencing the stroke receives prompt treatment in a hospital. In many cases, however, people do not reach hospital in time. Dr Carol Percy and Jacqueline Wilson, from Coventry University, have investigated the factors which seem to result in delay in getting medical attention. Their research focused on people of Afro-Caribbean origin, as this is an ethnic group at higher than average risk of experiencing a stroke (Forouhi and Sattar 2006).

Their research revealed that although there was some misinterpretation of the symptoms of stroke, the key factor resulting in delay was a reluctance to call emergency services for someone suspected of having a stroke. People said they would tend to phone their GP rather than call for an ambulance, as they expressed uncertainty about the interpretation of the symptoms and did not want to waste time and resources. There was also a general perception among participants that the ambulance would come more quickly if called by the GP. The results of this research can ensure that educational campaigns focus on the right factors. The research highlights that campaigns do not need to focus on the understanding of stroke symptoms in this group, but rather what to do if someone is suspected of having a stroke, emphasising the need to call an ambulance without delay.

Patient–practitioner communication

The importance of 'a good bedside manner' for health professionals and good communication skills which inspire confidence, has long been recognised. The success of the placebo effect, where people appear to show a medical improvement despite not being given any active treatment, is often explained as being due to the patient's faith in their doctor. Consultation style can influence another behaviour that is of importance to the smooth running of the health care system – whether patients follow the advice of health care professionals. Good communication skills can also contribute to satisfaction and minimise distress in situations where health care professionals have to give bad news. Increased understanding of the factors which lead to successful consultations has led to changes in the training given to health care professionals.

Adherence to treatment recommendations

The phrase 'doctor's orders' is often used and certainly carries with it the expectation that patients will comply with what the doctor (or other health care professional) tells them. It is evident that people are incredibly bad at following the advice of health care practitioners. For example, it has been estimated that approximately half of all those prescribed antibiotics do not complete the course (Ley 1988). Even in the more serious situation of having a kidney transplant, one in seven patients does not take the anti-rejection medicine as required. Wasted medication and missed appointment times represent a cost to the health service. Taking medication as prescribed is also important – at less than the prescribed dose, patients may miss out on therapeutic benefits and risk complications, which may require more serious and probably more expensive treatment.

So why are we so bad at following what is well-intended advice? Ley (1988) highlighted three key factors which influence adherence to advice: satisfaction, memory and understanding. Researchers distinguish between unintentional non-compliance, when people fail to adhere to treatment because they forget or misunderstand, and deliberate (or creative) non-compliance, when the patient varies the treatment on purpose – this is more related to the level of satisfaction with the health care interaction and illness representations. Interventions to target unintentional non-compliance have focused on making instructions clearer, treatment regimes simpler and using triggers or reminders. One necessary condition to following instructions is to understand and remember them at the time they are given. People are quite bad at remembering verbal information given in consultations and may benefit by writing their own notes or by being given leaflets. Alternatively, health care professionals can be trained to phrase instructions more simply to promote understanding. Second, we need to remember correctly the instructions at the appropriate time for action. Research has found that what is termed *event-based recall* is better than *time-based recall*. Thus an instruction such as 'Take your medication twice a day' is likely to be less effective than an instruction such as 'Take your medication before breakfast and before dinner' (Myers and Abraham 2005).

Interventions to tackle creative non-compliance need to understand fully the reasoning behind the decision to vary the treatment and are more related to our satisfaction with the health care interaction. Patients who vary their treatment may do so because they do not believe that the treatment is beneficial, they are worried about side-effects, they cannot afford it or they want to check the effect of stopping the treatment, for instance to see if their condition is still present. Health care professionals who address their patients' concerns are likely to reduce levels of creative non-compliance where patients deliberately do not follow advice.

Breaking bad news

Health care professionals are often called on to break bad news to people concerning their own health or that of loved ones. For example, a nurse may have to tell a father who has been called to the hospital after his son has been in a motorcycle accident that his child is now brain dead and that the doctors are seeking consent for organ donation; a consultant may have to tell a person that results of tests show that the cancer they thought they had beaten has returned; or a mother may be told that her unborn baby has a life-threatening disability. All these situations require great skill on the part of the person breaking the bad news, both to determine how much information is wanted at the time and the most sensitive way to convey this.

When asked to recall how bad news was broken to them, a significant number of patients recall that it was given badly. Finlay and Dallimore (1991) interviewed 150 bereaved parents about how they were told of their child's death. A third thought that the interviews had been handled badly, although their satisfaction with the interview was not linked to their grief reaction. Common sense suggests that insensitivity at this time may have long-term adverse effects, although no research evidence has been published at the time of writing (2006).

Although receiving bad news is difficult, it is also difficult to give bad news. The shocked and often upset reaction of the receiver of bad news is one aspect which makes breaking bad news an unpleasant and difficult task. Health professionals are seen as a caring profession, but when they need to give bad news, they are causing distress to the patient and sometimes removing the patient's hope that things might turn out better. Health professionals may feel uncomfortable dealing with the emotional reactions that ensue. Health professionals may also see giving bad news as an admission that they have failed, and they may fear not being able to answer all the questions they may be asked. Patients may react with anger towards the person giving them bad news – hence the phrase 'don't shoot the messenger'.

One way in which to avoid the adverse effects of having to give bad news is not to tell the person if it can be avoided. Although it might seem shocking, there was, and in some places still is, a commonly held view that patients are better off not knowing about a diagnosis, even (or especially) if it concerns a terminal illness. For example, in 1961, Oken found that in the USA, 90 per cent of doctors said they would not tell a patient of a cancer diagnosis. In general, not telling of a diagnosis was more often the case when the patient was perceived as not being likely to cope very well with the news, such as an elderly person or a young child – or, in the past, a woman! More 'robust' members of the patient's family were often told, and their advice was sought on keeping information from the patient.

Views on whether patients should always be told bad news have changed over time, with a move towards doctors being more open about bad news. This seems to have changed for cancer in particular – an area that has been studied extensively. Research by Vassilas and Donaldson (1998) in the late 1990s found that 90 per cent of UK GPs always or often would tell a person of a terminal cancer diagnosis. This has probably also been driven by the increasingly litigious nature of patients concerned about their rights. However, it seems that disclosure rates for other conditions lag behind. For example, Vassilas and Donaldson (1998) found that rates of disclosure for a dementia diagnosis were much lower than for cancer, with only 39 per cent of GPs in their sample saying they would always or often tell the patient. Clafferty et al. (2000) found similar rates of 44 per cent of consultants conveying a diagnosis of dementia. For schizophrenia, Clafferty, Brown and McCabe (1998) found that only 59 per cent of psychiatrists would provide a diagnosis after a first episode of schizophrenia, although this rose to 89 per cent after a second episode.

Keeping bad news from a patient was usually not done out of general secrecy or a desire to mislead the patient, but because the health care professionals or the patient's family believed that the patient should not be told in order to protect them, or because they believed that the patient did not really want to know. However, the standards we have for when we should keep information secret are not always the same as what we would wish for ourselves. An interesting study by Maguire et al. (1996) asked 100 people whether they would want a member of their family told about a diagnosis of Alzheimer's disease. The majority of participants, 83 per cent, said that their family member should not be told, giving reasons such as the knowledge of the diagnosis would depress the patient. However, 71 per cent of these participants said they would want to know if they were ever diagnosed with Alzheimer's disease, the most common reason cited being that they had a right to know! No wonder doctors have a difficult job. Research with a number of patient groups seems to support this, with the majority stating that they want to know their own diagnosis and have as much information as possible. For example, Benson and Britten (1996) interviewed 30 people who had received a diagnosis of cancer between one and seven years earlier, and found that 80 per cent of patients felt that information should only be given to their family with their consent, and 93 per cent opposed their family influencing the information given to them, although 23 per cent said that they would not have wanted to know a poor prognosis.

People do differ in the information they want. In some circumstances, it might be possible to discuss with patients in advance how and what level of information they might want regarding any future diagnosis (Keating et al. 2005).

As highlighted, conveying potentially bad news is very difficult and health care professionals often express a lack of confidence in their abilities. The SPIKES mnemonic (Baile et al. 2000) was devised as an easy way for health care professionals to remember the key points of best practice when breaking bad news. The six steps are:

- *S*etting up: The physical setting should be private and risks of interruption should be reduced. Attention should be paid to whether the person being given the bad news may want someone close with them. The person giving bad news should sit down to convey that they are not in a rush – if they do have limited time, this should be explained.
- *P*erception: The health professional should assess what the person already understands about the situation and the terminology that they use – this will help them to pitch their explanations at a level the patient will understand, without being overly technical or condescending.
- *I*nvitation: The health professional should explore what the person wants to know. For example, using phrases such as, 'How would you like me to give you the information about your test results? Would you like me to give you all the information or sketch out the results and spend more time discussing the treatment plan?' (Baile et al. 2000: 306). This enables the health professional to assess how much information may be wanted, and recognises that while some people do want all the details, others would be more comfortable with less information.
- *K*nowledge: A 'warning shot' should be given to the patient that bad news is to come (e.g. 'I have some bad news…'). When giving details of the bad news, health professionals should avoid being too blunt or using technical jargon, and should give information in small chunks and in language appropriate to the person's understanding.
- *E*xploring reactions: Time should be given not only to convey the bad news, but also to explore the person's reaction to it and acknowledge that it is okay to feel this way – whether it be shock, anger, denial or sadness.

➠ *S*ummary and strategy: The health professional should check that the person is ready to discuss next steps; if they are, a discussion of what will happen next is appropriate, whether this be treatment plans or, in the case of the death of a loved one, arrangements for the body.

The SPIKES protocol (and others like it) is widely used to train health care professionals and it has been demonstrated that health professionals can improve their practice in this area (Baile et al. 2000).

Being a patient and the health care environment

Hardly anyone looks forward to being in hospital, and for many people, fear of what being a patient may bring can even cause them to delay seeking medical attention. In the past, hospitals were feared places due to their association with death and dying, and also because of some of the depersonalising aspects of hospital care. Patients would have their home clothes removed and wear hospital gowns, have their personal possessions limited and be permitted only limited contact with their family. Even in more recent times, the hospital environment has been criticised. Sleep deprivation due to the hospital routine, lack of familiar environment and loss of control are highlighted as toxic aspects of hospital environments which may hinder recovery (Vögele 2004).

Research on the hospital environment has shown how this can impact on health. In a classic study, Ulrich (1984) examined the recovery rates of surgical patients who had had their gall bladders removed. Records were examined depending on whether patients were allocated to a room with a view of either trees or a brick wall. Those in the rooms with a view of trees had faster recoveries and needed less pain relief than those looking at the brick wall.

Research and insights from health psychology can be used to modify conditions in hospitals to make them more healing places (Mroczek et al. 2005). It has become recognised that designing spaces to make use of natural light and views, allowing longer visiting hours, shortening length of stay and permitting people to wear their own clothing does not increase infection rates and can in fact improve

outcome. Research on the impact of stress on wound healing (Glaser 2005) suggests that reducing the levels of stress and anxiety that a patient experiences will have an effect on outcome. In the first study of its kind, Janis (1958) demonstrated that patients who were given comprehensive information on what to expect of the surgical procedure required less pain relief and staff attention and were able to be discharged more quickly. Since then, researchers have established that adult patients who receive preparation for surgery experience less negative emotion and pain, require less pain relief and in-patient care, show enhanced recovery and are more satisfied (Johnston and Vögele 1993).

Particular advances have been made in the way children are treated in hospital. It used to be thought that having frequent visits from parents would cause additional stress. Research has established that having parents around actually reduces children's stress levels and therefore improves outcome (Justus et al. 2006). It was also thought that giving information about forthcoming medical procedures would frighten a child more and therefore it was better not to tell them what to expect. Interventions based on social learning theory, however, have used the example of a video of another child coping successfully with a medical procedure to reduce levels of pre-operative anxiety (ibid.). For adults too, a successful example seems to reduce stress and improve outcome. Kulik, Moore and Mahler (1993) found that people waiting for cardiac surgery showed less anxiety before surgery and had a quicker recovery if paired with a person who had just had the surgery, than if they were roomed with another patient also waiting for surgery.

Coping with long-term conditions or disability

The number of people living with a long-term chronic condition or disability has increased, as both the average age of the population has increased and the general pattern of illness has changed to one of fewer infectious diseases. There are approximately 17.5 million adults who report one or more long-term conditions in the UK (Department of Health 2001): this represents about four in ten of the adult population, and thus a considerable burden of disease. Long-term

Example of an intervention in health psychology

Chronic disease self-management courses are based on the work of Kate Lorig (e.g. Lorig et al. 1999). Although originally designed for people with arthritis, they have been extended to cover a wider remit of chronic conditions and have been embraced within the UK government's Expert Patients programme (Department of Health 2001). Courses last for six weeks and people with a range of chronic conditions (e.g. diabetes, haemophilia, myalgic encephalomyelitis) will attend the same group. The courses integrate stress management skills such as relaxation training, cognitive restructuring for symptom management, problem-solving and communication skills. As part of the course, participants are encouraged to make action plans and set themselves appropriate goals to extend their coping skills. There is a general focus on empowerment and control over the chronic condition.

Researchers at the Applied Research Centre in Health and Lifestyle Interventions at Coventry University have followed the changes seen in both participants and tutors on such programmes. They have documented dramatic improvements in psychological well-being, increases in self-efficacy, decreases in pain and fatigue, an improvement in physical functioning and a decrease in utilisation of health care, such as GP visits or attendances at Accident and Emergency departments.

Importantly, these improvements were sustained at follow-up a year later (Barlow et al. 2005), which demonstrates a lasting benefit of the courses on quality of life and use of health care beyond initial actual attendance. These improvements were not seen in a comparable group of patients who did not attend the courses.

conditions are more common as people become older: more than six out of ten of those aged over 75 years report one or more long-term conditions, compared to fewer than two in ten of those aged below 30 years.

In contrast to an acute condition, where the patient may be expected to get much better or much worse within a fairly short timeframe, a long-term condition may be stable for many years or show only slow deterioration. Symptoms may fluctuate, making diagnosis and prognosis difficult. Receiving a diagnosis can shatter a person's sense of who they are and their future. If symptoms impact on ability to take part in normal social interaction, there can be a real sense of isolation. Although people vary in the extent to which they are affected, there is no doubt that long-term conditions pose a challenge to those living with them, their friends and families. Long-term conditions can often require complex self-management, and reaction to unpredictable and changing symptoms. For example, high-action antiretroviral treatments for HIV involve a complex series of daily drug treatments, which must be taken within a strict timeframe, and insulin-dependent diabetes mellitus requires attention to diet and regular insulin injections. In the course of living with their condition, however, patients may

become more expert in their own symptoms and treatment than health care professionals.

The government's White Paper, *Saving Lives: Our Healthier Nation* (Department of Health 1999), introduced the term *Expert Patients*, which recognises that in long-term conditions the patient may be the person who knows most about their condition. The Expert Patients programme was set up to utilise this resource of knowledge and allow patients to have active input into their care. A key aspect of the programme is the provision of self-management courses, which aim to enhance coping abilities and self-confidence. Health psychologists have been influential in the design of such programmes and also in evaluating whether they are effective (see the box, 'Example of an intervention in health psychology').

CURRENT DIRECTIONS IN HEALTH PSYCHOLOGY

Health psychology's origins and the bulk of its current work lie in research and theory development. One of the current trends within health psychology is to move away from theory development and towards more applied work. At the time of writing (2006), the number of hospitals with a health psychologist post is very small. Nichols (2005: 26) describes his 'average-patient test', where in any hospital it is asked: 'Who is handling this patient's psychological care and how is it going?' He highlights that although patients may be surrounded in hospital by many caring health professionals, they frequently have no emotional support. He noted that many patients need psychological support, not particularly for 'mental health problems' as such, but more for the everyday worries that accompany being a patient. One of the most exciting new areas in health psychology, therefore, is the expansion of applied skills, often applying techniques established in clinical psychology to physical health conditions, to help people interact with the health care system and cope with challenges to health more successfully.

Another shift can be seen in the greater emphasis, not just on understanding the factors which relate to health behaviours, but on the efficient design and evaluation of interventions to change behaviour. Interventions have also evolved from provoking a change in behaviour while helping people to sustain their behaviour and not slip back to old ways. The more frequent use of strategies such as intervention mapping aims to enable lessons to be learned from both successful and unsuccessful health promotion interventions.

Health psychologists in the UK are also starting to engage more closely with the broader public health agenda (Abraham and Michie 2005). This development marks an exciting opportunity for lessons learned within the theory of health psychology to be translated into large-scale improvements in public health. In particular, health psychology can offer advantages of theory and evidence-based policies and rigorous evaluation, which can impact on the delivery of health care.

CONCLUSION

Health psychology is a vibrant and innovative area of applied psychology. The urgency and importance of the factors which have led to the rise of health psychology – poor health behaviours, increasing costs of treatment and changes in our interaction with the health care system – are likely to keep health psychology at the forefront of applied psychology.

RECOMMENDED FURTHER READING

Abraham, C. and Michie, S. (2005) Towards a healthier nation. *The Psychologist*, 18(11), 670–1.

Nichols, K. (2005) Why is psychology failing the average patient? *The Psychologist*, 18(1), 26–7.

Ogden, J. (2004) *Health Psychology: A textbook*, third edition. New York: Open University Press.

Sapolsky, R. M. (2004) *Why Zebras Don't Get Ulcers*, third edition. New York: Henry Holt.

USEFUL WEBSITES

Division of Health Psychology of the British Psychological Society: http://www.health-psychology.org.uk/

Division of Health Psychology of the American Psychological Association: http://www.health-psych.org/

Home of official UK statistics: http://www.statistics.gov.uk/ (look at the health theme for information on current health status and health behaviours within the UK population)

Exercises

1 How might each of the following impact on health? In coming to your conclusions, try to consider how factors may operate on our biology, thinking, behaviour and wider social environment.
➡ Being a generally happy person.
➡ Having no friends.
➡ Threat of redundancy.
➡ Family history of heart disease.
➡ Living in a high crime neighbourhood.
➡ Global poverty.

This exercise illustrates the interrelationship of determinants of health and the importance of an integrated biopsychosocial approach to understanding influences on health.

2 What effect on health behaviours does the conditioning have in each of the cases in the table below? Match each of the examples (A–E) to the conditioning process they represent (1–5). Answers are given underneath the table.

3 Create a life events checklist to measure sources of stress. Can you devise a reasonably short list of stressful events which will capture important sources of stress for people of all ages and from all walks of life? This exercise illustrates the subjective nature of stress and some of the problems in devising life events checklists to measure stress levels.

Example	Conditioning process
A. When running, your car has an annoying warning alarm which only stops when you wear the seatbelt.	1. Positive reinforcement
B. When you refuse a cigarette, you tend to be excluded from your group of friends.	2. Punishment
C. Your friends comment on how healthy you look since you improved your eating habits.	3. Time out
D. Your parents dock your allowance if they catch you drinking alcohol, as you are under age.	4. Extinction
E. You used to go to the gym to catch sight of a bloke you fancied, but he has now stopped working there so you do not go so often.	5. Negative reinforcement

Answers to Question 2. A5, B3, C1, D2, E4.

Occupational Psychology

8 chapter

You may have a healthy life, remain mentally balanced, not indulge in sport, not notice your environment, avoid crime or the courts and have no further involvement in statutory education. However, almost certainly you *will* be involved in the world of work, or perhaps with the consequences of not being employed. Occupational psychology attempts to answer such questions as:

➠ What makes us work harder?
➠ What makes us satisfied in our work?
➠ Do groups work differently from individuals?
➠ What produces effective leadership at work?
➠ What factors in the work environment facilitate or impede work performance?
➠ What makes one organisation more effective than another?

OCCUPATIONAL PSYCHOLOGY IN THE BRITISH PSYCHOLOGICAL SOCIETY (BPS)

Occupational Psychology is a division of the BPS, with a membership of 3259 in 2006. Members can gain the title Chartered Occupational Psychologist (the route to this title is described in the box on p.187: 'How would I become an occupational psychologist'). The BPS administers the Postgraduate Certificate in Occupational Psychology, which can be taken by those not studying for an MSc qualification, and which stands as evidence of 'sound knowledge and understanding of occupational psychology', as required in stage 1 of the three-stage journey towards chartered status. The BPS also gives accreditation to occupational psychology MSc courses.

PRINCIPLES OF OCCUPATIONAL PSYCHOLOGY

Occupational psychology is, quite simply, the study of human behaviour and experience in the workplace. In addition, it is the application of psychological principles and theory in order to help workers and organisations. Because occupational psychology includes this focus on organisations in general, we have to be careful when referring to the world of work. Because volunteers may work (very hard) for a charitable organisation, we cannot always assume that 'helping' an organisation involves anything to do with increasing profits (though it may well involve increasing productivity), and we cannot assume that money is the main motivator for all people working in organisations. We might say, then, that occupational psychology aims to improve – through the application of psychological principles and theory – the effectiveness of organisations, the effectiveness of work performed within organisations and the conditions and satisfaction of workers within organisations.

Terminology

Occupational psychology started off life in this country as *industrial psychology*, when the National Institute of Industrial Psychology was established in 1921 by C. S. Myers. We shall return to the history of occupational psychology shortly. By the 1950s the favoured term had become *occupational psychology* and this remains the title of the division of the BPS. However, a strong lobby within the BPS would prefer the commonly used European term, *work psychology*, and this is the title of many textbooks, as well as modules within British universities. This term will be used here when referring to general theory and research rather than the specific UK profession. Other academic titles can be *work and organisational psychology*, *organisational psychology* and *organisational behaviour*. Finally, the preferred US term is *industrial and organizational psychology*, or *I/O psychology* for short.

WHAT AN OCCUPATIONAL PSYCHOLOGIST DOES

In order to appreciate the scope of occupational psychology, we can look at the areas defined by the BPS's Division of Occupational Psychology in its Guidelines on Becoming a Chartered Occupational Psychologist (from the BPS website http://www.bps.org.uk). Here eight areas are defined and the occupational psychologist must demonstrate 'sound knowledge and understanding' in all.

1 Human–machine interaction
   This can also be called *ergonomics* and is about the study of how humans interact with machines. Some people may recall that we once pressed our foot on a floor button in order to dip the headlights in a car. This was not a good idea and was especially dangerous if the driver was changing gear at the same moment!
   It is reported (Kelso 2005) that London won the 2012 Olympics vote because of 'fat finger' syndrome, the use of too closely spaced buttons resulting in an easy error where a panel member apparently voted for Paris instead of Madrid; Paris won by two votes and London faced Paris rather than Madrid, against which city experts thought London would have lost. The syndrome is also blamed for several multimillion pound mistakes, for instance the buying of 50,000 shares rather than 50,000 pounds' worth of shares.

2 Design of environments and work: health and safety
   The second area concerns health and safety, and covers factors to do with noise, light, ventilation, general workspace, risk factors and occupational stress.

3 Personnel selection and assessment, including test and exercise design
   It is expensive to hire the wrong staff. Occupational psychologists have contributed strongly to this area and we shall start off here when we consider research and applications below.

4 Performance appraisal and career development
   Psychologists can assist and advise organisations on how to run staff appraisals so that they are two-way affairs which employees respect and value. Career development is essential, but how does an organisation avoid offering such good development that the employee is then extremely attractive to competing organisations?

5 Counselling and personal development
   The topics and skills used in this area will be many of those described in Chapter 3. Occupational psychologists may work as careers advisers or stress management counsellors, among other roles, and in these cases the emphasis is primarily on being a good listener, demonstrating empathy and being accepted as genuine.

6 Training

A trained workforce is one that is productive, but also one that avoids costly or dangerous errors. Many occupational psychologists spend the majority of their time identifying training needs, and in the design and delivery of training programmes.

7 Employee relations and motivation

Many aspects of mainstream social psychology were developed through the study of the ways that small groups interact and perform in a work context. This area includes research into conformity, obedience, teamwork, team building, attitudes, communication and, especially, leadership. It also investigates theories of work motivation.

8 Organisational development and change

Organisations are dynamic and continually evolving structures. External influences force change on organisations. For example, all organisations in the UK have had to comply with equal opportunities legislation and with health and safety directives such as those concerning smoking at work. Organisations may need to downsize or to overhaul their general culture. Occupational psychologists may help an organisation to institute change and alter attitudes, using findings and theory from social psychology and group dynamics, along with their own practical experience of organisational development.

The eight areas described above can be grouped into three broad categories of research and application in work psychology:

➡ human factors – areas 1 and 2;
➡ personnel work – areas 3 to 6;
➡ organisational psychology – areas 7 and 8.

Occupational psychologists may practise in all these areas, but very often they tend to specialise within one. Occupational psychologists in the human factors area might be involved in:

➡ designing or redesigning jobs;
➡ the design of equipment to match human features and capabilities;
➡ health and safety at work;
➡ introduction of new technology.

The services offered by an occupational psychologist in the personnel area might include:

➡ selection and assessment of personnel;
➡ appraisal of work performance;
➡ training programmes;
➡ careers guidance and counselling;
➡ issues of equal opportunity at work.

In the area of organisational development, occupational psychologists might run projects concerning:

➡ attitude and opinion surveys;
➡ team building, leadership and management;
➡ industrial relations;
➡ the changing of organisational culture;
➡ enhancing the quality of working life;
➡ improvement of the quality and effectiveness of communications.

How would I become an occupational psychologist?

In order to have the kitemark of the BPS you would want to become a Chartered Occupational Psychologist, and the first step would be to obtain a degree in psychology, which provides the Graduate Basis for Registration (see Chapter 1). Chartered status is acquired through three levels, which must take a minimum of three years from graduation. Level 1 requires a demonstration of knowledge and understanding in the eight areas of occupational psychology outlined above. Typically, you would enrol on a one-year full-time or two-year part-time MSc course in occupational psychology. At the same time, you would need to apply to become a member of the Division of Occupational Psychology of the BPS, with a status which is known as 'practitioner-in-training'. While achieving the three levels you need to be supervised. Supervisors may be found through the BPS website, through your place of employment or by other informal contact. Meetings occur on at least a three-monthly basis, and the supervisee completes a log over the practice period which is checked annually by the Board of Examiners of the BPS. Application to become a practitioner-in-training involves naming the supervisor and presenting a plan which details how you expect to gain the knowledge, skills and experience which will take you through the three years to chartered status.

Level 2 involves demonstrating practical application skills in five of the eight areas of occupational psychology outlined above. This is usually achieved partly on the Masters course (e.g. interviewing, test administration skills), partly through specialised workshops and training courses, and through your work as a trainee occupational psychologist, assuming that you have an appropriate position.

Finally, for Level 3 you need to demonstrate competence to practise independently with the public, under supervision, in at least one of the following four areas:

➠ work and the work environment (including health and safety);
➠ the individual (including assessment, selection, guidance and counselling);
➠ the organisation (including organisational development and change: employee relations and motivation);
➠ training.
(Source: BPS website, 23 July 2006)

On successful completion of Level 3 you would become a Practitioner Member of the Division of Occupational Psychology, and you would then apply to the BPS to become a Chartered Occupational Psychologist, a status for which you would now be fully eligible.

Different roles for the occupational psychologist

Occupational psychologists can be employed full-time by large organisations, such as the BT Group or Royal Mail, and government sectors such as the Department for Work and Pensions (over 100 psychologists) and the Ministry of Defence (40 psychologists). Very often, an occupational psychologist works as a consultant, either as a single individual or, more commonly, as a member of a consultancy, comprising anything from 2 or 3 to more than 50 occupational psychologists. Either way, the psychologist works as an adviser to organisations, charging a fee for specific projects. You will also find occupational psychologists in the psychology departments of many universities, in management or business departments, or in separate business colleges. They may teach and supervise students on MSc courses in occupational

psychology and will engage in academic research, but usually will generate additional income by providing services to industry and other organisations.

In occupational psychology it is possible that the practitioner-researcher tension is at its strongest because of the highly competitive and profit-based nature of the business world. Business managers may well become impatient with competing and ambiguous theories, prevarication and reluctance to call theories 'facts'. Occupational psychologists may feel a great pressure, therefore, to cut corners and to proceed without the research-based evidence that would normally be required to justify the interventions of psychological professionals (Briner 1998). In fact, a schism between researcher and practitioner in occupational psychology has indeed arisen, with the establishment of the Association of Business Psychologists in 2001. The complaint of the psychologists within this organisation has been that the Division of Occupational Psychology in the BPS is too academic and does not cater for the needs of consultants working in the business world. However, Fletcher (2003: 206) feels, from listening to these complaints, that the real problem

is that the academic side [for the complainants] is just all too difficult, and what they actually want are meetings and publications that are little more than experience exchanges and presentations of the latest tool-kits for consultants. Certainly if one talks to the typical practitioner in occupational psychology, they have usually read very few if any recent journal articles. For them continuous professional development seems to be about learning to use new tests or hearing about the latest business development practices, rather than enhancing and updating the scientific knowledge base which is the foundation of their professional identity.

This quotation encapsulates the divide: on the one hand, the development of broader and deeper scientific knowledge and evidence, to be used in the solution of practical problems in the field; on the other hand, the delivery of pragmatic (and profitable) solutions to the business world, never mind the science. Indeed managers and employers often take the view: 'Never mind the airy-fairy theory – give me something that works.' With this division in mind, we will look at the differing roles of occupational psychologists across the different types of position they might fill.

DEVELOPMENT OF OCCUPATIONAL PSYCHOLOGY

It is traditional to consider, as the first textbook of work psychology, Munsterberg's *Psychology and Industrial Efficiency*, published in the USA in 1913. In the UK in 1915, the wartime government established the Health of Munitions Workers Committee (HMWC), which addressed a number of interrelated topics, including fatigue at work, the health of workers, environmental conditions, organisation of the factory and methods of pay. Munitions factories were not good places to suffer from fatigue, carelessness or disgruntlement! This committee became renowned for reducing hours, improving conditions and yet increasing productivity, a result quite contrary to most factory owners' beliefs in more hours, less mollycoddling and more profit. However, as early as 1845, a broad-thinking Lancashire mill owner had reduced hours from 12 to 11 and, 'to the surprise of all concerned, the output was just as good' (Smith 1952: 19 in Hollway 1991: 35).

In post-war 1918 the Industrial Fatigue Research Board (IFRB) succeeded the HMWC, and in 1921 the National Institute of Industrial Psychology (NIIP) was established by C. S. Myers. The NIIP inherited the reputation of the IFRB and HMWC in bringing about positive changes, mainly through the work of psychologists. Its brief was: 'To promote and encourage the practical application of the sciences of psychology and physiology to commerce and industry by any means that may be found practicable' (Arnold 2005: 17).

Occupational psychology, then, was established and respected by British industry from just before 1920 onwards, sufficiently so for the first full-time occupational psychologist to be employed by Rowntree (the sweet manufacturer) in 1922.

The early years of work psychology – scientific management and philanthropy

In the early 1900s a radical and uncompromising approach to worker performance arose through the work of F. W. Taylor (1911). His view was that jobs could be analysed, using so-called *time-and-motion studies*, into the smallest actions as they were performed by the most efficient workers, and, having found the most economical way of performing the job, new workers could be trained to perform to this standard. The approach was very distrustful of workers, seeing them as selfish, irrational and not desirous of responsibility. The principles of Taylorism, or *scientific management* as it became known, were:

- systematically break job tasks into the smallest components;
- having found the most efficient way to perform a job task, set times and procedures as standards;
- train workers to perform to the standards and to exercise no discretion;
- reward workers only with money;
- set up procedures that prevent workers from any deception or shirking.

Scientific management in the UK

The strongest forms of Taylorism were resisted in early twentieth-century Britain, both by workers and by a group of powerful Quaker philanthropist employers, especially Sebohm Rowntree and the Cadbury family. Though interested in some aspects of scientific management, Cadbury (1914: 105 in Hollway 1991: 17) wrote:

> The reduction of the workman to a living tool, with differential bonus schemes to induce him to expend his last ounce of energy, while initiative and judgement and freedom of movement are eliminated, in the long run must either demoralise the workman, or more likely in England, produce great resentment and result in serious differences between masters and men.

The last point, less humanitarian and more protective of profits, is related to the power that British workers could now wield, using their newly formed but well-organised Trades Union movement, which enabled them to resist production increases far more successfully than workers were able to do in the USA. Nevertheless, Cadbury was genuinely and actively interested in worker welfare. He agreed with Taylorism's emphasis on worker training, but for him this extended to a general education of workers, which Cadbury supported on his own site. He also emphasised job design, fitting jobs to workers, and a scientific study of selection methods.

Rowntree believed, unfashionably, that staff satisfaction could be enhanced by asking workers to join in discussions on their work environment and conditions. He established a 'works council', with representatives from the various workers' groups within the factory, and also set up a factory Psychological Department, working closely with Charles Myers and the NIIP. Unlike Taylor, Rowntree viewed it as fundamental that organisations needed to consider their workers' thoughts, feelings, attitudes and job satisfaction *along with* their physical condition and training needs. For Rowntree, employers were performing a service to the public and profiting by it. They had a right to do so, but with rights come responsibilities, and owners therefore needed to be accountable to those who bolstered their enterprise. In particular, this meant looking after and nurturing workers. For many other employers, even today, this might sound like 'nanny' management, but no self-respecting large employer would now be able to ignore the philosophy and findings of the *human relations* movement which followed the early activities of the philanthropist sweet-makers, and to which we now turn.

Hawthorne and the human relations movement

In a famous series of studies carried out at the Hawthorne electrical plant in Chicago (Mayo 1933; Roethlisberger and Dickson 1939), from the mid 1920s and into the 1930s, psychologists 'discovered' (or rather, firmly established) that humans do not operate like machines, that feelings, attitudes and social relations have a very significant impact on productivity, and physical conditions, fatigue and monotony are only part of the story.

Probably the most famous experiment (Mayo 1927) concerned a group of five women who assembled telephone relays and who were placed in a separate room in order for the researchers to investigate, under carefully controlled conditions, how changes in rest breaks and working-day length would affect their work. The intriguing results showed, first, that productivity was independent of any changes. In general, productivity tended to go up, but, contrary to what is taught in most textbooks, the upward trend was not consistent (see Olson, Hogan and Santos 2006, for a critical examination of what many textbooks report about the Hawthorne studies). In fact, productivity dipped when two rest pauses of ten minutes were replaced by six breaks of five minutes. When conditions were returned to the original ones, however, the researchers recorded the highest productivity of all the variations. Methodologically the experiments were somewhat questionable. Effects were confounded by employer changes in incentives and supervisory style. The women also received feedback on their performance, which was a rarity in those days and has since been found to have a significant effect on worker motivation. In addition, two of the original five women were replaced by the researchers because they were thought to be uncooperative and too talkative. As Olson, Hogan and Santos (2006) point out, it is hard to single out one variable, from all those intentionally or inadvertently manipulated, that was responsible for productivity increases.

What emerged as crucial from these studies was the finding that the women had formed a close-knit social group, and to some extent this included their supervisor. They were working under far more positive conditions than previously, participating in discussions about their output, able to vary and discuss their assembly techniques, and they were participating freely in an interesting experiment. The experiment constituted one of the first on social processes within small groups.

Figure 8.1 a, b Workers at the Hawthorne plant

A separate study at the Hawthorne plant involved the observation of men whose job was to wire equipment. Once they had become accustomed to the presence of an observing researcher in the room, they began to show just how *social norms* (shared ideas about appropriate behaviour) were maintained in the group, especially those concerning production rates. If a worker went too quickly or too slowly the group used sanctions (such as 'binging' – thumping a person's arm with a knuckle) in order to get them into line. The groups in the room (there were two in competition) also tried to get supervisors to meet their preferred norm of being informal and affable.

The Hawthorne studies played a significant part in the introduction to social psychology of the study of group dynamics, group processes and the power of social norms. Within work psychology researchers had discovered what Hollway (1991) calls the 'sentimental worker', meaning that workers had feelings and were essentially social individuals, and management ignored this at its peril; without the social dimension, work behaviour is difficult to predict and its determinants are well beyond the narrow focus of rewards, control and task simplicity. This pioneering work can be seen as a launching point for the human relations movement, which dominated thinking in work psychology from the 1930s to the 1960s, and the principles of which still permeate much management thinking today. Its main principles were:

⟹ Physical features of the job and the individual, along with financial rewards, are not enough to explain worker performance and motivation.
⟹ Work is a social situation; workers are involved in a network of social relations and rewarding or unfavourable relationships with others.
⟹ The psychology of the informal small group is therefore of great importance in understanding work productivity.
⟹ Work motivation and attitudes can be enhanced by meeting some of the social and personal development needs of employees, *especially* where jobs are monotonous.

War – an engine of opportunity for occupational psychology

Cox (2001) has argued that war has been a significant driver in the development of occupational psychology. The First World War saw the first use of psychological tests on a very large scale, to both select and place US army recruits. In just over a year, more than a million men were tested, and this impressive efficiency generated large-scale public support for psychological tests. Post-war, in the UK, selection tests proliferated for weavers, solderers, engineers, and so on, and psychologists built on the credit they had gained from increasing production while improving working conditions. When the Second World War began, psychological tests had developed to a sophisticated level, enough not only to assess recruits' abilities to learn, but even to identify those who might make good spies. Human factors work also gained a foothold during the Second World War, as psychologists worked with engineers and manufacturers on the design of instrument displays and controls to suit human operators.

The 1960s brought a fusion of social psychologists, sociologists and business experts who collaborated in the study of behaviour in large organisations, giving rise to the discipline of organisational behaviour or organisational psychology. In general, the period from the 1960s to the 1990s was one of great expansion and productivity in work psychology. Most of the ground-breaking research and theory stems from this time, including as examples the study of job satisfaction, work motivation, goal setting, organisational culture, development and stress, group processes, leadership and politics and conflict. We will now move on to consider some of these ideas in detail.

RESEARCH, THEORY AND APPLICATIONS

In a book this size one can either skim every topic in work psychology or take some of the more central issues and consider these in some detail. This chapter takes the latter approach. Stress, a central topic, is omitted, since it occurs elsewhere (see Chapter 7). Human factors work is rather technical. Hence we will concentrate here on more accessible topics, which will put in context psychological research and theory that will often be familiar to the general psychology student. We will look at assessment and selection, training, motivation, people in groups and leadership. These last three topics are involved in organisational development, but the study of organisations as a whole is omitted since it relates to little mainstream psychology. However, the intervention study (see box on p. 213) is an example of an organisational development project.

Personnel issues: Selection and training

In this section we will look at how people are selected for jobs, among other things, and how they are trained for those jobs and for further development.

Work psychologists have probably contributed more to this area than to any other, and this reflects the crucial importance of getting the right people for the right jobs and how costly it is if the selection process is not effective. Personnel selection does not only concern selecting people *into* an organisation. It can also be the process which determines your

promotion, further training and even redundancy or retirement, as Figure 8.2 shows. In this section, though, we will concentrate on the selection of new employees for the most part.

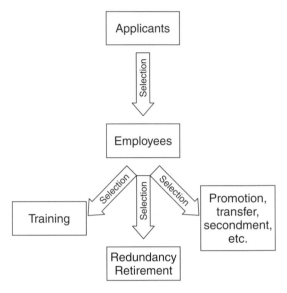

Figure 8.2 Uses of selection in personnel psychology

The psychology of person selection for jobs starts out with a few basic assumptions:

➡ There are individual differences in people's KSAOs (knowledge, skills, abilities/attitudes and other characteristics).
➡ It is possible to identify job requirements and to list the KSAOs that are required.
➡ It is possible to measure and differentiate between people's KSAOs.
➡ It is possible to match jobs and people.
➡ It is possible to predict job performance to some extent.

The process of selection for jobs is summarised in Figure 8.3. This process must be carried out under an overarching principle of equality of opportunity to be selected. If tests are unfavourable towards a minority ethnic group, for example, they are inherently unjust and companies will also face the threat of legal action. Overtly, very many people today will claim they are in no way discriminatory towards people of clearly different ethnicity, and many selection managers will believe this fervently. In spite of this, Dovidio and Gaertner (2000)

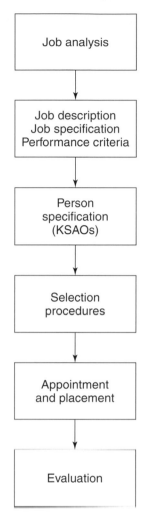

Figure 8.3 Stages in the selection process

involved, its location in the organisational structure, the responsibilities, equipment and duties involved and, eventually, a specification of the KSAOs needed to perform the job. Not all analyses are that thorough, but at the very least the analysis should provide the sound evidence needed when salaries are allocated, job redesign is being considered and, most importantly, when appointments are being made. The output of a job analysis is a *job description*, which details the expected tasks and output of the job, the job title, its location, work conditions, and so on, all of which may be linked to pay and promotion prospects for the job holder. From this a job specification is created (also known as a *person specification*), which will describe the qualities, qualifications and KSAOs required for the job, often divided into 'essential' and 'desirable'.

Types of job analysis

Some jobs are relatively easy to analyse in terms of specific tasks performed. Examples might be fitting exhausts on a production line or delivering milk. Many jobs, however, are better analysed in terms of required characteristics – a lecturer's or a lawyer's job, for instance, involves long periods where an observer might see virtually no tasks being performed at all, though if they stick around for long enough they might be able to record that the task of 'planning a sequence of lectures' or 'preparing a defence argument' had been performed. Such tasks are referred to as 'long-cycle'. Table 8.1 overleaf gives some of the more popular techniques of job analysis, along with some advantages and disadvantages of each one.

Finding criteria for job selection

Having conducted a job analysis and developed a job description and person specification, the task now is to find ways of assessing each applicant in a fair and unbiased way on each of the required KSAOs. Ideally we would find the best way to assess each characteristic. A traditional interview might be used to assess interpersonal skills and general job knowledge; a cognitive test might be administered to test problem-solving skills. Observation might be made of the applicant's specific skills, for example operating a lathe. This latter approach is known as taking a work *sample*, whereas the use of a cognitive test is seen as a *signs* approach – good performance on the test being only a sign that job performance might also be good.

showed experimentally that, although selectors did not discriminate when a black applicant's qualifications were high or low, they did discriminate towards an alternative white candidate when the black applicant's qualifications were ambiguous. Hence the process of selection needs to be clear and transparent at all stages, and we must start out first of all with sound knowledge of what the job specifically entails. Hence the first topic we turn to is that of *job analysis*.

Job analysis

If successful, a job analysis should produce a description of the scope of the job, the tasks

	Observation	Interview	Self-report – questionnaire, diary	Critical incident technique (Flanagan 1954)
Description	Trained observer records job holder's actions, decisions, etc.	Face-to-face questioning by analyst; can interview several job holders together	Job holders record day-to-day activities or keep a diary; some formal scales and inventories, such as McCormick et al.'s (1972) Position Analysis Questionnaire	Job holders describe specific incidents and behaviour characteristic of highly effective/ineffective job performance; workers may be described as high/low on that incident
Comments	Easy for simple, structured and manual jobs, but ineffective for long-cycle jobs	Good for long-cycle jobs; worker actively engaged in process; flexible and checkable; workers might exaggerate job, may feel intimidated; no information on what is not asked for	Cheap, quick and descriptive of job; depends on literacy skills; exaggeration possible; time-consuming and distracts from actual job	Highly relevant to job success; factual descriptions; high face validity for workers involved; focused on critical incidents, but not on mundane aspects of the job

Table 8.1 Types of job analysis technique, with advantages and disadvantages

Validity tests – how we know that selection procedures are good

How will we know that each of our assessments is a good predictor of future work performance? Psychologists have long worked with a concept of *validity*, which compares how a person scored at selection with what their performance turns out to be at a later date, once employed. This is known as *predictive validity*. *Concurrent validity* occurs when *existing* workers are tested on the predictors and these scores are compared with their current job performance. The comparison is made using *correlation* (see Chapter 11). A perfect relationship between predictor and performance would be 1, and no relationship at all would be 0. In practice, it is rare to get validities higher than 0.5 (e.g. Salgado, Viswesvaran and Ones 2001). One reason for this is that we only conduct validity studies on people who are selected, not those who are rejected. This is known as a *restriction of range* and it can have the effect of lowering the potential correlation that would occur if *all* applicants were used in the calculation. Obviously, psychologists would have a hard time getting organisations to employ the whole range of applicants simply in order to obtain more accurate validity data. Similarly, employers will not wait until psychologists have conducted validity studies on each predictor, but in principle this is what ought to happen, since unvalidated predictors might be unfair to applicants. In practice, it is more a matter of psychologists getting employers to adjust their existing methods in light of what validity studies tell them.

Selection methods

➡ *Interviews* are the most popular selection method, but have been found to have low validity (Huffcutt and Arthur 1994), probably because so many used to take the form of an informal chat, 'to see how you might fit in'.

Interviews have returned to favour, however, so long as they are *structured*, that is, questions are the same for all applicants, are based on job analysis and are consistently rated (Eder and Harris 1999). Huffcutt et al. (2001) have found validities to be comparable to other selection methods and sometimes as high as for cognitive tests (see below).

➡ *Observation* is sometimes used on work samples and, though costly to set up, according to traditional literature (e.g. Hunter and Hunter 1984), produces good validities around 0.55. Roth, Bobko and McFarland (2005), however, conducted a meta-analytic study and reported estimated validities of 0.33.

➡ *Psychological tests* are the work psychologist's strongest contribution to selection and can mostly be categorised into *cognitive ability* or *personality* tests. Cognitive ability tests (e.g. numeracy, general intelligence tests, logical reasoning tests) have become increasingly popular since their low point of distrust in the 1970s, and Robertson and Smith (2001) estimate their validity to be generally around 0.55. The more complex the job though, the higher the validity, according to Ones and Viswesvaran (2003). Personality tests do not enjoy the same level of validity or popularity and are probably best used in conjunction with other measures (see Hough and Furnham 2003 for a review).

Although selectors need to avoid all sources of discrimination, psychological tests have suffered specific criticism in terms of their effects on what is known as *adverse impact* (e.g. see Outtz 2002). This refers to a substantially different rate of selection that works to the disadvantage of members of a race, gender or ethnic group. The concept has legal implications under equal opportunity legislation. Various solutions have been offered to avoid selecting disproportionately more white than black applicants, for instance, without affecting the validities of selection tests. One can assess only the specific cognitive skills required and not overall cognitive ability, for example (Darany and Smith 2004). Creighton and Scott (2006) see the Situational Judgement Inventory (SJI) as an alternative to general cognitive tests and justify its use in terms of lowering negative impact. SJIs ask about job-relevant behaviour by presenting test takers with several scenarios (e.g.

You arrive at work and someone is using your computer…), and three or four possible responses to each in a multiple-choice format.

➡ *Assessment centres* involve a range of different selection methods, such as a cognitive test, a work sample test, an individual interview, a team-leading exercise and a group interview or group discussion. These are usually extremely costly to run, but come out with generally high validities of around 0.4 (Ones and Viswesvaran 2003).

Training

The training department of many organisations in the past was very much a sideshow – tolerated because someone had to teach new employees the basics. In the early twenty-first century they are often seen as central to the organisation and are integrated into all developments. Why might this be? Consider the question: 'Why is training so much more important today than it used to be?' and then look at some possible answers provided in Box 2.

Box 2 Reasons why training is so central today

➡ The speed of technological development means that employees need to be updated almost constantly with regard to changes.

➡ Many employees need training for work in different cultures in a world of increasing globalisation.

➡ Progression in an organisation is no longer always upwards; employees need to develop a breadth of competencies and experience.

➡ In many areas career advance can only be achieved by moving to a different organisation, hence a broad skills portfolio is essential; advance is no longer a case of Buggins's turn.

➡ Employers can attempt to retain valued employees by attending to their career development.

Training needs analysis

If your manager suddenly said to you, 'You ought to get some training', you would probably reply, 'For what?' Although some companies do believe that any training must be good, and some employees treat training courses as a company perk or a good break, training generally needs to be planned and focused. In fact, training is increasingly an integral part of an organisation's development plan, viewed as a training cycle, as depicted in Figure 8.4.

Training needs develop as a result of organisations introducing new technology, developing new products, changing their overall marketing strategy, expanding, and so on. An occupational psychologist might be called on to identify training needs once the development strategy has been decided. Commonly, a training needs analysis (TNA) can be conducted at three levels, as follows.

➠ *Organisational analysis*: the training needs of the organisation will flow directly from the kinds of developments just mentioned, or from a recognition that the organisation is weak or failing in some specific areas. It might be, for example, that callers to a university receive a gruff reception and are put off.

➠ *Task analysis*: task analysis determines the important elements in jobs or tasks and the KSAOs required to complete them. For instance, an overall objective of training positive caller reception can be broken down into specific tasks, such as answering the phone with the receptionist's first name and offering to help. Further specific behaviours will be required

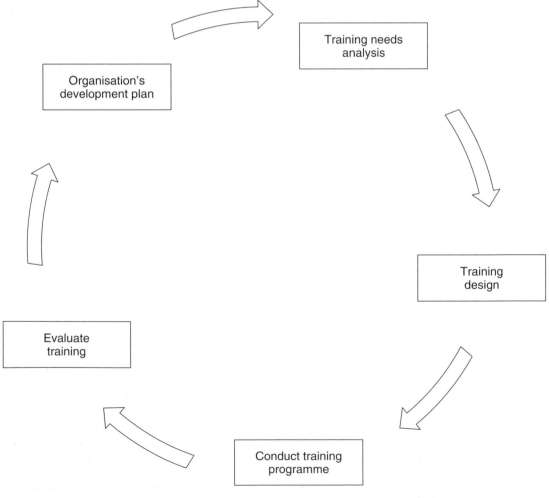

Figure 8.4 The training cycle

dependent upon what the caller wants. Some tasks, such as servicing a car, can be broken down into several levels and sub-levels, and such analysis is called *hierarchical.*

⟹ *Person analysis*: individual training needs are often identified as managers conduct a performance review with their staff. Usually the needs identified will be those that help the employee to meet the goals of the organisation. The process is marred, of course, if the individual does not agree with the reviewer's suggestions. Some needs will be identified by the employee, but are very often only met with training if they are in tune with organisational needs.

Training design

Having identified needs, the next requirement is to design programmes that will deliver the training. Programmes need to specify the precise objectives involved, set in measurable terms. 'The employee will be able to appreciate the role of health and safety regulations in their work' is too vague. How could we measure this appreciation? Something like, 'The employee will be able to identify at least three major causes of fire', along with several other similarly worded objectives, make it possible for assessment to show us whether or not the training has been successful.

Theories of learning

There is not space here to go into a detailed account of all the findings that have been developed through the major theories of learning. Chapter 10 provides an introduction to these approaches. A general textbook, such as Gross (2005), will provide a more thorough summary, and a specialist training text will go much further. Patrick (1992) is ageing a bit, but is still a valuable and extremely thorough text.

Considering the theories discussed in Chapter 10, a major contribution from *behaviourism* has been the emphasis on measurable behaviour and the phrasing of objectives. Another might be the concept of *programmed instruction* (Skinner 1958), in which learning is broken down into small units and the learner must proceed in a fixed order. Behaviourism's failure to deal effectively with cognitive processes makes its theory difficult to apply in a realistic workplace training setting, but its offshoot – *social learning theory* (SLT) – has enjoyed success with its concept of *behaviour modelling training* (BMT). This involves trainees being shown both appropriate and inappropriate work behaviour, observing the outcomes and then practising the observed task. Of course, workers have always learned by observation (in factories this was once called 'sitting by Nellie', that is, watching how the job was done as an expert performed it), but Bandura's work (e.g. Bandura, Ross and Ross 1963) explored many of the subtle links between observation, imitation and reinforcement. Simon and Werner (1996) showed BMT to surpass both programmed instruction and a lecture approach in training computer operators.

SLT's use of the term 'modelling' or 'imitation', however, begs the question of why people 'copy'. After observing a trainer using a new computer programme, trainees do not simply imitate at their own machine. They are likely to try to make the programme work and to say things like, 'Now how did he get that menu down?' and so on. That is, they use the trainer's actions as *information* in order to get the task done. Hence the *cognitive approach* has concentrated on our thinking patterns, how we use information and how we then plan our behaviour. An important aspect of learning is *feedback* (or knowledge of results) and trainers need to make sure that trainees receive immediate, not delayed, feedback on how they are doing – and it needs to be positive (what was done right) rather than negative (Martocchio and Webster 1992). Feedback is not 'reinforcement', as behaviourists used to argue, but information that the learner uses in order to adjust behaviour.

Other research over the years has shown that training needs to be well organised, well structured and run by credible trainers, that its aims need to be clear to the trainee and made practically relevant, and that this is accepted by the trainee who does in fact want to learn.

Evaluating training

A thorough evaluation of the effectiveness of training means taking measures of behaviour, preferably before and after training, and also preferably against the same measures for a group that has *not* been trained. In so many cases training is simply administered and the assessment is a matter of asking trainees how they did and what they got out of it. If we measure behaviour and other criteria, such as output or sales, only after training has taken place, we have no way of knowing whether change occurred. The results are uninterpretable, yet this is a common event in work training. Taking pre-post training measures (see Figure 8.5) will provide this evidence, but it will not tell us whether the change occurred only for trainees. Use of a control group *will* tell us this. For example, if a trained and control group are assessed for 'customer friendliness' and *both* groups improve, this might be because friendliness generally improves as new employees gain confidence with their work. Hence, without the control group we might think that training is improving friendliness when it is not.

Evaluation will also tend to demonstrate whether there has been *transfer of training*. This is a very important concept in training. Managers might go on an interesting team leadership weekend, but can we be certain that any of what they have experienced or learned will transfer to the workplace? Trainees might learn customer care skills in a training room or off-site; they may simulate their skills, but only with 'easy' clients. Have their skills transferred to the reception or call centre desk?

Work motivation

If you have worked in an organisation you have probably come across both the workaholic and the skiver, and wondered what motivates them to work at that level. Motivation is the drive to work harder or less so, to seek new horizons or to plod along. What interests psychologists (and managers, of course) are the factors leading to higher levels of motivation among employees.

Types of motivation theory

The study of motivation will be of intense interest to employers and managers *if* it comes up with clear answers. Apart from Taylorism's (and

behaviourism's) belief in tangible rewards as central motivators, there are theories based on a variety of *needs*, on the idea that humans *rationally* calculate what level of motivation is appropriate, and those based on the *design of the job* itself.

Need theories

Maslow argued that we have to satisfy the needs at the foot of his hierarchy (see Figure 8.6) before we can move on to satisfying those higher up – a quotation attributed to Dorothea Dix (1801–87) by Myers (2007) goes: 'Nobody wants to kiss when they are hungry'. A criticism of this point is that plenty of people try to satisfy status or aesthetic needs even when they are very hungry – for instance, the starving artist. We must also ask how we know when we can move up a level – how *much* satisfaction? Self-actualisation was thought to be a very fulfilled, unselfish higher state which may not last and occurs rarely for most people. There is very little empirical evidence for this ordering of needs, but the model appeals to many people's common sense.

Rowan (1998) suggests that there should also be a need for competence (to be able to master skills) and that the model does not distinguish between self-esteem and esteem from others.

Much empirical support has been provided for those theories that look only at *specific* need variables, such as McClelland's (1961) Need for Achievement, or NAch. McClelland argued that this was a personality variable which could be altered by life experiences, and several empirical measures of the construct have been developed, thus providing the opportunity to obtain direct evidence, which is hard to do with Maslow's theory. Although these theories are old, they often stimulate new research, such as the finding by

Figure 8.5 Types of evaluation design

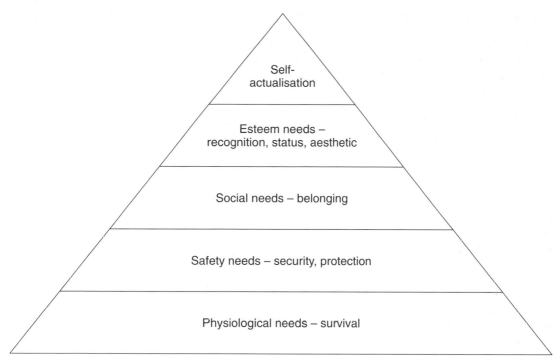

Figure 8.6 Maslow's hierarchy of needs

Baruch, O'Creevy and Hind (2004), among 846 workers from 41 organisations, of a direct relationship between need for achievement and job performance, but no relationship between workers' need for control and performance.

Rational theories

These include equity and expectancy theory. These grew up in the relatively new era of cognitive psychology and they assume that people are rational beings. Hence they make calculations about their work environments and from these deduce what level of motivation is appropriate. *Equity theory* (Adams 1965) assumed that people would feel uncomfortable when they perceived inequity in their working conditions and would adjust their behaviour (e.g. their output) accordingly. You might work less, for instance, if you perceived that others were being paid the same as you for less work. This theory has the counter-intuitive implication that people would work harder if they perceive that they are overpaid! In fact, Mowday (1991) found that empirical evidence was far weaker for equity predictions when people were overpaid than when underpaid – what a surprise!

In *expectancy theory*, Vroom (1964) argued that the motivation involved in a task is based on us calculating the probability that we will succeed in the task, the probability that success will bring rewards and the value of those rewards – hence, no reward or no chance of success gives no motivation.

Although these theories have been around for a while, with arguable degrees of evidence for them, they have served a useful function in the practical world of management. There are several messages implied by the two rational theories:

1 Equity
- Ensure people get equal rewards for equivalent work; and/or
- Make clear to workers what the criteria are for judging equivalence in work.

2 Expectancy
- Make sure workers know what task accomplishments will bring rewards.
- Make rewards (and costs) of task performance clear to all.
- Make sure workers can perform the tasks that carry rewards.

Job design theories

These look at the job itself and see in what ways it can be designed to increase *job satisfaction*. According to Herzberg (1966), job satisfaction can be divided into two components: satisfaction and dissatisfaction. Some things cause dissatisfaction, and these he termed *hygiene factors*. Things that increase satisfaction he termed *motivators*. He argued that satisfaction and dissatisfaction are two different states, not necessarily caused by the same things. The *absence* of hygiene factors (such as good supervision, good working conditions, salary) causes dissatisfaction, but their presence does not necessarily increase satisfaction; conversely, the presence of motivators (such as responsibility, promotion) causes satisfaction, but not necessarily dissatisfaction if absent. Teachers and nurses, for instance, are not highly paid, but they would probably argue that they get a lot of satisfaction from the importance, interest and responsibilities of their work in training young people's minds or saving lives. However, if salaries get too low, even these usually conscientious workers will start to take action.

The theory has not enjoyed a lot of empirical support, though it has been used to stimulate (or justify) innovations in management techniques, especially *job enrichment* (see below). A weak area of the theory appears to be the treatment of salary as a hygiene factor, when pay rises, and especially bonuses, are often linked to productivity deals. Bassett-Jones and Lloyd (2005), however, surveyed 3200 workers and found that, in the limited area of motivation to contribute ideas, money was not a prime motivator; so they argued that Herzberg's theory still had relevance 50 years on.

Hackman and Oldham's (1976:256) *Job Characteristics Model* (JCM) (depicted in Figure 8.7) is a much more complex theory, arguing that certain features of the design of jobs (core job characteristics, or JCs) lead to psychological states which in turn have an effect on work outcomes, including performance. *Skill variety* refers to the range of skills and tasks involved in a job. *Task identity* is the extent to which the employee sees a whole product from what they do. This would be low for production-line workers. *Task significance* refers to the impact the job

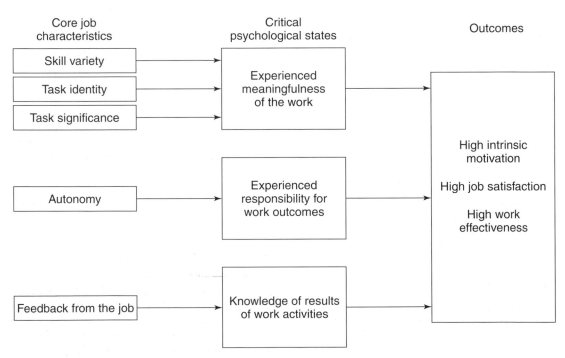

Figure 8.7 Hackman and Oldham's job characteristics model of motivation
Source: Hackman and Oldham (1976)

has on others: a manager's job has more task significance than that of a filing clerk. *Autonomy* is the degree of independence in the job – the amount of discretion permitted. *Feedback* is high where workers can tell from what happens in their job how well they are doing (and not just by being told by their line manager). For instance, a salesperson knows directly how many sales they are making, but a production-line fitter will not know about their performance until there is feedback from supervisors or quality checkers.

Figure 8.7 shows that Hackman and Oldham believed the first three of these characteristics had a causal effect on how meaningful we find our work. Autonomy connects with a sense of responsibility, while feedback gives us knowledge of the results of our work. These psychological states, in turn, were assumed to have effects on work performance through their influence on motivation and job satisfaction.

A lot of research work has been generated by this model, with much supportive evidence. However, many of the research designs have been correlational, so we do not know, for example, whether experienced meaningfulness of the job leads to greater job satisfaction or if those who are more satisfied find their work more meaningful as a consequence. The status of the psychological events between the job characteristics and the supposed outcomes has been much questioned. However, Behson, Eddy and Lorenzet (2000) conducted a complex meta-analysis and concluded that the core psychological states (CPS) should be retained as a valid part of the model, arguing:

> Failure to incorporate CPS into the JCM could lead to unexpected results and misdirected organizational interventions. This classic theory is quite complex and rich, and has implications for many of the workplace change initiatives ... in use in organizations today. Even though the two-stage model represents a more parsimonious model, important information may be lost if the CPS are not included.

Job enrichment

The hard-line approach of Taylorism led many people to be concerned about the *quality of working life*. The work of Herzberg, and Hackman and Oldham, was in part a response to the rigid job designs produced by scientific management principles. Both these approaches have stimulated job redesign initiatives, known as *job enrichment*, in which employers attempt to increase satisfaction, and hopefully motivation, by increasing existing levels of the job characteristics described above, particularly by:

- increasing autonomy by giving workers more responsibility and freedom to make decisions;
- encouraging workers to take on a wider variety of tasks;
- providing more feedback on worker performance;
- increasing the degree to which the worker sees the whole product on which they work.

These aims can be achieved through a number of initiatives, including *job rotation*, where people move round a number of similar types of job, perhaps on a week-to-week basis, and *semi-autonomous working groups*, where small groups of workers are allowed to organise themselves and make their own decisions in accomplishing a wider set of tasks than they would normally experience.

A problem occurs in job enrichment if it is seen mainly as job *enlargement* – more work for the same pay – but where there is a genuine increase in autonomy and interest, there are often positive effects on motivation and productivity. Volvo successfully introduced semi-autonomous work groups to their Kalmar plant in 1974. An early review of job enrichment initiatives (Warr 1982) concluded that those which went beyond the mere introduction of variety had shown some success. A review by Campion et al. (2005) argued that job enrichment can be successful, but there are several obstacles which need to be addressed. Some redesign, for example, has occurred as part of downsizing programmes, or among managers who are not completely supportive; measures of 'success' differ from case to case, so it is difficult to make clear comparisons and to untangle the sole effects of the redesign factor.

Socio-technical systems

A further impetus to job redesign was the work of psychologists associated with the psycho-analytically oriented Tavistock Institute in London. Their concern was the problems associated with introducing new technology without consideration for the social implications. A relatively recent example of this was the rapid introduction of emailing to organisations in the 1990s. Without adequate training and experience there were incidents of 'flame mail', as people sent ambiguous and curt messages that could be interpreted as hostile, and which lacked the interpersonal cues present in face-to-face meetings. Gotcher (1997) reported on this effect among lecturers and recommended training in both the expression of anger and in confidentiality issues. Burkeman reported in *The Guardian* (20 June 2001) that the lottery company Camelot had banned emailing among staff for a month. Much earlier, a seminal study by Trist and Bamforth (1951), working with the Tavistock Institute, reported on the serious problems in production and absenteeism created by the introduction of fast coal-cutting machines into the Durham coalfields, along with supervised large groups who worked on just one limited task at any one time. Previously, workers had operated in relatively autonomous three-man groups known as 'marrow groups'.

Goal-setting theory

A final and spectacularly successful approach to motivation has been that of *goal-setting theory* (Locke and Latham 2002). Locke basically looked at the effects on performance of setting clear targets. If you have an essay to write, the feeling of helplessness can be overpowering. However, if you sit down and decide what can be managed by tomorrow (e.g. do essay plan, read two articles), the task can appear a lot more manageable and therefore your motivation (and eventually your performance) goes up.

The counter-intuitive finding in Locke's research was that setting harder goals produced higher performance, *but* there were several required conditions. Workers require *clear, specific goals.* Setting general, 'do-your-best' goals is not effective. Goals must also be reachable, and the route to them must be clear to the worker concerned, who must also be committed to the goals. This finding that more difficult goals, if realisable, produce higher motivation and performance is contrary to expectancy theory, which would predict greater motivation the more likely the goal is to be achieved. It means that, within reason, we increase our effort at work when we can see there is a lot to be done. (Locke and Latham (2002) is a concise summary of all the different factors that affect performance as a consequence of goal setting.)

Specific goal setting does not appear to be effective when the task is new and complex, with no previously learned strategy for performing it. Here, Earley, Lee and Hanson (1990) found that a general, do-your-best goal was more effective. Specific goals were thought to encourage too much time being spent on devising strategies to achieve the goals, and not enough time spent actually performing the task itself. Specific goal setting is geared towards increasing motivation and performance when we do not have to learn what the task *is*.

Group processes in organisations

So far in this chapter we have concentrated on factors concerning the individual. Some of these have had social implications, but now we turn specifically to look at the ways in which groups in general operate within organisations. An organisation can be seen as comprising a collection of individuals, but, in this case, the whole is very much greater than the sum of its parts. We saw earlier, with the Hawthorne studies, the power of *social norms* in determining the behaviour of individuals in a group. An organisation comprises many formal groups, but also a number of *informal groups*. A new employee will soon experience these as colleagues introduce them to 'the Friday drinking club' or 'the gym squad'. The formal objectives of the organisation may not be met as expected because of the actions of informal groups, which, as at Hawthorne, to some extent determine what actually goes on in the workplace as against what is planned.

Influence of the group on the individual

Psychologists have provided plenty of evidence that individuals in groups behave differently from how we might expect them to behave on their own. Asch's (1956) work on conformity almost needs no introduction to psychology students. He showed that participants observing a group of confederates choosing an obviously wrong answer to very simple questions about lengths of lines, would also go along with these answers, though some did this much more than others. It is important to note, however, that the 'non-conformers' mostly felt uncomfortable with their public disagreement.

Managers and group leaders, then, need to be aware that group members can feel intimidated by making their decisions public and may feel obliged to go along with what may seem to them to be a bad idea.

Of particular relevance to work psychology is the finding by Crutchfield (1955) that 37 per cent of a group of US military officers on a training course agreed with the statement: 'I doubt whether I would make a good leader'. This was not a public decision, but one made after being given false feedback as to how four peers had chosen. Nevertheless, the situation was 'real' for the officers.

Box 3 Intimidation by the group – a fatal example

In the phenomenon of groupthink, to be discussed shortly, it is found that not only do people feel intimidated by a group and then perhaps not speak their mind, but also that other people loyal to the group leader, and/or his/her decisions, can use ridicule to make a dissenter's silence even more likely. This is made dramatically clear by an example from Brown (1988: 91) of a section of cockpit conversations between three crew members bringing a passenger plane in to land:

> Captain: (*in a relaxed voice*) Well, we know where we are; we're all right.
> Engineer: The boss has got it wired.
> Co-pilot: I hope so.
> Captain: No problem.
> Co-pilot: (*cautiously*) Isn't this a little faster than you normally fly this John?
> Captain: (*confidently*) Oh yeah, but it's nice and smooth. We're going to get in right on time. Maybe a little ahead of time. We've got it made.
> Co-pilot: (*uncertainly*) I sure hope so.
> Engineer: You know, John, do you know the difference between a duck and a co-pilot?
> Captain: What's the difference?
> Engineer: Well a duck can fly!
> Captain: Well said!

This was in the last few minutes before the plane crashed. Here a majority of just two, including some seniority of rank, managed to silence a very wise minority of one.

When minorities *can* win

There are times, as work teams tackle a problem, when a minority feels the need to convince a majority. According to the work of Moscovici (1985), a minority arguing for a position within a larger group needs to:

➡ disagree consistently with the majority on more issues than the crucial one;

➡ be seen as consistent, independent and confident; they do not win hearts by being liked or by being rational.

Nemeth (1986) suggested that minority arguments are good for majorities because generally groups solving more difficult problems tend to avoid conflict by settling for the minimal acceptable solution. He found that groups exposed to minority argument were more original in their thinking; they used a wider range of strategies and found novel solutions, *even when* the minority arguments were wrong! It seems that simply having to deal with contrary views will help employees to be more creative in their problem-solving.

Ng and Van Dyne (2001) studied the effects of a minority view on decision-making, but also took into account the extent to which participants espoused individualistic values (individual achievement is valued over duty to one's group) or collectivist values (one's role in supporting the group is paramount). They found that people with high collectivist values, and who reject individualistic values, were less influenced by minority views and made poorer quality decisions. However, this latter group made better decisions if the influencing minority was of high group status. Managers might well need to take into account the cultural values and orientation of employees, while recognising the general value of voicing minority opinion.

How groups solve problems

What generally happens, then, when a work team tackles a problem together? Early work by Maier and Solem (1952) set up some basic findings. They used problems like that shown in the box below, where there is a correct answer, but careful logic is required to demonstrate its validity. Try the problem now and check your answer against the solution.

Box 4 Logic problem

Natasha buys a car for £600 and sells it for £700. She then buys it back for £800 and sells it again for £900. How much profit has Natasha made overall?

(Many people say £100, but the correct answer is £200. Take it in two stages and treat the sales as being of two *separate* cars. The answer is then more obvious.)

Maier and Solem found that lower status group members had less influence in the group, even when they held the correct answer. Here we see that even when workmates take the courage to offer an answer, they may not be heard. A discerning group leader will ensure that everyone hears the logic of all members' solutions, but as Arnold (2005: 437) points out, because it needs someone else to recognise a low status group member's correct solution, '…the group is as good as its second best member'.

Brainstorming – a solution to group suppression

As long ago as 1954, Osborn suggested that groups might use a procedure of *brainstorming* to solve problems, and this was devised to counteract those group discussion effects that prevent good answers emerging. In brainstorming, the group is instructed that in the first period of problem-solving, all possible ideas, however bizarre, are welcome, and that no one is permitted to ridicule or even comment on an idea until all ideas have been aired. Early critical studies showed that *individuals* actually produced more ideas than brainstorming groups, and confirmations of this result have continued (e.g. Rietzschel, Nijstad and Stroebe 2006). However, as with minority views above, it appears that exposure to other people's creative ideas can improve creativity, so long as 'production blocking' is avoided. This was one of the explanations for the inferior performance of groups, where it was argued that, even in brainstorming groups, only one person can speak at a time, thus blocking some potentially creative ideas, especially if those giving way then forget theirs.

Group polarisation

In an organisation, when groups discuss any kind of future planning, such as new products or marketing strategies, there is usually an element of risk involved. In 1961, James Stoner inspired a completely new and very productive vein of research into groups and risky decisions, using an MA thesis which has never been formally published. In his experiment, individuals working alone made a decision about how much risk they would accept in taking a certain action. They then joined a group which discussed the same problem together and agreed on a group position. Surprisingly, these group decisions often carried more risk than the average of the decisions made by the individuals in the first part of the experiment. This is counter-intuitive because one might assume that groups would rein in any wild decision, and this was the received wisdom of the time – hence Stoner's findings caused a stir.

It was soon shown, however, that sometimes the group decision would be more *conservative* than the average individual decision (Fraser, Gouge and Billig 1971), so the phenomenon, originally termed 'risky shift', came to be known as *group polarisation*. Several explanations of the phenomenon have been offered and two of these have received good support. One (from Brown 1965) argues that individuals wish to appear as good as, or even better than, other group members, so if the group is valuing risk, they will be even riskier. An alternative explanation argues that individuals in the group sessions will be exposed to more of the dominant view (Burnstein and Vinokur 1977). If the tendency is towards caution, then numerically more cautious arguments will be heard. An antidote to this in a work setting would be to ensure that devil's advocates are always able to present opposing views, or at least have the chairperson give more time for the less favourable view.

Groupthink

Sometimes groups make appalling decisions and publicity is given to these if lives are lost or there is a financial disaster. Janis (1972) coined the term *groupthink*, referring to dreadful decisions made in the 1960s, some concerning Vietnam and, in particular, one which led to the so-called Bay of Pigs fiasco. In this incident, President Kennedy's government sent 1400 badly trained and unfit Cuban exiles to attempt a reinvasion of Cuba under a communist-led regime boasting at least 20,000 troops. In retrospect, this decision has been seen as ludicrous, and it is difficult to understand how anyone could have bought into it, not least the poor old exiles.

One feature of groupthink phenomena is the extreme confidence with which participants embark upon the calamitous actions. Recall that the captain's opening comment (see Box 3 on p. 203) makes it somewhat unlikely that the rest of the crew will easily and confidently challenge his flying of the plane.

Box 5 Features of groupthink

Factors leading to groupthink:

➡ Group is highly cohesive and has strong, respected leader who has a view on the issue.
➡ Members see each other as similar and are isolated from other influence.
➡ Group feels external threat, but problem is complex and difficult to solve.
➡ Group believes it is morally superior and invulnerable.

Behaviour within the group:

➡ Illusion of unanimous agreement within the group and belief that 'nothing can go wrong'.
➡ Members disagreeing are pressured to conform (e.g. by ridicule).
➡ 'Mind guards' protect leader from contrary information and hustle for support.
➡ Group does not consider all options – settles for solution from leaders or experts; tendency to seek only evidence that confirms the preferred solution.
➡ Proposed action is not questioned sufficiently – those who do question are silenced; dissent is seen as disloyal – food for the enemy.
➡ Possibly 'pluralistic ignorance' occurs (Latané, Williams and Harkins 1979), where, since others do not say anything, it is assumed that there is no problem.

Figure 8.8 Explosion of the Challenger *shuttle in 1986*

The Challenger disaster

Several features of groupthink were associated with the decisions that led to the loss of the US space shuttle *Challenger* in 1986, which for the first time carried a US civilian; a teacher who was to have spoken from the spaceship to the US President Ronald Reagan and to her pupils. The explosion occurred on live television and many of us who recall the event have the iconic shot (Figure 8.8) forever available as a 'flashbulb memory'.

The likely cause was a set of defective 'O' ring seals about which engineers had complained several times; they raised grave doubts about

launching, since the rings had never been used in temperatures as cold as that of the launch day. Nevertheless, a series of quite irrational group decisions was made and the launch proceeded. Warning signs, presented by the worried engineers, were explained away. A one-third 'burn out' (erosion) of the *Challenger* 'O' ring on previous launches was taken as a 'safety factor' of three (there would be two-thirds left, after all!) (Reason 1990).

Such irrational 'rationalising' is a feature of groupthink, and other phenomena were also present. No one wished to be responsible for delaying the launch and therefore disrupting the arrangement with President Reagan. The people in ultimate control were highly cohesive and to some extent separated from those with the doubts. 'Mind guards' ensured that the engineers' complaints were not heard by the decision-makers. The presidential commission investigating the decision-making process revealed that a major problem lay with the system of communication within the National Aeronautics and Space Administration organisation. The decision system was ambiguous; it was not clear which decision should go to the very top and it was consequently very hard to attribute clear responsibility.

Box 6 Weapons of mass destruction (WMD)?

In 2004 groupthink was cited by the chairman of a US Senate Select Committee which had investigated the failure to find WMD in Iraq. According to the chairman, the report found that the intelligence community had suffered from 'collective group think', by coming to the unsupported conclusion that Iraq was actively pursuing nuclear, chemical and biological weapons programmes. The report (*Report on the U.S. intelligence community's prewar intelligence assessment on Iraq*, 7 July 2004) was covered in a Canadian Broadcasting Corporation news discussion (CBC Online, 9 July 2004, http://www.cbc.ca/news/background/iraq/intelligencereport.html). According to CBS, the report accuses the intelligence community of interpreting ambiguous evidence as conclusively indicative of a WMD programme, and of ignoring and minimising evidence that Iraq did not have such a programme. Intelligence community managers did not encourage their analysts to challenge their assumptions. The analysts relied on information from defectors which was unreliable and likely to be highly biased. According to the report, an ex-defence analyst argued that the decision to go to war was made before, and independent of, any reports on WMD, and the US Senate committee's conclusions were an attempt to blame the problems in Iraq on poor intelligence. So strong and distorted was the collective government belief that nothing could go wrong, that the Deputy Secretary of Defence claimed that invading American troops would be welcomed with chocolates and flowers. When France and Germany refused to go along with the proposed invasion they were ridiculed as being 'old Europe' (the supportive UK, of course, was 'new Europe'). It is said that on Air Force One, the US President's jet, French fries were renamed 'freedom fries'.

How do groups avoid groupthink?

Janis (1982) suggested several strategies for the avoidance of groupthink decisions:

➡ permit members to discuss issues with people outside the group;
➡ break larger groups into smaller units to discuss different aspects of the problem;
➡ allow a period of second-chance reconsideration of doubts and alternatives;

➡ leader stays impartial and encourages *all* members to speak their mind and encourages criticism;
➡ have experts present to raise doubts, or at least appoint devil's advocates to take contrary positions (as Kennedy did for the Cuban Missile Crisis of 1962).

This last point has stimulated its own vein of research. Schulz-Hardt, Jochims and Frey (2002) found that having a devil's advocate (DA) among experimental groups of managers did lessen the tendency for like-minded groups to seek only evidence that confirmed their initial views. This tendency partly supported Janis. However, in groups where the researchers had deliberately put people with differing views together, the genuine disagreement exposed in those groups was more effective than the DA factor in preventing confirmation seeking.

Forming the optimum group – Belbin's team roles

Belbin (2004) is famous in team-building circles for a position he has held for some years on how to form the most productive team for solving complex problems. His research group started by putting together teams consisting entirely of members scoring highly on a mental ability test. These were a disaster and performed worst among differently composed teams. Each member wanted their own ideas to be implemented and found it difficult to listen to the ideas of others without finding weakness. Belbin argues that there are several roles which team members can take in problem-solving discussions and it is best if a team contains one person in each role. The roles are shown in Table 8.2. An important addition to Belbin's groups was that of a 'plant' – a creative person who can get the team off well-worn thinking rails and on to novel ideas and solutions. It would be problematic, however, to have more than one plant in a team, since their zany ideas might clash and cause distraction. Those with the cash to spare might like to discover their own Belbin preferred team role on Belbin's own website (http://www.belbin.com/testing.htm).

Group conflict

Before we denounce conflict as a 'bad thing', we should take a moment to consider the view of several work psychologists that a certain amount of conflict is not only inevitable when groups interact,

Coordinator (Chairman)	Impartial; clarifies goals, promotes decision-making, delegates well; may be seen as manipulative.
Plant	Creative, imaginative, unorthodox; solves difficult problems; ignores incidentals; may be too preoccupied to communicate effectively.
Monitor, evaluator	Soberly evaluates all suggestions; sees all opinions; judges accurately; may lack drive and ability to inspire others.
Implementer (company worker)	Turns ideas into practical actions; gets the team working; disciplined, reliable, conservative and efficient; may be somewhat inflexible.
Completer, finisher	Checks details for problems and errors; painstaking, conscientious, anxious; delivers on time; may worry unduly; reluctant to delegate.
Shaper	A driver; challenging, dynamic, thrives on pressure; helps overcome obstacles; may be prone to provocation and offensiveness.
Resource investigator	Works outside the group, developing contacts and checking possibilities; extrovert, enthusiastic, communicative; may be overoptimistic.
Team worker	Listens to others, shows empathy; is sensitive and can help avoid friction in the group using social lubrication; cooperative, perceptive and diplomatic; may be indecisive in crunch situations.
Specialist	Provides knowledge and skills in rare supply; single-minded, self-starting, dedicated; contributes only on a narrow front; dwells on technicalities.

Table 8.2 Belbin's (2004) team roles and their characteristics

but, within healthy organisations, it is also desirable. Conflict can help stimulate people and enable them to reach innovative solutions to problems (James, Chen and Goldberg 1992); it can improve the quality of decisions if the process involves individuals trying harder to express their own views, thereby exposing the group to a wider range of information and ideas (Cosier and Dalton 1990; also consider the discussion above about minority views). Conflict can also:

⟶ remove tension by bringing disgruntlements and underlying issues to the surface;
⟶ help avoid complacency, especially in successful teams;
⟶ motivate and energise generally.

Too little conflict, therefore, can be undesirable, but what is certainly destructive is too *much* conflict. Conflict very often occurs between different groups in the workplace. For example, the exhaust fitters can never rely on their parts being delivered – the drivers are thought to be always swigging tea by the roadside.

Realistic group conflict theory

In a famous field experiment, Sherif et al. (1961) produced evidence that group conflict is caused by competition for resources. They arranged for two groups of boys at a summer camp, previously kept separate from one another and relatively cooperative, to take part in a series of competitive events. The two groups quickly became highly hostile to one another and created derogatory names and stereotypes. The set-up was rather artificial, however, in that the boys did not know each other before the camp. Tyerman and Spencer (1983) showed that groups of English Boy Scouts, treated similarly to Sherif's boys, retained their friendships with one another across competing groups. This is more like the situation at work.

A challenge to the idea that competition creates inter-group hostility arose with the work of Tajfel and Turner (1985). They argued that simply knowing one is in a group is enough to create in-group favouritism and a stance against other groups. Our 'in-group' could be our family, our college class or the people at our local pub. In several classic experiments it was shown that people will favour a group that they have only just become a member of, even when allocation of members to the group was almost or completely arbitrary (e.g. a preference for a painting or even just the toss of a coin). After allocation to a group, participants then worked alone, awarding points to themselves and to one anonymous member of the other group. Participants usually favoured themselves, and the *difference* between what they and the other group received was crucial. They would prefer to allocate 13 points to themselves and 13 to the out-group, for instance, rather than give 25 to the out-group and receive 19 themselves! Here it seemed that merely being formed into a group caused an allegiance to it *prior to* any competition.

Tajfel's *social identity theory* has been criticised for seeming to assume that inter-group prejudice (and even racism) is a *natural* effect of group formation. However, it has stimulated a huge volume of research and later evolved into *self-categorisation theory* (Turner 1999),which argues that our sense of group membership is altered by the context of the other groups we are being compared with, and that this in turn affects our levels of self-esteem.

Reducing or managing conflict

Thomas (1992) identified five different strategies for the reduction of conflict and placed them on a grid composed of two dimensions: *Assertiveness,* the extent to which a group or individual tries to satisfy its own needs or desires, and *Cooperativeness,* the extent to which the other party's needs or desires are considered.

➠ *Competition,* a win-lose situation in which one party persists in obtaining their goals at the expense of the other.
➠ *Collaboration*: both parties try to find a resolution in a win-win manner by clarifying differences and considering a wide and complex range of alternatives. Where scarce resources are required by both sides, this solution may not be possible.
➠ *Compromise*: each party gives up part of their claim. This can be described as (and may often be) a lose-lose outcome. However, consider the common example of a union–management conflict over pay and conditions. Each side

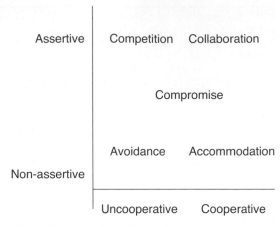

Figure 8.9 Types of conflict resolution
Source: Thomas (1976)

might start out with an unrealistic position from which they know they will have to move (as when two people haggle over a used car). If each side gets what they consider realistically to be a fair enough deal, then the situation is more win-win than lose-lose.
➠ *Avoidance*: the conflict is suppressed on both sides – a lose-lose tactic, which may be an appropriate tactic where the parties have to interact but the situation is too difficult to resolve. This might also occur as a 'cooling-off' period. However, the differences still exist and it may be necessary to resort to one of the other tactics later on, or simply part company, as when an employee resigns or is sacked, or when two partners split up a company.
➠ *Accommodation*: one side gives in to benefit the other. This is a lose-win situation, which might occur where one side sees it as too expensive to continue the dispute. Of course, they may be devising another strategy to regain their losses at a later date, with a different set of circumstances.

The role of superordinate goals

In Sherif et al.'s (1961) experiment described earlier, there was an attempt to resolve the artificially created conflict. The groups met up for various activities, such as seeing a film. This did not work, but when the two groups had to work together to restore the camp's water supply (secretly cut off), and to rescue a truck with a rope, the hostility diminished and the sets of boys started making friendship choices from the opposing group. The researchers assumed that common goals on which both sides had to cooperate would reduce conflict.

Can't we just get the workers all together? The 'contact' hypothesis

Psychologists have long believed (as do many lay people) that if only conflicting groups could be brought into normal contact with one another, they would let go of the damaging stereotypes they hold. The 'out-group' would be discovered to be just as human, error-prone, humorous and moral as we consider ourselves to be. Allport (1954) dubbed this the *contact hypothesis*. Perhaps the administrative staff would let go of the stereotype they hold of the lecturers if we held a Christmas party? Managers might believe, somewhat naively, that simply bringing together members of two conflicting teams in a formal discussion or a sporting event, for example, will reduce hostility through the destruction of inter-group myths. Previous research, especially that of Cook (1978), has suggested that contact may be successful, but only if:

⟹ out-group members do not behave in ways which confirm the existing stereotypes;
⟹ out-group members are seen as typical members (if not, we might get the classic response: 'I don't mean you, you're different');
⟹ group members meet in an informal setting so that interactions can be personal;
⟹ group members engage in tasks which require mutual cooperation;
⟹ the environment *supports* cooperative behaviour and stereotype reduction – the effort must not be seen as a token gesture;
⟹ group members have equal status – this will be the hardest criterion to meet in the real world of work, though some efforts can be made to reduce obvious signs of status difference, such as lack of uniform, first names, neutral territory, and so on.

Although there has always been a level of scepticism about contact theory, a meta-analytic review claims results which thoroughly support the hypothesis. The researchers reviewed 713 independent samples from 515 studies, and concluded that contact 'typically reduces intergroup prejudice... These contact effects typically generalize to the entire outgroup, and they emerge across a broad range of

outgroup targets and contact settings' (Pettigrew and Tropp 2006: 751). The effects were found to be similar whether or not the in-/out-groups were racial or ethnic. They also found greater prejudice reduction where the conditions above applied, but argued that the conditions themselves were not necessary for prejudice reduction.

Leadership

Organisations have always hoped that psychologists might some day deliver the Holy Grail of management – that is, to tell them what makes a good leader. However, there has also been much discussion about whether we really want managers to be leaders. Job adverts certainly ask that managers should be able to show 'true leadership qualities', but are the two concepts different? Managers can be leaders, but we do not usually think of leaders as managers. Have a think about the differences between the two and then take a look at how Statt (2004) sees the differences, in Table 8.3.

Of course, managers often demonstrate some of the 'leader' characteristics in Table 8.3, and leaders might also show some of the 'manager' characteristics. One important difference often

Manager	Leader
Motivates people and administers resources to achieve stated organisational goals	Motivates people to develop new objectives
Implements	Shapes
Narrows down horizons	Opens up horizons
Rational	Emotional
Does things right	Does the right thing
Transactional	Transformational
Concerned with means; for example: ⟹ Responsibility ⟹ Fairness ⟹ Maintaining agreements	Concerned with ends; for example: ⟹ Future direction of the organisation ⟹ Ultimate goals and values ⟹ Empowerment of staff
Static orientation	Dynamic orientation

Table 8.3 Differences between managers and leaders
Source: Statt (2004:299)

occurring between the two roles is that managers are *appointed*. They get their authority from their *assigned role*. Leaders, however, often get their power from what is called *legitimate authority*. They do not enjoy respect simply because of their allocated position; they gain the respect of others from what they do and how they perform.

What are leaders like? Leader characteristics

The most obvious approach to the study of leadership, and one of great interest to organisational management, has been to assume that leaders differ from others in certain personality characteristics, sometimes referred to as 'traits', and increasingly known in the twenty-first century as 'competencies'. Early studies tended to find some relationship between effective leadership and intelligence, dominance, need for power, self-confidence and a few other traits. The problem here is the usual one with studies that simply find variables that are related. Does self-confidence produce good leadership or does assumed leadership develop one's self-confidence? In addition, these early studies produced many contradictions, only small associations between variables and did not take into account the task involved. No single trait was found to be common to all good leaders (Hollander 1985). In the last decade of the twentieth century and the early years of the twenty-first, there has been an upsurge of interest in leader characteristics, but these have been more general factors, such as charisma (see overleaf) or flexibility.

Observing leader behaviour

Because of the difficulty in finding specific characteristics that marked out leaders, psychologists turned their attention towards the behaviour that leaders exhibited. After all, this is easier to observe and record, and in keeping with the empirical method. One of the earliest studies (Lewin, Lippitt and White 1939) was carried out in a number of boys' clubs, where the members attempted to construct models. Group leaders were asked to take on just one of three different styles, described in Table 8.4.

Contrary to the expected finding that democratic leadership would produce the best results, no one style proved to be consistently superior in all aspects. The autocratically led groups produced generally better models, but there was more fighting and the boys only worked with the leader present. In the democratically run groups the boys were more satisfied with the experience. Those in the laissez-faire groups displayed low morale *and* little productivity.

Leadership behaviour characteristics – Ohio and Michigan

A rare case of psychologists independently coming up with similar findings occurred at the Universities of Ohio and Michigan in the late 1950s. At Ohio, psychologists asked people to describe their leaders and then analysed the results, coming up with two major factors that they argued underlay most of the descriptions. These were:

➡ *Initiating structure*: The degree to which leaders organised people's roles, assigned tasks, maintained work standards, and so on.
➡ *Consideration*: The degree to which leaders considered the feelings of subordinates, demonstrated respect and trust for them and developed rapport with them.

The Ohio group found the two behaviour patterns first, and then sought to demonstrate differences in performance and satisfaction among workers under the two styles. Similarly to the Lewin, Lippitt and

Democratic	Autocratic	Laissez-faire
Discussed possible projects with the boys and involved them in decisions about activities. Explained his comments.	Issued orders and *told* the boys what to do. Did not invite their opinions. Sometimes praised or blamed. Did not explain comments.	Left the boys to themselves after instructing them to do the same as the others. Offered help only when asked. Did not praise or blame.

Table 8.4 Three leadership styles
Source: Lewin, Lippitt and White (1939)

White (1939) study, the most common finding was that structured leaders were associated with better job performance, while leaders higher on consideration produced greater satisfaction, both with jobs and with the leader. A review by Judge, Piccolo and Ilies (2004) validated these findings over a very large number of studies, but by rather small margins.

At Michigan the researchers *started* with the differences in effectiveness and then looked for related leader behaviour styles. They found that effective managers demonstrated more relationship-oriented behaviour, whereas non-effective leaders were largely task-oriented, that is, they concentrated mainly on getting the job done. Basically the two styles were very similar to those found by the Ohio group, but the Michigan group considered relationship-oriented style to be better.

Contingency theories

This preference for one apparently superior style is that for some situations it may be better to be task-oriented (e.g. dealing with an emergency) and for others to be person-oriented (e.g. during the restructuring of a department). This is the position taken by *contingency theories*, which argue that the best leadership will occur when the leader's behaviour is *contingent upon* the specific situation. The most influential approach has been that of Fiedler (1967), who accepted the basic dimensions of task and person orientation as relatively fixed in each individual, and assumed that they were two ends of a single dimension – if you were high on one, you would be low on the other. He invented an indirect measure to assess the degree to which a person was more task- or person-oriented. Called the Least Preferred Co-worker (LPC) measure, it asks the test taker to select the worker whom they have found it most awkward to work with (*not* their least liked worker). If the test taker assessed this worker quite harshly, Fiedler assumed they had a task orientation,

whereas a forgiving and understanding assessment indicated person orientation.

Next Fiedler considered the *interaction* between these two leadership behaviour patterns and the specifics of the task situation. Fiedler identified three key aspects of work situations that, depending on the type of leader involved, would make that situation either favourable or unfavourable to the leader:

➡ *Leader–member relations*: These are high where members like, trust and respect their leader.
➡ *Task structure*: The degree to which task goals, and procedures for reaching them are well defined, as well as the means of measuring output.
➡ *Position power*: The degree to which the leader holds authority, for example in the form of ability to reward, discipline or even sack.

Given that each of these situational variables can have two values (e.g. high/low), we get eight possible combinations of measures of situation variables (as shown in Table 8.5).

Now the task is to look at how the two extreme types of leader behaviour would interact with these eight possible combinations. For instance, Fiedler argued, where the situation is either very favourable or very unfavourable, a more task-oriented leader (low LPC score) is appropriate. In the former case, interpersonal relations are already high, so there is no need to work on these and the impetus can be towards getting the job done. Where things are highly unfavourable, there is probably no point in trying to improve relations and, again, the leader can concentrate on the job. Where favourability is in between, there is more of a need to nurture good relations in order to keep team members motivated towards the task, so a high-LPC leader is preferred.

	High	←		Situation favourability			→	Low
L–M relations	Good	Good	Good	Good	Poor	Poor	Poor	Poor
Task structure	High	High	Low	Low	High	High	Low	Low
Position power	Strong	Weak	Strong	Weak	Strong	Weak	Strong	Weak

Table 8.5 Aspects of situation favourability

Fiedler's theory stimulated a lot of research and the production of alternative theories. A meta-analytic study by Schriesheim, Tepper and Tetrault (1994) found general support, and, in particular, found that high-LPC leaders did better than low-LPC leaders in situations of moderate favourability, and much better in moderately unfavourable conditions. They argued that since most situations of management *are* moderately unfavourable, why not just assume that high-LPC leaders are better? Fiedler himself argued, in a sense, for fitting the job to the manager, and developed the Leader Match programme to this end. The programme helped managers to recognise their leadership style and suggested ways in which situations (rather than the leader's behaviour) could be altered to create greater favourability. Fiedler has since developed his *cognitive resource* theory out of the original one, but now includes the interaction of the leader's own intelligence and experience, along with the stress generated by the leadership role. Stress will make us think less clearly and act out of old habits, hence leaders with greater experience should do better under stress. Fiedler has claimed support from quite a number of studies (Fiedler 1995).

Transactional, transformational and charismatic leaders

If you look back to Statt's (2004) distinctions between managers and leaders in Table 8.3, you will see that the manager role concerns day-to-day activities like getting people to do their allotted tasks or ensuring that agreements are kept to. These are manger–employee transactions, so Burns (1978) suggested the term *transactional leadership*, and the term *transformational leadership* when leaders are more like the right-hand side of Table 8.3 (the 'Leader' column). A transformational leader is one who inspires their teams, gets them to think harder, be more creative and to make some self-sacrifice in the cause of the organisation or movement. Clearly these are going to be of interest to most managements! This has been a hugely successful concept in psychological research. Judge and Bono (2000) reported that over half the psychological literature on leadership in the 1990s concerned the transformational leadership concept. Across many studies, transformational leadership has been found to be superior to transactional leadership in promoting work effectiveness (Lowe, Kroeck and Sivasubramaniam 1996; Bass 1998). Alimo-Metcalfe and Alban-Metcalfe (2001) argued

that much transformational leadership research has been carried out on 'distant' managers or executives (i.e. high up in their organisation), and mostly on males in the USA. They developed the Transformational Leadership Questionnaire, which they present as valid for the measurement of 'nearby' leaders (i.e. including middle management) and equally across genders.

Charismatic leadership

One aspect of transformational leadership that has attracted a good deal of attention in recent years is that of *charisma*. There are some great leaders whom we feel would have generated loyalty and devotion no matter when or where they were born. Obvious candidates would be Nelson Mandela and Mahatma Gandhi. However, in talking of the ability to inspire large numbers of followers, we would also have to include the likes of Hitler. At work, however, leaders need not be quite so inspirational. Charismatic leadership qualities, identified by House (1977), would be: vision of the future; an attractive set of values and morals; and having an extraordinary effect on followers, who find it easy to identify with the leader. In addition, the leader is 'one of the people', often suffering more than they do (or working even harder) to achieve the overall goal. House, Spangler and Woycke (1991) showed that the more charisma possessed by US presidents, the more effective they had been in dealing with the economy. Conger and Kanungo (1998) discuss the value of charismatic leaders within organisations.

Do we need leaders at all?

Collins (2002) produced interesting data on 1435 companies, some of which he defined as 'great', if their performance was three times the average market performance for any one year. The data were collected for a 15-year period and he found that, contrary to what most management thinkers would predict, the companies' success did *not* depend on factors like large-scale organisational change, clever new business strategies or hiring a charismatic, expensive chief executive. It is this last point which is of interest here – the best companies did not have new, inspirational leaders. There has been a vein of thinking over the last 20 years which argues that leadership is *mainly* in the eye of the beholder. That is, for most of the concepts we have considered – transformational and charismatic leaders, contingency theory, trait theory – there is always contradictory evidence as to whether this or that leadership variable actually results in greater productivity or job satisfaction. Though there is not time to go into this debate here, it is well argued, and amusingly so, in Statt (2004). Meinzl (1985 in Statt 2004) claimed that leadership is a romance. We have deep-seated needs to feel we are being led, that someone is taking responsibility; and the more likeable and unselfish they are, the more charismatic they will seem to be.

Example of an intervention in occupational psychology: job redesign at a call centre

This is a summary of an intervention by organisational development consultants which was evaluated by Michael Workman and William Bommer, whose work was published in 2004. A large company, which sold computer operating systems and had revenues of $8 billion in the late 1980s, found it had problems at its call centres where support engineers (SEs) answer calls from system users experiencing problems with the software. The volume of calls had increased immensely because of the uptake in personal computers in the 1990s: the SEs could not keep up, customers were complaining about the time taken to respond to calls (sounds familiar!) and many solutions were hasty and inadequate.

The company's management perceived low morale, poor performance, negative staff attitudes, low commitment, was experiencing an alarming staff turnover rate and finally sought the help of external consultants. Three types of intervention programme were devised and a fourth group of SEs served as a control group. The programmes were:

⬛➡ Alignment job design (AJD)

Organisational and individual goals are 'aligned' by restructuring the rewards system. The authors claim that the approach is compatible with the Job Characteristics Model in that skill variety, task identity, individual autonomy and feedback are all targeted. New performance measures were introduced that took some of the pressure off SEs to answer as many calls as possible, in order for them to give more time to solutions. A job rotation scheme was also introduced, involving two days a week off the phones in order to work on especially difficult problems that the SE had queued up.

⬛➡ High involvement work processes (HIWP)

SEs were encouraged to participate in teams with their leader in restructuring some aspects of the job. These teams restructured the performance criteria and measures for their job and created a research team which SEs would work in on alternate weeks,

coming off the phones for that period. This team tackled the harder software problems, and junior members were paired with senior specialists as mentors. To start the programme, SEs attended a one-week training seminar that encouraged participation, and there were also regular lunch-and-learn workshops with managers, which included widening SEs' knowledge of the organisation. Quotas were set for the group rather than individuals, and individual bonuses were based on meeting objectives set by the team.

⬛➡ Autonomous work teams (AWT)

These were mentioned earlier when discussing job enrichment. In this case the group formed was entirely autonomous, and management gave up any involvement in setting and assessing performance measures. The group was responsible for assigning jobs to members and planning and scheduling all work. The group introduced a rotation scheme similar to that started in the AJD condition, and the group was awarded merit increases in wages, based on the team's own defined productivity and quality targets.

Measures of job satisfaction and organisational commitment were taken before the experiment started and again six months later. The consultants would have liked to extend this period, but the company needed to get on with putting in place the intervention that produced the best results. AJD produced a significant increase in job satisfaction, but not in commitment, whereas HIWP produced significant increases in both. There were no significant changes for the AWT condition or the control condition. The authors suggest that the individually based approach of AJD probably worked against any increase in commitment to the organisation. The study did not measure job performance directly, but the authors argue that, theoretically, increases in job satisfaction and commitment to the organisation are good indicators of likely increases in performance. Finally, being a quasi-experiment (see Chapter 11), it was difficult to control some possible confounding variables, especially that of management involvement, which was highest in the HIWP condition and lowest in the AWT condition, so here is an alternative explanation of the findings. However, the researchers also measured preference for working in a group, and what is impressive is the fact that in the HIWP

condition, even those *lowest* in preference for group work increased their job satisfaction and organisational commitment.

A day in the life of an occupational psychologist

If you would like to see how occupational psychologists spend their day, and read a lot more about their experience of work, you could look at the following website, which provides back issues of *People and Organisations at Work* (POW), a BPS Division of Occupational Psychology publication, which carries a regular 'Day in the life of...' feature: http://www.bps.org.uk/dop/division-publications/pow/previous-issues.cfm

An occupational psychologist might well spend the entire day training. This might be a course in test administration to give participants BPS Level A (skills and mental abilities) or Level B (personality) Competencies in Occupational Assessment. Let us suppose, though, that the day is more varied:

➠ 9.00–10.00: Deliver training module – part of Level A training course run by colleagues.
➠ 10.00–11.00: Work on reliability data from new psychometric instrument which assesses job satisfaction for call centre employees.
➠ 11.30–1.00: Visit estate agent wishing to create more motivated and tightly knit sales teams in branches. Suggest autonomous teams training and arrange for branch visits to staff prior to putting in a consultancy bid.
➠ 2.00–3.00: Drop in to local hospital where clinical staff have been taking part in a stress management programme delivered by specialist trainers. Our job here is to check that the experimental procedures are being adhered to so that we can evaluate the effects of two types of training, compared to a control group, in six months' time.
➠ 3.00–5.00: Back to the office to work on questionnaire data gathered from truck mechanics in a project conducted for the local council's transport department, investigating safety and risk factors in their maintenance depots which have been experiencing higher than usual accident figures.

CURRENT DIRECTIONS IN OCCUPATIONAL PSYCHOLOGY

One thing is for certain, occupational psychologists will need to keep adapting to the world of work which is changing very rapidly. What might be considered the most important changes are explored below.

Diversity

It is still the case that a mere 9 per cent of FTSE 100 company directors are female. Psychologists still have a lot to teach selectors about discrimination. Minority ethnic groups are still under-represented among graduate members entering large organisations. Companies themselves need to take note of increasingly successful litigation concerning discrimination and harassment at work, while psychologists are likely to be involved in training, organisational change and, particularly, in the development of improved selection techniques.

Flexible and home working

Information technology is creating all kinds of previously unimagined working arrangements. Fifteen years ago I would not have dreamed of being able to post lectures, talk with students, collect assessments, deliver feedback and post marks, all from a desk either at home or on the other side of the world. All this and much more is now possible. In addition, some 21 per cent of all full-time employees now work to some kind of flexible working pattern (Kandola 2005). Men are gradually taking up wider childcare options. Occupational psychologists, therefore, should become increasingly involved in adapting management and supervision systems to cope with more flexible work schedules and staff communications.

Flatter, leaner organisational structures

Jobs are no longer for life, and there is not such a steep, multi-levelled promotion structure within each organisation. Employees therefore need to develop a wider portfolio of competencies, and be prepared to train, develop, switch organisations and change working status – sometimes employed, sometimes contracted or self-employed. Career and counselling psychologists will have a lot of involvement here, but so will those advising management on selection, appraisal, development and motivational factors.

Ageing workforce

Partly because we simply live longer, but also because of changes in the financial security of pensions, people are working longer. This brings in the issue of age discrimination and stereotypes (along with gender and ethnicity), but it also means attention to differences across ages in what creates job satisfaction, the changing importance of the work–life balance, counselling for retirement and factors relating to learning and skill acquisition at different ages.

Globalisation and multinational organisations

Enquire about your computer, check on your insurance and you may well, without realising it, be talking to someone in India or China. A number of credit card companies and British Telecom also use call centre staff based in India to call you to remind you to pay your bill. Who trains these staff so that their conversations with UK dialect speakers is as smooth as possible? As business communication becomes more and more global, there is work to do in training staff how to communicate across cultures. In many Eastern cultures, for instance, it would be a huge mistake to start off calling your business host by his first name; directly challenging a much older person's point of view will be frowned upon also.

One of the biggest threats to occupational psychology is the practitioner–academic divide, which has seen many 'pure' practitioners split off into their own Association of Business Psychologists (see p. 188). Kandola (2005) argues that occupational psychologists are in danger of becoming seen as merely human 'assessment technicians', because assessment selection is the area in which they have made the biggest impression. However, psychologists are not influential enough, Kandola argues, when companies face major change, nor in the formulation of national policy and initiatives such as Investors in People. This is partly because of industry's stereotypes of occupational psychologists as psychological testers, and partly because of the need for occupational psychologists themselves to earn a living and therefore concentrate on what customers want. According to Kandola, however, there is an urgent need for practitioners to make more use of what the academics produce and to encourage them to produce more that is relevant to the profession. Otherwise the occupational psychologist can start to look more like a pure human resources consultant.

RECOMMENDED FURTHER READING

Arnold, J. (2005) *Work Psychology*. Harlow: Prentice Hall.

Hollway, W. (1991) *Work Psychology and Organizational Behaviour*. London: Sage.

McKenna, E. F. (2000) *Business Psychology and Organisational Behaviour: A student's handbook*. Hove: Psychology Press.

Riggio, R. E. (2006) *Introduction to Industrial/ Organizational Psychology*, fourth edition. New York: Prentice Hall.

USEFUL WEBSITES

BPS Division of Occupational Psychology. http://www.bps.org.uk/dop/dop_home.cfm

Society for Industrial and Organizational Psychology (American Psychological Association): http://www.siop.org/

Personnel Today magazine: http://www.personneltoday.com/Home/Default.aspx

Applied Psychology

Exercises

1 Look at Maslow's hierarchy of needs (p. 199) and think of ways in which an organisation can try to satisfy these needs for individual employees.

2 In term's of Fiedler's contingency theory of leadership, try to decide which kind of leader might be most appropriate in the following situations and explain why:

➠ *Uptown Rovers for the cup*

Uptown High football team just love and admire their coach[1]; she is the school Head of Sports[2] and the team are focused on winning the forthcoming cup final match with the Downtown Upper School first XI[3].

➠ *Much Whopping Cricket Club*

MWCC are led by someone who is just about tolerated by the team[1]. He is the local butcher and volunteered for the task many years ago[2]. At present the team is struggling for cash. They have decided that they need to generate a better image for the team in order to attract a local business into sponsorship, but they have little idea how to go about doing this[3].

➠ *Old Farm Primary School in Bedland County, a nice shire location*

Sheila is in the position of Deputy Head Teacher[1]. Some of the staff are resentful of the way in which Sheila was appointed over their old colleague Dan, who subsequently retired. Other, newer staff are very fond of and loyal to her because they find her very supportive and very forthcoming with valuable information[2]. The Head Teacher is known to be fairly strict in his approach, but is often away on work for the county. Sheila is responsible for developing the school's new multicultural policy and strategy. The local education authority has issued general guidelines, but each school must adapt these to its own particular circumstances[3].

3 Your tutor has asked you to lead a tutorial group which has to create a strategy for appointing a lecturer. List the factors you would take into account in helping the group come to the best solution.

Answers

1

➠ Physiological needs – temperature, food and drink on site, but also a good living wage to provide food, and so on.
➠ Safety needs – safety on the work site, but also enough pay to purchase good housing.
➠ Social needs – staff room, parties.
➠ Esteem needs – recognition of worth to organisation through appraisal and reward system; aesthetic need perhaps through work-based staff societies.
➠ Self-actualisation – facilitating autonomous working; giving employees power in decision-making, and so on.

2

➠ *Uptown Rovers for the cup*
[1] Leader–member relations are high; [2] leader has position power; [3] highly focused task, with clear goals. Hence situation favourability is high and task-oriented leader appropriate.

➠ *Much Whopping Cricket Club*
[1] Leader–member relations are poor; [2] leader has low position power; [3] task does not have clear goals. Hence situation favourability is low and task-oriented leader appropriate.

➠ *Old Farm Primary School in Bedland County, a nice shire location*
[1] Sheila has moderate position power, but this is not complete as she is only the deputy; [2] leader–member relations are mixed – some good, some not; [3] the task has moderate structure, with some general goals clear, but some goals unclear, needing development at the school. Hence situation favourability is moderate and a person-oriented leader is appropriate.

3
General answer revising all factors mentioned under group processes, including: conformity, brainstorming, group polarisation, minority influence, team and leadership roles.

Sport and Exercise Psychology

SPORT AND EXERCISE PSYCHOLOGY IN THE BRITISH PSYCHOLOGICAL SOCIETY (BPS)

In the early twenty-first century, sport and exercise psychology has gained recognition within the mainstream discipline. The British Psychological Society (BPS) formally acknowledged this in 2004 by establishing a Division of Sport and Exercise Psychology (http://www.bps.org.uk/spex/spex_home.cfm). At the time of writing (2006), the division has around 650 members. Integrating sport and exercise into the BPS gave sport and exercise psychologists the opportunity to apply for chartered status. Ultimately, this will lead to a career progression for the sport and/or exercise psychologist, from an undergraduate psychology degree, through postgraduate training in sport and exercise psychology, to becoming a Chartered Psychologist.

The sport and exercise psychology community appears divided on the relative advantages afforded by this route and the more traditional career path, through an undergraduate degree in sport and exercise science, followed by postgraduate studies in sport and/or exercise psychology, combined with supervised applied experience (explored in the box on p. 220: 'How would I become a sport or exercise psychologist?'). A recent trend has been the development of undergraduate sport and exercise psychology programmes offering graduate basis for registration with the BPS (see Chapter 1). These appear to offer a compromise, providing both depth of content in psychology and knowledge of the other areas of sport and exercise science.

Chartered status with the BPS (like accreditation from the British Association of Sport and Exercise, which comes from the more traditional route) is an important threshold attainment. It indicates a level of competence to practise. Under both schemes there is an expectation that a psychologist will engage in continuing professional development and training.

PRINCIPLES OF SPORT AND EXERCISE PSYCHOLOGY

Sport and exercise psychology is the scientific study of people and their behaviours in the context of sport and exercise (Gill 2000). In the first edition of this book (1996), there was a single chapter entitled 'Sport Psychology', which covered sport psychology, exercise psychology and skill acquisition/motor control. Since then, the two sub-disciplines of exercise psychology and sport psychology have diverged into two distinct areas of study. Skill acquisition and motor control was included in the first edition, but it has largely realigned itself with biomechanics and will not be included in this chapter.

What is exercise psychology?

Exercise refers to structured and relatively formal physical activity. Exercise behaviours are usually carried out in gyms, health clubs or sport centres. *Physical activity*, on the other hand, refers to unstructured and informal behaviours, such as walking, dancing and housework. Both are important aspects of health-enhancing physical activity.

Exercise psychology links with health and clinical psychology. Theoretical understanding about health-related behaviour has helped exercise psychologists to understand why some people adopt and maintain a physically active lifestyle, while others do not. Exercise psychology also examines the positive impact activity and exercise can have on psychological well-being.

What is sport psychology?

Sport psychology has links with organisational and occupational psychology, and also, perhaps surprisingly, with counselling psychology. Theoretical understanding from these areas can help the sport psychologist to address performance-related issues, such as poor team dynamics, low confidence and performance anxiety. The aims of sport psychology are to help athletes and teams to fulfil their potential as performers, and to develop a sense of personal satisfaction and development through their sport. Both aims are important. Many sport performers are outcome-oriented – winning and striving for excellence can obscure everything else in a committed performer. However, sport, especially elite sport, can be brutal. Many players have their careers affected, or even terminated, through injury, and the pool of talent in many sports is large; a poor run of form can easily see performers go from 'hero to zero' in a few weeks. The psychologist has a key role in helping players to develop mental skills that enable them to develop and fulfil their potential in performance and also manage the related stresses.

WHAT AN EXERCISE PSYCHOLOGIST DOES

All psychologists have the same aims: to observe, describe and explain behaviour, and to intervene to modify or control behaviour, where this is appropriate or necessary. Exercise psychologists conduct research to observe and describe exercise and physical activity behaviour. Research is conducted in a wide spectrum of settings (e.g. free living populations, exercise clubs, gyms) and with a wide array of populations, including clinical populations. Exercise psychologists are also very interested in understanding why people do not exercise or adopt physically active lifestyles. Conducting this type of research often involves working within primary health care settings. This is because around 95 per cent of the population will visit their family doctor in a three-year period (Taylor 1999). Researchers can be certain, therefore, that they will be gathering data from as large a sample pool as possible. From this research, theoretical models are developed to explain behaviour, and these are tested, refined and applied in public health interventions designed to encourage the adoption of physical activity.

Exercise psychologists may also be involved in dissemination of knowledge, either within colleges and universities, or, increasingly, working with health professionals who have day-to-day contact with patients who need to change or maintain change to a healthier lifestyle. These types of interventions are often delivered through the growing number of general practitioner exercise referral schemes, where people are prescribed exercise in preference to or in conjunction with other forms of treatment.

A day in the life of an exercise psychologist

This is the typical day of a research fellow in exercise psychology at a university:

➡ 9.00–11.00: Research meeting. I am part of a multidisciplinary research team investigating the role of exercise in the management of obesity. We are currently seeking funding for a large intervention project in socially deprived areas. In today's meeting we are reviewing an application prior to submission.

➡ 11.00–12.30: Return to the university to hold a tutorial for a group of postgraduate nurses studying the psychology of behavioural change.

➡ 12.30–1.00: I practise what I preach! I go for a 30-minute brisk walk with a colleague before lunch. This is my 10,000 steps for the day.

➡ 1.30–3.30: In-service training. I am running a training session for practice nurses involved in a GP referral programme. Today's session is covering motivational interviewing.

➡ 3.30–6.00: Exercise referral clients. As part of a trial of an intervention aimed at increasing physical activity, I am conducting interviews with people with type 2 diabetes referred to an exercise programme.

WHAT A SPORT PSYCHOLOGIST DOES

Sport psychologists have three main roles: research, consultancy and teaching. Until the late twentieth century, the majority of sport psychologists in the UK were based in universities, and combined research and consultancy roles with teaching undergraduate and postgraduate students. In the late 1990s, many sports received additional funding for world-class performance through the National Lottery. National and Regional Institutes of Sport were established around the UK, providing support services for athletes. Most of these institutes employ sport psychology support staff to work with elite and developing athletes. In this respect, the UK is following the pattern set in North America and

Australia, where applied sport psychologists work as full-time consultants outside educational settings. However, there is a still a great deal of basic research that needs to be carried out to explain psychological factors linked to performance. This research is critical, as it clarifies which interventions are appropriate and effective in helping athletes develop mental skills to support performance.

A day in the life of a sport psychologist

This is a typical day for a sport psychologist working in private practice:

➡ 7.00–8.00: Meeting with team prior to travelling to make first contact with a new client. The client is a motor sport racing team.

➡ 8.30–11.30: Presentation on performance psychology to motor sport team, followed by extensive question-and-answer session about the practicalities of service delivery to drivers and support teams around the world. This is a very important client.

➡ 11.30: Return to the office, check email and voicemail. All client contact leads followed immediately.

➡ 12.30–1.30: Lunch meeting with co-owner of the practice.

➡ 1.30–2.30: One-to-one session with professional golfer. She has recently won her tour card, but lacks really deep confidence. She is seeking ongoing support while on the tour.

➡ 3.00–5.00: Meeting with sport science support manager at the English Institute of Sport. They are seeking psychologists to work with the sports medicine team in athlete rehabilitation.

➡ 6.30–7.30: Attend training with a senior semi-professional soccer team. The coach has referred players to us in the past.

DEVELOPMENT OF SPORT AND EXERCISE PSYCHOLOGY

Sport and exercise psychology are often described as 'young' areas of specialisation within the parent discipline of psychology. However, sport psychology has roots that date back to the early years of mainstream psychology. Research into sport performance was carried out by Norman Triplett in 1897. These studies examined the effect of an audience on the performance of competitive cyclists. Early behavioural research in sport and exercise was mainly focused on the acquisition and retention of movement skills. This work was conducted primarily in the USA. In 1925, Coleman Griffiths founded a movement control laboratory at the University of Illinois, and his two seminal publications, The *Psychology of Coaching* (1926) and *Psychology and Athletics* (1928), established him as the leading theoretical and applied sport psychologist of his generation. The Second World War was a stimulus for further research efforts aimed at understanding how movement skills were learned and controlled. Psychologists were at the forefront of work seeking to understand how skills related to military operations could be learned in the most efficient manner possible. The post-war years, however, saw little specific development in sport and exercise psychology. The emphasis remained on educational aspects of skill acquisition and movement control.

The next significant developments were in the 1960s. In 1965, the International Society for Sport Psychology (ISSP) was founded. International meetings of academic sport psychologists were convened and national and international bodies, such as the British Society for Sport Psychology (BSSP) and Fédération Européenne de Psychologie des Sports et des Activités Corporelles (FEPSAC) were established. Another important milestone in the development of academic sport and exercise psychology was the founding of the ISSP's *International Journal of Sport Psychology* in 1970. This was followed, in 1979, by the *Journal of Sport Psychology*, allied to the North American sport psychology community. This journal later changed its title to the *Journal of Sport & Exercise Psychology*.

In the UK, the 1970s saw sport and exercise develop from roots within physical education to become an area of academic study in its own right. The first undergraduate sport and exercise science programmes were opened at Loughborough University and Liverpool Polytechnic, now Liverpool John Moores University. Sport psychology formed a significant part of the curriculum. In 1985, academics from other disciplines of sport and exercise science came together to form BASS (British Association of Sport Sciences). Research in the 1980s and early 1990s was characterised by a drive to take sport

psychology out of the laboratory and into the field. At this time, in the UK, applied sport psychologists were to be found increasingly working in support and consultancy roles in elite sports, and providing psychological support for athletes at major international competitions, such as the Olympic Games. On the theory development side, significant developments were made in our understanding of fundamental aspects of human performance, such as motivation, stress and performance, and group dynamics.

In 1993, BASS became BASES (British Association of Sport and Exercise Sciences), acknowledging the development of interest in health-related physical activity. One of the main developments since the first edition of this book has been the divergence of sport psychology and exercise psychology as distinct areas within applied psychology. *Exercise psychology*, where the focus is on behaviour related to health or self-presentation, differs from *sport psychology*, where the focus is on competition and performance enhancement. However, there is a commonality of approach in relation to application. Both sport psychology and exercise psychology confront important practical challenges, and aim to use well-researched techniques and interventions to resolve them.

How would I become a sport or exercise psychologist?

There are two methods of entry to careers in sport and exercise psychology. The newer route, which follows an undergraduate psychology degree with postgraduate training in sport and exercise psychology, and leads to chartered status with the BPS, is explored at the beginning of this chapter (see 'Sport and exercise psychology in the British Psychological Society'). The more traditional path is outlined here.

Many practitioners have entered the profession after an undergraduate degree in sport and exercise science. This usually entails study of sport and exercise psychology, along with exercise physiology, biomechanics and other related topics. Following this route, the aspiring sport and/or exercise psychologist goes on to postgraduate work, at either Masters or doctoral level, specialising in sport and/or exercise psychology. The applied training may start while the psychologist is undertaking postgraduate work. Postgraduate sport and exercise psychology programmes offer supervised applied experience as part of the programme. Supervised experience means working with an accredited sport or exercise psychologist within the criteria set out by the professional body for sport and exercise in the UK – BASES (http://www.bases.org.uk). Supervised experience usually lasts three years.

The advantage of this method of becoming a sport and exercise psychologist is that the trainee has a depth of knowledge and competence in all areas of sport and exercise science. The main disadvantage is that there may be significant gaps in their psychological knowledge. Also, most sport and exercise science degree programmes are unable to award Graduate Basis for Registration with the British Psychological Society (see Chapter 1), although this is slowly changing in the early twenty-first century.

RESEARCH, THEORY AND APPLICATIONS: EXERCISE PSYCHOLOGY

Life in the developed world changed dramatically during the course of the twentieth century. Active occupations became increasingly sedentary and mechanised, motorised transport became the norm and most people enjoyed more leisure time than previous generations. Food became more widely accessible, its relative cost fell and it was increasingly viewed and marketed as a commodity. Given these social changes, coupled with advances in health care, it would be reasonable to expect a period of unprecedented health for people in the developed world. In reality, in the first decade of the twenty-first century, we are entering a period of unprecedented ill-health. Evidence points to a tripling in the rates of obesity in adults and children (National Audit Office 2001). In addition, the Organization for Economic Cooperation and Development (OECD 2006) published data to show that the UK had the highest rate of obesity in Europe. Concomitant health concerns, such as heart disease,

hypertension, certain cancers and type 2 diabetes, are growing, and placing a significantly increased burden on the National Health Service in the UK (Haslam, Sattar and Lean 2006). The main difference between the current obesity epidemic and epidemics of previous ages is that this one is primarily caused by lifestyle choices that we all make on a daily basis: choices about what we eat, how we travel and whether we see physical activity as integral to our lives.

The present public health challenge has two elements: first, the human genetic heritage, and second, the nature of our environment. Our early ancestors had to work very hard to find or cultivate food. They also had to endure long periods where no food was available. It is reasonable to conclude that those who were able to store fat effectively to service periods of famine were at an evolutionary advantage. In present-day conditions in the developed world, food is plentiful, cheap and accessible, but unsuccessful dieters often report an inability to control their behaviour concerning food. This is thought to be the same gene expressing itself, preparing for famine. However, there is evidence to suggest that calorific intake in the year 2000 was very similar to that of previous generations. The situation is made worse by the reduction in physical activity. In most cases, obesity is caused by an interaction between predisposing genes and living in an environment where we are encouraged to over-consume food and be under-active. Physical activity and exercise have been shown to have a central role, not only in the maintenance of good health, but also in the prevention and treatment of numerous medical conditions. Research evidence confirming the long-term protection that regular exercise can afford is incontrovertible (Biddle, Fox and Boutcher 2000; Hillsdon and Thorogood 1996). These findings have resulted in health policy advisers recommending a threshold of physical activity that is required for the maintenance of health. The American College of Sports Medicine advocates that 'every US citizen should accumulate 30 minutes or more of moderate intensity physical activity on most, preferably all days of the week' (ACSM 1995: 406). This advice has also been adopted as policy in the UK, with the modification that children should aim to accumulate 60 minutes of activity. For definitional purposes, moderate intensity equates to brisk walking.

There have been a number of large-scale epidemiological surveys examining the proportion of the population that achieves the recommended levels of physical activity. Figure 9.1 shows data collected as part of the 2003 Health Survey for England. The data do have some methodological weaknesses, but give an overall impression of the low level of compliance in terms of the recommended levels for physical activity, particularly among women and older people.

Why do people choose to adopt an active lifestyle?

Weight management

In 2001, the National Audit Office (NAO) presented evidence showing that one in five adults in England is obese, and that the incidence of obesity had trebled in the past 20 years. Nearly two-thirds of men and more than one-half of women are either overweight or obese. The NAO report went

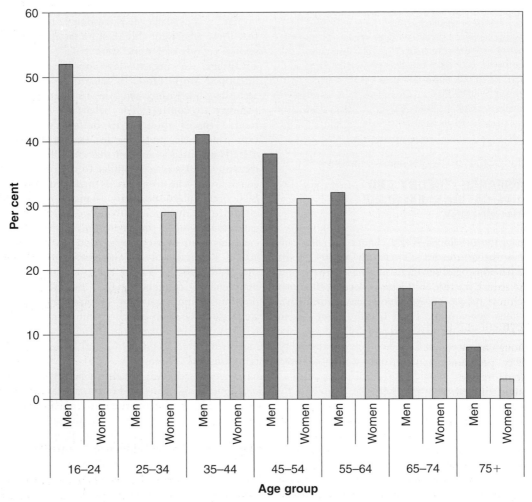

Figure 9.1 Proportion of the population achieving the 30 minutes' accumulated moderate-intensity physical activity on most days of the week
Source: Health Survey for England (Department of Health 2003)

on to identify the financial cost to the economy of ill-health associated with overweight and obesity, concluding that the annual cost to the National Health Service is around £500 million pounds, and the additional cost to the economy through absenteeism is around £2 billion pounds. There is also a human cost. Many people who perceive themselves to be overweight experience psychological distress, either because of the direct impact of being overweight on self-esteem, or because of the behaviour of others towards them. For example, children who are overweight may be bullied by their peers (Griffiths et al. 2006).

The first response when people realise they are becoming overweight is to attempt to manage their diet. Dieting can be effective on its own. However, exercise and dietary control together are the most effective approaches to weight loss. People sometimes worry that exercise can increase their appetite, but this is not the case, particularly if there is sound knowledge of what should be consumed, and when. Weight loss also has the potential to bring with it other psychological benefits in terms of self-esteem (Wadden et al. 1996).

Reduced risk of cardiovascular disease

Exercise and physical activity have the potential to help manage the primary risk factors for heart disease: hypertension and high levels of low-density lipids like cholesterol. Exercise can also help to manage stress, another important risk factor in cardiovascular disease. The exact nature of the dose response (i.e. how much exercise you need to do to reduce the risk of heart disease) is the focus of much research in the early twenty-first century.

Enjoyment and intrinsic motivation

Although many people begin an exercise or physical activity programme for some extrinsic, health-related reason, such as losing weight or rehabilitating after a heart attack, it is rare to continue with a programme if you do not experience enjoyment. This transition is crucial. Long-term adherence to activity and exercise is necessary for health benefits. Adherence is much more likely where intrinsic motives, such as satisfaction and enjoyment, are experienced. This is the application of an extremely important line of motivational theory called self-determination theory (Deci and Ryan 1985), which will be discussed in more detail later in the chapter.

Building self-esteem

Exercise, particularly when the programme has been adhered to for a sustained period, has the potential to increase an individual's self-esteem and confidence. The sense of accomplishment in achieving targets is believed to be at the root of this change.

Socialising

Another significant motive for many people adopting exercise is to increase their opportunities for social interaction. It is common for people of all ages to report that they would prefer to exercise as part of a group or with a specific exercise buddy. Exercising with others can also heighten a person's sense of personal commitment to their activity, as well as building social support. Both are important for maintaining behavioural change (Willis and Campbell 1992).

Why do people not engage in physical activity and exercise?

The major barriers preventing exercise are lack of time, lack of energy and lack of motivation. Less significant barriers may include the high cost of joining a gym, fear of embarrassment, not having access to facilities and other personal and situational factors. It is important to recognise that the decision not to be active is usually a complex one. Understanding and addressing this decisional process is critical for public health professionals aiming to facilitate lifestyle changes.

Theoretical models of physical activity and exercise behaviour

Earlier it was stated that one of the roles of the exercise psychologist is to undertake research aimed at developing models of exercise behaviour. The next section will outline four key theories that have been developed and applied to explain exercise behaviour.

Health belief model (Becker and Maiman 1975)

The health belief model is one of the most enduring theoretical approaches to preventative health behaviour. Specifically, it identifies two factors that predict the likelihood of a person adopting health-related behaviours. These are the person's perception of the severity of the potential illness and the appraisal of the personal costs of adopting the behaviour balanced against the benefits. Although there has been some success in applying the model, results have been equivocal, as it was originally developed to explain behaviour in disease states rather than exercise (Godin 1994).

Theory of planned behaviour (Ajzen and Madden 1986)

The theory of planned behaviour developed from an earlier theory of reasoned action (Ajzen and Fishbein 1980). Both state that the strongest predictors of actual behaviours are intentions. Intention is the product of two complex cognitive processes: the attitude towards the behaviour and the subjective norm of the behaviour. The subjective norm is composed of the beliefs and opinions of other people and the person's motivation to comply with them.

Transtheoretical model (Prochaska, DiClemente and Norcross 1992)

The models discussed above are very useful descriptions of the relationship between attitudes and behaviour, but they tend to be viewed as static models. The transtheoretical model recognises that people do not go from being entirely sedentary (i.e. not being physically active at all) to adopting the recommended levels of physical activity, and maintaining this change for a sustained period, in one single step. The transtheoretical model identifies five stages in the process:

1 *Pre-contemplation*: People in this stage have not really considered changing their lifestyle to adopt more activity. They may be in this stage because they actively choose to avoid exercise, perhaps through embarrassing or stressful experiences in the past (e.g. at school) or through lack of knowledge.
2 *Contemplation*: People in this stage can see the benefits of changing their behaviour and now have serious intentions about adopting a more active lifestyle. Despite these intentions, many people never get any further and become 'chronic contemplators'.
3 *Preparation*: In this stage, people begin to act on their contemplation. Preparation may be joining an exercise class or buying a pair of running shoes. This is a key stage, as it is very common to see relapse back to contemplation.

4 *Action*: In the action stage, a clear change in behaviour is seen – the individual has made a behavioural transition towards adopting and maintaining the behaviour. Again, the stability of the behavioural change is an issue. Many people begin their exercise programme (or indeed any programme of behavioural change) and expect to see immediate results. When these do not occur, there is a risk of disillusion and relapse to earlier stages.
5 *Maintenance*: This is the final stage in the model and has been defined as when physical activity has been maintained for a period of six months.

It should be noted that relapse to a previous stage is possible anywhere within the model. It is also important to note that the types of 'intervention' required to make transitions from one stage to the next are different. Helping someone gain information about the benefits of physical activity is an important aspect in pre-contemplation and contemplation, but is much less significant for someone at the action stage. In later stages, other interventions, such as social support or offering rewards for continued participation in a programme, are much more pertinent. This differential approach to interventions is known as 'stage matching' (Marcus et al. 1992). Stage matching is an integral part of the application of this model.

There are two more elements to the transtheoretical model. These are *decisional balance* and *self-efficacy*. Decisional balance is the process by which an individual audits their own personal pros and cons for behavioural change. This is a highly subjective process. Self-efficacy, in this context, relates to the extent to which a person believes they can successfully maintain their physical activity in the face of 'risky' situations or events. For example, will the person maintain their physical activity while on holiday, during poor weather (if the activity is outside) or when exercise buddies are not available?

Self-determination theory (Deci and Ryan 1985)

In terms of exercise and physical activity, people who are intrinsically motivated are seeking to be competent and self-determining in their quest to remain healthy. However as Markland (2006) shows, the contemporary view is that intrinsic and extrinsic motivation exist on a continuum, and there are different forms of both (see Figure 9.2).

Amotivation is the situation where an individual is neither intrinsically nor externally motivated. They can see no reason why they should undertake the behaviour.

A person who is *externally regulated* has their behaviour entirely driven by external motives. In an exercise context, this could be the individual who is driven to exercise more in order to be a little lighter for their next slimming club weigh-in.

Moving further in the direction of intrinsic motivation, *introjected regulation* is still, according to Deci and Ryan, extrinsic, but the external pressures translate into behaviours that are more closely linked to intrinsic motivation. An example of a behaviour that is introjected is the exerciser whose main motive for exercise is to impress other people with their physique. This could be a young male beginning a weight-training programme solely to improve his physical appearance.

Identified motivation is another form of extrinsic motivation that is very common in sport and exercise. The activity or exercise behaviour is willingly engaged in and is highly valued, but is not perceived as being pleasant in its own right.

The closest form of extrinsic motivation to intrinsic motivation is *integrated regulation*. These are behaviours that are valued for their outcome, to state that they have been achieved. For example, many people who would not call themselves runners diligently train through the winter months to complete the London Marathon each spring. A proportion have never run in a race before the marathon and will never run a race after it. The outcome, the medal, the experience, being able to say, 'I've run the London Marathon', is what drives their training and competing, not the pleasure and satisfaction of running.

Crossing the divide into intrinsic motives, there are three main categories: motivation to know, to accomplish and to experience stimulation. The key to intrinsic motivation is that the behaviour is engaged in for the personal satisfaction, enjoyment and challenge of the activity itself. Motivation to know is the motive to learn, explore or understand a new activity or skill. Motivation to accomplish relates to the desire to overcome a challenge or master a difficult task. Motivation to experience stimulation is derived from the pleasure or satisfaction when exercising or being active. Sport and exercise are full of excellent examples of intrinsically motivated individuals. Rock climbing (see Figure 9.3) is a particularly good example of intrinsic motivation. The challenges are self-chosen and usually attempted in a very private context. Most climbers compete only with themselves and a problem on a rock face.

Exercise psychology is not only concerned with understanding the reasons why people engage in or

Degrees of self-determination in behavioural regulation

Figure 9.2 The self-determination continuum
Source: Markland (2006)

Figure 9.3 Intrinsic motivation in action: rock climbing in Verdon Gorge
Source: Jon Graham Collection

avoid physical activity and exercise. It also aims to describe and explain the physical effects of exercise. One of the most commonly experienced is the effect of exercise on mood – the so-called 'feel-good factor' (Buckworth and Dishman 2002).

Exercise and the 'feel-good factor'

While the physical benefits of exercise and activity are unequivocal, the relationship between exercise and psychological well-being is less well researched. Where research has been undertaken, there are some important methodological problems limiting the findings. This section will review the literature linking exercise and physical activity with psychological well-being, and discuss some of the problems associated with research in this area.

Physical activity can improve mood

The relationship between exercise and mood has been researched in many settings, with many different populations (Yeung 1996). Providing that some important caveats are acknowledged, the finding that exercise enhances positive mood has been widely supported and is extremely robust. These caveats were discussed by Berger and Motl (2001). They include the following:

➡ The activity should involve closed and predictable activities.
➡ There should be a minimum of interpersonal competition.
➡ The duration and intensity of the activity should be chosen by the individual.
➡ There should be rhythmical abdominal breathing.

The link between exercise and mood has stimulated a great deal of research into the mechanism or mechanisms of influence. Two broad categories have been proposed: physiological mechanisms and psychosocial mechanisms (see Table 9.1).

It is beyond the scope of this chapter to study in detail the mechanisms underlying the relationship between exercise and mood. It is worth noting, however, that there is evidence indicating multiple causality (Buckworth and Dishman 2002). Given the complexity of mood and the very broad scope for exercise and physical activity to influence it, it should not be surprising to discover that there is no simple mechanism underlying the relationship between exercise and mood.

Exercise and depression

Since the late 1980s, there has been developing evidence that exercise has an antidepressant effect that in most studies is at least as effective as other treatment modes. The evidence for this comes primarily from meta-analyses (McDonald and Hodgdon 1991; North, McCullagh and Tran 1990).

Hypothesised physiological mechanisms	Hypothesised psychosocial mechanisms
Increases in cerebral blood flow	Enhanced feelings of control
Changes in brain neurotransmitters (e.g. NA, 5-HT)	Enhanced feelings of competence and self-efficacy
Increased oxygenation of cerebral tissue	Positive social interactions
Reduction in muscle tension	Improved self-concept and self-esteem
Release of endorphins	Opportunities to take time out from sources of stress

Table 9.1 Physiological and psychosocial mechanisms

The use of exercise in the treatment of depression received a further impetus in 2005, when a major mental health charity in the UK published a report entitled *Up and Running? Exercise therapy and the treatment of mild or moderate depression in primary care* (Mental Health Foundation 2005). The report acknowledged the body of evidence showing that exercise is an effective treatment. It also reported that most general practitioners are aware of the value of exercise in treating their patients and have established mechanisms by which exercise prescriptions can be delivered. Despite this level of awareness and the relative ease of prescription, most GPs will select drugs or psychotherapy as their main forms of treatment. It is clear from the Mental Health Foundation report that the potential for exercise referral to make an impact on the mental health of the nation has yet to be realised.

Although exercise as treatment for depression has been the main focus of the clinical research, various psychiatric and other disorders have been examined. For example, there is strong evidence for the reduction of anxiety through exercise. Once again, there have been meta-analytic studies confirming this effect (e.g. Petruzzello et al. 1991). However, in common with the depression research, there have been several critiques that indicate methodological problems with this research. Biddle and Mutrie (2001) conclude that in comparison to what we know about exercise and depression, very little is known about the relationship between exercise and anxiety disorders. There is a clear need for further, well-controlled and large-scale research to be undertaken on clinical populations.

Can exercise go wrong?

I have presented the case for exercise in the maintenance of good physical and psychological health. From the text you may get the impression that exercise and physical activity are a panacea. Sceptics of the efficacy of exercise are keen to point out cases where exercisers have died prematurely of heart disease or experienced other debilitating physical conditions. However, the risks of adopting a sedentary lifestyle far outweigh the risks associated with being active. Can the same be said of the *psychological* risks associated with exercise?

There is a small population of exercisers who present with exercise-related psychological disorders, such as exercise dependence, exercise-related eating disorders and body dysmorphia. These are examined briefly below.

Exercise dependence

Exercise dependence is a rare condition where a person presents with an overvalued view of exercise. Similar to other forms of dependence, a person who is exercise dependent has a profound need for exercise. Exercise 'addicts' differ from those who have a healthy commitment to exercise in that addicts manage withdrawal from exercise very badly. Healthy exercisers recognise the importance of rest in a training programme and can manage without exercising for a few days. Exercise dependence can be particularly problematic when it is a secondary aspect to another disorder. The most complex of these is seen where exercise dependence is secondary to eating disorders such as anorexia nervosa or bulimia nervosa.

The link between *eating disorders* and exercise has received a good deal of research attention. One of the earliest published studies reported strong similarities between the psychological make-up of anorexic women and very committed, male, long-distance runners (Yates, Leehey and Shisslak 1983). Szabo (2000) reviewed this rather controversial and equivocal body of literature, and concluded that there is a relationship between high levels of athleticism or exercise and some symptoms of eating disorders, but not in all populations or all sports. Women are at higher risk of developing exercise-related eating disorders, particularly in sport or exercise forms where body shape is directly or indirectly associated with performance, for example, in endurance sports like running, dance and gymnastics. However, males may also be at risk, particularly in sports where weight is an issue; for example, jockeys may spend the majority of their professional career trying to maintain a body weight several kilos below their normal weight. Similarly, boxers, power lifters, martial artists and rowers are required to make weight. This complex relationship between sport and exercise and eating disorders has been summarised by Williamson et al. (1995) (see Figure 9.4).

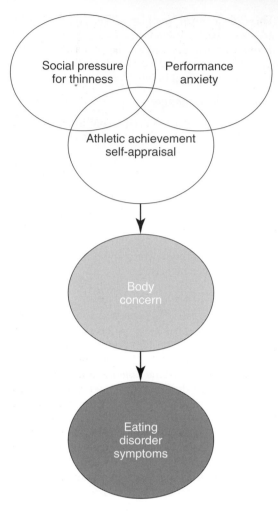

Figure 9.4 A psychosocial model for the development of eating disorder symptoms in athletes and committed exercisers
Source: Based on Williamson et al. (1995)

Body concern

Body concern is also an extremely important issue. It may manifest itself in people (particularly women) displaying social physique anxiety (Crawford and Eklund 1994), and avoiding exercise and physical activity settings where they feel their bodies will be negatively evaluated by others. Another manifestation of body concern is *muscle dysmorphia*. This is a very serious disorder that occurs almost exclusively in men and is characterised by a preoccupation that one's body is too small, 'puny'

and inadequately muscular. In reality, many of these men are unusually muscular and large. Behavioural muscle dysmorphics are often characterised by compulsive working out at the gym, and painstaking attention to diet and dietary supplements. Muscle dysmorphia may lead to abuse of anabolic steroids. Studies in the USA indicate that 6–7 per cent of high school boys have used these drugs in an effort to grow bigger, rather than to improve athletic performance (Pope, Phillips and Olivardia 2000).

Helping more people to become more active, more often

In concluding this section, I would like to discuss briefly the challenge that exercise psychologists face in trying to understand and explain why the majority of the population appears to be reasonably well informed about the health benefits of exercise, but much less able to transfer knowledge into action.

How do we encourage people to adopt physical activity, without lecturing them and making them resentful about being told what is good for them? How do we encourage people to do a little more exercise and eat a little less unhealthy food, without make them anxious about how their bodies appear and thus undermining their self-esteem or promoting unhealthy eating behaviours?

The leading sports medicine body in the world is the American College of Sports Medicine (ACSM). In their 1998 position stand (ACSM 1998: 976), they adopted a graded approach to their advice. A key part of this is active living.

> The ACSM now views exercise and physical activity for health and fitness in the context of an exercise dose continuum… Many significant health benefits are achieved by going from a sedentary state to a minimal level of physical activity.

The current message for the promotion of physical activity is a staged approach, outlined in Table 9.2.

In the UK, there have been media campaigns advocating this type of staged approach. These have yet to be evaluated fully. When they are, the results are likely to replicate the campaign run in Scotland in the mid 1990s. This campaign promoted the

Recommendation	Advice	Target group
Stage one: Active living	Add activity into your daily routine	Sedentary or irregularly active people
Aim to accumulate 30 minutes of moderate-intensity activity on most days of the week	e.g. use stairs rather than the lift; park your car a little further from work	
Stage two: Regular exercise	Gradually increase your fitness by increasing the intensity or duration of activity	Those achieving stage one and aiming to improve fitness
Aim to include three bouts of vigorous-intensity activity, lasting at least 20 minutes, into your weekly routine	e.g. be more active and build on the intensity of what you already do	

Table 9.2 The promotion of physical activity
Source: Adapted from Biddle and Mutrie (2001: 260)

idea that walking is sufficient activity for health. By the fourth week, 70 per cent of the population reported being aware of the campaign, indicating effective recognition of the message. However, there was no notable change in the intention of the population to change their behaviour and adopt walking as a health-related activity (Wimbush, Macgregor and Fraser 1997). This is a common problem in health-related media campaigns. Exercise psychologists are at the forefront of work to design interventions that change information and knowledge into action. Two approaches that have proved effective are the *transtheoretical model* and *motivational interviewing*.

The transtheoretical model was introduced earlier in this chapter as one of the main theoretical pillars of exercise psychology. Its status as such is magnified by the fact that it is highly practical. The transtheoretical model identifies specific interventions related to each stage.

Pre-contemplators need information about the risks and benefits of exercise, so interventions should be aimed at raising awareness. Contemplators need opportunities to have their questions answered and their personal needs met. They need information about how they could integrate physical activity into their lives without major disruption. Personalised advice from primary health care workers, such as GPs, nurses and physiotherapists, could be effective interventions here. Preparers are often already active, but not regularly so. They need more opportunities and a reduction in the perceived barriers. A consultation with a member of exercise staff might help, for example, with time management. Those in the action stage have recently become regularly active and need the social support of fellow exercisers to prevent them falling back into their old patterns of behaviour. They may also need the stimulus of variety in how they exercise. Finally, those in the maintenance group need ongoing support from an infrastructure of provision, for example, ensuring that exercise clubs or groups are not seasonal.

Many health and exercise clubs offer fitness assessment or testing as an incentive for members. This is often used as a method of initially assessing fitness levels in order to develop a 'prescription' of exercise. However, there is little evidence to suggest that this is effective in developing long-term motivation or adherence to activity. A technique developed by Miller and Rollnick (1991), called *motivational interviewing*, has proved to be a much more effective method. Motivational interviewing is a cognitive-behavioural strategy, aimed at identifying and changing behaviours that place people at risk of developing health problems. It has been applied to smoking cessation and addiction, and to exercise and physical activity. Interviewers are trained to respond to clients by helping them to understand their thought processes in relation to their choice of a sedentary lifestyle, examining their choices and challenging existing patterns of behaviour. Motivational interviewing can be seen to dovetail well into physical activity promotion campaigns based on the transtheoretical model. However, it is essential that providers of the infrastructure for exercise and physical activity ensure that their staff are trained not only in safe practice in relation to exercise, but also in the psychology of behavioural change. This may lead to a whole new breed of highly trained exercise professionals, capable of responding to the challenge of a sedentary population.

> The relationships between food, physical activity, body shape and happiness have become confused and contradictory. We see food as one of many commodities that we must buy in order to further personal happiness and economic growth. At the same time we're trying to buy health, fitness, weight-loss and the perfect body. We don't seem to be able to handle the choices we have created for ourselves.

This quote, from Obesity Scotland (2006: 6), is a challenge to psychologists interested in exercise, physical activity and health. There is immense scope to explore human behaviour around exercise and to design interventions with the potential to lead to great personal and social benefit.

Exercise psychology: A case study in behavioural change

Case notes

Linda is a 51-year-old woman. She has a demanding job in a large city. She drives her car to work. She gave up smoking ten years ago when she returned to work full-time. Her current health is reasonably good. Her body mass index (weight in kilos divided by height in metres squared) is 28.4, placing her in the overweight, approaching obese, classification. Her blood pressure is slightly elevated. Her family history gives her some cause for concern. Her mother died of heart disease in her early 60s and her 56-year-old brother has had cardiac bypass surgery. However, her father, who is 80 years old, is healthy and leads an active life.

In a recent consultation with her doctor, Linda was referred to a physical activity counsellor. In the counselling session she said that she knew she should lose weight. She explained that she hated sport and exercise and still had bad memories of

'sadistic' PE teachers at school. She stated: 'I just don't see myself as a gym person.' She went on to say that her father was never a great one for exercise, but 'He's doing great at 80.' When asked about her physical activity routine, she explained that she was often too rushed to walk to meetings, and that work extended into the evenings most nights. At weekends she liked to 'catch up on sleep' and 'meet with friends'. Asked how often she managed to accumulate 30 minutes of moderate physical activity, she said she did not know. When pressed, she thought it might be once a week. When the counsellor asked about her motives for becoming more physically active, she said that she would like to lose weight and help herself stay healthy. At the end of the interview she joked that she might become more active, 'but don't expect me to enjoy it!'

Identifying the issues

Linda presents with several health issues:

- overweight;
- elevated blood pressure;
- approaching menopause – this means she will gradually lose the protective influence of oestrogen on her cardiovascular system;
- family history of heart disease.

In terms of physical activity behaviours, Linda:

- is not habitually active;
- does not see physical activity as an important part of her life;
- views herself as not having time to be active;
- is not intrinsically motivated to be active.

Designing an intervention

Linda is at the pre-contemplation stage of behavioural change, according to the transtheoretical model. Her decisional balance sees the disadvantages of adopting physical activity outweighing the advantages. The first aim of an intervention to help Linda adopt physical activity would be to raise her awareness about the health benefits of even relatively small amounts of activity. In motivational interviews, the psychologist might probe around what would have to change for Linda in order for her to adopt more activity.

The second aim would be to raise Linda's awareness about how much physical activity she currently does. At this stage, suggesting that Linda should join a gym would probably not be effective. However, a simple process of giving her a pedometer and asking her to record how many steps she takes daily for a week would provide some idea about current levels and a baseline for incremental increase.

Third, once a baseline assessment of present activity has been made, we would aim for Linda to achieve 30 minutes of physical activity on most days of the week, ultimately aiming for 10,000 steps on her pedometer. This could be accumulated in three 10-minute bouts. Time is an issue, so perhaps this could be achieved by parking her car in a car park slightly further away from work, although here we would be mindful of personal safety. We would aim to establish the habit of walking between floors in the office, rather than taking the lift, and perhaps taking a walk away from the office at lunchtime or during other breaks. She should receive regular prompts and support from the counsellor.

At the weekend there would be an opportunity to have family or friends support the adoption of activity. Adherence is improved where there is good social support. Again, we are not advocating formal exercise. It might be that Linda walks to the newsagent for her Sunday newspaper rather than taking the car.

This intervention would require close monitoring in the early stages. Linda would receive regular prompts to increase adherence. Her medical status would also be monitored, so that she would receive feedback on how her increased activity was impacting on her health.

Ultimately, once the increased activity had been adhered to for a sustained period, the psychologist might introduce Linda to a more formal exercise prescription (if appropriate), based on stage 2 of the ACSM advice (see Table 9.2).

RESEARCH, THEORY AND APPLICATIONS: SPORT PSYCHOLOGY

Singer (1996) schematically summarised the primary areas of concern in sport psychology. These are shown in Table 9.3.

In the space available in this chapter, I cannot cover all these areas. I intend to outline and discuss the principles of applied sport psychology support work; demonstrate commonly used interventions; and show links with aspects of the theoretical basis of the discipline. I cannot stress strongly enough the importance of integration between theory and practice. However, due to the applied emphasis of this text, and the limited space available, I will be highly selective about the material covered. For a more complete summary of the theoretical basis of sport psychology in the areas identified by Singer (1996), I recommend Singer, Hausenblas and Janelle's *Handbook of Sport Psychology* (2001). This authoritative work provides a comprehensive overview of the 'state of the art' in sport psychology theory, although given the speed of theoretical development, some areas may already be dated.

Understanding the sport performance context

Essentially, all sports can be mapped onto four factors:

1 Physical factors: Broadly, 'fitness' – different sports demand different physical fitness characteristics.
2 Technical factors: What are the requisite skills required for performance in the sport?
3 Tactical factors: A characteristic of experts is their ability to 'do the right thing at the right time'.
4 Mental factors: From a psychological perspective, which factors allow the physical, technical and tactical to be expressed optimally, allowing the performer to fully exploit their performance potential?

Modern sport science recognises an equal contribution to performance of each of these factors. Optimal mental preparation is just as important to performance as physical and technical preparation. When a sport performer engages in physical training to develop fitness or technical skills, we often see a change in their physique or the skills they are using in performance. Developing mental skills often results in more subtle changes, but the processes and aims are the same. The purpose of engaging in systematic and consistent mental skills training is to enhance performance, increase enjoyment and achieve greater satisfaction from performance.

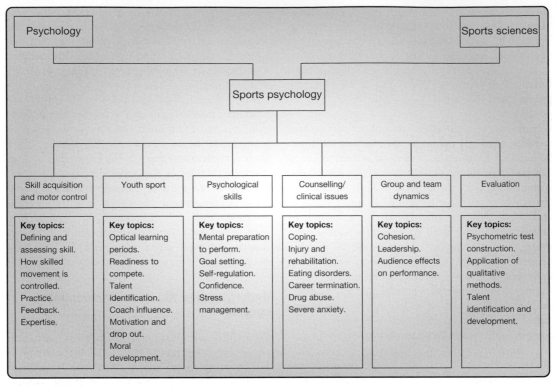

Table 9.3 The influences of psychology and the sport sciences on key areas in sport psychology.
Source: Adapted from Singer, Hausenblas and Janelle (eds) (2001: xviii)

The optimal performance state in sport

Psychological research into the characteristics of optimal performance has focused on two slightly different questions. First, what are the characteristics of optimal or peak performance, and second, what are the characteristics of peak performers? Peak performances can occur to any performer at any level of performance. They are those memorable moments all sport performers experience when everything seems to 'come together'. Typically, athletes describe this as an involuntary state; the more they seek it, the less likely it is to be achieved. Jackson and Csikszentmihalyi (1999) have developed the idea of peak performance and integrated it into the concept of 'flow'. Flow is a psychological state first described by Csikszentmihalyi (1985) as an intrinsically motivated state where there is total involvement in the task at hand. When athletes are in a flow state, they are thought to be experiencing the following:

- An optimal balance between the challenge of the task and their skills.
- A merging of action and awareness. There is an effortless integration of action.
- Clarity and simplicity of goals.
- Unambiguous feedback.
- Total immersion in the task.
- Paradoxical feelings of control, where the athlete feels in control of what they are doing, but is in no way forcing their actions.
- A loss of self-consciousness and evaluation.
- A transformation in time perception, either speeding up or slowing down.
- Pleasure and enjoyment in the task.

To try to build sport psychology interventions that would help athletes get into flow state regularly would be difficult. Rather than try to intervene to recreate flow, it is more realistic for sport psychologists to identify the characteristics of performers who appear to consistently perform at, or very close to, their physical, technical and tactical potential. Once these characteristics have been identified, we can design interventions that can be integrated into 'mental training' aimed at developing these characteristics or attributes.

Orlick and Partington (1988) investigated the psychological characteristics of high-level sport performers. Their research, in which 75 Olympians were interviewed and a further 160 completed questionnaires, identified what athletes believed to be the key mental links to excellence across all sports. At the top of the list was 'Total commitment to pursuing excellence'. Other characteristics were described as 'success elements', and these differentiated the successful from the unsuccessful performers (although it should be noted that 'unsuccessful' in this context still refers to an Olympic athlete!). These elements described daily routines, such as the use of imagery, goal setting and simulation training, mental preparation for competition, including focusing and refocusing plans, and effective post-competition review. Orlick and Partington's work has served to provide a platform for mental skills interventions undertaken by sport psychologists. In this section I aim to show how sport psychologists support athletes in the development of these success elements and achieve the goal of applied sport psychology – to help athletes consistently perform at or as close to their potential as possible.

Applying theory to practice in sport psychology

We saw earlier how sport performance is a composite of four elements: physical fitness, technical development, strategy and mental skills. Historically, the coach has been responsible for the development of all these. A modern trend, especially in elite sport, is for a multidisciplinary team of specialist coaches to collaborate in providing a comprehensive programme of preparation and support. Therefore, it is not uncommon for an individual or team to have a coaching team that includes technical coaches, video analysts, strength and conditioning coaches and, increasingly, a sport psychologist.

Steve Bull is a sport psychologist who has provided psychological support to the England cricket team since 1997. He described a staged model applied to work with teams and athletes (Bull 1989: 262).

- Stage one – Rapport building: building trust and respect between the psychologist and the performer.
- Stage two – Assessment of athlete needs: identifying performer's mental training needs.
- Stage three – Designing a programme of interventions and mental skills training: prioritising the areas of development which are most important in enhancing performance.
- Stage four – Ongoing monitoring and adjustment: identifying what has been effective and monitoring adherence.
- Stage five – Evaluation: withdrawal, but maintaining contact.

I will use this as a framework and provide some insight into the day-to-day work of a sport psychology consultant.

Prior to stage one: introduction/gaining entry

How does a sport psychologist begin to work with an individual or team? How the athlete initially makes contact with the psychologist appears an insignificant point. In practice, it often provides an indicator of how effective the work will be. An athlete who seeks out the advice of a psychologist often has a high degree of motivation and willingness to embrace new ideas, leaving no stone unturned in their quest for excellence. On the other hand, where the athlete feels they have been 'sent by the coach to see the shrink', there is often low motivation and a resistance to ideas presented. This may lead to ineffective interventions, low adherence and poor results.

Professional sport psychologists in the UK are bound by a code of ethical principles, either through BASES or the BPS. As early as possible in sport psychology support work, it is critical for all parties to understand the ethical and practical basis of the work. Some aspects of this are as follows:
1 *Who is the client?* If a sport psychologist begins working with the players on an individual basis, who 'owns' the knowledge gathered? If a club is paying the psychologist, does this give the coach or other club officials the right to know the details of consultations? If so, the players need to be aware of this and understand that information may be disclosed. This may compromise the work of the psychologist.

2 *Recognition of boundaries and competencies.* The psychologist is responsible for the mental development of the player, not coaching technique or developing strength and conditioning. In some sports, the technical and mental overlap, such as golf or equestrian sports. This can cause problems if there is not a strong interaction between the psychologist and the coach. Another example concerns the competence of the sport psychologist to deal with clinical issues. Unless the sport psychologist is clinically trained, it should be made clear that they must be referred to the appropriate professional and not dealt with 'in house'.

3 *What are the criteria for successful support work?* It is important for the psychologist, the coach and the athlete to agree the outcomes they are working towards. Coaches and athletes are often motivated by performance outcomes, like winning a competition. The sport psychologist needs to be careful not to pander to this and claim that 'sport psychology can help you win' – athletes and coaches like to hear this, but the reality of sport is that such claims can turn into disastrous hostages to fortune if the winning outcome is not achieved. In the early stages of their work, sport psychologists aim to identify clear, process-related goals from the athletes they work with. For example, if an athlete says, 'I would like to learn to control my anxiety before and during an important competition', there is a clearer end point to work towards.

The BASES code of conduct can be viewed on the BASES website: www.bases.org.uk/newsite/pdf/code%20of%20conduct.pdf

Stage one – Rapport building

Sport psychologists work to develop a warm, supportive, non-judgemental and solution-focused relationship with their clients. The relationship is very similar to the therapeutic alliance developed in counselling and clinical psychology and psychotherapy. It is significant that training in counselling is now obligatory for sport psychologists undergoing supervised experience towards accreditation with BASES. An important question in this phase of work is the extent to which the psychologist is required to be expert in the sport in which they are working. On one hand, expert knowledge of the sport gives the psychologist credibility and authority; on the other hand, too much insight and expertise can get in the way. The psychologist may begin to coach technique.

Stage two – Assessing the mental training needs of the performer

There are four methods of assessing the mental training needs of the performer:

➡ performance profiling;
➡ interviewing;
➡ psychometric testing;
➡ observing training and performance.

Performance profiling

Performance profiling was developed by Butler and Hardy (1992). It is adapted from personal construct theory (Kelly 1955; Bannister and Fransella 1986). In developing a profile, the psychologist asks the athlete to identify the characteristics or qualities of the best performers from their sport. Usually, athletes will identify characteristics from one world-class individual, but they can develop a composite picture of several if they prefer. These are the constructs or qualities that are important for that individual athlete. The athlete may name characteristics across all four performance areas – physical, technical, strategic and mental – or just one, mental. The next step is for the athlete to rate the relative importance of each construct.

Finally, the athlete will rate himself or herself on the same constructs, thereby mapping their qualities on those of a world-class performer.

As the constructs have been identified by the performers themselves, profiling clarifies what is important and indicates where they see their areas of relative strength and weakness (although a sport psychologist would not describe them as 'weaknesses' – the preferred description would be 'areas of greatest potential gain'). Skilled profiling involves 'unpacking' the constructs to gain clear understanding of meaning. If profiling is accurate, the next stage – designing an intervention – becomes more straightforward. Performance profiles are often more effective when the athlete and the coach collaborate. The athlete and coach can complete profiles independently and then compare the results. This often leads to a heightened awareness for both parties. It is not uncommon for the coach and athlete to communicate in an entirely new way after completing a profiling exercise. This knowledge often leads to more effective coaching.

Interviewing

A psychologist may adopt a more traditional counselling approach in their assessment of an athlete's need. A skilled psychologist will question and probe in order to develop a sense of what motivates the athlete, what they want to achieve and how they aim to fulfil these ambitions. It is common for interviewing to be used in conjunction with profiling. Good interviewing can also aid the building of rapport between athlete and psychologist.

Psychometric testing

In the 1960s and 1970s, there were a number of studies that used a psychometric approach to find out if sport performers, in particular the elite, presented a consistently different psychological profile to the non-athletic population. These early studies (e.g. Kane 1970) used psychometric tests developed in either the general population (e.g. 16PF) or in clinical populations (e.g. EPI). While this research was flawed on methodological grounds and yielded equivocal results, it did establish a tradition of psychometric testing in sport. Since the late twentieth century, the trend has been to develop sport-specific tests and questionnaires. Ostrow's (1996) *Directory of Psychological Tests in the Sport and Exercise Sciences* contains over 300 psychological tests, questionnaires and inventories available to the researcher and practitioner. Some important examples of these are the Test of Performance Strategies (TOPS) (Thomas, Murphy and Hardy 1999), the Competitive Sport Anxiety Inventory 2 (CSAI-2) (Martens, Vealey and Burton 1990), the Task and Ego Orientation in Sport Questionnaire (TEOSQ) (Duda 1989) and the Test of Attentional and Interpersonal Style (TAIS) (Nideffer 1976). These questionnaires, and many others, have been exposed to rigorous testing of their reliability and validity. As is the case in mainstream psychology, some are considered to be more psychometrically robust than others. Despite the ongoing debate and lack of consensus about psychometric tests, many sport psychologists continue to use pencil-and-paper tests in their research and applied practice (Andersen 2000). Others prefer not to use them.

Observing performance in training and competition

A final angle on assessing the needs of sport performers is to view them in their natural habitat. As already discussed, an important aspect of applied work is helping athletes gain self-awareness. This can be achieved by behavioural observation in training and performance. This provides powerful evidence, enabling the psychologist to make the athlete aware of typical and atypical behaviour.

Time taken to assess accurately the psychological needs of the performer helps the psychologist design an intervention. If the needs assessment is right, there is a good chance that the intervention will be right and will reap the performance and well-being benefits that the athlete and coach are aiming to achieve.

Stage three – Designing an intervention

How does a sport psychologist design interventions aimed to enhance performance and build a deeper level of satisfaction in the athlete?

Many of the interventions used by applied sport psychologists have been developed for use in other contexts. In the following section I will outline the main intervention tools that a sport psychologist may use (see Table 9.4), discussing how they are used and providing a brief theoretical background.

Motivation and volitional control: the theoretical basis of goal setting

Goal setting was developed for use in occupational settings. It is common in business for employees to be incentivised by the setting of goals and the prospect of financial or other rewards if the goals are achieved. Sport psychologists have applied the same idea, but with some modifications. Most sport performers spontaneously set themselves goals, whether it is to win certain games or competitions, or to complete a race in a certain time. Unfortunately, not all goal setting is helpful or beneficial. In order to understand why this is the

Applied Psychology

Intervention aim	Derivation	Intervention
Motivation and volitional control	Occupational and organisational psychology	Goal setting
Developing and maintaining effective attention	Cognitive psychology	Concentration training, e.g. developing performance routines, simulation and cueing responses
Stress and anxiety management	Cognitive psychology, clinical and counselling psychology	Somatic relaxation and thought management, e.g. cognitive restructuring
Confidence building	Clinical and counselling psychology	Affirmations, self-talk and positive reviewing
Building mental practice and imagery skills	Cognitive psychology	Mental rehearsal and imagery

Table 9.4 Derivation of interventions commonly used in applied sport psychology

case, we need to examine two areas: first, how motivation is conceptualised in sport, and second, the research that has clarified how best to use goal setting in sport.

Motivation in sport

Motivation has been of central interest to psychologists from the earliest days of the discipline (James 1890). However, this has not necessarily led to a good understanding of the concept by laypeople. This also occurs in sport. Sport psychologists and sport performers sometimes differ in their understanding of what motivation is and how it influences behaviour. In common usage, motivation is used simplistically as a synonym for 'psyching-up' routines that coaches or managers use in team talks or warm-ups. The sport psychologist also has a simple definition of motivation: it is the 'direction and intensity of behaviour' (Gill 2000). By direction we mean what we choose to do, and by intensity we mean how much effort or energy is invested in that choice. However, the simplicity of this definition belies a theoretical complexity due to the many models aimed at explaining the nature of motivation. I will outline some key contemporary models.

Self-determination theory

The distinction between *intrinsic* and *extrinsic motivation* is important. Intrinsic motivation is where a performer is primarily motivated to participate in their sport for enjoyment and personal satisfaction, while extrinsic motivation is

driven by external rewards and incentives. *Self-determination theory* proposes that we have an innate and spontaneous desire to display competence, autonomy/self-determination and relatedness in our sport behaviour (Frederick and Ryan 1995; Deci and Ryan 2000). Sport is often regarded as behaviourist in context. From the start of a young sport performer's career, a climate of reinforcement and punishment develops. Good performance brings recognition, selection, praise and often tangible rewards, such as trophies and money. These shape behaviour, but may also undermine intrinsic motivation. Motivationally, the following problematic scenario is one commonly seen in youth sport. A young, talented performer, at the top of an age group category, may be successful and receive recognition and other extrinsic rewards for being successful. The following season they go from being the oldest (and often the biggest and strongest) in the age group to being the youngest (and often the smallest and weakest) in the next age group. The extrinsic rewards they enjoyed the previous season may disappear. Unless the athlete has a high level of intrinsic motivation, he or she will be very vulnerable to a motivational crisis. The extrinsic rewards they enjoyed have come to drive their motivation; when these are not forthcoming, there is no intrinsic motivation to replace them. The same sort of motivational crises can occur in professional sport, where extrinsic rewards effectively turn 'play' into 'work'.

Linked to self-determination theory is the concept of *perceived competence*. In Deci and Ryan's (2000) model, a desire to demonstrate competence is a feature of intrinsic motivation. Harter (1978) developed this further. She argued that people will engage in an activity with the motivation to demonstrate mastery. Following the attempt, they receive feedback from a number of sources – peers, family and coaches. The information received will inform their perceptions of their own competence and, in turn, will affect responses. These perceptions, in Harter's model, determine whether someone will repeat or avoid the activity. However, it fails to account for how people attribute competence. For some people, competence may be defined as demonstrating skills, irrespective of outcome; in others, however, the outcome is the important element. In these people, competence is defined by whether you win, not by how skilfully you play. This is where another model, achievement goal theory (Nicholls 1984), can be applied.

Achievement goal theory

Achievement goal theory was developed by Nicholls (1984) to explain academic motivation. Duda (1989) developed and modified this approach, which now provides one of the most important lines of motivation theory in sport psychology. In her model there are two goal orientations: *ego*, where achievement is defined in terms of demonstrating superiority over others, and *task*, where the goal is to achieve personal mastery over a task. Motivationally, the task-oriented performer seeks ongoing development of skills, they are not concerned with how others are performing, they maintain a high work rate, persist after failure and seek challenges that allow them to gather feedback on how they are improving. On the other hand, ego-oriented individuals are primarily motivated by selecting competition where superiority can be demonstrated. High perceived ability and high effort will only be seen if the person feels that she or he can demonstrate superior ability. Where this cannot be achieved, the person will either choose goals that are extremely hard or avoid the situation altogether. Task orientation and ego orientation are not mutually exclusive. It is common to see a high level of both. In that case, a person is motivated by both the development of skills and also outcomes. This is an important issue that we need to consider when we return to discussing the sort of interventions that a sport psychologist might develop for an athlete. Setting mastery goals for a performer who is primarily ego-oriented is unlikely to be effective.

A weakness of the achievement goal orientation model is its emphasis on personal motives. Other people, such as peers, parents, coaches or teachers, can contribute to a 'motivational climate' (Newton 1994) around a person. This can reinforce or conflict with a person's own motivational orientation. The motivational climate around an athlete is extremely important in the development of motivation, particularly in young athletes.

Theory into practice: goal-setting interventions in sport

Goal setting is probably the single most widely used sport psychology intervention. Locke and Latham (1994) argued that it works by way of four performance-enhancement mechanisms. Goals:

➡ focus attention on key elements of performance;
➡ mobilise effort in response to the task;
➡ enhance persistence; and
➡ have an indirect effect, in that they encourage new learning strategies.

It is very common for performers to focus only on *outcome goals*, such as winning an event or being selected for a team. Supporting outcome goals are *performance goals*, such as a race time or, in games, pass completion percentages or tackle counts. Supporting performance goals are *process goals*. Process goals are the day-to-day behaviours that make the achievement of performance and outcome goals more likely. For example, if a soccer team is aiming to win a league, they need to win more games. A performance goal might be to ensure that the opposing team does not score goals. The process goals leading to this relate to how the defensive organisation works and the development of sound defensive skills in the players. The process goals are specific behaviours that are under the volitional control of the players themselves. Therefore, these can be evaluated independently of external factors.

Does goal setting actually work? Kyllo and Landers (1995) conducted a meta-analysis on a sample of 36 studies and found that goal setting enhances performance by around 0.34 of a standard deviation. This appears to be a very small amount; however, in performance terms, this may take an athlete from being tenth to being first in the world, or may lower a personal best performance by 2 or 3 per cent. Most athletes would welcome this order of improvement. However, this is nothing like the magnitude of gain reported in the occupational psychology literature. Locke and Latham (1990) report significantly greater gains in their survey of goal setting in commerce. There are a number of methodological and practical reasons why this is the case. Burton, Naylor and Holliday (2002) provide an excellent overview of these issues.

Developing and maintaining effective attention

Abernethy (2001: 53) stated that it is difficult to imagine anything more important in sport than 'paying attention to the task at hand'. Paying attention means different things in different sports. Football goalkeepers must be centrally aware of the flight of the ball while ignoring the jostling of players around them; gymnasts must be aware of feedback from their limbs indicating their position and speed as they make transitions from move to move; and marathon runners need to maintain attention on running quickly, while ignoring the fatigue of accumulated miles. In our earlier discussion of the ideal performance state, it was noted that, paradoxically, peak performance is often associated with **not** thinking about what you are doing, just allowing the mind and body to run automatically, without conscious control of either. Applied sport psychologists are faced with a dilemma in trying to help athletes achieve optimal attention – too many explicit rules and thought management can mitigate against achieving this 'bubble' of concentration; too little attentional control and the mind can lose focus, taking attention in directions that are unhelpful to the athlete. Cognitive psychology has researched attention since the 1950s, and sport psychology research into attention has been strongly rooted in this cognitive tradition. The issue of applying theory to practice is to help the athlete identify and maintain a focus on the most task-relevant aspects of performance. From this perspective, Nideffer's (1976) model of attentional style in sport classified attention according to two dimensions – *width* (analogous to the 'spotlight' or 'zoom lens' models) and *direction*, a distinction between an internal and external attentional focus (see Figure 9.5).

Theory into practice: interventions to develop and maintain optimal attention

Moran (1996) presented a simplified summary of the principle components of attention in sport:

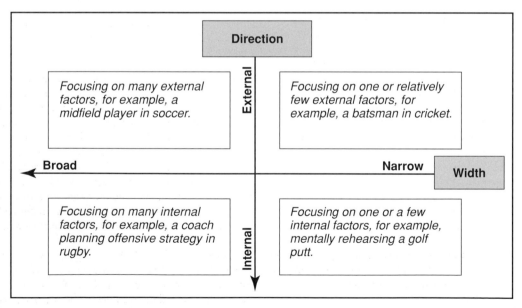

Figure 9.5 Nideffer's model of attentional style
Source: Adapted from Nideffer (1976)

1 Concentration requires mental effort.
2 One can only concentrate on one thought at a time.
3 Athletes are focused when they concentrate on actions that are specific, task relevant and under their own volitional control.
4 Athletes 'lose' concentration when they focus on task-irrelevant factors or things which are not under their own volitional control.
5 Performance-related anxiety, particularly worry, is a problem because it influences the width and direction of attention.

When psychologists question athletes about what optimal concentration 'feels' like, their replies generally coincide with the ideal performance elements: movements are automatic, there is little perception of effort, time appears distorted, etc. They often go on to examine what can interrupt this state. Some examples of factors interrupting optimal concentration are set out in Table 9.5.

Internal factors	External factors
Fatigue	Officiating decisions
Over-analysis	Intimidating opponents
Worry about mistakes	Weather or environmental conditions
Excitement about good play	Crowd noise

Table 9.5 Factors interrupting optimal concentration

Performers need to develop mental skills to cope with both internal and external distractions, and to enable them to maintain concentration. Moran (2004) advocates a four-step approach to the development of attentional control.
1 Specific 'process' goals – actions under one's own control.
2 Using performance routines.
3 Using trigger words
4 Mental rehearsal.

We have already examined the role of process goals in maintaining attention by directing the athlete to task-relevant elements of performance.

Performance routines develop from simulation training (Orlick 1990). This is where training is designed to mimic actual performance in as many ways as possible. Mike Atherton, the former England cricket captain, gave an excellent example of this in Selvey (1998: 2):

> It is a conscious thing, a full dress rehearsal. I treat nets as a match situation. So as you walk into the net, you give yourself the same thought processes as you might in a match, you take guard and do all your trigger movements the same and you are very hard on yourself.

Figure 9.6 Mike Atherton regularly used simulation to make practice more like real competition

Simulation can address internal distractions, such as worry or fatigue, very well, as they are relatively easy to recreate in training. External distractions are much more difficult to simulate. An excellent case in point is the simulation of taking penalties in important soccer matches. Many players and coaches argue that there is no point practising penalty shoot-outs because of the marked environmental differences between practice and competition. While the skills are technically identical, the attentional demands are very different.

In 'closed skills', such as golf, where the environment remains constant, performance routines are commonly used. Tiger Woods' putting routine is an excellent example. In both practice and competition, he follows his routine of examining the putt from every angle, every time he putts.

Trigger words help athletes to maintain task-relevant thinking. A gymnast may say 'tuck' as he goes into a somersault, or a hurdler might say 'flow' to herself as she attacks a barrier. These are all elements of an athlete's 'self-talk'. To be effective, cue words should be brief, energising and emphasise what the athlete is aiming to do, not what they are aiming to avoid. A sport psychologist may work with an athlete to modify their self-talk and cue words in a very similar way to that in which a cognitive behavioural therapist works to modify the self-talk of a person with a phobia or with depression.

The final attentional intervention Moran (2004) suggested is mental rehearsal. This will be discussed in detail later in the text.

Stress management interventions

If you play sport, you have probably experienced performance-related nerves. It comes as a surprise to many recreational performers to discover that professional and elite sport performers are also prone to nervousness and anxiety.

Jack Nicklaus (cited in Patmore 1986: 75), considered to be the greatest golfer in the history of the game, said:

> It doesn't take much technique to roll a 1.68 inch ball along a smooth, level surface, into the immediate vicinity of a 4.5 inch hole. With no pressure on you, you can do it one-handed most of the time. But there is always pressure on the shorter puts ... 90% of the rounds I play in Major championships I play with a bit of shake.

Poczwardowski and Conroy (2002: 313) noted that 'excellence in coping precedes excellence in performance'; therefore, it is an important part of the sport psychologist's support role to help performers develop skills that help them to cope with stress and anxiety related to performance.

Competitive sport provokes anxiety because it involves some or all of the following:

- Performance: The sport demands performance of a skill or activity, which may provoke worry or fear (e.g. running 26.2 miles in a marathon or facing a 90 mph bowler in cricket).
- Evaluation: The performance is public and will be evaluated in some way. A performer's perceived 'worth' may be bound up in the performance or outcome. Worth may also be linked to intrinsic or extrinsic rewards.
- Uncertainty: In sport there is much uncertainty about what will happen – a player may become injured, they may lose when they expect to win and a whole array of other unpredictable scenarios may be played out.

Sport psychology interventions aimed at managing stress need to address these factors.

The theoretical basis of stress and performance in sport

At the outset, it is important to define key terms: arousal, anxiety and stress.

Arousal is the level of activation in the autonomic nervous system. Many performers view increased physiological arousal as a good thing, and aim, through their pre-performance routine, to gain the benefits of circulating adrenalin. However, increased physiological arousal may affect gross motor skills and fine motor skills differently. Gross motor skills involve the whole body and usually require high energy expenditure, for example power lifting. Increased physiological arousal may facilitate performance of these. Fine motor skills usually involve fine control of small body parts and require little energy output. Increased arousal may lead to performance errors.

Spielberger (1966: 17) defined *anxiety* as a 'negative emotional state with feelings of worry, nervousness, and apprehension associated with activation or arousal of the body'. He also differentiated trait and state elements – trait anxiety being a stable and enduring proneness to view situations as threatening, and state anxiety being viewed as transient and situationally specific. The contemporary view of anxiety in sport is that it is a multidimensional construct composed of two elements. One is a cognitive element, characterised by fear, apprehension, negative expectations and doubt. The other element is defined as *somatic anxiety*. This is the complex of autonomic symptoms experienced in the body and negatively perceived. Typically, these are dry mouth, increased sweating of the palms and butterflies in the stomach.

The modern view of *stress* is that it is a process whereby the perceived demands of a situation are weighed against the perceived ability to cope (Woodman and Hardy 2001). The key word here is 'perceived'. The actual demands and the actual coping resources are often unknown. A person may under- or overestimate the demands of the task and, equally, may under- or overestimate their ability to cope. Another aspect of the stress 'process' is the notion of 'value'. If an athlete does not really care about the outcome, or their performance, it is unlikely that they will experience stress. Where performers have invested value in their performance, they are much more likely to experience stress. The stress response is thought to be graded, depending on the degree of imbalance between perceived demands and perceived ability to cope. If the imbalance is perceived as a high level of challenge and low level of coping, extreme stress may be experienced, leading to high levels of cognitive and somatic anxiety and a desire to avoid the challenge. Interestingly, the model suggests that anxiety is also experienced when the challenge is low and the perceived ability to cope is very high. This is seen in sport, where high-ranking teams or players are drawn to play weaker opponents. Here, the performance anxiety is generally more profound for the stronger opponents.

The link between stress and performance

Prior to the late 1980s, sport psychology accepted a simplistic, unidimensional theoretical basis to the stress–performance relationship – the inverted-U hypothesis (Yerkes and Dodson 1908) (see Figure 9.7). Hardy and his co-workers (Fazey and Hardy 1988; Hardy 1990; Hardy and Parfitt 1991) developed a multidimensional approach. In their

'catastrophe' model (see Figure 9.8), physiological arousal interacts with state anxiety to determine performance. In the simplest model, the cusp-catastrophe model, they accept that there is an inverted-U relationship between arousal and performance, **but** only when cognitive anxiety is low. When cognitive anxiety is high, increases in arousal serve to facilitate performance, improving it up to a certain threshold point. Beyond this threshold, or cusp, further increases in arousal or cognitive anxiety lead to a sudden, dramatic and catastrophic drop in performance. Unlike the inverted-U hypothesis, which suggests symmetry in the performance curve, the catastrophe model suggests that a great deal of effort is required to return to optimal levels of arousal and anxiety, and thereby regain previous performance. This theory has generated a great deal of research interest (e.g. Hardy, Parfitt and Pates 1994; Edwards et al. 2002). However, it is complex and difficult to test empirically. It should be noted that ecologically valid as catastrophe theory is, it remains a descriptive model. It does not explain the mechanism by which anxiety influences performance. To do this, we need to refer to mainstream cognitive psychology.

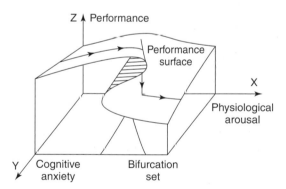

Figure 9.8 Hardy and Fazey's (1987) catastrophe model of the relationship between anxiety and performance
Source: Jones and Hardy (eds) (1990: 88)

Explanatory models of the stress–performance relationship

Sport psychology has adopted two aspects of cognitive psychology theory to clarify the mechanism by which stress influences sport performance.

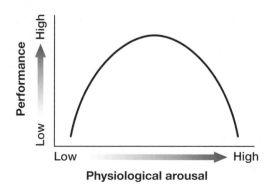

Figure 9.7 The inverted-U hypothesis
Source: Weinberg and Gould (2003: 86)

1 *Processing efficiency theory* (Eysenck and Calvo 1992) proposes that state anxiety, particularly the cognitive component of it, has two functions. The first function is that cognitive anxiety or worry uses processing capacity in working memory. This leads to poorer performance, particularly in tasks that also demand processing space in working memory. However, worry also has a motivational function. Eysenck and Calvo (1992: 415) explained this as worry 'motivating the performer to invest more effort into avoiding the consequences of poor performance'. This is why state anxiety has the potential to both enhance and undermine performance.

2 *Conscious processing or reinvestment theory* (Masters 1992) addresses the anxiety–performance question from a skill acquisition angle. Masters argued that sudden drops in skilled performance were due to a regression to an earlier stage of learning under conditions of increased anxiety. When a person practises a skill and it becomes well learned, it makes a transition from being controlled on a conscious level, through 'explicit rules', to being controlled automatically. Under conditions of increased anxiety, Masters argued, the performer tends to introduce conscious control of the movement by isolating and focusing on specific components. This tends to undermine smooth automatic execution. This idea is one that is familiar to sport performers – if you think too much about what you are doing, it may undermine performance.

Theory into practice: interventions aimed at managing stress

You may have noted two important performance-related issues in this discussion of stress and performance.

1 The balance required between performers benefiting from increased physiological arousal and performance not being undermined by cognitive anxiety.

2 That the applied challenge in managing anxiety is not an emotional one, but an attentional one. The anxious athlete usually experiences lower levels of performance because cognitive anxiety is encouraging thought which is not task relevant.

Managing physiological arousal

Most sport performers recognise that they have their own, highly personal, emotional or arousal state at which they perform best. Performers need skills that enable them to fine-tune arousal in order to gain maximum performance benefit. Behaviourally, over-aroused athletes tend to speed up their actions. Psychologists often observe performance and give feedback on this. Cues can be used to slow down and relax whenever they become aware of over-arousal. Relaxation techniques, such as centring and progressive muscle relaxation (PMR), can be very useful, particularly in sports where there are natural breaks, like tennis or golf. Centring is a breathing technique where the athlete aims to reduce arousal by slowing the heartbeat. The technique develops slow, diaphragmatic breathing, aimed at calming and relaxing. PMR is a technique that involves the systematic clenching and relaxing of muscle groups through the body. Knowing when and how to deploy these interventions is important. It would be a mistake for rugby players to do extensive physiological relaxation prior to a game. During a game, however, they may need to calm themselves prior to taking an important kick or throwing to an important line-out. Centring could be incorporated in a pre-kick or pre-throw routine.

Interventions aimed at managing cognitive anxiety

Many of the techniques sport psychologists use to manage cognitive anxiety are derived from clinical interventions. Cognitive restructuring may be used to help people who experience anxiety when they recognise that the demands placed on them exceed their perceived ability to cope. For example, a football player may dread taking a penalty in an important shoot-out. The player may be focusing on the anticipated negative outcome – 'What happens if I fail?' By restructuring their thinking – 'Taking this kick is a chance to show how good I am' – anxiety may be reduced. This appears straightforward, but in reality it is often a long and difficult job encouraging athletes to see competition as an opportunity rather than a threat.

Interventions aimed at building self-confidence

Performers will often describe their best performances in terms of deep and unshakeable confidence, and their worst in terms of low or non-existent confidence. A deep, robust and enduring self-belief was seen to be one of the main characteristics of the 'mentally tough' performer described in the work of Bull et al. (2005) and also Jones, Hanton and Connaughton (2002). Our understanding of confidence in sport draws heavily on two lines of theory: first, self-efficacy theory (Bandura 1986), and second, sport confidence theory (Vealey et al. 1998).

Self-efficacy theory developed from Bandura's (1986) clinical work on phobias. He found that a subjective, highly task-specific expectation, indicating the level of belief that a person could cope with in a situation related to their phobia, was the strongest predictor of actual behaviour. Hence the widely accepted definition of self-efficacy is an individual's personal judgement of his or her capability or skill to perform (efficacy expectations) and judgements about the outcome of performance (outcome expectations) (Bezjak and Lee 1990). Bandura identified four sources of efficacy information:

➡ Performance accomplishments (things that I have done well or achieved and attributed to myself).
➡ Vicarious experiences (watching others whom I perceive to be similar to me).
➡ Verbal encouragement (encouragement from a coach or self-talk).
➡ Physiological arousal (excitement, fatigue).

Bandura argued that these sources of efficacy information are organised hierarchically. The strongest and most direct form of information used to build self-efficacy is therefore performance accomplishment; the weakest and least direct is physiological arousal. Bandura argued that self-efficacy predicts the actual level of performance, provided the necessary skills and incentives are in place. He also suggested that when self-efficacy is high, athletes will persist in the face of failure and invest higher levels of effort.

The other model of confidence that informs sport psychology interventions is the *sport confidence model*, first proposed by Robin Vealey in 1986, and subsequently developed by Vealey et al. (1998). Vealey argued that some people were generally more confident than others. She went on to argue that trait confidence interacted with situational factors to derive the situational confidence 'state'. In the 1998 development of the model, Vealey and her co-workers identified the nine factors that contributed to sport confidence.

It is evident that there is overlap between Bandura's and Vealey's models. Although they differ fundamentally in what they are assessing – Bandura is aiming to predict very specific and narrow behaviours, and Vealey is aiming to predict a more global, outcome-related confidence – both models do place previous performance accomplishment at the centre of developing robust 'efficacy', or confidence.

To this end, when sport psychologists develop interventions aimed at building confidence, they aim to help an athlete build a sense of what they have achieved personally. In doing this, they also need to guard against overconfidence, complacency and arrogance.

Theory into practice: interventions to develop robust self-belief

Like the interventions used in managing anxiety, those aimed at building confidence are based on clinical and counselling interventions, such as self-talk and cognitive restructuring. In developing confident self-talk, there is an awareness-building phase, where performers become aware of the inner dialogue they have when they compete. For example, rugby players often report confidence being lost after making a mistake, such as dropping a pass or missing a tackle. The next stage of the intervention is to gain awareness of the consequences of the low-confidence thought. Players who have just made a mistake get angry with themselves and then try to avoid situations where they could make another mistake. So they avoid receiving passes or making tackles. The final phase is to replace the 'faulty', low-confidence thought with a positive, action-related thought. What would a confident player do now? Look for the ball, look for a tackle to make an impact. Psychologists may also seek to restructure thinking by teaching the players to keep perspective on how skilled they are. Elite players do not drop the ball very often – having done it once, the probability of doing it a second time is extremely low.

Another intervention that can be used to develop confidence is an attribution-based technique that links goal setting and confidence. Most sport performers conduct post-performance reviews.

Factor	Example
Mastery	Previous good performance – demonstrating high levels of skill
Demonstration of ability	Previous winning performance – demonstration of ability relative to others
Physical/mental preparation	Feeling physically or mentally prepared
Physical self-presentation	Perception of one's physical self – how one looks to others
Social support	Perceiving support from team mates, coach and other important others
Vicarious experience	Watching others being successful
Coach's leadership	Believing that the coach is skilled in decision-making and leadership
Environmental comfort	Feeling like the competitive venue is familiar and 'known'
Situational favourableness	Getting the breaks or rub of the green

Table 9.6 Sources of sport confidence in Vealey et al.'s (1998) model
Source: Adapted from Vealey et al. (1998)

However, many of them are distorted because they rely on players' subjective recall of what happened in the game or event. Usually players recall mistakes rather than things they did well. This technique helps players to develop a much more objective review process.

Issues related to confidence are some of the most common reasons athletes seek psychological assistance. A psychologist cannot give an athlete confidence; what they can do is to help the athlete develop the skills to start the 'fire of confidence' within themselves. However, sometimes athletes develop complex thought processes that mitigate against building confidence. These require skill and patience to understand, and the design of interventions to overcome.

Interventions to develop mental rehearsal and imagery skills

On initial inspection, imagery and sport performance appear to be distantly related.

However, research has indicated that imagery is used by sport performers in both competition and training (Orlick and Partington 1988). Imagery can be used in a number of ways, relating to performance enhancement and skill acquisition. Therefore, imagery tends to be used in training to assist the process of skill acquisition, and in competition to assist with mental readiness to perform.

Hall, Rodgers and Barr (1990) showed that imagery is used by athletes immediately prior to performance. These results were confirmed by Munroe et al. (2000). Other researchers have found that imagery is used extensively by injured athletes to help retain skills that cannot be consolidated through physical practice. Throughout rehabilitation, mental practice and imagery can help maintain skills.

Paivio (1985) presented a framework demonstrating how imagery influences motor skills. He suggested that imagery serves two functions and that these operate on either specific or general levels (see Table 9.7).

A recent modification of this model was proposed by Moritz et al. (1996). They suggested that the motivational-general aspect (MG) of imagery function should be further divided into two elements: MG – mastery, and MG – arousal. Their rationale for this separation was that if athletes want to develop, regain or maintain their confidence, it is important that they imagine performing skills confidently. To Moritz et al., this type of imagery is MG – mastery imagery. MG – arousal imagery relates to the experience of arousal and competitive anxiety. Some performers like to include imagery as part of their warm-up for performance. In this context, images of arousal may help the performer to 'psych up'. Equally, some performers prefer to use calming imagery as

	General	Specific
Motivational	General motivational imagery – relating to the physiological state of the performer – arousal and mood	Specific goal achievement – imagining winning an event
Cognitive	General cognitive imagery – imagining executing a strategy successfully to gain an advantage	Specific cognitive imagery – imagining successful execution of a specific skill

Table 9.7 Framework of imagery function
Source: Adapted from Paivio (1985)

part of their pre-performance routine. The study by White and Hardy (1998) found evidence of both types of imagery use within samples of athletes in the same sport. The nature of the imagery content is highly subjective and driven by the goals of the performer.

An important distinction is the adoption of different imagery perspectives. Some performers prefer to imagine themselves from the outside, as if watching a video of their performance. Others prefer a more kinaesthetic approach and adopt an internal perspective, as if viewing their performance through their own eyes. Hardy and Callow (1999) examined this and found that both perspectives have important roles. An internal perspective encourages the performer to rehearse what the movement *feels* like, while an external perspective encourages the athlete to focus on what the movement *looks* like. The feeling aspect is important when learning a skill; the looking aspect is important when the skill is learned. Hardy and Callow (1999) make the point that in some sports, like gymnastics and dance, what the skill looks like is critical. Integration between internal and external perspectives can be very effective.

How does imagery work?

There are a number of proposed mechanisms aimed at explaining how imagery and mental rehearsal impact on performance.

➡ *Psychoneuromuscular theory*: Carpenter (1894) suggests that imagery facilitates the learning of a skill by enhancing the neuromuscular connections controlling the movement.
➡ *Symbolic learning theory*: Sackett (1934) argues that imagery helps people acquire skills by creating a mental 'blueprint' for the movement.

Where a motor programme is being developed through physical practice, mental rehearsal or imagery reinforces learning, creating a more durable memory trace.

➡ *Bioinformational theory*: Lang (1977, 1979) proposes that images are functionally organised in the central nervous system and can be triggered by different types of 'propositions'. Stimulus propositions are statements about the stimulus features of the scene to be imagined, for example: 'You are preparing to take a penalty kick in front of 25,000 people.' Response propositions, on the other hand, relate to the imager's response to the scenario, so: 'You are preparing to take a penalty kick in front of 25,000 people. You feel your heart thumping in your chest, but you calm it.' In Lang's model, it is the response propositions that are central to the effectiveness of imagery.
➡ *Functional equivalence or PETTLEP model* (see below): Holmes and Collins (2001) developed Langs' bioinformational approach further by arguing that for mental practice to be effective, it must be as functionally similar to physical practice as possible. In short, it must engage the same parts of the central nervous systems as actual physical practice.

Theory–practice integration: imagery interventions

Weinberg and Gould (2003) outline several uses for imagery, including imagery to improve concentration, to build confidence, to control emotional responses, to acquire and practise skills, to acquire and practise strategy, to solve problems and, finally, to cope with pain and injury. A sport psychologist integrates theory and practice by composing and adapting 'scripts' that enable performers to mentally rehearse key technical or tactical skills, or practise their attentional control, stress management or confidence skills. Holmes and Collins's (2001) PETTLEP approach prescribes that effective imagery scripts should include all (or as many as possible) of the *P*hysical, *E*nvironment, *T*ask, *T*iming, *L*earning, *E*motion, *P*erspective aspects of the task or skill. We will see an example of this in the case study. The PETTLEP model has received little empirical testing, but it does provide a very useful framework for designing imagery-based interventions.

Stage four – Ongoing monitoring and adjustment

Rowan (1997) identified three phases in long-term counselling.

- In phase one, the initial 'symptoms' or issues are dealt with, often with an immediate positive effect.
- In phase two, deeper issues, which may not have been evident at the start of the work, are identified and addressed.
- In the third phase, the person undergoing counselling works through the daily implications of their raised knowledge and awareness. This may be evident in changed behaviour or in their emotional responses to situations.

In sport psychology support work, similar phases are seen. If the psychologist adopts a 'pedagogic' mental skills approach to their support work, their contact with the athlete may stop at the end of phase one. From an ethical and practical perspective, this may be satisfactory. The athlete may be satisfied that their mental training goals have been achieved and that the psychologist has operated within their competency. However, if support for the athlete is maintained over a prolonged period, the work may develop into phases two and three. If this is the case, the ongoing monitoring of the effectiveness of the interventions needs to be examined closely. In doing this, the psychologist may well uncover issues that were not evident at the start of the programme of work – it may be that these fall outside their area of competence. This is a crucial point. It is potentially abusive for a psychologist to raise an athlete's awareness of issues and then not help them towards resolution. To this end, it is very important that the sport psychologist has access to peer support, and clinical or counselling psychology colleagues who can offer advice and accept referrals.

An important aspect of the ongoing monitoring process concerns adherence. Adherence, in this case, refers to the extent to which an athlete is sticking to their mental training programme. No training programme, physical or mental, will be effective if the athlete fails to adhere, or undermines their training by being a 'super-adherer'. Ongoing contact and regular prompts can help adherence. This is important if the interventions require athletes to learn skills, such as imagery training, or to modify well-learned habits or routines, such as managing self-talk. There has been little research examining adherence of athletes on mental skills training programmes. Studies that have been undertaken show that adherence rates are often poor (Bull 1991).

Stage five – Evaluation, withdrawal but maintain contact with athlete or team

Evaluating the effectiveness of sport psychology interventions has become a very important issue. In professional sport, many coaches adopt the multidisciplinary approach to preparation discussed earlier, and they are very keen to see what aspects of the team 'add value' to performance. Similarly, in Olympic sports, many performers are funded by the National Lottery. Part of a sport's budget will be spent on the provision of sport psychology support. It is quite justified to check if that money is benefiting performance. The problem is that specifically evaluating the effectiveness of one aspect of a performer's preparation is very difficult to do. The reasons for an athlete's performance in competition are often complex and interlinked.

The most effective evaluations involve comprehensive objective and subjective data. An example of objective assessment would be to return to the aims of the programme discussed in stage one. If the athlete and coach aimed to increase one area of performance, such as free-throw shooting under pressure, the trend in this through the period of the mental skills training can readily be mapped. However, this is not the whole story. The subjective reports of those who underwent the mental training should also be assessed. Information about which techniques worked or were useful to them, whether there was enough time for, or emphasis on mental training, and information about the personal approach or philosophy of the psychologist are all valuable in generating an overall impression of a programme's worth. Usually, evaluations adopt a qualitative methodology. However, Partington and Orlick (1987a, b) developed a quantitative tool, the Sport Psychology Consultant Effectiveness Form, which has been widely used.

One final aspect of evaluation concerns the ethical obligation of sport psychologists to review their own practice. Sport psychologists should engage in an ongoing review of their practice, with a view to developing service delivery. Recently, considerable emphasis has been placed on 'reflective practice' as a method of doing this. Anderson, Knowles and Gilbourne (2004) provide an excellent overview of this.

In withdrawing from a direct support role, the psychologist needs to ensure that the performer is not left with any 'unfinished business', and that they understand that contact is suspended rather than terminated.

Example of a sport psychology intervention: an imagery intervention

The aims of this study were:

- to examine the use made of mental imagery by an elite rugby forward;
- to assess the impact of mental imagery on actual playing performance.

This study has been selected because it highlights the importance of grounding applied research in theoretical foundations. The researchers (Evans, Jones and Mullen 2004) have adopted the framework of imagery function developed by Hall et al. (1998). This framework identifies five uses for imagery:

- cognitive-general (CG, e.g. imagining strategies in play);
- cognitive-specific (CS, e.g. imagining executing skills perfectly);
- motivation-general – arousal (MG – arousal, e.g. imagining the arousal and anxiety associated with performance);
- motivation-general – mastery (MG – mastery, e.g. imagining being mentally tough);
- motivation-specific (MS, e.g. imagining a specific goal being achieved).

The study also highlights the importance of using appropriate research methodology. This study was field based, over a 14-week period. A mixture of methods was used. Quantitative assessment of the imagery ability was conducted using the Sports Imagery Questionnaire (Hall et al. 1998). Qualitative methods were used in the form of semi-structured interviews, to understand what imagery was being used and how effective it was. The player also maintained an imagery diary over the period of the intervention.

The intervention had three phases:

1 The aims of phase one were to improve the clarity and vividness of the images and, specifically, to 'defuzz' the images the player had of his scrimmaging. Finally, the player sought to introduce opposition into his imagery practice of tactics. The diary recorded substantial improvements in all areas within two weeks.

2 In phase two of the study, the player sought to refine his imagery further. Depending on his training and playing schedule, he was doing imagery practice two or three times a day, for between five and ten minutes.

3 The final phase of the intervention coincided with a transition between the end of the domestic season and an overseas tour. By this stage, the interview and diary data recorded that the player was skilled and confident in his use of imagery, and that mental practice had become firmly established as part of his routine.

In discussing the intervention, Evans, Jones and Mullen (2004) give examples of where the data supported the Hall et al. (1998) framework. For example, the use of MG – mastery and CS imagery to develop scrimmaging skills; and the use of CS imagery content to develop tactical aspects of play. However, there were some contradictions; for example, the player appeared to use cognitive imagery to manage arousal and anxiety. In relation to performance, it appears that imagery had a positive effect on performance. However, it is not possible to infer cause and effect due to the non-experimental design. It would be possible to give alternative explanations for the data collected.

In conclusion, this is a very good example of applied research. It highlights the importance of theory-practice integration and also problems of field-based research in sport psychology.

Importantly, the research team worked hard to draw conclusions that will serve to stimulate both future research and applied practice.

Source: Evans, Jones and Mullen (2004)

FUTURE DIRECTIONS FOR SPORT AND EXERCISE PSYCHOLOGY

Although it is difficult to predict how an area will develop over time, there are significant issues and events in both sport and exercise that will shape the immediate future for psychologists working in those areas.

In sport, the London Olympics will provide a stimulus for sport psychology. The stated aim of the organising committee is for Great Britain to achieve its highest ever medal tally. As I write this (in December 2006), sport psychologists are involved not just in research and service delivery, but also in the key area of talent identification and development. In sport there is a saying that 'being an overnight success takes about ten years of preparation'. Sport psychologists are at the forefront of this process.

In exercise, the public health problems related to obesity will be a central focus for the foreseeable future. Exercise psychology has a key role to play in developing cost-effective interventions to increase health-enhancing physical activity across the whole population and across the whole lifespan. Exercise psychologists will have a major part to play in the radical thinking and bold decision-making required if the obesity epidemic is to be checked.

CONCLUSION

The public awareness of sport psychology has never been higher. Many sport performers and coaches accept and value the contribution that it can make to success in sport. However, it is important to recognise that sport psychology is practised by highly trained and professional psychologists – who do not profess to endow performers with superhuman powers. The continuing development of applied sport psychology depends on the ongoing development of a scientifically robust theoretical basis, and the willingness of researchers to integrate theory and practice. Applied sport psychology still has a great deal to learn from counselling and clinical psychology about the delivery of effective interventions. It also has the potential to teach other areas of psychology about optimal human functioning.

RECOMMENDED FURTHER READING

Andersen, M. (2000) *Doing Sport Psychology*. Champaign, IL: Human Kinetics.

Biddle, S., Fox, K. and Boutcher, S. (2000) *Physical Activity and Psychological Well-being*. London: Routledge.

Buckworth, J. and Dishman, R. (2002) *Exercise Psychology*. Champaign, IL: Human Kinetics.

Lavallee, D., Kremer, J., Moran, A. and Williams, M. (2004) *Sport Psychology: Contemporary themes*. Basingstoke and New York: Palgrave Macmillan.

Weinberg, R. and Gould, D. (2007) *Foundations of Sport and Exercise Psychology*. Champaign, IL: Human Kinetics.

Exercises

1. Define sport psychology and exercise psychology. Explain how they differ in their aims.

2. Visit the BASES and BPS websites (http://www.bases.org.uk and http://www.bps.org.uk). Compare the breadth and scope of the two organisations. Outline three ways in which they are similar and three ways in which they are different.

3. Despite the fact that exercise and physical activity can make a significant contribution to health, why do you think that so few people engage in it?

4. Do you achieve the target of 30 minutes of moderate-intensity physical activity on most days of the week? If yes, why have you made the decision to be active? If no, why do you not do so?

5. Interview a friend who exercises about their exercise behaviour. Explore the reasons why they exercise – are their motives intrinsic or extrinsic? What are the longer-term motivational implications if (a) their motives are mainly extrinsic? (b) their motives are mainly intrinsic?

6. Think about a sport that you play or are familiar with. Identify the main characteristics of elite performers in the following four areas: physical, technical, tactical, mental.

7. What do you think are the psychological characteristics of sport performers who consistently perform at or close to their potential?

8. Think of a sport performer who you know well. What do you think are their most pressing mental training needs? How would you go about confirming your thoughts?

9. Differentiate between task orientation and ego orientation. Review your own motives for playing sport. Do you tend to display ego orientation or task orientation?

10. List the things that undermine your concentration when you play sport. What interventions could you adopt to manage these?

11. Are you prone to nervousness in sport? Does it tend to help you play better or cause you to play worse? Imagine you have been invited to a sport radio programme as an expert guest. The presenter asks you to explain why nervousness helps some performers but hinders others – how would you respond?

12. What advice would you give to a performer who sought your advice about how to build confidence?

Major Theoretical Approaches

10 chapter

A theoretical approach in psychology is an overall perspective on how to study and how to understand human minds and behaviour. Very often a classical approach is seen as revolutionary and has sought to overthrow a previous approach, or at least to break new ground or make a distinct change of direction. An approach usually brings with it new methodology – preferred ways of investigating humans in order to demonstrate the newer way of understanding. Behaviourists sought to reject psychoanalytic and earlier mystical approaches. They also put faith in objective measurement of behaviour. Humanism sought a third way between behaviourism and psychoanalytic thought, and used more qualitative methods. The 'cognitive revolution', which several authors claim did not actually occur, was taken to be a scientifically-based reinstatement of mental processes back into the agenda of psychological investigation. No single approach or theory has become *the* approach in psychology. Some appear to be complementary, but do not be deceived by textbooks which present them as a matter of 'take your pick – they are all equally valid'. Many uncomplimentary words have been uttered, and even careers lost, in the frequently bitter battles between the different 'schools' of psychology.

WHY ARE THERE DIFFERENT APPROACHES? LEVELS OF EXPLANATION

The aim of psychological theorising is to provide the most productive and enlightening explanation of human thought and behaviour. Part of the difference between major approaches to theorising can be attributed to differing *levels of explanation*. Consider the following example. Suppose we are asked why a certain train disaster occurred. A superficial explanation might run: 'The signal was red, but the driver was asleep and did not see the signal.' A different perspective says: 'This kind of accident has been increasing because management is trying to cut corners. They refuse to update signalling equipment and they demand more work of drivers.' An additional perspective might be: 'The driver had been under tremendous domestic pressure; he had been up all night, arguing with his wife about the settlement for their separation.' Notice here that the first explanation sticks close to the immediate facts. The other two speculate about the wider context of causes, all relevant, but in two quite different directions.

Another concrete example might be: 'Why did your car stop?' A nuts-and-bolts explanation might concentrate on what happens in a car engine when there is no more petrol coming to the carburettor. A completely different level of explanation occurs when the driver explains: 'I had asked my partner to fill it up. I noticed this had not been done, but I was distracted by the urgency of picking up my son from school and the foul weather.' Notice here that the second explanation is not a wider explanation leading up to the immediate facts of the case. It serves quite a different purpose, and the nuts-and-bolts mechanical explanation is irrelevant here.

Reductionism

The nuts-and-bolts explanation is an example of *reductionism* – an attempt to reduce an explanation at one level (e.g. psychological) to an explanation at a more basic level (e.g. physiological). It is not useful to explain why a snooker player won a match in terms of the Newtonian mechanics of every collision of balls in the match. Similarly, if we are trying to explain social behaviour, it is not useful generally to be told what physiological factors or what individual string of thoughts preceded a

certain pattern of behaviour. For instance, if we are piloting a programme to give workers more job satisfaction through increased responsibility in order to raise factory output, then an explanation in terms of each workers' arm and leg movements, or in terms of their every single thought, will not be useful. We shall probably want to consider communication and interaction patterns, and possibly the workers' general assessment of the new working conditions. On the other hand, within clinical psychology, in some circumstances, we may be interested in individual thoughts which trigger certain problematic behaviour. Psychologists differ in the level at which they are explaining behaviour, from the *molar* to the *molecular*.

From molar to molecular

Across all the social sciences, as we seek to explain human behaviour at various levels, we are said to move from the *molar*, through the *micro*-level and on to the *molecular* level of explanation. At each level, different kinds of factors are seen as influential, and behaviour is analysed at different levels of complexity. In the train crash example above, the explanation of the management cutting corners is at a molar level and is somewhat beyond individual-level psychology, using organisational and economic analysis. On the other hand, an explanation focusing on the family moves towards the micro-level; and to say that his hand slipped through a combination of tiredness and alcohol would be to use a molecular analysis. Table 10.1 outlines various levels of analysis and explanation, with different areas of psychology associated with each, though of course there is overlap. Developmental psychology, for instance, is sometimes about the social factors surrounding the child, and sometimes about individual issues such as self-esteem or problem-solving style.

The holistic view

A substantial number of psychologists hold the view that one cannot sensibly isolate *aspects* of an individual (such as their 'intelligence' or a particular, measured attitude). They argue that an individual only makes sense *as* a whole individual. They are opposed to understanding people as the sum of various characteristics or mental processes 'isolated' by psychological research. They are opposed to reductionism in the explanation of

Molar		Micro	Molecular
Societal/ organisational focus	**Group (inter-individual) focus**	**Individual focus**	**Intra-individual focus**
Social structures: political and economic factors, legal system, social ideology. (Organisational psychology, sociology, politics, economics) *Cultural factors:* ideology and values of identified culture. (Anthropology, cross-cultural studies) *Organisational factors:* Authority structures at work.	*Formal and informal groups:* Work groups, social groups, peer groups, family. (Sociology, social psychology, developmental psychology, communication studies)	*External and interpersonal factors.* (Social psychology, differential psychology, developmental psychology, humanistic psychology) *Behavioural goals, large-scale behaviour.* (Behaviourism)	*Individual responses.* (Behaviourism) *Internal or intrapersonal factors.* (Biological psychology, cognitive psychology, psychodynamics)

Table 10.1 Levels of analysis

human experience and behaviour, and are seen as taking a *holistic* approach.

INDIVIDUAL DIFFERENCES/ DIFFERENTIAL PSYCHOLOGY

Some psychologists make general statements and theories about how humans work per se. That is, they are not so much interested in individual differences between people, but are keen on explaining how the mind works or how people acquire (i.e. learn) behaviour in *general*. Piaget, for instance, developed theories of the pattern in which almost all children's thinking develops, irrespective of any advantages one child has in mathematical or verbal skills. Skinner (1953) developed an overall model of the way in which people's behaviour is shaped, irrespective of any particular personality characteristics they might possess. The cognitive psychologist is interested in general features of human thought.

Individual differences – nomothetic and idiographic

In contrast, the study of *individual differences* is an area in which specific differences *between* individuals are the very subject of interest. Some of these differences can be *generalised*. It is thought possible to measure any individual on the particular characteristic. Examples might be the traits (characteristics) of anxiety, assertiveness or extraversion. Such measurement and generalising is known as a *nomothetic* approach. Some psychologists, however, feel it is important to recognise the existence of traits which, though they might seem similar superficially, have a *unique existence* in each individual – an *idiographic* position. Aggression may look similar on the outside, for instance (it usually involves hitting and shouting), but its causes, its exact content and its pattern of occurrence vary in important ways from one person to the next. Clinical, counselling and educational psychologists, in particular, often express a need to analyse their clients' behaviour at this level.

Individual differences – traits or situations?

A further debate concerns the issue of whether there is any justification for assuming that people's behaviour varies largely as a result of individual differences. In some situations virtually everyone will behave in a similar manner. Most people will stop to help when an elderly person falls down beside them, for instance. Some have argued (Hartshorne and May 1928; Mischel 1968) that most individual behaviour is not consistent across various settings. This position puts more emphasis on *situations* in controlling our behaviour, and argues that individual differences do not account for as much variation in behaviour as most people think. An *interactionist* position accepts that individuals are not consistent across situations – but it also argues that each situation does not produce the same behaviour in each individual. The situation means different things to different individuals, and because of *some* differences in personality traits, different people will behave differently in the *same* situation. Mischel moved towards this position in his later work (Mischel and Shoda 1995). From the mid 1990s onwards, however, there has been something of a rejuvenation of the idea that we can describe human personality adequately using consistent traits, especially those often referred to as the 'big five': extroversion (to introversion), agreeableness, conscientiousness, emotional stability (or neuroticism) and openness to experience (Costa and McRae 1992).

THE PSYCHOANALYTIC APPROACH

This perspective generally sees human behaviour as the product of forces within us, many of them largely beyond our conscious control. Athletes' motivation is explained, not in terms of social and financial rewards, not in terms of natural talent, but in terms of what success and winning mean or *symbolise* to the person concerned. The athlete may well be unable to recognise these deeper meanings, and may refer to something like 'feeling good' as an explanation. Beneath the surface of consciousness, however, in psychoanalytic thought, there is a causally related set of associations, all linked by past (and especially emotional) experience, which can be investigated with the willing participation of the client. Stressful thoughts and events, buried in our 'unconscious' mind, tend to surface in the form of symbols. Humans make strong use of symbols in their ordinary thinking – a particular car, for example, can be a symbol of success. One notorious source of symbolic material is our dream life, but our unexplained and out-of-the-ordinary behaviour, slips, accidents, failed memories,

outbursts, and so on, are all similar sources. These give a (rather obscured) 'window' through to our psychological type, our deeper reasons for behaviour and our driving forces. Several of the major principles on which most psychoanalytic thinkers would agree are as follows:

- The very early life of the infant, especially its relationship with its parents, has an all-important effect on later personality and general approach to the world.
- Development leaves most of us with unresolved, strong emotional conflicts, which continue to affect our thoughts and behaviour at an unconscious level. Young children cannot reason about their emotions. Consequently, powerful forces are laid down in childhood which are hard to recover in adulthood, yet they may guide our behaviour and we may need to get in touch with them in order to solve a psychological problem and progress with normal life.
- A near universal feature of human life is the employment of *defence mechanisms* in order to deal with and suppress underlying *conflicts* between thoughts and urges; conflicts too threatening to be admitted to oneself consciously are suppressed.
- Early psychoanalysts emphasised sexual feelings and emotions, but later theorists embrace the full range of emotionality and some de-emphasise the role of sex. Others also put more emphasis on people's ability to be rational and think forwards towards change, lessening the pessimistic Freudian focus on unconscious control.

Applications of the psychoanalytic approach

Psychoanalysis and motivation

In terms of motivation and conscious life, it will be useful to understand Freud's major components of the mind – the *id, ego* and *superego*. The *id* refers to our basic biological drives, including the important sexual one, and may be seen as Freud's concession to biological determinants in our behaviour, largely overwritten by social and emotional *learned* patterns of behaviour. Only at an early age are we honestly and unambiguously driven by hunger and pain to respond instantly and automatically as we feel at the moment. The *ego* develops, according to Freud, to protect us from the consequences of acting on the spur of the moment. It is not a moral or socialised force, but simply our rational sense which tells us that the consequences of acting just as we wish can be uncomfortable and our immediate impulses need to be tempered with caution and forward planning. The ego is what we are mostly aware of when we talk about our self and our reasons for doing things. The *superego*, developing from our highly emotionally charged relationship with our parents, is a mightily powerful 'conscience' in Freud's thinking. It contains the ideal self, possibly an 'introjected' (taken in) image of a parent, and a model of perfection we can never achieve. It also acts as a source of morality, controlling our behaviour even when it will produce no immediate negative consequences. Contravening these moral standards produces guilt and consequent anxiety. This alone will eventually control impulses to act against moral norms, and even impulses to think guilt-provoking thoughts.

The ego has the role of 'protecting' us from the anxiety which follows from serious conflicts, mostly those occurring between the id and superego. This is achieved with the use of defence mechanisms. For instance, a highly paid executive might 'rationalise' that his salary is justified in order to keep him with the company, making good profits for all to benefit from, rather than admit that his salary is excessive and that he is basically greedy. Hence, according to Freud, in general psychology, we might often speculate about the *real* reasons for a person's behaviour rather than accept those *apparent* reasons put forward by the ego and which are accepted even by the individual concerned. The athlete, for instance, may not be motivated simply by financial or social reward. It may be that the athlete's father's strict expectations, now part of the athlete's superego, can never be satisfied. The athlete may not realise that attempting the near impossible is aimed at damaging the father's image by showing him to be wrong.

Figure 10.1 overleaf shows diagrammatically how the ego has the job of suppressing conflicts using defence mechanisms. The conflicts are often between desires of the id and the superego. The id might demand sex, but the superego recoils in horror. The ego sorts it out, but symbols of the conflict might occur in dreams or in our behaviour, via slips of the tongue for instance.

Psychoanalysis and therapy

The most prevalent use of psychoanalytic principles is encountered in Chapter 2. It can be said that the approach is the foundation of all modern individual and group therapy, but much evolution has occurred and the diversity of what is now available can be quite bewildering. It is also important to note here that psychoanalytic therapy techniques are not reserved for the clearly psychologically disturbed. They are or have been employed in versions of stress management, in play therapy with children, in training sports participants, in the 'treatment' of interpersonal problems at work and in work with offenders.

THE BEHAVIOURIST APPROACH

Let us take another look at the motivation for athletes' behaviour. In normal conversation it is common to hear an explanation in terms of 'the will to achieve' or 'killer instinct'. At the beginning of the last century, psychologists too used such explanatory concepts as 'instinct' and 'will'. However, we learn nothing new, when we hear that someone has a 'will to achieve', *after* we have discovered that they do indeed enjoy a lot of success. The explanation is a 'pseudo' one, often prompting the reply, 'Well, what exactly do you *mean* by a "winning instinct"?' The reply might be: 'That which helps athletes to supremacy, to victory over their competitors.' The 'explanation' is now seen for what it really is – a re-description of what we already know and a statement of ignorance about what really drives successful athletes. The speaker says no more than that successful athletes succeed because they have something which makes them succeed! Inventing a 'will to win' adds no more to the explanation of events, and behaviourists denounced such pseudo-explanatory concepts as 'mystical'. They also dismissed cognitive processes (mental events) with the same justification. This was partly why so much of their work centred around laboratory experiments with animals. They were concerned not to *assume* what they could not verify directly and began with the investigation of the simplest behaviour patterns. For instance, they were concerned not to *assume* that a dog 'expected' food just because it salivated at the sound of a bell which had accompanied the presentation of food several times. 'Expectancy' was

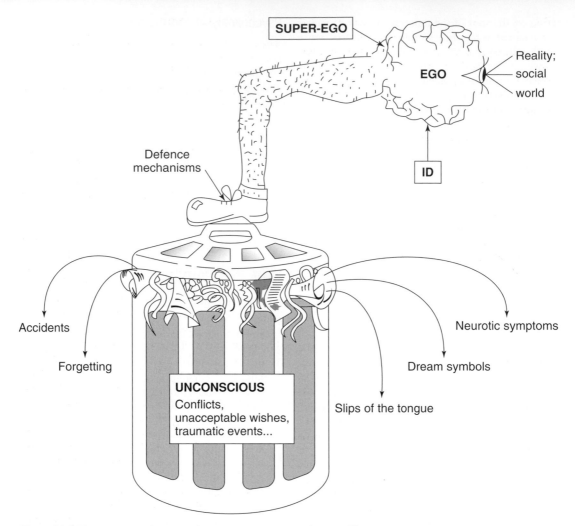

Figure 10.1 The ego not quite managing to suppress unconscious conflicts

a non-observable, non-physical event, which could not *cause* behaviour to occur – the issue of the mind-body problem.

Behaviourists believed one should only use as scientific data the facts of observed behaviour. It was argued in a reductionist manner that learning was built up out of the same basic processes, no matter what the species – it was more detailed and complex in humans, but the same bricks were used. Some common threads of fundamental behaviourist belief are outlined below:

➠ Almost all human behaviour is learned, that is, developed through experience with and feedback

from our environment. It is not the result of biological 'instinct'. 'Mentalistic' events (such as thoughts or ideas) and 'mystical' concepts (such as 'instinct', 'will', 'feeling' or 'mental event'), which cannot be observed or measured, cannot form part of an objective, scientific explanation of human behaviour.

➠ 'Problem' behaviour, such as that of a psychiatric patient, 'difficult' worker or disruptive school pupil, is not explained by giving it a label (such as 'mental illness', 'alienation' or 'delinquency'); it is best analysed and modified by treating it as a set of individually observable and changeable responses to the events in our immediate environment.

⮕ Behaviour can be investigated scientifically through very careful observation and measurement; the principles of learning thus derived (many from the study of laboratory animals) can be applied to learning in humans and therefore to the treatment of abnormal or unwanted behaviour patterns.

⮕ Behaviour is largely influenced by situations, not personality traits (see above).

⮕ Behaviour is best analysed as a set of relatively 'molecular' (small unit) responses under the control of events in the immediate environment which have been associated with these responses in the past.

⮕ A person's 'feelings' may only be assessed by *public* evidence, such as a verbal report from the individual (e.g. 'I feel a level 9 stress on a scale of 1 to 10').

The classical tradition

Few westerners with even a vague interest in human behaviour in the second half of the twentieth century can have remained unaware of Pavlov's (1927) experiments and demonstrations. From these there developed the scientific formulation of a principle which must surely have been known to Roman dog handlers, that dogs, who generally salivate at the sight of food, will also do this at the sound or sight of any stimulus which has regularly accompanied their food in the recent past. However, in the behaviourist model, one must resist the temptation to say that the dog 'expects' or anticipates its food (though the sight of a dog cocking its head on one side, twitching its ears and holding itself like a coiled spring is rather compelling). This notion of 'expectancy' is unobservable – what can be *observed* are the dog's specifically 'conditioned' responses. 'Conditioning' is the term used for the experimental demonstration that an animal's behaviour can be altered systematically. However, the term quickly became generalised to any behaviour, including human, where it is assumed that conscious control is irrelevant and the responses are reliably triggered by some environmental stimulus. One is not 'conditioned' *against* one's will. It is simply that 'will' is an irrelevant concept for explaining behaviour patterns. It is easiest to grab hold of the original behaviourist position by accepting the *empty organism model* depicted in Figure 10.2, where

Figure 10.2 The empty organism model of behavioural control

the circle represents the person/organism, whose inner workings we cannot observe, and where the raw data of scientific observation are the stimuli impinging on the individual and that individual's consequent responses.

In the classical model, a new, previously neutral stimulus (e.g. a bell), producing no particular response, was presented just before giving a dog food (an unconditional stimulus – UCS). The dog's natural salivation to the food (unconditional response – UCR) became paired with the bell, so that eventually the bell alone would produce salivation and is now called a conditional stimulus (CS), the salivation becoming a conditional response (CR). The natural stimulus and response are unconditional, but the new stimulus and associated response are conditional upon them.

To take an example, following Figure 10.3, phobia of buses, after falling from one, is explained by the *association* of an originally painful event (hitting one's head on the ground – the UCS), with the stimulus (originally neutral) of a bus (CS). Initially, the blow naturally caused pain behaviour and fear (UCR), which may include purely physiological reactions, such as sweating and adrenaline secretion. Now, after conditioning, buses alone (CS) produce the fear (*part* of the UCR) and this response (now the CR) is beyond the control of the individual concerned. Similarly, anxiety may become associated with mealtimes where trouble has occurred in the past, or with public places where humiliation has been experienced (e.g.

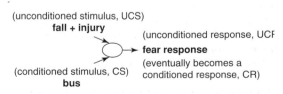

Figure 10.3 The classical conditioning model

school), and so on. In this model, from Figure 10.2, S1 originally produces R and, after association, S2 now produces R.

In Pavlov's original model, failure to have the CS and UCS associated over several trials resulted in the dog's salivation response gradually dying away – known as *extinction*. A departure from this, and a reason to suspect that the explanation is too rigid and simple, is the fact that people can become phobic about buses or spiders after just *one* traumatic exposure, even though there are *no more* similar associations. Later adjustments to theory explained the maintenance of fear in terms of 'hidden' reinforcement (of the *operant* kind – see below). For instance, whenever the individual *avoids* situations which just *might* involve buses, they would experience a form of reward because their feelings of anxiety would be reduced (an example of *negative reinforcement* – see below). However, this begs the question of why they should continue to experience anxiety, though this *might* be because, by avoiding the CS, they never give themselves the chance to *unlearn* their responses to the bus stimulus.

The operant or instrumental model

Classical conditioning offers some sort of an explanation of why we should come to associate a new stimulus with an old feeling or reaction. However, it offers little understanding of how new and relatively complex patterns of behaviour are developed. *Instrumental learning* is the process by which the *result* of responding *strengthens that response*. If a child is regularly rewarded for crying, by being picked up, it is not surprising that the child should develop a strong and swift crying response, especially on sight of a parent. In the operant model later developed by Skinner (1953), following Figure 10.2, the crucial elements are a response (R) and its consequences (or *reinforcement*, denoted by 'r'). A stimulus (e.g. S2) may permit the animal to *discriminate* the circumstances in which a reward will be likely to occur. If only the baby's mother picks it up when it is crying, then mother will become a *discriminative stimulus* for the baby, who may learn to cry forcefully when she is around, but not (or not so hard) on sight of anyone else. According to this system of explanation, a 'maladaptive' response, for instance, petty shoplifting, may be maintained by the succession of

reinforcements (admiration of friends, goods obtained, thrill) in the face of the odd aversive consequence, such as being told off and banned from a shop, or even a court appearance with warning, especially where this, too, makes one important among peers. Again, 'extinction' occurs where reinforcement ceases to follow responses.

Skinner's work with *schedules of reinforcement*, or *intermittent reinforcement*, demonstrated that animals would work even harder when they were not reinforced for *every* response, but only after several had been produced. For instance, on a *fixed ratio* schedule, an animal (or human) is reinforced for every *n* responses produced, for example after every tenth response. A *variable ratio* schedule gives reinforcement for every *n*th response *on average*. *Interval* schedules are based on time elapsed since responding. A two-minute *fixed-interval* schedule delivers reinforcement for the first response produced after two minutes from the last response, while a two-minute *variable-interval* schedule uses an *average* of two minutes. Not surprisingly, animals (and humans in some circumstances) work harder towards the end of a fixed interval, but hardest of all with a variable ratio schedule, where more responses produce more but somewhat unpredictable reinforcements. This system can explain why a baby may learn to cry very loudly indeed if its parents, trying to withhold reinforcement in order to 'extinguish' its crying, in fact give in and go to the baby after it has cried for quite some time. Many responses are rewarded only after they have occurred several times – for instance, a boy talking to girls in the hope of a date, a charity collector, a high-jump athlete.

A further strength of this model was its apparent ability to explain the development of fairly complex patterns of behaviour. A reinforced response will continue to occur for some time without reinforcement. If, during this time (the 'extinction' period), another response is produced with the first, and reinforcement follows this *combination*, the two *together* will now be produced reliably. On this explanation – that of *shaping* – the origin of the excessive rituals of the compulsive or obsessive person become easier to explain. The notion of shaping would also be useful, at first glance, in explaining an athlete's gradual learning of a skill requiring an intricate combination of well-rehearsed movements. However, as we shall see, the cognitive model argues that simply joining together a set of responses would result in a rather jerky performance, without *feedback* and constant, controlled refinement.

Negative reinforcement and punishment

A common confusion occurs, even in some textbooks, between *negative reinforcement* and *punishment*. The problem can be avoided if the reader always links reinforcement with the *strengthening* of a response. A negative reinforcer strengthens behaviour, but in a *negative* manner. The reinforcement here is the *removal* of an uncomfortable stimulus. If it is noisy, and shutting the window removes the noise, then window shutting is reinforced. If my anxiety *reduces* because I engage in rapid breathing, then I am more likely to breathe rapidly when I next feel anxiety coming on.

Punishment is the delivery of an uncomfortable event to the individual as a *consequence* of their behaviour, and it is intended to *weaken*, not strengthen, the response it follows. Punishment, especially physical, has many unwanted side effects, especially those of humiliation and of learning (by the punished) that power is a way to control others. Partly for these reasons, partly because it is often pretty ineffective in reducing behaviour, and partly for basic humane reasons, it has not been used much in therapeutic or organisational applications.

Applications of behaviourist psychology

We meet behaviouristic approaches everywhere in applied psychology, from the reductionist and reward-oriented Taylorism in early work psychology, through the revolution in psychotherapy occurring in the 1960s, and on to behaviour modification for children and adults with learning difficulties, which is a very common and powerful approach in the early twenty-first century. Health psychology includes methods of *bio-feedback* (based on the operant principle), and educational psychology includes the use of shaping and reward systems in order to keep 'difficult' children in their seats and on tasks. Wherever we can raise the question: 'What motivates people to… (work hard; keep to positive health behaviour patterns; keep trying in sport)?' there will be a behaviourist position invoking reinforcement.

COGNITIVE PSYCHOLOGY

The terms 'cognitive psychology' and 'cognitive psychologist' have ambiguous meaning. As a *topic*, cognitive psychology is the study of mental processes such as memory, attention, perception, language, thinking. As a theoretical position, however, a cognitive *approach* reflects a radical alternative to behaviourism, a 'school' which, unlike the approaches above, has no 'great names' familiar to the general public. In a nutshell, the approach lays great emphasis on the *central role of mental events* (or 'cognitive processes') in determining our subsequent behaviour. These were the very events dismissed as mythical and non-explanatory by the original behaviourists. The picture is muddied somewhat by the fact that many researchers studying cognitive processes over the last two to three decades have called themselves 'behaviourists'. By this they mean that, although they conduct research designed to verify models of human cognitive processes, the evidence they use is *observable behaviour*. They share the behaviourists' strong emphasis on the careful definition of variables and analysis of public evidence – people's responses to various stimuli, usually controlled in a laboratory setting. However, what we shall consider here is the cognitive *model* – a perspective which considers our behaviour to be guided by internal, structured planning processes. Notice that, above, we skimmed the issue of *how* an animal can discriminate one stimulus from another. This, for the cognitive psychologist, is an extremely interesting and important issue, and will involve theories of how we *process information* internally, with no obvious external behaviour being produced.

The shift to cognitive psychology – social learning theory

By the 1960s the behaviourist reliance on reinforcement as the main factor in learning new behaviour was becoming burdensome. Any casual observer could see that children often short-circuited the supposed learning process by imitating other people, and that this could be a quick way to the production of novel responses. The *social learning* theorists, led by Albert Bandura, also tried to move the emphasis of pure behaviourism towards the inclusion of mental events as explanatory concepts. Their major principles were:

➡ operant and classical learning processes are not enough to explain the development and maintenance of complex human behaviour;

➡ other processes, especially *modelling* (imitation), contribute to human development – children spontaneously imitate and then may be reinforced for doing so;

➡ *vicarious reinforcement* – observing others being rewarded or punished – may also contribute to the development of our regular patterns of behaviour;

➡ between a *stimulus* and a *response*, we *must* assume that other internal processes occur; social learning theorists called these *internal mediating responses*.

Bandura's studies (e.g. Bandura, Ross and Ross 1963) demonstrated that children spontaneously imitate specific adult behaviour, and adjust their imitation depending on whether the adult 'model' is rewarded or punished. This may be obvious to most parents or childcare workers, but Bandura's work is important for demonstrating empirically that there need be no reinforcement, however subtle, involved in the emergence of new behaviour. Rewarding it once it *has* emerged, of course, may well help to maintain it.

Early studies by social learning theorists attempted to bring aspects of Freudian theory into the world of checkable scientific testing. For instance, psychoanalytic theory held that if a child experienced loss of love from a warm, nurturant mother, anxiety would be produced that would motivate the child to 'introject' its mother's behaviour. Social learning theorists recast *introjection* as *modelling* – imitating and learning from a significant person. Especially significant would be parents who withdrew affection as part of normal child training. Imitation would supply an *image* of the warmth lost by the child. Research supported this notion, but also showed that children copy aggression irrespective of the warmth of the person modelling it (Bandura and Huston 1961). Here, psychologists were not completely rejecting earlier useful psychoanalytic ideas. They were attempting to *support* those ideas with *empirical evidence*. When ideas did not appear to fit, further explanation and research were attempted.

Later, Bandura (1989) emphasised the role of internal expectations in guiding our behaviour, especially those concerning *self-efficacy* – our sense of competence in tasks. People with higher self-efficacy (higher levels of belief in their competence) tend to work harder at problems, and tackle them more thoroughly, irrespective of their actual ability. These effects can be seen even when self-efficacy is raised artificially by giving false information to participants (Weinberg, Gould and Jackson 1979).

The cognitive revolution – humans as information processors

The so-called 'cognitive revolution' in psychology was kick-started from a symposium on information theory held at the Massachusetts Institute of Technology in September 1956, at which George Miller discussed his famous 'Magical number 7 +/- 2', Newell and Simon presented their general problem-solving model, and Chomsky discussed linguistic competence and the rules of grammar. A seminal development was the publication in 1960 of Miller, Galanter and Pribram's *Plans and the Structure of Behaviour*. The driving force behind a lot of this work was the advent of the powerful computer, which could simulate human thinking processes.

Computers made it possible to show that even an inanimate object could 'act with a purpose', that is, have a 'goal' to work towards. Computers were capable of self-adjustment, learning and the gradual movement towards a specific goal, using *feedback* (data giving information on how the action is progressing). Behaviourists had argued that 'goals' were unmeasurable, unscientific concepts. Changes in behaviour were simply under the control of external, perhaps subtle reinforcement. The cognitivists argued that, as with computers, an internal goal could form part of an explanation of organised sequences of an organism's behaviour.

In addition, humans were seen (like computers) as rapid interpreters of large amounts of incoming information. Computers receive stimuli, but do not need to respond immediately. They can receive information from a variety of different *kinds* of source, deal with the information as so many electrical impulses, then act appropriately to the analysis of information. The human information-processing system does much the same thing. The physical processes may be different, but the important point is that our reactions are not direct, simple responses to incoming stimuli. Information is filtered and analysed, mostly by our cortex, and we can respond both appropriately and flexibly. Our more complex actions are not automatic, but the product of *decision-making*. However, even the simple act of putting down a teacup is under the control of many cycles of incoming information, analysis and consequent fine adjustment of movement.

Operant and cognitive explanations of problem-solving

Tolman (1932) described research in which rats who had learnt to turn right to get food in a cross maze, turned *left* when they were started from the other side of the maze. Tolman argued that this would not be possible if only their *physical responses* had been acquired in the learning process. If right turning had been conditioned, then a right turn should occur even if it did not lead to food. The rats, he felt, must be adjusting their behaviour according to an *internal 'map'* of the maze's turns. This map would now be referred to as a *schema* – a set of rules for understanding aspects of the world and for guiding our behaviour within it. A feel for the working of schemas can be gained by considering how both behaviourists and cognitivists would account for solving the problem set in Figure 10.4. In the pure behaviourist model, it is difficult to see how a person would come up with the right answer other than by trying numbers at random until a 'hit' is obtained. It is interesting that, in solving this problem, 'no' sometimes has its usual negative connotation, and at other times is reinforcing, but one would not know this without a plan. The reinforcement paradigm did not do justice to the reasoning powers which humans possess and use many times every day, very often without realising it consciously. A very young child can work out instantly, and yet for the first time, that if No. 13 buses go from one street and No. 14 buses go from another, the logical choice is to change streets if a No. 13 comes along and a No. 14 is required.

To understand complex human behaviour, then, it seems necessary to work with the concept of a *plan* or *schema*. Our individual responses are guided by the plan and its goal in a quite flexible manner. For example, if I want you to pass me the water, I can ask for it with very many possible sentences. I can also point urgently at it or do something like hang

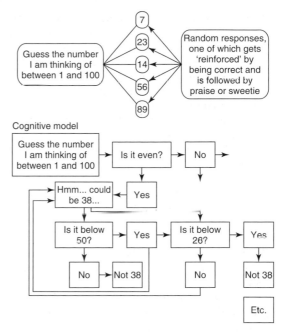

Figure 10.4 Operant and cognitive models of problem-solving

out my tongue in obvious need of it. I can even lasso it or siphon it out of the jug! Most importantly, *I can produce behaviour which I have never used before* (and which, therefore, has never been reinforced). *All* these amount to my 'obtaining a glass of water'. Here, the only common factor is the eventual *goal* that I had in mind. Likewise, with no prior reinforcement, when driving to work, I can suddenly change my actions and achieve my goal if one morning I find that my way is blocked by road digging or fallen trees. What is important to maintain my guided behaviour is *feedback*. Even observation of very young infants will reveal that they adjust their movements, perhaps not so subtly at first, to incoming stimuli which inform them of the results of their actions. Infants only a few days old can quickly learn just how hard to suck on a specially made and electronically connected 'pacifier' in order to hear their mother's voice in preference to another woman's voice (DeCasper and Fifer 1980).

Molar and molecular

We have said that behaviour analysed at the level of fine movements, as with sucking or driving movements, or the *gradual* placement of a teacup, is said to be treated at the *molecular* level. The behaviourists, by contrast, might treat putting down a cup and saucer as a *single* response under the control of reinforcement – presumably the feeling of success in setting it down right, or, as a child, parental responses of 'well done!', and so on. Behaviour can be treated in ever larger units, such as 'driving to work', 'riding a bicycle', 'digging the garden', or even 'bringing up a child'. These examples, especially the last, are much more towards the molar end of the molecular-molar continuum described earlier.

In a sense, the behaviourists tended to treat behaviour at a more molar level and to tell us *why* a person produces responses (for reinforcement), whereas cognitive analyses tended to work at a more molecular level and consider the effects of constant feedback on behavioural adjustment towards a planned goal. In the teaching of maths, for example, a behaviourist orientation might emphasise effective and timely rewards for correct answers. A cognitive approach might concentrate on the most effective structuring of information in order for the child to be able to develop logical schemas for working with numbers. What is essential is that, in the cognitive view, a child *is not passively responding to rewards*, but *is actively seeking information* in order to solve the huge number of problems there are in simply understanding how the world works. Most parents will find it hard to deny that their babies are naturally curious. It is very difficult to stop a child learning, and the rewards we *do* employ are often entirely ineffective – for instance, rewarding a young speaker for saying 'went' rather than 'goed'. If the child is at the 'goed' stage, it will persist with 'goed' until it incorporates special rules for irregular verbs. As adults, unless depressed, we are still curious when confronted with problems – information not fitting our existing schemas. This is the great attraction of magic, puzzles, speculation about other people ('gossip') and do-it-yourself tasks.

Cognitive psychology and the scientific ('hypothetico-deductive') method

Behaviourists might object that schemas and cognitive models are unmeasurable, internal concepts. Cognitivists would answer that, if well defined, they serve the same purpose as hypothetical concepts in any other science. Physicists can propose a model of what properties a 'quark' has, for instance, but they will never directly observe a quark, because this is impossible, in principle and in practice. What they do is to argue that *if* their model is correct, certain results should follow. If those results occur, their model is *supported* (but not 'proven true'). Models survive while evidence supports them. Models may be refined in the light of contrary evidence, but if that evidence becomes too great and too unruly, the models are jettisoned in favour of alternative ones which deal with all the evidence more effectively and economically. This is the basis of the *hypothetico-deductive method* in science.

The scope of cognitive psychology

Since the 1960s cognitive psychology has investigated many areas of human ability and mental operation. In addition, it has had an influence across the whole spectrum of psychological research, including the areas of social psychology, abnormal psychology and therapy. Therefore, we find that by far the most popular treatment used by clinical psychologists today is that of cognitive or cognitive-behavioural therapy. This form of therapy is also very often used in work with the rehabilitation of offenders. We shall also find a cognitive approach embedded within all other applied areas. Cognitive psychology has had particular effect within the 'ergonomics' and 'human factors' areas of work psychology. Ergonomics covers the area of human–machine interaction, and clearly it is well worth studying the ways in which humans perceive their environment, and the limits of their attention and other mental capacities, in order to design human-friendly technology, to organise work efficiently and to set reasonable limits to human work expectations.

THE BIOLOGICAL APPROACH

This book generally concentrates on *psychological* approaches to predicting and altering human behaviour in constructive ways. However, there is certainly a need, at times, to consider biological effects on human behaviour, if only to recognise that biological processes, states and constitutions may modify or limit any changes which a psychologist may wish to produce, or may help us to understand why a certain principle does not work in the same way for all people. However, it is important to recognise that a reduction to biological explanation can never be entirely appropriate, as there will always remain a social and psychological context in which to understand behaviour. For instance, just as explaining a snooker game in terms of ball collisions is not appropriate, nor is it useful or productive to understand neurotic behaviour solely in terms of the biological processes underlying anxiety. We shall want to know why *this* neurotic behaviour is directed towards dogs, while another person's is very much concerned with dinner parties. There will be a social history which may guide us to the reasons for another person being terrified of travel.

We know that chemical and biological events can affect human behaviour directly. In the nineteenth century, the disease syphilis was eventually found to be responsible for decaying cognitive faculties. Lithium certainly reduces some extreme reactions in schizophrenics, though it by no means 'cures' them. We also know that human behaviour affects biological bodily events, as when a person's stressful life habits eventually create problems of ulcers and heart deterioration. We know that memory can be affected by physical events (bullets, drugs, nerve decay) and that memory can, in turn, affect behaviour. According to Freud's original findings, a repressed memory or fantasy can manifest itself in pathological behaviour (neurotic symptoms, defensive reactions, accidents, and so on). There is two-way traffic, then, between our behaviour and its effects on our biology, and our biology's effects on our behaviour.

The nature–nurture debate

One important aspect of the biological perspective influences debate on many topics in psychology. This is the question of the extent to which our enduring characteristics or personality are the result of genetic forces (the 'nature' view) or are developed within our lifetime through experience with our environments (the 'nurture' view). If a certain personality feature is largely inherited, this would have implications for employment selection (only select those with/without the feature) and training. It would presumably be futile to train people in something for which they do not have innate, genetic potential. Similarly, therapists will

have little success if certain states of psychological disturbance are largely caused by a natural disposition.

Intelligence and twin studies

One of the first and most illustrious applied psychologists this century, Sir Cyril Burt, Britain's first employed educational psychologist, contributed enormously to the nature–nurture debate concerning intelligence (e.g. Burt 1972). He tested many pairs of identical twins, reared in separate families, and correlated their scores. Identical twins have identical genetic material, so if they are separated near birth and reared in different families, it is argued that any similarity between their two intelligence scores must be largely genetic in origin. This argument, however, only works if each pair of twins is randomly allocated to family types. This never happens in practice. Adoption agencies tend to place twins in similar environments (socio-economic position, religion, etc.). Many of the separated identical twins who were studied were only separated into different parts of the same family – for example, one twin would be reared by an aunt because the mother could not cope with both. Many such flaws occurred with the original twin data, but in addition, Burt's findings, which showed very strong correlations, were later alleged to be fraudulent and were certainly too inconsistent to count any longer as suitable scientific data.

Twin study data are used to make estimates of heritability of traits such as intelligence or of mental conditions such as schizophrenia. Most workers in the field have estimated heritability of intelligence to be somewhere between 40 per cent and 70 per cent. However, it is easy to misunderstand what a heritability estimate of 50 per cent is telling us. It is *not*, contrary to common belief, telling us that *for any individual* 50 per cent of their intelligence can be related to genetic causes. A heritability estimate is an estimate of the degree to which variation *within a population* can be attributed to genetic factors. Even with a heritability estimate of 90 per cent, it is still possible that a difference between populations is entirely caused by environmental factors. Suppose that virtually every black child in a country were deprived of access to the full education which whites received, as was the case in South Africa up to 1993. Here the difference in intelligence *between* black and white populations is going to be caused almost exclusively by this important *environmental* factor, irrespective of any difference *within* populations. Think of this as two fields of carrots, where carrot length is 90 per cent heritable, but where one field receives growth fertiliser and the other does not. Differences in carrot length *within* each field may be largely predictable from the length of the 'parent' carrots, but the difference *between* the two fields is due almost entirely to the application of fertiliser. Many psychologists hold to an *interactionist* position on the relative influences of nature and nurture in the development of intelligence (e.g. Scarr 1991). That is, to talk of heritability on its own is not at all useful, and it is the interaction of any genetic inheritance with the environment in which the person develops, which will determine intellectual ability.

THE HUMANISTIC APPROACH

This has often been termed the 'third force' within mainstream psychology. This was intended to mean that it took a new direction, away from both psychoanalysis and behaviourism. It is still true that humanism is a uniquely different way, since the cognitive approach too shares a concentration on scientific investigation and quantitative assessment of variables. Carl Rogers, one of humanism's founders, did promote a quantitative scientific evaluation of the results of psychotherapy (1957), but overall the approach is opposed to the piecemeal investigation of aspects of cognition or behaviour. It concentrates on the *whole self* and is at the other extreme from any reductionism in understanding humans. The approach is *phenomenological*, which, in a crude definition, means that priority is given to whatever people *experience*, whether or not we would agree that their experience is actually valid. Objective assessment of 'facts' is a suspect activity in this approach, since each person's view of the world is unique and no one has a claim to a 'better', more accurate understanding of reality. Echoes of this original position are very strong today in applied psychology. Those researchers who take a *qualitative* approach to research methods (see Chapter 11) would largely agree with this analysis of people's view and understanding of their world.

Within the fields of applied psychology covered in this book, the influence of humanism has been largely confined to the practice of therapy, with Rogers' *client-centred therapy* having great influence on the practice of counselling and on many psychologists in clinical work, even though their preferred approach might not be humanist. Hence, discussion of Rogers' main contribution, his theory of *self*, is to be found in Chapter 3 which discusses Councelling Psychology.

WHAT IS THE VALUE OF DIFFERENT APPROACHES WITHIN APPLIED PSYCHOLOGY?

In the world of academic psychological research, the approaches just described developed at different points in the twentieth century and were influenced by the philosophies of the researchers and the technology of the times. Each movement was often very hostile to its competitors. Psychologists defended (and still do) their favoured approach and conducted research designed to support their view over another. In the applied world too it is quite possible to find energetic defence of one approach against another. For instance, psychoanalysts and the original behaviour therapists were completely irreconcilable in their arguments over which technique was the most appropriate, beneficial and effective in treating psychological disturbance. Today, this gulf between proponents of the two views has hardly been bridged and heated debates continue between them, though there are a few meeting points.

Eclecticism

On the other hand, each approach has given rise to various forms of application, not necessarily closely linked to the original theory which produced them. Very many practising psychologists are *eclectic* in their outlook. Thus a clinical psychologist might employ aspects of psychoanalysis with some of their clients, or at certain points in treating one client, yet also find behaviour therapy techniques more effective at other stages of treatment or for different conditions. An occupational psychologist might take a cognitive approach to a problem of organisational communication, yet employ the concept of reinforcement when dealing with issues of incentive and disincentive and their effects on production.

One cannot always adopt a 'supermarket' approach to the different schools of thought within psychology. In some areas there are just two rival theories or explanations, and both cannot be true, or appropriate, at the same time. In other areas, however, one can see the two explanations as operating more at two different levels, and hence both can be partly valid at their respective levels. More often than not, though, the various approaches represent quite radically different ways of viewing the human being in the environment. For instance, the child is seen as passively responding to cues and reinforcements by behaviourists, but as an active information processor by cognitivists. For some psychologists working with children, the early emotional stages of development are all-important. For others, they are not, and the emphasis is on practical change in the here and now. It is very important indeed then, that the student reader (and the practising psychologist) is quite clear about the differing implications for behaviour and change which two or more perspectives on the same topic or issue have to offer.

Methods for the Production of Research and Practice Data

In several applied areas discussed in this book it will be found that there is quite a separation between psychologists who carry out a 'hands-on' applied role in their normal working day and those who concentrate on pure research. Some psychologists manage to balance these two roles, but very often practitioners report finding little opportunity to conduct research. However, most practitioners also report that, in their everyday work with clients, they are often grateful for their training in investigative methods and find these central to the task of gathering data in order to tackle practical problems. The occupational psychologist, for instance, may conduct a survey of staff in a large company, using the same methods as would be employed to conduct pure research on attitude. The following section provides a very brief summary of the major research procedures and concepts used by psychological researchers. Much of the time these are the procedures which are applied to tackling practical human problems in the field.

PLACES FOR RESEARCH – FIELD vs LABORATORY

It is far more likely that applied psychologists will carry out their research in the 'field' than in a laboratory or on research premises. Their research will be conducted with people who are the usual focus of that practitioner – this might be in a hospital, school, factory, office, shopping precinct or clinic. Research designs in the field, however, may employ conventional experimental designs. An example would be the field experiment conducted by Workman and Bommer (2004), described in Chapter 8 (see Box on p. 213).

There are times, though, when research may be best carried out in the rarefied but controlled environment of a psychological laboratory. If we wish to determine exactly what effect caffeine has on performance levels, it is worth testing selected participants carefully in a well-controlled environment so that unwanted variables can be ruled out as effects. In an everyday environment it is difficult to control such unwanted variables. In Workman and Bommer's study, for instance, there were possible 'contamination' effects because workmates talked to each other about the different treatments they were receiving. We shall soon define such an unwanted factor as a *confounding* variable (see p. 273). In the laboratory we can be fairly certain that caffeine level is the *only* factor to vary and that it is therefore the cause of any observed changes in our participants' behaviour.

General problems with laboratory studies

Serious problems are incurred, however, with the use of laboratory studies in psychological research. We shall consider a few of these below.

Artificiality

Laboratory studies have been much criticised for the artificial environment in which participants perform what is required of them. The whole point of laboratory studies, however, *is* to create an artificial environment. If we want to demonstrate that a piece of coal and a feather fall to the earth at the same rate in a vacuum – which they do – it is no use trying to do this in a natural environment. Laboratories are used to control variables and strip down processes to their basic elements.

We must also remember that many of the flaws in psychological research which people tend to associate with the artificial laboratory experiment are also present in most field studies. Expectancy effects, for example, have been demonstrated frequently in field settings (see below). The effects of social desirability, need for approval, demand characteristics, and so on (all explained below) will all occur in a field setting so long as participants know that they are the subjects of a research project. What a laboratory *might* do is to intimidate participants more than would be the case in their own natural environment, especially if complicated equipment is involved – but people can feel intimidated easily when taking a test given by a psychologist, *even if* it is administered in their own factory or school, for example.

Expectancy – the participant

A difficulty in comparing groups, such as students experiencing different teaching methods or clients receiving different therapies, is that, very often, in applied work, it is difficult to keep hidden from participants what is the expected outcome of the research. The effect of participant expectancy gained notoriety through the applied occupational work of the Hawthorne studies (Roethlisberger and Dickson 1939). A factory work team of five women generally increased their productivity, no matter how their rest breaks and working day length were manipulated, except for certain exceptions. It even increased when conditions were returned to the most adverse ones in operation at the start of that section of the research. History has given us the 'Hawthorne effect', now generally interpreted as *the effect that simply being the focus of investigation has on the participants.* It is sometimes more specifically assumed that the workers here raised their output because they *expected* this to be the desired outcome. However, there were several other *confounding variables* present in the study which might have explained the dramatic increase in output (see below, and Chapter 8).

Placebo groups

It is for this reason that experiments often include a 'placebo' group. The idea is borrowed from medical and pharmacological research, where some patients are given an actual drug which is on trial, while another group is given a substance such as a salt pill, with absolutely no effect – the 'placebo'. Should this latter group show any improvement, it will indicate that perhaps something other than the drug, for instance the mere *thought* of having received treatment, can have an effect on the progress of the illness. Similarly, in psychological experiments, we may give one group training – the variable actually under research – while we give a placebo group some attention or simulated training, but nothing we truly believe to be effective. If an experimental group is given a training programme designed to reduce racial prejudice, for instance, we might give the placebo group a neutral experience such as a session on team building. If members of this placebo group change their racial prejudice (as measured before and after by questionnaire) as much as the trained group, we might suspect that mere training is enough to affect expressed attitudes; we would suspect that the race training itself is *confounded*, perhaps by participant expectancy effects.

Expectancy – the researcher

It has been argued that the expectancy of *researchers* also has its effect on participants' responses. Rosenthal (1966) showed that students told that their experimental rats were either 'dull' or 'bright' obtained results in accordance with the rats' label. Transferring this 'Pygmalion effect' to humans, Rosenthal and Jacobson (1968) famously showed that when teachers were led to believe that some of their children were 'late bloomers' and likely to accelerate in their learning, the children did in fact do significantly better than their peers, even though the names of the children had been selected at random. Many studies since have failed to provide strong evidence for experimenter expectancy effects. However, Eden (1990) demonstrated the Pygmalion effect in a work psychology context. In defence force platoons where leaders were told their subordinates were above average (when they were not), platoon members significantly outperformed control groups where the leader was not so informed.

Demand characteristics

Closely linked to the concept of expectancy are the 'demand characteristics' of a research situation (Orne 1962). This refers to the features of an experimental situation that are clues, for enquiring humans, as to what the experimental aims are. As a consequence, participants *may* try to behave according to experimenter expectations – sometimes referred to as 'pleasing the experimenter' – though the effect could occur in non-experimental research situations, of course.

TYPES OF RESEARCH

There are three major ways in which psychologists, and social scientists in general, can obtain data from people. They can watch, ask questions or meddle. Watching people behave is better known as observation. This may be used in an observation study, where observation is the main vehicle for gathering data, or as part of an experiment in which observation is the method used to measure one of the variables – for instance, aggression after mild frustration. Questioning comes in the form of the interview and the survey, and also as the administration of psychological measuring instruments. By 'meddling' I meant, facetiously, engaging in an experiment. It is generally considered true that, where an experiment can be carried out, we have stronger evidence of the direction of a *causal relationship* (i.e. A caused B, not B caused A) than can be obtained by other means. I hope the following will clarify this point.

Correlational studies (or data)

A vast amount of information gathered in applied psychology is not gathered in the laboratory and is not obtained from an experiment (though there are many 'field' experiments). As a result, research designs very often gather *field data* and are *correlational*. As an example, suppose we gathered data on A Level students and found that students' confidence, prior to exams, *correlated* highly with subsequent exam success. That is, people who scored highly on one measure (confidence) also scored highly on the other measure (exam grade), *and* vice versa. In general, scores on one measure could be *predicted* fairly well from scores on the other measure. Correlation is the degree of 'agreement' between pairs of scores. For example, in most organisations, salary level will tend to correlate with level of responsibility. The degree of correlation is measured on a scale stretching from −1, through 0, to +1. It is important to note the following:

➡ the nearer a correlation is to +1, the closer is the agreement between pairs of values;
➡ the nearer a correlation is to 0, the more purely random is the association between pairs of values.

Negative correlation

What is to be made, then, of a correlation near to −1? In this case, there is a strong tendency for *positive* scores on one measure to be associated with *negative* scores on the other. This might occur in the case of anxiety and performance – the higher the anxiety a person experiences, the lower may be their performance.

Applied Psychology

Problems with correlational data

A psychologist carrying out research in a factory might notice that people who produce high stress scores on a certain test tend to make more errors in their work. On further investigation, a strong correlation between these two variables is found. The researcher might hold the view that stress increases error, and these data would certainly support that view. The trouble is, the data *also* support the view that those making more errors (perhaps because of their inferior working conditions) become more stressed as a *result*. A correlation does not give unambiguous evidence of a *causal link* between variable A and variable B. If we *believe* that A is a cause of B, and predict a correlation between them, any resulting high correlation will support *both* the A-causes-B and the B-causes-A possibility explanations.

A correlation can also be misleading where there is an association for people at the *extremes* of each variable, but little relationship for those with average to moderate scores only. For instance, highly stressed people might do particularly badly on a test and extremely calm people might do particularly well. This might produce a moderately strong correlation among a group where, for the *mid range* of people, there is little association between stress and performance. This exemplifies the need to *inspect* any data where an effect is found to see whether it is the product of certain portions of the sample rather than the group as a whole, and then to investigate further.

A related problem is that of *restriction of range* (see Chapter 8, p. 194). Usually, we can only correlate the level of work performance and interview test score for those employees who are actually employed by a company. We cannot assess those whose low scores caused them to fail the interview (since they are no longer available and have not produced any work performance). Hence the *range* of people we assess is restricted, and the correlation we obtain may be higher or lower than that which we would obtain if we could include a wider range in our sample. This is one of the problems associated with conducting research in a real-life, as against an academic, setting. Correlations between maths and English grades at a UK public school would be similarly restricted to a narrow sample range.

The experiment

One way to obtain unambiguous evidence for the stress-creates-errors view is to run a proper *experiment*. One would manipulate stress (create stress for one group by giving them more work to complete in a shorter time, for example) and observe its consequent effect on error (see Figure 11.1). Here, stress level would be termed the *independent variable* and error rate the *dependent variable*. To make this a *true* experiment, we would *randomly allocate* participants to either of the two groups (high stress and low stress). Why? Well, imagine what might happen in a real factory. We probably could not randomly allocate and might have to go along with the manager's suggestion of using the day shift for the high stress condition and the night shift for the low stress condition. Suppose the day shift workers produce more errors under stress. It could be argued that these participants had worse skills initially and therefore made more errors. This design issue is known as the problem of *non-equivalent groups* and it is a common one in applied situations, where, very often, we cannot randomly allocate all our participants to different conditions. In a *true experiment*, only the independent variable is varied and all other variables are held constant or balanced, including the allocation of participants to groups on a random basis. This way we can be more certain that only the independent variable is responsible for any changes in the dependent variable. One way to check whether the stress conditions actually produced the higher error rate would have been to compare the two shifts *before* the experiment, by taking *pre*-experiment error scores to compare with *post*-experiment scores.

Control groups

In the stress experiment we might call the group given extra pressure the *experimental group*, while the group working normally is a *control group*. We need the latter in order to have a *baseline performance* with which to compare the manipulated, higher stress group. In some situations, the use of a control group can create ethical dilemmas. Suppose a school pilots a new reading scheme and compares the performance of reading scheme and control groups, with the experimental group doing much better after one

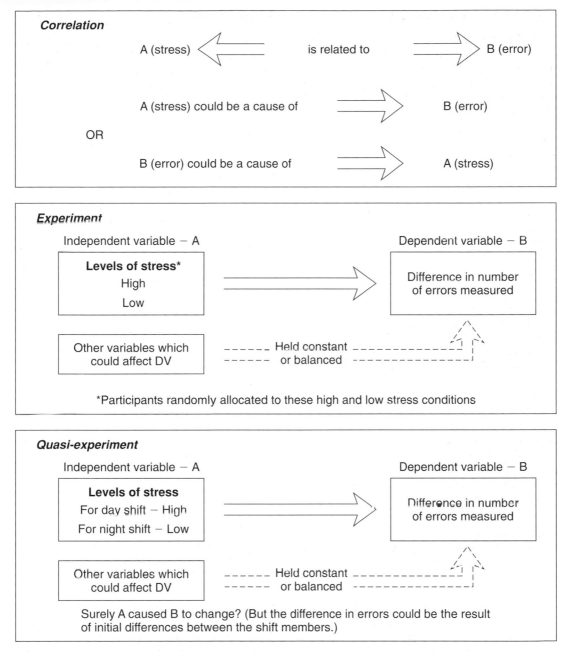

Figure 11.1 Experiments, quasi-experiments and correlation

month's trial. Should the experimenters continue to the previously planned six-month stage (perhaps to compare with other similar experiments), or should the control group now start on the programme in order not to get too far behind?

Quasi-experiments (compared with true experiments)

In the stress experiment described above, we said that *pre-existing groups* (day and night shift workers) might need to be used as experimental and control groups. Where random allocation to conditions cannot occur, we refer to the study as a *quasi-experiment*, and these are common in applied psychology. It would have been unreasonable to ask an employer to randomly allocate employees to shifts, but applied psychologists can sometimes randomly allocate. Keogh, Bond and Flaxman (2006) randomly allocated UK school pupils either to a cognitive behaviourally-based stress management programme or to a control group. The children who received the stress management training performed one grade better at GCSE overall and had higher mental health scores than the children in the control group.

Another type of quasi-experiment occurs where the researcher does not manipulate the independent variable, as for example when a clinic administers two different types of drug rehabilitation programme and the psychologist *uses* the circumstances as a kind of *natural experiment*. Because the psychologist is not in control of the study there could be other variables, not controlled by the clinicians, which could be responsible for any difference found between the two programmes. The point about the term 'quasi-experiment' is that we have a research design which is a kind of experiment, but in which certain variables are left uncontrolled, and doing this can make interpretation of results more ambiguous. (For more information see Coolican 2004; and for a thorough review see Cook and Campbell 1979.)

Internal and external validity

Cook and Campbell were also largely responsible for the introduction of these validity terms into the terminology of experimental and applied psychology research. In general, *validity* is the question of how confident we are that the effect we have appeared to demonstrate is in fact a real effect. In general science this would be like asking: 'Do all metals really expand when you heat them?' *Internal validity* questions whether the effects shown are truly caused by manipulation of the independent variable (e.g. did the high stress condition really cause more errors?) or whether another variable could be responsible (e.g. the existing difference between day and night shift workers discussed above).

External validity questions the extent to which the effect shown can be generalised to a wider or different population ('population validity'), to other contexts or places ('ecological validity') or across different time periods. If an effect only works in one place, then it is peculiar to that place and not a general scientific principle or 'law'. Do not get trapped into thinking, as many textbooks state, that ecological validity is automatically higher if a study is carried out in 'naturalistic' surroundings. If the effect shown does not appear anywhere else, the study does *not* have ecological validity. A good example is the study of Hofling et al. (1966), which showed that in a real hospital setting (as compared with Milgram's (1963) laboratory), nurses obeyed instructions to administer an unknown medicine under several conditions which broke hospital safety policy. This has never been replicated and consequently has *low* ecological validity, whereas Milgram's ecological validity is high since his results have been confirmed in many contexts, not least in a downtown commercial company office, as compared with Milgram's original Yale University laboratory (see Coolican 2004).

Sampling

Good population validity depends on good sampling. Applied psychologists would obviously like to be able to *generalise* the results of studies from the sample of people used to a wider but similar population. A *population* is a tricky concept – it is not just *everybody*. For example, it could be limited to office workers, female bus drivers, violent criminals, truants, javelin throwers or rheumatism sufferers. Suppose we hear of a therapy which has been successful on children with school phobia, or a management technique which increases job satisfaction among telephone operators. We would hope that each technique could be generalised to the population of all school-phobic children or all telephone operators. Of course, this is an optimistic notion. In the first example, the therapy may well be limited in its usefulness to children of a certain age where the phobia is the result of something quite specific, such as incidents of bullying.

It is important that any sample used in a study where we wish to generalise is not a specially drawn sample, such as only those children who expressed great interest in the therapy. This would be an example of *sampling bias*. By the nature of applied psychology, in many studies the sample *is* biased, because we are working with pre-established groups, or simply those we can get hold of or persuade to take part. What we must know then, in each case, is how *representative* each sample is of any wider population to which we would wish to generalise.

A large sample drawn on a *random* basis from a population will normally be fairly representative of the population as a whole. Poll companies attempting to predict election outcomes rely heavily on this principle. The strict meaning of a *random sample* is that *any person and combination of persons within the target population has an equal chance of being selected*. Since this is an unrealistic criterion, many samples in applied studies are made representative not by random sampling, but by some form of well-organised *selection strategy* or *sampling technique* (see Coolican 2004).

Controlling extraneous and confounding variables

If our school phobia study includes only children who are interested in the therapy, we would have an example of bias in the sample *confounding* the result. We may get very positive results here, but not when all types of school-phobic child are included. *Confounding variables* are the heart of research analysis. We are constantly asking the question: 'What *else* might be responsible for this difference or trend in results?' Confounding variables are either variables (*other than those intended*) which are producing effects, or they are variables which *obscure* real effects. For example, people performing a task first without caffeine and then with caffeine, may perform at the same level on the second trial because, although caffeine enhances their performance, they are also more tired on the second attempt. Their improvement is obscured by fatigue.

Problems in gathering authentic data in the field

Social desirability

Social desirability is the tendency to want to 'look good' socially. Few parents will want to admit to a strange interviewer that they sometimes wish they had not had their children. Parents know that physical punishment of children is frowned upon by professionals and so may be reticent about the

extent of its use in their household. Few will expose their racist attitudes willingly in a street survey. Few people will easily discuss fears about their relationship or their sexual fantasies and behaviour.

Local pressures

From an ethical point of view, the applied researcher must always keep in mind that those interviewed or observed are not acting in a vacuum. Research in organisations invariably raises the ethical issue of *confidentiality*. Even where anonymity is guaranteed for the individual, it cannot be assumed that workers will answer truthfully or fully. It will be difficult for the visiting psychologist to appear neutral between management and workforce, and, in any case, an individual can tell when the information they give is precise enough to pinpoint them, with or without anonymity.

Observer and interviewer bias

Researcher or experimenter expectancy was outlined above. Observers and interviewers, to some extent, can also see or hear what they expect to see or hear, given their prior expectations and social stereotypes. They are trained in standardised *rating systems* intended to remove much of the individual bias in perception.

Blinds and double blinds

A further safeguard often employed is to have raters give quantitative values to observation or interview data 'blind' to its source. For instance, a *single blind* occurs where participants do not know whether they received a stimulant or a placebo. Where performance is rated by trained observers who are *also* unaware of the substance given to each participant, the study uses a *double blind*.

Standardised procedures

Generally, within mainstream experimental psychology research, it has been the norm to use *standardised procedures* with each participant, in the interest of controlling all extraneous variables which could affect different participants differently. This concept has usually been carried through into the areas of test administration and, to a lesser extent, interviewing. However, there is a powerful argument against this approach in some areas of applied work; where what is required are the different accounts and impressions people have of their health or work situation, it would be far more important to conduct what are known as *clinical interviews*, in which the interviewer employs the skills of *unstructured* or *semi-structured interviewing* (see page 277) in order to extract the full richness of each person's perspective.

The qualitative-quantitative debate

The last point has brought us to a huge and often hostile debate within psychological research: whether there should always be an attempt to control variables and *quantify* (i.e. measure numerically) psychological phenomena. The alternative position argues that the attempt to quantify all psychological variables, and follow a conventional scientific method, frequently leads to rather arid findings, divorced from everyday reality. For example, it is argued that IQ scores give an extremely narrow impression of a person's full range of mental capacity, just as measuring attitude to authority or the quality of group cohesiveness as a numerical value, creates a quite artificial notion that such qualities exist in quantities ranging from one end of a unidimensional scale to the other. Incorporated into this debate, on the generally 'qualitative' side, is the argument that the experimental 'scientific' model creates an inappropriate and artificial body of knowledge quite unrelated to the real world of human interaction. Laboratory studies on small, short-lived groups, into leadership or team cooperation and performance, are seen as quite unlike these phenomena as they operate in the real world of work and recreation.

There is not space here to enter into this now classic debate, but the interested reader might refer to Coolican (2004) for a brief account, or to the several fuller arguments mentioned in that text. Examples of contemporary qualitative data analysis can be found in Willig (2001) and Smith (2003). The debate is especially important within applied psychology, however, since it is mainly the applied areas which have promoted the debate and developed qualitative methods. The following paragraphs give some flavour of these approaches.

Action research

Initiated by Kurt Lewin in the mid 1940s, this approach calls for psychological research to deal with practical social issues: to enter a situation, attempt to change it and to monitor results –

often known as an *intervention study*. An important guiding principle is to involve the participants (often members of a work group) in the process of change. The approach sees the researcher–researched (or consultant–client) role as central to any attempted intervention. In contrast, the traditional scientific research model tends to see the researcher or consultant in a neutral position, observing 'the facts', and sees social interaction factors, such as 'participant expectation' or 'social desirability', as 'nuisance variables' in need of control. In the UK, especially for work psychology, action research principles are strongly associated with the Tavistock Institute of Human Relations.

Participative and collaborative research

In applied areas of psychology (especially occupational, health and educational), since the 1980s, it has become more common for research to include participants as active enquirers in the research process, as Lewin and the Tavistock Institute have recommended. At the extreme, 'collaborative' end of this approach, the researcher takes the role of 'consultant', while facilitating work group members to conduct their own production of theories, data gathering, analysis and recommendations for change (see Reason 1994).

Qualitative data

Qualitative research generates qualitative data. Some researchers argue that any attempt to quantify the data will destroy much of its richness and meaning. A popular approach is the employment of 'grounded theory' (see Strauss and Corbin 1990; Smith 2003), by which it is argued that theory can develop from the data one has gathered. This is to be contrasted with the conventional scientific model in which one sets out to *test* a theory by gathering data. Other researchers gather qualitative data and then, as part of the project, reduce this to some set of categories in order to report on the generalities found during the study. One compromise achieved in dealing with initially non-numeric data is to subject it to some form of *content analysis*. The data may have arrived from:

- open-ended questionnaire items;
- relatively unstructured observation (participant or non-participant);
- relatively unstructured interviews;

➡ projective test responses;

➡ already recorded data, such as children's school essays, lavatory graffiti (this *has* been done!), personal advertisements, television advertisements, news items, politicians' speeches, and so on.

(The first four sources are all described below.)

In content analysis a *coding system* is devised, and raters are trained to use the system to categorise information, initially in qualitative form. A *rating scale* is often used to apply some quantitative assessment. Raters' level of agreement can then be subjected to *reliability analysis* (also explained below).

A further use of content analysis has been in work with *verbal protocols*, where, in the work situation, an operative is asked to state aloud the silent speech they would use to help themselves carry out a task, *or* to mention *any* thoughts which occur while carrying out the task. Martin and Klimoski (1990) used this method to study managers' evaluations of personnel. The managers were asked to speak aloud while evaluating their own and their subordinates' performances. It was found that the subordinates' performance was attributed to their relatively permanent personality characteristics, whereas for the managers themselves, performance was more likely to be seen as a product of the surrounding situation. Roberts and Fels (2006) used 'think-aloud' protocols to show that deaf participants assessing software usability could viably use the same method, but with gestures (sign language) rather than vocal language.

HOW DO PSYCHOLOGISTS ASK QUESTIONS?

There are two major approaches to asking questions, first, by *interview*, and second by questionnaire or *psychometric test* (or 'scales'). Many interviews incorporate the use of a test, scale or questionnaire. Even experiments may involve the use of a questionnaire or scale, often to measure the dependent variable. Patients randomly assigned to two different programmes for dietary control might be assessed on their dietary behaviour, pre- and post-training, using a questionnaire. However, the vast majority of test and questionnaire usage is in non-experimental field studies.

Questionnaires, scales and psychometric tests

Psychologists use a variety of questionnaires, scales and tests in order to obtain information from people. In general (borrowing terminology from the natural sciences and technology), these measures are known as *instruments*. Those that request information from people about themselves are commonly known as *self-report measures*. Below are listed and defined the general categories of measure which a psychologist might use.

Questionnaire

This is the correct name for a measure which asks several questions, unlike many *attitude* and *personality scales*, which are described below. Questionnaires are often used for survey work in order to obtain current views on a particular issue. They are also used to obtain information about regular behaviour, such as modes of child discipline, sexual habits, typical leisure activities, moral principles and voting behaviour.

Attitude scales

These are intended to measure a relatively permanent and habitual position (rather than an opinion) of an individual on a particular issue. Attitude scales often employ a set of *statements* (not questions) with which the respondent indicates their level of agreement or disagreement.

Personality scales

These are intended to measure a relatively enduring feature of a person's regular behaviour (such as their general anxiety level, extraversion or typical approach to crises). For the most part, they also use statements with which to agree or disagree. Personality scales may use a set of descriptive terms from which the respondent has to select those most closely describing him or her. A few use only 'yes' or 'no' responses.

Psychometric tests

These are instruments of 'mental measurement', and include personality and attitude scales, along with measures of mental ability such as intelligence, creative thinking and linguistic ability. It is important here to distinguish between the following measures:

➡ *personality trait*: what you are normally like most of the time (e.g. your friendliness);

➠ *personality state*: what you are like at this moment (e.g. your current state of anxiety);

➠ *ability*: what you are generally able to do (e.g. your numerical ability);

➠ *achievement*: what you have achieved so far (e.g. your performance in a school or college test in psychology);

➠ *aptitude*: your *potential* performance (e.g. a general logic test, which aims to predict how good you would be at computer programming).

Like interviews, psychological scales and tests can vary along the dimensions of *structure* and *disguise*. Psychometric tests are highly structured, since they are viewed as accurately constructed measurement instruments and are subject to rigorous testing for reliability and validity (see below). Some questionnaires used in an interview or general survey, however, contain *open-ended* questions (e.g. 'Please describe any sexual harassment or disadvantage you feel you have suffered in your employment'). Here, results are difficult to quantify, but can be subject to content analysis. The specific aim of some scales or questionnaires can be disguised in order to avoid social desirability effects. In other scales there is no disguise, but it would not be clear to the participant what is covered, simply because of the highly theoretical nature of the variables assessed and the complexity of the overall test.

Projective tests

These are based on the psychoanalytic notion that, when confronted by ambiguous stimuli, we tend to reveal our inner, normally defended thoughts, by projecting them into what we perceive in the display. Those who interpret what is reported in projective testing claim to be able to assess such factors as concealed aggression, sexual fantasy, anxiety, and so on. Being unstructured and disguised, they are seen as providing rich data, with no bias from people guessing the researcher's intentions (except by clients experienced in therapy!). *Rorschach ink blots* are one well-known type of projective test, still often used in clinical psychology. These are symmetrical, abstract patterns, rather like the 'butterfly' paintings produced in nursery classes. Another example is the *Thematic Aperception Test* (TAT), which is a set of generally ambiguous visual scenes. In each case, people are asked what they see and, for the TAT, what may happen next.

Why should we trust psychological measures?

Reliability and validity

The description above of projective tests might leave the reader asking two related questions: How do we know the Rorschach test really *does* measure aspects of personality? Surely I could produce a different result one day to the next? The first question is one of *validity* and the second is a question of *reliability*.

We would ask of any measure, for instance our bathroom scales, that it produces the same reading each time the same amount is measured, and that it gives us a true measure of what we want. Psychologists expect their measures to be:

➠ *reliable* – they are consistent and stable;
➠ *valid* – they measure what is intended;
➠ *standardised* – we can make comparisons with other people measured on the same scale or instrument.

Reliability

An assessment of the *reliability* of a test or scale can be obtained in two ways.

1 *External reliability* is assessed by comparing results on the measure for the *same* group of people at two different times. Comparison is conducted using correlation (as described above).

2 *Internal reliability* is assessed either by comparing people's scores on two halves of the test, or (using *item analysis*) by comparing their scores on each item with their score overall.

Inter-rater reliability refers to the level of agreement between two raters of projective test data or essay content, for example, as in content analysis. *Inter-observer reliability* is assessed by correlating the ratings of two different observers assessing the same behaviour events.

Validity

These methods may satisfy us that the test or assessment schedule is consistent in its measurement effects (*reliable*), but not necessarily that it measures what we want it to measure (is *valid*). A test of children's word knowledge, presented in written form, may fail because the children *know* the words, but are not able to *read* them. There are many ways of checking the validity of a psychological measure, but a common practice is to check that it predicts what we would expect. For instance, people scoring highly on an intelligence measure would be expected to do well in academic tests and exams; people scoring highly on a work motivation test would be predicted to be more successful and productive; an anxiety test should discriminate between people with anxiety-related problems and a group with no such problems.

Standardisation

We would also expect any useful measure to be *transferable* from one test situation to another. A measure of reading ability developed to distinguish between the various years of pupils in a very high-ability school will not be useful for assessing performance in many other ordinary schools. *Standardisation* is the process of making a test transferable. This is done by taking large enough representative samples from the population with which individual cases are to be compared in future use of the test. Then a good deal of item analysis, adjustment of content and improvement in reliability is carried out, until (usually) a *normal distribution* of scores is obtained. This is a symmetrical spread of scores, with most lying near the central point. It is now possible to assess individuals who come from the same population as that on whom the test was standardised. Scores can be compared with the general distribution, very often in terms of the individual's *deviation* from the mean (average) of the population.

Operational definitions

It is important to recognise that psychologists do not work with a set of measuring instruments which have the universal acceptance that, say, physical measures of electrical current or liquid volume enjoy. For any particular research project it is important to ask: what was the measure employed? If a psychologist is attempting to reduce aggression in disturbed children, and claims to have demonstrated this with a new technique, it is important for that researcher to report the *measure* of aggression employed. An *operational definition* is *a description of the steps taken in measuring an entity*. This is true in any science. In the psychological example given, the researcher would need to state how 'aggression' was measured, *for the purposes of the present study*. This might be in terms of the specific observations made of children's behaviour

(number of hits, number of aggressive verbal responses, and so on), or by means of a questionnaire. Many variables mentioned in this book – for example, stress, anxiety, personality characteristics, motivation, verbal intelligence – are measured in terms of an operational definition.

Test factors and factor analysis

With reference to some of the tests mentioned in this book, there may be talk of some 'factors' associated with the test. This is especially true for so-called general intelligence tests, where, on analysis, it is argued that the test measures several (at least partially) distinct 'factors'. As we said earlier, a written word knowledge test also partially tests reading ability. Both word knowledge and reading ability, then, might be *factors* contributing to an individual's overall test score. Some would argue that performance on a general intelligence test is determined by factors of numerical reasoning, verbal reasoning, verbal knowledge, thinking speed, and so on. Psychologists use the statistical procedure of *factor analysis* to analyse results for the likely number of factors that are assessed by a complex psychological instrument.

Interviews

An interview is a face-to-face encounter (though video and telephone 'interviews' are possible) in which data are recorded using notes, audio- or videotape recording. Interview types vary from being pretty unstructured, as is often the case in counselling psychology, to completely structured, as is the case in the social survey. Some of the types of interview commonly in use are described below.

- *Non-directive*: used frequently by counsellors and 'client-centred' therapists, where the aim is not so much to gather data as to help the client. No specific direction is given. The interviewer supports the client in personal growth, reflects back their statements and helps them to solve their own problems as far as possible.
- *Informal*: quite unstructured, but with an overall data-gathering aim. The interviewee is prompted to talk, while the interviewer listens patiently and sympathetically, offering useful comments, but no advice or argument. The interviewer may prompt further expansion on a point and offer a direction or support in further exploration by the interviewee.

➠ *Informal but guided*: the interviewer has a set of topics to cover and perhaps some specifically worded questions, but the interview is conducted as a friendly, natural conversation. The interviewer 'plays it by ear', and works in the various questions or topics as the discussion progresses. Also known as *semi-structured*. Piaget used a version of this in his *clinical method* (or interview), which follows up a child's answers to set questions with spontaneous new enquiries, which are intended to do justice to his or her pattern of thought.

➠ *Structured but open-ended*: there is a fixed set of questions to ask, but replies are open-ended. Interviewees may answer in any terms they wish. The interviewer will search for further information using prompts and probes.

➠ *Fully structured*: there is a fixed set of questions and a fixed set of possible responses for the interviewee to choose from. This is the type of interview mostly used in *surveys*.

Observation

Controlled and naturalistic observation

Although non-experimental studies lack some control over the independent and extraneous variables, nevertheless researchers usually *control* their data gathering as far as possible. Ways to exert this control in an observation study are:

➠ creating a structured assessment system;
➠ creating good inter-rater reliability, with further training and practice if necessary;
➠ control, where possible, over the environment in which the observation takes place – perhaps an observation room at the research centre.

Most applied psychology observational studies take place in the natural environment of the people observed and are therefore known as *naturalistic studies*. Bandura's famous research (1969) on the ways children model adult behaviour took place in a controlled laboratory setting, but most applied work is not so generalised. Naturalistic observation may occur on the shop floor, in the office, in the classroom, at the hospital clinic, and so on. Because the observed behaviour would have occurred anyway, if the observer is discreet, realism is likely to be high. However, where a researcher or video camera follows family members around the house

for extended periods, for example, behaviour might be distorted by the observation.

To avoid this effect of the observer's presence, researchers can become a familiar part of the work, school, leisure or medical environment. Charlesworth and Hartup (1967) made several visits to a nursery school, talked to the children and learnt their names. They found they could also test out the reliability of their proposed observation scheme prior to formal data gathering.

Participant observation

A major method of preference for psychologists who tend to reject the traditionally scientific and experimental model of psychological research has been to get in among the people who are the object of investigation. In 'action research' this means also involving the participants as co-researchers, but in classic versions of *participant observation*, an observer would make observations while being a member of the group under study, often without the observed people being aware of the observer's role. This can be queried on ethical grounds, since participants do not have the power to censor information which they might not wish to be published. On methodological grounds there have always been doubts about the possible objectivity of the observer under such circumstances, to say nothing of the strain involved in memorising information or somehow recording observations without 'blowing cover'. Very many applied research projects, however, involve the researcher in working or living with the group studied and attempting to see the world from their point of view.

Case studies

Compared with mainstream psychological research, a good deal of the work within applied psychology involves individual *case studies*. Much of Freud's theory was developed from work with individual patients. Today, in clinical psychology, a great deal of the literature concerns individual clients and their specific problems. An individual case study would generally include several of the following:

➠ a case history – notes and evidence concerning the individual's prior history, exam grades, schools attended, medical history, and so on;

- detailed observation of the individual, for instance at school or in the hospital ward;
- interviews, perhaps at regular intervals;
- administration of psychometric tests (anxiety, personality, verbal ability, etc., as appropriate);
- information from diaries written by the person studied;
- reports from those working with the individual, such as teachers or social workers.

Case studies are extremely important in applied psychology. It may be that just one case of a person *not* developing as expected sheds light on a completely new area of thinking or expectation. One seriously deprived child who nevertheless develops well academically and socially is of particular interest. One success with a new therapy used on a case of bulimia will be a good lead. Disasters and serial murders do not occur to order or in sufficient frequency for generalisations to be made easily, but we can learn from in-depth study of such cases that *do* occur. Many studies in occupational psychology are of one particular organisation in depth.

There is sometimes a form of knee-jerk reaction within psychology that investigative work must always be carried out on fairly large groups of people. This is true only where the final aim is to generalise at least to the population from which the people are drawn. There is no problem, though, in using a statistical significance test (see below) on a set of data drawn from *one* person. For example, in clinical psychology a therapist might want to target several aspects of a client's behaviour for change. Suppose we want to assess whether therapy has effected any such changes. If we observe 12 aspects of behaviour before therapy commences, and again after a test period of three months, and find that 11 aspects *have* changed for the better, we can confidently reject the expectation from the null hypothesis (see below) that the changes varied only at chance level. Under the null hypothesis we would predict small random changes in each behaviour (no two measures are exactly the same), but half of these should be in one direction and half in the other. The result here allows us to present evidence *supporting* (but *not* proving) our hypothesis that the therapy had some effect on the client's behaviour.

MEASUREMENT AND STATISTICS

Descriptive and inferential statistics

Much work in applied psychology involves the gathering of what are known as *descriptive statistics*. In educational psychology we may wish to know the average reading age of a group of children on a run-down housing estate, and we may wish to know the variation within this group. Statistics are summaries of measurements taken of individuals or groups. They simply *describe* those people. Very often, though, we want to know whether a *difference* exists. For example, we might want to know whether the housing estate children differ *significantly* from the general average for children this age. In the development of theory, as we have seen, we deduce a hypothesis, then test it, making use of what are known as *inferential* statistics (we use them to infer that a difference exists). These will tell us to what extent we can claim that a difference, or a correlation, we have measured can be taken seriously. We hope to be able to claim with some confidence that the estate children's mean differs markedly from the usual mean for children this age – that their much lower score is not simply a matter of random variation. We want to convince others that the difference is not just a 'fluke'. *We do this by showing how unlikely it is that any two average (randomly selected) groups of children would differ by so much.*

The concept of significance

Most quantitative research articles make use of *statistical significance* testing. A concrete example should illustrate this. A clinic announced that it could help couples to have a baby of the sex they desired. A radio interview produced the claim that four out of six couples so far treated had left satisfied. Even the most non-mathematical of readers will probably find this a rather dubious claim for support. The most likely outcome for six couples who have a desire for a baby of a specific sex is that three will be satisfied and three will not, assuming that the clinic is entirely ineffective. Four out of six is the next most likely outcome, *by chance* alone. It is therefore a *likely* outcome in normal (non-treated) conditions. The clinic is *not* doing well so far.

Suppose an occupational psychologist claims to employ a highly effective stress-reducing technique.

You, as an employer considering purchase of the psychologist's services, will want evidence that the technique is indeed effective. The psychologist might present evidence that 10 out of 12 people who took the programme in a controlled study showed a lower stress score (measured by questionnaire) after the sessions than they had before the programme began. To understand the logic of significance testing, take the sceptical position. Assume that the stress technique does *not* work. If this is so, the results will be at chance level only. What would results obtained at chance level look like? If we measure people's scores on a complex test twice, there will usually be *some* slight difference. As with the toss of a coin, there is an equal chance that the difference from time 1 (before programme) to time 2 (after programme) will be positive or negative. By chance alone, then, half the differences in stress level should be an increase and half should be a decrease, and this is what *will* happen most of the time *if* the programme is entirely ineffective. In other words, if the technique has no effect *at all*, the most likely effect we could expect would be that 6 of the 12 people will 'improve' and 6 will 'worsen'. We must remember that *if* the technique does not work, these are not 'improvements' at all, just random fluctuations. The assumption that there is absolutely no effect is known as the *null hypothesis*, and the outcome of 6 'improvements' and 6 'worsenings' is the most likely result *if* the null hypothesis is true. The null hypothesis refers to the *population* of scores from which we are sampling.

What the psychologist *actually* obtained was 10 improvements, and only 2 not improving. The probability of getting 10 results in one direction, when there was an equal chance of each result going either way (the null hypothesis), are around 4 in 100. For instance, if you tossed 12 coins together, you would only get 10 heads or 10 tails about 4 times in every 100. In other words, 10 out of 12 tails, 10 boys out of 12 babies, or 10 'successes' out of 12 tries (*if each try depends only on luck*) are pretty unlikely events. We have established that *if the stress results are just chance outcomes*, the likelihood of getting these results is pretty low. The psychologist here would take the step of assuming that the null hypothesis *is not* true, and proceed to accept that the therapy works, at least provisionally. It is important to recognise that when researchers obtain significant differences or correlations they do *not* 'prove that their theory is correct', but simply provide themselves with evidence. This evidence says that if they are *wrong*, then the outcomes they obtained are a remarkable coincidence.

Conventional levels of significance – $p<0.05$ and $p<0.01$

Probability is not conventionally stated in the way that betting odds are. Probability is written as '*p*' and can take any value between 0 (absolutely no likelihood whatever) to 1 (absolutely certain). The probability that the stress results above would occur, *if the technique has no effect*, is 0.04. On a scale of 0 to 1, this is very low. Conventionally, researchers make the decision to reject the null hypothesis when the probability (*p*) of the results occurring, *if the null hypothesis is true*, is less than 0.05. Hence our result above would be counted as 'significant'. Traditionally, it is usual to report results where $p<0.05$ as 'significant' and results where $p<0.01$ as 'highly significant', though some dislike this habit. What matters for your understanding of research outcomes reported in this book is that researchers *cannot* claim to have support for their theory, or to have an effective technique, unless, statistically, their results would be highly unlikely *if* the null hypothesis is true – they *must* have a significant result. This is the basis on which results are reported in this book. If a difference or correlation is reported, it can be assumed that the result *has* been tested *and* found to be significant, even if this is not stated specifically.

Combining hypothesis tests – meta-analysis

Some studies support one theory, others do not. *Meta-analysis* is a way to solve the problem of assessing the *overall* direction of possibly hundreds of tests of the same or very similar hypotheses. It employs a set of statistical techniques in order to use the results of many studies as a new 'data set'. Only studies that are similar enough and meet certain criteria are included, but the end result is a more certain estimate of 'effect size', based on sample sizes and significance levels. That is, we can combine the results of as many goal-setting research studies as possible, and we can be more certain that goal setting has real effects and can get a better idea of just what the sizes of those effects are. Meta-analysis takes account of sample size and various statistical features of the data from each study. Specific examples are encountered in several chapters of this book.

References

CHAPTER 1: INTRODUCTION

Anderson, N., Herriot, P. and Hodgkinson, G.P. (2001) The practitioner-researcher divide in industrial, work and organizational (IWO) psychology: Where are we now, and where do we go from here? *Journal of Occupational and Organizational Psychology*, 74, 391–411.

Binet, A. and Simon, T. (1915) *A Method of Measuring the Development of Intelligence of Young Children*. Chicago, IL: Chicago Medical Book Company.

Bowlby, J. (1980) *Attachment and Loss*. New York: Basic Books.

Briner, R.B. (1998) What is an evidence-based approach to practice and why do we need one in occupational psychology? *British Psychology Society Occupational Psychology Conference Book of Proceedings*. Leicester: British Psychological Society.

Coolican, H. (2004) *Research Methods and Statistics in Psychology*. London: Hodder & Stoughton.

Doyle, C. (2003) Occupational and organizational psychology. In Bayne, R. and Horton, I. (eds) *Applied Psychology*. London: Sage.

Harper, D., Mulvey, R. and Robinson, M. (2003) Beyond evidence-based practice: Rethinking the relationship between research, theory and practice. In Bayne, R. and Horton, I. (eds) *Applied Psychology*. London: Sage.

Hovland, C.I., Lumsdaine, A.A. and Sheffield, F.D. (1949) *Experiments on Mass Communication. (Studies in Social Psychology in World War II, Vol. 3)*. Princeton, NJ: Princeton University Press.

Mayo, E. (1927) Cited in Rose, M. (1975) *Industrial Behaviour: Theoretical developments since Taylor*. Harmondsworth: Penguin.

Norcross, J.C., Brust, A.M. and Dryden, W. (1992) British clinical psychologists. II. Survey findings and American comparisons. *Clinical Psychology Forum*, 40, 25–9.

CHAPTER 2: CLINICAL PSYCHOLOGY

Bandura, A. (1997) *Self-Efficacy: The exercise of self-control*. New York: Freeman.

Bateson, G. (1972) *Steps to an Ecology of Mind*. New York: Ballantine Books.

Bebbington, P.E., Johnson, S. and Thornicroft, G. (2002) Community mental health care: Promises and pitfalls. In Sartorius, N., Gaebel, W., Lopez-Ibor, J.J. and Maj, M. (eds) *The Changing Social Contexts of Psychiatry*. London: Wiley.

Beck, A.T., Steer, R.A. and Brown, G.K. (1996) *Manual for the Beck Depression Inventory II*. San Antonio, CA: Psychological Corporation.

Bowlby, J. (1969) *Attachment*. London: Hogarth Press.

Brallier, S.A. and Tsukuda, R.A. (2002) Organizational and team structure. In Heinemann, G.D. and Zeiss, A.M. (eds) *Team Performance in Health Care: Assessment and development*. London: Springer.

Bruch, M. and Bond, F. (1998) *Beyond Diagnosis: Case formulation approaches in CBT*. London: Wiley.

Chadwick, P. and Trower, P. (1996) Cognitive therapy for punishment paranoia: A single case experiment. *Behaviour Research and Therapy*, 34(4), 351–6.

Chadwick, P., Williams, C. and Mackenzie, J. (2003) Impact of case formulation in cognitive behaviour therapy for psychosis. *Behaviour Research and Therapy*, 41, 671–80.

Cochrane, R. and Sashidharan, S.P. (1995) *Mental Health and Ethnic Minorities: A review of the literature and implications for services*. University of Birmingham and Northern Birmingham Mental Health Trust. Available at http://www.academicarmageddon.co.uk/library/ETHMENT.htm (accessed 20 December 2006).

Compas, B. and Gotlib, I. (2002) *Introduction to Clinical Psychology*. New York: McGraw-Hill.

Ellis, A. (1962) *Reason and Mention in Psychotherapy*. New Jersey: Lyle Stewart.

Ellis, A. (1973) *Humanistic Psychotherapy: The rational emotive approach*. New Jersey: McGraw-Hill.

Emmelkamp, P.M.G., Bowman, T.K. and Blaauw, E. (1994) Individualized versus standardized therapy: A comparative evaluation with obsessive-compulsive patients. *Clinical Psychology and Psychotherapy*, 1, 95–100.

Eysenck, H.J. (1952) The effects of psychotherapy: An evaluation. *Journal of Consulting and Clinical Psychology*, 60, 659–63.

Fairbairn, W.R.D. (1952) *An Object-Relations Theory of the Personality*. New York: Basic Books.

Fernando, S., Ndegwa, D. and Wilson, M. (1998) *Forensic Psychiatry, Race and Culture*. London: Routledge.

Jackson, L., Tudway, J.A., Smith, J. and Giles, D. (2005) Social Identity Maintenance Strategies in Mental Health In-Patient Service Users. Poster presentation. Breaking the Boundaries, Medical Sociology Conference, University of Nottingham, UK.

Jacobson, N.S., Schmaling, K.B., Holtzworth-Munroe, A., Katt, J.L., Wood, L.F. and Follette, V.M. (1989) Research-structured vs clinically flexible versions of social learning-based marital therapy. *Behaviour Research and Therapy*, 27, 173–80.

Kinderman, P. and Lobban, F. (2000) Evolving formulations: Sharing complex information with clients. *Behavioural and Cognitive Psychotherapy*, 28(3), 307–10.

McCormack, J., Hudson, S.M. and Ward, T. (2002) Sexual offenders' perceptions of their early interpersonal relationships: An attachment perspective. *The Journal of Sex Research*, 39(2), 85–93.

Meichenbaum, D. (1977) *Cognitive Behavioral Modification: An integrative approach*. New York: Plenum Press.

Minuchin, S. (1968) *Families of the Slums*. New York: Basic Books.

Mowrer, O.H. (1956) Two factor learning theory reconsidered, with special reference to secondary reinforcement and the concept of habit. *Psychological Review*, 63, 114–28.

Nicholson, P. (1992) Gender issues in the organisation of clinical psychology. In Ussher, J.M. and Nicholson, P. (eds) *Gender Issues in Clinical Psychology*. London: Routledge.

Oltmanns, T. and Emery, R. (2006) *Abnormal Psychology*, fifth edition. Englewood Cliff, NJ: Prentice Hall.

Parjares, F. and Miller, M.D. (1994) Role of self-efficacy beliefs and general math ability in mathematical problem-solving: A path analysis. *Journal of Educational Psychology*, 86, 193–203.

Perls, F.S. (1969) *Ego, Hunger and Aggression*. New York: Vintage Books.

Perls, F., Hefferline, R.F. and Goodman, P. (1951) *Gestalt Therapy: Excitement and growth in the human personality*. New York: The Julian Press.

Pilgrim, D. (2003) Six threats to the sustainability of clinical psychology. *Clinical Psychology*, 28, 6–8.

Romme, M. and Escher, S. (2000) *Making Sense of Voices*. London: Mind Publications.

Rutter, M. (1981) *Maternal Deprivation Reassessed*, second edition. Harmondsworth: Penguin.

Schulte, D. (1997) Behavioural analysis: Does it matter? *Behavioural and Cognitive Psychotherapy*, 25, 231–49.

Schulte, D., Kunzel, I.L., Pepping, G. and Schulte-Bahrenberg, T. (1992) Tailor-made versus standardized therapy of phobic patients. *Advances in Behaviour Research and Therapy*, 14, 67–92.

Seligman, M. (1975) *Helplessness: On depression, development, and death*. San Francisco, CA: W.H. Freeman.

Skinner, B.F. (1955) The control of human behavior. *Transactions of the New York Academy of Sciences*, 17, 547–51.

Sturmey, P. (1996) *Functional Analysis in Clinical Psychology*. London: Wiley.

Szasz, T.S. (1960) The myth of mental illness. *American Psychologist*, 15, 113–18.

Winnicott, D. (1953) Transitional objects and transitional phenomena. *International Journal of Psychoanalysis*, 34, 89–97.

Wolpe, J. (1958) *Psychotherapy by Reciprocal Inhibition*. Stanford, CA: Stanford University Press.

CHAPTER 3: COUNSELLING PSYCHOLOGY

Beutler, L.E. Machado, P.P. and Neufeldt, S.A. (2004) Therapist variables. In Bergin A.E. and Garfield, S.L. (eds) *Handbook of Psychotherapy and Behaviour Change*. New York: Wiley.

Bowen, M. (1966) The use of family theory in clinical practice, *Comprehensive Psychiatry*, 7, 345–74.

Bowen, M. (1976) Theory in the practice of Psychotherapy. In Guerin, Jr. P.J. (ed.) *Family Therapy: Theory and practice*. New York: Gardner Press.

Breuer, J. and Freud, S. (1895) *Studies on Hysteria,*

Standard Edition of the Complete Psychological Works of Sigmund Freud, Vol. 2. Edited and translated J. Strachey (1955), London: Hogarth Press and the Institute of Psychoanalysis.

British Association for Counselling (1984) *Code of Ethics and Practice for Counsellors*. Rugby: BAC.

Butler, A.C. and Beck, J.S. (2000) Cognitive therapy outcomes: a review of meta-analyses, *Journal of the Norwegian Psychological Associations*, 37, 1–9.

Cartwright, D.S. (1957) Annotated bibliography of research and theory construction in client-centred therapy. *Journal of Counselling Psychology*, 4(1), 82–100.

Coppersmith, E. (1980) The family floor plan: A tool of training, assessment, and intervention in family therapy. *Journal of Marital & Family Therapy*, 6, 141–5.

Dare, C., Eisler, I., Russell, G., Treasure, J. and Dodge, I. (2001) Psychological therapies for adults with anorexia nervosa: randomised controlled trial of out-patient treatments. *British Journal of Psychiatry*, 178, 216–21.

Department of Health (1999) National service framework for mental health: modern standards and service models. London, DOH, 1999. Available at www.dh.gov.uk/publicationsAndStatistics/Publications.

DeRubeis, R.J., Amsterdam, J.D., Shelton, R.C., Young, P.R., Salomon, R.M., O'Reardon, J.P., Lovett, M.L., Gladis, M.M., Brown, L.L. and Gallop, R. (2005) Cognitive therapy vs medications in the treatment of moderate to severe depression. *Archives of General Psychiatry*. 62(4), 409–16.

Dryden W. and Mytton J. (1999) *Four Approaches to Counselling and Psychotherapy*. London: Routledge.

Duhl, F.J., Kantor, D. and Duhl, B.S. (1973) Learning space and action in family therapy: A primer of sculpting. In D. Bloch (ed.) *Techniques of Family Psychotherapy: A Primer*. New York: Grune & Stratton.

Egan, G. (1986) *The Skilled Helper*, third edition, California: Brooks Cole.

Ellis, A. (1962) *Reason and Emotion in Psychotherapy*. New York: Lyle Stuart.

Emery, G. (1981) *A New Beginning: How you can change your life through cognitive therapy*. New York, Simon and Schuster (Touchstone).

Fiedler, F. (1950) The concept of an ideal therapeutic relationship. *Journal of Consulting Psychology*, 14, 243.

Goldenberg, I. and Goldenberg, H. (1996) *Family Therapy: An Overview*, fourth ed. Pacific Grove, CA: Brooks Cole.

Greenberg, L.S, Elliott, R.K. and Lietaer, G. (1994) Research on experiential psychotherapies. In Bergin, A.E. and Garfield, S.L. (eds) *Handbook of Psychotherapy and Behavior Change*, fourth edition, New York: Wiley.

Guerin, P.J. and Chabot, D.R. (1992) Development of family systems theory. In Freedheim, D.K. (ed.) *History of Psychotherapy: A Century of Change*. Washington DC: American Psychological Association.

Haley, J. (1973) *Uncommon Therapy*. New York: Norton.

Jacobs, M. (1988) *Psychodynamic Counselling in Action*. London: Sage.

Leichsenring, F. and Leibing, E. (2003) The effectiveness of psychodynamic therapy and cognitive behavior therapy in the treatment of personality disorders: a meta-analysis. *American Journal of Psychiatry* 160, 1223–32.

Maslow, A. (1968) *Towards a Psychology of Being*, second edition. New York: Van Norstrand.

McColdrick, M. and Gerson, R. (1985). *Genograms in Family Assessment*. New York: Norton.

Mearns, D. and Thorne, B. (1988) *Person-Centred Counselling in Action*. London: Sage.

Minuchin, S. (1974) *Families and Family Therapy*. London: Tavistock.

Minuchin, S. and Fishman, C. (1981) *Family Therapy Techniques*. Cambridge, MA: Harvard University Press.

Minuchin, S. and Fishman, H. (1981) *Techniques of family therapy*. Cambridge, MA: Harvard University Press.

Nelson-Jones, R. (1993) *Practical Counselling and Helping*, third edition. London: Cassell.

Patterson, C. (1974) *Relationship Counselling and Psychotherapy*. New York: Harper Row.

Perls, F.S., Hefferline, R.F. and Goodman, P. (1951) *Gestalt Therapy*. New York: Julian Press.

Rogers, C. (1942) *Counseling and Psychotherapy*. Boston: Houghton Mifflin.

Rogers, C. (1951) *Client-Centred Therapy*. Boston: Houghton Mifflin.

Rogers, C. (1957) The necessary and sufficient conditions of therapeutic personality change. *Journal of Counseling Psychology*, 21(2), 95–103.

Rogers, C. (1961) *On Becoming a Person*. Boston: Houghton Mifflin.

Rogers, C. (1975) Empathic: an unappreciated way of being, *The Counselling Psychologist*, 5(2), 2.

Roth, A, and Fonagy, P. (2004) *What Works for Whom? A critical review of psychotherapy research*, second edition. New York: Guilford Press.

Selvini-Palazzoli, M., Cirillo, S., Selvini, M. and Sorrentino, A.M. (1989) *Family Games: General*

Models of Psychotic Processes in the Family. London: Karnac.

Shadish, W., Ragsdale, J., Glaser, R. and Montgomery, L. (1995) The efficacy and effectiveness of marital and family therapy: a perspective from meta-analysis *Journal of Marital and Family Therapy*, 21(4), 345–60.

Sherman, R. and Fredman, N. (1986) *Handbook of Structural Techniques in Marriage and Family Therapy*. New York: Brunner/Mazel.

Stuart, R. (1989) *Helping Couples Change*. New York: Guildford Press.

Wachtel, E.F. and Wachtel, P.L. (1986) *Family Dynamics in Individual Psychotherapy: A Guide to Strategies*. New York: Guilford Press.

Wampold, B., Minami, T., Baskin, T. and Callen Tierney, S. (2002) A meta-(re)analysis of the effects of cognitive therapy versus other therapies for depression. *Journal of Affective Disorders*, 68, 159–65.

Wolpe, J. (1969) *The Practice of Behaviour Therapy*, Oxford: Pergamon Press.

CHAPTER 4: EDUCATIONAL PSYCHOLOGY

Andersen, J.R. (2005) *Cognitive Psychology and its Implications*, sixth edition. New York: Worth.

Archives of Disease in Childhood (2004) Blindness in the UK, 2000. *Archives of Disease in Childhood*, 89, 352. Available at: http://adc.bmj.com/cgi/content/full/archdischild%3b89/4/352 (accessed 20 December 2006).

Aronson, E., Bridgeman, D., and Geffner, R. (1978) The effects of cooperative classroom structure on student behaviour and attitudes. In D. Bar Tal and L. Saxe (eds), *Social Psychology of Education*. Washington, D.C.: Hemisphere.

Ashton, R. and Roberts, E. (2006) What is valuable and unique about the educational psychologist? *Educational Psychology in Practice*, 22(2), 111–23.

Bandura, A. (2001) Social cognitive theory: An agentic perspective. *Annual Review of Psychology*, 52, 1–26.

Baron-Cohen, S. (2000) Theory of mind and autism: A 15 year review. In Baron-Cohen, S., Tager-Flusberg, H. and Cohen, D.J. (eds) *Understanding Other Minds*. Oxford: Oxford University Press: 3–22.

Baumrind, D. (1991) The influence of parenting style on adolescent competence and substance use. *Journal of Early Adolescence*, 11, 56–95

Berk, L.E. (2006) *Child Development*, seventh edition. Boston, MA: Allyn & Bacon.

Brophy, J. (2004) *Motivating Students to Learn*, second edition. Boston, MA: McGraw-Hill.

Brouwers, A. and Tomic, W. (2001) The factorial validity of the Teacher Interpersonal Self-efficacy Scale. *Educational and Psychological Measurement*, 61, 433–45.

Bruner, J. (1966) *Toward a Theory of Instruction*. New York: Norton.

Bruning, R.H., Schraw, G.J., Norby, M.M. and Ronning, R.R. (2004) *Cognitive Psychology and Instruction*, fourth edition. Upper Saddle River, NJ: Merrill/Prentice Hall.

Burns, C. (2006) Autism 'rise' – Changes in diagnosis, or something more? *The Psychologist*, 19(9), 517.

Carruthers, P. and Smith, P.K. (1996) *Theories of Theories of Mind*. Cambridge: Cambridge University Press.

Collins, W.A., Maccoby, E.E., Steinberg, L, Hetherington, E.M. and Bornstein, M.H. (2000) Contemporary research on parenting: The case for nature and nurture. *American Psychologist*, 55, 218–232

Contact a Family (2004) *The Contact a Family Directory: Specific conditions, rare disorders and UK family support groups*. London: Contact a Family.

Cowie, H. and Ruddock, J. (1991) *Cooperative Group Work in the Multi-ethnic Classroom*. London: BP Publications.

Crick, N.R., Grotpeter, J.K. and Bigbee, M.A. (2002) Relationally and physically aggressive children's intent attributions and feelings of distress for relational and instructional peer provocation. *Child Development*, 73, 1134–42.

Dapretto, M., Davies, M.S., Pfeifer, J.H., Scott, A.A., Sigman, M., Bookheimer, S.Y. and Iacoboni, M. (2006) Understanding emotions in others: Mirror neuron dysfunction in children with autism spectrum disorders. *Nature Neuroscience*, 9(1), 28–30 (published online 4 December 2005: doi:10.1038/nn1611).

Davenport, G.C. (1994) *An Introduction to Child Development*, second edition. London: Collins Educational.

Denham, A., Hatfield, S., Smethurst, N., Tan, E. and Tribe, C. (2006) The effect of social skills interventions in the primary school. *Educational Psychology in Practice*, 22(1), 33–51.

De Rosnay, M. and Hughes, C. (2006) Conversation and theory of mind: Do children talk their way to socio-cognitive understanding? *British Journal of Developmental Psychology*, 24, 7–37.

DES (1975) *Circular 2/75*. London: HMSO.

Dessent, T. (1978) The historical development of school psychological services. In Gillham, B. *Reconstructing Educational Psychology*. London: CroomHelm.

Dessent, T. (1992) Educational psychologists and 'The Case for Individual Casework'. In Wolfendale, S., Bryans, T., Fox, M., Labram, A. and Sigston, A. *The Profession and Practice of Educational Psychology: Future directions*. London: Cassell Education.

DfES (2000) *Educational Psychology Services (England): Current role, good practice and future directions. The report of the working group*. London: HMSO.

DfES (2003) *Every Child Matters: Change for Children*. London: HMSO.

DfES (2004) *The Children Act*. London: HMSO.

DfES (2006) National Statistics First Release. 18 January. Available at: http://www.dfes.gov.uk/ rsgateway/ (accessed 20 December 2006).

Douglas, J.W.B. (1964) *The Home and the School*. London: MacGibbon and Kay.

East Region SEN Benchmarking (2004) *Regional Partnerships: Who we are and what we do*. Available at: http://www.easttogether.org.uk/pages/viewpage.asp?uniquid=348 (accessed 20 December 2006).

Eggen, P. and Kauchak, D. (2007) *Educational Psychology: Windows on Classrooms*, seventh edition. Upper Saddle River, NJ: Pearson Education.

Elliot, A. and Thrash, T. (2001) Achievement goals and the hierarchical model of achievement motivation. *Educational Psychology Review*, 13, 139–56.

Elliott, C.D., Smith, P. and McCullock, K. (1996) *British Ability Scales*, second edition (BAS-II). London: nferNelson.

Farrell, P., Crutchley, C. and Mills, C. (1999) The educational attainments of pupils with emotional and behavioural difficulties. *British Journal of Special Education*, 26(1), 50–3.

Farrell, P., Woods, K., Lewis, S., Rooney, S., Squires, G. and O'Connor, M. (2006) A review of the functions and contribution of educational psychologists in England and Wales in light of 'Every Child Matters: Change for children'. Research Report RR792. School of Education, University of Manchester.

Fau, X. and Chen, M. (2001) Parental involvement and student's academic achievement: A meta-analysis. *Educational Psychology Review*, 13, 1–22.

Fawcett, L.M. and Garton, A.F. (2005) The effect of peer collaboration on children's problem-solving ability. *British Journal of Educational Psychology*, 75(2), 157–70.

Feinstein, L. and Symons, J. (1999) Attainment in secondary school. *Oxford Economic Papers*, 51, 300–21.

Flavell, J.H. (1985) *Cognitive Development*, second edition. Englewood Cliffs, NJ: Prentice-Hall.

Flouri, E. (2006) Parental interest in children's education, children's self-esteem and locus of control, and later educational attainment: Twenty-six year follow up of the 1970 British Birth Cohort. *British Journal of Educational Psychology*, 76, 41–55.

Flouri, E. and Buchanan, A. (2004) Early father's and mother's involvement and child's later educational outcomes. *British Journal of Educational Psychology*, 74, 141–53.

Fuerstein, R., Rand, Y., Hoffman, M. and Miller, R. (1980) *Universal Enrichment: An intervention program of cognitive modifiability*. Baltimore, MD: University Park Press.

Gillborn, D. and Mirza, H. (2000) *Educational Inequality*. HMI 232.

Gillham, B. (ed.) (1978) *Reconstructing Educational Psychology*. London: CroomHelm.

Good, T. and Brophy, J. (2003) Looking in Classrooms, ninth edition. Boston, MA: Allyn and Bacon.

Gray, C. (2000) *Writing Social Stories with Carol Gray*. Arlington, TX: Future Horizons.

Hardman, M., Drew, C. and Egan, W. (2005) *Human Exceptionality*, eighth edition. Needham Heights, MA: Allyn & Bacon.

Harrop, A. and Swinson, J. (2000) Natural rates of approval and disapproval in British infant, junior and secondary classrooms. *British Journal of Educational Psychology*, 70, 473–83.

Hill, N.E. and Taylor, L.C. (2004) Parental school involvement and children's academic achievement: Pragmatics and issues. *Current Directions in Psychological Science*, 13, 161–4.

Jarvis, M. (2005) *The Psychology of Effective Learning and Teaching*. Cheltenham: Nelson Thornes.

Johnson, D.W. and Johnson, R. (2006) *Learning Together and Alone: Co-operation, competition and individualization*, eighth edition. Needham Heights, MA: Allyn and Bacon.

Johnston, R., Wilson, D. and Burgess, S. (2006) Ethnic segregation and educational performance at secondary schools in Bradford and Leicester. ESRC Working Paper No 06/142. University of Bristol.

Jonasson, D.H. (1991) Objectivism versus constructivism: Do we need a new philosophical paradigm? *Educational Technology Research and Development*, 39(3), 5–14.

Kelly, G.A. (1955) *The Psychology of Personal Constructs*, vols 1 and 2. New York: Norton.

Klahr, D. and Nigram, M. (2004) The equivalence of learning paths in early science instruction. Effects of direct instruction and discovery learning. *Psychological Science*, 15(10), 661–7.

Labram, A. (1992) The educational psychologist as

consultant. In Wolfendale, S., Bryans, T., Fox, M., Labram, A. and Sigston, A. (1992) *The Profession and Practice of Educational Psychology: Future directions.* London: Cassell Education.

Larney, R. (2003) School-based consultation in the United Kingdom. Principles, practice and effectiveness. *School Psychology International*, 4(1), 5–19.

Leadbetter, J. (2006) Investigating and conceptualising the notion of consultation to facilitate multi-agency work. *Educational Psychology in Practice*, 22(1), 19–31.

Leahy, T. and Harris, R. (2001) *Learning and Cognition*, fifth edition. Upper Saddle River, NJ: Merrill/Prentice-Hall.

Levesque, C., Stanek, L., Zuehlke, A.N. and Ryan, R. (2004) Autonomy and competence in German and American university students: A comparative study based on self-determination theory. *Journal of Educational Psychology*, 96(1), 68–84.

Ma, X. (2001) Bullying and being bullied: To what extent are bullies also victims? *American Educational Research Journal*, 38(2), 351–370.

Maughan, A. and Ciccetti, D. (2002) Impact of child maltreatment and interadult violence on children's emotion regulation abilities and socioemotional adjustment. *Child Development*, 73, 1525–42.

McCall, L. and Farrell, P. (1993) The methods used by educational psychologists to assess children with emotional and behavioural difficulties. *Educational Psychology in Practice*, 9(3), 164–9.

National Children's Bureau (2000) *Bullying in Schools*, Highlight no. 174. London: National Children's Bureau.

Newton, C., Taylor, G. and Wilson, D. (1996) Circles of friends: An inclusive approach to meeting emotional and behavioural needs. *Educational Psychology in Practice*, 11(4), 41–8.

NICHCY (National Dissemination Center for Children with Disabilities) (2004) *Visual Impairments*, Fact Sheet 13. Washington, DC: NICHCY. Available at: http://www.nichcy.org/pubs/factshe/fs13txt.htm (accessed 20 December 2006).

Olweus, D. (1993) *Bullying at School: What we know and what we can do*. Oxford: Blackwell.

Perner, J. and Wimmer, H. (1985) 'John thinks that Mary thinks that…': Attribution of second order beliefs by 5–10 year old children. *Journal of Experimental Child Psychology*, 39, 437–71.

Peterson, B. (2003) Cortical abnormalities in children and adolescents with attention-deficit hyperactive disorder. *The Lancet*, 22 November.

Pettibone, T.J. and Jernigan, H.W. (1989) Applied psychology in education. In Gregory, W.L. and Burroughs, W.J. (eds) *Introduction to Applied Psychology*. Glenview, IL: Scott Foresman.

Piaget, J. (1954) *The Construction of Reality in the Child*. New York: Basic Books.

Piaget, J. (1963) *Origins of Intelligence in Children*. New York: Norton.

Rees, C., Farrell, P. and Rees, P. (2003) Coping with complexity: How do psychologists assess students with emotional and behavioural difficulties? *Educational Psychology in Practice*, 19(1), 35–47.

Reynell, J.K. and Gruber, C.P. (1990) *Manual of the Reynell Developmental Language Scales*. Greenville, SC: Super Duper Educational Materials.

Ruffman, T., Slade, L., Devitt, K. and Crowe, E. (2006) What mothers say and what they do: The relation between parenting, theory of mind, language and conflict/cooperation. *British Journal of Developmental Psychology*, 24, 105–24.

Schoon, I., Bynner, J., Joshi, H., Parsons, S., Wiggins, R.D. and Sacker, A. (2002) The influence of context, timing and duration of risk experiences from the passage of childhood to midadulthood. *Child Development*, 73, 1486–504.

Schunk, D. (2004) *Learning Theories: An educational perspective*, fourth edition. Upper Saddle River, NJ: Merrill/Prentice-Hall.

SENCO Week (2006) E-bulletin for SEN professionals, Issue 14, 17 October 2006. Available at: http://www.sen-for-schools.co.uk/backissues/161006.html (accessed 20 December 2006).

Sharp, P. (2001) *Nurturing Emotional Literacy: A practical guide for teachers, parents and those in the caring professions*. London: David Fulton.

Singh, B.R. (1991) Teaching methods for reducing prejudice and enhancing academic achievement for all children. *Educational Studies*, 17(2), 157–71.

Sivan, E. (1986) Motivation in social constructivist theory. *Educational Psychology*, 21(3), 209–33.

Slavin, R.E. (1994) *Educational Psychology: Theory and practice*. Boston, MA: Allyn and Bacon.

Smith, P.K. and Sharp, S. (eds) (1994) *School Bullying: Insights and perspectives*. New York: Routledge.

Steiner, H.H. and Carr, M. (2003) Cognitive development in gifted children: Toward a more precise understanding of emerging differences in intelligence. *Educational Review*, 15, 215–46.

Stipek, D. (2002) *Motivation to Learn*, fourth edition. Boston, MA: Allyn & Bacon.

Stott, D.H. (1987) *The Social Adjustment of Children: Manual to the Bristol Social Adjustment Guides*. London: Hodder & Stoughton.

Tollefson, N. (2000) Classroom applications of cognitive

theories of motivation. *Educational Psychology Review*, 12, 63–83.

Vygotsky, L.S. (1978) *Mind in Society: The development of higher psychological processes*. Cambridge, MA: Harvard University Press.

Vygotsky, L.S. (1986) *Thought and Language*. Cambridge, MA: MIT Press.

Wagner, P. (2000) Consultation: Developing a comprehensive approach to service delivery. *Educational Psychology in Practice*, 16(1), 9–18.

Warnock Report (1978) *Special Educational Needs: Report of the Committee of Enquiry into the Education of Handicapped Children and Young People*. London: HMSO.

Wechsler, D. (1993) *Wechsler Objective Reading Dimensions* (WORD). San Antonio, CA: The Psychological Corporation, Harcourt Assessment, Inc.

Wechsler, D. (1996) *The Wechsler Objective Language Dimensions* (WOLD). San Antonio, CA: The Psychological Corporation, Harcourt Assessment, Inc.

Wechsler, D (2003) *Wechsler Intelligence Scale for Children*, fourth edition (WISC-IV). San Antonio, CA: The Psychological Corporation, Harcourt Assessment, Inc.

Wedge, P. and Essen, J. (1982) *Children in Adversity*. London: Pan.

Weiner, B. (2000) Intrapersonal and interpersonal theories of motivation from an attribution perspective. *Educational Psychology Review*, 12, 1–14.

Weinstein, R. (2002) *Reaching Higher: The power of expectations in schooling*. Cambridge, MA: Harvard University Press.

Wellman, H.M. and Bartsch, K. (1988) Young children's reasoning about beliefs. *Cognition*, 30, 239–77.

Wilson, R. and Branch, R. (2006) *Cognitive Behavioural Therapy for Dummies*. London: Wiley and Sons Ltd.

Wood, D. (1998) *How Children Think and Learn*, second edition. Oxford: Blackwell.

CHAPTER 5: ENVIRONMENTAL PSYCHOLOGY

Altman, I. (1975) *The Environment and Social Behaviour: Privacy, personal space, territoriality and crowding*. Monterey, CA: Brooks/Cole.

Altman, I. and Chemers, M. (1980) *Culture and Environment*. Monterey, CA: Brooks/Cole.

Arnon, S., Shapsa, A., Forman, L., Regev, R., Bauer, S., Litmanovitz, I. and Dolfin, T. (2006) Live music is beneficial to preterm infants in the Neonatal Intensive Care Unit environment. *Birth: Issues in Perinatal Care*, 33(2), 131–6.

Bamberg, S. (2006) Is a residential relocation a good opportunity to change people's travel behaviour? Results from a theory-driven intervention study. *Environment and Behaviour*, 38(6): 820–40.

Barker, R.G. (1968) *Ecological Psychology: Concepts and methods for studying the environment of human behaviour*. Stanford, CA: Stanford University Press.

Barker, R.G. and Wright, H. (1955) *Midwest and its Children*. New York: Row & Petersen.

Baron, R.A. (1972) Aggression as a function of ambient temperature and prior anger arousal. *Journal of Personality and Social Psychology*, 21, 183–9.

Baron, R.A. (1978) Aggression and heat: The 'long hot Summer' revisited. In Baum, A., Valins, S. and Singer, J.E. (eds) *Advances in Environmental Research*, vol. 1. Hillsdale, NJ: Erlbaum: 186–207.

Branthwaite, A. and Trueman, M. (1989) Explaining the effects of unemployment. In Hartley, J. and Branthwaite, A. (eds) *The Applied Psychologist*. Milton Keynes: Open University Press.

Brown, G.W. and Harris, T.O. (1978) *The Bedford College Life Events and Difficulty Schedule: Directory of contextual threat ratings of events*. London: Bedford College, University of London.

Burroughs, W.J. (1989) Applied environmental psychology. In Gregory, W.L. and Burroughs, W.J. (eds) *Introduction to Applied Psychology*. London: Scott, Foresman and Company.

Byerley, W.F., Brown, J. and Lebeque, B. (1987) Treatment of seasonal affective disorder with morning light. *Journal of Clinical Psychiatry*, 48, 447–8.

Calhoun, J.B. (1962) Population density and social pathology. *Scientific American*, 206, 136–48.

Canter, D. (1968) *The Measurement of Meaning in Architecture*. Unpublished manuscript. Glasgow Building Performance Research Unit.

Canter, D. (1969) An intergroup comparison of connotative dimensions. *Environment and Behaviour*, 1, 37–48.

Canter, D. (1983) The purposive evaluation of places: A facet approach. *Environment and Behaviour*, 15, 659–98.

Canter, D. and Thorne, R. (1972) Attitudes to housing: A cross cultural comparison. *Environment and Behaviour*, 4, 3–32.

Cassidy, T. (1997) *Environmental Psychology: Behaviour and experience in context*. Hove: Psychology Press.

Cassidy, T. (1999) *Stress, Cognition and Health*. London: Routledge.

Cialdini, R.B. (1980) Full cycle social psychology. In

Bickman, L. (ed.) *Applied Social Psychology Annual*, vol. 1. Beverly Hills, CA: Sage.

Cohen, D.A., Scott, M., Overton, A., Evenson, K.R., Voorhees, C.C., Bedimo-Rung, A. and McKenzie, T.L. (2006) Proximity to school and physical activity among middle school girls: The Trial of Activity for Adolescent Girls Study. *Journal of Physical Activity and Health*, 3(1), 129–38.

Coolican, H. (2004) *Research Methods and Statistics in Psychology*, fourth edition. London: Hodder & Stoughton.

Davies, D.R., Lang, L. and Shackleton, V.J. (1973) The effect of music and task difficulty on performance of a visual vigilance task. *British Journal of Psychology*, 64, 383–9.

Deisenhammer, E.A. (2003) Weather and suicide: The present state of knowledge on the association of meteorological factors with suicide. *Acta Psychiatrica Scandinavia*, 108, 455–9.

D'Urso, S. (2006) Who's watching us at work? Towards a Structural-Perceptual Model of Electronic Monitoring and Surveillance in Organizations. *Communication Theory*, 16(3), 281–303.

Evans, G.W. (2006) Child development and the physical environment. *Annual Review of Psychology*, 57, 423–51.

Evans, G.W. and Stecker, R. (2004) Motivational consequences of environmental stress. *Journal of Environmental Psychology*, 24(2), 143–65.

French, S.A., Story, M., Fulkerson, J.A. and Hannan, P. (2004) An environmental intervention to promote low-fat food choices in secondary school: Outcomes of the TACOS study. *American Journal of Public Health*, 94(9), 1507–12.

Gaffney, D.A. (2006) The aftermath of disaster: Children in crisis. *Journal of Clinical Psychology*, 62(8), 1001–16.

Galle, O.R., Gove, W.R. and McPherson, J.M. (1972) Population density and pathology: What are the relationships for man? *Science*, 176, 23–30.

Gibson, J.J. (1979) *The Ecological Approach to Visual Perception*. Boston, MA: Houghton Mifflin.

Gifford, R. (1987) *Environmental Psychology: Principles and Practice*. Boston, MA: Allyn and Bacon.

Gist, R. and Lubin, B. (1989) *Psychosocial Aspects of Disasters*. Chichester: Wiley.

Gregory, R.L. (1966) *Eye and Brain*. New York: McGraw-Hill.

Hall, E.T. (1966) *The Hidden Dimension*. Garden City, NY: Doubleday.

Halpern, D. (1995) *Mental Health and the Built Environment*. London: Taylor & Francis.

Hawking, S. (1992) *A Brief History of Time*. Cambridge: Cambridge University Press.

Holmes, T.H. and Rahe, R.H. (1967) The social readjustment rating scale. *Journal of Psychosomatic Research*, 11, 213–18.

Kanner, A.D., Coyne, J.C., Schaefer, C. and Lazarus, R.S. (1981) Comparisons of two modes of stress management: Daily hassles and uplifts versus major life events. *Journal of Behavioural Medicine*, 10, 19–31.

Kaplan, S. and Kaplan, R. (1982) *Cognition and Environment: Functioning in an uncertain world*. New York: Praeger.

Kelly, G.A. (1955) *The Psychology of Personal Constructs*. New York: Norton.

Kimhy, D., Harlap, S., Fennig, S., Deutsch, L., Draiman, B.G., Corcoran, C., Goetz, D., Nahon, D. and Malaspina, D. (2006) Maternal household crowding during pregnancy and the offspring's risk of schizophrenia. *Schizophrenia Research*, 86(1–3), 23–9.

Lee, S.Y. (2005) Effects of control over office workspace on perceptions of the work environment and work outcomes. *Journal of Environmental Psychology*, 25(3), 323–33.

Lee, T. (1976) *Psychology and the Environment*. London: Methuen.

Levy-Leboyer, C. (1982) *Psychology and Environment*. London: Sage.

Lewin, K. (1951) *Field Theory in Social Science*. New York: Harper.

Linley, P.A. and Joseph, S. (2003) Trauma and personal growth. *The Psychologist*, 16(3), 135.

Magnivita, N. (2001) Cacosmia in health workers. *British Journal of Medical Psychology*, 74(1), 121–7.

Maher, A. and von Hippel, C. (2005) Individual differences in employee reactions to open-plan offices. *Journal of Environmental Psychology*, 25(2), 219–29.

McKechnie, G.E. (1974) *ERI Manual: Environmental Response Inventory*. Berkeley, CA: Consulting Psychologists Press.

Mendelson, M.B., Catano, V.M. and Kelloway, K. (2000) The role of stress and social support in Sick Building Syndrome. *Work and Stress*, 14(2), 137–55.

Midveit, E. (2005) Crime prevention and exclusion: From walls to opera music. *Journal of Scandinavian Studies in Criminology and Crime Prevention*, 6(1), 23–38.

Milfont, T.L. and Duckitt, J. (2006) A cross-cultural study of environmental motive concerns and their implications for proenvironmental behaviour. *Environment and Behaviour*, 38(6): 745–67.

Murray, H.A. (1938) *Explorations in Personality*. New York: Oxford University Press.

Neisser, U. (1976) *Cognition and Reality: Principles and Implications of Cognitive Psychology*. San Francisco, CA: W.H. Freeman.

Newman, O. (1972) *Defensible Space*. New York: Macmillan.

Parker, C., Barnes, S., McKee, K., Morgan, K., Torrington, J. and Tragenza, P. (2004) Quality of life and building design in residential and nursing homes for older people. *Ageing & Society*, 24(6), 941–62.

Proshansky, H.M., Ittelson, W.H. and Rivlin, L.G. (eds) (1976) *Environmental Psychology*, second edition. New York: Holt, Rinehart and Winston.

Robinson, M.B. (2000) From research to policy: Preventing residential burglary through a systems approach. *American Journal of Criminal Justice*, 24, 169–79.

Rosen, S. (1985) The weather: Windy and grouchy. *The Catholic Digest*, 94–7.

Rotton, J. (1990) Stress. In Kimble, C.E. *Social Psychology*. Iowa: W.C. Brown.

Runeson, R. and Norback, D. (2005) Associations among sick building syndrome, psychosocial factors and personality traits. *Perceptual and Motor Skills*, 100(3), 747–59.

Salame, P. and Baddeley, A.D. (1989) Effects of background music on phonological short-term memory. *Quarterly Journal of Experimental Psychology*, 41, 107–22.

Seligman, M.E.P. (1975) *Helplessness: On depression, development and death*. San Francisco, CA: W.H. Freeman.

Sloan, D.M. (2002) Does warm weather climate affect eating disorder pathology? *International Journal of Eating Disorders*, 32(2), 240–4.

Stansfield, S.A., Berglund, B., Clark, C., Lopez-Barrio, I., Fischer, P., Ohrstrom, E., Haines, M.M., Head, J., Hygge, S., van Kamp, I. and Berry, B.F. (2005) Aircraft and road traffic noise and children's cognition and health: A cross-national study. *Lancet*, 365(9475), 1942–9.

Stokols, D. (1972) On the distinction between density and crowding: Some implications for future research. *Psychological Review*, 79, 275–7.

Thogersen, J. and Olander, F. (2006) To what degree are environmentally beneficial choices reflective of a general conservation stance? *Environment and Behaviour*, 38(4): 550–69.

Timperio, A., Ball, K., Salmon, J., Roberts, R., Giles-Cort, B., Simmons, D., Baur, L.A. and Crawford, D. (2006) Personal, family, social, and environmental correlates of active commuting to school. *American Journal of Preventive Medicine*, 30(1), 45–51.

Turnbull, C. (1961) Some observations regarding the experiences of the Bambuti pygmies. *American Journal of Psychology*, 74, 304–8.

Veitch, R. and Arrkelin, D. (1995) *Environmental Psychology: An interdisciplinary perspective*. Englewood Cliffs, NJ: Prentice Hall.

Warr, P. (1987) Job characteristics and mental health. In Warr, P. (ed.) *Psychology at Work*, third edition. Harmondsworth: Penguin.

Wertheimer, M. (1944) *Productive Thinking*. New York: Harper.

Williams, R. (2006) The psychosocial consequences for children and young people who are exposed to terrorism, war, conflict and natural disasters. *Current Opinion in Psychiatry*, 19(4), 337–49.

CHAPTER 6: FORENSIC PSYCHOLOGY

Abwender, D.A. and Hough, K. (2001) Interactive effects of characteristics of defendant and mock juror on US participants' judgement and sentencing recommendations. *Journal of Social Psychology*, 141(5), 603–15.

Ainsworth, P.B. (1981) Incident perception by British police officers. *Law and Human Behavior*, 5, 231–6.

Ainsworth, P.B. (2001) *Offender Profiling and Crime Analysis*. Cullompton: Willan Publishing.

Alison, L.J. (2005) *The Forensic Psychologist's Casebook: Psychological profiling and criminal investigation*. Cullompton: Willan Publishing.

Alison, L.J. and Barrett, E.C. (2004) The interpretation and utilisation of offender profiles: A critical review of 'traditional' approaches to profiling. In Adler, J. (ed.) *Forensic Psychology: Concepts, debates and practice*. Cullompton: Willan Publishing.

Alison, L.J., West, A. and Morgan, K. (2003) Interpreting the accuracy of offender profiles. *Psychology, Crime and Law*, 9(2), 185–95.

Allport, G.W. and Postman, L. (1947) *The Psychology of Rumor*. New York: Henry Holt.

Bamfield, J. (2005) *Female Offenders*. Centre for Retail Research. Available at http://www.retailresearch.org/crime_and_fraud/female_offenders.php (accessed 20 December 2006).

Barclay, C.D., Cutting, J.E. and Kozlowski, L.T. (1978) Temporal and spatial factors in gait perceptions that influence gait recognition. *Perception and Psychophysics*, 23, 145–52.

Bartlett, F. (1932) *Remembering: A study in experimental and social psychology*. Cambridge: Cambridge University Press.

Blackburn, R. (2000) Risk assessment and prediction. In

McGuire, J., Mason, T. and O'Kane, A. (eds) *Behaviour, Crime and Legal Processes*. Chichester: Wiley.

Bornstein, B.H. (1995) Memory processes in elderly eyewitnesses: What we know and what we don't know. *Behavioral Sciences and the Law*, 13, 337–48.

Bothwell, R.K., Brigham, J.C. and Pigot, M.A. (1987) An exploratory study of personality differences in eyewitness memory. *Journal of Social Behaviour and Personality*, 2, 335–43.

Brown, R. and Kulik, J. (1977) Flashbulb memories. *Cognition*, 5, 73–93.

Bruck, M. and Ceci, S.J. (1999) The suggestibility of children's memory. *Annual Review of Psychology*, 50, 419–39.

Buckhout, R. (1974) Eyewitness testimony. *Scientific American*, 231, 23–31.

Bull, R. and Green, J. (1980) The relationship between physical appearance and criminality. *Medicine, Science and the Law*, 20, 79–83.

Campbell, C. (1976) Portrait of a mass killer. *Psychology Today*, 9, 110–19.

Canter, D. (1994) *Criminal Shadows*. London: HarperCollins.

Canter, D. (2000) Offender profiling and criminal differentiation. *Legal and Criminological Psychology*, 5(1), 23–46.

Canter, D. (2004) Offender profiling and investigative psychology. *Journal of Investigative Psychology and Offender Profiling*, 1, 1–15.

Canter, D. and Alison, L.J. (1999) *Profiling in Policy and Practice*. Aldershot: Ashgate.

Canter, D. and Youngs, D. (2003) Beyond offender profiling: The need for an investigative psychology. In Carson, D. and Bull, R. (eds) *Handbook of Psychology in Legal Contexts*. Chichester: Wiley.

Christiansen, R.E., Sweeney, J.D. and Ochalek, K. (1983) Influencing eyewitness descriptions. *Law and Human Behavior*, 7, 59–65.

Christianson, S.A. (1992) Emotional stress and eyewitness memory: A critical review. *Psychological Bulletin*, 112, 284–309.

Christianson, S.A., Karlsson, I. and Persson, L.G.W. (1998) Police personnel as eyewitnesses to a violent crime. *Legal and Criminological Psychology*, 3, 59–72.

Craik, F.I. M. (1977) Age differences in human memory. In Birren, J.E. and Schaie, K.W. (eds) *Handbook of the Psychology of Aging*. New York: Van Nostrand Reinhold.

Crighton, D. (2006) Methodological issues in psychological research in prisons. In Towl, G. (ed.) *Psychological Research in Prisons*. Oxford: Blackwell.

Crombag, H.E.M., Wagenaar, W.A. and Van Koppen, P.J. (1996) Crashing memories and the problem of 'source monitoring'. *Applied Cognitive Psychology*, 10, 95–104.

Cutler, B.L. and Penrod, S.D. (1988) Improving the reliability of eyewitness identification: Lineup construction and presentation. *Journal of Applied Psychology*, 73, 281–90.

Cutler, B.L. and Penrod, S.D. (1995) *Mistaken Identification: The eyewitness, psychology and the law*. Cambridge: Cambridge University Press.

Davies, A. (1997) Specific profile analysis: A data-based approach to offender profiling. In Jackson, J.L. and Bekerian, D.A. (eds) *Offender Profiling: Theory, research and practice*. Chichester: Wiley.

Davies, G. and Noon, E. (1991) *An Evaluation of the Live Link for Child Witnesses*. London: Home Office.

Davies, J. (2005) *DFP Membership Survey 2004*. Leicester: British Psychological Society.

Dernevik, M., Johansson, S. and Grann, M. (2000) Prediction of violent behaviour in mentally disordered offenders in forensic psychiatric care. Paper presented at European Association of Psychology and Law Conference, Cyprus.

DeSantis, A. and Kayson, W. (1997) Defendants' characteristics of attractiveness, race and sex on sentencing decisions. *Psychological Reports*, 81(2), 679–83.

Devonport, J.L., Studebaker, C.A. and Penrod, S.D. (1999) Perspectives on jury decision-making: Cases with pre-trial publicity and cases based on eyewitness identifications. In Durso, F.T. (ed.) *Handbook of Applied Cognition*. New York: Wiley.

Diges, M., Rubio, M.E. and Rodriguez, M.C. (1992) Eyewitness memory and time of day. In Losel, F., Bender, D. and Bliesenerm, T. (eds) *Psychology and Law: International perspectives*. New York: Walter de Gruyter.

Dion, K., Berscheid, E. and Walster, E. (1972) What is beautiful is good. *Journal of Personality and Social Psychology*, 24(3), 285–90.

Dixon, M., Reed, H., Rogers, B. and Stone, L. (2006) *Crimeshare: The unequal impact of crime*. London: Institute for Public Policy Research.

Douglas, J.E., Burgess, A.W., Burgess, A.G. and Ressler, R.K. (1992) *Crime Classification Manual*. New York: Lexington.

Dunning, D., Li, J. and Malpass, R. (1998) Basketball fandom and cross-race identification among European Americans: Another look at the contact hypothesis. Paper presented at the American Psychology and Law Society Biennial Conference, Relondo Beach, California. Cited by Memon, A. and Wright, D.B. (2000) Factors influencing witness evidence. In McGuire, J., Mason, T. and O'Kane, A. (eds) *Behaviour, Crime and Legal Processes: A guide for forensic practitioners.* Chichester: Wiley.

Dunning, D. and Perretta, S. (2002) Automaticity and eyewitness accuracy: A 10- to 12-second rule for distinguishing accurate from inaccurate positive identifications. *Journal of Applied Psychology,* 87, 818–35.

Ellsworth, P.C. (1993) Some steps between attitudes and verdicts. In Hastie, R. (ed.) *Inside the Juror: The psychology of juror decision making.* Cambridge: Cambridge University Press.

Ellsworth, P.C. and Mauro, R. (1998) Psychology and law. In Gilbert, D., Fiske, S. and Lindzey, G. (eds) *The Handbook of Social Psychology.* Chicago, IL: McGraw-Hill.

Eysenck, H.J. (1964) *Crime and Personality.* London: Routledge and Kegan Paul.

Farrell, G. and Pease, K. (1993) *Once Bitten, Twice Bitten.* Crime Prevention Unit Paper 46. London: HMSO.

Farrall, S. and Gadd, D. (2004) The frequency of fear of crime. *British Journal of Criminology,* 44, 127–32.

Fein, S., Morgan, S.J., Norton, M.I. and Summers, S.R. (1997) Hype and suspicion: The effects of pre-trial publicity, race, and suspicion on jurors' verdicts. *Journal of Social Issues,* 53(3), 487–502.

Feingold, A. (1992) Good-looking people are not what you think. *Psychological Bulletin,* 111(2), 304–41.

Felson, M. (2002) *Crime and Everyday Life,* third edition. Thousand Oaks, CA: Sage.

Festinger, L. (1957) *A Theory of Cognitive Dissonance.* Stanford, CA: Stanford University Press.

Finch, E. and Munro, V.E. (2005) Juror stereotypes and blame attribution in rape cases involving intoxicants. *British Journal of Criminology,* 45, 25–38.

Flin, R.H. and Shepherd, J.W. (1986) Tall stories: Eyewitnesses' ability to estimate height and weight characteristics. *Human Learning,* 5, 29–38.

Flood-Page, C., Campbell, S., Harrington, V. and Miller, J. (2000) *Youth Crime – Findings from the 1998–99 Youth Lifestyles Survey.* Home Office Research Study 209. London: HMSO.

Friedman, W.J. (1993) Memory for time of past events. *Psychological Bulletin,* 113, 44–66.

Furnham, A. (2003) Belief in a just world: Research progress over the past decade. *Personality and Individual Differences,* 34(5), 795–817.

Garland, D. (1994) The development of British criminology. In Maguire, M., Morgan, R. and Reiner, R. (eds) *The Oxford Handbook of Criminology.* Oxford: Clarendon Press.

Garrison, A. (2000) Rape Trauma Syndrome: A review of the behavioural science theory and its admissibility in criminal trials. *American Journal of Trial Advocacy,* 23, 591.

Gieselman, R.E., Fisher R.P., Firstenberg, I., Hutton, L.A., Sullivan, S., Avetissian, I. and Prosket, A. (1984) Enhancement of eyewitness memory: An empirical evaluation of the cognitive interview. *Journal of Police Science and Administration,* 12, 74–80.

Godwin, M. (2000) Geographic profiling. In Godwin, M. (ed.) *Criminal Psychology and Forensic Technology.* Boca Raton, FL: CRC Press.

Golding, J.M., Fryman, H.M., Marsil, D.F. and Yozwiak, J.A. (2003) Big girls don't cry: The effect of child witness demeanour on juror decisions in a child abuse trial. *Child Abuse and Neglect,* 27, 1311–21.

Gretenkord, L. (2000) How to use empirical findings for the prognosis of mentally disordered offenders. Paper presented at the 10th European Conference of Psychology and Law, Limassol, Cyprus. Cited in Howitt, D. (2005) *Introduction to Forensic and Criminal Psychology.* Harlow: Pearson.

Gudjonsson, G.H. (1992) *The Psychology of Interrogations, Confessions and Testimony.* Chichester: Wiley.

Gudjonsson, G.H. and Copson, G. (1997) The role of the expert in criminal investigation. In Jackson, J.L. and Bekerian, D.A. (eds) *Offender Profiling: Theory, research and practice.* Chichester: Wiley.

Haegerich, T.M. and Bottoms, B.L. (2000) Empathy and jurors' decisions in patricide trials involving sexual assault allegations. *Law and Human Behavior,* 24(4), 421–48.

Hastie, R. (ed.) (1993) *Inside the Juror: The psychology of juror decision making.* Cambridge: Cambridge University Press.

Hastie, R., Penrod, S.D. and Pennington, N. (1983) *Inside the Jury.* Cambridge, MA: Harvard University Press.

Hogg, G. and Vaughn, M.A. (2002) *Social Psychology.* London: Sage.

Hope, L., Memon, A. and McGeorge, G. (2004) Understanding pre-trial publicity. *Journal of Experimental Psychology,* 10(2), 111–19.

Howard, P. (2006) *The Offender Assessment System: An evaluation of the second pilot.* Home Office Findings

278. London: HMSO. Available at http://www.homeoffice.gov.uk/rds/pdfs06/r278.pdf (accessed 20 December 2006).

Jackson, J.L. and Bekerian, D.A. (eds) (1997) *Offender Profiling: Theory, research and practice.* Chichester: Wiley.

Kalven, H. and Zeisel, H. (1966) *The American Jury.* Chicago, IL: University of Chicago Press.

Kapardis, A. (2003) *Psychology and the Law: A critical introduction.* Cambridge: Cambridge University Press.

Kassin, S.M. (1998) Eyewitness identification procedures: The fifth rule. *Law and Human Behavior,* 22, 649–53.

Kebbell, M.R. and Milne, R. (1998) Police officers' perceptions of eyewitness performance in forensic investigations. *Journal of Social Psychology,* 138(3), 115–29.

Kebbell, M.R., Wagstaff, G.G. and Covey, J.A. (1996) The influence of item difficulty on the relationship between eyewitness confidence and accuracy. *British Journal of Psychology,* 87, 653–62.

Kelly, L., Temkin, J. and Griffiths, S. (2006) *Section 41: An evaluation of new legislation limiting sexual history evidence in rape trials.* Home Office Online Report 20/06. London: HMSO.

Kemshall, H. (2001) *Risk Assessment and Management of Known Sexual and Violent Offenders: A review of current issues.* Police Research Series Paper 140. London: Home Office.

Kocsis, R.N., Cooksey, R.W. and Irwin, H.J. (2002) Psychological profiling of sexual murders: An empirical model. *International Journal of Offender Therapy and Comparative Criminology,* 46(5), 532–54.

Konecni, V.J., Ebbeson, E.B. and Nehrer, E. (2000) Retrospective implications for the probative value of psychologists' testimony on eyewitness issues of exonerations by DNA evidence. In Czerederecka, A., Jaskiewicz-Obdzinska, T. and Wojcikiewicz, J. (eds) *Forensic Psychology and Law: Traditional questions and new ideas.* Krakow: Institute of Forensic Research Publishers.

Kovera, M.B. (2002) The effects of general pre-trial publicity on juror decisions. *Law and Human Behavior,* 26(1), 43–72.

Langlois, J., Kalakanis, L., Rubenstein, A., Larson, A., Hallam, M. and Smoot, M. (2000) Maxims or myths of beauty: A meta-analytic and theoretical review. *Psychological Bulletin,* 126(3), 390–423.

Leichtman, D. and Ceci, S.J. (1995) The effects of stereotypes and suggestions on pre-schoolers' reports. *Developmental Psychology,* 31, 568–78.

Lerner, M.J. (1965) Evaluation of performance as a function of performer's reward and attractiveness. *Journal of Personality and Social Psychology,* 1, 355–60.

Lerner, M.J. and Miller, D.T. (1978) Just world research and the attribution process: Looking back and ahead. *Psychological Bulletin,* 85, 1030–51.

Lerner, M.J. and Simmons, C.H. (1966) The observer's reaction to an innocent victim: Compassion or rejection? *Journal of Personality and Social Psychology,* 4, 203–10.

Levine, J.P. (1992) *Juries and Politics.* Pacific Grove, CA: Brooks/Cole Publishing Company.

Levine, J.P. and Tapp, J. (1971) The psychology of criminal identification: The gap from Wade to Kirby. *University of Pennsylvania Law Review,* 121, 1079–132.

Lieppe, M.R. (1994) The appraisal of eyewitness testimony. In Ross, D.F., Read, J.D. and Toglia, M.P. (eds) *Adult Eyewitness Testimony: Current trends and developments.* Cambridge: Cambridge University Press.

Light, L.H. (1991) Memory and aging: Four hypotheses in search of data. *Annual Review of Psychology,* 42, 333–76.

Loftus, E.F. (1979) *Eyewitness Testimony.* Cambridge, MA: Harvard University Press.

Loftus, E.F. (1993) The reality of repressed memories. *American Psychologist,* 48, 517–37.

Loftus, E.F. (2003) Our changeable memories: Legal and practical implications. *Nature,* 46, 231–4.

Loftus, E.F. and Guyer, M. (2002) Who abused Jane Doe? *The Skeptical Inquirer,* 26(3), 24–32. Available at http://faculty.washington.edu/eloftus/Articles/JaneDoe.htm (accessed 20 December 2006).

Loftus, E.F., Loftus, G.R. and Messo, J. (1987) Some facts about 'weapon focus'. *Law and Human Behavior,* 11, 55–62.

Loftus, E.F. and Palmer, J.C. (1974) Reconstruction of automobile destruction: An example of the interaction between language and memory. *Journal of Verbal Learning and Verbal Behavior,* 13, 565–89.

Lombroso, C. (1911) *Crime, its Causes and Remedies.* Boston, MA: Little, Brown.

Lonsway, K. (2005) The use of expert witnesses in cases involving sexual assault. Violence Against Women Online Resources. Available at http://www.mincava.umn.edu/documents/commissioned/svandexpert witnesses/svandexpertwitnesses.html (accessed 20 December 2006).

Maass, A. and Kohnken, G. (1989) Eyewitness identification: Simulating the 'weapon effect'. *Law and Human Behavior,* 13, 397–408.

MacLeod, M.D., Frowley, J.N. and Shepherd, J.W. (1994) Whole body information: Its relevance to eyewitnesses. In Ross, D.F., Read, J.D. and Toglia, M.P. (eds) *Adult Eyewitness Testimony: Current trends and developments.* Cambridge: Cambridge University Press.

Matthews, R., Hancock, L. and Briggs, D. (2004) *Jurors' Perceptions, Understanding, Confidence and Satisfaction in the Jury System: A study of six courts.* Home Office Research Findings 227. London: HMSO.

Mauet, T.A. and McCrimmon, L.A. (1993) *Fundamentals of Trial Techniques.* Melbourne: Longman.

McGuire, J., Mason, T. and O'Kane, A. (eds) (2000) *Behaviour, Crime and Legal Processes: A guide for forensic practitioners.* Chichester: Wiley.

Memon, A. and Higham, P. (2000) A review of the cognitive interview. *Psychology, Crime and Law*, 5, 177–96.

Memon, A. and Wright, D.B. (1999) Factors influencing witness evidence. In McGuire, J., Mason, T. and O'Kane, A. (eds) *Behaviour, Crime and Legal Processes.* Chichester: Wiley.

Mirrlees-Black, C. and Budd, T. (1997) *Policing and the Public: Findings from the 1996 British Crime Survey.* London: HMSO.

Muller, D. (2000) Criminal profiling: Real science or just wishful thinking? *Homicide Studies*, 4(3), 234–64.

Murray, J.D., Spadafore, J.A. and McIntosh, W.D. (2005) Belief in a just world and social perception: Evidence for automatic activation. *Journal of Social Psychology*, 145(1), 35–47.

Neisser, U. and Harsch, N. (1992) Phantom flashbulbs: False recollections of hearing the news about Challenger. In Winograd, E. and Neisser, U. (eds) *Affect and Accuracy in Recall: Studies of flashbulb memories.* Cambridge: Cambridge University Press.

Office for Criminal Justice Reform Consultation Paper (2006) *Convicting Rapists and Protecting Victims – Justice for victims of rape.* London: Home Office.

Orcutt, H.K., Goodman, G.S., Tobey, A.E., Batterman-Faunce, J.M. and Thomas, S. (2001) Detecting deception in children's testimony: Factfinders' abilities to reach the truth in open court and closed-circuit trials. *Law and Human Behavior*, 24(4), 339–72.

Peelo, M., Francis, B., Soothill, K., Pearson, J. and Ackerley, E. (2004) Newspaper reporting and the public construction of homicide. *British Journal of Criminology*, 44, 256–75.

Pennington, N. and Hastie, R. (1990) Practical implications of psychological research on juror and jury decision-making. *Personality and Social Psychology Bulletin*, 16(1), 90–105.

Penrod, S.D. (2003) Eyewitness identification evidence: How well are witnesses and police performing? *Criminal Justice Magazine*, Spring, 36–47, 54.

Penrod, S., Solomon, M., Fulero, J.D. and Cutler, B.L. (1995) Expert psychological testimony on eyewitness reliability before and after *Daubert*: The state of the law and science. *Behavioral Sciences and the Law*, 13, 229–59.

The Portman Group Quarterly Review of Alcohol Research (2005) Winter, 13(4). Available at http://www.portmangroup.org.uk (accessed 20 December 2006).

Prime, J., White, S., Liriano, S. and Patel, K. (2001) Criminal careers of those born between 1953 and 1978. *Statistical Bulletin* 4/01. London: HMSO.

Rhodes, G. and Zebrowitz, L. (2002) *Facial Attractiveness: Evolutionary, cognitive and social perspectives.* London: Ablex Publishing.

Rose, D. (2006) Crime rates soar as criminals walk free. *The Observer*, 28 May.

Sandys, M. and Dillehay, R.C. (1995) First ballot votes, predeliberation dispositions, and final verdicts in jury trials. *Law and Human Behavior*, 19, 175–95.

Sarason, I. and Stroops, R. (1978) Test anxiety and the passage of time. *Journal of Consulting and Clinical Psychology*, 70, 1103–39.

Scheck, B., Neufeld, P. and Dwyer, J. (2000) *Actual Innocence.* New York: Random House.

Schill, T. (1966) Effects of approval motivation and varying conditions of verbal reinforcement on incidental memory for faces. *Psychological Reports*, 19, 55–60.

Smart Justice (2006) *Victims of Crime Survey.* Available at http://www.smartjustice.org/pressfullvictimsurvey.shtml (accessed 20 December 2006).

Statistics Commission (2006) *Crime Statistics: User perspectives.* Report no. 30. Available at http://www.statscom.org.uk (accessed 20 December 2006).

Steblay, N.M. (1992) A meta-analytic review of the weapon focus effect. *Law and Human Behavior*, 16, 413–24.

Steblay, N.M., Dysart, J., Fulero, S. and Lindsay, R.C.L. (2003) Eyewitness accuracy rates in police show-up and line-up presentations: A meta-analytic comparison. *Law and Human Behavior*, 27(5), 523–40.

Steele, C.M. and Josephs, R.A. (1990) Alcohol myopia:

Its prized and dangerous effects. *American Psychologist*, 45, 921–33.

Stephenson, G.M. (1992) *The Psychology of Criminal Justice*. Oxford: Blackwell.

Stern, L.B. and Dunning, D. (1994) Distinguishing accurate from inaccurate eyewitness identifications: A reality monitoring approach. In Ross, D.F., Read, J.D. and Toglia, M.P. (eds) *Adult Eyewitness Testimony: Current trends and developments*. Cambridge: Cambridge University Press.

Sternberg, K., Lamb, M., Orbach, Y., Esplin, P. and Mitchell, S. (2001) Use of a structured investigative protocol enhances young children's responses to free-recall prompts in the course of forensic interviews. *Journal of Applied Psychology*, 86(5), 997–1005.

Stewart, J. (1980) Defendants' attractiveness as a factor in the outcome of criminal trials: An observational study. *Journal of Applied Social Psychology*, 10(4), 348–61.

Temkin, J. (2000) Prosecuting and defending rape: Perspectives from the bar. *Journal of Law and Society*, 27, 219–35.

Thomas-Peter, B. (2006) The modern context of psychology in corrections: Influences, limitations and values of 'what works'. In Towl, G. (ed.) *Psychological Research in Prisons*. Oxford: Blackwell.

Thomson, D.N. (1995) Eyewitness testimony and identification tests. In Brewer, S. and Wilson, C. (eds) *Psychology and Policing*. Hillsdale, NJ: Erlbaum.

Tinsley, Y. (2001) *Juror Decision-making: A look inside the jury room*. Selected Proceedings (Volume 4) from the British Society of Criminology, July 2000, University of Leicester.

Towl, G. (ed.) (2006) *Psychological Research in Prisons*. Oxford: Blackwell.

Van Koppen, P.J. and Lochun, S.K. (1997) Portraying perpetrators: The validity of offender descriptions of witnesses. *Law and Human Behavior*, 21, 661–85.

Walker, A., Kershaw, C., and Nicholas, S. (2006) *Crime in England and Wales 2005–06*. London: HMSO.

Weaver, C.A. (1993) Do you need a 'flash' to form a flashbulb memory? *Journal of Experimental Psychology: General*, 122, 39–46.

Wells, G.L. (1993) What do we know about eyewitness identification? *American Psychologist*, 48, 553–71.

Wells, G.L. and Olson, E.A. (2003) Eyewitness testimony. *Annual Review of Psychology*, 54, 277–95.

Wells, G.L., Small, M., Penrod, S., Malpass, R., Fulero, S.M. and Brimacombe, C.A.E. (1998) Eyewitness identification procedures: Recommendations for line-ups and photospreads. *Law and Human Behavior*, 22, 603–47.

Westcott, H. and Davies, G.M. (2002) *Children's Testimony: A handbook of psychological research and forensic practice*. Chichester: Wiley.

Westcott, H. and Kynan, S. (2006) Interviewer practice in investigative interviews involving suspected child sexual abuse. *Psychology, Crime and Law*, 12(4), 367–82.

Williams, K.D., Loftus, E.F. and Deffenbacher, K.A. (1992) Eyewitness evidence and testimony. In Kagehiro, D.K. and Laufer, W.S. (eds) *Handbook of Psychology and Law*. New York: Springer.

Wogalter, M.S., Malpass, R.S. and McQuiston, D.E. (2004) A national survey of US police on preparation and conduct of identification line-ups. *Psychology, Crime and Law*, 10(1), 69–82.

Wright, D.B. (1993) Recall of the Hillsborough disaster over time: Systematic biases of 'flashbulb' memories. *Applied Cognitive Psychology*, 7, 129–38.

Wright, D.B. and McDaid, A.T. (1996) Comparing system and estimator variables using data from real line-ups. *Applied Cognitive Psychology*, 10, 75–84.

Yarmey, A.D. (1986) Verbal, visual and voice identification of a rape suspect under different conditions of illumination. *Journal of Applied Psychology*, 71, 363–70.

Yuille, J.C. and Cutshall, J.L. (1989) Analysis of the statements of victims, witnesses and suspects. In Yuille, J.C. (ed.) *Credibility Assessment*. Holland: Kluwer.

CHAPTER 7: HEALTH PSYCHOLOGY

Abraham, C. and Michie, S. (2005) Towards a healthier nation. *The Psychologist*, 18(11), 670–1.

Abraham, C. and Sheeran, P. (2005) The health belief model. In Conner, M. and Norman, P. (eds) *Predicting Health Behaviour*, second edition. Maidenhead, UK: Open University Press: 28–80.

Ajzen, I. (1991) The theory of planned behavior. *Organizational Behavior and Human Decision Processes*, 50, 179–211.

Armitage, C.J. and Conner, M. (2001) Efficacy of the theory of planned behaviour: A meta-analytic review. *British Journal of Social Psychology*, 40(4), 471–99.

Baile, W.F., Buckman, R., Lenzi, R., Glober, G., Beale, E.A. and Kudelka, A.P. (2000) SPIKES – A six-step protocol for delivering bad news: Application to the patient with cancer. *The Oncologist*, 5(4), 302–11.

Barlow, J.H., Wright, C.C., Turner, A.P. and Bancroft,

G.V. (2005) A 12-month follow-up study of self-management training for people with chronic disease: Are changes maintained over time? *British Journal of Health Psychology*, 10(4), 589–99.

Bartholomew, L.K., Parcel, G., Kok, G. and Gottlieb, N.H. (2006) *Planning Health Promotion Programs: Intervention mapping*, second edition. New York: Jossey Bass Wiley.

Becker, M.H. (1974) The health belief model and personal health behavior. *Health Education Monographs*, 2, 324–508.

Belloc, N.B. and Breslow, L. (1972) Relationship of physical health status and health practices. *Preventative Medicine*, 1, 409–21.

Benson, J. and Britten, N. (1996) Respecting the autonomy of cancer patients when talking with their families: Qualitative analysis of semistructured interviews with patients. *British Medical Journal*, 313, 729–31.

Berkman, L.F. and Syme, S.L. (1979) Social networks, host resistance, and mortality: A nine-year follow-up study of Alameda County residents. *American Journal of Epidemiology*, 109(2), 186–204.

Breslow, L. (1998) Musings on sixty years in public health. *Annual Review of Public Health*, 19, 1–15.

Bridle, C., Riemsma, R.P., Pattenden, J., Sowden, A.J., Mather, L., Watt, L.S. and Walker, A. (2005) Systematic review of the effectiveness of health behavior interventions based on the transtheoretical model. *Psychology and Health*, 20(3), 283–301.

Brown, G.W. and Harris, T. (1978) *Social Origins of Depression: A study of psychiatric disorder in women*. New York: Free Press.

Cannon, W.B. (1932) *The Wisdom of the Body*. New York: Norton.

Carroll, D., Ebrahim, S., Tilling, K., Macleod, J. and Smith, G.D. (2002) Admissions for myocardial infarction and World Cup football: Database survey. *British Medical Journal*, 325(7378), 1439–42.

Carver, C.S., Scheier, M.F. and Weintraub, J.K. (1989) Assessing coping strategies: A theoretically based approach. *Journal of Personality and Social Psychology*, 56, 267–83.

Checkley, S. (1996) The neuroendocrinology of depression. *International Review of Psychiatry*, 8(4), 373–8.

Clafferty, R.A., Brown, K.W. and McCabe, E. (1998) Under half of psychiatrists tell patients their diagnosis of Alzheimer's disease. *British Medical Journal*, 317, 603.

Clafferty, R.A., McCabe, E., Brown, K.W. and Fisher, M. (2000) Telling patients with schizophrenia their diagnosis. *British Medical Journal*, 321, 384.

Clark, A. (2004). Want to feel less stress? Become a fighter pilot, not a commuter. *The Guardian*, 30 November.

Cohen, S., Kamarck, T. and Mermelstein, R. (1983) A global measure of perceived stress. *Journal of Health and Social Behavior*, 24, 385–96.

Cohen, S., Tyrrell, D.A.J. and Smith, A.P. (1991) Negative life events, perceived stress, negative affect and susceptibility to the common cold. *Journal of Personality and Social Psychology*, 64, 131–40.

Conner, M. and Sparks, P. (2005) The theory of planned behaviour and health behaviour. In Conner, M. and Norman, P. (eds) *Predicting Health Behaviour*, second edition. Maidenhead, UK: Open University Press: 223–75.

Department of Health (1999) *Saving Lives: Our healthier nation*. London: The Stationery Office.

Department of Health (2001) *The Expert Patient: A new approach to chronic disease management for the 21st century*. London: The Stationery Office.

DHP (British Psychological Society, Division of Health Psychology) (2006) *A Survey of the Diversity and Variability of Employment of Health Psychologists in the UK*. Available at http://www.health-psychology.org.uk/downloads/Survey_of_the_employment_of_health_psychologists_-_summary.pdf (accessed 20 December 2006).

Doll, R. and Hill, A.B. (1950) Smoking and carcinoma of the lung: Preliminary report. *British Medical Journal*, 2(4682), 739–48.

Doll, R., Peto, R., Boreham, J. and Sutherland, I. (2004) Mortality in relation to smoking: 50 years' observations on male British doctors. *British Medical Journal*, 328(7455), 1519–28.

Engel, G.L. (1977) The need for a new medical model: A challenge for biomedicine. *Science*, 196(4286), 129–36.

Finlay, I. and Dallimore, D. (1991) Your child is dead. *British Medical Journal*, 302(6791), 1524–5.

Forouhi, N.G. and Sattar, N. (2006) CVD risk factors and ethnicity – A homogenous relationship? *Atherosclerosis Supplements*, 7(1), 11–19.

Glaser, R. (2005) Stress-associated immune dysregulation and its importance for human health: A personal history of psychoneuroimmunology. *Brain, Behavior, and Immunity*, 19(1), 3–11.

Gollwitzer, P.M. and Schaal, B. (1998) Metacognition in action: The importance of implementation intentions. *Personality and Social Psychology Review*, 2(2), 124–36.

Hagger, M.S. and Orbell, S. (2003) A meta-analytic review of the common-sense model of illness representations. *Psychology and Health*, 18(2), 141–84.

Hawe, P., McKenzie, N. and Scurry, R. (1998) Randomised controlled trial of the use of a modified postal reminder card on the uptake of measles vaccination. *Archives of Disease in Childhood*, 79(2), 136–40.

Hochbaum, G. (1958) *Public Participation in Medical Screening Programs*. Washington, DC: US Government Printing Office.

Janis, I. (1958) *Psychological Stress*. New York: Wiley.

Johnston, M. and Vögele, C. (1993) Benefits of psychological preparation for surgery: A meta-analysis. *Annals of Behavioral Medicine*, 15, 245–56.

Justus, R., Wyles, D., Wilson, J., Rode, D., Walther, V. and Lim-Sulit, N. (2006) Preparing children and families for surgery: Mount Sinai's multidisciplinary perspective. *Pediatric Nursing*, 32(1), 35–43.

Karasek, R.A. (1979) Job demands, job decision latitude, and mental strain: Implications for job redesign. *Administration Science Quarterly*, 24, 285–307.

Keating, D.T., Nayeem, K., Gilmartin, J.J. and O'Keeffe, S.T.O. (2005) Advance directives for truth disclosure. *Chest*, 128(2), 1037–9.

Kellar, I. and Abraham, C. (2005) Randomized controlled trial of a brief research-based intervention promoting fruit and vegetable consumption. *British Journal of Health Psychology*, 10(4), 543–58.

Kiecolt-Glaser, J.K., Marucha, P.T., Malarkey, W.B., Mercado, A.M. and Glaser, R. (1995) Slowing of wound healing by psychological stress. *Lancet*, 346, 1194–6.

Knight, K.M., McGowan, L., Dickens, C. and Bundy, C. (2006) A systematic review of motivational interviewing in physical health care settings. *British Journal of Health Psychology*, 11(2), 319–32.

Knowles, J.H. (1977) The responsibility of the individual. *Daedalus*, 106, 57–80.

Kulik, J.A., Moore, P.J. and Mahler, H.I. (1993) Stress and affiliation: Hospital roommate effects on preoperative anxiety and social interaction. *Health Psychology*, 12, 118–24.

Lazarus, R.S. and Folkman, S. (1984) *Stress, Appraisal and Coping*. New York: Springer.

Leventhal, H., Meyer, D. and Nerenz, D. (1980) The common sense representation of illness danger. In Rachman, S. (ed.) *Contributions to Medical Psychology*, vol. 2. Oxford: Pergamon Press: 7–30.

Lewin, K. (1951) *Field Theory in Social Science: Selected theoretical papers*. New York: Harper & Row.

Ley, P. (1988) *Communicating with Patients*. London: CroomHelm.

Lorig, K., Sobel, D.S., Stewart, A.L., Brown, B.W., Bandura, A., Ritter, P. et al. (1999) Evidence suggesting that a chronic disease self-management program can improve health status while reducing hospitalization. *Medical Care*, 37(1), 5–14.

Maguire, C.P., Kirby, M., Coen, R., Coakley, D., Lawlor, B.A. and O'Neill, D. (1996) Family members' attitudes toward telling the patient with Alzheimer's disease their diagnosis. *British Medical Journal*, 313, 529–30.

Matarazzo, J.D. (1982) Behavioural health's challenge to academic, scientific and professional psychology. *American Psychologist*, 37, 1–14.

McEwen, B.S. (1998) Stress, adaptation and disease. Allostasis and allostatic load. *Annals of the New York Academy of Sciences*, 840, 33–44.

Michie, S. and Abraham, C. (2004) Interventions to change health behaviours: Evidence-based or evidence inspired? *Psychology and Health*, 19, 28–49.

Michie, S. and Williams, S. (2003) Reducing work related psychological ill health and sickness absence: A systematic literature review. *Occupational and Environmental Medicine*, 60(1), 3–9.

Michie, S., Wren, B. and Williams, S. (2004) Reducing absenteeism in hospital cleaning staff: Pilot of a theory based intervention. *Occupational and Environmental Medicine*, 61(4), 345–9.

Miller, W.R. and Rollnick, S. (2002) *Motivational Interviewing: Preparing people for change*, second editon. New York: Guilford Press.

Mroczek, J., Mikitarian, G., Vieira, E.K. and Rotarius, T. (2005) Hospital design and staff perceptions: An exploratory analysis. *The Health Care Manager*, 24(3), 233–44.

Myers, L. and Abraham, C. (2005) Beyond 'doctor's orders'. *The Psychologist*, 18(11), 680–3.

Nichols, K. (2005) Why is psychology failing the average patient? *The Psychologist*, 18(1), 26–7.

Ogden, J. and Mtandabari, T. (1997) Examination stress and changes in mood and health related behaviours. *Psychology and Health*, 12, 289–99.

Oken, D. (1961) What to tell cancer patients: A study of medical attitudes. *Journal of the American Medical Association*, 175, 1120–8.

Petrie, K.J., Cameron, L.D., Ellis, C.J., Buick, D. and Weinman, J. (2002) Changing illness perceptions following myocardial infarction: An early intervention randomized controlled trial. *Psychosomatic Medicine*, 64(4), 580–6.

Prochaska, J.O., DeClemente, C.C. and Norcross, J.C.

(1992) In search of how people change: Applications to addictive behaviours. *American Psychologist*, 47(9), 1102–14.

Rahe, R.H., Mahan, J.L. and Arthur, R.J. (1970) Prediction of near-future health change from subjects' preceding life changes. *Journal of Psychosomatic Research*, 14(4), 401–6.

Richard, R., Van der Pligt, J. and de Vries, N. (1995) Anticipated affective reactions and prevention of AIDS. *British Journal of Social Psychology*, 34, 9–21.

Ruidavets, J.-B., Peterniti, S., Bongard, V., Giroux, M., Cassadou, S. and Ferrières, J. (2006) Triggering of acute coronary syndromes after a chemical plant explosion. *Heart*, 92(2), 257–8.

Sapolsky, R.M. (2004) *Why Zebras Don't Get Ulcers*, third edition. New York: Henry Holt.

Saposnik, G., Baibergenova, A., Dang, J. and Hachinski, V. (2006) Does a birthday predispose to vascular events? *Neurology*, 67(2), 300–4.

Schroeder, D.H. and Costa, P.T. (1984) Influence of life event stress on physical illness: Substantive effects or methodological flaws? *Journal of Personality and Social Psychology*, 46(4), 853–63.

Selye, H. (1956) *The Stress of Life*. New York: McGraw-Hill.

Sheeran, P., Milne, S., Webb, T.L. and Gollwitzer, P.M. (2005) Implementation intentions and health behaviour. In Conner, M. and Norman, P. (eds) *Predicting Health Behaviour*, second edition. Maidenhead, UK: Open University Press: 276–323.

Strike, P.C. and Steptoe, A. (2005) Behavioral and emotional triggers of acute coronary syndromes: A systematic review and critique. *Psychosomatic Medicine*, 67(2), 179–86.

Stuteville, J.R. (1970) Psychic defenses against high fear appeals: A key marketing variable. *Journal of Marketing*, 34(2), 39–45.

Sutton, S. (2005) Stage theories of health behaviour. In Conner, M. and Norman, P. (eds) *Predicting Health Behaviour*, second edition. Maidenhead, UK: Open University Press: 223–75.

Ulrich, R.S. (1984) View through a window may influence recovery from surgery. *Science*, 224(4647), 420–1.

Vassilas, C.A. and Donaldson, J. (1998) Telling the truth: What do general practitioners say to patients with dementia or terminal cancer? *British Journal of General Practice*, 48, 1081–2.

Vögele, C. (2004) Hospitalisation and stressful medical procedures. In Kaptein, A. and Weinman, J. (eds) *Health Psychology*. Oxford: Blackwell.

Wallace, L.M., Evers, K.E., Wareing, H., Dunn, O.M., Newby, K., Paiva, A. and Johnson, J.L. (2007) Informing school sex education using the Stages of Change construct: Sexual behavior and attitudes towards sexual activity and condom use of children aged 13–16. *Journal of Health Psychology*, 12(1), 179–83.

Webb, T.L. and Sheeran, P. (2006) Does changing behavioral intentions engender behavior change? A meta-analysis of the experimental evidence. *Psychological Bulletin*, 132(2), 249–68.

Weinstein, N.D. (1984) Why it won't happen to me: Perceptions of risk factors and susceptibility. *Health Psychology*, 3, 431–57.

Witte, K. and Allen, M. (2000) A meta-analysis of fear appeals: Implications for effective public health campaigns. *Health Education and Behavior*, 27(5), 591–615.

World Health Organization (WHO) (1948) Preamble to the Constitution of the World Health Organization as adopted by the International Health Conference, New York, 19–22 June 1946; signed on 22 July 1946 by the representatives of 61 states and entered into force on 7 April 1948. *Official Records of the World Health Organization*, 2, 100.

CHAPTER 8: OCCUPATIONAL PSYCHOLOGY

Adams, J.S. (1965) Inequity in social exchange. In Berkowitz, L. (ed.) *Advances in Experimental Social Psychology*, 69, 334–45.

Alimo-Metcalfe, B. and Alban-Metcalfe, R.J. (2001) The development of a new Transformational Leadership Questionnaire. *Journal of Occupational and Organizational Psychology*, 74(1), 1–27.

Allport, G.W. (1954) *The Nature of Prejudice*. Reading, MA: Addison-Wesley.

Ansari, M.A. and Shukla, R. (1987) Effects of group performance and leader behaviour on leadership perceptions. *Psychological Studies*, 32(2), 111–18.

Arnold, J. (2005) *Work Psychology: Understanding human behaviour in the workplace*. Harlow: Prentice Hall.

Asch, S. (1956) Studies of independence and conformity: A minority of one against a unanimous majority. *Psychological Monographs*, 70.

Bandura, A., Ross, D. and Ross, S.A. (1963) Imitation of film-mediated aggressive models. *Journal of Abnormal and Social Psychology*, 66, 3–11.

Baruch, Y., O'Creevy, M.F. and Hind, P. (2004) Prosocial behavior and job performance: Does the need for control and the need for achievement make a difference? *Social Behavior and Personality*, 32(4), 399–411.

Bass, B.M. (1998) *Transformational Leadership: Industrial, military, and educational impact.* Mahwah, NJ: Erlbaum.

Bassett-Jones, N. and Lloyd, G.C. (2005) Does Herzberg's motivation theory have staying power? *Journal of Management Development*, 24(10), 929–43.

Behson, S.J., Eddy, E.R. and Lorenzet, S.J. (2000) The importance of the critical psychological states in the job characteristics model: A meta-analytic and structural equations modeling examination. *Current Research in Social Psychology*, 5(12), 170–89. Available at http://www.uiowa.edu/~grpproc/crisp/crisp.5.12.htm (accessed 20 December 2006).

Belbin, R.M. (2004) *Management Teams: Why they succeed or fail.* Oxford: Butterworth-Heinemann.

Briner, R.B. (1998) What is an evidence based approach to practice and why do we need one in occupational psychology? *British Psychological Society Occupational Psychology Proceedings*. Leicester: British Psychological Society.

Brown, R. (1965) *Social Psychology*. New York: Macmillan.

Brown, R. (1988) *Group Processes*. Oxford: Blackwell.

Burkeman, O. (2001) Post Modern. *The Guardian*, 20 June.

Burns, J.M. (1978) *Leadership*. New York: Harper & Row.

Burnstein, E. and Vinokur, A. (1977) Persuasive argumentation and social comparison as determinants of attitude polarisation. *Journal of Experimental Social Psychology*, 13, 315–32.

Campion, M.A., Mumford, T.V., Morgeson, F.P. and Nahrgang, J.D. (2005) Work redesign: Eight obstacles and opportunities. *Human Resource Management*, 44(4), 367–90.

Collins, D.B. (2002) Performance-level evaluation methods used in management development studies from 1986 to 2000. *Human Resource Development Review*, 1(1), 91–110.

Conger, J.A. and Kanungo, R.N. (1998) *Charismatic Leadership in Organizations*. London: Sage.

Cook, M. (1978) *Perceiving Others*. London: Routledge.

Cosier, R.A. and Dalton, D.R. (1990) Positive effects of conflict: A field assessment. *The International Journal of Conflict Management*, 1, 81–92.

Cox, T. (2001) What? Occupational psychology: Making a difference. Address to the British Psychological Society's centenary event, *Psychology – A science for society*, 5 January 2001, at the Royal Society.

Creighton, P. and Scott, N. (2006) An introduction to Situational Judgement Inventories. *Selection and Development Review*, 22(3), 3–6.

Crutchfield, R.S. (1955) Conformity and character. *American Psychologist*, 10, 191–8.

Darany, E. and Smith, K. (2004) *Adverse Impact: History, concepts and testing concerns.* Presentation to the International Personnel Management Association Assessment Council, 22 June 2004. Available at http://www.ipmaac.org/conf/04/darany1.pdf (accessed 20 December 2006).

Dovidio, J.F. and Gaertner, S.L. (2000) Aversive racism and selection decisions: 1989 and 1999. *Psychological Science*, 11(4), 315–19.

Earley, P.C., Lee, C. and Hanson, L.A. (1990) Joint moderating effects of job experience and task component complexity: Relations among goal setting, task strategies and performance. *Journal of Organizational Behaviour*, 11(1), 3–15.

Eder, R.W. and Harris, M.M. (1999) *The Employment Interview Handbook*. London: Sage.

Fiedler, F.E. (1967) *A Theory of Leadership Effectiveness*. New York: McGraw-Hill.

Fiedler, F.E. (1995) Cognitive resources and leadership performance. *Applied Psychology: An International Review*, 44, 5–28.

Flanagan, J.C. (1954) The critical incident technique. *Psychological Bulletin*, 51, 327–58.

Fletcher, C. (2003) Occupational and organizational psychology. In Bayne, R. and Horton, I. (eds) *Applied Psychology*. London: Sage.

Fraser, C., Gouge, C. and Billig, M. (1971) Risky shifts, cautious shifts and group polarisation. *European Journal of Social Psychology*, 1, 7–30.

Gotcher, J.M. (1997) Perceptions and uses of electronic mail: A function of rhetorical style. *Social Science Computer Review*, 15(2), 145–58.

Gross, R.D. (2005) *Psychology: The science of mind and behaviour*, fifth edition. London: Hodder & Stoughton.

Hackman, J.R. and Oldham, G.R. (1976) Motivation through the design of work: Test of a theory. *Organizational Behavior and Human Performance*, 16(2), 250–79.

Herzberg, F. (1966) *Work and the Nature of Man*. Cleveland, OH: World Publishing.

Hollander, E.P. (1985) Leadership and power. In Lindzey, G. and Aronson, E. (eds) *The Handbook of Social Psychology*, third edition. New York: Random House: 485–538.

Hollway, W. (1991) *Work Psychology and Organizational Behaviour*. London: Sage.

Hough, L.M. and Furnham, A. (2003) Use of personality

variables in work setting. In Borman, W.C., Ilgen, D.R., Klimoskwi, R.J. and Weiner, I. B. (eds) *Handbook of Psychology*. Hoboken, NJ: Wiley: 131–69.

House, R.J. (1977) A 1976 theory of charismatic leadership. In Hunt, J.G. and Larsen, L.L. (eds) *Leadership: The cutting edge*. Carbondale, IL: Southern Illinois University Press: 189–207.

House, R.J., Spangler, W.D. and Woycke, J. (1991) Personality and charisma in the US presidency: A psychological theory of leader effectiveness. *Administrative Science Quarterly*, 36, 364–96.

Huffcutt, A.I. and Arthur, W. (1994) Hunter and Hunter (1984) revisited: Interview validity for entry-level jobs. *Journal of Applied Psychology*, 79, 184–90.

Huffcutt, A.I., Conway, J.M., Roth, P.L. and Stone, N.J. (2001) Identification and meta-analytic assessment of psychological constructs measured in employment interviews. *Journal of Applied Psychology*, 86, 897–913.

Hunter, J. and Hunter, R. (1984) Validity and utility of alternative predictors of job performance. *Psychological Bulletin*, 96, 72–98.

James, K., Chen, J. and Goldberg, C. (1992) Organizational conflict and individual creativity. *Journal of Applied Social Psychology*, 22, 545–66.

Janis, I.L. (1972) *Victims of Groupthink: A psychological study of foreign-policy decisions and fiascoes*. Boston, MA: Houghton Mifflin.

Janis, I.L. (1982) *Groupthink*. Boston, MA: Houghton Mifflin.

Judge, T.A. and Bono, J.E. (2000) Five factor model of personality and transformational leadership. *Journal of Applied Psychology*, 85(5), 751–65.

Judge, T.A., Piccolo, R.F. and Ilies, R. (2004) The forgotten ones? The validity of consideration and initiating structure in leadership research. *Journal of Applied Psychology*, 89(1), 36–51.

Kandola, B. (2005) The future of occupational psychology. Conference presentation (invited speaker), BPS Division of Occupational Psychology Conference 2005. Available at http://www.bps.org.uk/downloadfile.cfm?file_uuid=DD00D361-306E-1C7F-B616-E1E610DC6A2B&ext=pdf (accessed 20 December 2006).

Kelly, C. and Kelly, J. (1994) Who gets involved in collective action? Social psychological determinants of individual participation in trade unions. *Human Relations*, 47(1), 63–88.

Kelso, P. (2005) The fat finger that may have helped London win Olympics. *The Guardian*, 23 December: 3.

Latané, B., Williams, K. and Harkins, S. (1979) Many hands make light work: The causes and consequences of social loafing. *Journal of Personality and Social Psychology*, 37, 822–32.

Lewin, K., Lippitt, R. and White, R. (1939) Patterns of aggressive behaviour in experimentally created 'social climates'. *Journal of Social Psychology*, 10, 271–99.

Locke, E.A. and Latham, G.P. (2002) Building a practically useful theory of goal setting and task motivation: A 35 year odyssey. *Scientific American*, 57(9), 705–17.

Lowe, K.B., Kroeck, K.G. and Sivasubramaniam, N. (1996) Effectiveness correlates of transformational and transactional leadership: A meta-analytic review of the MLQ literature. *Leadership Quarterly*, 7(3), 385–425.

Maier, N.R.F. and Solem, A.R. (1952) The contribution of a discussion leader to the quality of group thinking: The effective use of minority opinions. *Human Relations*, 5, 277–88.

Martocchio, J.J. and Webster, J. (1992) Effects of feedback and cognitive playfulness on performance in microcomputer software. *Personnel Psychology*, 45(3), 553–78.

Mayo, E. (1927) Cited in Rose, M. (1975) *Industrial Behaviour: Theoretical Developments Since Taylor*. Harmondsworth: Penguin.

Mayo, E. (1933) *The Human Problems of an Industrial Civilisation*. New York: Macmillan.

McClelland, D.C. (1961) *The Achieving Society*. New York: Van Nostrand.

McCormick, E.J., Jeanneret, P. and Meacham, R.C. (1972) A study of job characteristics and job dimensions as based on the position analysis questionnaire. *Journal of Applied Psychology*, 36, 347–68.

Moscovici, S. (1985) Social influence and conformity. In Lindzey, G. and Aronson, A. (eds) *The Handbook of Social Psychology*, third edition. New York: Random House.

Mowday, R.T. (1991) Equity theory predictions of behaviour in organisations. In Steers, R.M. and Porter, L.W. (eds) *Motivation and Work Behaviour*, fifth edition. New York: McGraw-Hill: 111–31.

Munsterberg, H. (1913) *Psychology and Industrial Efficiency*. Boston, MA: Houghton Mifflin.

Myers, D.G. (2007) *Psychology*, eighth edition. New York: Worth.

Nemeth, C.J. (1986) Differential contributions of majority and minority influence. *Psychological Review*, 93, 23–32.

Nemeth, C., Brown, K. and Rogers, J. (2001) Devil's

advocate versus authentic dissent: Stimulating quantity and quality. *European Journal of Social Psychology*, 31(6), 707–20.

Ng, K.Y. and Van Dyne, L. (2001) Individualism-collectivism as a boundary condition for effectiveness of minority influence in decision making. *Organizational Behavior and Human Decision Processes*, 84(2), 198–225.

Olson, R., Hogan, L. and Santos, L. (2006) Illuminating the history of psychology: Tips for teaching students about the Hawthorne studies. *Psychology Learning and Teaching*, 5(2), 110–18.

Ones, D.S. and Viswesvaran, C. (2003) Job specific applicant pools and national norms for personality scales: Implications for range-restriction corrections in validation research. *Journal of Applied Psychology*, 88(3), 570–7.

Osborn, A.F. (1954) *Applied Imagination*. New York: Scribner.

Outtz, J.L. (2002) The role of cognitive ability tests in employment selection. *Human Performance*, 15(1–2), 161–72.

Patrick, J. (1992) *Training: Research and practice.* London: Academic Press.

Pettigrew, T.F. and Tropp, L.R. (2006) A meta-analytic test of intergroup contact theory. *Journal of Personality and Social Psychology*, 90(5), 751–83.

Reason, J. (1990) *Human Error*. Cambridge: Cambridge University Press.

Rietzschel, E.F., Nijstad, B.A. and Stroebe, W. (2006) Productivity is not enough: A comparison of interactive and nominal brainstorming groups on idea generation and selection. *Journal of Experimental Social Psychology*, 42(2), 244–51.

Riggio, R.E. (2002) *Introduction to Industrial/ Organizational Psychology*. Upper Saddle River, NJ: Prentice Hall.

Robertson, I.T. and Smith, M. (2001) Personnel selection. *Journal of Occupational and Organizational Psychology*, 74(4), 441–72.

Roethlisberger, F.J. and Dickson, W.J. (1939) *Management and the Worker*. Cambridge, MA: Harvard University Press.

Rose, M. (1975) *Industrial Behaviour: Theoretical developments since Taylor*. Harmondsworth: Penguin.

Roth, P.L., Bobko, P. and McFarland, L.A. (2005) A meta-analysis of work sample test validity: Updating and integrating some classic literature. *Personnel Psychology*, 58(4), 1009–37.

Rowan, J. (1998) Maslow amended. *Journal of Humanistic Psychology*, 28, 81–92.

Salgado, J.F., Viswesvaran, C. and Ones, D. (2001)

Predictors used for personnel selection: An overview of constructs, methods, techniques. In Anderson, N., Ones, D.S., Sinangil, H.K. and Viswesvaran, C. (eds) *Handbook of Industrial, Work and Organizational Psychology*. London: Sage.

Schriesheim, C.A., Tepper, B.J. and Tetrault, L.A. (1994) Least preferred co-worker score, situational control, and leadership effectiveness: A meta-analysis of contingency model performance predictions. *Journal of Applied Psychology*, 79, 561–73.

Schulz-Hardt, S., Jochims, M. and Frey, D. (2002) Organizational productive conflict in group decision making: Genuine and contrived dissent as strategies to counteract biased information seeking. *Behavior and Human Decision Processes*, 88(2), 563–86.

Sherif, M., Harvey, O.J., White, B.J., Hood, W.R. and Sherif, C. (1961) *Intergroup Cooperation and Competition: The robbers cave experiment*. Norman, OK: University of Oklahoma.

Simon, S.J. and Werner, J.M. (1996) Computer training through behavior modelling, self-paced, and instructional approaches: A field experiment. *Journal of Applied Psychology*, 81(6), 648–59.

Skinner, B.F. (1958) Teaching machines. *Science*, 128, 969–77.

Statt, D.A. (2004) *Psychology and the World of Work*. New York: Palgrave Macmillan.

Stoner, J.A.F. (1961) *A Comparison of Individual and Group Decisions Involving Risk*. Unpublished MA dissertation. Cambridge, MA: Massachusetts Institute of Technology.

Tajfel, H. and Turner, J.C. (1985) The social identity theory of inter-group behaviour. In Worchel, S. and Austin, W.G. (eds) *Psychology of Inter-group Relations*, second edition. Chicago, IL: Nelson-Hall.

Taylor, F.W. (1911) *The Principles of Scientific Management*. New York: Harper & Row.

Thomas, K. (1976) Conflict and conflict management. In Dunnette, M.D. (ed.) *Handbook of Industrial and Organizational Psychology*. Chichester: John Wiley: 889–935.

Thomas, K.W. (1992) Conflict and negotiations processes in organizations. In Dunnette, M.P. and Hough, L.M. (eds) *Handbook of Industrial and Organizational Psychology*, second edition. Palo Alto, CA: Consulting Psychologists Press: 651–717.

Triandis, H.C., Bontempo, R.V. and Marcelo J. (1988) Individualism and collectivism: Cross-cultural perspectives on self-ingroup relationships.

Journal of Personality and Social Psychology, 54(2), 323–38.

Trist, E.A. and Bamforth, K.W. (1951) Some social and psychological consequences of the longwall method of coal-getting. *Human Relations*, 4, 3–38.

Turner, J.C. (1999) Some current themes in research on social identity and self-categorization theories. In Ellemers, N., Spears, R. and Doosje, B. (eds) *Social Identity: Context, commitment, content*. Oxford: Blackwell: 6–34.

Tyerman, A. and Spencer, C. (1983) A critical test of the Sherifs' Robber's Cave experiment: Intergroup competition and cooperation between groups of well-acquainted individuals. *Small Group Behaviour*, 14, 515–31.

Vroom, V.H. (1964) *Work and Motivation*. Chichester: Wiley.

Wall, T.D. (1982) Perspectives on job redesign. In Kelly, J.E. and Clegg, C.W. (eds) *Autonomy and Control in the Workplace*. London: CroomHelm.

Warr, P.B. (1982) A national study of non-financial employment commitment. *Journal of Occupational Psychology*, 55, 297–312.

Workman, M. and Bommer, W. (2004) Redesigning computer call center work: A longitudinal field experiment. *Journal of Organizational Behavior*, 25(3), 317–37.

CHAPTER 9: SPORT AND EXERCISE PSYCHOLOGY

Abernethy, B. (2001) Attention. In Singer, R., Hausenblas, H. and Janelle, C. (eds) *Handbook of Sport Psychology*, second edition. New York: Wiley.

ACSM (American College of Sports Medicine) (1995) Position stand: The recommended quantity and quality of exercise for developing and maintaining cardiorespiratory and muscular fitness in healthy adults. *Medicine and Science in Sport and Exercise*, 22, 265–74.

ACSM (American College of Sports Medicine) (1998) Position stand: The recommended quantity and quality of exercise for developing and maintaining cardiorespiratory and muscular fitness, and flexibility in healthy adults. *Medicine and Science in Sport and Exercise*, 8 June, 30(6), 975–91.

Ajzen, I. and Fishbein, M. (1980) *Understanding Attitudes and Predicting Social Behaviour*. Englewood Cliffs, NJ: Prentice Hall.

Ajzen, I. and Madden, T.J. (1986) Prediction of goal-directed behaviour: Attitudes, intentions and perceived behavioural control. *Journal of Experimental Social Psychology*, 22, 453–74.

Anderson. A.G., Knowles, Z. and Gilbourne, D. (2004) Reflective practice for sport psychologists: Concepts, models, practical implications, and thoughts on dissemination. *The Sport Psychologist*, 18, 188–203.

Andersen, M.B. (ed.) (2000) *Doing Sport Psychology*. Leeds: Human Kinetics Europe.

Bandura, A. (1986) *Social Foundations of Thought and Actions: A social cognitive theory*. Englewood Cliffs, NJ: Prentice Hall.

Bannister, D. and Fransella, F. (1986) *Inquiring Man*, third edition. London: Routledge.

BASES (British Association for Sport and Exercise Sciences) (2002) Code of Conduct. Available at http://www.bases.org.uk/newsite/pdf/code%20of%20conduct.pdf (accessed 20 December 2006).

Becker, M.H. and Maiman, L.A. (1975) Socio-behavioral determinants of compliance with health and medical care recommendations. *Medical Care*, 13(1), 10–24.

Berger, B. and Motl, R. (2001) Physical activity and quality of life. In Singer, R., Hausenblas, H. and Janelle, C. (eds) *Handbook of Sport Psychology*, second edition. New York: Wiley.

Bezjak, J. and Lee, J. (1990) Relationship of self-efficacy and locus of control constructs in predicting college students' physical fitness behaviors. *Perceptual Motor Skills*, 71, 499–508.

Biddle, S.J.H., Fox, K.R. and Boutcher, S.H. (2000) *Physical Activity and Psychological Well-Being*. London: Routledge.

Biddle, S.J.H. and Mutrie, N. (2001) *Psychology of Physical Activity: Determinants, well-being and interventions*. London: Routledge.

Buckworth, J. and Dishman, R. (2002) *Exercise Psychology*. Champaign, IL: Human Kinetics.

Bull, S.J. (1989) The role of the sport psychology consultant: A case study of ultra distance running. *The Sport Psychologist*, 3, 254–64.

Bull, S.J. (1991) Personal and situational influences on adherence to mental skills training. *The Sport Psychologist*, 13, 121–32.

Bull, S.J., Shambrook, C.J., James, W. and Brooks, J.E. (2005) Towards an understanding of mental toughness in elite English cricketers. *Journal of Applied Sports Psychology*, 17, 209–27.

Burton, D., Naylor, S. and Holliday, B. (2002) Goal setting in sport: Investigating the goal effectiveness paradigm. In Singer, R., Hausenblas, H. and Janelle,

C. (eds) *Handbook of Sport Psychology*, second edition. New York: Wiley.

Butler, R. and Hardy, L. (1992) The performance profile. Theory and application. *The Sport Psychologist*, 6, 253–64.

Carpenter, W. (1894) *Principles of Mental Physiology*. New York: Appleton.

Crawford, S. and Eklund, R. (1994) Social physique anxiety, reasons for exercise and attitudes towards exercise settings. *Journal of Sport & Exercise Psychology*, 16, 70–82.

Csikszentmihalyi, M. (1985) *Beyond Boredom and Anxiety*. London: Jossey-Bass.

Deci, E.L. and Ryan, R.M. (1985) *Intrinsic Motivation and Self-Determination in Human Behavior*. New York: Plenum Press.

Deci, E.L. and Ryan, R.M. (2000) The what and why of goal pursuits: Human needs and the self-determination of behavior. *Psychological Inquiry*, 11(4), 227–68.

Department of Health (2003) Health Survey for England, Vol. 2: Risk factors for cardiovascular disease. Available at http://www.dh.gov.uk/assetRoot/04/09/89/11/04098911.pdf (accessed 20 December 2006).

Duda, J.L. (1989) The relationship between task and ego orientation and the perceived purpose of sport among male and female high school athletes. *Journal of Sport & Exercise Psychology*, 11, 148–65.

Edwards, T., Kingston, K., Hardy, L. and Gould, D. (2002) A qualitative analysis of catastrophic performances and the associated thoughts, feelings, and emotions. *The Sport Psychologist*, 16, 1.

Evans, L., Jones, L. and Mullen, R. (2004) An imagery intervention during the competitive season with an elite rugby union player. *The Sport Psychologist*, 18, 252–71.

Eysenck, M.W. and Calvo, M.G. (1992) Anxiety and performance: The processing efficiency theory. *Cognition and Emotion*, 6, 409–34.

Fazey, J.A. and Hardy, L. (1988) *The Inverted-U Hypothesis: A Catastrophe for Sport Psychology*. Leeds: National Coaching Foundation.

Frederick, C. and Ryan, R. (1995) Self-determination in sport: A review using cognitive evaluation theory. *International Journal of Sport Psychology*, 26, 5–23.

Gill, D.L. (2000) *Psychological Dynamics of Sport and Exercise*, second edition. Champaign, IL: Human Kinetics.

Godin, G. (1994) Social-cognitive models. In Dishman, R. (ed.) *Advances in Exercise Adherence*. Champaign, IL: Human Kinetics: 113–36.

Griffiths, C. (1926) *The Psychology of Coaching*. New York: Charles Scribner's.

Griffiths, C. (1928) *Psychology and Athletes*. New York: Charles Scribner's.

Griffiths, L., Wolke, D., Page, A. and Horwood, J. (2006) Obesity and bullying: Different effects for boys and girls. *Archives of Disease in Childhood*, 91, 121–5.

Hall, C., Mack, D., Paivio, A. and Hausenblas, H. (1998) Imagery use by athletes: Development of the sport imagery questionnaire. *International Journal of Sport Psychology*, 29, 73–89.

Hall, C., Rodgers, W. and Barr, K. (1990) The use of imagery by athletes in selected sports. *The Sport Psychologist*, 4, 1–10.

Hardy, L. (1990) A catastrophe model of performance in sport. In Jones, G. and Hardy, L. (eds) *Stress and Performance in Sport*. Chichester: John Wiley: 81–106.

Hardy, L. and Callow, N. (1999) Efficacy of external and internal visual imagery perspectives for the enhancement of performance on tasks in which form is important. *Journal of Sport & Exercise Psychology*, 21, 95–112.

Hardy, L. and Parfitt, G. (1991) A catastroph`e model of anxiety and performance. *British Journal of Psychology*, 82, 163–78.

Hardy, L., Parfitt, G. and Pates, J. (1994) Performance catastrophes in sport: A test of the hysteresis hypothesis. *Journal of Sports Sciences*, 12, 327–34.

Harter, S. (1978) Effectance motivation reconsidered. *Human Development*, 21, 34–64.

Haslam, D., Sattar, N. and Lean, M. (2006) ABC of obesity – Time to wake up. *British Medical Journal*, 23 September, 333(7569), 640–2.

Hillsdon, M. and Thorogood, M. (1996) A systematic review of physical activity promotion strategies. *British Journal of Sports Medicine*, 30, 84–9.

Holmes, P. and Collins, D. (2001) The PETTLEP approach to motor imagery: A functional equivalence model for sport psychologists. *Journal of Applied Sport Psychology*, 13, 60–83.

Jackson, S. and Csikszentmihalyi, M. (1999) *Flow in Sports: The keys to optimal experiences and performances*. Champaign, IL: Human Kinetics.

James, W. (1890) *Principles of Psychology*. New York: Holt, Rinehart and Winston.

Jones, G., Hanton, S. and Connaughton, D. (2002) What is this thing called mental toughness? An investigation of elite sport performers. *Journal of Applied Sport Psychology*, 14, 205–18.

Jones, G. and Hardy, L. (eds) (1990) *Stress and Performance in Sport*. Chichester: John Wiley.

Kane, J. (1970) Personality and physical abilities. In Kenyon, G.S. (ed.) *Contemporary Psychology of Sport*. Chicago, IL: Athletic Institute: 131–41.

Kelly, G. (1955) *The Psychology of Personal Constructs*, vols 1 and 2. New York: Norton.

Kyllo, L. and Landers, D. (1995) Goal setting in sport and exercise: A research synthesis to resolve the controversy. *Journal of Sports and Exercise Psychology*, 17, 117–37.

Lang, P. (1977) Imagery in therapy: An information-processing analysis of fear. *Behaviour Therapy*, 8, 862–86.

Lang, P. (1979) A bio-informational theory of emotional imagery. *Psychophysiology*, 17, 495–512.

Locke, E.A. and Latham, G.P. (1990) *A Theory of Goal Setting and Task Performance*. Englewood Cliffs, NJ: Prentice-Hall.

Locke, E.A. and Latham, G.P. (1994) Goal setting theory. In O'Neil, H.F. and Drillings, M. (eds) *Motivation: Theory and Research*, Hillsdale, NJ: Erlbaum: 13–29.

McDonald, D.G. and Hodgdon, J.A. (1991) *Psychological Effects of Aerobic Fitness Training*. New York: Springer.

Marcus, B.H., Banspach, S.W., Lefebvre, R.C., Rossi, J.S., Carleton, R.A. and Abrams, D.A. (1992) Using the change model to increase the adoption of physical activity among community participants. *American Journal of Health Promotion*, 6, 424–9.

Markland, D. (2006) Self-determination theory: The self-determination continuum. Available at http://www.bangor.ac.uk/~pes004/exercise_psych/sdt/contin.htm (accessed 20 December 2006).

Martens, R., Vealey, R. and Burton, D. (1990) *Competitive Anxiety in Sport*. Champaign, IL: Human Kinetics.

Masters, R.S.W. (1992) Knowledge, knerves and know-how: The role of explicit versus implicit knowledge in the breakdown of complex motor skill under pressure. *British Journal of Psychology*, 83, 345–58.

Mental Health Foundation (2005) *Up and Running? Exercise therapy and the treatment of mild or moderate depression in primary care*. London: Mental Health Foundation.

Miller, W.R. and Rollnick, S. (1991) *Motivational Interviewing: Preparing people to change addictive behaviour*. New York: Guilford Press.

Moran, A. (1996) *The Psychology of Concentration in Sports Performers: A cognitive analysis*. Hove: Psychological Press.

Moran, A. (2004) *Sport and Exercise Psychology*. London: Routledge.

Moritz, S.E., Hall, C.R., Martin, K.A. and Vadocz, E. (1996) What are confident athletes imaging? An examination of image content. *The Sport Psychologist*, 10, 171–9.

Munroe, K., Giacobbi, P., Hall, C. and Weinberg, R. (2000) The four w's of imagery use: Where, when, why and what. *The Sport Psychologist*, 10, 171–9.

National Audit Office (2001) Tackling Obesity in England. Available at http://www.nao.org.uk/publications/nao_reports/00-01/0001220.pdf (accessed 20 December 2006).

Newton, M. (1994) The relationship between perceived motivational climate and dispositional goal orientations to indices motivation among female volleyball players. Unpublished doctoral dissertation, West Lafayette, IN: Purdue University.

Nicholls, J. (1984) Concepts of ability and achievement motivation. In Ames, C. and Ames, R. (eds) *Research on Motivation in Education. Student motivation*. New York: Academic Press.

Nideffer, R. (1976) Test of attentional and interpersonal style. *Journal of Personality and Social Psychology*, 34(3), 394–404.

North, T.C., McCullagh, P., Tran, Z.V. (1990) Effects of exercise on depression. *Exercise and Sport Science Reviews*, 19, 379–415.

Obesity Scotland (2002) Why diets, doctors and denial won't work. Available at http://www.gla.ac.uk/services/estates/obesity.pdf#search=%22www.obesityscotland.com%22 (accessed 20 December 2006).

OECD (Organization for Economic Cooperation and Development) (2006) Obesity. Available at http://caliban.sourceoecd.org/vl=18448768/cl=11/nw=1/rpsv/factbook/10-01-03.htm (accessed 20 December 2006).

Orlick, T. (1990) *In Pursuit of Excellence*. Champaign, IL: Human Kinetics.

Orlick, T. and Partington, J. (1988) Mental links to excellence. *The Sport Psychologist*, 5, 322–34.

Ostrow, A. (ed.) (1996) *Directory of Psychological Tests in the Sport and Exercise Sciences*. Morgantown, WV: Fitness Information Technology.

Paivio, A. (1985) Cognitive and motivational functions of imagery in human performance. *Canadian Journal of Applied Sport Sciences*, 10, 22S–28S.

Partington, J. and Orlick, T. (1987a) The sport psychology consultant: Olympic coaches' views. *The Sport Psychologist*, 1, 95–102.

Partington, J. and Orlick, T. (1987b) The sport psychology consultant evaluation form. *The Sport Psychologist*, 1, 309–17.

Patmore, A. (1986) *Sportsmen Under Pressure*. London: Stanley Paul.

Petruzzello, S.J., Landers, D.M., Hatfield, B.D., Kubitz, K.A. and Salazar, W. (1991) A meta-analysis on the anxiety-reducing effects of acute and chronic exercise: Outcomes and mechanisms. *Sports Medicine*, 11, 143–82.

Poczwardowski, A. and Conroy, D.E. (2002) Coping responses to failure and success among elite athletes and performing artists. *Journal of Applied Sport Psychology*, 14, 314–40.

Pope, H., Phillips, K. and Olivardia, R. (2000) *The Adonis Complex: The secret crisis of male body obsession*. New York: The Free Press: 11.

Prochaska, J.O., DiClemente, C.C. and Norcross, J.C. (1992) In search of how people change. *American Psychologist*, 47, 1102–14.

Rowan, J. (1997) Transpersonal counselling. In Feltham, C. (ed.) *Which Psychotherapy?* London: Sage.

Sackett, R. (1934) The influences of symbolic rehearsal upon the retention of a maze habit. *Journal of General Psychology*, 13, 113–28.

Selvey, M. (1998) Getting up for the Ashes. *The Guardian*, 20 November, p.2 (Sport).

Singer, R. (1996) Future of sport and exercise psychology. In Van Raalte, J. and Brewer, B. (eds) *Exploring Sport and Exercise Psychology*. Washington, DC: American Psychological Society: 451–68.

Singer, R., Hausenblas, H. and Janelle, C. (eds) (2001) *Handbook of Sport Psychology*, second edition. New York: Wiley.

Spielberger, C. (1966) Theory and research on anxiety. In Spielberger, C. (ed.) *Anxiety and Behaviour*. New York: Academic Press: 3–22.

Sports Council and Health Education Authority (1992) *Allied Dunbar National Fitness Survey: Summary*. London: Sports Council and Health Education Authority.

Szabo, A. (2000) Physical activity and psychological dysfunction. In Biddle, S.J.H., Fox, K.R. and Boutcher, S.H. (eds) *Physical Activity and Psychological Well-Being*. London: Routledge.

Taylor, A. (1999) Adherence in primary health care exercise promotion schemes. In Bull, S.J. (ed.) *Adherence Issues in Sport and Exercise*. Chichester: John Wiley.

Thomas, P.R., Murphy, S.M. and Hardy, L. (1999) Test of performance strategies: Development and preliminary validation of a comprehensive measure of athletes' psychological skills. *Journal of Sports Sciences*, 17, 697–711.

Vealey, R. (1986) Conceptualisation of sport confidence and competitive orientation: Preliminary investigation and instrument development. *Journal of Sport Psychology*, 8, 221–46.

Vealey, R., Hayashi, S., Garner-Homan, G. and Giacobbi, P. (1998) Sources of sport confidence: Conceptualisation and instrument development. *Journal of Sport and Exercise Psychology*, 20, 54–80.

Wadden, T., Steen, S., Wingate, B. and Foster, G. (1996) Psychosocial consequences of weight reduction: How much weight loss is enough? *American Journal of Clinical Nutrition*, 63, 461S–465S.

Weinberg, R. and Gould, D. (2003) *Foundations of Sport and Exercise Psychology*. Champaign, IL: Human Kinetics.

White, A. and Hardy, L. (1998) An in-depth analysis of the uses of imagery by high-level slalom canoeists and artistic gymnasts. *The Sport Psychologist*, 12, 387–403.

Williamson, D., Netemeyer, R., Jackman, L., Anderson, D., Funsch, C.L. and Rabalais, J. (1995) Structural equation modeling of risk factors for the development of eating disorder symptoms in female athletes. *International Journal of Eating Disorders*, 17, 387–93.

Willis, J. and Campbell, J. (1992) *Exercise Psychology*. Champaign, IL: Human Kinetics.

Wimbush, F., Macgregor, A. and Fraser, E. (1997) Impacts of a national mass media campaign on walking in Scotland. *Health Promotion International*, 13, 45–53.

Woodman, T. and Hardy, L. (2001) Stress and anxiety. In Singer, R., Hausenblas, H. and Janelle, C. (eds), *Handbook of Sport Psychology*, second edition. New York: Wiley.

Yates, A., Leehey, K. and Shisslak, C.M. (1983) Running: An analogue of anorexia? *New England Journal of Medicine*, 308, 251–5.

Yerkes, R.M. and Dodson, J.D. (1908) The relation of strength of stimulus to rapidity of habit formation. *Journal of Comparative Neurology and Psychology*, 18, 459–82.

Yeung, R. (1996) The acute effects of exercise on mood state. *Journal of Psychosomatic Research*, 2, 123–41.

CHAPTER 10: THE MAJOR THEORETICAL APPROACHES WITHIN APPLIED PSYCHOLOGY

Bandura, A. (1989) Perceived self-efficacy in the exercise of personal agency. *Psychologist*, 2, 411–24.

Bandura, A. and Huston, A.C. (1961) Identification as a process of incidental learning. *Journal of Abnormal and Social Psychology*, 63, 311–18.

Bandura, A., Ross, D. and Ross, S.A. (1963) Imitation of film-mediated aggressive models. *Journal of Abnormal and Social Psychology*, 66, 3–11.

Bion, W.R. (1968) *Experiences in Groups*. London: Tavistock Publications.

Burt, C. (1972) The inheritance of general intelligence. *American Psychologist*, 27, 175–90.

Costa, P.T., Jr. and McRae, R.R. (1992) *NEO PI-R Professional Manual*. Odessa, FL: Psychological Assessment Resources.

de Board, R. (1978) *The Psychoanalysis of Organizations*. London: Tavistock Publications.

DeCasper, A.J. and Fifer, W.P. (1980) Of human bonding: Newborns prefer their mothers' voices. *Science*, 208, 1174–6.

Gross, R.D. (1995) *Themes, Issues and Debates in Psychology*. London: Hodder & Stoughton.

Hartshorne, H. and May, M.A. (1928) *Studies in the Nature of Character: Vol. 1, Studies in Deceit*. New York: Macmillan.

Krahé, B. (1992) *Personality and Social Psychology: Towards a Synthesis*. London: Sage.

Miller, G.A., Galanter, E. and Pribram, K.H. (1960) *Plans and the Structure of Behaviour*. New York: Holt, Rinehart and Winston.

Mischel, W. (1968) *Personality and Assessment*. New York: Wiley.

Mischel, W. and Shoda, Y. (1995) A cognitive-affective system theory of personality: Reconceptualising situations, dispositions, dynamics and invariance in personality structure. *Psychological Review*, 102, 246–68.

Pavlov, I. P. (1927) *Conditioned Reflexes*. London: Oxford University Press.

Rogers, C.R. (1957) The necessary and sufficient conditions of therapeutic personality change. *Journal of Consulting Psychology*, 21, 95.

Scarr, S. (1991) Theoretical issues in investigating intellectual plasticity. In Brauth, S.E., Hall, W.S. and Dooling, R. (eds) *Plasticity of Development*. Cambridge, MA: MIT Press.

Skinner, B.F. (1953) *Science and Human Behaviour*. New York: Macmillan.

Tolman, E.C. (1932) *Purposive Behaviour in Animals and Man*. New York: Century.

Weinberg, R.S., Gould, D. and Jackson, A. (1979) Expectations and performance: An empirical test of Bandura's self-efficacy theory. *Journal of Sport Psychology*, 1, 320–31.

CHAPTER 11: METHODS FOR THE PRODUCTION OF RESEARCH AND PRACTICE DATA

Bandura, A. (1969) *Principles of Behaviour Modification*, New York: Holt Rinehart Winston.

Bruner, J.S. (1973) *Beyond the Information Given*. New York: Norton.

Charlesworth, R. and Hartup, W.W. (1967) Positive social reinforcement in the nursery school peer group. *Child Development*, 38, 993–1002.

Cook, T.D. and Campbell, D.T. (1979) *Quasi-experimentation: Design and analysis issues for field settings*. Chicago, IL: Rand McNally.

Coolican, H. (2004) *Research Methods and Statistics in Psychology*, fourth edition. London: Hodder & Stoughton.

Eden, D. (1990) Pygmalion without interpersonal contrast effects: Whole groups gain from raising manager expectations. *Journal of Applied Psychology*, 75(4), 394–8.

Hofling, C.K., Brotzman, E., Dalrymple, S., Graves, N. and Pierce, C.M. (1966) An experimental study in nurse–physician relationships. *Journal of Nervous and Mental Disease*, 143, 171–80.

Keogh, E., Bond, F.W. and Flaxman, P.E. (2006) Improving academic performance and mental health through a stress management intervention: Outcomes and mediators of change. *Behaviour Research and Therapy*, 44(3), 339–57.

Luria, Z. and Rubin, J.Z. (1974) The eye of the beholder: Parents' views on sex of newborns. *American Journal of Orthopsychiatry*, 44, 512–19.

Martin, S.L. and Klimoski, R.J. (1990) Use of verbal protocols to trace cognitions associated with self- and supervisor evaluations of performance. *Organizational Behavior and Human Decision Processes*, 46(1), 135–54.

Milgram, S. (1963) Behavioral study of obedience. *Journal of Abnormal Psychology*, 67, 371–8.

Orne, M.T. (1962) On the social psychology of the psychology experiment: With particular reference to demand characteristics and their implications. *American Psychologist*, 17, 776–83.

Reason, P. (ed.) (1994) *Participation in Human Inquiry*. London: Sage.

Roberts, V.L. and Fels, D.I. (2006) Methods for inclusion: Employing think aloud protocols in software usability studies with individuals who are deaf. *International Journal of Human-Computer Studies*, 64(6), 489–501.

Roethlisberger, F.J. and Dickson, W.J. (1939)

Management and the Worker. Cambridge, MA: Harvard University Press.

Rosenthal, R. (1966) *Experimenter Effects in Behavioural Research*. New York: Appleton-Century-Crofts.

Rosenthal, R. and Jacobson, L. (1968) *Pygmalion in the Classroom*. New York: Holt.

Smith, J.A. (2003) *Qualitative Psychology: A practical guide to research methods*. London: Sage.

Strauss, A. and Corbin, J. (1990) *Basics of Qualitative Research*. London: Sage.

Willig, C. (2001) *Introducing Qualitative Research in Psychology*. Buckingham: Open University Press.

Workman, M. and Bommer, W. (2004) Redesigning computer call center work: A longitudinal field experiment. *Journal of Organizational Behavior*, 25(3), 317–37.

Zuber-Skerritt, O. (1992) *Action Research in Higher Education*. London: Kogan Page.

Index